The Essential
MILTON

*an annotated bibliography
of major modern studies*

A
Reference
Publication
in
Literature

James L. Harner
Editor

The Essential
MILTON

*an annotated bibliography
of major modern studies*

P. J. KLEMP

G.K.HALL&CO.
70 LINCOLN STREET, BOSTON, MASS.

Library of Congress Cataloging-in-Publication Data

Klemp, P. J.
      The essential Milton : an annotated bibliography of major modern
studies / P. J. Klemp.
          p. cm. -- (A Reference publication in literature)
      Bibliography: p.
      Includes index.
      ISBN 0-8161-8730-4
      1. Milton, John, 1608-1674--Bibliography. I. Title. II. Series.
Z8578.K57 1989
[PR3581]
016.821'4--dc19
                                        89-30984
                                          CIP

This publication is printed on permanent/durable acid-free paper
MANUFACTURED IN THE UNITED STATES OF AMERICA

Contents

Contents

The Author

A member of the editorial staff of *Milton Quarterly*, *Literary Research*, and *Seventeenth-Century News*, P. J. Klemp teaches at the University of Wisconsin, Oshkosh. His publications include articles on Milton (*Milton Quarterly*), Donne (*Renaissance and Reformation*), Spenser (*Studia Neophilologica* and *Spenser Encyclopedia*), Dante (*Italica*), and Andrewes (*Bodleian Library Record*). He has published a bibliography titled "Numerology and English Renaissance Literature" in the *Bulletin of Bibliography*, and *Fulke Greville and Sir John Davies: A Reference Guide* (G. K. Hall, 1985).

Preface

No English author can match Milton's love of argument and free intellectual inquiry, which both search for the truth, as *Areopagitica* asserts, by imitating Isis and gathering up the scattered limbs of Osiris. As one who believes in such a messy process in which "much arguing, much writing, [and] many opinions" lead to "knowledge in the making," who holds firm convictions, and who writes masterpieces about the most important subjects, Milton sets an example for those who would write about his life and works. Milton scholarship, not surprisingly, has been characterized for three centuries by firmly held opinions, generally high quality, and combativeness among scholars holding diverse views. As John R. Mulder notes, "Scholars may agree to differ about Chaucer, or Spenser, but about Milton they differ passionately."[1] Especially in the twentieth century, some scholars identify Milton as a misogynist, while others believe he takes up the feminist cause; according to some, he is a political conservative or an advocate of war, but others view him as a liberal or a pacifist; on religious matters, he has been called a heretic, a defender of orthodoxy, and everything in between. Because these contradictory positions are defended with vigor and a variety of critical approaches, ranging from historical criticism (old and new) to deconstruction, from feminist to numerological to psychoanalytic criticism, we cannot readily dismiss any.

The variety of interpretations Milton provokes has led not only to "knowledge in the making" but also to confusion, which is compounded by the vast amount of scholarship about him. Despite Malcolm Mackenzie Ross's assertion in 1954 that "Further novelties in the reading of the poem [*Paradise Lost*] are not possible"[2] and E. M. W. Tillyard's confident claim in 1951 that

"By now a great deal has been found out [about Milton's thought]; and one suspects that there is not much more to find,"[3] one estimate indicates that over one hundred works about Milton have appeared, on average, during each year of the twentieth century. Attempting to sift this material, the following bibliography includes the most significant Milton scholarship published between 1900 and 1987, though coverage of the final year is necessarily sketchy. As I read over 3,000 studies of Milton, I selected those that best illuminate our understanding of the man, his writing, and his relationship to his age and others. Highly specialized or narrowly focused studies, regardless of their quality, are generally omitted, as are theses, dissertations, and works in foreign languages. The works annotated in this bibliography are available in a good university library or through interlibrary loan, but in some entries I provide information, by no means thorough, about reprints (particularly of key essays or sections of books) in order to make some of these studies more accessible.

In this bibliography, each essay or book is cited with the details of its first appearance in print. When dealing with essays later incorporated as chapters in a book devoted to Milton by a single author, I required some flexibility. To cite only the essays would use up many of the pages that I was allotted, and this procedure might omit those parts of the book not reprinted from elsewhere; to cite both the essays and the book would use up many entries and be largely redundant. So in most cases, I cite the book in which an author's essays are included if that book is devoted to Milton and makes a significant contribution to scholarship. For example, a number of important articles by Barbara Lewalski or Balachandra Rajan or John Steadman appear to have been overlooked in this bibliography when in fact readers who consult their books cited herein will find those essays and much more of value (unfortunately, space limitations prevent me from indicating which books reprint which essays). Sometimes an author publishes an article, has it included in a collection of essays by diverse hands, and later incorporates it in a book. When I cite that book, I also try to note when part of it (the original article) is reprinted in a critical anthology, even if my citation looks suspicious because the anthology antedates the book.

In the annotations, I try to do justice to the works included here and rely on the index to compensate for the brevity of each annotation. The index, which is more thorough than the cross references in the body of this bibliography, frequently calls attention to names and subjects that are important in a given scholarly work but could not be squeezed into the annotation. If a work presents an argument, I summarize it, but if it is a reference tool or edition, I briefly describe its contents. When an annotation refers to Milton studies "today" or a "current debate," these temporal markers should be understood as coming from the original author's point of view.

The process of selection is, of course, subjective, so I welcomed guidance from many sources. Besides reading every essay in every volume of *Milton Studies* and *Milton Quarterly* (formerly *Milton Newsletter*), I relied on bibliographies by Stevens (see entry 77), Fletcher (see entry 73), and Huckabay (see entry 75), and the annual bibliographies that appear in the *MLA International Bibliography*, the Modern Humanities Research Association's *Annual Bibliography of English Language and Literature*, and the *Year's Work in English Studies*. I paid special attention to each entry that Hanford's bibliography designated as "a work of 'special importance' in the field" (1966; the second edition [see entry 74] drops this designation), other selective bibliographies, surveys of Milton scholarship, works reprinted in anthologies of Milton criticism, and the Milton Society of America's annual awards for distinguished scholar and scholarship. The anxiety of influence kept C. A. Patrides's *Annotated Critical Bibliography of John Milton* (New York: St. Martin's Press, 1987) unopened on a bookshelf until my work was finished. Because the annotations in Patrides's selected bibliography are brief and general, I have not included it here, though we seem to agree about the merits of over two-thirds of our selections and though his critical writings on Milton are among the most valuable of our century.

I chose to include many works because of the frequency with which scholars cite them as well as the comments accompanying those citations. One scholar's denunciation of another's work was as likely to catch my attention as praise, for energetic negative assessments--one thinks of responses to Empson's work (see entry 772), for example--often greet works of authentic, if controversial, value. So I was not surprised to find that this bibliography contains entries for what A. S. P. Woodhouse refers to as "what must surely be (among many strong competitors) the worst book on Milton ever written"[4] and what he believes is "the best single brief study of Milton ever written."[5] Finally, I felt free to disregard any of this guidance because the choices ultimately reflect my judgment of how these studies will benefit an audience that ranges from an undergraduate who encounters Milton for the first time to a scholar who has devoted a lifetime to the study of the poet.

To help such a wide range of students of Milton locate or be reminded of scholarly materials, this bibliography is organized in such a way that the two forms in which he wrote--verse and prose--are kept discrete, though this arrangement disturbs the chronological sequence of his writings. The opening general section includes background studies of Milton's thought and his relationship to his age, editions, biographies (with biographical studies of his canon), reference works, and discussions of Milton scholarship. After a subsection devoted to broad studies that cover most of Milton's verse, the second section focuses on his poetry, with the more important short poems and the three long poems receiving their own subsections. Because the subsection on *Paradise Lost* is the largest in this bibliography, I divided it into subject areas (such as style and the narrator) and then into the epic's three main geographical regions--hell (including chaos and the limbo of vanity), earth, and heaven. These geographical subdivisions contain studies that focus on a single region, its residents, and the events that occur there (even if those events are narrated far from where they happen, as is the case with the war in heaven). The third and final section of this bibliography deals with Milton's prose. By placing his poetry and prose in separate sections, and thus not dividing the verse into short and long works, I hope that this bibliography is easier to use and that it gives a sense of the coherence, even with its great diversity, of Milton scholarship.

While working on this bibliography, I accumulated many debts that I can only begin to repay by offering my gratitude. Professor James L. Harner, the editor of this volume, gave me both guidance and independence, as well as the benefit of his estimable editorial skills. Along with a number of efficient interlibrary loan workers who could locate virtually anything, two librarians, Kim Fisher and Terry Basford, helped me find material and resolve some difficult questions. For assistance with computers, I owe thanks to Professor Leonard Leff and Deborah Bransford, to Professor Stan Larson and Sandy Wendt. Professor Albert Labriola kept me informed about the annual awards made by the Milton Society of America. Saving me from embarrassment, Professor Edward Jones managed--usually when I thought my work was nearly finished and thus sometimes to my exasperation--to keep finding books and essays that I had overlooked. His efforts, both professional and personal, made a difference in many ways. The members of my Milton seminar in the fall of 1987 alerted me to a few critical works and, through their enthusiasm, reminded me of why I read Milton. Three research assistants helped a great deal: Stephen Haney transcribed citations for the initial list of a few thousand works, which guided my reading and led to the selections that appear in this bibliography; Aimee Piotrowski proofread the index; and Julie Reed double-checked many citations and proofread some of the text.

NOTES

1. John R. Mulder, "The Lyric Dimension of *Paradise Lost*," *Milton Studies* 23 (1987):145. Many readers of Milton scholarship would agree, I think, that it shows a remarkable amount of discipline, intelligence, and conviction; there seems to be little justification for complaints such as those lodged by Christopher Hill in *Milton and the English Revolution* (London: Faber and Faber, 1977; New York: Viking Press, 1978):

> . . . Milton needs to be defended from his defenders almost more than from the declining band of his enemies. There is the immensely productive Milton industry, largely in the United States of America, a great part of whose vast output appears to be concerned less with what Milton wrote (still less with enjoyment of what Milton wrote) than with the views of Professor Blank on the views of Professor Schrank on the views of Professor Rank on what Milton may or may not have written. Milton has been described as "the poet of scholars and academic critics" --no longer either a people's poet or a poet's poet. What a fate for the arch-enemy of academic pedantry: better dead than buried alive, surely! (P. 3)

In the same year and spirit, A. L. Rowse offered similar criticism twice in *Milton the Puritan: Portrait of a Mind* (London: Macmillan, 1977):

> There is an overweighty Milton industry as there is about Shakespeare, burying the man and his work beneath a mountain of dead academicism. The intelligent reader will hardly need to burden himself with this and can safely ignore most of it, in both cases. (P. 9)

> In this appalling egalitarian age, without sense of quality or distinction, without taste or savour, in which so much writing is characterless chaff, there is an inflationary Milton industry as there is a Shakespeare industry, neither of which illuminates the writer, but buries him under a mountain of commentary without significance. (P. 219)

2. Malcolm Mackenzie Ross, *Poetry and Dogma: The Transfiguration of Eucharistic Symbols in Seventeenth Century English Poetry* (New Brunswick, N.J.: Rutgers University Press, 1954), 206.

3. E. M. W. Tillyard, *Studies in Milton* (London: Chatto and Windus; New York: Macmillan, 1951), 137.

4. A. S. P. Woodhouse, "The Historical Criticism of Milton," *PMLA* 66 (1951):1042.

5. A. S. P. Woodhouse quoted in *John Milton, Poet and Humanist: Essays by James Holly Hanford*, foreword by John S. Diekhoff (Cleveland, Ohio: Press of Case Western Reserve University, 1966), vii.

General Studies

BACKGROUND

1   ARTHOS, JOHN. *Milton and the Italian Cities*. London: Bowes and Bowes; New York: Barnes and Noble, 1968, 235 pp. 10 illustrations.

Stifled by repression, the Florence that Milton visits sees most of its leading intellectual leaders drawn away to Rome, Venice, and Paris. Although Rome means a great deal to Milton, Naples more than any other Italian city propagates Galileo's ideas. Milton realizes, while in Naples, what he is going to make of himself. No records survive to indicate his acquaintances in Venice. *Samson Agonistes* is influenced by Italian musical drama, the *sacra rappresentazione* (such as Andreini's *L'Adamo*), and the developing *melodramma*. But the play has many parallels with Monteverdi's *favole in musica* and is most indebted to the type of drama that Buchanan establishes, which adapts the classical tragic form and biblical stories.

2   BARKER, ARTHUR E. *Milton and the Puritan Dilemma, 1641-1660*. University of Toronto Department of English Studies and Texts, no. 1. Toronto and Buffalo, N.Y.: University of Toronto Press, 1942, 464 pp. Frequently reprinted.

1

Background

Instead of being a digression from Milton's poetry, his prose records his development from the young Horton poet to become the great writer of his long poems. His anti-episcopal tracts consistently argue that divine law supersedes all human judgment in determining the form of church government and discipline. The definition of Christian liberty, which ultimately divides Milton from orthodox Puritanism and the Separatists, is at the heart of his prose. In the early 1640s, he is impressed by the consistent perversity, not the power, of human reason. But the theory of indifferency, which deals with matters about which divine authority is silent, requires the use of human conscience. Milton eventually joins the extremists against the Assembly and argues not only for freedom of conscience in things indifferent, but also for the right to determine what matters are indifferent. Beginning in 1644, with the appearance of *Areopagitica*, Milton shifts from emphasizing reason's depravity to emphasizing its potential. In *Areopagitica*, he pleads not for liberty in all things but for Christian liberty in indifferent things, while in *Tetrachordon*, he emphasizes personal liberty from all external authority. His final prose works--*Civil Power, Hirelings*, and *Christian Doctrine*--most clearly reveal the pattern that dominates his thinking about civil and theological matters for twenty years. The final civil and ecclesiastical pamphlets indicate what remains to be done for Christianity; *Christian Doctrine* shows that only the establishment of Christ's kingdom will bring about a utopia on earth. Adopting the Puritan extremist position, Milton abandons reformation in favor of liberty and individualism in religion.

3 BUSH, DOUGLAS. "Milton." In *The Renaissance and English Humanism*. Toronto: University of Toronto Press, 1939, pp. 101-34. Frequently reprinted.

The last great voice of the Christian humanist tradition that extends back to the middle ages, Milton is no longer an active force in poetry because his lofty themes seem remote and irrelevant. Christian humanism fades in his age, but Milton displays it in his youthful optimism and faith that he is about to enter a new era, his dedication to heroic poetry and the classical office of poet-priest, and his views on education and free choice. Pessimism appears near the end of *Paradise Lost* and grows extreme in *Samson Agonistes*. The conflicts inherent in Christian humanism are most apparent in *Paradise Regained*, when Christ denounces classical learning, and in *Paradise Lost*, when Adam learns that the pursuit of knowledge has limits.

Background

4   DIEKHOFF, JOHN S., ed. *Milton on Himself: Milton's Utterances upon Himself and His Works*. New York: Oxford University Press, 1939, 333 pp. Reprint. New York: Humanities Press, 1965; London: Cohen and West, 1966.

Diekhoff prints extracts from the prose and poetry in which Milton discusses such matters as a plan of life, love, and blindness.

5   FIXLER, MICHAEL. *Milton and the Kingdoms of God*. [Evanston, Ill.]: Northwestern University Press; London: Faber and Faber, 1964, 293 pp.

Setting unrealistic expectations for himself as Christian and as poet, Milton would have been satisfied only with "the apocalyptic fulfilment which at the close of his long period of celibacy and self-preparation loomed over the horizon" (47). Identifying himself with the revolutionary leadership, Milton in the antiprelatical tracts envisions the visible kingdom of Christ as a politically immutable society dominated by religion. Although recognizing that perfection would not be attained in human affairs, he believes in spiritual perfectibility (the creation of a national holy community) through the exercising of Christian liberty. He prefers a Christian humanistic republicanism distinct from political millenarianism. While Milton once believed that a just God would deal righteously with the English by vouchsafing them extraordinary grace, *Christian Doctrine*, emphasizing the second coming and individual regeneration, demonstrates his movement toward Arminianism. In *Paradise Lost* and *Paradise Regained*, Milton establishes an equivalence among three kingdoms--in heaven, on earth, and in man's soul--over which Satan covets dominion but over which the Son is king.

6   GAIR, W. REAVLEY. "Milton and Science." In *John Milton: Introductions*. Edited by John Broadbent. Cambridge: Cambridge University Press, 1973, pp. 120-44.

Living in an age that sees a transition from the old to the new science, Milton shares Bacon's dislike of scholasticism and his belief that studying the natural sciences can lead one to reassume the command over the creation that Adam lost when he fell. Milton, however, does not want science separated from religion, which places him in agreement with Sir Thomas Browne. Though Milton originally accepts determinism, in the 1640s he turns to a belief in free will, so he

3

Background

stands opposed to Hobbes's views. Milton believes in the four elements and humors, three souls and spirits, and both the Ptolemaic and the Copernican systems of astronomy. See entries 18, 212, 459, 476, 489, 512, 521, 579, 728.

7   HALLER, WILLIAM. "'Hail Wedded Love.'" *ELH* 13 (1946):79-97.
    Milton's quasi-religious, romantic attitude toward love and marriage shapes his attitude toward divorce. Love, according to his age, must lead to marriage, and love and marriage call to the soul as means of grace. Although men are viewed as superior to women, in marriage they are spiritual equals, and one's choice of a spouse is final. Milton's views on love and marriage are shaped primarily by preachers and reading, particularly the Bible and Spenser's *Faerie Queene*. If *Comus* advocates celibate chastity, it runs contrary to this training. The divorce tracts express Milton's ideals about marriage and its emphasis on spiritual satisfaction. He argues that, if the soul is not satisfied, divorce should be allowed.

8   HALLER, WILLIAM, and HALLER, MALLEVILLE. "The Puritan Art of Love." *Huntington Library Quarterly* 5 (1942):235-72.
    As the marriage of Adam and Eve in *Paradise Lost* reveals, Milton's knowledge of love comes from Scripture, the Puritan pulpit, and such writers as Plato, Xenophon, Ovid, Dante, Petrarch, and especially Spenser. Condemning the requirement of a celibate clergy, Puritan preachers are dedicated to the conjugal life, and they speak about how aspiring saints should act in marriage, one of the most important calls to the soul. Marriage, from the Puritan perspective, focuses on "the procreation of children, the relief of concupiscence, and the consolation of loneliness" (242). The family is a little church or state, in which all members have specific roles and in which woman is man's subordinate but makes equal claims to grace and salvation. Milton in his divorce tracts and *Paradise Lost* asserts the Puritan preachers' view, but he pursues its extreme implications, including an emphasis on marriage as spiritual consolation.

9   HILL, CHRISTOPHER. *Milton and the English Revolution*. London: Faber and Faber, 1977; New York: Viking Press, 1978, 559 pp.

Milton's character and work are shaped less by the church fathers and ancient poets than by contemporary radicals. Throughout his life, Milton engages in a dialogue with Levellers, Diggers, Ranters, and especially Muggletonians. He embraces some of their unorthodox positions, such as anti-clericalism, millenarianism, antinomianism, anti-Trinitarianism, mortalism, and materialism. A profoundly political animal, Milton connects *Paradise Lost*, *Paradise Regained*, and *Samson Agonistes* to the events of the English Revolution. The three major poems wrestle with the problems created by the failure of God's cause in England and by the failure of the millenium to arrive.

Appendixes: "The Date of Samson Agonistes"; "John and Edward Phillips"; "Nathan Paget and His Library."

10   HUGHES, MERRITT Y. "Milton as a Revolutionary." *ELH* 10 (1943):87-116. Reprinted in *Ten Perspectives on Milton* (New Haven, Conn., and London: Yale University Press, 1965), pp. 240-75.

We may be dissatisfied with Milton as a revolutionary because he believes the Puritan Revolution is a late, perhaps final stage in the Reformation, because he does not grant toleration to Catholics or atheists, or because the Arianism of *Christian Doctrine* distracts attention from his more startling heterodox views. Based on a respect for the individual's dignity, Milton's anti-episcopal tracts have a utopian element. The Puritan Revolution's conception of liberty is based on right reason. In *Paradise Lost*, the Son is politically significant as an effective leader, which is what all parliaments must have. Moderns have difficulty accepting the aristocratic nature of Milton's political thinking. From his perspective, however, it is an aristocracy based not on birth but on talent.

11   LEAVIS, F. R. "In Defence of Milton." *Scrutiny* 7 (1938):104-14. Reprinted in *The Common Pursuit* (London: Chatto and Windus, 1952), pp. 33-43; frequently reprinted.

Tillyard (see entry 216) produces a Milton of his own, a man of no greatness who is concerned with being up to date. This portrait robs the English tradition of a unique heroic figure, a lonely figure who remains aloof and self-sufficient. The medium that Milton invents denies itself the vitality of the living language. See entry 117.

Background

12   MacCALLUM, H. R. "Milton and Figurative Interpretation of the Bible." *University of Toronto Quarterly* 31 (1962):397-415.

        Agreeing with Calvin and Luther that the life-giving Spirit of 2 Corinthians 3:6 should be conceived in terms of grace, Milton abandons much of the ancient tradition of polysemous figurative interpretation of the Bible. He believes in the doctrine of compound sense but is suspicious of metaphor and the symbolic use of images. His theory of accommodation focuses on the Bible itself and defines the boundaries of human comprehension: we must accept what we cannot understand. Even the Son does not bridge human understanding and the divine nature. Milton distinguishes among types, examples, and prophecy; he usually identifies typology explicitly by scriptural authority. He opposes Renaissance Neoplatonism's conception of symbolism as the mark of the poetic office and of multiple-sense interpretations of the Bible. See entries 25, 166, 176, 956.

13   MAJOR, JOHN M. "Milton's View of Rhetoric." *Studies in Philology* 64 (1967):685-711.

        Though he masters its rules, Milton always distrusts rhetoric. He agrees with two key views of rhetoric: Cicero's argument that a skilled orator must use his power for good ends and must be a good man; and Isocrates's belief that a rhetorical education should "train able, intelligent statesmen, rulers, and counselors of rulers" (690). Eloquence, Milton says, promotes and is nurtured by liberty. Although his prose is not polished, his poems present carefully constructed debates between smooth, sophistical rhetoricians (Comus, Satan, Eve, and Dalila, for example) and characters who argue from reason and with true eloquence (the Lady, Christ, Adam, Samson). Milton's antagonism to rhetoric may come from his Platonism, his reading of Augustine, and contemporary attitudes toward it.

14   MARTIN, JOHN RUPERT. *The Portrait of John Milton at Princeton and Its Place in Milton Iconography.* Princeton, N.J.: Princeton University Press, 1961, 40 pp. 25 illustrations.

        Four portraits of Milton, made during his lifetime, are of great significance: the portrait of him at the age of ten, by an unknown artist; the Onslow portrait of Milton at twenty-one; the inept Marshall engraving for the 1645 volume of *Poems*, representing Milton at the age of about thirty-seven; and the Faithorne engraving of Milton from 1670, which is the most important because of the artist's competence and its appearance in print during Milton's lifetime. The Faithorne engraving, which others frequently imitated, has some claim to being Milton's "official image" (8). Formerly known as the Baker or Bayfordbury portrait, the crayon drawing at Princeton was identified by Milton's daughter, Deborah Clarke, as being a true likeness of her father. The Princeton portrait may be by Faithorne, who may have based it on the same preparatory study that produced his 1670 engraving or, more likely, who may have made the crayon drawing from life and revised it to produce the 1670 engraving. See entries 17, 26, 156.

15   MAYNARD, WINIFRED. "Milton and Music." In *John Milton: Introductions*. Edited by John Broadbent. Cambridge: Cambridge University Press, 1973, pp. 226-57.

As he grows up, Milton has music all around him, though it is regarded as a social accomplishment rather than an academic subject. But his father takes music seriously and finds a good pupil in his son. Besides learning about music at home and during his Italian journey, Milton studies the inaudible music of the spheres. Song and harmony are very important in *Paradise Lost*, especially in Eden and heaven. Some eighteenth-century musical arrangements draw on *Comus*, *L'Allegro*, and *Paradise Lost*. See entries 22, 142, 290, 321, 337, 370, 430, 861.

16   MILLER, LEO. *John Milton among the Polygamophiles*. New York: Loewenthal Press, 1974, 390 pp.

Although Milton makes notes about polygamy before he marries Mary Powell, his thoughts become clear after she deserts him. Old Testament patriarchs are polygamous, as he points out in his *Commonplace Book* and *Christian Doctrine*, and neither Testament condemns plural marriage. Milton's is not an idiosyncratic view in Renaissance Europe: prominent people, theologians, and legal authorities define the issue as he does, consider similar proposals, and fail to resolve the matter. Because divorce doctrine and polygamy doctrine are commonly linked in Milton's age, his reputation as a divorcer leads to his association in print with polygamophiles.

Background

17   MILLER, LEO. *Milton's Portraits: An "Impartial" Inquiry into Their Authentication*. Special issue of *Milton Quarterly*. Athens: Ohio University, 1976, 43 pp. 6 illustrations.

The Onslow portrait ("At age 21") and members of its group are authentic representations of Milton as a Cambridge scholar. If one is not satisfied with this view, another hypothesis is possible: Elizabeth Minshull Milton owned a genuine portrait of Milton as a Cambridge student, along with the painted coat of arms of his forbears, but the location of these items--if they are extant--is unknown. See entries 14, 26, 156.

18   NICOLSON, MARJORIE. "Milton and the Telescope." *ELH* 2 (1935):1-32. Reprinted in *Critical Essays on Milton from "ELH"* (Baltimore, Md., and London: Johns Hopkins Press, 1969), pp. 15-45.

Milton's imagination is stimulated not just by books about the new astronomy, but especially by the actual experience of telescopic observation. The astronomy of his early poems is old, derived from Aristotle and the classics. Although Milton meets Galileo, we need not think that the Italian's telescope is the first to make the poet aware of new realms of vision. Milton's sense of cosmic distance and perspective, through which he expands space in his verse, is the result of the telescope. See entries 6, 212, 459, 476, 489, 512, 521, 579, 728.

19   POWELL, CHILTON L. "Milton Agonistes." *Sewanee Review* 34 (1926):169-83.

Milton's readers today see a liberalism and modernism in his work, but the foundation of his beliefs, indeed the most important reason why we may call him a Puritan, is always the binding covenant between God and man. He judges all things--including divorce, truth, human action, and the monarchy--according to how they conform to the covenant's contractual terms. If liberalism means individualism, Milton's belief in the contract between God and man denies individualism, asserts a disciplined mutual relationship, and defines a particular kind of conservatism.

20 SAMUEL, IRENE. *Plato and Milton*. Cornell Studies in English, vol. 35. Ithaca, N.Y.: Cornell University Press, 1947, 192 pp. Reprint. 1965.

The Platonic dialogues and work of Xenophon, particularly their assertions of the Socratic doctrine of love, influence Milton after 1637 (at the latest), when Platonism first pervades his thought. Before 1637, he shows enthusiasm for Platonism but no serious independent study of it. Milton pays almost no attention to the pagan Neoplatonists, but he and his contemporary Cambridge Platonists share many interests, particularly concerning writers who first tried to reconcile Plato and the Bible. Like Plato, Milton in *Reason of Church-Government* emphasizes poetry's ethical and educational nature, while criticizing its abuses. In his prose, he often notes his debts to Plato; in the three major poems, he absorbs Plato's ethics. But Plato's highest good is ethical knowledge, while Milton's is the vision of the truth. When Milton uses the word "Idea," he associates it with Plato's usage--a pattern in the human or divine creative mind that shapes things in our world. By substituting love for knowledge as the foundation of happiness, Milton eventually transcends Platonic thought.

21 SIMS, JAMES H. "Milton, Literature as a Bible, and the Bible as Literature." In *Milton and the Art of Sacred Song*. Edited by J. Max Patrick and Roger H. Sundell. Madison and London: University of Wisconsin Press, 1979, pp. 3-21.

Literature, defined as all branches of knowledge presented in the reading program in *Of Education*, is for Milton a secular Bible, which--however incomplete and misleading--can be beneficial. Because everything in the Bible is not good, the best knowledge comes from a reciprocal relationship between sacred and pagan literature. The Renaissance argument in favor of divine poetry gains strength as more people accept the assumption that all great art is in some sense inspired.

22 SPAETH, SIGMUND GOTTFRIED. *Milton's Knowledge of Music: Its Sources and Its Significance in His Works*. Princeton, N.J.: The University Library, 1913, 192 pp.

A native English school and golden age of music begin under Henry VIII, a formal style emerges under Elizabeth, and Milton's age inherits a valuable musical tradition, which develops into polyphony and

Background

a monodic style. John Milton, Senior, who ranks with the better composers of his time, raises his son in a musical atmosphere. Milton's substantial musical education continues at St. Paul's and Cambridge, as well as during his Italian journey. While Milton refers to a number of musical instruments in his writings and plays some, the organ is his favorite. A mystical faith is at the heart of Milton's theory of music. See entries 15, 142, 290, 321, 337, 370, 430, 861.

23   SUMMERS, JOSEPH H. "Milton and the Cult of Conformity." *Yale Review* 46 (1957):511-27. Reprinted in *Milton: Modern Judgements*, ed. Alan Rudrum (London: Macmillan, 1968), pp. 29-43.

Anyone who attempts to label Milton's personality and thought ends up with a series of paradoxes; any member of a religious, nationalistic, or ideological group who embraces Milton soon discovers that his views offer little comfort. Yet his works reveal a singleness of purpose: to further the cause of liberty. In order to be a heroic poet, he must live a heroic life, though he recognizes that this will be difficult in a decadent age. But even a heroic life is not sufficient, for a heroic poet requires but cannot will inspiration from God. With a revolution taking shape, Milton cannot exile himself to write poetry; he turns to prose to voice his arguments for liberty. When in 1660 the English people choose to be slaves, Milton regains his artistic freedom. *Paradise Lost*, *Paradise Regained*, and *Samson Agonistes* include trials that require heroic action.

24   WILDING, MICHAEL. "Regaining the Radical Milton." In *The Radical Reader*. Edited by Stephen Knight and Michael Wilding. Sydney: Wild and Woolley, 1977, pp. 119-43.

In the 1930s and 1940s, some critics take the seemingly radical position of attacking Milton's verse, a stance that turns into the orthodox view of the 1950s when young, radical readers see Milton as oppressive, orthodox, and traditional. We now recognize that the attackers are formalists and conservatives, even reactionaries, but their opponents defend Milton "from a standpoint of chilling boredom and conservatism" (120). With the American escalation of the Vietnam War, readers find that the New Criticism is not a value-free method to study the poem itself but a method that apprehends only technique, while omitting all of the troubling meanings of a literary work. Now we can rediscover Milton the radical who actually writes about something:

the execution of a king, the Commonwealth, divorce, censorship. As *Paradise Regained* demonstrates, Milton is a pacifist.

25   WILLEY, BASIL. "Milton and Scriptural Interpretation" and "The Heroic Poem in a Scientific Age: Milton." In *The Seventeenth Century Background: Studies in the Thought of the Age in Relation to Poetry and Religion*. London: Chatto and Windus, 1934, pp. 75-82, 219-62. Frequently reprinted; part reprinted in *Milton: "Paradise Lost," a Casebook*, ed. A. E. Dyson and Julian Lovelock (London and Basingstoke: Macmillan, 1973), pp. 73-76.

Milton believes that Scripture often reveals truth figuratively and never acts as an obstacle to anything he seeks. Freeing himself from the authority of tradition, he--like most seventeenth-century Protestants--interprets the Bible according to an inner, individual principle. He is a rationalist. See entries 12, 166, 176, 956.

In an age of scientific enlightenment, a heroic poem claims great authority because it aims for a form of truth, moral instruction. Because God chooses to be a poet in the Bible, scriptural poetry as prophecy is the perfect vehicle for Milton to convey truth. In his handling of the fall in *Paradise Lost*, Milton encounters the contemporary conflict between conceptual and visual thinking. But he cannot believe that a person in any state should avoid the pursuit of moral knowledge. The real fall is not the indifferent act of eating the apple, which Milton rationalizes as disobedience, but the act of obscuring reason and losing liberty through passion.

26   WILLIAMSON, G. C. *The Portraits, Prints and Writings of John Milton*. Cambridge: Cambridge University Press, 1908, 175 pp. 28 illustrations. Reprint. New York: Burt Franklin, 1968.

Two authentic portraits of Milton are extant (by Cornelius Janssen and by William Faithorne), along with the copy of a third (the Onslow portrait, copied by Benjamin Van der Gucht). The Woodcock portrait should now be added to the list of authentic portraits of Milton. See entries 14, 17, 156.

Williamson catalogues statuary work, miniatures, portraits, drawings, and engravings of Milton; manuscripts; and early editions.

Background

27 WOLFE, DON M. *Milton in the Puritan Revolution*. New York and
London: Thomas Nelson and Sons, 1941, 510 pp. Reprint. New
York: Humanities Press; London: Cohen and West, 1963.
    Radicals see that, under the Stuarts, the quest for religious
liberty is closely linked to opposition to the monarchy. Milton is slow to
make this connection: his antiprelatical tracts argue against the bishops
because they weaken the monarchy; later, his attacks join prelacy with
King Charles. With *Areopagitica*, Milton's thinking moves dramatically
toward contemporary radicalism. Rejecting Presbyterianism, he
becomes an Independent, though this group would have disapproved of
his views on divorce, polygamy, mortalism, and anti-Trinitarianism. No
sect agrees with all of Milton's thoughts. The strongest, most consistent
element in Milton's personality is his arguing from first principles,
especially the individual conscience. Although he was a constitutional
monarchist, after the start of the Civil Wars, his comments on kings
grow more negative. He believes that a leader should rule by virtue of
superior integrity and wisdom. In *Paradise Lost*, heaven's government is
consistent with Milton's Commonwealth principles.
    Appendixes: "Light for the Benighted: Comenius and Milton";
"William Walwyn, *A Still and Soft Voice* [1647]"; "Gerrard Winstanley,
A Watch-Word to the City of London [1649]"; "Lilburne, Overton, and
Prince, *The Second Part of Englands New-Chaines Discovered* [1649]";
"John Saltmarsh, *Shadows Flying Away* [1646]."

28 WOLFE, DON M. "Milton's Conception of the Ruler." *Studies in
Philology* 33 (1936):253-72.
    Throughout his life, Milton believes in the idea of a leader who
holds his position only through his superior integrity. This perception is
behind not only his rejection of Charles and acceptance of Cromwell,
but also the governments of heaven and hell in *Paradise Lost*. A royalist
until the age of thirty-four, Milton is silent on the subject for seven
years, when he argues that a constitutional monarchy is acceptable, that
power resides in the people, and then that the monarchy itself is not a
good idea. Charles's execution is legal, Milton states, because it
represents the will of the people. For a while, Milton supports
Cromwell, even at his most tyrannical, as an agent of God who will
bring freedom of speech and conscience. Since free men can govern
themselves and others, any form of single-person rule, including
Cromwell's, is unnecessary.

29 WOODHOUSE, A. S. P. "Milton, Puritanism, and Liberty." *University of Toronto Quarterly* 4 (1935):483-513.

Christian liberty, according to the orthodox view, frees humans from the condemnation of the Mosaic Law and elevates them to a position as Christ's heirs through faith in him. People who live in Christian liberty voluntarily obey the higher service of God's will. As a basis for revolution, Puritans emphasize revolutionary aspects of the doctrine. Milton believes in the radical idea that the Gospel abrogates the entire Mosaic Law but not the fundamental moral law. Where Roger Williams uses Christian liberty to lead to democracy and the separation of church and state, Milton believes in the latter but stops at individualism. Interested exclusively in the regenerate, Milton wants the state's positive laws reduced to a minimum. He does not believe in equality for all, since--according to the aristocratic principle in Puritanism--only the regenerate possess Christian liberty, which he sees in ethical rather than spiritual terms.

EDITIONS

30 BROOKS, CLEANTH, and HARDY, JOHN EDWARD, eds. *Poems of Mr. John Milton. The 1645 Edition with Essays in Analysis.* New York: Harcourt, Brace & Co., 1951, 375 pp.

In *Nativity Ode*, Milton maintains aesthetic distance by using a stanza form and by presenting a cosmic sweep. "Passion" fails because of the poet's self-consciousness. If the "Mountain Nymph sweet Liberty" presides over *L'Allegro* and the cherub Contemplation presides over *Il Penseroso*, these characters tend to merge into the same figure; the poems' use of light imagery also ties together the opposites. In *Lycidas*, when Milton hints that the muse cannot save her followers, he questions the efficacy of the tears of grief. Rather than providing an allegorical exposition of a philosophical doctrine, *Comus* emphasizes virtue and grace. The young Milton feels the influence of the sixteenth-century Ovidian poets, the seventeenth-century Spenserians, and the metaphysicals, yet he finds none completely satisfying. See entry 361.

Appendixes: "A Note on Reading the Longer Poems"; Shorter Poems Not Found in the 1645 Edition; "Glossary."

Editions

31 BUSH, DOUGLAS, ed. *The Complete Poetical Works of John Milton*. Boston, Mass.: Houghton Mifflin, 1965, 604 pp. 6 illustrations.

Bush modernizes spelling and punctuation, translates poems in foreign languages (and provides the originals), and gives brief but thorough annotations.

32 CAREY, JOHN, and FOWLER, ALASTAIR, eds. *The Poems of John Milton*. London and Harlow: Longmans, 1968, 1203 pp.

This is the most fully annotated edition of Milton's complete poems. Carey provides translations of Milton's poems in foreign languages. In this edition, spelling is modernized but punctuation is not.

33 FLETCHER, HARRIS FRANCIS, ed. *John Milton's Complete Poetical Works*. 4 vols. Urbana: University of Illinois Press, 1943-48, 1870 pp. Photographic facsimile.

With the facsimiles, Fletcher presents thorough discussions of the printing history of Milton's poems, especially the three long ones.

Vol. 1: *Poems* (1673), *Poems* (1645), *A Mask* (1637 and manuscripts), *Lycidas* (1638), *Epitaphium Damonis* (ca. 1640), Poems Printed by Others, Verses from the Prose Works, the Trinity College Manuscript, Manuscript of *Ad Joannem Rousium*.

Vol. 2: *Paradise Lost* (1667).

Vol. 3: *Paradise Lost* (1674).

Vol. 4: *Paradise Regained* and *Samson Agonistes* (1671).

34 HUGHES, MERRITT Y., ed. *John Milton: Complete Poems and Major Prose*. Indianapolis, Ind., and New York: Odyssey Press (Bobbs-Merrill), 1957, 1078 pp. Frequently reprinted.

Hughes's edition provides useful introductions for almost every work (they are especially thorough for the three major poems), modernized spelling and punctuation with the retention of Milton's "most conspicuous seventeenth century typographical peculiarities" (vii), references to selected critical studies, complete but brief annotations, translations of Milton's work in foreign languages (with the original, if it is poetry), and an appendix that reprints "Some Early Lives of Milton" (by John Aubrey, Edward Phillips, and the Anonymous Biographer).

35   HUGHES, MERRITT Y., gen. ed. *A Variorum Commentary on the Poems of John Milton*. 3 vols. in 5 to date (6 vols. projected). New York: Columbia University Press, 1970-75, 400; 1082; 503 pp.
        The *Variorum*, keyed to the Columbia edition (see entry 39), summarizes previous interpretations of Milton's poetry.

        Vol. 1 : The Latin and Greek Poems (Douglas Bush); The Italian Poems (J. E. Shaw and A. Bartlett Giamatti).

        Vol. 2 : Parts 1-3: The Minor English Poems (A. S. P. Woodhouse and Douglas Bush).

        Vol. 4 : *Paradise Regained* (Walter MacKellar); With a Review of Studies of Style and Verse Form (Edward R. Weismiller).

36   PATRICK, J. MAX, gen. ed. *The Prose of John Milton*. Garden City, N.Y.: Anchor Books, Doubleday, 1967, 710 pp.
        Patrick's edition of selected prose works by Milton uses old spelling and provides full annotations.

37   PATRIDES, C. A., ed. *John Milton: Selected Prose*. Rev. ed. Columbia: University of Missouri Press, 1985, 463 pp.
        Based on the Columbia edition's old-spelling text (see entry 39), Patrides's edition is divided into three sections: Milton on Milton; The Major Premises; and Extracts, Mainly on Literature. Patrides includes John Aubrey's and Edward Phillips's biographies of Milton, as well as a selective bibliography of studies of Milton's prose.

38   PATTERSON, FRANK ALLEN, ed. *The Student's Milton*. Rev. ed. New York: Appleton-Century-Crofts, 1933, 1338 pp.
        Patterson includes Milton's complete poems (with translations of those in foreign languages, along with the originals), a large selection

15

Editions

of prose, textual notes, glossary, and explanatory notes. The original spelling and punctuation of the poems are preserved, but the prose is modernized. Patterson's revised edition includes some early biographies of Milton (such as those by Edward Phillips and the Anonymous Biographer), *Prolusions*, and *Letter to a Friend*.

39 PATTERSON, FRANK ALLEN, gen. ed. *The Works of John Milton*. 18 vols. in 21. New York: Columbia University Press, 1931-38, 620; 556; 594; 377; 361; 380; 594; 273; 315; 396; 551; 426; 660; 410; 417; 389; 595; 577 pp.

Patterson's edition provides an old-spelling text, translations of Milton's writings in foreign languages (with the originals), and textual notes. The *Index* to the Columbia edition (2 vols; New York: Columbia University Press, 1940, 2167 pp.), by Patterson and French Rowe Fogle, indexes explicit references and allusions to proper names, biblical passages, and subjects.

Vol. 1: Part 1: Minor Poems. Part 2: *Samson Agonistes*.

Vol. 2: Part 1: *Paradise Lost*, Books 1-8. Part 2: *Paradise Lost*, Books 9-12, *Paradise Regained*.

Vol. 3: Part 1: *Of Reformation, Of Prelaticall Episcopacy, Animadversions, Reason of Church-Government, Apology against a Pamphlet*. Part 2: *Doctrine and Discipline of Divorce*.

Vol. 4: *The Judgement of Martin Bucer, Tetrachordon, Colasterion, Of Education, Areopagitica*.

Vol. 5: *Tenure of Kings and Magistrates, Eikonoklastes*.

Vol. 6: *A Treatise of Civil Power, Considerations Touching the Likeliest Means to Remove Hirelings, A Letter to a Friend, The Present Means, and Brief Delineation, The Readie & Easie Way, Brief Notes upon a Late Sermon, Of True Religion, Observations on the Articles of Peace, A Declaration or Letters Patents*.

Vol. 7: *Pro Populo Anglicano Defensio*.

Vol. 8: *Pro Populo Anglicano Defensio Secunda*.

Editions

Vol. 9: *Pro Se Defensio*.

Vol. 10: *The History of Britain, A Brief History of Moscovia*.

Vol. 11: *Artis Logicae*.

Vol. 12: Familiar Letters, *Prolusions*, An Early *Prolusion* and Miscellaneous Correspondence in Foreign Tongues, English Correspondence.

Vol. 13: *State Papers*.

Vol. 14: *De Doctrina Christiana*, Book 1, Chapters 1-6.

Vol. 15: *De Doctrina Christiana*, Book 1, Chapters 7-20.

Vol. 16: *De Doctrina Christiana*, Book 1, Chapters 21-33.

Vol. 17: *De Doctrina Christiana*, Book 2.

Vol. 18: Uncollected Writings (including Additional State Papers, *Commonplace Book, Character of the Long Parliament*, Additional Correspondence, Marginalia, and Legal Documents).

40   SHAWCROSS, JOHN T., ed. *The Complete English Poetry of John Milton (Excluding His Translations of Psalms 80-88)*. Garden City, N.Y.: Doubleday, 1963, 591 pp.
      Shawcross retains the original spelling and punctuation, translates Milton's poems in foreign languages (but omits the originals), and provides annotations and textual notes.

41   TILLYARD, PHYLLIS B., trans., and TILLYARD, E. M. W. *Milton: Private Correspondence and Academic Exercises*. Cambridge: Cambridge University Press, 1932, 183 pp.
      This edition includes thirty-one of Milton's letters and seven academic exercises.
      Milton's private correspondence seems overly rhetorical and formal because he conceived of the Latin letter as a set form of writing.

Editions

Prolusions enrich our understanding of life at Cambridge University from 1625 to 1632.

42 WOLFE, DON M., gen. ed. *Complete Prose Works of John Milton*. 8 vols. in 10. New Haven, Conn., and London: Yale University Press, 1953-82, 1089; 852; 664; 1782; 1445; 887; 560; 640 pp.
The Yale *Complete Prose Works* provides extensive introductions, thorough annotations, old-spelling texts (though only translations, not Milton's Latin originals, are included), and doubtful works.

Vol. 1 (1624-42): Edited by Don M. Wolfe. *Prolusions*, Private Correspondence, *Commonplace Book*, *Of Reformation*, *Of Prelatical Episcopacy*, *Animadversions*, *Reason of Church-Government*, *An Apology against a Pamphlet*.

Vol. 2 (1643-48): Edited by Ernest Sirluck. *Doctrine and Discipline of Divorce*, *Of Education*, *The Judgement of Martin Bucer*, *Areopagitica*, *Tetrachordon*, *Colasterion*, Private Correspondence.

Vol. 3 (1648-49): Edited by Merritt Y. Hughes. *The Tenure of Kings and Magistrates*, *Observations upon the Articles of Peace*, *Eikonoklastes*.

Vol. 4 (1650-55): Edited by Don M. Wolfe. Part 1: *A Defence of the People of England, A Second Defence of the English People*. Part 2: *Pro Se Defensio*, Milton's Private Correspondence.

Vol. 5 (1648?-71): Edited by French Fogle. Part 1: *History of Britain*, The Digression, *Character of the Long Parliament*.

Vol. 5 (1649-59): Edited by French Fogle. Part 2: *The Miltonic State Papers*.

Vol. 6 (ca. 1658-ca. 1660): Edited by Maurice Kelley. *The Christian Doctrine*.

Vol. 7 (1659-60): Rev. ed., edited by Robert W. Ayers. *A Treatise of Civil Power, Considerations Touching the Likeliest Means to Remove Hirelings, A Letter to a Friend, Proposalls of Certaine*

Biographies

Expedients, The Readie & Easie Way (1st ed.), *The Present Means and Brief Delineation of a Free Commonwealth, The Readie and Easie Way* (2d ed.), *Brief Notes upon a Late Sermon*, Private Correspondence.

Vol. 8 (1666-82): Edited by Maurice Kelley. Private Correspondence, Prose Accompanying *Paradise Lost* (1668 and 1674), *Accedence Commenc't Grammar*, Prose Preliminary to *Samson Agonistes, The Art of Logic, Of True Religion, A Declaration, or Letters Patents, A Brief History of Moscovia*.

See also entries 73-77, 115, 172, 304, 359-60, 396-97, 436, 571, 926.

BIOGRAPHIES

43   BAILEY, JOHN. *Milton*. The Home University Library of Modern Knowledge, vol. 103. London: Oxford University Press; London: Williams and Norgate, 1915, 256 pp. Frequently reprinted.

Milton's sublimity comes from a will determined to achieve great deeds, one that also produces a disagreeable personality. Milton profits from his undergraduate education at Cambridge, where he is highly regarded. During the Civil Wars, his prose cannot contain the hatred he feels for his political opponents. Although his divorce tracts are scorned, his defense of regicide makes him, along with Cromwell, England's greatest celebrity for foreign visitors. Milton's 1645 volume of *Poems* assures him of a rank among England's six finest poets. When he justifies God's ways in *Paradise Lost*, his argument is consistently literal and legalistic. *Paradise Regained* contains fine speeches that are not dramatically convincing. Critics admire *Paradise Regained* only because Milton sets himself a difficult task when he chooses its subject. Unlike *Paradise Regained, Samson Agonistes* is a very emotional work.

44   BELLOC, HILAIRE. *Milton*. Philadelphia, Pa., and London: J. B. Lippincott Co., 1935, 313 pp.

Milton's life falls into three distinct periods: lyric until the age of thirty-four; polemic between thirty-four and fifty-two; and epic thereafter. Egotism and excessive seriousness possess him, but his virtues include industriousness and tenacity. As *Comus* reveals, he is a Puritan who shares that group's "nervous terror bred by excess of

Biographies

sensual enjoyment" (110). The divorce tracts show his grievances against women, whom he regards as having an atrocious nature; Mary Powell turns him into a subject for mockery. *Areopagitica* is generally turgid, dull, and confused about which subjects should enjoy a free press and to what degree. *Paradise Lost* is a magnificent work flawed by terrestrial descriptions of spiritual creatures and settings, and by excessive displays of learning. *Paradise Regained*, a truly bad poem, is merely a foil to *Paradise Lost*, but *Samson Agonistes* stands as "the strongest monument to Milton's genius" (271). Probably written in the 1640s, *Christian Doctrine* reveals Milton's authentic convictions, which are unorthodox.

45　BROWN, ELEANOR GERTRUDE. *Milton's Blindness*. Columbia University Studies in English and Comparative Literature. New York: Columbia University Press; London: Milford, 1934, 168 pp. Reprint. New York: Octagon Books, 1968.

　　　　We lack sufficient evidence to draw final conclusions about the cause of Milton's blindness. Contemporaries and later writers put forward a number of theories, some relevant and some fantastic; for example, it is a judgment from God; a drop of King Charles's blood quenches the poet's eyesight; Milton is an albino. Contrary to what others argue, Milton does not have syphilis. His blindness is probably caused by glaucoma or myopia and detachment of the retina. He often refers to his blindness in his poetry and prose, where he sounds a note of sacrifice without regret. *Samson Agonistes* is not autobiographical. Even after he becomes blind, Milton continues to stay active and to study.

46　BUSH, DOUGLAS. *John Milton: A Sketch of His Life and Writings*. Masters of World Literature. New York: Macmillan; London: Collier-Macmillan, 1964, 224 pp. Reprint. New York: Collier Books, 1967.

　　　　Milton's early poems (before *Lycidas*) are characterized by idealism and susceptibility to beauty. The inexplicable death of Edward King tests Milton's idealism and faith for the first time. Attaining order through struggle is a dominant theme in *Lycidas* and in the long poems. The Italian journey fortifies his confidence in himself and his career. When he writes his prose in his thirties, Milton conducts his education in public, embracing antiprelacy only to reject Presbyterianism within a few years. With the Restoration, he feels a sense of defeat that he answers by summoning up the heroic past and ignoble present in his long poems. *Paradise Lost*'s subject is the war between good and evil in man's soul; though it contains a tragic vision of human experience, its total scheme, ending with some hope, is that of a divine comedy. A cold poem only to cold readers, *Paradise Regained* shows Milton in his old age relying more and more on humble faith. *Samson Agonistes* is experimental in form and style.

47 CAREY, JOHN. *Milton*. London: Evans, 1969, 154 pp. Reprint. New York: Arco, 1970.
        Milton feels insecure among common young men, but he craves their approval. His two opposed dreams, to be a secluded scholar with spiritual peace or to be a famous man with the praise of heaven and the public, contribute to the tension of his thought. The Italian journey gives him a new self-confidence. Although *Comus*'s original audience no doubt approves of what they see, the masque questions their complacency. The classical air of *Lycidas* stifles authentic grief, and the poem's various movements guarantee a split in structure. Milton's prose represents his attempt to win liberty for himself, for he has a low opinion of those who are not like him. *Paradise Lost* "bristles so irresistibly with questions because by its own moral standards it is a failure" (122). *Paradise Regained* is an anti-epic with an anti-hero and rejections rather than temptations. Instead of portraying the protagonist's gradual regeneration, *Samson Agonistes* shows the changing circumstances that allow his building resentment to lash out. In general, Milton is preoccupied with "Sage and Hero" and his poetry is about "Good Conduct" (147).

48 CLARK, DONALD LEMEN. *John Milton at St. Paul's School: A Study of Ancient Rhetoric in English Renaissance Education*. New York: Columbia University Press, 1948, 279 pp. Reprint. Hamden, Conn.: Shoe String Press, 1964.
        Renaissance instruction in rhetoric aims to train the whole man for public affairs as an orator-statesman. In grammar school, Milton learns to read, speak, and write Latin poetry and prose; to read and write Greek poetry and prose; and to read Hebrew. At home, tutors must have trained him in French and Italian. Milton's late

Biographies

entrance into Cambridge may be attributed to a heavy load of
extracurricular work assigned by tutors, devotion of time to writing
poetry, ill health, and eye problems. The ideal school that he describes
in *Of Education*, though notably unlike Cambridge, is very similar to St.
Paul's, but Milton recommends reading the ancients before practicing
exercises in Latin themes. His curriculum also differs from St. Paul's by
emphasizing such subjects as agriculture, arithmetic, geometry, and
natural philosophy.

49   DAICHES, DAVID. *Milton*. London: Hutchinson University
     Library, 1957, 254 pp.
         Starting in his youth, Milton prepares to be a great writer who
will combine the roles of poet and prophet. Although he begins his
career by separating classical and Christian elements, he soon mixes
them, as in *Nativity Ode*. He turns away from entering the church
because of his dissatisfaction with the clergy and his developing poetic
ambitions. Not concerned simply with King or Milton, *Lycidas*'s
subjects are man as creator, fame, and mortality. In *Paradise Lost*,
Milton shows some of the main paradoxes of the human situation and
"the tragic ambiguity of man as a moral being" (145). The poem's moral
pattern is concerned with our world, and *Paradise Lost* is weak only
when the argument, imagery, or narrative detail is too specific. *Paradise
Regained* is a necessary sequel because Milton has to show another
Adam's facing and resisting temptation. He reconciles his humanism
and Christianity by writing *Samson Agonistes*, a Greek tragedy with the
biblical theme of Samson's recovery process.

50   DARBISHIRE, HELEN, ed. *The Early Lives of Milton*. London:
     Constable & Co., 1932, 414 pp. 6 illustrations.
         Some of Milton's early biographers know him, many derive
their information from credible sources, and all have a living sense of
his personality. They portray him as a cultured, friendly, and generous
man who loves music and intelligent conversation. The Anonymous
Biographer is John Phillips.
         Darbishire prints the biography of Milton in Anthony Wood's
Fasti Oxonienses (1691) and the biographies by John Aubrey (1681),
John Phillips, Edward Phillips (1694), John Toland (1698), and
Jonathan Richardson (1734).

51 DAVIES, GODFREY. "Milton in 1660." *Huntington Library Quarterly* 18 (1955):351-63.

During the second half of 1660, Milton must have worried about whether he would be executed for his part in the revolution. The Act of Oblivion is approved on 19 August, pardoning almost all treasons and offenses of the Civil Wars. Because the Act does not name Milton as an exception, he is pardoned. With the return of Charles's court, Milton goes into hiding, which suggests that he and his friends believe he is in danger. On 16 June, the House of Commons requests that Charles issue a proclamation to recall John Goodwin's *Obstructors of Justice* and Milton's *First Defence* and *Eikonoklastes*, and that he indict their authors. Goodwin is one of the twenty men excluded from the pardon, yet when Milton's name is raised to be the final person excluded, no one supports the motion, though his misdeeds are greater than Goodwin's. Milton's friends conspire to remain silent. Milton is arrested, probably in August, and released in mid-December. His friends may have agreed that he should submit to the disgrace of the 16 June recall proclamation, but that he suffer no other punishment.

52 EMERSON, EVERETT H. "A Note on Milton's Early Puritanism." In *Essays in Honor of Esmond Linworth Marilla*. Edited by Thomas Austin Kirby and William John Olive. Louisiana State University Studies, Humanities Series, no. 19. Baton Rouge: Louisiana State University Press, 1970, pp. 127-34.

Though the word "Puritan" is used in many ways between 1550 and 1650, Milton in the 1640s identifies himself with the Smectymnuans, the Presbyterians who lead the Puritan attack on episcopacy. Milton's antiprelatical tracts endorse part of the current Puritan agenda (attacking prelatical episcopacy), but he also opposes the royalists' social, economic, and political practices. In the 1630s and 1640s, Puritanism deals with both religious and secular reform. After 1642, Milton's thinking develops more rapidly than do the political and social orders to which he belongs.

53 FLETCHER, HARRIS FRANCIS. *The Intellectual Development of John Milton*. 2 vols. Urbana: University of Illinois Press, 1956-61, 475 pp. (15 illustrations); 697 pp. (9 illustrations).

A mixture of two educational traditions--one to raise a future prince, the other to raise a future scholar--characterizes Milton's school

Biographies

and university careers, as well as the context for *Of Education*. He receives extensive training in languages, music, mathematics, and astronomy, and maintains an interest in them throughout his life. Such recreational activities as dancing, fencing, and horse riding probably occupy the young Milton. At Cambridge, he studies such subjects as logic, ethics, metaphysics and theology, and rhetoric. He decides to become a poet, not a clergyman or lawyer, as early as 1627 or 1628. He could choose to be a biblical, Semitic, or classical scholar, for he excels in each of these fields; but he wants to become a different kind of man of letters.

54　FRENCH, J. MILTON, ed. *The Life Records of John Milton*. 5 vols. Rutgers Studies in English, no. 7. New Brunswick, N.J.: Rutgers University Press, 1949-58, 456; 401; 472; 484; 525 pp. Reprint. New York: Gordian Press, 1966.
　　　French edits "a source book, designed to provide a day-by-day guide to the known facts" in Milton's life (vol. 1, p. v). He provides the information, from the record of Milton's birth to the title page of the posthumous publication of *Christian Doctrine*, in a chronological sequence and without commentary.

55　GRIERSON, Sir HERBERT J. C. "John Milton: The Man and the Poet." In *Cross Currents in English Literature of the Seventeenth Century; or, The World, the Flesh and the Spirit, Their Actions and Reactions*. London: Chatto and Windus, 1929, pp. 232-73. Frequently reprinted.
　　　Milton knows for much of his life that he is preparing for a great task, though he does not see its exact nature and though the preparation leaves him ill-suited to face the rough world. His position with respect to every issue of the day comes from personal experience and high idealism. An egotist, he never doubts his infallibility. His youthful poetry is already Miltonic in both its strengths (such as elaborate, carefully constructed verse) and weaknesses (such as self-centered emotions). The Civil Wars produce Milton's great awakening; the Restoration, the ruin of his hopes. In *Paradise Lost*, Satan is a great literary creation but no hero. Instead of working in harmony, Milton's creative imagination portrays a grand Satan while his critical intellect gives a rational justification of God's ways. *Paradise Regained* tries to correct the imbalance; *Samson Agonistes* continues the disharmony.

But *Paradise Lost*'s real argument, based on the narrative, is that a man must learn to control his wife. See entry 120.

56   HANFORD, JAMES HOLLY. "The Chronology of Milton's Private Studies." *PMLA* 36 (1921):251-314. Reprinted in *John Milton, Poet and Humanist: Essays by James Holly Hanford* (Cleveland, Ohio: Press of Western Reserve University, 1966), pp. 75-125.

The notes in Milton's *Commonplace Book* are made at various times and in various hands. Certain evidence--handwriting and spacing of entries, for example--allows us to approximate the dates of the entries and hence of Milton's reading. During the Horton period (1632-38), Milton devotes himself to reading secular and church history as well as political works, many of which contain the seeds of his republicanism. He studies these works not to prepare to write in a similar vein or to search for poetic material, but to broaden and mature his mind. After the Horton period, he continues his reading with studies of French history, political philosophy, and Italian literature.

57   HANFORD, JAMES HOLLY. "Creative Personality: The Case of John Milton." *Johns Hopkins Alumni Magazine* 15 (1927):329-52.

The type of man Milton is links him with other men of action who are emotionally unstable, hypersensitive, and temperamental. As he develops at Cambridge and Horton, he watches carefully and feels apprehensive about his confidence as a poet, a reaction that he answers with a strong religious commitment. He expresses his sense of sexuality in refined erotic fantasies in verse until he turns twenty-one, when he suppresses his imagination as his ideals halt his awakening passion. He experiences an increasing "anxiety for the safety of the idealized image" of himself (341). Milton's poems portray these major internal conflicts. He comes to expect the veneration that his parents provide, but Mary Powell and her children do not offer it to him. Using associative patterns of thinking, Milton connects himself with the objects of his thought--Orpheus, St. Paul, and Edward King, for example. Late in Milton's life, hatred and rebellious pride threaten his idealized self-image.

58   HANFORD, JAMES HOLLY. *John Milton, Englishman*. New York: Crown Publishers, 1949, 283 pp. 11 illustrations.

Biographies

After entering school at the normal age, Milton probably experiences eye trouble, which--combined with heavy curricular demands--slows him and leads him to enter university late. This retarding of progress may affect him for the rest of his life; it is "the 'secret of John Milton'" (12). His Italian journey confirms his sense of belonging to Europe's intellectual elite. He returns to England believing that his long poetic apprenticeship is finished. *Paradise Lost*, in biographical terms, is two poems, since it is written before and after personal and public crises strike. The main characters--God, Christ, Adam, and Satan--show various parts of Milton's personality as it is or as he wishes it to be. *Paradise Regained* portrays a part of his consciousness, right reason's subjugation of passion, that *Paradise Lost* treats only in a wavering form. In *Samson Agonistes*, Milton states a great deal about his character that he suppresses elsewhere: the drama allows human will, not right reason, to triumph.

59 HANFORD, JAMES HOLLY. "The Youth of Milton: An Interpretation of His Early Literary Development." In *Studies in Shakespeare, Milton and Donne*. By Members of the English Department of the University of Michigan. University of Michigan Publications, Language and Literature, vol. 1. New York and London: Macmillan, 1925, pp. 89-163. Reprinted in *John Milton, Poet and Humanist: Essays by James Holly Hanford* (Cleveland, Ohio: Press of Western Reserve University, 1966), pp. 1-74.

Between the ages of eighteen and thirty-two, Milton shows the influences of home (particularly music), education (which teaches him to value his native tongue), and such literary figures as Du Bartas and Giles and Phineas Fletcher. If Milton's later thought is radical, the early works point to its roots in humanistic culture. In the early poems, he shows his awakening imagination and sensual desires, as well as idealism and ambition. He sublimates his emotional urges in the Italian sonnets, turning from Ovid's to Petrarch's influence. With *Elegy 6* and *Nativity Ode*, Milton, with Virgil's career as his model, sets a loftier goal, though it is not yet attainable. He then comes under the influence of Renaissance romance epics, especially the *Faerie Queene*, and Platonism when he writes *Comus*. Religious discipline is the foundation for his restraint in this period, as he integrates sensuous and ideal experience.

Biographies

60 HILL, JOHN SPENCER. *John Milton: Poet, Priest and Prophet. A Study of Divine Vocation in Milton's Poetry and Prose*. London and Basingstoke: Macmillan, 1979, 247 pp.

Reformation theology defines two kinds of vocation or calling, both relevant to Milton's life and writing: the Old Testament call to public works or service and the New Testament call to personal faith or salvation. Vocation, for Milton, is an aspect of only natural renovation, embracing both the Old and New Testament views. From 1641 to 1660, his vocation shifts to that of poet-prophet, as his mission coincides with that of the nation. In his major poems, Milton reassesses his calling in light of the Puritan failure and presents heroes who, like Milton, learn about the limits of power, knowledge, and vocational expectations. Since the national cause has collapsed, in *Paradise Lost* Milton turns from public to individual vocation and regeneration in an internal paradise. As Samson goes through the regenerative process in *Samson Agonistes* (written in 1660-61), he changes from a self-motivated to a divinely-motivated agent. Christ in *Paradise Regained* experiences trials of his self-knowledge and vocational insight, which lead to a denial of self.

Appendix: "Milton Agonistes: The Date of *Samson Agonistes*."

61 KERMODE, FRANK. "Milton in Old Age." *Southern Review*, n.s. 11 (1975):513-29.

Milton's friends help him after the Restoration by delaying the order for his arrest, contriving an announcement that he has fled, and making a deal by which he will not be named in the Act of Oblivion but will have two of his books burned. Because a mishap in this scheme causes his arrest, he has to acknowledge the King's authority by suing for pardon. *Samson Agonistes* shows Milton's interest "in the problems created by the peculiar conduct of God toward his elected heroes, including Milton" (519). Because his impulses come from God, Samson's sufferings are not his fault, and what appears to be a punishment is no such thing. As one of God's elected champions, Milton knows that his life fits a pattern, but one event violates his purity: submission to King Charles II when suing for a pardon. Milton concludes that this submission fits the pattern and proves the authenticity of his impulses. God's justice is vindicated.

General Studies

Biographies

62 KRAMER, JEROME A. "'Virtue, Religion, and Patriotism': Some Biographies of Milton in the Romantic Era." *Milton and the Romantics* 3 (1977):1-7.

Biographers of Milton in the Romantic period, from Hayley in 1796 to Carpenter in 1836, preserve older views of the poet and reshape him for their own age. To them, Milton is a superhuman, heroic figure; a man of integrity and justifiable pride who defends liberty; and a zealous Puritan and defiant individual. They do not exclusively emphasize his roles as Christian poet or interpret his personality as objectionable. Rather, they revere the whole Milton--as man, thinker, and poet. No biographer from this period associates Milton and Satan.

63 MACAULAY, ROSE. *Milton*. London: Duckworth, 1933, 161 pp. Frequently reprinted.

With his love of liberty of speech and thought, Milton is a misfit, "a superb and monstrous alien" (2), in his age and country. He disapproves of Cambridge's scholastic curriculum and finds the intellectual company inadequate. By isolating himself at Horton and avoiding literary coteries, Milton chooses an unusual direction for his life: to train for the future. Returning to England after an important Italian journey, he teaches and continues his interrupted studies. He then attempts to save his nation by writing pamphlets, for he enjoys a good fight. The failure to attain liberty for England leaves Milton permanently embittered. His low estimate of women is inconsistent with his ideals of marriage. *Christian Doctrine* reveals Milton as an Arminian, an Arian, and an advocate of polygamy. All of his experiences and dreams appear in *Paradise Lost*. The heroes of *Paradise Regained* and *Samson Agonistes* are modeled on their author.

64 MILLER, LEO. "Milton's Clash with Chappell: A Suggested Reconstruction." *Milton Quarterly* 14 (1980):77-87.

A reconstruction of the events of spring, 1627, may explain the conflict between Milton and his tutor, William Chappell. When the tutor gives Milton an assignment involving Aristotelian metaphysics, Milton is forced, in what becomes *Prolusion 4*, to regurgitate a mass of obscurities derived from Francisco Suarez. Milton cannot perform such a recitation, so he jokes, teases, and speaks his own views about "being compelled to blather such twaddle" (79). Perhaps Chappell keeps calm while Milton speaks, but *Prolusion 3*--which insults Aristotle while using him to define a new curriculum--must have enraged the tutor. After his exile from Cambridge, Milton returns in the winter of 1627-28 and states that he expects trouble with his audiences as he discourses on the silly topic assigned by his new tutor: whether day is better than night. In *Prolusion 6*, he speaks contritely yet securely, for his quarrel with Chappell is at least a draw.

Appendix: "The Occasion of Milton's *Elegia VII*." *Elegy 7* is based on the same girl-watching period recorded in *Elegy 1*.

65 PARKER, WILLIAM RILEY. *Milton: A Biography*. 2 vols. Oxford: Clarendon Press, 1968, 1510 pp. 4 illustrations.

The idealistic Milton enters Cambridge with high hopes, only to be disappointed. After leaving, though he is not ready to reject taking Holy Orders, he postpones them because he feels disappointed in his education and not yet prepared. Perhaps his interest in writing poetry also sways him. The invitation to write *Comus* must have revealed the shift in Milton's direction, and *Ad Patrem* shows his response to parental disapproval. The Italian journey heightens Milton's patriotism, self-confidence, and Protestantism, and he is viewed as an ambassador of English letters. But events in England turn him to writing prose, which he never regards as a diversion from writing poetry. Sharing much with the biblical Samson, Milton in 1647, as his vision grows worse, starts to write *Samson Agonistes*. He develops an exaggerated view of his own accomplishments, believing that his *First Defence* saved the nation. *Paradise Lost* shows how politics educates Milton, for his poem indicates that tyranny must exist because Adam loses true liberty. Religious experience is inward, each individual being responsible for his own freedom. Most of *Paradise Regained* may have been dictated before 1665, the rest between 1667-70.

Appendixes: "Milton's Publications, 1628-1700, in the order of their appearance, and with the number of surviving copies located in public, institutional, or private libraries"; "Surviving copies of seventeenth-century editions of Milton located in public or institutional libraries."

66 RALEIGH, WALTER. *Milton*. London: Edward Arnold; New York: Knickerbocker Press, G. P. Putnam's Sons, 1900, 306 pp. Part reprinted in *Milton Criticism: Selections from Four Centuries*, ed. James Thorpe (New York: Rinehart & Co., 1950), pp. 114-42.

Biographies

Milton's poems reflect contemporary life and politics, as well as the severe and self-centered life of a Puritan. His personal experience is the first motive for writing tracts on marriage, freedom of the press, education, and political and religious liberty. Throughout his life, Milton's main concern is liberty, his main flaw "a confidence too absolute in the capacity and integrity of the reasonable soul of man" (59). His prose is that of a poet. The theme and style of *Paradise Lost* are vaster than those of any preceding epic. Rather than expressing contemporary ideas, Milton seeks to impose an imaginative scheme on his age. "The *Paradise Lost* is not the less an eternal monument because it is a monument to dead ideas" (85). When he portrays Satan, Milton needs to draw a worthy adversary for God, but the poet soon finds himself serving Satan. Milton's skill lies not in character analysis, but in describing "some noble or striking attitude, some strong or majestic action, in its outward physical aspect" (153). Although the success of *Paradise Lost* in 1667 is immediate, Milton does not change English poetry: "He imitated no one, and founded no school" (229). See entry 664.

67 RICHMOND, HUGH M. *The Christian Revolutionary: John Milton.* Berkeley, Los Angeles, and London: University of California Press, 1974, 215 pp.

Milton's views shift from a Platonic insistence on human rationality to a skeptical tolerance of the individual's unreliable intelligence, from a conservative moderation to a real innovation and rebellion. His life is marked by hasty, idealistic action leading to shocked disillusionment and failure. The ideology of his prose is Platonic, relying on human reason to construct a new social order, but his last major poems undercut this naive optimism. Indeed, the political pamphlets disprove the values of rational reform. *Paradise Lost* teaches us about failure: how wrong choices are made and how we should respond to them. Rather than preaching Platonic optimism, *Paradise Lost* seeks to clarify what happens to readers after a failure they cannot rectify. *Paradise Regained* and *Samson Agonistes* explore the extremes of mental experience, ranging from an awareness of ruin to a demonstration of divine capacities. Unlike Milton's short poems, *Paradise Regained* and *Samson Agonistes* show the triumph of God's will over man's will.

Biographies

68   ROWSE, A. L. *Milton the Puritan: Portrait of a Mind*. London: Macmillan, 1977, 297 pp. Reprint. Lanham, Md.: University Press of America, 1985.

Born into an obstinate family, Milton enjoys being out of step. His personality is a curious combination of genius and naivete, and it has a femininity that he seeks to repress by overemphasizing the masculine qualities, which leads to bitterness and a sharpening of the senses. "Not very heterosexual," Milton would benefit from "a little rolling in the hay" (31). His political treatises show that he is out of touch with ordinary human nature. Milton overcompensates aggressively for his inferiority complex. His nasty Puritanism turns an otherwise decent man into a disagreeable and inhuman person. *Paradise Lost* is dominated by its hero, Satan, and by political themes, as it conveys all of Milton's hopes and frustrations from the Civil Wars on. Christ in *Paradise Regained* has Milton's personality, especially as it turns toward the Quakers' pacificism. *Samson Agonistes* is "the most autobiographical work of this most autobiographical of writers" (255).

69   SAURAT, DENIS. *Milton: Man and Thinker*. London: Jonathan Cape; New York: Dial Press, 1925, 380 pp. Frequently reprinted; part reprinted in *Milton Criticism: Selections from Four Centuries*, ed. James Thorpe (New York: Rinehart & Co., 1950), pp. 169-77.

Milton's personality is based on sensitivity, moral intractability, and a belief in personal independence. Recognizing his greatness at an early age, he takes it for granted and never learns that others are not like him. Milton does not believe in many of the events related in *Paradise Lost*. Using dogma as myth, he turns Christ into the force of reason and Satan into the opposing force of passion or sensuality. Because Milton identifies his pride and defeat with Satan's, we feel sympathy and admiration for the devil. *Paradise Regained* is a failure, but *Samson Agonistes* succeeds in bringing out the main themes of *Paradise Lost*: sensuality and regeneration. *Samson Agonistes* avoids dogma and emphasizes psychology to resolve problems that disturb Milton throughout his life. His blindness is caused by retinitis, complicated by glaucoma from eye strain, all resulting from generally bad health probably produced by hereditary syphilis. See entry 226.

Biographies

70 SEARS, DONALD, trans. "*La Tina*: The Country Sonnets of
Antonio Malatesti as Dedicated to Mr. John Milton, English
Gentleman." *Milton Studies* 13 (1979):277-317.
   Malatesti gives and dedicates to Milton the manuscript of fifty
Italian sonnets when the Englishman departs from Florence in April of
1639. Considering that these poems addressed to a rural mistress are
filled with bawdy images and double entendres, we should give Milton
credit for having a broad social wit. Malatesti does not miscalculate
Milton's wit and sensibility, for Milton believes that honorable men can
deal with obscene material in obscene terms. Indeed, *Second Defence*
and *Pro Se Defensio* show that he can write sexual puns, and he may
even see an analogy between Malatesti's comic story of an affair with a
country girl and the several scandals of Milton's opponent, Alexander
More.
   Sears provides a translation of *La Tina*.

71 THORPE, JAMES. *John Milton: The Inner Life*. [San Marino,
Calif.]: Huntington Library, 1983, 201 pp.
   The values that dominate Milton's inner life are his sense of
his relationship to God, viewed as a personal taskmaster overseeing a
man suffering from original sin; his sense of his mission as a poet,
which requires training, for it is the highest calling for man; and his
sense of virtue, the standard of human conduct that he is obliged to
extend to the world around him. Perhaps writing about the failure of
others, such as Satan and Samson, helps Milton deal with his own
failures. In his poetry, Milton dwells on crises that humans face and the
triumphs that can emerge from failure. His heroes are separated from
their worlds, and the villains are alienated. Milton has to face three
major crises: desertion by Mary Powell, blindness, and the Restoration.
Guidance, an important theme for Milton, comes from the Bible as
interpreted by right reason or conscience, the Spirit of God. Final truth
resides in the inner life.

72 WILSON, A. N. *The Life of John Milton*. Oxford and New York:
Oxford University Press, 1983, 279 pp.
   Milton grows up in an environment that sees no conflict
between Christianity and high literary standards. Witnessing future
clergymen make fools of themselves in some bad university drama,
Milton realizes that he cannot be ordained with such idiotic characters.

Suddenly, he has no interest in his career at Cambridge. During the Horton period, Milton discovers that he has a divine vocation. His deliberate isolation from the English literary scene, where he is unknown, works to his advantage on the Continent, where he is lionized. Radical and republican tendencies, previously latent in Milton, come to the front of his mind, and his Protestantism is redefined. Until the Italian journey, his training is traditional, his thinking orthodox. Rather than expressing Milton's doubts about orthodox views, *Christian Doctrine* asserts his faith and constancy. Since his attempts to change the world fail, Milton removes himself from it as he writes his epic poem. Like Milton's personality, *Paradise Lost* has a dark side that we should not exaggerate. *Samson Agonistes* is autobiographical in its reflections of Milton's inner journey. The Christ of *Paradise Regained* embodies all that Milton believes to be good.

See also entries 4, 34, 37-38, 74, 91, 146, 156, 169-70, 180, 183, 191, 201, 213.

BIBLIOGRAPHIES

73 FLETCHER, HARRIS FRANCIS. *Contributions to a Milton Bibliography 1800-1930, Being a List of Addenda to Stevens's "Reference Guide to Milton."* University of Illinois Studies in Language and Literature, vol. 16. Urbana: University of Illinois Press, 1931, 166 pp. Reprint. New York: Russell and Russell, 1967.

   Fletcher supplements Stevens's *Guide* (see entry 77) with over 1,030 annotated entries of studies, editions, and translations of Milton's works. The index covers scholars, authors mentioned in annotations, subjects, and titles of Milton's works.

74 HANFORD, JAMES HOLLY, and McQUEEN, WILLIAM A. *Milton*. Goldentree Bibliographies in Language and Literature. 2d ed. Arlington Heights, Ill.: AHM Publishing Corp., 1979, 121 pp.

   This selected bibliography omits few entries from the first edition (1966) and adds about 400 entries to Hanford and Crupi's original bibliography. McQueen drops the asterisks that marked the most significant works, but the organization is nearly the same as in the first edition (including Special Topics sections on versification, style and imagery, and translations).

Bibliographies

75 HUCKABAY, CALVIN. *John Milton: An Annotated Bibliography, 1929-1968.* Rev. ed. Duquesne Studies, Philological Series, vol. 1. Pittsburgh, Pa.: Duquesne University Press; Louvain: Editions E. Nauwelaerts, 1969, 409 pp.

Huckabay's bibliography provides brief annotations for almost 4,000 studies, editions, and translations of Milton's works, with an index of scholars. This book is a revised and updated version of Huckabay's *John Milton: A Bibliographical Supplement, 1929-1957* (Pittsburgh, Pa., and Louvain: Duquesne University Press, 1960).

76 SHAWCROSS, JOHN T. *Milton: A Bibliography for the Years 1624-1700.* Medieval and Renaissance Texts and Studies, vol. 30. Binghamton, N.Y.: Medieval and Renaissance Texts and Studies, 1984, 466 pp.

Divided into a primary and a secondary bibliography, Shawcross's work "tries to bring together all manuscripts and editions of the works [by Milton] and all studies and critical statements concerning Milton's life and works, all allusions and quotations, and all significant imitations during the years 1624-1700" (ix).

77 STEVENS, DAVID HARRISON. *Reference Guide to Milton from 1800 to the Present Day.* Chicago, Ill.: University of Chicago Press, 1930, 312 pp. Reprint. New York: Russell and Russell, 1967.

Covering the years 1800-1928, Stevens's *Guide* provides brief annotations for almost 2,800 studies, editions, and translations of Milton. The index covers scholars, authors mentioned in annotations, and titles of Milton's works. For a supplement, see entry 73.

See also entries 254, 271, 926.

REFERENCE WORKS

78 BOSWELL, JACKSON CAMPBELL. *Milton's Library: A Catalogue of the Remains of John Milton's Library and an Annotated Reconstruction of Milton's Library and Ancillary Readings.* New York and London: Garland Publishing, 1975, 279 pp.

Calling his work preliminary, Boswell catalogues over 1,500 books, identifying each as one that Milton owned or read, may have owned, or probably did not own. See entry 156.

79   COOPER, LANE. *A Concordance of the Latin, Greek, and Italian Poems of John Milton*. Halle: Max Niemeyer, 1923, 226 pp.
     Cooper prints a separate concordance for the poems in each foreign language.

80   GILBERT, ALLAN H. *A Geographical Dictionary of Milton*. Cornell Studies in English, 4. Ithaca, N.Y.: Cornell University Press; New Haven, Conn.: Yale University Press; London: Oxford University Press, Humphrey Milford, 1919, 330 pp.
     By referring to books that Milton read, Gilbert explains almost all of the place names in Milton's poetry and prose.

81   HUNTER, WILLIAM B., Jr., gen. ed. *A Milton Encyclopedia*. 9 vols. Lewisburg, Pa.: Bucknell University Press; London: Associated University Presses, 1978-83. 208; 206; 199; 218; 206; 216; 208; 205; 170 pp.
     From "Abdiel" to "Zwingli," the *Milton Encyclopedia* contains the work of over 150 scholars. Volume 9 includes a few new entries, bibliographies for some entries in the previous eight volumes, an index of names, and an index of subjects.
     Selected entries (some revised) about biography and the English poems are reprinted in *Milton's English Poetry; Being Entries from "A Milton Encyclopedia,"* introduction by William B. Hunter, bibliography by John T. Shawcross (Lewisburg, Pa.: Bucknell University Press; London and Toronto: Associated University Presses, 1986), 248 pp.

82   INGRAM, WILLIAM, and SWAIM, KATHLEEN, eds. *A Concordance to Milton's English Poetry*. Oxford: Clarendon Press, 1972, 700 pp.
     From "Aaron" to "Zorah," this concordance is based on printed and manuscript texts of Milton's English poems.

Reference Works

83   Le COMTE, EDWARD. *A Dictionary of Puns in Milton's English Poetry*. New York: Columbia University Press, 1981, 259 pp.
     Listing about 1,630 puns found by himself and by Milton's editors, Le Comte notes that puns need not be comic. While Milton favors the etymological pun, he also uses syntactic punning.

84   Le COMTE, EDWARD S. *A Milton Dictionary*. New York: Philosophical Library, 1961, 362 pp.
     Le Comte's dictionary covers difficult words in Milton's poetry and prose; his correspondents and named friends and opponents; geographical, mythological, biblical, literary, and historical allusions; each work by Milton (in a descriptive entry); and biographical matters related to Milton, his family, editors, and leading critics.

85   STERNE, LAURENCE, and KOLLMEIER, HAROLD H., gen. eds. *A Concordance to the English Prose of John Milton*. Medieval and Renaissance Texts and Studies, vol. 35. Binghamton, N.Y.: Medieval and Renaissance Texts and Studies, 1985, 1510 pp.
     From "Aaron" to "Zwinglius," Sterne and Kollmeier's concordance is based on the Yale *Complete Prose Works*.

See also entries 54, 65, 73-77, 96, 129, 156, 254, 271, 926.

REPUTATION AND INFLUENCE

86   BARKER, ARTHUR. "'. . . And on His Crest Sat Horror': Eighteenth-Century Interpretations of Milton's Sublimity and His Satan." *University of Toronto Quarterly* 11 (1942):421-36.
     In order to understand the development of nineteenth-century interpretations of Milton, and our own, we need to examine the neoclassical readings of *Paradise Lost*. Milton shows eighteenth-century poets that sublimity beyond art's regular reach (because of its irregularity) can be achieved in English verse, though most writers agree that it lacks polish and a true epic subject. With increasing frequency, writers cite sections of *Paradise Lost*'s opening books or the war in heaven to illustrate the poem's sublimity, which becomes more

and more connected to the dreadful and terrible during the century. As terror is mixed with sympathetic admiration for Satan in the eighteenth century, we see the beginnings of the Romantics' perspective on *Paradise Lost*.

87 BRISMAN, LESLIE. *Milton's Poetry of Choice and Its Romantic Heirs*. Ithaca, N.Y., and London: Cornell University Press, 1973, 348 pp.

While presenting alternatives, *L'Allegro* and *Il Penseroso* actualize the choice when one makes the spiritual and stylistic progression from the former poem to the latter, from a world of multiplicities toward a higher vision. *Comus* and the sonnets follow a similar pattern. In *Paradise Lost*, Milton takes us through the experience of alternatives, such as the temptation, by presenting them as if they were still options. He thus recaptures choice, as he does in *Lycidas* by using art to arrest time. Milton's silences in *Paradise Lost* point to a higher order redemptive of time, as Keats sees when he faces Milton. Shelley embraces the Miltonic moment of arrest but does not let it lead to an awareness of loss. On the pinnacle in *Paradise Regained*, an arrest occurs and choice opens out into imaginative space, an idea from which all of Blake's myths are derived. Recognizing the gap between Milton's voice and his own, Wordsworth revisits the Miltonic paradigm as a superior spirit.

88 DOWDEN, EDWARD. "Milton in the Eighteenth Century (1701-1750)." *Proceedings of the British Academy* 3 (1907-8):275-93.

In the eighteenth century, writers are influenced by the poetic style of *Paradise Lost*, the sentiment and style of Milton's earlier poems, and the thought of his prose works. The extensive eighteenth-century Milton scholarship includes editions, translations, critical commentaries, musical and theatrical adaptations, biographies, translations, and illustrations.

89 ELIOT, T. S. *Milton*. Oxford: Oxford University Press, 1947, 19 pp. Reprinted in *Sewanee Review* 56 (1948):185-209; *Milton Criticism: Selections from Four Centuries*, ed. James Thorpe (New York: Rinehart & Co., 1950), pp. 310-32; *On Poetry and Poets* (London and New York: Faber and Faber, 1957), pp. 165-83; *The Modern Critical*

Reputation and Influence

Spectrum, ed. Gerald Jay Goldberg and Nancy Marmer Goldberg (Englewood Cliffs, N.J.: Prentice-Hall, 1962), pp. 175-86; *Milton: "Paradise Lost," a Casebook*, ed. A. E. Dyson and Julian Lovelock (London and Basingstoke: Macmillan, 1973), pp. 77-84.

If one poet exerts a bad influence over others, the later writers bear the responsibility. Milton does not cause the "dissociation of sensibility" that occurs in the seventeenth century. His is a personal style, "a perpetual sequence of original acts of lawlessless" (*On Poetry and Poets* 175), in which we find his greatness. Just as his verse is remote from ordinary speech, so his poetic language is his own invention. In Milton's verse, visual elements are weak, but this becomes a strength in *Paradise Lost*. He emphasizes sound, not sight or idea. While placing limitations on blank verse, Milton perfects it. Future poets should study him as "the greatest master in our language of freedom within form" (183). See entries 111, 118, 467, 615.

90   FERRY, ANNE DAVIDSON. *Milton and the Miltonic Dryden*. Cambridge, Mass.: Harvard University Press, 1968, 241 pp.

If Dryden's *State of Innocence* is "an offensive vulgarization" of *Paradise Lost* (21), *Absalom and Achitophel* is an analogy of *Paradise Lost* that transforms it into a new vision, using allusion, imitation, and parody to describe a contemporary example of the universal temptation and fall. *Absalom and Achitophel* follows *Paradise Lost*'s model in showing language and style to be the powers of both sin and restoration. *Samson Agonistes* emphasizes unutterable truths. Because *Samson Agonistes* lacks descriptions of visual impressions and instead relates what the hero feels or hears, the reader grows close to Samson and seems to share the enclosed space and isolation of his body. As the betrayer of his own secret, Samson committed a verbal sin rather than a sexual one. He must restore internal, heroic silence. In *All for Love*, Dryden follows *Samson Agonistes* as a model by presenting a world of relationships and inexpressible feelings that are meaningless because they depend on threatening and arbitrary language. Dryden's hero seeks a silent oblivion.

91   GOOD, JOHN WALTER. *Studies in the Milton Tradition*. University of Illinois Studies in Language and Literature, vol. 1, nos. 3-4. Urbana: University of Illinois, 1915, 310 pp.

Reputation and Influence

Milton is never as unpopular or ignored as eighteenth-century writers suppose, and their view is overcorrected by the nineteenth-century emphasis on the influence of his shorter poems. The publishing history of his works reveals that most are consistently in demand. Early biographers of Milton often vilify him because of his politics, though some admire his poetry. After about 1726, the biographies become more favorable, turning in mid-century to Milton as a genius and a source of national pride. Until 1730, critics devote their attention to establishing his rank as a man of letters based on *Paradise Lost*; they are indifferent toward his short poems and negative toward his prose, which become popular between 1730 and 1765, as writers try to chart the development of Milton's genius.

Appendixes: "Milton's *History of Britain*"; "Milton's Blindness"; "Mrs. Macaulay on Milton"; "Addison's Critique upon the *Paradise Lost*, in the Eighteenth Century"; "Milton's Religion"; "Notes on Milton's Sources"; "Religious Titles"; "Some Educational Titles Bearing upon Milton's Influence upon Education"; "Milton's Eden and English Landscape Gardening"; "Milton's Monument, Grave, and Family."

92 GRIFFIN, DUSTIN. *Regaining Paradise: Milton and the Eighteenth Century*. Cambridge: Cambridge University Press, 1986, 310 pp.

In a sense, Milton "set the poetic agenda" for the eighteenth century (2), as writers respond creatively to his myth of a lost garden of innocence, defiant stance against opponents, celebration of marriage, and themes of choice, freedom, and responsibility. The most interesting imitations of and allusions to Milton in this period assert both affinity and difference. Although they emphasize the relationship between Milton's biography and writing, eighteenth-century writers feel no anxiety about Milton's influence. He helps them define their politics, gives them ideals of public virtue and moral values, and above all serves as their literary hero. Many of Milton's works are adapted, translated, and illustrated in order to honor him, make his works accessible to a wide audience, and improve his verse. Some new literary genres are prompted by Milton's writings. The major writers of this period--Dryden, Pope, Thomson, Johnson, and Cowper--show a creative response to Milton's presence.

Reputation and Influence

93   HAVENS, RAYMOND DEXTER. *The Influence of Milton on
     English Poetry*. Cambridge, Mass.: Harvard University Press, 1922,
     734 pp. Reprint. New York: Russell and Russell, 1961.
          Paradise Lost is far more popular and highly regarded in the
     eighteenth century than scholars realize. Because of its religious value
     and novelty, the epic is translated, rewritten, annotated, parodied,
     alluded to, imitated, and published with great frequency. Milton's love
     of freedom, especially as illustrated by his use of blank verse rather
     than rhyme, attracts the most attention, and unrhymed poems in the
     Miltonic style are suddenly popular and numerous, though Milton
     never influences dramatic blank verse. *Paradise Lost*'s influence
     continues until 1915. Although *L'Allegro* and *Il Penseroso* exert a slight
     influence on English verse before 1740, Milton's other minor poems
     have virtually none. As the lyric impulse is revived after the 1740s, his
     shorter poems grow popular.
          Appendixes: "Parallel Passages Showing Expressions Probably
     Borrowed from Milton [by Pope, Thomson, Young, Warton, Cooper,
     Wordsworth, and Keats]"; "Poems in Non-Miltonic Blank Verse, 1667-
     1750"; "Loco-Descriptive Poems Not Known To Be Miltonic"; "Rimed
     Technical Treatises"; Bibliographies: "Poems Influenced by *Paradise
     Lost* [1685-1915]"; "Poems Influenced by *L'Allegro* and *Il Penseroso*
     [1647-1832]"; "Poems Influenced by the Remaining Works of Milton
     [*Lycidas*, *Comus*, the translation from Horace, and *Nativity Ode*]";
     "Eighteenth-Century Sonnets."

94   LOCKWOOD, DEBORAH H. "The Eighteenth-Century Response
     to *Paradise Lost*'s Last Two Books." *English Language Notes* 21
     (1984):22-32.
          From 1667 to 1800, *Paradise Lost* is praised, with the exception
     of Books 11 and 12, which do not suit eighteenth-century taste because
     they are considered low. Some of Adam and Eve's emotional speeches
     and the epic's concluding lines appear in collections of poetic beauties,
     and critics admire the content, if not the execution, of Books 11 and 12.
     In general, eighteenth-century critics see a falling off and an absence of
     the sublime in the final two books.

95   NELSON, JAMES G. *The Sublime Puritan: Milton and the
     Victorians*. Madison: University of Wisconsin Press, 1963, 222 pp. 3
     illustrations.

Reputation and Influence

During the Victorian age, not only do many literary artists see Milton as "a power amongst powers" and *Paradise Lost* as "a central force among forces," in De Quincey's words, but literate members of the laboring class read *Paradise Lost* because of its religious positions or its author's republican views. High Churchmen, Catholics, and Tories condemn Milton. He and Mary Powell are cast as fictional characters in various works of the period. Evidence of imitation appears in the many religious books indebted to *Paradise Lost* and *Paradise Regained* in the 1820s and 1830s. By placing a new emphasis on Milton's prose, editors and biographers help shatter the image of him promulgated by eighteenth-century Tories. Tennyson, the major Victorian poet most influenced by Milton, anticipates the later Victorian view by focusing on Milton's artistry and ignoring his theology and philosophy.

96 PARKER, WILLIAM RILEY. *Milton's Contemporary Reputation: An Essay, Together with a Tentative List of Printed Allusions to Milton, 1641-1674, and Facsimile Reproductions of Five Contemporary Pamphlets Written in Answer to Milton.* Columbus: Ohio State University Press, 1940, 308 pp.

Although Milton and his poems are appreciated in Italy when he travels there, he knows that he lacks a reputation in England. The antiprelatical pamphlets bring some response, largely mockery, from his countrymen, but Milton is still little known until the publication of *Doctrine and Discipline of Divorce*, which catches the public's attention and brings him grief. This is why the volume of *Poems* appears in 1645, complete with tributes from Italian friends. It sells poorly, is rarely imitated by contemporaries, and is alluded to in no book or manuscript collection of poems. *Tenure of Kings and Magistrates* and Milton's limited reputation as "an eloquent *enfant terrible*" (26) are the credentials that encourage the Council of State to employ him as Secretary for Foreign Tongues. With his response to Salmasius in *First Defence*, he finally acquires fame. After the Restoration, Milton is probably seen as a legendary figure, but there is a dearth of published allusions to *Paradise Lost* from 1667 to 1674.

Parker includes facsimiles of *A Modest Confutation* (1642), *An Answer to the Doctrine and Discipline of Divorce* (1644), Sir Robert Filmer's *Observations on Master Milton against Salmasius* (1652), *The Censure of the Rota upon Mr. Milton's Book* (1660), and Sir Roger L'Estrange's *No Blinde Guides* (1660).

Reputation and Influence

97   ROBERTSON, J. G. "Milton's Fame on the Continent." *Proceedings of the British Academy* 3 (1907-8):319-40.

The first English poet to gain respect for English literature on the Continent, Milton influences European ideas about epic poetry, German writers of the eighteenth century, and French Romanticism in the early nineteenth century. But his reputation first spreads to Europe because of his duties as the Secretary for Foreign Tongues and the defender of regicides. In 1727-28, Milton's poetic reputation overtakes his political reputation on the Continent, though Voltaire turns from praising to attacking Milton because he fears that a foreign poet might endanger Europe's good taste. Milton's influence on French poetry is minimal in the eighteenth century. Italian critics initially approve of Milton's epic, but they eventually ridicule it. Spain remains indifferent, while Germany and Holland are interested in *Paradise Lost*. In nineteenth-century Europe, Milton's fame is purely bookish, except in France, where he exerts a great influence on poetry.

98   SAGE, LORNA. "Milton in Literary History." In *John Milton: Introductions*. Edited by John Broadbent. Cambridge: Cambridge University Press, 1973, pp. 298-341.

No matter what the norms at any given moment during the past three centuries, Milton's constant function is to create divergence from those norms. Seen as a polemicist before the Restoration, Milton then writes an epic that claims classical status while opposing the contemporary ideal of the classical. Eighteenth-century writers define the relationship between Milton's classicism and current poetry, and many poets imitate Milton's pastoral works. The Romantics see Milton as contained by his epic characters, while nineteenth-century novelists view *Paradise Lost* as a source to bring the cosmic scope of epic into prose fiction. The Victorian Milton, as passed down by Wordsworth and Keats, is an author whose poetry, however admirable, offers an example of how not to write. In our century, Milton is the subject of sharp controversy.

99   SENSABAUGH, GEORGE F. *Milton in Early America*. Princeton, N.J.: Princeton University Press, 1964, 332 pp.

In America's youth, as it searches for national identity and a voice to express its greatest concerns, Milton has a great influence until about 1815, when his fame diminishes. Starting in about 1714, colonialists praise Milton's poetic skill, especially its sublimity and divine inspiration. Later, Americans give him the mantle of scriptural writers and place him in the hierarchy of angels. *Paradise Lost* provides a model for the language and form of American epics, as well as a standard for comparison. The American Revolution brings Milton's work on civil and ecclesiastical liberty to center stage and transforms him into a cultural hero leading America toward a utopia. Milton is imitated by poets, plagiarized by political writers, and cited in sermons, grammar books, diaries, almanacs, and periodicals. As the early Republic's authors move from neoclassical to Romantic principles, Milton's supremacy is sometimes questioned. His influence is much reduced in American life of the nineteenth century.

100 SENSABAUGH, GEORGE F. *That Grand Whig Milton*. Stanford University Publications. University Series, Language and Literature, vol. 11. Stanford, Calif.: Stanford University Press; London: Oxford University Press, 1952, 222 pp.
  During the Civil Wars, Milton writes about the power of kings and liberty of conscience, but he does not immediately change Englishmen's thinking or attain the political stature he wants. After the Restoration, nonconformists draw from his work in their disputes with the Cavalier-Church party (later called Tory) that hates and fears Milton, and Whigs in the eighteenth century consider him an oracle as they adapt his writings and thought in their attempt to break Tory power. The Whigs also use Milton's voice to contribute to the Revolutionary Settlement, which repudiates old Tory doctrines. With the triumph of Whig principles in about 1700, the party gives Milton his proper acclaim. He becomes the Whig party's voice, though the Tories continue to oppose it.

101 SHAWCROSS, JOHN T., ed. *Milton: The Critical Heritage*. London: Routledge and Kegan Paul; New York: Barnes and Noble, 1970, 287 pp.
  Besides providing some of Milton's statements about literature, Shawcross prints excerpts from commentaries about Milton's work to 1731. See entry 102.
  Appendixes: "Publication of the Works"; "Selected Secondary References and Collections Similar to the Present Volume"; "Noteworthy Criticism Omitted in This Selection."

Reputation and Influence

102   SHAWCROSS, JOHN T., ed. *Milton, 1732-1801: The Critical Heritage*. London and Boston, Mass.: Routledge and Kegan Paul, 1972, 450 pp.

The companion volume of entry 101, this book contains a long introduction that surveys commentary about Milton from 1732 to 1801 and excerpts from critical works.

Appendixes: "Selected Secondary References"; "Additional Significant Criticism Omitted in This Selection"; "Important Editions, 1732-1801."

103   SHERBURN, GEORGE. "The Early Popularity of Milton's Minor Poems." *Modern Philology* 17 (1919):259-78; 17 (1920):515-40.

Although literary historians claim that Milton's minor poems are neglected until the mid-eighteenth century, these works--especially *L'Allegro, Il Penseroso, Comus*, and *Lycidas*--are steadily reprinted, widely echoed, and highly regarded before that period.

104   STAVELY, KEITH W. F. *Puritan Legacies: "Paradise Lost" and the New England Tradition, 1630-1890*. Ithaca, N.Y., and London: Cornell University Press, 1987, 308 pp.

As the most distinctly Puritan literary figure, Milton shares a cultural identity with New England, the most distinctly Puritan society. Milton, like early New Englanders, experiences the attempt to eliminate Puritanism, the revolutionary milieu of the mid-seventeenth century, and the emergence of the spirit of capitalism and the Protestant ethic into socioeconomic prominence. In *Paradise Lost*, Adam and Eve's relationship--complete with its quarrels, opportunities for learning, and individual independence--enacts Puritan domestic doctrine, provides a microcosm of the relationships within the Puritan church and state, and is mirrored by convoluted relationships in colonial New England. *Paradise Lost* acknowledges the polarities that exist within Puritanism (such as egalitarianism and elitism, enthusiasm and order) and that persist in New England.

See also entries 45-46, 58, 62, 65-66, 74, 76, 114, 117, 121, 156, 201, 217, 228, 239, 449, 487, 535, 565, 615, 717, 926, 983.

STUDIES OF TRANSLATIONS, ILLUSTRATIONS, AND ADAPTATIONS

105 ENGLAND, MARTHA WINBURN. "John Milton and the Performing Arts." *Bulletin of the New York Public Library* 80 (1976):19-70.

Presenting no burden of the past for eighteenth-century actors, *Comus* and *Samson Agonistes* are living works and good box office. Milton's plans include writing musical drama for the public stage in which he would link ideas about biblical exegesis and Italian music theory about opera and oratorio. Patriots, women, and performers are excited about adaptations of his dramas (*Comus* and *Samson Agonistes*), *Paradise Lost*, *Paradise Regained*, *L'Allegro*, and *Il Penseroso*. When adapting Milton's work for a musical or dramatic performance, every artist faces the problem of making public what are private matters in Milton's poetry. He also influences English hymnody.

106 HUNT, JOHN DIXON. "Milton's Illustrators." In *John Milton: Introductions*. Edited by John Broadbent. Cambridge: Cambridge University Press, 1973, pp. 208-25. 6 illustrations.

Medina, Milton's first and only contemporary illustrator, reads *Paradise Lost* carefully and provides a visual interpretation of it. In the late eighteenth century, Fuseli isolates the epic's dramatic effects, and Blake masters gestures that reveal spiritual life. John Martin has a sense of the cosmic scale of *Paradise Lost*, and he connects the poem to Victorian life. By creating illustrations that are far too literal, Doré may account for the general lack of illustration of Milton since the late nineteenth century. Good illustrations can sharpen our responses to Milton's poetry by leading us to critical insights.

107 POINTON, MARCIA R. *Milton and English Art*. Manchester: Manchester University Press; Toronto and Buffalo, N.Y.: University of Toronto Press, 1970, 319 pp. 218 illustrations.

Medina, the first illustrator of *Paradise Lost* (1688), uses his plates to explain and enlighten. Louis Charon introduces a grandeur and sophistication to the illustration of Milton's works. In the work of

Studies of Translations

Hogarth and Hayman, the baroque appears in Milton illustrations. Two styles characterize illustrations of Milton in the late eighteenth century: the decorative prettiness of the rococo (Mortimer, Smirke, and Wright) and the elegance of the sublime (Fuseli). Blake, unlike any other illustrator, "incorporated into his designs his own interpretations of the poem" (137); he also follows the details of Milton's text, using a symbolic rather than a representational method to focus on ideas instead of narrative. From 1800 to 1860, while Turner develops the romantic aspects of the late nineteenth-century artists of the sublime, others conventionalize the classical side of Fuseli's and Barry's work.

     Appendixes: "Illustrations of Milton's Poetry from the 1870s to the Present Day"; "Sculpture on Miltonic Themes"; "Pictures of Milton's Life"; "J. H. Fuseli's Milton Gallery, 1799"; "Blake's Illustrations to *Paradise Lost*."

108   THALER, ALWIN. "Milton in the Theatre." *Studies in Philology* 17 (1920):269-308.
     From the early eighteenth to the middle of the nineteenth century, a surprising range of Milton's work is adapted to music or the stage: *Comus, Arcades, Paradise Lost, L'Allegro, Il Penseroso, Samson Agonistes, Lycidas,* "On Shakespeare," and parts of *Nativity Ode*. Milton enjoys the theatre.
     Thaler lists the productions of *Comus* in Britain from 1738-1843.

See also entries 73-75, 77, 92-93, 97, 100, 103, 439, 457, 474, 482.

CRITICS ON MILTON CRITICISM

109   ADAMS, ROBERT MARTIN. *Ikon: John Milton and the Modern Critics*. Ithaca, N.Y.: Cornell University Press, 1955, 252 pp. Reprinted 1966; part reprinted in *"A Maske at Ludlow": Essays on Milton's "Comus,"* ed. John S. Diekhoff (Cleveland, Ohio: Press of Case Western Reserve University, 1968), pp. 78-101.
     Critics "overread" *Comus*, which should be examined not as a metaphysical poem but as an allegorical masque with a temptation scene at its center. The text, unlike some critics, makes no distinction between virginity and chastity. Archetypal criticism of *Lycidas* and

Paradise Lost often argues from similarities between works, though the parallels are sometimes farfetched and require a huge leap to any conclusion. Despite editors' attempts to make systematic the use of emphatic and unemphatic pronouns (he-hee and she-shee, for example) in *Paradise Lost*, Milton does not intend these spellings. In a number of places in *Paradise Lost*, however, he intentionally fractures English grammar, alters spelling, and shifts levels of diction in order to make a point. By analyzing clusters of images, the New Critics can dismiss Milton's work, which succeeds because of more broadly conceived elements, such as plot, character, diction, scenic balances, and structural analogies. None of these can be effective without a sweeping, energetic style.

110 ALPERS, PAUL J. "The Milton Controversy." In *Twentieth-Century Literature in Retrospect*. Edited by Reuben A. Brower. Harvard English Studies, 2. Cambridge, Mass.: Harvard University Press, 1971, pp. 269-98.
     Leavis's essay on Milton's verse (see entry 614), along with Eliot's "Note" (see entry 239), initiates the first developed argument against Milton's preeminence in English poetry. Finally, thirty years later, the poet's defenders meet the attack, though Ricks's work (see entry 620) does not offer a sufficiently comprehensive response. As Leavis argues, Milton's descriptions lack concreteness; yet this is caused not by his inability to write detailed sensuous description, but by his questioning whether fallen humans and their poetic skills can apprehend Eden. Milton's view of human nature, as both individual and linked by a common relation to God and the world, leads him to use intrusive comments to guide the reader's judgment. Waldock (see entry 558) thinks such narratorial interpreting denies thematic vitality, but the narrator accurately brings out the story's implications in terms of human nature. By holding *Paradise Lost*'s poetry up to the highest standards, Leavis does Milton honor; insofar as Leavis's critics never fully answer him, they have been untrue to *Paradise Lost*'s single-mindedness and scope.

111 BROOKS, CLEANTH. "Milton and the New Criticism." *Sewanee Review* 59 (1951):1-22.
     Douglas Bush (see entry 451) fears that New Critics, with T. S. Eliot's help (see entry 89), exalt Donne over Milton. From Bush's

Critics on Milton Criticism

perspective, Milton is a great poet because he is a great moralist; Eliot says Milton is great because of his mastery of free verse. Bush's point is irrelevant, Eliot's partial. In many areas, Milton's verse resembles Donne's. *Comus*, for example, contains witty conceits and condensed images. Even *Paradise Lost*, which generally creates grand pictorial effects, uses imagery and metaphor in ways that resemble Donne's practice. Milton uses similes and images as microcosms of his entire epic. Intensely dramatic, *Paradise Regained* shows two characters in a debate about means and ends. We are always aware of the complexities of Donne's poetry, as we are not with Milton's, and this makes Milton's easier to misread.

112 HUGHES, MERRITT Y. "The Seventeenth Century." In *Contemporary Literary Scholarship: A Critical Review*. Edited by Lewis Leary. New York: Appleton-Century-Crofts, 1958, pp. 67-82.
　　　Contemporary scholarship on Milton emphasizes an understanding of the poems that does not necessarily depend on or reflect his personality. This is particularly clear in studies of Milton's cosmology, use of science, and imagery. *Areopagitica* has a great deal to say to us, and we should turn to it both for its defense of free expression and its ability to cure us of the undue influence that some scholars exert on our thinking about Milton.

113 McALISTER, FLOYD L. "Milton and the Anti-Academics." *JEGP: Journal of English and Germanic Philology* 61 (1962):779-87.
　　　While Milton scholars answer his detractors, they ignore the nature of the modern reaction to Milton, which is caused by changes in poetic theory, new critical approaches, and a conflict between the generation before World War I and that after it. The prevailing climate includes a distrust of academics, whose special interest Milton becomes in the second half of the nineteenth century. For the detractors, Milton represents all that they hate about the academy: a faulty curriculum with a philosophical orientation, too much respect for the past and its opinions, and a lack of innovation.

114 MURRAY, PATRICK. *Milton: The Modern Phase. A Study of Twentieth-Century Criticism*. London: Longmans; New York: Barnes and Noble, 1967, 172 pp.

Critics on Milton Criticism

For two centuries, Milton is seen as Shakespeare's "compeer," but in the second decade of the twentieth century this view is challenged with the first sustained attack on his poetry rather than on his politics or personality. Such poet-critics as Eliot and Pound have reservations about Milton's diction and syntax, and they argue that he has a negative influence on young poets. Focusing on Milton's ideas, instead of on the grand style, and discovering the value of his early editors and biographers, other modern critics rehabilitate his reputation. From the 1920s to about 1951, the "intellectual" tradition-- which includes Donne, Jonson, and Marvell--is considered the mainstream of English literature, while Milton is seen as operating outside of it. Basing their thoughts on Milton's role in seventeenth-century political struggles, anti-Miltonists frequently embrace very old notions about the poet's supposedly inhuman personality and simple-minded ideas; other critics try to rehabilitate our view of these areas.

115   ORAS, ANTS. *Milton's Editors and Commentators from Patrick Hume to Henry John Todd (1695-1801): A Study in Critical Views and Methods*. London: Oxford University Press; Tartu: University of Tartu (Dorpat), 1931, 381 pp. Reprint. New York: Haskell House, 1964.

The first commentary on Milton, probably by Patrick Hume, appears in 1695, its size indicating that the poet will be treated as an authentic classic. The next commentary, more methodical and based on textual criticism, is by Richard Bentley. Far less scholarly and more impressionistic, the two Richardsons speak as enthusiastic common readers. Francis Peck is a philologist and pedant. After more than fifty years of commentary accumulates, Bishop Newton compiles the first variorum edition of Milton. Warton's edition of the minor poems is the best of the eighteenth-century commentaries; this work influences Dunster's edition of *Paradise Regained* and Todd's edition of Milton's *Poetical Works*.

116   PETER, JOHN. "Reflections on the Milton Controversy." *Scrutiny* 19 (1952):2-15.

In the guerrilla warfare between the critics and the scholars who deal with Milton, too many people assume that the scholars have prevailed and that the critics' attempts to analyze the poet's deficiencies have been discredited. But the assessment of Milton is not a closed

Critics on Milton Criticism

matter. No one has yet offered a rejoinder to Leavis's (see entry 614) or Waldock's (see entry 558) arguments about the weaknesses in *Paradise Lost*'s verse and structure. Rather than carefully refuting these positions, such critics as Lewis (see entry 506) and Rajan (see entry 532) avoid direct value judgments, though they want to vindicate Milton as a personal friend by distracting attention from his faults. Tillyard's (see entry 217) and Grierson's (see entry 151) defenses of Milton's verse are dogmatic, reckless, and impressionistic.

117　SMITH, LOGAN PEARSALL. *Milton and His Modern Critics*. London: Oxford University Press, 1940, 87 pp. Reprinted (Boston, Mass.: Little, Brown, 1941); (Hamden, Conn.: Shoe String Press, 1967).

Until recently, Milton holds a secure place in the ranks of great poets. The praise grows louder from 1900 to 1920, when critics see him as no mere Puritan author and examine his age, character, influence, and sources. Then Pound and Eliot (see entry 239) express their contempt for Milton's poetry, a view that soon finds adherents in England (Murry and Leavis [see entries 11, 614], for example). Those who argue that *Paradise Lost* reveals Milton's unconscious at work believe that the epic shows his spite for Mary Powell or that Satan, embodying the unconscious Milton, is *Paradise Lost*'s hero. However, we should treasure poetry not for what it says but for how it says something.

118　STARKMAN, M. K. "The Militant Miltonist; or, The Retreat from Humanism." *ELH* 26 (1959):209-28.

A dispassionate Miltonist is no Miltonist, for the true one is militant and committed. The history of Milton criticism reflects the major concerns of literary criticism in general. After a period of anti-Miltonism in the 1920s and 1930s, scholars write Milton apologetics, as new New Critics blossom and suddenly approve of Milton and old New Critics become scholars. Distorting Milton, such writers as Knight (see entry 499) and Eliot (see entry 89) are less interested in literary criticism than in the poet's usefulness in the name of propagandistic zeal. Lewis's conversion to orthodox Anglicanism is simultaneous with his conversion to Milton, who now appears without heterodox views (see entry 506). In our century, quarrels about Milton begin on critical grounds but are resolved on religious ones. Even Ross (see entry 197), a sound Miltonist, is too interested in promoting dogma via Milton's poetry. Miltonists have retreated from humanism.

119 THORPE, JAMES, ed. *Milton Criticism: Selections from Four Centuries*. New York: Rinehart & Co., 1950, 384 pp. Frequently reprinted.

Milton receives relatively little attention in his lifetime, but in the last quarter of the seventeenth century he is often praised in critical asides. The eighteenth century, while emphasizing his religious teaching and having doubts about his style, generally exalts him. In the nineteenth century, the cult of Satan attacks the religious ideas in *Paradise Lost*; some critics split his verse into expression, of which they approve, and thought, with which they are dissatisfied. The dismissal of Milton's thought continues through the nineteenth century even as his artistry is praised more than ever. Though increasingly complex, criticism in the first half of the twentieth century continues earlier traditions: some scholars define Milton's thought as humanistic and original rather than as Puritan, while others try to fuse these views; some scholars reject the Victorians' praise of Milton's artistry and condemn his style and influence according to a newer critical theory. Other scholars attempt to refute these positions.

Thorpe provides selections from the most significant studies of Milton from 1674 to 1947.

120 WILLIAMS, ARNOLD. "Conservative Critics of Milton." *Sewanee Review* 49 (1941):90-106.

In our age, as in the eighteenth century, Milton's critics frequently bring their own religious, social, and political values into their criticism. Critics who color their scholarship with their own conservatism offer testimony to Milton's continued vitality. Rather than being honest about ideological differences, Eliot (see entry 239) and others allow this bias to affect their judgment of Milton's poetic practice. Other critics, such as Grierson (see entries 55, 151), Tillyard (see entry 216), and Whiting (see entry 228), use their philosophies of life to find a pessimistic meaning in *Paradise Lost*; they probably want Milton to emerge from the English Revolution as a pessimist. Over and over, *Paradise Lost* shows the temporary victory of evil leading to a greater good. Too many critics fail to recognize that Milton has a radical mind and character.

Critics on Milton Criticism

121   WITTREICH, JOSEPH ANTHONY, Jr., ed. *The Romantics on Milton: Formal Essays and Critical Asides*. Cleveland, Ohio, and London: Press of Case Western Reserve University, 1970, 617 pp.

New Critics who want to dethrone Milton often turn to Romantic criticism for support; historical critics consider the Romantics unfit critics, though they helped reestablish the Milton tradition. If Blake, Byron, and Shelley find Milton's Satan admirable, other Romantics--including Wordsworth and Coleridge--should not suffer guilt by association. While Keats's criticism has received some attention, that of Lamb, Landor, Hazlitt, De Quincey, and Hunt has largely been ignored.

Wittreich prints critical essays and material from such sources as diaries, letters, and poems that the Romantics wrote about Milton.

Appendixes: "A Supplementary Bibliography [of Lamb, Landor, Hazlitt, Hunt, and De Quincey]"; "The Lectures of Samuel Taylor Coleridge."

122   WOODHOUSE, A. S. P. "The Historical Criticism of Milton." *PMLA* 66 (1951):1033-44. Reprinted in *The Modern Critical Spectrum*, ed. Gerald Jay Goldberg and Nancy Marmer Goldberg (Englewood Cliffs, N.J.: Prentice-Hall, 1962), pp. 233-43.

New Criticism thus far concentrates on only the individual poem, usually a shorter lyric poem, while historical criticism examines all poems by an author in an attempt to advance from the knowledge of a poem to the entire body of poems. When considering *Samson Agonistes*, the historical critic recognizes that Milton works within a Greek and a Christian tradition. As is typical of historical criticism, we can only hypothesize about the extent to which Milton's extra-aesthetic experience enters *Samson Agonistes*. Milton bases the aesthetic patterns of his poems on a foundation of conceptual thought; the historical critic studies both. Historical criticism and New Criticism need each other.

See also entries 11, 24, 86-104, 174, 320, 361, 363, 487, 500, 535, 541, 558, 563, 609, 615, 620, 657, 661, 664, 674, 681, 683-84, 686, 786, 868, 921, 923.

Poetry

GENERAL CRITICISM OF THE CANON

123 ALLEN, DON CAMERON. *The Harmonious Vision: Studies in Milton's Poetry*. Enlarged ed. Baltimore, Md., and London: Johns Hopkins Press, 1970, 166 pp. Part reprinted in *Milton: Modern Essays in Criticism*, ed. Arthur E. Barker (London, Oxford, and New York: Oxford University Press, 1965), pp. 177-95; part reprinted in *Twentieth Century Interpretations of "Samson Agonistes,"* ed. Galbraith M. Crump (Englewood Cliffs, N.J.: Prentice-Hall, 1968), pp. 51-62; part reprinted in *"A Maske at Ludlow": Essays on Milton's "Comus,"* ed. John S. Diekhoff (Cleveland, Ohio: Press of Case Western Reserve University, 1968), pp. 58-71; parts reprinted in *On Milton's Poetry*, ed. Arnold Stein (Greenwich, Conn.: Fawcett Publications, 1970), pp. 183-89, 257-73; part reprinted in *Milton: "Comus" and "Samson Agonistes," a Casebook*, ed. Julian Lovelock (London and Basingstoke: Macmillan, 1975), pp. 185-97.

An instrument for expressing the divine will, the poet-prophet, in Milton's view, reveals a vision of universal harmony. *L'Allegro* and *Il Penseroso* show an ascending movement from the slavery of dissatisfaction to gratification. *Nativity Ode* transcends conflicts between two views to create a unity of a higher order. Because *Comus* fails to reconcile aesthetic and emotional responses into a higher

General Criticism of the Canon

compromise, it results in confusion. *Samson Agonistes* focuses on theological views about the origin of and cure for despair, a state through which Samson passes to achieve regeneration. Throughout his career, Milton turns to the myths of Orpheus and Hercules as anticipations of biblical events and as reflections of his ideals. Both characters follow the movement that governs *Paradise Lost*: a descent into darkness and an ascent to light. The Christ and Satan of *Paradise Regained* are not the same characters we see in *Paradise Lost*.

124   BANKS, THEODORE HOWARD. *Milton's Imagery*. New York: Columbia University Press, 1950, 274 pp. Reprint. New York: AMS Press, 1969.

Milton draws some images from the public life of London (monarchy, business, urban sights and sounds, for example), though he shows his puritanical nature by generally avoiding images of tavern scenes, sport, and rich clothes. He is notably aware of the body only in terms of motion and of hands. From the private life of London, Milton uses images of the house and household activities, food, and medicine. Images of travel to and from London and to the Continent are drawn from his reading and experiences, just as war imagery comes both from his surroundings and books. In Milton's view, nature, the expression of God's will, is orderly and appears as *natura naturata* and *natura naturans*. After he loses his eyesight, Milton's other senses improve. He displays his learning in images associated with writing or books, science, the Bible, the supernatural, and classical literature.

125   BARKER, ARTHUR E. "Structural and Doctrinal Pattern in Milton's Later Poems." In *Essays in English Literature from the Renaissance to the Victorian Age Presented to A. S. P. Woodhouse*. Edited by Millar MacLure and F. W. Watt. [Toronto and Buffalo, N.Y.]: University of Toronto Press, 1964, pp. 169-94. Part reprinted in *Twentieth Century Interpretations of "Samson Agonistes,"* ed. Galbraith M. Crump (Englewood Cliffs, N.J.: Prentice-Hall, 1968), pp. 74-83.

Milton's doctrine of Christian liberty, associated with his radical statements on private or domestic liberty, contributes to the structure of his later poems and the way their representation of experience develops its meaning. Although the later poems' structure shows the incompleteness of earlier dispensations and thus a discontinuity between successive dispensations, the mimetic action in these poems points to the developing response to the continuity of God's ways through all dispensations. In *Samson Agonistes*, Samson recognizes that his failure and despair lead to an understanding of God's renovating calling; he must respond by contradicting and undermining the Law while fulfilling his earlier calling to national and physical heroism. Christ in *Paradise Regained* shows the abrogation of the Law and the fulfillment of the prophetic spirit through his fulfillment of the redemptive act. In the final books of *Paradise Lost*, we see the rhythm of Adam's response to renovation.

126   BLAU, SHERIDAN D. "Milton's Salvational Aesthetic." *Journal of Religion* 46 (1966):282-95.

Because Milton's prose uses the eloquent style embraced by the Anglicans and cavaliers rather than the Puritan plain style, many people think he compromises his Puritan beliefs. The Elizabethan aesthetic is didactic, and an author shows his nobility by teaching and delighting in an opulent style. But seventeenth-century Puritans believe that mankind is divided into the elect and the damned, and that the only valid aesthetic is one that leads to salvation by teaching religious truth. In his poetry, Milton transforms the Elizabethan aesthetic to serve the purposes of a Puritan theocracy. He equates salvational and aesthetic goals in such works as *Comus*, "At a Solemn Music," and *Paradise Lost*.

127   BRODWIN, LEONORA LEET. "Milton and the Renaissance Circe." *Milton Studies* 6 (1974):21-83.

As Ariosto, Tasso, Spenser, and Sandys's Ovid reveal, Renaissance poets work within the Homeric tradition in which Circe presents three temptations with three levels of degradation: she captures the mind, degrades through sexual enslavement, and promises carefree happiness. Even at the age of eighteen, Milton gives the name of Circe to the main temptation to his sense of a higher vocation. *Comus* contains his most important treatment of the myth, for Comus, a personification of Circe, follows the pattern of Tasso's and Spenser's temptations by reversing the second and third and offering the third in two forms. With the start of the Civil Wars, Milton gives the Circe myth political significance. In *Paradise Lost*, the myth provides an analysis of the tyranny man suffers by subordinating reason to lower powers. All three forms of Circean temptation appear in *Paradise Lost, Paradise*

General Criticism of the Canon

Regained, and *Samson Agonistes*. The portrait of Dalila evokes the image of Circe.

128   BUDICK, SANFORD. *The Dividing Muse: Images of Sacred Disjunction in Milton's Poetry*. New Haven, Conn., and London: Yale University Press, 1985, 222 pp.

Milton in *Nativity Ode* shows how the Logos, functioning as a discriminator, creates a harmony structured according to the divided parts with the Word at its center. This is a special kind of dialectic, based on continuous separation at its stabilizing center. Derived from the biblical image of the mercy seat (or throne) of God, Milton's analytic images of sacred disjunction are related to the Ramist method of dichotomization, as well as to Philo's and Grotius's biblical commentaries on the dividing Word of God. God's self-imaging in *Paradise Lost* creates the impulse for all creativity and imaging; Satan can image only himself, for he cannot admit exclusion. In *Paradise Regained*, Milton has a new, untold story to sing: the recovery of paradise through the renewal of Christ's sacrifice in the reader's mind. *Paradise Regained* shows that the sum of Christian knowledge is the Logos-divided form.

129   BUSH, DOUGLAS. "Milton." In *English Literature in the Earlier Seventeenth Century, 1600-1660*. Vol. 5, *Oxford History of English Literature*. Rev. ed. London, Oxford, and New York: Oxford University Press, 1962, pp. 377-420. Reprinted 1973; part reprinted in *Milton Criticism: Selections from Four Centuries*, ed. James Thorpe (New York: Rinehart & Co., 1950), pp. 289-309; parts reprinted in *On Milton's Poetry*, ed. Arnold Stein (Greenwich, Conn.: Fawcett Publications, 1970), pp. 80-88, 238-46.

Throughout his career, Milton recreates traditional literary genres and conventions. His poetry develops as part of the mainline Renaissance tradition, moving from the richness of Elizabethan and Jacobean verse to a classical sobriety, though the metaphysical style hardly affects him. *Comus* reveals his Christian Platonic idealism, but in 1637 *Lycidas* shows signs of a spiritual disturbance. Besides developing many of Milton's ethical and religious positions (particularly his love of liberty and reason), some of his prose works are monumental, but in too many he fails to rise to philosophic principles of lasting wisdom. In *Paradise Lost*, Satan is indeed a hero--a traditional epic hero, with a conscience and unfulfilled tragic potential. The use of blank verse for a heroic poem is an innovation, and *Paradise Lost*'s style is more varied and simple than some scholars allow. Christ in *Paradise Regained* is the perfect hero; Samson in *Samson Agonistes*, a Greek and Christian work, is wholly human.

Bush provides selective bibliographies of Milton (pp. 615-22), "The Background of Literature" (pp. 496-523), and other subjects.

130   BUSH, DOUGLAS. "Milton." In *Mythology and the Renaissance Tradition in English Poetry*. Rev. ed. New York: W. W. Norton, 1963, pp. 260-97.

Like no other English poet before him except Jonson, Milton is a true classical scholar. Ovid exerts a great influence on Milton, placing him squarely in the Renaissance tradition. While the mythology of some of Milton's early poems shows Spenser's influence, with *L'Allegro* and *Il Penseroso* we see the purer, more classical influence of Jonson acting as a corrective to the Elizabethan ornateness. Milton arrives at his own *via media*. Embellishing his sacred subject with material from classical sources, Milton in *Paradise Lost* usually insists that the pagan material is untrue. He occasionally indicates that classical myth is a distorted version of biblical history. *Samson Agonistes* refers to classical myths as Gentile fables, and *Paradise Regained* uses myth to construct an argument or to portray opulence or bareness. As Milton's poetic career develops, he uses classical mythology with an increasing power and complexity.

131   BUSH, DOUGLAS. "Virgil and Milton." *Classical Journal* 47 (1952):178-82, 203-4.

Like others, Milton sees that Virgil's career progresses from pastoral to georgic and finally to epic. *Lycidas* is a pastoral work, but *Nativity Ode*, *L'Allegro*, and *Il Penseroso* belong to both the pastoral and georgic traditions. If no gap exists between Homer's theme and material, for Virgil a gap develops because his theme is somewhat symbolic and abstract. For Milton, the problem is even more acute because his theme is abstract and his characters are not ordinary humans. The *Aeneid* is an important source for *Paradise Lost*, especially in terms of structure and such epic conventions as catalogues, councils, epic similes, recapitulation of the past, and prophecy. By adapting Virgil's poetry, Milton recreates it.

General Criticism of the Canon

132   CARRITHERS, GALE H., Jr. *"Poems (1645): On Growing Up."*
      Milton Studies 15 (1981):161-79.
            From *Nativity Ode* to *Lycidas*, the English poems in Milton's
      1645 volume constitute a coherent fictive sequence, framed by the
      Greek comment on the engraving of the poet, about the writer's
      development as he becomes "a priestly poet in the priesthood of all
      believers" (161). Beginning with a birth of consciousness in *Ode*, and
      even in the next three poems, the speaker lacks a sense of human
      causality and change. The next three poems recognize but do not
      wrestle with dark negatives and adversities. Soon the speaker learns to
      assimilate peripheral facts, but not death. *L'Allegro* and *Il Penseroso*,
      ironic poems both, continue to evade life's trials and commitment, a
      stance reversed in the final movement of *Poems* (including *Lycidas*, the
      last poem), where the speaker sees that reforming the self can lead to
      reforming the world.

133   CAWLEY, ROBERT RALSTON. *Milton and the Literature of*
      Travel. Princeton Studies in English, no. 32. Princeton, N.J.:
      Princeton University Press, 1951, 167 pp.
            Peter Heylyn's *Cosmographie* (1652) provides Milton with
      many of the geographical details in *Paradise Lost*, particularly in Book
      9, when Michael shows Adam the future world, and in Book 3 of
      Paradise Regained, where Satan shows Christ the kingdoms of the
      world. Milton's interest in Russia, a country he despises for many
      reasons, is based on its religious tolerance, attitude toward
      incompatible marriage partners, and willingness to rise up and kill
      immoral monarchs. In *A Brief History of Moscovia*, Milton relies on
      books by Hakluyt and Purchas, which he was able to read ten years
      earlier and which are relevant to his epics. Satan in *Paradise Lost* is
      occasionally associated with the Tartars, known for their deceptive
      fighting tactics. More traditional, the geographical references in
      Milton's early poems are based on biblical and classical works. In his
      middle period, he adds to this knowledge with travel and contemporary
      sources. Milton finally assimilates all of this material.

134   CHRISTOPHER, GEORGIA B. *Milton and the Science of the*
      Saints. Princeton, N.J.: Princeton University Press, 1982, 276 pp.
            By shifting the emphasis from things to words as the
      sacramental medium, the Reformers make religious experience a

"literary" experience, the passionate reading of a divine text and the identification of its figures. In *Comus*, the Lady may be *virginitas fidei*, faith unadulterated, which Milton wants to keep distinct from love. As the creation scene in *Paradise Lost* illustrates, God speaks a *verbum reale*; his dramatic voice encourages us to view his speech as an event. Adding to God's command by calling for unremitting work in the garden, Eve commits a proto-sin that is by nature interpretive. She errs in the temptation scene by believing the creature's words against the creator's. In the final two books, Adam learns about the inadequacy of the visual and the superiority of the verbal. The struggle in *Paradise Regained* is between spirit and flesh, in Reformation terms, whereby flesh is not the body but the self set in opposition to God. *Samson Agonistes* presents a Hebrew hero who is an honorary Puritan saint.

135   CONDEE, RALPH WATERBURY. *Structure in Milton's Poetry: From the Foundation to the Pinnacles*. University Park and London: Pennsylvania State University Press, 1974, 211 pp.

Milton juxtaposes the careers of Satan and Adam, two of *Paradise Lost*'s heroes, to create a structure and definitions of heroism. As Satan fades, Adam emerges as the hero of patient martyrdom. In *Elegy 1*, *Elegy 3*, *Ad Patrem*, and *Lycidas*, Milton defines structure through similar patterns of contrast. Rather than dealing with extra-poetic material or beginning with one attitude and leading to another, *L'Allegro* and *Il Penseroso* examine a situation present as each poem begins. *Comus*, which continues the masque tradition while redefining it, has both a phantastic center in the freeing of the Lady and an icastic center in the reunion of the Egerton family. Like some of the early poems, *Samson Agonistes* tries to reconcile an apparently unjust world with God's just ways. But in *Samson Agonistes*, Milton more successfully creates a transition from initial conflicts to a resolution. By avoiding action and adventure, *Paradise Regained* boldly renounces and transcends the epic form. *Paradise Regained*'s dynamic structure is based on internal struggles.

136   CORNS, THOMAS N. "Ideology in the *Poemata* (1645)." *Milton Studies* 19 (1984):195-203.

When the volume of *Poems* appears in 1645, Milton has the reputation of a prose controversialist. Many of this volume's Latin poems fossilize Milton's ideology from another era: the elegies on the

General Criticism of the Canon

bishops of Ely and Winchester, written in the mid-1620s, are included, though Milton's respect for these men decreases and he publishes antiprelatical tracts in 1641-42. In poems celebrating the fifth of November and in *Elegy 4*, Milton appears reactionary in his praise of King James and in his lack of serious concern over the Thirty Years' War. The Ovidian eroticism and voyeuristic persona of some poems do not square with Milton's personality in 1645, when his prose reveals a different persona--that of a learned man pulled against his will into controversies. The enemies of Milton's prose paint him as a "low-class sectary" (201), an image that *Poems* confronts. The poems in the 1645 collection are offered as a series of documents tracing his evolution.

137   DAICHES, DAVID. "Some Aspects of Milton's Pastoral Imagery."
      In *More Literary Essays*. Edinburgh and London: Oliver and Boyd,
      1968, pp. 96-114.
      The classical tradition emphasizes the pastoral poem as art or an example of formal excellence. This attitude, rather than the desire to write didactic literature, influences Milton's early work. Often exhibitionistic pieces of art, Milton's Latin elegies show how he deals playfully or exuberantly with classical influences while displaying some personal feeling. Though *Nativity Ode* and "Epitaph on the Marchioness of Winchester" use pastoral imagery in a conventional way, the imagery in "Song: On May Morning" has a medieval English feel. The atmosphere of *L'Allegro* is English, even when we are in the world of classical mythology; *Il Penseroso* is more consistently based on classical sources. *Arcades* classicizes an English setting, but *Comus* counterpoints classical and English elements.

138   DANIELLS, ROY. *Milton, Mannerism and Baroque*. [Toronto]:
      University of Toronto Press, 1963, 239 pp. 11 illustrations.
      To produce strange and unsettling effects, mannerist art simultaneously imitates and distorts classical models, while portraying spatial movement within rigid boundaries. An example of mannerism, *Comus* does not fulfill our expectations. Similarly, *Lycidas* establishes expectations of form and central figures only to alter them. The monody's mannerist effects are most explicit when it manipulates space with rapid shifts and avoids an ordered landscape in which a broad, harmonious perspective should appear. Emphasizing openness and a diagonal penetration of space, baroque art perpetuates traditional

General Criticism of the Canon

forms even as it reacts against them. Every part of a baroque structure points to, and resists, the source of authority and power. The argument of *Paradise Lost* moves forward in the concepts of unity, power, and will, all coming from and returning to God. Both intellectually and dynamically, each of the five locales of *Paradise Lost* flows into the rest. Like other baroque artists, Milton makes extensive use of paradox and ambiguity, along with some humor. *Paradise Regained* and *Samson Agonistes* use many techniques associated with baroque art. See entries 147, 178, 206, 537.

139 DIEKHOFF, JOHN S. "Critical Activity of the Poetic Mind: John Milton." *PMLA* 55 (1940):748-72.
      Milton's revisions in the Trinity manuscript show the poetic process at work as the author clarifies thought by changing diction or syntax, fills in comparatively empty lines with material of substance, and heightens a phrase's poetic effect by inversion. He writes drafts fluently and then carefully revises them.

140 ENTZMINGER, ROBERT L. *Divine Word: Milton and the Redemption of Language.* Duquesne Studies, Language and Literature Series, vol. 6. Pittsburgh, Pa.: Duquesne University Press, 1985, 198 pp.
      Milton believes that the Reformation theology of the Word, by linking spiritual and verbal redemption, will lead to a recovery from original sin and a reversal of the effects of Babel. Early in the seventeenth century, Puritan detractors of eloquence and poetry, to be followed by the Royal Society's linguists, argue for a plain style and a congruence between words and things. Milton, aware of this climate of suspicion about language, explores the nature of redeemed speech and shows its opposite, demonic speakers or false prophets. To prepare them against temptation, Raphael must show Adam and Eve how false language works and how they can resist it. Satan, having introduced duplicity to the cosmos, violates Eden's linguistic standards. In *Paradise Regained*, Christ's vocation uses the primary tool of language to fulfill his heavenly warrant. *Samson Agonistes* most fully articulates the pattern of spiritual renewal and verbal redemption.

General Criticism of the Canon

141 FALLON, ROBERT THOMAS. *Captain or Colonel: The Soldier in Milton's Life and Art.* Columbia: University of Missouri Press, 1984, 282 pp.

　　Largely bookish and traditional, except in *Elegy 4*, the martial imagery in Milton's early poems is decorative, useful for portraying conflicting abstractions, or present to define his interest in writing a British martial epic. Milton later sees war from two perspectives: as a London citizen who identifies with the Puritan cause and as the servant of a government that directs military operations. Sonnet 8 shows his involvement in the confrontation at Turnham Green: as a bard, he will serve the warrior by praising his valor, as poets have traditionally done. Even if Milton finds war an unsuitable topic for his heroic song, *Paradise Lost* is filled with martial imagery. *Paradise Lost* issues a promise and a warning about military matters: martial imagery defines evil, shows the disobedience that leads to war and the obedience that protects against war's fatal appeal, and illustrates war's consequences for humans. Many of the military episodes and diplomatic missions in *Paradise Lost* are influenced by contemporary events. In Samson, Milton gives us the image of God's faithful soldier.

142 FINNEY, GRETCHEN LUDKE. "Speculative Musical Imagery in Milton's Poems." In *Musical Backgrounds for English Literature: 1580-1650.* New Brunswick, N.J.: Rutgers University Press, 1962, pp. 161-74. Reprint. Westport, Conn.: Greenwood Press, 1976.

　　Milton uses contemporary speculative ideas about music not to explain man's relationship to God or to man, but to turn to as a book of knowledge. He avoids a literalistic use of musical imagery, and his musical metaphors are not especially specific. Through many of his poems sounds a musical world spirit that refines or gives life. Besides this spiritual approach to music, Milton uses a Platonic approach, defining music primarily as words. He has changing ideas about the relation of love and music. Though *Paradise Lost* is written at a time when the mechanical view of the universe replaces the musical one, Milton resists this by filling the cosmos with the divine spirit's musical breath. The universe of *Samson Agonistes* is not musical. See entries 15, 22, 290, 321, 337, 370, 430, 861.

143 FISH, STANLEY. "The Temptation to Action in Milton's Poetry." *ELH* 48 (1981):516-31.

General Criticism of the Canon

In Milton's poetry, many characters' desire for action is disappointed because it is withheld ("At a Solemn Music"); is unnecessary or has already occurred (*Nativity Ode*); is not decisive in the way the characters hoped; or is decisively disastrous. *Christian Doctrine*'s definition of Christian liberty leads Milton to redefine action as interior. He seeks to detach us from expectations about actions by returning us to "a moment when nothing and everything is happening, to work us, after the example of Christ, a perpetual peace" (530). We see that the urge to ask questions about action shows our desire to shed moral responsibilities and to place them in the world of circumstance.

144   FISHER, PETER F. "Milton's Theodicy." *Journal of the History of Ideas* 17 (1956):28-53.

In theory, according to his convictions, Milton is always a monist; in practice, or in ethical experience, he is a dualist. Yet his metaphysics form the basis for and example of his ethics. Christ in *Paradise Regained* exemplifies Milton's metaphysical monism, while Satan in *Paradise Lost* bears the ethical dilemma. As a representative of the rational and metaphysical superiority of human nature, Christ conquers evil, but Satan--representing the moral tragedy of human nature--atones for evil. Metaphysical evil, in Milton's view, is the separation from the knowledge of and obedience to God's will. Natural evil is found not in the natural world but in man's nature: through sin, the individual is ultimately responsible for the suffering that comes with existence. Milton attempts to deal with ethical evil, which is rooted in man's conflict with God, by positing a theocracy that returns humans to a prelapsarian social structure. In Milton's final vision, in *Paradise Lost*, *Paradise Regained*, and *Christian Doctrine*, one achieves liberty "as a state of spiritual realization" (53).

145   FLETCHER, HARRIS FRANCIS. *Milton's Rabbinical Readings.* Urbana: University of Illinois Press, 1930, 344 pp. Frequently reprinted.

As indicated by passages in *Apology for Smectymnuus* and *Doctrine and Discipline of Divorce*, Milton uses rabbinical commentaries, particularly Buxtorf's rabbinical Bible and its marginal variants and commentaries. Part of Milton's account of the creation is based on Proverbs 8, but he makes further changes based on the commentary on Proverbs in Buxtorf's Bible written by Ibn Ezra, Rashi,

General Criticism of the Canon

and Ben Gerson. Milton follows Ben Gerson by making the muse in Book 7 of *Paradise Lost* the spirit of understanding and of wisdom, personifications of the two forces accompanying God during the creation; he follows Rashi's account of the sequence of events in the creation, the adversary's jealousy of the first couple's conjugal relations, and the development of Adam's mind. Loosely constructed and eclectic, Milton's angelology is derived from medieval Christian and Jewish sources. In general, Milton uses rabbinical sources more frequently in his poetry than in his theological prose. See entries 210, 226.

146 FLETCHER, HARRIS FRANCIS. *Milton's Semitic Studies and Some Manifestations of Them in His Poetry.* Chicago, Ill.: University of Chicago Press, 1926, 165 pp. Reprint. New York: Gordian Press, 1966.

Milton acquires a good grounding in Hebrew before attending Cambridge, where Gill, Young, and Mede help him advance his language studies. During the Horton period, he continues to focus on languages and literatures. He has the Hebrew Bible read to him after he goes blind, but his Semitic studies advance no more. Earlier, Milton can read New Testament Syriac, Aramaic (Chaldee), and the pointed text of the Hebrew canon. He uses a rabbinical Bible, probably the Buxtorf edition of ca. 1620. That he alludes to its marginal commentary (Masorah) indicates that he also reads unpointed rabbinical Hebrew, which mixes Hebrew and Aramaic. Despite his assertion in *Christian Doctrine*, he probably cannot read Arabic and Ethiopic versions of the New Testament. Milton's metrical Psalms reveal no deviations caused by a misunderstanding of the Hebrew text. Ultimately of Semitic origin, the material that forms *Paradise Lost* comes to Milton indirectly, through Continental and English literatures.

147 FRANK, JOSEPH. "The Unharmonious Vision: Milton as a Baroque Artist." *Comparative Literature Studies* 3 (1966):95-108.

As Milton's theology becomes less assured, his poetry becomes more baroque. Milton imposes obstacles to make his poetic task difficult. His urge to exploit tradition and his ability to overcome artistic obstacles make him a baroque artist. By adhering to the nativity poem tradition, *Nativity Ode* is not baroque, while *L'Allegro* and *Il Penseroso* stretch convention toward its breaking point. With *Comus*, Milton approaches full baroque work. In *Paradise Lost*, he uses traditional epic materials but stretches them in a daring way, thus isolating himself from the epic tradition. *Paradise Lost*'s use of a vast scope, humor, complex ideological matters, difficult theodicy, and literalism all point to the stretching of conventions. *Paradise Regained* is just as baroque as *Paradise Lost*, and *Samson Agonistes* is essentially baroque in the way it stretches traditional form. See entries 138, 178, 206, 537.

148   FRIEDMAN, DONALD. "Harmony and the Poet's Voice in Some of Milton's Early Poems." *Modern Language Quarterly* 30 (1969):523-34.

As Milton pushes toward the goal of writing epic poetry, he experiments with the use of a persona, which often draws its energy from the recognition of the musical symbol's power over the poet's imagination. The poet's persona shifts from the role of explainer to questioner of death in "Fair Infant." In *Nativity Ode*, the poet defines his persona by a stance in time rather than by a social role or fictive place. In "Epitaph on the Marchioness of Winchester," *L'Allegro*, and *Il Penseroso*, the persona's statements flow from his perspective rather than from any special insight or knowledge. Sonnet 7 shows Milton's thoughts about his poetic preparation, and "At a Solemn Music" shows his actions based on that preparation. He finds a way to place the human voice in relation to the universal harmony.

149   GARBER, MARJORIE B. "Fallen Landscape: The Art of Milton and Poussin." *English Literary Renaissance* 5 (1975):96-124. 3 illustrations.

In *Mansus*, Milton praises Marino, the friend and patron of the painter Nicolas Poussin. Milton shares with Poussin a respect for Tasso's poetry and theoretical writings. Like Poussin, whose syncretism may come from Marino, Milton synthesizes Christian and pagan elements in order to comment on the present. His use of allegory, mythology, and visual imagery in *Paradise Lost* is much like Poussin's. In Milton's poetry, we find two kinds of landscapes: unfallen ones, which are based on the medieval and Renaissance tradition of the earthly paradise; and fallen ones, which are elegiac, pictorial, historical, and filled with men of action. The former kind appears in the prelapsarian Eden of *Paradise Lost*, the latter in *Lycidas*, *Nativity Ode*, and *Paradise Lost*'s hell and fallen earth. Like Poussin's *Four Seasons*,

General Criticism of the Canon

Milton's *Paradise Lost* charts man's movement from an unfallen to a fallen landscape and his search for the paradise within.

150   GRACE, WILLIAM J. *Ideas in Milton*. Notre Dame, Ind., and London: University of Notre Dame Press, 1968, 213 pp.

Despite his great debt to classical and modern traditions, Milton adheres to a kind of humanism that recognizes the limitations of human knowledge. His reading of Scripture is remarkably unrevolutionary--literal and exact. While *Paradise Lost* places its aesthetic emphasis on Eve's fall, Adam's fall receives the epic's theological emphasis. The ironic hero of the epic, Satan has good qualities--he is perceptive, courageous, and a strong leader--that he perverts. In terms of one of *Paradise Lost*'s main themes, glory, Satan searches wildly for what he already has; when he loses true glory, he searches for the false version. *L'Allegro* and *Il Penseroso* examine the natures of true joy and melancholy; *Comus* deals with the natures of moderation and excess. Beginning with a sense of tragedy and frustration, *Lycidas* goes on to establish harmony and reconciliation through providence. In *Paradise Regained*, we find an author who is less lyrical and more stern. *Samson Agonistes* shows Milton rejecting humanism and embracing Puritanism.

151   GRIERSON, Sir HERBERT J. C. *Milton and Wordsworth: Poets and Prophets. A Study of Their Reactions to Political Events*. Cambridge: Cambridge University Press; New York: Macmillan, 1937, 195 pp. Part reprinted in *Milton Criticism: Selections from Four Centuries*, ed. James Thorpe (New York: Rinehart & Co., 1950), pp. 239-51.

Inspiration becomes more and more central to Milton's conception of poetry. When he decides to become a poet, it is not a decision about a career; rather, it is an admission of a sacred calling. Milton postpones the composing of *Paradise Lost* until as late as 1658 because he still dreams of creating a nationalistic epic. When he writes *Second Defence*, he realizes that he has already produced his nationalistic work in the political, revolutionary tracts, and thus needs to redefine the goal and subject of his planned epic poem. *Paradise Lost* is didactic rather than prophetic. It contains the same pessimism that we find in evangelical Christianity and Puritanism. While moving into a more restrained style, *Paradise Regained* maintains *Paradise Lost*'s didactic view of human nature and history. Milton in *Samson Agonistes* vindicates his own life. See entries 116, 120.

152   GROSS, KENNETH. "'Each Heav'nly Close': Mythologies and Metrics in Spenser and the Early Poetry of Milton." *PMLA* 98 (1983):21-36.

Milton makes the alexandrine the place of his revision of Spenser, who uses the alexandrine in the *Faerie Queene*, *Epithalamion*, and *Prothalamion* to balance ending and continuity, memory and anticipation. Rather than using the hexameter to achieve such a balance, the visionary Milton creates oxymoronic unions that are oriented, in a vertical dimension, toward the certainty of revelation, as we see in *Comus* and "Death of a Fair Infant." In *Nativity Ode*, Milton turns the hexameter's resources against Spenser by using the line "to contain images of discontinuity, departure, and vacancy" (32). *Ode* banishes both pagan deities and the worlds of mythographic Spenserian poetry with its infolded tales. The use of a hexameter line in almost all of Milton's early strophic poetry points directly to Spenser.

153   GUIBBORY, ACHSAH. "John Milton: Providential Progress or Cyclical Decay." In *The Map of Time: Seventeenth-Century English Literature and Ideas of Pattern in History*. Urbana and Chicago: University of Illinois Press, 1986, pp. 169-211.

Finding a cyclical pattern within a progressive, linear pattern, Milton believes we must break with the past rather than repeat the patterns of previous ages. His hope for future happiness, expressed in the antiprelatical and divorce tracts, vanishes after the Civil Wars and Interregnum: he loses faith in people's willingness to alter the pattern of history. Such poems as *Comus*, *Paradise Lost*, *Paradise Regained*, and *Samson Agonistes* use the journey motif to illustrate the importance of a progressive, linear movement. Change, in Milton's view, is potentially good, with Satan and human beings often condemning things for being new, while God and the Son use change and creation to bring progress. But his late prose works show signs of disillusionment as he sees that the English nation has not seized the providential opportunity and that humans are prone to relapse.

General Criticism of the Canon

154 HANFORD, JAMES HOLLY. "The Temptation Motive in Milton."
Studies in Philology 15 (1918):176-94. Reprinted in *John Milton, Poet
and Humanist: Essays by James Holly Hanford* (Cleveland, Ohio:
Press of Western Reserve University, 1966), pp. 244-63.

Because Milton sees moral conflict in virtually every aspect of
human existence, the temptation theme is dominant in his poetry. In his
early verse, he reveals little tension between his strongly sensuous
nature and Puritan asceticism. *Lycidas* and *Elegy 6* show such a conflict
based not on moral grounds but as a choice Milton faces in seeking to
write lofty poetry. If the conflict in *Comus* is clearly between abstract
sensuality and virtue, in *Paradise Lost* it occurs within the soul; both
works define temperance as a possible reconciling force. The ascetic
point of view is victorious in *Paradise Regained* and *Samson Agonistes*,
but the reality of the temptation has disappeared. Milton also
recognizes the related temptation presented by the abstract love of
knowledge and fame. Part of Milton's heroic personal struggle is
against despair, the loss of confidence in self and providence; the
temptation to distrust becomes dominant in *Samson Agonistes*.

155 HANFORD, JAMES HOLLY. "That Shepherd, Who First Taught
the Chosen Seed: A Note on Milton's Mosaic Inspiration." *University
of Toronto Quarterly* 8 (1939):403-19.

In his drafts for a drama on the fall of man contained in the
Trinity manuscript, Milton frequently changes his mind about who will
speak the prologue. Moses is the speaker in some versions, and
Milton's contemplation of him is connected to an interest in the
relationship between body and spirit, for Moses--like Enoch and Elijah
--prefigures the Resurrection by possessing his true body after death.
But Milton is ambiguous, perhaps believing that Moses lives on, after
his earthly life, in a terrestrial paradise because he is preserved by his
association with God. This episode influences Milton's use of guardian
angels in "Fair Infant," *Comus*, and *Lycidas*, as well as his discussion of
spirits and paradise in *Paradise Lost*. Milton is capable of Platonizing
Moses by showing that he has the vision required to see the truth.
Moses thus becomes Milton's original, the most important of the poet-
prophets who are his ancestors.

156   HANFORD, JAMES HOLLY, and TAAFFE, JAMES G. *A Milton Handbook*. 5th ed. New York: Appleton-Century-Crofts, 1970, 386 pp. 14 illustrations.

Materials about Milton's biography are abundant because he is a public figure and because his desire for fame leads him to present a self-portrait in many of his works. His prose is characterized by a savage joy in attacking opponents and by endless haggling over previous written authorities. Although his minor poems do not amount to a large body of work, Milton publishes them to show evidence of youthful poetic promise. *Paradise Lost* contains his views about cosmology, ethics, and doctrine. In *Paradise Regained*, he shifts much of the dramatic weight to Satan. *Samson Agonistes* too is a counterpart to *Paradise Lost*.

Appendixes: "Miscellaneous Prose Items of Uncertain Date"; "Milton's 'Biographia Literaria'"; "The Milton Portraits" (see entries 14, 17, 26); "Milton's Private Library" (see entry 78); "Milton and His Printers"; "Milton in Italy."

157   HELGERSON, RICHARD. "Milton and the Sons of Orpheus." In *Self-Crowned Laureates: Spenser, Jonson, Milton, and the Literary System*. Berkeley, Los Angeles, and London: University of California Press, 1983, pp. 185-282.

Unlike their Elizabethan predecessors, poets of Milton's age do not write out of frustrated ambition or the self-conscious sense that their accomplishments have never before been done in England. Milton, though apparently part of this belated generation that lacks a sense of literary mission and identity, is divided from his contemporaries because of his antimonarchial Puritanism, which helps to define his self-presentation. He may have examined the cavaliers' writing with care, especially work produced by poets exiled after Charles's execution. When the monarch controls the laureate, poetry becomes trivial flattery. Reversing the tradition, the new laureate is a poet of alienation and exile. Milton's 1645 *Poems* is an important self-presentational gesture, though collecting one's works and including a frontispiece no longer have the power to convey a laureate identity. With *Paradise Lost*, Milton gains autonomy, for God is his only literary patron.

General Criticism of the Canon

158   HENINGER, S. K., Jr. "Sidney and Milton: The Poet as Maker." In
      Milton and the Line of Vision. Edited by Joseph Anthony Wittreich,
      Jr. Madison: University of Wisconsin Press, 1975, pp. 57-95.
            Sidney's *Defence* underlies Milton's poetic theory in his best
      work. Du Bartas, Sidney's and Milton's favorite French author, in *La
      Sepmaine* shows a devotion to the Word (Logos) and operates within a
      Platonic framework in which he praises God as a "Work-man" creating
      with a "Forme" or "Idea." Milton Christianizes Plato's cosmogony in his
      account of the creation in *Paradise Lost*. As a true maker, the poet
      creates an icon of the zodiac (and hence of time and eternity). Milton
      begins his epic just as Spenser started his, with a statement of the fore-
      conceit: "Man's first Disobedience." He then fulfills his obligation as a
      true maker by creating a universe of time and space with a hero at its
      center. The earthly or temporal view and the divine or atemporal views
      coexist in *Paradise Lost*, forcing us to analyze every episode in two
      paradoxical ways.

159   HIEATT, A. KENT. "Spenser and Milton." In *Chaucer, Spenser,
      Milton: Mythopoeic Continuities and Transformations*. Montreal and
      London: McGill-Queen's University Press, 1975, pp. 153-270.
            Even early in his life, Milton recognizes Spenser's use of
      mythic patterns, the poetic and narrative embodiments of ideas. In
      Comus, Paradise Lost, and *Paradise Regained*, Milton finds Spenser's
      mythic framework useful (particularly that of *Faerie Queene*, Book 2),
      though he transforms its surface and terms. The conflict between
      Comus and the Lady is related to Guyon's assault on Acrasia's Bower
      of Bliss. Comus is even more closely connected to Spenser's False
      Genius. Throughout *Faerie Queene*, Book 2, the Platonist Spenser
      presents his myth through various kinds of temperance in dichotomous
      relationships, a pattern that reappears in *Paradise Lost* and *Paradise
      Regained* as Milton preserves Spenser's mythology and psychology of
      temptation. *Paradise Lost* is connected to Spenser's Garden of
      Proserpina and Acrasia's Bower. Eve's anguish and Satan's despair and
      defiance are modeled on the conduct of characters in the *Faerie
      Queene*. If *Paradise Lost*'s Satan matches Spenser's Mammon, *Paradise
      Regained*'s Satan is even closer to Spenser's character. The brief epic is
      connected to Spenser's episode about Mammon's cave.

General Criticism of the Canon

160   HUGHES, MERRITT Y. "Milton and the Sense of Glory."
       Philological Quarterly 28 (1949):107-24. Reprinted in *Ten
       Perspectives on Milton* (New Haven, Conn., and London: Yale
       University Press, 1965), pp. 12-34.

       In every major poem, Milton uses some aspect of the theme of
glory. *Lycidas* and *Paradise Regained* follow St. Augustine's lesson that
one should hold fame or glory in contempt because human judgment is
worthless. Milton conceives of the glorification of the saints either as
the beatific vision or as the fame that God gives. In the hell of *Paradise
Lost*, Milton uses light and dark imagery to show the reversal of
heaven's glory. He defines a sectarian view of glory in which an
aristocracy of grace is opposed to the majority who remain outside the
invisible church.

161   HUNTER, WILLIAM B., Jr. "John Milton: Autobiographer." *Milton
       Quarterly* 8 (1974):100-104.

       Just as Milton allows an inferior work ("Passion") to appear in
his 1645 volume of poems, so in the 1673 collection he publishes the
embarrassing "Fair Infant" because he shares the Calvinist belief that
every experience carries religious significance. This view leads to an
emphasis on autobiography to record the working of God's will on the
individual, an impulse that explains not only Milton's dating and nearly
chronological arrangement of the poems in these volumes, but also his
inclusion of poor poems. "Spiritual autobiography thus seems explicitly
or implicitly meant in everything that he wrote" (101). But Milton's
work contains no account of a spiritual conversion, an omission that
points to his Arminianism.

162   JOHNSON, LEE M. "Milton's Blank Verse Sonnets." *Milton Studies*
       5 (1973):129-53.

       In his three major works, Milton uses fourteen-line blank-verse
units as sonnets to clarify moral purport and structural design. They
Christianize classical heroism and conventions in *Paradise Lost* and
Samson Agonistes, while in *Paradise Regained* they mark each speaker's
identity and summarize the main movements in the debate about public
versus private life.

General Criticism of the Canon

163   KERRIGAN, WILLIAM. "The Heretical Milton: From Assumption
       to Mortalism." *English Literary Renaissance* 5 (1975):125-66.
            Milton's acceptance of mortalism helps rid him of the
       confusion that sometimes harms such early poems as "Fair Infant" and
       Lycidas, where evoking bodily assumption does not provide consolation
       but instead leaves him searching for a double consolation and hesitant
       about the apparent separation of body and soul. Because it preserves
       the unity of body and soul, the mortalist heresy intensifies Milton's
       sense of the dead body's dignity and gives him a clear perspective with
       which he reshapes the drama of Christian history in the eschatology of
       Paradise Lost, Paradise Regained, and *Samson Agonistes*.

164   KERRIGAN, WILLIAM. *The Prophetic Milton*. Charlottesville:
       University Press of Virginia, 1974, 294 pp.
            Renaissance literary theorists never seek to clarify the
       relationship between the roles of *vates*, which connotes madness, and
       propheta, a Christian role dealing with a complex form of inspiration.
       Linking inspiration and anarchy, Davenant in 1650 suggests that a
       poetry of reason is connected to conservative politics while a poetic
       furor is connected to the English Revolution. Calvin's doctrine that
       divides the ministry of Christ into the roles of priest, king, and prophet
       attracts Milton. In *Paradise Lost*'s first invocation, he wishes to become
       a new vessel for the Word. The poet joins the company of those Old
       Testament prophets who receive the wisdom of Christ; he shares the
       cumulative wisdom of the prophetic tradition. Satan is an inverted
       version of the narrator. Lacking a prophetic guide, readers of *Samson
       Agonistes* must be their own mediators, though Samson evokes the
       figure of the inspired narrator. The prophet becomes a zealous warrior
       rather than a divine visionary.

165   KNIGHT, G. WILSON. "The Frozen Labyrinth: An Essay on
       Milton." In *The Burning Oracle: Studies in the Poetry of Action*.
       London, New York, and Toronto: Oxford University Press, 1939, pp.
       59-113. Revised in *Poets of Action* (London: Methuen, 1967), pp. 18-
       69.
            In such poems as *Nativity Ode, L'Allegro, Il Penseroso*, and
       Comus, Milton's nature imagery is impressionistic, mechanized, and
       without energy. *Paradise Lost*, "a magnificent failure" (70), focuses on
       Adam and Eve's fortunes as Milton boldly analyzes the relationship

between the divine and the shameful. Because characters must reject something positive in order to avoid ugly lasciviousness, the repression that Milton champions leads to ethical confusion. In *Paradise Lost*, the Son is too often a figure of stark force, and Satan is unnecessarily heroic. The imagery used to describe Eden resembles that of Milton's early poems, stony and lifeless. Just as the theme of *Paradise Lost* is cosmic disharmony, so the poem itself is disharmonious. The Miltonic style, an example of verbal music, comes from the author's scholarly and romantic mind: he is a successful technician who fails as a maker.

166   KNOTT, JOHN R., Jr. "Milton and the Spirit of Truth." In *The Sword of the Spirit: Puritan Responses to the Bible*. Chicago, Ill., and London: University of Chicago Press, 1980, pp. 106-30.
        Milton's style is influenced by his stance as the defender of pure and plain Scripture, calling people to hear the Word and avoid the tainted ecclesiastical tradition. He is the heroic Christian knight, armed with the spirit and the pure Word to do battle with error. In his later controversial writings, where he needs to develop painstaking arguments from texts, Milton turns from celebrating Scripture to calling for renewed study of it. As a supplement to Scripture and as a guide, the rule of charity becomes an important interpretive tool for Milton. He sees the Spirit performing a dynamic operation in the Christian's life. At the end of *Paradise Lost*, Milton no longer emphasizes the pure Word as he does in the antiprelatical tracts. Adam's descendants will receive more guidance from the Spirit than from pure written records. Exploring the right understanding of Scripture through faith, *Paradise Regained* shows Christ both nourished by and becoming the Word. See entries 12, 25, 176, 956.

167   LABRIOLA, ALBERT C. "Portraits of an Artist: Milton's Changing Self-Image." *Milton Studies* 19 (1984):179-94.
        In *Epitaphium Damonis*, Milton's image of himself is derived from the Italian journey, which shows both his unwillingness to dissociate Diodati from the role of intimate friend and his willingness to associate himself with the ideal, enlightened culture of Italy. Had he not died, Diodati would have supported Milton's literary aspirations as the Italians did; instead, when Milton returns to England, he is isolated. The poem is his way of sharing his hopes with his friend: self-image is a necessary means to gaining self-worth. Milton is at a transitional stage

General Criticism of the Canon

in his career as he follows Virgil's example and shifts from pastoralism to higher genres, particularly an Arthurian epic. A new self-image, that of an alienated man who has failed or been interrupted, appears in other works, including Sonnet 19, *Paradise Lost*, and *Samson Agonistes*. During the Interregnum, Milton in a letter argues that the poet can change society, as he uses a stance that looks back to that of *Epitaphium Damonis*. Milton in the 1650s portrays himself in terms reminiscent of such heroes in *Paradise Lost* as Abdiel and Noah.

168   LAWRY, JON S. *The Shadow of Heaven: Matter and Stance in Milton's Poetry*. Ithaca, N.Y.: Cornell University Press, 1968, 431 pp.
        In his early poems, Milton's stance is that of a joyously confident writer, and the audience is participative. He turns for subject matter to the ideal of the monochord in his early poems, celebrating a Neoplatonic harmony while admitting that such a postlapsarian celebration is illusory. *Paradise Lost* demonstrates the one eternal act of creation, fall, and renewal, leading the audience to a godlike stance in which divine and human action must be one. The condition of all existence is reduced to the single requirement of heroic choice. Instead of facing a single choice, Christ in *Paradise Regained* faces the flow of choices that lead him to becoming perfected in knowledge. The audience must learn to will and understand, but not to do. In *Samson Agonistes*, the hero's two stances--the hell of physical and spiritual enslavement and the place of deliverance--enact the natures of Adam and Christ.

169   Le COMTE, EDWARD. *Milton and Sex*. London and Basingstoke: Macmillan, 1978, 164 pp.
        Not puritanical and certainly not prudish, Milton is outspoken about sex. He can tell coarse jokes (*Prolusion 6*), mix erotic Ovidian allusions into a poem about a bishop's death (*Elegy 3*), and fall in love with an Italian lady living in England. Milton and Mary Powell consummate their marriage, for otherwise he could claim annulment and not call for a new divorce law. Never is he a misogynist, and he privately approves of polygamy. In life and in his verse and prose, Milton disapproves of "female pride." He portrays the creation, Edenic life, and the temptation in sexual terms, treats Satan and Sin in images of sexual organs and copulation, and associates hell with entrails. Belial in *Paradise Regained* suggests tempting Christ with sexual pleasures. If

General Criticism of the Canon

Dalila receives harsh criticism in *Samson Agonistes*, other characters--not Milton--are speaking in their dramatic roles.

170   Le COMTE, EDWARD. *Milton's Unchanging Mind: Three Essays*. National University Publications. Series in Literary Criticism. Port Washington, N.Y., and London: Kennikat Press, 1973, 131 pp.
       Milton's obsession with time can be traced through all of his early poems. Instead of following the convention of portraying oneself as older and more mature that one actually is, he often presents himself as younger and less mature than he must have been. Reluctance and self-deprecation, paradoxically mixed with pride, characterize Milton's view of himself. In the prose, his rationalizations include the belief that, if an epic does not appear, this is because he needs more preparation. His prose and, to a lesser degree, his poetry show that Milton prefers grim humor or satirical wit. He uses satire as a mode, while his successors--Dryden, Pope, and Swift--use it as a form. We, not Milton, are too solemn.

171   Le COMTE, EDWARD S. *Yet Once More: Verbal and Psychological Pattern in Milton*. New York: Liberal Arts Press, 1953, 201 pp.
       Although critics often divide Milton's artistic career into three periods, the work of any one period contains verbal parallels with and other similarities to work of the other periods. "Milton's work abounds in autoplagiarisms" (10), and he frequently serves as his best commentator. In poem after poem, he shows his training in rhetoric and logic with such stylistic devices as repetition through parallelism and refrains. As we move from one poem to the next, some 300 duplicate phrases help us see how he writes and thinks; the prose works also echo one another, and the verse and prose are connected by verbal parallels. Like Milton's English work, his Latin works in verse and prose exhibit borrowings. His attitude toward women can be summed up in one phrase: female pride. Neither a feminist nor a misogynist, Milton holds the common view of his day--that women have an unequal role that they should maintain.

172   LEISHMAN, J. B. *Milton's Minor Poems*. Edited with a preface by Geoffrey Tillotson. London: Hutchinson & Co., 1969, 360 pp. Part

General Criticism of the Canon

reprinted in *Milton: Modern Judgements*, ed. Alan Rudrum (London: Macmillan, 1968), pp. 58-93.

Milton starts his career as poet under Spenser's influence, which produces the ambition to write patriotic, public, and long poems. In his minor poems, Milton, like Spenser but unlike Donne and Jonson, is very pictorial. Not constructed according to sharp contrasts, *L'Allegro* and *Il Penseroso* display the most delightful characteristics of Stuart poetry, such as octosyllabic couplets and dialectical argument. These poems and others show that Shakespeare taught Milton "not merely to see but to say" (148). Although *Arcades* closely resembles Jonson's masques, *Comus* does not because it is a self-sufficient piece of literature and it lacks spectacle and a masque proper. It is more closely related to the pastoral drama, featuring the fullest exposition of the young Milton's moral and religious idealism. A far more original poem than many have supposed, *Lycidas* transforms the pastoral elegy.

173   McCANLES, MICHAEL. "Signs of Power and the Power of Signs in Milton's Last Poems." *Southern Humanities Review* 17 (1983):327-38.

In his final poems, Milton focuses more closely on "the problematic relation of physical power to divine, spiritual power" (327). Physical power and spiritual power form a dialectic in which each negates the other and, from the negation, one gains the capacity to manifest the other. This dialectic is paralleled by the dialectic between invisible spiritual reality and its outward physical symbol. In *Paradise Regained*, the kingdom of God has a dialectical nature, both of and not of this world. Satan sees and offers only the political kingdoms of the earth. The Son refuses to accept dichotomistic categories, so he cannot react to Satan by opting for a wholly spiritual kingdom. If the Son in *Paradise Regained* is tempted to separate dialectical categories, Samson in *Samson Agonistes* is an idolater, one who reduces divine power to its physical incarnation. Milton in *Samson Agonistes* is equivocal: he does not fuse or separate human physical power and divine spiritual power.

174   MacKENZIE, PHYLLIS. "Milton's Visual Imagination: An Answer to T. S. Eliot." *University of Toronto Quarterly* 16 (1946):17-29.

Comparing Milton unfavorably with Shakespeare, Eliot (see entry 239) finds Milton's imagery not sufficiently particularized and his words not carefully married in descriptive passages. But Eliot fails to consider these descriptions in their contexts and he assumes that Milton seeks the same effects that Shakespeare achieves. Although Milton's imagery is often general, he is always attentive to the cumulative effects of specifics as parts of a larger whole. Shakespeare aims for realistic descriptions, Milton for a broader evocative design. If heaven and hell in *Paradise Lost* are both real settings and states of mind, then the mixture of abstractness and concreteness in the descriptions is appropriate. Milton generates emotional atmosphere, but his similes are visual and concrete. In the description of Eden, he fully shows his ability to control descriptive effects at long range.

175 MACKLEM, MICHAEL. "Love, Nature and Grace in Milton." *Queen's Quarterly* 56 (1949-50):534-47.

Like his contemporaries, Milton sees two levels of existence: nature and grace. Humanists keep the two separate, but Christians synthesize them with the idea of love. Milton's early poetry moves on the level of nature, with *Elegy 5*, Sonnet 7, and *Nativity Ode* revealing his initial understanding of the conflict between the humanist and Christian responses to those worlds. In the final version of *Comus*, though not in the Trinity manuscript version, Milton uses love to integrate "all levels of experience in a unified world-view" (539). *Paradise Lost* furthers this view of love as a force that unites the realms of nature and grace.

176 MADSEN, WILLIAM G. *From Shadowy Types to Truth: Studies in Milton's Symbolism*. New Haven, Conn., and London: Yale University Press, 1968, 208 pp.

Seventeenth-century theories of biblical interpretation and the doctrine of typology illuminate Milton's symbolism. He believes that through the Law God speaks obscurely, using types and shadows that are abandoned when Christ comes to earth. Except when referring to God, Milton distrusts metaphor and therefore does not use the method of accommodation in *Paradise Lost* since only God may use it. Although critics see Raphael speaking in terms of Neoplatonic accommodation, asking if earth is like heaven, Adam says that nothing on earth prepares him to understand the war in heaven. The shadow to which Raphael refers, and all the symbolism of *Paradise Lost*, is in fact Christian and typological rather than Platonic. In Raphael's speech, "shadow" means foreshadowing, adumbration, or type. Unlike Milton's Christ, his Samson cannot feel contempt about aspiring to victorious

General Criticism of the Canon

deeds. The Christian significance of *Samson Agonistes*, which is both a Hebraic and Christian play, adds irony to the speakers' literal statements. See entries 12, 25, 166, 956.

177 MADSEN, WILLIAM G. "The Idea of Nature in Milton's Poetry." In *Three Studies in the Renaissance: Sidney, Jonson, Milton*. By Richard B. Young, W. Todd Furniss, and William G. Madsen. Yale Studies in English, vol. 138. New Haven, Conn.: Yale University Press, 1958, pp. 181-283.

The figure of Comus comes from a literary tradition of naturalists. The masque's nature imagery supports the Lady's Christian attitude that nature's dictates are the same as those of reason and God. Comus and the Lady agree that nature is fertile; they disagree about its use. On one level a symbol of Christian purity in its broadest sense, virginity on another level symbolizes the transforming of the natural order by grace (Sabrina). Although Raphael tells Adam that man may someday participate with angels, *Paradise Lost* in general holds out a different goal: rather than spiritualizing the body, humans should learn to accept their condition, their place in the cosmic scheme. The ethical content of *Paradise Lost* does not involve a simple conflict between reason and passion, for both are present in varying degrees when Adam and Eve fall. Milton's epic deals with the conflict between pride and charity. As God created it, matter is not involved with disorder or evil.

178 MAHOOD, M. M. "Milton: The Baroque Artist." In *Poetry and Humanism*. New Haven, Conn.: Yale University Press, 1950, pp. 169-206.

A number of Milton's poems--particularly "Fair Infant," *Nativity Ode*, and "Passion"--are indebted to Giles Fletcher for their conceits, personifications, and baroque amplitude of conception. In *Paradise Lost*, a correspondence links the poem's shape, cosmology, and spiritual forces. Milton's cosmos, structured like a vortex, places Adam and Eve in the calm, protected center with the frantic motions of hell and the orderly motions of heaven on the perimeter. With the fall, the symmetry of this world-picture is marred as the physical and moral worlds become disordered. The historical dimension of Books 11-12 suggests the restoration of the world-order. Milton's imagery comes from a baroque awareness of the tension between the actual and the transcendental. See entries 138, 147, 206, 537.

General Criticism of the Canon

179   MARTZ, LOUIS L. *Poet of Exile: A Study of Milton's Poetry*. New Haven, Conn., and London: Yale University Press, 1980, 366 pp.
      Milton's 1645 *Poems* shows a progress toward maturity as he strives to create an impression of a youthful era and of a young, precocious poet. Both the Latin and English sections end with an assertion of Milton's attachment to Britain's history or language. Written by a man exiled by his blindness and politics, *Paradise Lost* sustains hope amid a sense of loss. Books 1-2 and 11-12 form the poem's dark border by presenting the world we know; the center contains the voice of the poet, who journeys backward and inward to discover the center of creativity. The poet's consciousness is the poem's unifying force. *Paradise Regained* reveals the Son's internal function as the voice of truth in the illuminated mind. Milton's three major volumes of 1645, 1667, and 1671 form a triptych: the youthful, joyous, pastoral work; the masterpiece, with pastoral at its center and visions of tragic failure and redemptive hope at its borders; and the austere, reasoned, rigorous work of age.
      Appendixes: "*Paradise Regain'd* and the *Georgics*"; "*Amor* and *Furor*: Anti-heroic Themes and the Unity of Ovid's *Metamorphoses*."

180   MUIR, KENNETH. *John Milton*. London: Longmans, 1955, 205 pp.
      Influenced more by the Spenserian poets than by Spenser himself, Milton in his early poems transforms their work through greater concentration and careful diction. *Nativity Ode* shows his interest in baroque imagery, and *Comus* reveals that he goes through a period of obsession with the idea of virginity. By the time he writes *Paradise Lost*, the fall is the one theme perfectly suited to his experience, ideas, and talents. After the first two books of magnificent poetry, the quality of *Paradise Lost*'s verse deteriorates when his stern and legalistic God starts to speak; the poetry of Books 11 and 12 is even weaker, but the temptation scene in Book 9 is a fine achievement. By making no concessions to readers who love poetic ornament, Milton in *Paradise Regained* creates a poem more perfect, but not greater, than *Paradise Lost*. *Samson Agonistes* deals with the recovery of faith after the hero experiences doubt and disillusionment.

181   MUIR, KENNETH. "Personal Involvement and Appropriate Form in Milton's Poetry." *Études Anglaises* 27 (1974):425-35.

General Criticism of the Canon

Milton sets goals for himself as a poet, and he reaches most of them. Although it appears that he never writes a poem until its subject (such as blindness) becomes personally important to him, in three works--*Samson Agonistes, Paradise Lost* (the invocation to Book 3), and *Second Defence*--blindness is less important as autobiography than as a matter of literary propriety, which always tempers Milton's personal feeling. The idea of premature death, though it interests Milton, appears in *Lycidas* to emphasize the loss of a poet and clergyman; the theme of chastity is appropriate to a masque. Until the 1640s, Milton does not have the experience of war, politics, and disillusionment that he needs to write *Paradise Lost* as we have it. If his epic shows human susceptibility to temptation and *Paradise Regained* portrays the Son's resistance of it, *Samson Agonistes* presents a sinful man's rehabilitation through grace. Milton's works are not fundamentally autobiographical.

182   NEUSE, RICHARD. "Milton and Spenser: The Virgilian Triad Revisited." *ELH* 45 (1978):606-39.
　　　Renaissance authors see the Virgilian triad of poetic forms (pastoral, georgic, and epic) as an autobiographical sequence that charts the poet's intellectual, technical, and personal progress; as a scheme of cultural or human evolution, ambivalently moving forward with joy into Augustan civilization but also longing for the past in a golden-age Arcadia; and as a journey back through literary history, from Theocritus to Hesiod and then to Homeric origins. As Milton recognizes, Spenser is the first English writer to shape his poetry into a record of his life's history, which moves from pastoral to epithalamium to epic. Milton's works follow the progressions of Virgil and especially Spenser: he begins with the pastoral *Poems* of 1645, whose persona develops a poetic identity as he goes through an abbreviated Christian calendar, and moves to *Paradise Lost*, which is an epic exploration of both the pastoral and epithalamium.

183   NICOLSON, MARJORIE HOPE. *John Milton: A Reader's Guide to His Poetry*. New York: Farrar, Straus, 1963, 400 pp. Frequently reprinted.
　　　All Milton's juvenilia serve as exercises in his poetic apprenticeship, bearing fruit in his later work from *Nativity Ode* on. With *L'Allegro* and *Il Penseroso*, the poet comes of age, while *Lycidas* is

one of the greatest poems of any period. Milton's prose illuminates both his early poems and the works that follow the Civil Wars. Falling into three groups--conventional, personal, and political--his sonnets reach a climax of artistic skill in the poem on the Piemont massacre. In *Paradise Lost*, Satan is a great literary creation who experiences a steady degradation, which we see in both his moral and physical nature. Inconsistent in his portrayal of God, Milton lets us visualize a character we cannot see, a character who is more often Hebraic than Christian. *Paradise Lost* is a divine comedy. Because the material for *Paradise Regained* comes from the Gospels, where Christ's style is simple and direct, Milton chooses just that style for his brief epic. Mixing Greek and Hebraic elements, *Samson Agonistes* is almost without Christian elements. All of Milton's major poems seek to justify God's ways to men.

184   NITCHIE, GEORGE W. "Milton and His Muses." *ELH* 44 (1977):75-84.
        When the birth of Christ signals the passing of the pagan gods in *Nativity Ode*, Milton tries to accomplish two incongruent things: to portray a divine hero and defeated devils (a prefiguring of *Paradise Regained*) and to present an almost dialectical opposition that we assimilate (as in *L'Allegro* and *Il Penseroso*). The English poet of *Ode* in 1629 appears to be denigrating the Latin poet of *Elegy 5*, written earlier the same year. Milton may have gone through the process of abandoning Latin and embracing English verse three times. Though the shift to English does not work during the first two attempts, Latin for Milton eventually becomes less serious and personal, a language rather than a role or gesture. His 1645 *Poems* is a collection of roles that the artist attempts, masters, and abandons. After 1645, only the roles of sonnet writer, Psalm translator, and Latin poet survive. Just as *Ode* answers and denigrates *Elegy 5*, so *Paradise Lost* deals with the *Poems* of 1645, reprinted in 1673 to respond to Milton's late work.

185   NORBROOK, DAVID. "The Politics of Milton's Early Poetry." In *Poetry and Politics in the English Renaissance*. London and Boston, Mass.: Routledge and Kegan Paul, 1984, pp. 235-85.
        Repression, Milton's early poems tell us, creates a false harmony that we should not trust. More of an experimenter than is usually acknowledged, Milton in his early verse (such as *Nativity Ode*)

turns to unfashionable literary traditions, but he also imitates the experiments of courtly writers, pushing their innovations even further to expose the conservatism behind their superficial modernity. Besides criticizing Jonson's politics, for example, *Comus* nearly crumbles the foundation of the masque form. Showing a commitment to the Spenserian tradition, *Lycidas* offers a critique of contemporary politics and poetry. Milton remains committed to the poet's prophetic role and always connects literary form and religious or political institutions that advance the cause of reformation.

186   ORAM, WILLIAM A. "Nature, Poetry, and Milton's Genii." In *Milton and the Art of Sacred Song*. Edited by J. Max Patrick and Roger H. Sundell. Madison and London: University of Wisconsin Press, 1979, pp. 47-64.

"The central theme of Milton's *Poems* (1645) is poetic conversion--the power of poetry to lead 'pagan' man toward Christian truth" (47). Through the use of genii or guardian spirits who mediate between the natural and supernatural worlds, Milton examines the nature of nature and the functions of poetry. In *Nativity Ode*, Milton banishes the genius, showing the opposition of earth and heaven, but in *Il Penseroso* and *Arcades* he stresses the reconciliation of heaven and earth. *Comus* and *Lycidas* elaborate this pattern of union, showing poetry's power to convert. After Milton's 1645 *Poems*, he uses no genii, which reflects his distrust of pagan myth and awareness of the spiritual danger of locating the sacred in created things. The guiding spirit is internalized in *Paradise Lost* and *Samson Agonistes*.

187   OSGOOD, CHARLES GROSVENOR. *The Classical Mythology of Milton's English Poems*. Yale Studies in English, vol. 8. New York: Holt, 1900, 196 pp. Reprint. New York: Gordian Press, 1964.

In his poems, Milton introduces classical mythology by using similes, incorporating a myth into a setting of his own creation, or by bringing in myth to describe nature. Because classical myths contain qualities and truths that appeal to all people, they help to give his poetry a universal appeal. We see Milton's range as he synthesizes myths and transforms them into something large and exalted. His view of myth is inconsistent: in *Paradise Regained*, he is antagonistic, regarding classical legends as hollow lies; in other poems, he indicates that myths contain hidden truths. The second half catalogues the sources of Milton's classical mythology.

188   PATRIDES, C. A. "'Something Like Prophetic Strain': Apocalyptic Configurations in Milton." *English Language Notes* 19 (1982):193-207. Revised in *The Apocalypse in English Renaissance Thought and Literature: Patterns, Antecedents and Repercussions*, ed. C. A. Patrides and Joseph Wittreich (Ithaca, N.Y.: Cornell University Press, 1984), pp. 207-37.

Milton's contemporaries believe that Revelation applies to "history" past and "history" future. In *Paradise Lost*, Satan's character contains many facets of the Antichrist, including acting as a parody of God. The revelations of Satan's imitative role point to his ambitions and the impossibility of extending them beyond parody. The Book of Revelation is only one among many models for *Paradise Lost*'s language, structure, and imagery. Such early works as "On Time," "At a Solemn Music," *Comus*, and *Lycidas* are apocalyptic even as they keep their distance from the Apocalypse. As some of Milton's prose works indicate, in the late 1630s and early 1640s he and many of his countrymen believe the Last Judgment is imminent. Milton sees the Apocalypse as Christocentric, teleologically oriented, and relentlessly eschatological. History, as *Paradise Lost* shows, is best apprehended from God's perspective: the past and present anticipate the future, which is inherent in the past; future and past are in the present.

189   RADZINOWICZ, MARY ANN. "'To Make the People Fittest To Chuse': How Milton Personified His Program for Poetry." *CEA Critic* 48-49 (1986):3-23.

Critics too frequently see Milton as political before 1660 and then as transcendent and sublime. Defining poetry as an instrument in his political attempt to educate the nation, Milton repeatedly draws a poet-figure who "experiences the process of writing as a process of self-education" (4). This persona acts as a mediator who, as the subject of education, is not a stern teacher but a friendly guide; Milton thus takes the authority from his poetry and gives a collaborative energy to his readers. The 1645 *Poems* presents the persona as a gifted, self-critical artist who works through a poetic program to master his craft. In the volume's first and last poems, *Nativity Ode* and *Lycidas*, he reaches his

General Criticism of the Canon

full mediatorial status. *Paradise Lost*'s prologues address his people, judge their society, and assert their responsibility for it.

190   RAJAN, BALACHANDRA. *The Lofty Rhyme: A Study of Milton's Major Poetry*. Coral Gables, Fla.: University of Miami Press, 1970, 198 pp.
        In *Comus*, the Lady rejects the tempter instead of arguing with him. *Lycidas* shows an assault on and a strengthening of the poem's own assumptions. The threads of *Paradise Lost*'s narrative always lead to the central moment of freedom and responsibility in the garden. Books 11 and 12 reveal that true knowledge and patience must take into account God's progressive commitment to history. In *Paradise Lost*, Milton elevates the style in order to intensify the poem's inherent pressures. Every retreat Christ makes from Satan in *Paradise Regained* marks an advance into self-realization. To bring into history the light of grace, Christ must refuse Satan's offer of the light of nature. *Samson Agonistes* completes both Milton's literary program and the pattern of a life that moves from innocence to engagement to withdrawal.

191   RAND, E. K. "Milton in Rustication." *Studies in Philology* 19 (1922):109-35.
        The youthful Milton who writes Latin verse absorbs Ovid's style, though the experiences of these poets have little in common, except that the reasons for the English poet's rustication and the Roman poet's exile are surrounded by mystery. From an early age, Milton, like Ovid and Virgil, knows he is destined to write a great work. His development shows important similarities with Virgil's. Perhaps Milton's proposed Arthuriad was intended to glorify contemporary England in an ancient, mythic setting. From Ovid, Milton receives his asceticism.

192   RAPAPORT, HERMAN. *Milton and the Postmodern*. Lincoln and London: University of Nebraska Press, 1983, 284 pp.
        An iconoclast who plays off many idealisms, Milton does not view the text as an idol that reveals meaning or spirit; rather than being logocentric, Milton's texts deconstruct themselves so they will undermine the ideology of text as presence and not accede to the idea of Scripture as the incarnate text. The allegory of Satan, Sin, and Death

General Criticism of the Canon

presents a *thanatopraxie* of writing, the praxis of the death drive. *Paradise Lost*'s pastoral imagery has a dark side, and Eve's status is linked with analogues of indeterminacy. In *Lycidas*, Milton uses the classical tradition of scattering flowers to engage in a *thanatopraxie* that deconstructs the classical metaphysics of death. The text itself is antherected, decapitated, decapitalized. Milton's imagination in his prose anticipates the rise of modern states based on the deconstruction of sovereignty. God's kingdom, from the poet's perspective, is a quasi-fascist antistate. The impotence of Milton's castrated discourse gives access to reserves of strength.

193   REESING, JOHN. *Milton's Poetic Art: "A Mask," "Lycidas," and "Paradise Lost."* Cambridge, Mass.: Harvard University Press, 1968, 219 pp.

   The Lady in *Comus*, an unfallen creature living in an unfallen natural order that she calls nature, is not drawn toward Comus's fallen world and nature. Sabrina acts as a mediator bringing grace to the Lady when she is in desperate need. The speaker in *Lycidas* shifts suddenly to the consolation of "Weep no more" because the poem suggests that artistic, poetic, and religious endeavors are cultivated in a community, which is part of the cosmic order that gives the speaker a sense of justice provided by divine governing. With Michael's help, Adam in *Paradise Lost* experiences an internal drama of moral consciousness that transforms his feelings about loss. Adam and Eve view death as endless woe or annihilation until, through a radical change in perspective, they learn that God redeems mankind through death. Milton's canon is dominated by the theme of divine rescue. His poems reveal characters who are tempted to believe that God is unjust, but who attain a knowledge and joy of God's just dealing with men.

194   RICKS, CHRISTOPHER. "Milton: Part I. *Poems* (1645)." In *English Poetry and Prose, 1540-1674*. Edited by Christopher Ricks. Vol. 2, *Sphere History of Literature in the English Language*. London: Sphere Books, 1970, pp. 249-81. Revised in *English Poetry and Prose, 1540-1674*, ed. Christopher Ricks, vol. 2, *The New History of Literature* (New York: Peter Bedrick Books, 1987), pp. 245-75.

   An awareness that he is thirty-six years old and notorious for his divorce tracts, and perhaps an awareness that he is going blind, prompts Milton to publish his *Poems* (1645), which shows a healthy

General Criticism of the Canon

tension between literary models (or traditional expectations) and what he must accomplish to surprise expectations. *Lycidas*'s first section (lines 1-164) asserts that Lycidas is dead and provides partial consolation to those who do not believe in an afterlife. Milton then denies this premise and substitutes a new consolation, which subsumes the other, based on a belief in the afterlife. *Nativity Ode*'s greatest strength is also its greatest weakness: an emphasis on the divine Christ and a minimizing of his humanity. In *Comus*, a correspondence between each character's acting and actions points to the Earl's success at inculcating values in his children, which is relevant to his role as the Lord President of Wales.

195   RIVERS, ISABEL. "The Making of a Seventeenth-Century Poet." In *John Milton: Introductions*. Edited by John Broadbent. Cambridge: Cambridge University Press, 1973, pp. 75-107.

Milton sees all of his training and experience as preparation for becoming a guide or educator of his nation. The humanist education at St. Paul's School, the scholastic education at Cambridge University, and Milton's personal reading program prepare him to perform "all the offices both private and public." In his view, poetry must achieve beneficial social effects, and the true poet is an inspired prophet. Never drawing on the English tradition in his early search for a poetic identity, Milton turns instead to Ovid. At Cambridge, he starts to experiment with contemporary native traditions, including devotional and metaphysical poetry. He sees his involvement in writing political pamphlets as a way to reconcile the active public life with the apparently passive, retired life of the poet.

196   ROSCELLI, WILLIAM JOHN. "The Metaphysical Milton (1625-1631)." *Texas Studies in Literature and Language* 8 (1967):463-84.

Milton's early verse differs from Donne's and Herbert's in terms of imagery, the purposes for using it, the treatment of ideas, and language and versification. After he enrolls at Cambridge, and before he writes *L'Allegro* and *Il Penseroso*, Milton experiments with metaphysical imagery in "Fair Infant," "Passion," "On Shakespeare," the two Hobson poems, and "Epitaph on the Marchioness of Winchester." He uses the metaphysical image to help him cope with death, a subject he has difficulty treating in verse. *Nativity Ode*'s imagery is not indebted to the metaphysicals.

General Criticism of the Canon

197 ROSS, MALCOLM MACKENZIE. "Milton and the Protestant Aesthetic: The Early Poems." In *Poetry and Dogma: The Transfiguration of Eucharistic Symbols in Seventeenth Century English Poetry*. New Brunswick, N.J.: Rutgers University Press, 1954, pp. 183-204.

Milton is not an Anglo-Catholic poet, for his rhetoric destroys ritual. His Christian symbols cease to be ritualistic as soon as he externalizes them. While remaining distinctively Protestant, Milton's art at its highest borders on the secular. Detaching the Christ symbol from traditional associations, Milton never presents him as an incarnational symbol. In *Nativity Ode*, Christ is a symbol of abstract values rather than a person, the Son of God not of man. The Anglican ritual appears in a positive light for the last time in *L'Allegro* and *Il Penseroso*; *Comus* attempts to move toward a transcendent conception of victorious grace, but confused and inadequate symbolism spoils it. *Lycidas* turns away from sacramental symbolism and toward the purified imagery of a new Protestant aesthetic. See entry 118.

198 ROSS, MALCOLM MACKENZIE. *Milton's Royalism: A Study of the Conflict of Symbol and Idea in the Poems*. Cornell Studies in English, vol. 34. Ithaca, N.Y.: Cornell University Press; London: Oxford University Press, 1943, 163 pp.

While he attends Cambridge, Milton is unaware of the disintegration of the Elizabethan cultural synthesis, so his mind--but not his world--holds classical, Elizabethan, and Puritan elements in suspension. The conflicts among these elements become clear in *Lycidas*, though Milton may have sided with Parliament as early as 1628, defended the monarchy (with reservations) in 1642, and kept silent on the subject from then until 1649. The belated Elizabethan apprenticeship of a man in search of a lost Spenserian ideal accounts for *Paradise Lost*'s conflict between royalist imagery and antiroyalist ideology. In his epic, "God is Caesar," and cosmic order is "a mighty tyranny" (75). Instead of distinguishing between the king of heaven and the kings of earth, Milton makes God more despotic than Charles I. Avoiding the royalist contradiction, *Paradise Regained* dramatizes the aristocratic triumph of the elect, and *Samson Agonistes* shows the apotheosis of power and vengeance.

General Criticism of the Canon

199 RØSTVIG, MAREN-SOFIE. "The Hidden Sense: Milton and the Neoplatonic Method of Numerical Composition." In *The Hidden Sense and Other Essays*, by Maren-Sofie Røstvig, Arvid Løsnes, Otto Reinert, and Diderik Roll-Hansen. Norwegian Studies in English, no. 9. Oslo: Universitetsforlaget; New York: Humanities Press, 1963, pp. 1-112.

Numerical composition results from applying Neoplatonic principles to artistic creation. In *Paradise Lost* and *Christian Doctrine*, Milton uses numerical composition to provide a structure and as an allegorical device. His discussion of the "two great sexes" in Book 8 visualizes the Platonic One, in which the odd numbers are associated with the active male principle of form and the even numbers with the passive female principle of matter. *Nativity Ode* follows the pattern of the Platonic lambda, and such works as Milton's Psalm translations, *Comus*, and "At a Solemn Music" are based on numerical composition.

200 SAGE, LORNA. "Milton's Early Poems: A General Introduction." In *John Milton: Introductions*. Edited by John Broadbent. Cambridge: Cambridge University Press, 1973, pp. 258-97.

By publishing *Poems* (1645), which carefully summarizes his early career, Milton announces that he is a poet, but one with a very small audience. While Cowley's and Cleveland's popular verse is witty and contemporary, Milton's early poems are serious and old-fashioned, looking back to Stuart writers who praise the monarch in the Elizabethan tradition of poetry. But Milton subverts this tradition by associating pastoral with revolution. The 1645 volume is intended to convey the picture of a self-sufficient author, acting as a Neoplatonic high priest who presents only polished work. If *Nativity Ode* and "Passion" are Neoplatonic, such poems as *Arcades*, *L'Allegro*, and *Il Penseroso* examine our world and speak to a broad community. In *Comus*, the explicit myth of community disguises an allegory of the individual's spiritual journey, which ultimately leads not to community but to autonomy. *Lycidas* validates individualism as it turns society into the outsider.

201 SAINTSBURY, GEORGE. "Milton." In *The Cambridge History of English Literature*. Edited by A. W. Ward and A. R. Waller. Vol. 7, *Cavalier and Puritan*, Cambridge: Cambridge University Press, 1911, pp. 95-141. Frequently reprinted.

General Criticism of the Canon

Milton offers us his life and work to explain each other. An indulgent father and lack of obstacles allow him to lead a studious life until he turns to writing pamphlets during the Civil Wars. His extensive reading and insufficient experience with life lead to a disdain for women and a traumatic marriage to Mary Powell. If Milton's early poems show signs of uncertainty, from *L'Allegro* to *Samson Agonistes* he is in complete control. Although *Paradise Lost* cannot maintain the height of its first two books, it is still a magnificent and unique work, and *Paradise Regained* is little inferior. *Samson Agonistes* brilliantly combines personal and poetic appeal. In his prose, Milton almost always fights for a prize that is not, in a literary sense, worth the competition. Sometimes abusive and offensive, he makes his opponents fight on his grounds, with his premises. His Latin poems show many signs of being exercises.

Appendix: "A Conspectus of Milton's Prose Works, with a Note on the Text of the Poems."

202 SAMUEL, IRENE. "The Development of Milton's Poetics." *PMLA* 92 (1977):231-40.

Very concerned about the theory of poetry, even though he never devotes a tract to the subject, Milton leaves fragmentary and various views. He is consistent in his view of poetry as a high office, the poet's need for inspiration, and the reader's need for fitness. While the younger Milton turns to Ficino's idea of a *furor poeticus* and the Horatian notion of developing one's own poetic skills, the mature Milton, as a reformer, looks to poetry's social and didactic utility, as Tasso had done. In the 1640s, Milton has a faith in the judgment of plain men that fades during the Interregnum and Restoration. The poet, he concludes, may teach only the teachable. Milton uses an Aristotelian poetics in *Paradise Lost, Paradise Regained,* and *Samson Agonistes,* in which poetry is mimesis, along with the Platonic view of poetry as paideutic. Concerning Milton's poetics, his three major poems tell us more by implication than do all of his prose statements on the subject.

203 SAMUEL, IRENE. "Milton on Comedy and Satire." *Huntington Library Quarterly* 35 (1972):107-30.

Based on reason, according to Milton, comedy imitates an action to produce laughter, and satire castigates, though it may also

General Criticism of the Canon

produce laughter in order to correct. The talent for laughter has a place
in Milton's notion of an urbane, virtuous individual. His early poems
use comedy and jests, but the latter appear in his prose, along with the
anger and laughter that he uses as corrective devices against opponents.
Horace influences his thinking about comedy and satire. *Paradise Lost*,
Paradise Regained, and *Samson Agonistes* contain more comedy than
critics usually acknowledge.

204   SCHULTZ, HOWARD. *Milton and Forbidden Knowledge*. New
      York: Modern Language Association of America; London: Oxford
      University Press, 1955, 316 pp.
         Milton probably doubts the prevalence and perhaps the
      existence of witchcraft in his age. Legitimate knowledge, as Bacon
      asserts, squares with the revealed truth of religion and is useful. In *Of
      Education*, Milton avoids Comenius's and the occultists' dream of
      education, turning instead to vocational training and the pagan ideal of
      humility. He follows tradition in reconciling learning with piety. In
      Paradise Lost, Raphael teaches Adam that self-knowledge is the
      beginning and end of wisdom; all other knowledge is curiosity. Uriel
      limits natural knowledge to the service of faith and worship, while
      Michael provides a lesson about self-knowledge in a context of original
      sin. The supposed rejection of knowledge in *Paradise Regained* is in fact
      consistent with *Of Civil Power* and *Likeliest Means To Remove
      Hirelings*: a minister needs to know God's Word; all other knowledge is
      inferior and dispensable.

205   SHAWCROSS, JOHN T. "Milton and Covenant: The Christian
      View of Old Testament Theology." In *Milton and Scriptural
      Tradition: The Bible into Poetry*. Edited by James H. Sims and
      Leland Ryken. Columbia: University of Missouri Press, 1984, pp.
      160-91.
         According to Milton, prelapsarian Adam is full of the law of
      nature, so no covenant of grace is needed. A prohibition or command
      never involves a covenant; thus, as *Paradise Lost* argues, man cannot
      accuse God of failing to uphold his part of the covenant when Adam
      and Eve sin. After the protevangelium comes a mutual covenant of
      grace between God and man, with Adam and Eve's posterity partaking
      of both the sin and the covenant. The old covenant posits the future
      Messiah; fully supplanting the old, the new covenant begins with the

General Criticism of the Canon

Incarnation. Although man abrogates the covenant of grace, it continues in perpetuity. *Paradise Regained* examines the means by which man can fulfill his covenant with God, as the brief epic's tension is between the old covenant and the new. *Samson Agonistes*, on the other hand, studies a prideful man who does not hold faith but whose humiliation leads to renovation. While Samson voids the covenant, God maintains it.

206 SHAWCROSS, JOHN T. "Pictorialism and the Poetry of John Milton." *Hartford Studies in Literature* 13 (1981):143-64. 6 illustrations.
     Many baroque elements--particularly verticality, syntactic ambiguity, and expansion--appear in *Paradise Lost*'s war in heaven, while Michael goes against baroque conventions by carefully framing human history. Like *Nativity Ode*, *Paradise Lost* has a form and boundary that are apparent when we view the total work; within each poem, however, the form and boundary move. Baroque works exist to glorify God. The important aspect of pictorialism is not the imitation of pictures but the imitation of the process of visual perception, in which the author uses analogues of vision to partake of "past, present, and future affectiveness" (155). *Paradise Regained* uses analogues of vision in a late baroque manner, along with a sense of verticality. See entries 138, 147, 178, 537.

207 STARNES, DeWITT T., and TALBERT, ERNEST WILLIAM. "Milton and the Dictionaries." In *Classical Myth and Legend in Renaissance Dictionaries: A Study of Renaissance Dictionaries in Their Relation to the Classical Learning of Contemporary English Writers*. Chapel Hill: University of North Carolina Press, 1955, pp. 226-339. Reprint. Westport, Conn.: Greenwood Press, 1973.
     Although Milton uses many dictionaries, he most frequently draws proper names and place names from Robert Stephanus's *Thesaurus* and Charles Stephanus's *Dictionarium*. Some of the geographical references in *Comus* and *Paradise Lost* come from Natalis Comes's *Mythologiae*.

General Criticism of the Canon

208 STEADMAN, JOHN M. *Milton's Biblical and Classical Imagery*.
     Duquesne Studies, Language and Literature Series, vol. 5.
     Pittsburgh, Pa.: Duquesne University Press, 1984, 270 pp.
         Milton uses the classical and biblical traditions in two ways: to
     show analogies between them that reveal classical literature to be a
     figurative commentary on Scripture, or to show the two traditions as
     antithetical. In *Paradise Lost*, he alludes to classical heroes to link his
     epic with those of his predecessors, even while affirming the truth of his
     subject and the superiority of his view of spiritual heroism. The muse in
     the invocations to Books 3 and 7 (and in 9.21) is identical; however, the
     Spirit of the opening invocations of *Paradise Lost* and *Paradise
     Regained* is not Urania but a related Spirit of God. If Dalila in *Samson
     Agonistes* is associated with such temptresses as Circe and the sirens,
     Samson is the Odysseus figure who refuses their charms. In *Paradise
     Lost*, Satan's assaults on Eve, especially in her dream, suggest sorcery.

209 STEADMAN, JOHN M. *Milton's Epic Characters: Image and Idol*.
     Chapel Hill: University of North Carolina Press, 1968, 356 pp. Part
     reprinted in *Milton: Modern Essays in Criticism*, ed. Arthur E.
     Barker (London, Oxford, and New York: Oxford University Press,
     1965), pp. 467-83; part reprinted in *Twentieth Century Interpretations
     of "Samson Agonistes*," ed. Galbraith M. Crump (Englewood Cliffs,
     N.J.: Prentice-Hall, 1968), pp. 106-7.
         Milton's portrayals of Adam, Satan, and the Son provide
     contrasting patterns of heroic virtue to show the difference between
     divine and secular criteria for heroism and heroic poetry. At the center
     of true heroism and true heroic poetry is the divine image, lost with the
     fall and recovered through Christ's satisfaction. Christ is thus the heroic
     norm, and the supreme heroic act is in his ministry of heroic
     redemption and its dual aspects of humility and exaltation. The secular
     hero seeks the opposite, high repute for the self on earth. In Milton's
     epics, the idea of felicity or beatitude is intrinsic to each poem's
     meaning, argument, and structure. Milton's three major poems present
     heroic idols whose personalities parallel those of classical heroes. Any
     virtues the devils in *Paradise Lost* possess are Gentile, not Christian, in
     nature.

210 STOLLMAN, SAMUEL S. "Milton's Rabbinical Readings and
     Fletcher." *Milton Studies* 4 (1972):195-215.

General Criticism of the Canon

Neither Milton nor Harris Francis Fletcher (see entry 145) is able to deal with the complexities of rabbinical Hebrew. Fletcher's evidence that Milton uses rabbinical sources is largely irrelevant because Fletcher frequently mistranslates these texts and because many of the parallels can be traced to other sources. There is evidence that Milton makes very limited use of the Buxtorf rabbinical Bible. See entry 226.

211   STROUP, THOMAS B. *Religious Rite and Ceremony in Milton's Poetry*. Lexington: University of Kentucky Press, 1968, 94 pp.

Liturgical ceremony or ritual structures Milton's poetry and provides an important theme, despite his objections to it in later life. Such poems as *Nativity Ode* and "At a Solemn Music" describe rituals of praise even as they become rituals of praise. The conflict of two double rites, Comus's and Sabrina's, defines the plot of *Comus*. By adapting classical conventions to suggest a Christian burial rite, *Lycidas* becomes a ritualistic poem. Among the many genres in *Paradise Lost* are such ritualistic lesser genres as the mystery and morality play, sermon, anthem, prayer, canticle, and oration. Christ's mission in *Paradise Regained* begins with the new baptism, which joins men's spirits with that of God. In *Samson Agonistes*, the last day of Samson's life follows a pattern that generally corresponds to the liturgy, moving from despair to confession of sins, and then to trial, wisdom, absolution, sacrifice, and salvation.

212   SVENDSEN, KESTER. *Milton and Science*. Cambridge, Mass.: Harvard University Press, 1956, 314 pp.

Many of Milton's ideas about mineralogy, botany, biology, and cosmology are derived from popular encyclopedias of science. In most of his work, except for Raphael's speech in *Paradise Lost*, Milton presents a geocentric universe, which acts as "one massive metaphor for its Maker and his ways to the first man" (85). *Paradise Lost* is a cosmological epic because it assimilates the particulars of natural properties and relationships through classical, medieval, and contemporary images. Whether composed of stones, plants, or beasts, hierarchies exist in Milton's works to teach man his place in the grand scheme, so he can ascend to God. His poetry and especially his prose works are filled with images drawn from medicine and anatomy. *Doctrine and Discipline of Divorce* is based on a comparison between

General Criticism of the Canon

the distortion of nature and the diseases in society caused by legal impediments to divorce. See entries 6, 18, 459, 476, 489, 512, 521, 579, 728.

213   TAYLER, EDWARD W. *Milton's Poetry: Its Development in Time*. Duquesne Studies, Language and Literature Series, vol. 2. Pittsburgh, Pa.: Duquesne University Press, 1979, 283 pp.
      Typology allows us to reason back and forth, from type to antitype to the Second Advent, to recognize the eternal patterns of past, present, and future events. Unlike Milton's successful poetry, "Fair Infant," "Circumcision," and "Passion" fail because they do not relate their central events to the past and future. *Nativity Ode* and *Lycidas*, however, define the eternal significance of their main events by recognizing them as types with a rhythm of prefiguration and fulfillment. Working through two movements of six books each and three movements of four books each, *Paradise Lost* illustrates how time reveals through types and *kairoi*. The epic is progressive revelation, unfolding the movement of providential history. *Samson Agonistes* relies on proleptic form, the anticipation of a known fulfillment. The lesson of *Paradise Regained* is patience or delay as the Incarnation brings the time of God into the time of man.

214   TAYLOR, DICK, Jr. "Grace as a Means of Poetry: Milton's Pattern for Salvation." *Tulane Studies in English* 4 (1954):57-90.
      Milton's major poems are based on the shaping principle that, for fallen man in the world of nature, victory in trial leads to grace and salvation. Though it is not required, a miraculous event always accompanies this victory. The unbending Lady in *Comus* resists temptation and, with the miraculous appearance of Sabrina, receives grace. Concerned with the trial and affirmation of the poet's creative faith, *Lycidas* contains more tension and another miracle, the deification of Lycidas, showing the extension of grace. *Paradise Lost* prepares for the fall by showing Adam's and Eve's weaknesses and Satan's opportunism, but the couple faces greater temptation--to despair and evade responsibility--in Book 10. Because they are victorious, prevenient grace descends. Like Milton's other protagonists, Samson experiences an inner struggle, which teaches him through "rousing motions" to make God's will his will. Of all his major poems,

General Criticism of the Canon

Paradise Regained shows the closest adherence to the pattern of trial and victory.

215 TILLYARD, E. M. W. *The Metaphysicals and Milton*. London: Chatto and Windus, 1956, 95 pp.

In its self-centered thought, logical structure, rhetoric, and voice, Donne's sonnet on his dead wife ("Since she whom I lov'd") reveals a different poetic personality from the one we find in Milton's Sonnet 23 on his dead wife. Milton's is not self-centered, and its logic never turns back on itself. Writing personal poetry, Donne is always an individualist, while Milton, more interested in action and public matters, submits himself to the literary conventions of his age. *Nativity Ode*, which seems closest to the metaphysical style, does not match the contortions of Donne's poems; it is more like Marvell's work in its use of fanciful comparisons. Unlike Donne, Milton rarely uses the rhythms of familiar speech in his verse. His epics use the elements of surprise and irony, but never on a small scale.

216 TILLYARD, E. M. W. *Milton*. London: Chatto and Windus; New York: Dial, 1930. Rev. ed. London: Chatto and Windus; New York: Collier Books, 1967, 348 pp. Part reprinted in *Milton Criticism: Selections from Four Centuries*, ed. James Thorpe (New York: Rinehart & Co., 1950), pp. 178-210.

Sometime around Christmas, 1629, Milton dedicates himself to the calling of epic poet. The nominal subject of *Lycidas* is Edward King's death; its real subject, Milton himself. His prose provides an almost tragic display of the changes in his thinking and preserves fragments of the epic that he would have written if political events had been different. *Paradise Lost* is really about "the true state of Milton's mind when he wrote it" (201). The human drama is at the center of the epic: Eve falls because of her mental triviality or lack of awareness of the issues; Adam's gregariousness leads to his fall, and he then plunges into mental levity and finally into sensuality. Satan, especially in the first half of *Paradise Lost*, best expresses the heroic energy in which Milton strongly believes. Milton never convinces us that a state of innocence is superior to an unregenerate state of sin; instead, we imagine that Milton, "stranded in his own Paradise, would very soon have eaten the apple on his own responsibility and immediately justified the act in a polemical pamphlet" (239). There is an underlying pessimism in

General Criticism of the Canon

Paradise Lost. Paradise Regained corrects features of *Paradise Lost* that Milton came to disapprove of: inconsistency of tone, unbalanced structure, and uncontrolled characters. See entries 11, 120, 361, 657.

217 TILLYARD, E. M. W. *The Miltonic Setting Past and Present.* Cambridge: Cambridge University Press; New York: Macmillan, 1938, 219 pp. Frequently reprinted.
    L'Allegro and *Il Penseroso* have a friendliness of tone that invites us to share the poet's experiences. *Lycidas* reinforces the idea of the poet's reconciliation to life as it is and reveals the patterns of rebirth and tragedy. In his poetry, Milton moves from one form of consciousness to another, as he deals with myths or archetypal patterns to express primitive feeling. His grandeur of sound and general descriptions are complemented by a powerful visual imagination and specific, sensuous details. As he grows older, Milton does not lose the tenderness and Elizabethan opulence of style that mark some of his work; such characteristics appear in various places, as the subject demands, in *Paradise Lost*. His style is organic, with substance and style conceived together. *Paradise Lost* combines the medieval epic's emphasis on religion, the Renaissance epic's political foundation, and a neoclassical compression of form. Milton could not write his proposed Arthuriad because he believed England had failed in its time of crisis. See entry 116.

218 TILLYARD, E. M. W. *Studies in Milton.* London: Chatto and Windus; New York: Macmillan, 1951, 184 pp. Frequently reprinted; part reprinted in *Milton: A Collection of Critical Essays*, ed. Louis L. Martz (Englewood Cliffs, N.J.: Prentice Hall, 1966), pp. 156-82; part reprinted in *"A Maske at Ludlow": Essays on Milton's "Comus,"* ed. John S. Diekhoff (Cleveland, Ohio: Press of Case Western Reserve University, 1968), pp. 43-57; part reprinted in *Milton: "Paradise Lost," a Casebook*, ed. A. E. Dyson and Julian Lovelock (London and Basingstoke: Macmillan, 1973), pp. 122-28.
    In order to bring Adam and Eve from innocence to sin in a plausible way, Milton anticipates the fall in *Paradise Lost* with Eve's dream and Adam's statement about how feminine beauty affects him. Technically innocent but virtually fallen, they cross the line that separates innocence from experience before eating the apple. There is no single moment of crisis; rather, the narrative differs from theology

General Criticism of the Canon

by showing a psychological movement toward sin. When the processes of destruction and despair culminate in Book 10, the regenerative process has actually started. Eve's conciliatory speech and Adam's acceptance of it mark the crisis of *Paradise Lost*. Adam and Eve are the heroes of *Paradise Lost*. Both stupid and splendid, Satan is not inconsistent just because he acts out different roles in different situations. Comus and the Lady both make erroneous arguments, or--if they are right--they are right in ways they do not see. Throughout his life, Milton is interested in the themes of action and contemplation. *Paradise Regained* stresses the latter, reflecting his inner state of mind at the time. See entry 657.

219   TOLIVER, HAROLD E. "Milton: Platonic Levels and Christian Transformation." In *Pastoral Forms and Attitudes*. Berkeley, Los Angeles, and London: University of California Press, 1971, pp. 151-76.

If one's place in the hierarchy is fixed in *Paradise Lost*, in Milton's early poetry--including *Arcades*, *Nativity Ode*, *L'Allegro*, *Il Penseroso*, and *Comus*--Platonic cycles of descent and return are prominent. Milton explores patterns of ascent that bring paradise within reach, and with each level of ascent comes an appropriate level of style. After the 1640s, he can no longer allow political emblems to show divine manifestations or to lead one's ascent, as in *Arcades*. Experience itself is hierarchical in *L'Allegro* and *Il Penseroso*, and the passive poet undergoes a metamorphosis in which his spiritual journey is fulfilled in an idyllic vision. In *Comus*, temptation links transformation and moral trial; the Lady knows about virtue or grace, but through music and song, which must be guided by reason, she learns how to make harmony functional. Art and Platonic harmony have no efficacy in *Lycidas*, which begins with innocent pastoralism and counters it with realism. Only a combination of apocalyptic and pastoral conventions can answer nature's disruptive power in the monody.

220   TUVE, ROSEMOND. *Images and Themes in Five Poems by Milton*. Cambridge, Mass.: Harvard University Press, 1957, 161 pp. Frequently reprinted; part reprinted in *Milton: Modern Essays in Criticism*, ed. Arthur E. Barker (London, Oxford, and New York: Oxford University Press, 1965), pp. 58-76; part reprinted in "*A Maske at Ludlow*": *Essays on Milton's "Comus*," ed. John S. Diekhoff

General Criticism of the Canon

(Cleveland, Ohio: Press of Case Western Reserve University, 1968), pp. 126-64; part reprinted in *On Milton's Poetry*, ed. Arnold Stein (Greenwich, Conn.: Fawcett Publications, 1970), pp. 60-73; part reprinted in *Milton: "Comus" and "Samson Agonistes," a Casebook*, ed. Julian Lovelock (London and Basingstoke: Macmillan, 1975), pp. 76-83.

The subject of *L'Allegro* is not merely Milton's gladness but the female personification Gladness, the grace named Euphrosyne. The subject of *Il Penseroso* is the goddess Melancholy. Mirth and melancholy are the dominant symbols in the two poems, which show how to comprehend different things. *Nativity Ode* is in fact about the mystery of the Incarnation, which controls its imagery. As a hymn, this poem uses music as a key symbol; accompanying this are harmony, time, and light. *Lycidas* poses questions about the end of a poet's and a priest's effort that are more suited to tragedy, from which Milton descends into pastoral. The poem's figurative imagery carries throughout the theme of Christian consolation. But consolation is figured in *Lycidas* by love's conquest of hostility and death. Masques, which have designs instead of plots, start out as images because they dramatize ideas. *Comus* uses pastoral imagery because the pastoral and masque have a similar metaphoric base: "that sense of unifying harmony between all creatures of 'Nature,' human or not" (124). Seldom do the images of *Comus* convey description or argument; instead, they reveal by imitating the coherence or incoherence of what they symbolize.

221   ULREICH, JOHN C., Jr. "The Typological Structure of Milton's Imagery." *Milton Studies* 5 (1973):67-85.

Not dissociative but reassociative, Milton's language recreates metaphor as a process of typological fulfillment. Milton, a rationalist when dealing with analogies, uses types that undercut their own meaning. From the medieval world view, he preserves the structure of typology but not the sacramental type. He destroys the image's letter in order that it may be reborn in the spirit of his symbolic intent; he thus unifies by recreating concrete meaning.

222   VICARI, PATRICIA. "The Triumph of Art, the Triumph of Death: Orpheus in Spenser and Milton." In *Orpheus: The Metamorphoses of*

a Myth. Edited by John Warden. Toronto, Buffalo, N.Y., and London: University of Toronto Press, 1982, pp. 207-30.

Orpheus appears frequently in Milton's work, carrying both a personal and emblematic significance. In *L'Allegro* and *Il Penseroso*, Orpheus is the consummate poet, but even in *Comus*, which never alludes to him, the triumph of music is Orphic, and the theme of chastity's power to overcome lust is similar to medieval allegorical treatments of the Orpheus myth. Like the chastity of Book 3 of the *Faerie Queene*, chastity in *Comus* will lead to fertility and marriage. All characters except Comus reflect part of the Orphic persona. In *Lycidas*, Orpheus is a symbol of the failure of even miraculous poetry to control people; in *Paradise Lost*, Milton rejects the Orpheus myth while identifying himself with Orpheus and contrasting Orpheus's poetry with his own.

223 WADDINGTON, RAYMOND B. "Milton among the Carolines." In *The Age of Milton: Backgrounds to Seventeenth-Century Literature.* Edited by C. A. Patrides and Raymond B. Waddington. Manchester: Manchester University Press; Totowa, N.J.: Barnes and Noble Books, 1980, pp. 338-64.

Although Milton's *Poems* and Waller's *Poems*, both printed by Moseley in 1645, appear to be twins, there are key differences in organization, voice or persona, and implied audience. Milton's prophetic stance and vatic voice place him outside the mainstream of fashionable Caroline poetry. A passage in *Reason of Church-Government* signals a shift in emphasis from Platonic poetics to strictly religious poetics; the design and persona of the 1645 *Poems* convey this sense of a newly confirmed vocation. As Milton turns to writing epics, the Orphic maker of symbolic, harmonizing images yields to the Mosaic expounder of types. His religious verse is influenced primarily by Spenser, his social verse by Jonson. But Milton is also influenced by his own work, leading to "self-plagiarism" that helps create an image of himself as poet while placing his earlier work in the established literary tradition.

224 WATKINS, W. B. C. *An Anatomy of Milton's Verse.* Baton Rouge: Louisiana State University Press, 1955, 162 pp. Part reprinted in *Milton: A Collection of Critical Essays,* ed. Louis L. Martz (Englewood Cliffs, N.J.: Prentice-Hall, 1966), pp. 121-47.

General Criticism of the Canon

Starting with *Comus*, Milton's verse appeals to all of the senses, which--if used correctly--lead to a knowledge of God. Milton uses sound to reproduce song and vision to dramatize events. Because it presents the opportunity to celebrate the gift of life, creation is the most completely realized theme in his work. He is less convincing when he deals with temptation in the major poems, for we do not share his elaboration of dogma when virtue triumphs. The rigid victory of reason in *Comus* and *Paradise Regained* demonstrates that, in Milton's poems, passion is always the stronger force, a fact that he accepts in *Paradise Lost* and *Samson Agonistes*.

225 WEBBER, JOAN. "The Son of God and Power of Life in Three Poems by Milton." *ELH* 37 (1970):175-94.

In three poems, Milton focuses on three events in Christ's life: *Nativity Ode* deals with his birth, *Paradise Lost* with his begetting, and *Paradise Regained* with his assumption of identity and vocation. Milton's poetic theology emphasizes not the Son's gift of life through death but "simply that he is life" (175). Life is synonymous with goodness, death with evil. In *Nativity Ode*, the poem's birth and our experience of that event imitate the effects of Christ's birth: the Word transforms sound, fulfills time, and initiates a revolution of life. *Paradise Lost* presents a Christ who is both God's instrument of life and incomprehensible to humans. Focusing on the relationship of Christ and Satan, *Paradise Regained* shows us the difficulty of knowing good from evil in our fallen world, and of using the Word to achieve transcendence. The Word meets the father of lies in *Paradise Regained*. If Christ in *Nativity Ode* and *Paradise Lost* is life, in *Paradise Regained* he also teaches us how to accept that gift.

226 WERMAN, GOLDA. "Milton's Use of Rabbinic Material." *Milton Studies* 21 (1985):35-47.

Such scholars as Fletcher (see entries 145, 146), and Saurat (see entry 69) assume, with no biographical evidence, that Milton is an accomplished Judaic scholar. Like the critics, he uses translations. Although he can read the Hebrew Bible and the Targums (Aramaic translations of the Bible), he cannot read the rabbinic texts, whose methodology and language are very difficult. Milton's prose tracts show his understanding of rabbinic material to be superficial. See entry 220.

General Criticism of the Canon

227 WEST, MICHAEL. "The *Consolatio* in Milton's Funeral Elegies." *Huntington Library Quarterly* 34 (1971):233-49.

In the *consolatio* of *Elegy 3*, Milton uses many Ovidian details and describes heaven in terms of an earthly paradise. His pose as a Latin elegiac poet partially invalidates the heavenly vision, for he sees the discrepancy between his Christian and classical material and uses this discrepancy to limit the *consolatio*'s grandeur. He follows much the same procedure in the elegies on the Bishop of Ely and the Vice-Chancellor of Cambridge, though *Elegy 2* lacks a *consolatio*. "Fair Infant" shows Milton's uneasiness about using classical mythology to describe the Christian heaven. "Epitaph on the Marchioness of Winchester" marks an advance, with the classical material not limiting the Christian material. In *Lycidas*, classical and Christian are opposed, for in the conclusion Milton dissociates himself from the audience of shepherds and the pastoral genre. The *consolatio* in *Epitaphium Damonis* does not convey any sense that Damon's personality and capacity for friendship can be expressed in heaven.

228 WHITING, GEORGE WESLEY. *Milton's Literary Milieu*. Chapel Hill: University of North Carolina Press; London: Oxford University Press, 1939, 415 pp. 6 illustrations. Reprint. New York: Russell and Russell, 1964.

The hexameral tradition, not the Zohar or rabbinical commentaries, provides Milton with many of *Paradise Lost*'s ideas about the creation, which blends Neoplatonic and Christian views. His treatment of providence and fate, as well as his description of Eden, is indebted to Ralegh's *History of the World*; other histories, especially those by Pliny and Diodorus Siculus, contribute details to *Paradise Lost*. While they inspire Milton, Renaissance maps and atlases, particularly Ortelius's *Theatrum*, also illustrate geographical passages in *Paradise Lost*, *Paradise Regained*, and *Lycidas*. The philosophy of Comus is based on Erasmus's *Encomium Moriae*. When Milton writes *Samson Agonistes*, he recalls Quarles's *Historie of Samson*. Milton's prose shares many of Bacon's views on religion and church reform. In *Of Reformation*, Milton refutes George Digby. *Eikonoklastes* is based not on *Eikon Alethine* but on state papers and current events. See entry 120.

General Criticism of the Canon

229   WILDING, MICHAEL. "Milton's Early Radicalism." In *Dragons Teeth: Literature in the English Revolution*. Oxford: Clarendon Press, 1987, pp. 7-27.

While New Critics remove the socio-political context of Milton's 1645 *Poems*, that volume contains signs of his early radicalism, such as the prefatory lines for *Lycidas* and the assertion that *Nativity Ode* was "Compos'd 1629," a pre-revolutionary period when the poet anticipates a better future. Milton uses the Apocalypse for political purposes in each poem, as he becomes a prophetic poet. *L'Allegro* and *Il Penseroso* deny the political in such a way as to suggest significant repression.

230   WILLIAMS, CHARLES. "Milton." In *The English Poetic Mind*. Oxford: Clarendon Press, 1932, pp. 110-52. Reprint. London: Russell and Russell, 1963.

Almost all of Milton's verse portrays sensuous satisfactions rejected by chastity, and this war between good and evil unifies his poetic canon. Hence he may be accused of dualism, but war is a reconciling force. Milton's poetry is self-conscious: his epic characters express their knowledge of their state of being. Accepting his internal contradiction, his divided consciousness, Satan knows he cannot destroy God but can only hate him. No great distance separates God and Satan, for each accepts and is fully conscious of himself and the other. In *Paradise Regained*, Satan does not just tempt Christ; rather, he attempts to discover whether he is tempting God. Milton's subordinationism leads him to focus on Christ's human will in *Paradise Regained*. *Samson Agonistes* marks the first time (though *Comus* may also qualify) that Milton uses poetry in a dramatic form that partly conceals his art.

231   WILLIAMSON, GEORGE. "Milton the Anti-Romantic." *Modern Philology* 60 (1962):13-21. Reprinted in *Milton and Others* (London: Faber and Faber, 1965), pp. 11-25.

Milton rejects romance because of its moral foundation not because of its unhistorical nature: its interest in extramarital defilement violates his theme of chastity. All ages need to learn the lesson of the fall and the role of providence in history; a Christian hero, not an Arthurian one, is Milton's vehicle, for liberty is essential to this character's virtue. In *Paradise Lost*, the devils and war are associated with romance. Adam learns a code of patience and heroic martyrdom.

Romance elements color Satan's temptations in *Paradise Regained*, while in *Samson Agonistes* the Harapha incident receives the full irony of romantic contrast.

232   WITTREICH, JOSEPH ANTHONY, Jr. *Visionary Poetics: Milton's Tradition and His Legacy*. San Marino, Calif.: Huntington Library, 1979, 348 pp. 12 illustrations.

During the Renaissance, prophecy is viewed as the noblest of poetic kinds in style and structure. The Book of Revelation is the sacred model of an epic-prophecy written in word-pictures. Milton, unlike Spenser, recognizes the ideological discrepancies between epic, which is conservative, and prophecy, which attempts to create revolutionary political action. *L'Allegro* and *Il Penseroso* anticipate Milton's progress toward prophecy or vision, while he accomplishes it in *Lycidas* and expands it in *Paradise Lost*. The monody's allusive style resembles that of Revelation, and each work rereads its context and rewrites it in light of prophecy. The pastoral in *Lycidas* ascends the hierarchy of genres and assimilates the styles and perspectives of lyric, dramatic, and epic forms. As it moves from narrative to lamentation and finally to consolation, *Lycidas* establishes a tripartite structure in which each part is further divided into three sections. Based on the English madrigal, the poem's circular rhyme scheme is single and continuous, developing from apparent irregularity to a regular rhyme.

Appendixes: "Henry More's Explanation of His Own, and of Joseph Mede's, Table of Synchronisms"; "The English Poems from *Justa Edovardo King Naufrago*."

233   WOODHOUSE, A. S. P. "Milton." In *The Poet and His Faith: Religion and Poetry in England from Spenser to Eliot and Auden*. Chicago, Ill., and London: University of Chicago Press, 1965, pp. 90-122.

Alienated from his age because of his poetic power, religion, and individualism, Milton is deliberate about his career and poetry. *Comus* fuses the religious and aesthetic experiences, just as in *Lycidas* Milton moves from occasional poem to religious experience. In the three major poems, he turns back to scriptural and classical sources, though his Christian Platonism fades and his Christian humanism changes direction and emphasis. Milton is an Arian, and he presents a radical development of the idea of Christian liberty. *Paradise Lost's*

General Criticism of the Canon

classical structure and Christian theme reinforce its main tragic episode, which is set against the pattern of a divine comedy. Christ is the poem's hero. The success of *Samson Agonistes* is attributable to the protagonist's dual role as God's instrument and as an individual tragic hero. Christ in *Paradise Regained* is the second Adam and the perfect pattern of Christian heroism.

234   WOODHOUSE, A. S. P. "Notes on Milton's Early Development." *University of Toronto Quarterly* 13 (1943):66-101. Revised in *The Heavenly Muse: A Preface to Milton*, ed. Hugh MacCallum, University of Toronto Department of English Studies and Texts, no. 21 (Toronto and Buffalo, N.Y.: University of Toronto Press, 1972), pp. 15-54.

In Sonnet 7, Milton records a renewal of self-dedication from which he never retreats, and he remains silent about favoring religious themes over erotic ones. Some of his Latin poems, such as *Elegy 5* and *Elegy 7*, show his shaping experience with an aesthetic pattern and thus establishing his ascendancy over experience. *Nativity Ode* and Sonnet 7 record Milton's equivalent of what the Puritans call conversion, though his version substitutes aspiration and renewed dedication for abasement and repentance. With the writing of *Ode*, he repudiates the elegiac vein and turns toward the heroic. *Ode*'s acceptance of the order of grace and its supremacy over nature begins Milton's movement toward becoming a religious poet. From the spring of 1631 to the summer of 1632, his mind and art mature rapidly with the composition of *L'Allegro*, *Il Penseroso*, and other works. The renewed dedication that Milton shows in Sonnet 7 is crucial to the rest of his career.

This essay includes Woodhouse's "Note on the Date of *Arcades* and Other Poems in the Cambridge MS."

For the concordance to the English poems, see entry 82. See also entries 9, 43, 46, 49, 52, 59, 65, 71-72, 81, 83-84, 89, 91, 96, 103, 115, 236-37, 239-41, 244, 266, 899, 938.

PROSODY

235   BRIDGES, ROBERT. *Milton's Prosody*. Oxford: Clarendon Press, 1921, 127 pp. Rev. ed. 1965.

The normal poetic line of *Paradise Lost* is made up of ten syllables with a stress on each of the five even-numbered ones. Some lines have three or four stresses, but no line in *Paradise Lost* has more than five. No line in *Paradise Lost* has fewer than ten syllables, though some lines have more, often because they contain elisions. In Milton's age, some words do not have a fixed number of syllables. Metrical inversions are most common in the first foot of a Miltonic line, followed in frequency by the third and fourth feet; they are very rare in the second and most rare in the fifth foot. Milton varies the location of the caesura, sometimes placing two breaks in a line. In *Paradise Regained* and *Samson Agonistes*, Milton relaxes his rules for elision and extends his experiments with rhythm. The spelling in *Paradise Lost*'s early editions is intentionally peculiar, even when it is inconsistent. See entry 243.

236   BURNETT, ARCHIE. *Milton's Style: The Shorter Poems, "Paradise Regained," and "Samson Agonistes."* London and New York: Longman, 1981, 201 pp.
       As the poems' pronouns and verbs indicate, the speaker in *L'Allegro* is effaced by the public experience he throws himself into, and the speaker in *Il Penseroso* celebrates a private experience. In *Nativity Ode*, Milton gives mankind only a small role in the redemptive plan as he diverts attention away from the humanity and naturalness of the Nativity and toward scheme and symbol. If moral issues are sharply delineated in *Comus*, the light imagery does not apply exclusively to good characters any more than dark imagery applies to bad ones. In *Lycidas*, an adjectival style, along with repetition, conveys the speaker's obsession with death. Milton's sonnets and metrical Psalms show his tendency to reduce the number of adjectives in his poetry. Not written consistently in the plain style, *Paradise Regained* uses a great deal of conjoining, cataloguing, and repetition. *Samson Agonistes*'s style is similar to *Paradise Regained*'s, especially in terms of adjective use and frequency.

237   DARBISHIRE, HELEN. "Milton's Poetic Language." *Essays and Studies*, n.s. 10 (1957):31-52.
       Using images of all the senses to apprehend the world, Milton in his *Poems* (1645) turns to ordinary diction. The language of *Lycidas* shifts from level to level as decorum demands. Although archaisms are

Prosody

scattered throughout *Paradise Lost*, Milton's vocabulary generally
consists of plain English words, yet he also uses Anglicized Greek and
Latin ones. Latin affects his syntax throughout his career. He allows
sound to determine his choice of words.

238 DIEKHOFF, JOHN S. "Milton's Prosody in the Poems of the
     Trinity Manuscript." *PMLA* 54 (1939):153-83.
          In the blank verse of *Comus*, as in *Paradise Lost*, Milton
     regards his verse as regularly iambic and decasyllabic, though he needs
     to use elision and the theoretical stress to maintain the fiction of a ten-
     syllable line. The revisions of *Comus* in the Trinity manuscript support
     this view of his prosody. The earlier, rhymed poems in the manuscript
     show less metrical freedom. In *Lycidas*, Milton uses the verse
     paragraph as a kind of stanza but without the restrictions that a stanza
     imposes.

239 ELIOT, T. S. "A Note on the Verse of John Milton." *Essays and
     Studies* 21 (1936):32-40. Reprinted in *On Poetry and Poets* (London
     and New York: Faber and Faber, 1957), pp. 156-64; *The Modern
     Critical Spectrum*, ed. Gerald Jay Goldberg and Nancy Marmer
     Goldberg (Englewood Cliffs, N.J.: Prentice-Hall, 1962), pp. 169-74;
     Milton: A Collection of Critical Essays, ed. Louis L. Martz
     (Englewood Cliffs, N.J.: Prentice-Hall, 1966), pp. 12-18; *Milton:
     "Paradise Lost," a Casebook*, ed. A. E. Dyson and Julian Lovelock
     (London and Basingstoke: Macmillan, 1973), pp. 77-84.
          As a man, Milton is unsatisfactory, and his bad influence on
     poets extends to the present. Artificial and conventional, his images
     give no strong sense of particularity; rather, they have a sensuous effect
     on the ear. Milton complicates his style in order to create a sound
     rather than to make sense, an emphasis that leads to the dislocation of
     sound and sense. See entries 110, 117, 120, 174, 467, 615.

240 EMMA, RONALD DAVID. "Grammar and Milton's English Style."
     In *Language and Style in Milton: A Symposium in Honor of the
     Tercentenary of "Paradise Lost."* Edited by Ronald David Emma and
     John T. Shawcross. New York: Frederick Ungar Publishing Co.,
     1967, pp. 233-51.

Milton's grammatical practice is based on traditional English. Critics should stress the general influence of Latin on English rather than on Milton. Although certain grammatical constructions sound strange to us, and are hence often called Latinate, they are fully acceptable to the Elizabethans. Milton's style uses fewer verbs, more passive constructions, and more adjectives than do Shakespeare's or Eliot's styles. The use of qualifiers gives precision to Milton's assertions while enriching them. In good colloquial English, we avoid inverted word order and redundant or nonfunctional adjectives; Milton conforms to both standards. His poetry shows a preference for loose, periodic sentences, which occur even more frequently in his prose. These sentences are essentially English in structure. The Ciceronian formal balance of parallel or antithetical elements appears rarely in Milton's prose and almost never in his verse. He may have been a radical in politics, but in his use of English he is traditional and conservative.

241 EMMA, RONALD DAVID. *Milton's Grammar*. Studies in English Literature, vol. 2. London, The Hague, and Paris: Mouton, 1964, 164 pp.

A sample of 1,000 words from each of eight poems and prose works by Milton shows that he uses nouns with the same frequency as do Elizabethans and contemporaries. Although a greater frequency of qualifiers (adjectives, adverbs, verbs) implies less concern with action in Milton's writing, he uses proportionally more action verbs and fewer copulatives. In prose and verse, Milton's Latinate style has been overstated.

242 GOLDSTEIN, LEONARD. "The Good Old Cause and Milton's Blank Verse." *Zeitschrift für Anglistik und Amerikanistik* 23 (1975):133-42.

In light of the closed couplet's stature in the mid-seventeenth century as the best and only adequate form of poetic expression, Milton defies neoclassical aesthetic norms by defending blank verse. Since this neoclassical literary theory also expresses a royalist and conservative political view, Milton's defense of blank verse is a defense of the good old cause. Arithmetical and regular, the closed couplet is counter-revolutionary because it stands for order, reason, and the status quo; Milton's refusal to use this form is a revolutionary act, as is his frequent

Prosody

use of enjambment. Couplets imply closure, an idea that a defeated revolutionary who hopes for future victory cannot embrace. Milton's resistance to the Restoration links him to the lower-class opponents of Charles's return. Milton resists not the bourgeoisie but the exploitation of that group, and his prosody reflects this resistance.

243   HUNTER, WILLIAM BRIDGES, Jr. "The Sources of Milton's Prosody." *Philological Quarterly* 28 (1949):125-44.
        Contrary to Bridges's claims (see entry 235), Milton's prosody in *Paradise Lost* and *Paradise Regained* is not derived from the syllabic structure of romance verse as Chaucer uses it. Neither the dramatic blank verse of Shakespeare and Jonson nor the narrative blank verse of Surrey and Gascoigne provides a model for Milton. But Sylvester's translation of Du Bartas, a work Milton knows well, establishes many of the prosodic rules that *Paradise Lost* follows, though in terms of elisions, feminine endings, and enjambment, Milton's practice differs from Sylvester's. The one truly syllabic poetry that influences Milton's prosody is the genre of the Puritan metrical Psalm translation. The prosody of *Paradise Lost* combines the principles of Sylvester and the metrical Psalms.

244   MILES, JOSEPHINE. *The Primary Language of Poetry in the 1640's.* Issue no. 1 of *The Continuity of Poetic Language: Studies in English Poetry from the 1540's to the 1940's.* University of California Publications in English, vol. 19. Berkeley and Los Angeles: University of California Press, 1948-51, pp. 28, 30-36, 86-92.
        Milton's poetry continues the intensification of the metaphysical norm, as seen in Crashaw's poems, and the movement of a mode far from the norm, as seen in Henry More's work. The 1645 *Poems* greatly shifts the tone and content of the poetry of the 1640s: compared to his contemporaries in that decade, Milton uses fewer standard epithets and other major terms, more adjectives and fewer verbs, and about the same proportion of four- and five-stress line lengths. For its decade, Milton's style is extreme because it uses few conceptual terms and employs nouns and verbs for scenic or sensory purposes.

245 ORAS, ANTS. *Blank Verse and Chronology in Milton*. University of Florida Monographs, no. 20. Gainesville: University of Florida Press, 1966, 81 pp.

Milton's style changes after *Comus* and remains consistent for about the first seven books of *Paradise Lost*. Then a more austere style appears for the rest of the epic and continues to develop in his final works, *Paradise Regained* and *Samson Agonistes*.

246 ORAS, ANTS. "Milton's Blank Verse and the Chronology of His Major Poems." In *SAMLA Studies in Milton: Essays on John Milton and His Works*. Edited by J. Max Patrick and James Holly Hanford. Gainesville: University of Florida Press, 1953, pp. 128-97.

Instead of undergoing any radical changes, a poet's stylistic and prosodic tendencies alter only as he incorporates new techniques into his old patterns. Moving from *Comus* to *Paradise Lost* and then from *Paradise Regained* to *Samson Agonistes*, one finds an increasing use of strong pauses, a decreasing tendency to run lines together and to place medial pauses in lines after Book 8 of *Paradise Lost*, and a shift in the location of strong pauses, which move from the first to the second half of the line. Milton's style changes between *Comus* and Books 1-6 of *Paradise Lost*, but Books 7-12 show a return to earlier tendencies, which are revealed even more clearly in *Paradise Regained* and *Samson Agonistes*. *Comus* contains the lowest frequency of polysyllabic words; they increase in *Paradise Lost*, drop slightly in *Paradise Regained*, and rise again in *Samson Agonistes*. *Comus* and, to a much greater extent, *Samson Agonistes* have a higher number of lines with feminine endings than do *Paradise Lost* or *Paradise Regained*. The traditional chronology of Milton's major poems is correct, though portions of those works may have been composed in a different sequence. See entry 250.

Appendix: "Prosodical Development in *Samson Agonistes*."

247 PARTRIDGE, A. C. "Milton." In *The Language of Renaissance Poetry: Spenser, Shakespeare, Donne, Milton*. London: Andre Deutsch, 1971, pp. 261-89.

Not idiomatic or Latinate, Milton's poetic style is still English, with such idiosyncrasies as poetic compression and periodic sentence structures. His style is Latinate only in its use of epithets, natural imagery, and tone. In the sonnets, the influence of Spenser and Shakespeare is apparent, as is that of recent Italian sonneteers. *Comus*

Prosody

is very Shakespearean in style. With *Lycidas*, which is based on the canzone, Milton refines his pentameter line and makes sustained use of compound epithets.

248 PRINCE, F. T. *The Italian Element in Milton's Verse*. Oxford: Clarendon Press, 1954, 198 pp. Rev. ed. 1962. Reprinted 1969; part reprinted in *Milton: A Collection of Critical Essays*, ed. Louis L. Martz (Englewood Cliffs, N.J.: Prentice-Hall, 1966), pp. 56-60; part reprinted in *On Milton's Poetry*, ed. Arnold Stein (Greenwich, Conn.: Fawcett Publications, 1970), pp. 151-66.

The Italians show Milton that a modern language can reproduce the techniques of Latin verse. In his sonnets, Milton imitates Bembo's intricate, Latinate syntax, Della Casa's loosening of the sonnet's rhythmic patterns, and both Italians' disregard for the division between quatrain and tercet. Milton's style profits from Tasso's epic verse and theory, which emphasizes *asprezza* (roughness) to create a difficulty of expression achieved through complex diction and suspended rhythm. Written in blank verse, the *Mondo Creato* is *Paradise Lost*'s model for diction and syntax. Before 1638, in his minor poems, Milton is less interested in absorbing Italian techniques than in assimilating his English literary heritage. But through Spenser and his school, Milton feels the Italian influence and shows it in the prosody of some poems. With *Lycidas*, he turns away from native and toward classical and Italian models for the rest of his career. After his journey to Italy, Milton confidently adopts the style of epic magnificence, which influences the blank-verse style--particularly the diction, syntax, and prosody--of *Paradise Lost*. In *Samson Agonistes*'s choruses, he uses a prosodic basis and other elements found in sixteenth-century Italian drama.

249 SAMUEL, IRENE. "Milton on Style." *Cornell Library Journal* 9 (1969):39-58.

Rather than limiting rhetoric to style or *elocutio*, Milton believes that the study of a vast body of knowledge, followed by the study of logic, poetics, and rhetoric, produces style. From *Prolusion 1* to *Paradise Regained*, he insists that matter makes manner. Only *Reason of Church-Government* reverses this by arguing that eloquence can make matter great. In other works, the quality of the matter (for example, Hebrew learning in *Paradise Regained*, the university in

Prolusion 3, or the unreformed church in *Of Reformation*) dictates the quality of the style in which it is expressed. Because style and its author are closely related, Milton in some treatises spends time defending his style. In his view, his opponents prove by their shabby style that their arguments' substance has no truth.

250   SHAWCROSS, JOHN T. "The Chronology of Milton's Major Poems." *PMLA* 76 (1961):345-58.

Oras's study of the chronology of Milton's major poems (see entry 246), which argues for the traditional sequence of *Paradise Lost*, *Paradise Regained*, and *Samson Agonistes*, is seriously flawed. Adopting *Comus*'s blank verse of 1638 as a standard, we should use prosodic evidence to determine the chronology of the major poems rather than to confirm our assumptions about the traditional sequence. According to prosodic data, *Samson Agonistes* is an early work, written perhaps around 1646-48. Book 2 of *Paradise Regained* may have been written at the same time, though Books 4 and 3 are written in 1647-48, and then come *Paradise Lost*'s Books 8, 9, 10, 1, 3, 12, and 11. Book 1 of *Paradise Regained* is written after 1648, and finally *Paradise Lost*'s Books 5, 7, 4, 2, and 6. This sequence generally corroborates the findings of Gilbert (see entry 477) and Parker (see *Philological Quarterly* 28 [1949]:145-66). *Paradise Regained* is initially planned as a drama made up of the main speeches in Books 1, 2, and 4, to which Book 3 is added; after the publication of *Paradise Lost*, Milton decides to make *Paradise Regained* a brief epic.

251   SPROTT, S. ERNEST. *Milton's Art of Prosody*. Oxford: Basil Blackwell, 1953, 158 pp.

Milton's phonetic spelling points to the correct pronunciation and meter, though his first printers do not consistently follow his wishes. There are similar inconsistencies in his punctuation. In its early stages, Milton's verse is fundamentally syllabic, rarely altering the number of syllables required in a line. He uses few inverted feet or enjambed lines in pentameter couplets. His octosyllabic couplets do not adhere to syllabic rules; they use many seven-syllable lines and inverted initial feet. His unhappiness with rhymed verse leads to his chief prosodic innovation: generally avoiding rhyme in *Paradise Lost* and *Paradise Regained*. In blank-verse lines, metrical inversions are most

Prosody

common in the first foot and very rare in the fifth. *Samson Agonistes* shows Milton at the height of his prosodic skill.

252   TRICOMI, A. H. "Milton and the Jonsonian Plain Style." *Milton Studies* 13 (1979):129-44.

Some of Milton's early poems are written in the elaborate Spenserian style, but "On Shakespeare" (1630) marks the beginning of Jonson's influence on Milton. When Henry Lawes--who knows Jonson, sets three of his lyrics to music, and acts in one of his masques--gives Milton the opportunity to contribute to Shakespeare's second folio, Milton studies Jonson's epigrams and elegiac epitaphs as models. Using a broad conception of the epigram, the poems on Hobson and the Marchioness of Winchester continue the movement into the plain style, though Milton avoids its stark diction. In *L'Allegro* and *Il Penseroso*, he successfully blends his rich poetic voice with the plain style.

253   WHALER, JAMES. *Counterpoint and Symbol: An Inquiry into the Rhythm of Milton's Epic Style*. Anglistica, vol. 6. Copenhagen: Rosenkilde and Bagger, 1956, 226 pp.

Despite its high percentage of enjambed lines, *Paradise Lost* maintains its basic unit of the five-stress line. Each verse paragraph of *Paradise Lost* is conceived as a finished contrapuntal piece, with the normal five-stress unit held stable throughout, even when it spills over from one line to the next. Related to the principles of contrapuntal music, numerological principles govern Milton's prosody in *Paradise Lost*. In its first edition (1667), *Paradise Lost* is divided into ten books because Milton associates that number with contrapuntal music. The structure of the ten-book *Paradise Lost* is based on thematic units, and we can group the books in units of 4, 3, 2, and 1, which is the descending primary Pythagorean progression. Milton uses the second edition (1674) to pay tribute to Virgil and the epic tradition.

Appendixes: "Patterns of Quick-Paced Integral Pentameters"; "Cross-Rhythmic Construction in *PL* and *PR*"; "The Rhythmic Method of Contrapuntal Music"; "Symbolic Series and Punctuation."

See also entries 35, 46, 93, 129, 152, 201, 265, 918.

LATIN AND GREEK POEMS:

BIBLIOGRAPHY

254 DILLON, JOHN B. "Milton's Latin and Greek Verse: An Annotated Bibliography." *Milton Studies* 19 (1984):227-307.

Dillon's selective bibliography of 492 items lists significant editions, translations, illustrations, and studies of Milton's Latin and Greek poems from their first appearance to 1982.

CRITICISM

255 ALLEN, DON CAMERON. "Milton as a Latin Poet." In *Neo-Latin Poetry of the Sixteenth and Seventeenth Centuries*. Papers by James E. Phillips and Don Cameron Allen. Los Angeles: William Andrews Clark Memorial Library (University of California, Los Angeles), 1965, pp. 30-52. Reprinted in *Image and Meaning: Metaphoric Traditions in Renaissance Poetry*, enlarged ed. (Baltimore, Md.: Johns Hopkins Press, 1968), pp. 115-37; *Stuart and Georgian Moments*, ed. Earl Miner, Clark Library Seminar Papers on Seventeenth and Eighteenth Century English Literature (Berkeley, Los Angeles, and London: University of California Press, 1972), pp. 23-45.

Milton's *Elegy 5* is part of a long tradition of poems about spring, including *Pervigilium Veneris* and works by Lucretius, Bion, Virgil, and Buchanan. Piecing together the fragments of this tradition, Milton creates a new poem that is connected to *Elegy 7*. Rather than focusing on the renewal of life in the spring, *Elegy 5* deals with poetic insight.

256 CAMPBELL, GORDON. "Imitation in *Epitaphium Damonis*." *Milton Studies* 19 (1984):165-77.

An example of the *elegos* or *epikedion*, *Epitaphium Damonis* declares its genres in its title: an *epitaphos logos* (funeral oration or poetic lament). In the title and opening lines, Milton identifies himself as an imitator of Theocritus and thus asks for comparison with

Latin and Greek Poems

Theocritus's greatest imitator, Virgil. Milton borrows the poem's refrain from Virgil, adapting a coarse line to a solemn setting. Many of Milton's imitations of phrases are derived from Latin imitations of Greek passages. While he is willing to take second place to Theocritus here, in *Paradise Lost* he announces his superiority over all competitors.

257 CHEEK, MACON. "Milton's *In Quintum Novembris*: An Epic Foreshadowing." *Studies in Philology* 54 (1957):172-84.

Much neglected, *In Quintum Novembris* shows Milton's earliest conception of Satan, the epic technique, and the epic style. This poem turns to Virgil as a model for phrasing, style, and techniques to describe motion. The Satan of this poem resembles Milton's Satan in *Paradise Lost*.

258 CONDEE, R. W. "The Latin Poetry of John Milton." In *The Latin Poetry of English Poets*. Edited by J. W. Binns. London and Boston, Mass.: Routledge and Kegan Paul, 1974, pp. 58-92.

By the time he turns twenty-one, Milton writes almost 1,400 lines of poetry, of which more than 1,000 are in Latin; by 1654, he stops writing Latin verse. His Latin poems frequently borrow phrases from Ovid, but in *Elegy 1* Milton presents a parallel between his exile and Ovid's. *Elegy 5*, one of his greatest short poems in Latin or English, gives proper emphasis to his classical learning and allusions; it also achieves a clear structure, which is one area where *Ad Patrem* is weak, though this poem's strength lies in the personae of Milton and his father. While following the encomium or panegyric tradition, *Mansus* also departs from it and transcends the occasion to celebrate the universe's harmony. Similarly, *Epitaphium Damonis* quickly grows restless with the traditional pastoral metaphor, but it turns restlessness into a dynamic force that lifts the poem from pastoral to hymn.

259 KENNEDY, WILLIAM J. "The Audiences of *Ad Patrem*." *Milton Studies* 19 (1984):73-86.

Milton's humor in *Ad Patrem* pays tribute to his father's ability to appreciate its hidden jokes. As an example of the family poem, *Ad Patrem* develops this genre by mixing it with tribute, satire, autobiography, and a defense of poetry. If the father is the primary audience, lines 93-94 address those who seek worldly ambition. Milton's own anxieties make up a third audience, and he addresses his literary works, including *Ad Patrem*, as a fourth audience in an attempt to disarm anticipated criticism from his father and to proclaim his dedication to poetry. The poem's opening lines indulge in self-mockery. In an ironic allusion to Ovid, Milton wittily compares himself and his father to Phaethon and Apollo, another son and father who were foolish in different ways. *Ad Patrem* asserts Milton's independence from his father.

260 KNEDLIK, JANET LESLIE. "High Pastoral Art in *Epitaphium Damonis.*" *Milton Studies* 19 (1984):149-63.

Not mixing pagan and Christian elements as in *Lycidas*, Milton in *Epitaphium Damonis* allows classical and Italian elements to maintain their integrity and to take on Christian and Neoplatonic significance. In its attempt to justify providence, *Lycidas* is filled with questionings; in its portrayal of gain through grief and loss, *Epitaphium Damonis* is filled with affirmations. The Latin poem resolves the issue of whether one should cultivate one's mind, a question that *Lycidas* raises only briefly. With each repetition, the refrain reinforces Thyrsis's disorientation and mental dilemma. The superior value of Damon becomes the criterion with which Thyrsis measures the values of the pastoral life. Forming his resolution, Thyrsis decides to pursue his epic even after life has lost its appeal. Consolation comes from within the pastoral experience.

261 LOW, ANTHONY. "*Elegia Septima*: The Poet and the Poem." *Milton Studies* 19 (1984):21-35.

Before the twentieth century, critics see in *Elegy 7* evidence of Milton's "exquisite sensibility" (22); modern scholars, though they replace this expression with psychological terminology, still read the poem as autobiography. Milton explores and exploits the tensions between experience and artistic play. In the first part, he uses a conventional situation, Cupid's vow of revenge, to establish a comic tone through which he laughs at the folly of humans (for the speaker will experience a comic downfall) and Cupid (the victim of the poem's satire). The poem's moral is clear: "don't boast your superiority to love, or you will suffer the consequences" (27). Its style verges on the mock-epic, and Milton's vision is almost Chaucerian.

Latin and Greek Poems

262 LOW, ANTHONY. "The Unity of Milton's *Elegia Sexta*." *English Literary Renaissance* 11 (1981):213-23.

Elegy 6 first addresses Diodati, then it praises wine drinking poets and water drinking ones, and finally--in what many see as an abrupt shift--it discusses what Milton has been doing, writing a poem about the Nativity. The elegy progresses from pagan, worldly gods to an exalted Jove, who is a typological representation of God. The basic metaphor for this elegy comes from St. Paul's admonition to "be not drunk with wine . . . but be filled with the Spirit" (Ephesians 5:18-19). But Milton denies that a conflict exists between the two kinds of poets and their poetry. St. Paul's metaphor prepares us for Milton's conclusion, where he announces that he has written a divine poem (*Nativity Ode*), an example of the second kind of poetry, which can accommodate the first or secular kind. Typology joins convivial and religious poetry, giving *Elegy 6* its unity of spirit and structure.

263 LOW, ANTHONY. "*Mansus*: In Its Context." *Milton Studies* 19 (1984):105-26.

Manso's distich to Milton alludes to Gregory the Great's words, thus establishing parallels between Manso and Gregory, and Milton and the barbarous English youths brought to Rome for sale. The distich contains a dig, however civilized, at Milton for his Protestantism. In an atmosphere of mutual respect, the Englishman returns both Manso's kindness and ambiguous compliment. Mixing genres, *Mansus* is a kind of panegyric, an epistle, a variation on the poet-patron poem, and above all a philosophical work. It represents Milton's call for recognition as an author, attempts to bridge the religious gap between the two men, and perpetuates Manso's fame. Perhaps *Mansus* avoids mentioning resurrection and eternal life because the Protestant Milton is not responsible for assuring the Catholic Manso's salvation.

264 McCOLLEY, DIANE KELSEY. "Tongues of Men and Angels: *Ad Leonoram Romae Canentem*." *Milton Studies* 19 (1984):127-48. 5 illustrations.

The epigram to Leonora Baroni has a place in Milton's development as an artist because of its emphasis on inspiration, the proper use of art, and the regaining of paradise. Like Leonora's song, the poet's art is inspired by the Spirit, links heaven and earth, and accustoms mortal hearts to divine music. Milton's epigram follows the tradition in the visual arts and literature of portraying angelic and human communication. The "mens tertia" of line 5, rather than referring to the Holy Spirit or the sphere of Venus, may allude to a third mind that is neither "Deus" nor "Angelus"; to the third and highest of the three angelic hierarchies; or to an angel who mediates between God and the inspired singer. As God or this third mind "steals on his way" ("serpit agens") through Leonora's heart, we are warned that inspiration can work and even sound like the serpent. We can thus distinguish good art from bad.

265   OBERHELMAN, STEVEN M., and MULRYAN, JOHN. "Milton's Use of Classical Meters in the *Sylvarum Liber.*" *Modern Philology* 81 (1983):131-45.

In the Latin poems of Sylvarum Liber, Milton's grasp of the principles of classical meters is so firm that he experiments with them and carefully matches a poem's meter with its subject and classical usage. The poem on John Gostlin's death, "In Obitum Procancellarii Medici," uses the Alcaic strophe, which Horace employs to explore the idea of death and the attitude of the living toward it. The oldest of classical meters, the dactylic hexameter form appears in half of the poems in the collection. To convey their serious and argumentative intent, three poems use iambic meters: "De Idea Platonica" (iambic trimeters), "In Obitum Praesulis Eliensis" (iambic strophe), and "Ad Salsillum" (choliambic, though Milton's reason for choosing this meter is not clear). The final poem in Sylvarum Liber, "Ad Joannem Rousium," follows the structure of the Pindaric ode.

Oberhelman and Mulryan provide a complete scansion for the Rouse ode.

266   PARKER, WILLIAM RILEY. "Notes on the Chronology of Milton's Latin Poems." In *A Tribute to George Coffin Taylor.* Edited by Arnold Williams. [Chapel Hill]: University of North Carolina Press, 1952, pp. 113-31.

When he prepares his 1645 and 1673 collections of verse, Milton dates many of the poems at the time of publication rather than composition, a practice that produces errors. His expression "Anno aetatis" refers not to his age but to the year of his life (or "at the age of"). In the 1645 volume, the Latin and Greek poems in three groups--

117

Latin and Greek Poems

Elegiarum Liber, Sylvarum Liber, and epigrammata--are, so far as we know for certain, in strictly chronological order within each group. Milton sometimes assigns poems dates that are erroneously early; the undated poems are generally written after he turns twenty.

267 PECHEUX, MOTHER M. CHRISTOPHER. "The Nativity Tradition in *Elegia Sexta*." *Milton Studies* 23 (1987):3-19.
    In *Elegy 6*, Milton's account of the poem he has just written does not correspond precisely with *Nativity Ode*. With such authors as Hilary, Juvencus, and Prudentius as his models, Milton declares that a Christian poet can serve God by using what he learns from classical masters. These writers are part of the school curriculum because they combine excellent classical verse and lofty matter, particularly in their nativity hymns. *Nativity Ode* participates in the hymn tradition, which looks back to the classical works of these writers.

268 REVARD, STELLA P. "*Ad Joannem Rousium*: Elegiac Wit and Pindaric Mode." *Milton Studies* 19 (1984):205-26.
    Mixing elegiac wit with the stately Pindaric manner, Milton's ode to Rouse addresses the role of the poet and poetry in a troubled society. In the ode, Milton progresses from the gentleman-poet's elegiac mode, which sees poetry as a quiet, peaceful occupation, to the Pindaric mode, which is more active in speaking to society about its problems. Like Ovid and Propertius, who both write about lost tablets, Milton in strophe 1 portrays himself as a private individual who finds entertainment in pastoral settings and verse. The heroic poet speaks in strophes 2 and 3, turning to the problem of a nation that has strayed from learning and the muses. Like Pindar, Milton believes that only the poet can purge the land. Milton says farewell to his role as a pastoral or elegiac poet.

269 SESSIONS, WILLIAM A. "Milton's *Naturam*." *Milton Studies* 19 (1984):53-72.
    Organizing the theme of "Naturam" in the form of an oration, Milton presents an *exordium*, a *reprehensio* (an alteration of the oration form), a *confirmatio* containing a *propositio*, and a *peroratio*. He begins by alluding to myths that show the limits of the human mind, which the absurd analogies show to be fragmented. In the first two sections,

Milton uses one premise as a foundation: "if the Oedipus-mind is so foolish as to identify its laws as those engraved by the fates, then what might one expect?" (58). When Milton moves from the negative instances to the positive view of the third section, he leaves behind sarcasm and absurdity as he turns to a climactic affirmation of the Father who unifies all the myths he has presented. As astral order prevails, this Father leads the auditor from Oedipus-madness to salvation. But the fourth section asserts that all forms of order must burn in order to reach the final conflagration and the Transfiguration figured by Christ.

270 SHAWCROSS, JOHN T. "Form and Content in Milton's Latin Elegies." *Huntington Library Quarterly* 33 (1970):331-50.
Precursors of Milton's later greatness, his Latin elegies are written in elegiac distichs composed of one line of dactylic hexameter and one line of dactylic pentameter. We may classify his seven elegies as verse epistles (1, 4, and 6), funeral tributes (2 and 3), and amatory works (5 and 7). Parts of *Elegy 1* anticipate aspects of *Lycidas* and *Paradise Lost*. The epideictic *Elegy 4* provides a vehicle for showing off Milton's poetic skills and anticipates his later views, in *Reason of Church-Government*, about providence and the prophetic role. Certain aspirations presented in *Elegy 6* are achieved in *Nativity Ode*. *Elegy 2* and *Elegy 3*, like *Elegy 6*, show a tension between occasion and content. While the imagery of *Elegy 5* makes it a good poem, *Elegy 7* superficially attempts to recapture a mood.

For the variorum, see also entry 35; for the concordance to the Latin, Greek, and Italian poems, see entry 79. See also entries 46, 53, 58-59, 64-65, 79, 130, 135-37, 163, 167, 169, 171, 175, 179, 191, 198, 202, 205, 207-8, 216-17, 227, 234, 274, 356, 376, 379, 395, 429, 462, 592, 596, 599, 637, 1005, 1013.

NATIVITY ODE:

BIBLIOGRAPHY

271   MacLAREN, I. S. "Milton's Nativity Ode: The Function of Poetry and Structures of Response in 1629 (with a Bibliography of Twentieth-Century Criticism)." *Milton Studies* 15 (1981):181-200.

The generic and stanzaic forms of *Nativity Ode* are mimetic functions of poetry's purpose, to recreate the rhythms of human experience (to hear, to consider, and to reform oneself). The proem is in two parts, followed by the hymn, giving the poem a tripartite structure like that of a Pindaric ode. As the proem's dualistic view comes into harmony, the hymn shows "the process by which the narrator learns to respond to the Nativity" (184). With its unique stanza form, the hymn uses varied line-lengths to reenact the narrator's oscillating responses to the Nativity. Milton juxtaposes the events of the year 1629, particularly the silencing of the people and the anticipation of a secular prince's birth, with the pattern of history described in his poem.

MacLaren compiles a checklist of eighty-eight studies of *Nativity Ode* from 1906-79.

CRITICISM

272   BARKER, ARTHUR. "The Pattern of Milton's *Nativity Ode*." *University of Toronto Quarterly* 10 (1941):167-81. Reprinted in *Milton: Modern Judgements*, ed. Alan Rudrum (London: Macmillan, 1968), pp. 44-57.

Rather than experiencing a typical Puritan moment of religious illumination, Milton rises above despair because of his conviction that he has a special calling to be a poet-prophet. He expresses the moment of impact, which corresponds to his fellow Puritans' conversions, in *Nativity Ode* in 1629. In between its four introductory stanzas and a concluding stanza, *Ode*'s three movements are related by a variation of image patterns of light and harmony contrasted with gloom and discord. By recognizing the significance of Christ's Incarnation and sacrifice, as well as the potential of complex symbols of illumination and harmony, Milton gives his thought and art a new unity of feeling.

273   CULLEN, PATRICK. "Imitation and Metamorphosis: The Golden-Age Eclogue in Spenser, Milton, and Marvell." *PMLA* 84 (1969):1559-70.

Milton's *Nativity Ode* is a variation of the golden-age eclogue genre as it appears in Virgil's fourth or messianic eclogue. This genre celebrates a figure, often a child, and his parents "in terms of the return of the golden age and the reign of Saturn" (1559), which is usually completed under the son's reign as nature and man are perfected. Reinterpreting Virgil's eclogue, Milton converts the genre to Christian truth and use. According to Virgil's cyclical view of history, the new golden age is a return to the old one; the meditator of Milton's eclogue is tempted by this very perspective.

274   DAVIES, H. NEVILLE. "Laid Artfully Together: Stanzaic Design in Milton's *On the Morning of Christ's Nativity*." In *Fair Forms: Essays in English Literature from Spenser to Jane Austen*. Edited by Maren-Sofie Røstvig. Cambridge: D. S. Brewer; Totowa, N.J.: Rowman and Littlefield, 1975, pp. 85-117.

After the proem, Milton's ode is arranged in a pattern of 15-11-1 stanzas. The number fifteen is often associated with a ladder, Christ's role as mediator, and heaven's gates. Eleven, the number of sin, is appropriate for a section concerned with the Crucifixion and pagan gods. The final stanza turns eleven into twelve and emphasizes the two numbers (four and three) of the proem. Milton uses similar structural principles in *Elegy 3*, "In Obitum Praesulis Eliensis," and *Lycidas*. The center of the entire *Nativity Ode*, stanza 12 of the hymn is the only stanza in the imperative mode; stanza 13 contains the thematic center; the hymn's central stanza (14) is preceded by forward movement and followed by backward movement. Other stanzas may be paired as we move away from these center stanzas (11 and 15, 10 and 16, and so forth).

275   DOBIN, HOWARD. "Milton's Nativity Ode: 'O What a Mask Was There.'" *Milton Quarterly* 17 (1983):71-80.

Nativity Ode

In *Nativity Ode*, Milton Christianizes the masque genre and "unmasks" it, removing the earthly level of metaphor calculated "to praise the glory of kings, and instead offering praise directly to the King of Glory" (71). The main masque begins with Christ's birth, and--at the final judgment--masquers and audience (God, angels, and men) will join for an everlasting revels.

276 FRY, PAUL H. "Milton's Light-Harnessed Ode." In *The Poet's Calling in the English Ode*. New Haven, Conn., and London: Yale University Press, 1980, pp. 37-48.

   Nativity Ode displays Milton's nervousness about claiming prophetic authority because it may promote illusion. We should consider the poem's allusion to Lucifer to signify a writer of odes rather than hymns. In the hymn section of the poem, until its last stanza, light exorcises darkness only to be followed by darkness and enclosure. But, as we expect from a poem about the Incarnation, descent and enclosure do not imply diminution. In the proem, the poet wonders whether he can rise to the task of creating a hymn, a job that becomes possible when he descends in humility and improves his prophetic hopes. If the oracles are dumb, only the poet's oracular voice remains. Milton wishes to restore all that the poem banishes or rejects, but in a redeemed form and on a new foundation. The poet does not enter the choir; rather, he eclipses the light with his own inward, ominous darkness.

277 GOEKJIAN, GREGORY F. "Deference and Silence: Milton's Nativity Ode." *Milton Studies* 21 (1985):119-35.

   As do all of Milton's poems, *Nativity Ode* asks how the human, especially the poetic, logos will function in the context of God's Logos. Milton struggles with the question of poetic authority, with *Ode* illustrating the analogy between the Incarnation and the divine poet's act. The poem's structure, marked by abrupt shifts in focus and direction (even by self-negation), reflects a sense of human inadequacy contrasted with divine power. By using convention as poetic fiction, Milton avoids infringing on the truth. Each claim of human authority in the poem is countered by a denial of that authority. The poem finally asserts its own silence in the face of Christ's speechless infancy, which is truly eloquent.

278 KASTOR, FRANK S. "Miltonic Narration: *Christ's Nativity." Anglia* 86 (1968):339-52.

Milton works with a view of history, from the creation to the judgment day, that provides a narrative framework for God's cosmic drama. He develops different parts of this story in *Nativity Ode, Paradise Lost*, and *Paradise Regained*. Christ's redemptive mission--the quelling of Satan and returning of man to eternal paradise--is important in *Ode* and *Paradise Lost*. In *Ode*, Milton establishes the time scheme, from the beginning to the end, in the first stanza. The hymn describes the Nativity and the larger framing story, but Milton tells the larger story in an unchronological sequence, which emphasizes and vivifies the Redeemer.

279 MacCALLUM, HUGH. "The Narrator of Milton's *On the Morning of Christ's Nativity*." In *Familiar Colloquy: Essays Presented to Arthur Edward Barker*. Edited by Patricia Bruckmann. [Toronto]: Oberon Press, 1978, pp. 179-95.

When Milton publishes *Nativity Ode*, he emphasizes his youth by stating the date of composition, placing the poem first in a volume that generally follows a chronological sequence, and giving it a title that suggests occasional poetry. Unlike "Passion," *Ode* never uses the first-person singular pronoun or refers to a young author. Instead, it uses the hymn's or carol's decorum, including plural pronouns. The poet suppresses his individuality so that he can speak, in a timeless present, for Christian worshipers and create a gift for them. The narrator is conspicuous as poet-priest, prophet, and silent attender of God's will in three places that mark the poem's beginning, middle, and end, precisely the places where the poem calls to mind the Nativity scene. If the narrator is initially too optimistic, he soon expresses a view of sin, mercy, and justice, and finally he joins the angelic choir.

280 MORRIS, DAVID B. "Drama and Stasis in Milton's *Ode on the Morning of Christ's Nativity*." *Studies in Philology* 68 (1971):207-22.

From Milton's perspective, the Nativity is both an isolated, static event that occurred at a particular moment and "an essential episode in the comprehensive drama of history" (207). As history proceeds from fall to Redemption, the Nativity marks its turning point. The Nativity is a stopped action, as is all time, from the perspective of eternity; seen from a temporal perspective, it is a moving, dramatic

Nativity Ode

event. Milton's *Ode* reconciles these two views. Pindar provides the form for a victory ode that celebrates a moment, while the Old Testament prophets establish the spirit for a prophetic poem. In *Ode*, Milton uses temporal ambiguity, abrupt shifts, and allusion to reconcile the divine and human perspectives.

281   NELSON, LOWRY, Jr. "Milton's *Nativity Ode*." In *Baroque Lyric Poetry*. New Haven, Conn., and London: Yale University Press, 1961, pp. 41-52.

In *Ode*'s introduction, Milton makes two time planes--that of the Nativity and that marking its anniversary--contemporaneous. The poem's shifting verb tenses thus come as no surprise. Milton eventually stretches time to its fullest limits, from creation to the future union of heaven and earth, without disturbing the two main time planes of the poem. *Ode* ends in "a vivid momentaneous present" (45), fusing the old past and present, in which Christ was an infant, is an infant, must be crucified, and paradoxically has already been crucified. Every Christmas and the day of Christ's birth are unified. Such an emphatic use of time is a baroque element in *Ode*.

282   PECHEUX, MOTHER M. CHRISTOPHER. "The Image of the Sun in Milton's *Nativity Ode*." *Huntington Library Quarterly* 38 (1975):315-33.

All of *Nativity Ode*'s key motifs--light and dark, timelessness and time, Christianity and paganism--come into focus in stanza 7 with the contrast between the "greater Sun" (Christ) and the created sun. Besides providing light, the sun is man's means to measure time and, at the winter solstice, the commemoration of the sun (Christ) replaces the pagan festival of the unconquered sun. The poem's liturgical context reinforces this emphasis on the sun image.

283   ROLLINSON, PHILIP. "Milton's Nativity Poem and the Decorum of Genre." *Milton Studies* 7 (1975):165-88.

Although Milton's poem, even the part that he identifies as the hymn, is usually classified as an ode, the Nativity poem belongs to the literary hymn tradition, along with neo-Latin, French, Italian, Latin, Greek, another English examples. Odes, Scaliger says, celebrate men;

hymns traditionally praise God. In a private, devotional sense, Milton's poem is liturgical.

284   RØSTVIG, MAREN-SOFIE. "Elaborate Song: Conceptual Structure in Milton's *On the Morning of Christ's Nativity.*" In *Fair Forms: Essays in English Literature from Spenser to Jane Austen*. Edited by Maren-Sofie Røstvig. Cambridge: D. S. Brewer; Totowa, N.J.: Rowman and Littlefield, 1975, pp. 54-84.

In order to make his ode reflect the structure of Christ's acts as creator and redeemer, Milton uses images of the center, the circle, and the balanced world hung on hinges. Following the organization of Psalm 119 and Lamentations 1-4, *Nativity Ode* is arranged in two sequences, one of 12-3-12 stanzas and the other of 1-9-7-9-1 stanzas. The introductory section relies on the numbers four, seven, and twenty-eight to enact time's weekly and seasonal cycles. Stanzas 13-15, the poem's center, depict the heavenly Jerusalem, while the earlier and later stanzas are dominated by the theme of rule. Christ stands at the beginning, middle, and end. Sidney and Cowley use similar structures.

285   SMITH, GEORGE WILLIAM, Jr. "Milton's Method of Mistakes in the Nativity Ode." *Studies in English Literature, 1500-1900* 18 (1978):107-23.

The culmination of mistakes made by nature, the stars, and the sun in stanzas 1-10 of *Nativity Ode*, the central stanzas describe a mistaken millennial vision. Stanzas 18-26 catalogue the objects and places to which deity was attributed before Christ's birth. In *Ode*, Milton's strategy is to show a series of mistakes that are corrected by apocalyptic intelligence in order to celebrate the mysteries of the Incarnation and Redemption. "Our fancy" creates our mistakes about Christ's role or appearance, and the poem corrects these erroneous visions.

286   STAPLETON, LAURENCE. "Milton and the New Music." *University of Toronto Quarterly* 23 (1954):217-26. Reprinted in *Milton: Modern Essays in Criticism*, ed. Arthur E. Barker (New York: Oxford University Press, 1965), pp. 31-42.

Nativity Ode has both an aesthetic center (the music of the spheres) and an intellectual core (the effect of Christ's birth,

Nativity Ode

particularly the routing of the pagan gods). Unlike most paintings of the Nativity, Milton's poem presents an uncluttered scene at Christ's birth, which allows the poet to emphasize other aspects of the event, including the expectancy produced by our very presence at the scene before anything occurs. Milton uses music as a sign for the two kinds of enchantment whose contrast forms the structure of *Ode*: the enchantment of good (in the descent of Peace), which leads to a *raptus* of contemplation based on the "new music" of the Word (as Clement of Alexandria describes it), or the music of the spheres, by which we can ascend to God. By banishing the pagan gods, Christ conquers a negative form of enchantment.

287   SWAIM, KATHLEEN M. "'Mighty Pan': Tradition and an Image in Milton's Nativity *Hymn*." *Studies in Philology* 68 (1971):484-95.
         Pan's name, which means "all," connects him to the physical universe and, in many interpretations, to Christ, the sun, and pastors. In *Nativity Ode*'s hymn, Pan conveys comprehensive unity. Milton uses the pagan, pastoral deity to show that, from the shepherds' limited perspective, a new order (Christ) has arrived, but they lack the correct name for it. The hymn's sound imagery moves from an expectant quiet in the first eight stanzas to a celebration of a supernal music outside of time in the next seven stanzas, and finally to harmony in time in stanzas 21-26. Under the order of nature, Pan embodies some aspects of deity that can be transformed under the new order.

For the variorum, see entry 35. See also entries 30, 43, 46-47, 49, 53, 58-60, 65, 67, 93, 108, 123, 128-32, 134-35, 137, 142-43, 147, 149, 152, 158, 164-65, 168, 172, 175, 178-80, 183-87, 189-90, 194, 197-97, 199-200, 205-6, 211, 213, 215-16, 219-20, 225, 229-30, 234, 236-37, 248, 252, 262, 267, 318, 429, 789, 1005.

L'ALLEGRO AND *IL PENSEROSO*

CRITICISM

288   BABB, LAWRENCE. "The Background of *Il Penseroso*." *Studies in Philology* 37 (1940):257-73.

L'Allegro and Il Penseroso

According to a perspective that goes back to Greek medicine and Galen, the melancholic humor black bile is dry, heavy, cold, and black, and it produces sluggish thought and movement, fear, and a fondness for darkness and solitude. The Renaissance notion of melancholy looks back to Aristotle, however, and indicates that melancholy comes in three forms: hot, which leads to madness; cold, which produces despondency and torpidity; and of a mean temperature, leading to superior mental activity. *L'Allegro* presents the melancholy of the Galenic tradition, *Il Penseroso* the melancholy of the Aristotelian tradition.

289 BROOKS-DAVIES, DOUGLAS. "The Early Milton and the Hermetics of Revolution: *L'Allegro* and *Il Penseroso* and *Comus*." In *The Mercurian Monarch: Magical Politics from Spenser to Pope*. Manchester: Manchester University Press, 1983, pp. 124-49.

Based on Hermes, a reforming intention appears in *L'Allegro* and *Il Penseroso*, the former portraying a corrupt court and the latter arguing for a private contemplative ideal as an alternative. The king's Mercurian power is seen as monarchial delusion, a perverted version of the Hermetic philosopher king, to be replaced with the Hermetic philosopher poet. The companion poems show a progression from youth to maturity (not necessarily accompanied by wisdom), from sanguinic to melancholic, and from Venus to Saturn. If Hermes Trismegistus can be summoned up, Britain may be restored and enjoy a golden age. Continuing the Hermetic theme, *Comus* contrasts the pure celestial court and the corrupt earthly one. *Comus* fuses Giordano Bruno's theme of an Egypt that must be purged of barbarians with the British myth of the return of Arthur and a golden age. As the herb haemony shows, Milton's masque is in part about achieving the alchemical quest.

290 CARPENTER, NAN COOKE. "The Place of Music in *L'Allegro* and *Il Penseroso*." *University of Toronto Quarterly* 22 (1953):354-67.

Musical references in the companion poems indicate that each poem presents a cycle of twenty-four hours and that neither poem focuses exclusively on city or country scenes. The climax of *L'Allegro*'s largely urban delight is Lydian music, which is soft, effeminate, and even lascivious. As an "air," it is music for a solo voice in a closed form, calling to mind the Italian aria and its associations with romantic love.

127

L'Allegro and Il Penseroso

Starting in the underworld, *L'Allegro* rises to Olympus, reaches a peak with the aria, and returns with Orpheus to the underworld. In *L'Allegro*, mirth offers urban entertainments, but in *Il Penseroso* pleasures appear only in thoughts and books, not in actuality. The climax of *Il Penseroso* occurs in the references to ecclesiastical music, particularly the great service and anthem. Musical imagery appears in many of Milton's works. See entries 15, 22, 142, 321, 337, 370, 430, 861.

291   EMBRY, THOMAS J. "Sensuality and Chastity in *L'Allegro* and *Il Penseroso*." *JEGP: Journal of English and Germanic Philology* 77 (1978):504-29.

Interested in chastity from the time he writes *Elegy 6*, Milton makes it a prerequisite for poetic inspiration in *Il Penseroso* and, in *L'Allegro* and *Il Penseroso*, focuses on the dichotomy between sensuality and chastity. He chooses his side by making *L'Allegro* ironic and *Il Penseroso* didactic. Not only does Milton associate mirth with sensuality and melancholy with chastity, but the imagery and allusions in both poems point in these directions.

292   FISH, STANLEY E. "What It's Like to Read *L'Allegro* and *Il Penseroso*." *Milton Studies* 7 (1975):77-99.

In line 46 of *L'Allegro*, Milton leaves readers free not to choose who comes to the window. The experience of reading *L'Allegro* is the pleasure of the absence of responsibility, including the pressure to interpret it. Preventing us from making sense of the poem, the non sequiturs leave us carefree. *Il Penseroso* exerts a pressure for us to interpret, to choose not one but every reading. The poem's clear transitions focus attention on the nature of melancholy. The activities in the poems and the activity of reading them correspond.

293   FIXLER, MICHAEL. "The Orphic Technique of *L'Allegro* and *Il Penseroso*." *English Literary Renaissance* 1 (1971):165-77.

Written in the genre of incantation, *L'Allegro* and *Il Penseroso* celebrate technique and thus symbolically affirm what Milton believes is the secret in creativity. The Orphic incantation, according to Pico, harnesses a power that can inspire or animate spirits and the human soul, restoring the latter to its divine nature (or, in Christian terms, to participation in Christ). As outlined in Orphic thought, the creative forces of Saturn and his daughter Venus, the presiding powers of *Il Penseroso* and *L'Allegro*, are conjoined in opposition and potential harmony. Milton's companion poems reveal the creative elements apparently disengaged, for the poems present but do not resolve various tensions and correspondences, which are left for our minds to complete in our own act of creative conception.

294   GECKLE, GEORGE L. "Miltonic Idealism: *L'Allegro* and *Il Penseroso.*" *Texas Studies in Literature and Language* 9 (1968):455-73.
         Milton's Platonic idealism is an important part of his early development. The companion poems symbolize the single principle of happiness in two modes of existence and on two levels of perfection. Based on a structure that Milton uses in his *Prolusions*, each of the companion poems contains an encomium and a vituperation within the framework of a thesis. At the end of *L'Allegro*, he points to dissatisfaction with the life of mirth, a life that is redefined in a negative way at the beginning of *Il Penseroso*, which concludes by exalting the melancholy man. In the epilogue of *Il Penseroso*, the speaker moves from stasis to action, achieving "an eternal moment in the absolute world of art" (473).

295   GREENE, THOMAS M. "The Meeting Soul in Milton's Companion Poems." *English Literary Renaissance* 14 (1984):159-74.
         In *L'Allegro* and *Il Penseroso*, the soul moves forward to select, apprehend, order, and assimilate, ultimately creating itself. As it chooses activities and sensations, the soul defines itself. But when the soul meets something, that thing's appearance changes as it becomes internalized. The alert soul keeps drifting into dreams and innerness, though *Il Penseroso* may do a better job of resisting the spell of appearances. The final couplet of each poem presents a conditional, introduced not by L'Allegro or Il Penseroso but by a third person susceptible to both yet committed to neither.

296   GROSE, CHRISTOPHER. "The Lydian Airs of *L'Allegro* and *Il Penseroso.*" *JEGP: Journal of English and Germanic Philology* 83 (1984):183-99.
         Halfway through *L'Allegro*, the speaker's authority develops when he turns from his role as spectator to active singer or maker. This

L'Allegro and Il Penseroso

event creates immediacy and achieves a "secure delight," letting us experience the Lydian airs of the poem. The delight becomes distant, a narrative event that points to but cannot invoke a prior experience of soul-lapping delight. *Il Penseroso* goes through the same process, attempting to recapture melancholy, here in the presence of a cherub. In both poems, the speakers attempt to prolong a moment of presence, only to pursue an elusive sense.

297   HUNTLEY, JOHN F. "The Poet-Critic and His Poem-Culture in *L'Allegro* and *Il Penseroso*." *Texas Studies in Literature and Language* 13 (1972):541-53.

   L'Allegro and *Il Penseroso* project a world of "the harmonious interaction of aesthetic criticism, worldly culture, and human destiny" (541), in which desire guides critical response. In the companion poems, a man's act of creation leads to choosing, which leads to becoming; and this becoming either receives the light of understanding (in *L'Allegro*) or dispenses it (in *Il Penseroso*). Through his desire to penetrate, the speaker or postulant creates his experience (culture) just as it is created for him. In the conclusion of *L'Allegro*, we await Orpheus's awakening; in *Il Penseroso*, the maturing of wisdom in a prophetic strain.

298   MILLER, DAVID M. "From Delusion to Illumination: A Larger Structure for *L'Allegro-Il Penseroso*." *PMLA* 86 (1971):32-39.

   Forming a single structure, *L'Allegro* and *Il Penseroso* merge the claims of God and the world. *Il Penseroso*'s conclusion is superior to all of *L'Allegro* because it is more useful in leading the individual to the contemplation of God. Though the poems appear to be balanced, *Il Penseroso* incorporates the virtues of *L'Allegro*, which has limitations. Every parallel between the poems shows that *Il Penseroso* is nearer to the contemplation of God. Together, they form a progression, a vertical structure that starts with black melancholy and leads to God. The educational pattern established in *Il Penseroso* is the same as the one articulated in *Prolusion 7*.

299   PHELAN, HERBERT J. "What Is the Persona Doing in *L'Allegro* and *Il Penseroso*?" *Milton Studies* 22 (1986):3-20.

L'Allegro and Il Penseroso

While the persona is physically present in some scenes in *L'Allegro* and *Il Penseroso*, in other scenes he is an off-screen narrator or he presents scenes that are merely figments of his imagination. He also uses quick cuts from scene to scene, flashbacks, and--in *Il Penseroso*, the more verbally sophisticated of the two poems--dissolves to melt scenes together. After line 78 of *L'Allegro*, the persona is no longer present in the scene; after line 85 of *Il Penseroso*, he relates dream visions in which he places himself. The persona of these poems does not reach his ultimate goals.

300   REVARD, STELLA P. *"L'Allegro* and *Il Penseroso*: Classical Tradition and Renaissance Mythography." *PMLA* 101 (1986):338-50.
        Milton's companion poems are modeled on the classical hymn or ode, which follows the pattern of invocation, description, supplication, and praise. *L'Allegro* is closely related to Pindar's Olympia 14. As inspirers of poetry, the muses are traditionally associated with mind and memory, and Milton's Melancholy must be the muse herself. *L'Allegro* and *Il Penseroso* examine the different kinds of poetic inspiration appropriate for the elegiac or the epic poet. One need not choose between the two accounts of the beginning and development of poetic inspiration.

301   SWAIM, KATHLEEN M. "Cycle and Circle: Time and Structure in *L'Allegro* and *Il Penseroso*." *Texas Studies in Literature and Language* 18 (1976):422-32.
        Concerned with more than just the daylight world, *L'Allegro* follows a careful chronology, moving from pre-dawn to night, when references to four bedtime stories complete the twenty-four-hour day. A second group of activities, urban and social, uses chronology as duration rather than as sequence, presenting different days instead of a continuation of the rustic day. The main character and the poem celebrate time and its patterns. Following no sequential pattern, *Il Penseroso* relates the subjective experience of an individual consciousness of timeless events. Together, the poems form a cycle.

302   WILLIAMSON, MARILYN L. "The Myth of Orpheus in *L'Allegro* and *Il Penseroso*." *Modern Language Quarterly* 32 (1971):377-86.

L'Allegro and Il Penseroso

In Renaissance mythology, Orpheus has two roles: poet-musician (his main role in *L'Allegro*) and priest-prophet (the emphasis of *Il Penseroso*). The former role stresses civil order, which is celebrated in *L'Allegro*; the latter role deals with philosophy or religious worship, and *Il Penseroso* is thus preoccupied with understanding the cosmos and divinity.

For the variorum, see entry 35. See also entries 15, 30, 43-44, 46-47, 53, 58-59, 65, 67, 71, 87-88, 91, 93, 99, 103, 105, 107-8, 123, 127, 129-32, 135, 137, 142, 147, 149-50, 158, 165, 168-69, 172, 174, 179-80, 183, 186-87, 196-97, 200, 207, 216-17, 219-20, 222, 228-29, 232, 234, 236, 251-52, 318, 324, 333, 342, 356, 592, 599, 829.

COMUS:

TEXTUAL STUDIES

303 DIEKHOFF, JOHN S. "The Text of *Comus*, 1634 to 1645." *PMLA* 52 (1937):705-27. Reprinted in *"A Maske at Ludlow": Essays on Milton's "Comus,"* ed. John S. Diekhoff (Cleveland, Ohio: Press of Case Western Reserve University, 1968), pp. 251-75.

Cancellations and insertions in the Trinity manuscript of *Comus* are copying errors, indicating that most of the verse is copied from rough drafts. During transcription, Milton revises passages earlier considered finished. Before his blindness, Milton's composing method is to write a hasty draft, greatly revise it, copy it (revising again if necessary), and make a clean copy, which he continues to revise. The 1645 edition of *Comus* is set from the 1637 text with constant reference to the Trinity manuscript, probably by an amanuensis.

304 SPROTT, S. E., ed. *John Milton: "A Maske," the Earlier Versions.* Toronto and Buffalo, N.Y.: University of Toronto Press, 1973, 230 pp.

Comus exists in five versions from Milton's lifetime--the Trinity manuscript, Bridgewater manuscript, and 1637, 1645, and 1673 editions--along with later adaptations. Sprott provides a parallel-text edition of the masque's "three earliest and most dissimilar versions" (3).

Sprott also reconstructs "a hypothetical fair copy of *A maske* probably written by Milton in 1634" (199).

Appendixes: "Words of Songs in Music Manuscripts"; "Reconstructed Text of [MS[1]]."

CRITICISM

305 ARTHOS, JOHN. "Milton, Ficino, and the *Charmides*." *Studies in the Renaissance* 6 (1959):261-74.

Though the meaning of chastity shifts in *Comus* (sometimes it is temperance, sometimes continence, and occasionally virtue in general that leads to immortality), this virtue consistently gives one the power to resist temptation, transforms body to spirit, changes the world, and links one to heaven. The practice of chastity is the same as the mind's activity in contemplation. Ficino's commentary on the *Charmides*, with its focus on *sophrosyne* (translated as *temperantia*), provides the source and explanation of the meaning of chastity in *Comus*. Like divine philosophy, chastity causes one to turn inward to the divine light within oneself.

306 ARTHOS, JOHN. *On "A Mask Presented at Ludlow-Castle" by John Milton.* University of Michigan Contributions in Modern Philology, no. 20. Ann Arbor: University of Michigan Press, 1954, 95 pp.

Beginning as a folk tale, Homer's story of Circe becomes a romantic episode in the following centuries, a development that influences Milton's alteration of Circe into Comus. The important sources of *Comus* are Peele's *Old Wives Tale*, which mingles folklore and romance, and Fletcher's *Faithful Shepherdess*, which presents the pastoral as sophisticated world. But Milton adds God to Peele's dramatic world and refines Fletcher's idea of chastity. Comus and the Attendant Spirit, both divine and disguised as shepherds, fight for the souls of the Lady and her brothers. Throughout Milton's Platonic masque of faith, the pastoral setting and conventions are governed by the idea of a distant heaven, though evil has invaded. The masque emphasizes the element of chance in its episodes, and the Lady's virtue is serene and confident.

Comus

307 BAKER, STEWART A. "Eros and the Three Shepherds of *Comus*."
     Rice University Studies 61 (1975):13-26.
          In *Comus*, Milton identifies the shepherd's role with the power
     to actualize desire through language. He explores the role of language,
     poet, and poetry through the opposition of the three main shepherds:
     the Attendant Spirit, a providential agent who subsumes the poet's role
     and who uses language to create; Thyrsis, the Attendant Spirit's second
     identity, who uses poetry to transform or recreate with his Orphic
     power; and Comus, who uses language in a Satanic parody of
     transformation that turns good to evil. The gardens of Hesperus
     transvalue many of the masque's themes and images by showing that
     true pleasure is identified with the process of generation and the cosmic
     cycle of process and change that forms its foundation. As revealed by
     connections between the myth of Cupid, Psyche, and her two sisters
     and the story of a celestial Cupid, the Lady, and her two brothers,
     physical love and spiritual love create true pleasure as expressions of
     each other.

308 BARBER, C. L. "*A Mask Presented at Ludlow Castle*: The Masque
     as a Masque." In *The Lyric and Dramatic Milton*. Edited by Joseph
     H. Summers. Selected Papers from the English Institute. New York
     and London: Columbia University Press, 1965, pp. 35-63. Reprinted
     in "*A Maske at Ludlow*": *Essays on Milton's "Comus*," ed. John S.
     Diekhoff (Cleveland, Ohio: Press of Case Western Reserve
     University, 1968), pp. 188-206; *Milton: "Comus" and "Samson
     Agonistes,"* a *Casebook*, ed. Julian Lovelock (London and
     Basingstoke: Macmillan, 1975), pp. 84-105.
          Presented rather than performed, a masque gives meaning to
     noble people, places, and occasions; it extends reality by fictions that
     are present and then points back to the reality. Masques seek to
     transform the situation at an entertainment: in *Comus*, Milton extends
     Ludlow Castle's environment to reveal or express a Christian situation;
     by playing roles, the Egerton children have their identities extended and
     educated. Chastity, as Milton presents it, is an intact disposition to love
     that depends on inner resources and on an outside world that reflects
     the Lady's reserved ardor. Comus gives only a false echo. Milton's
     masque is about sexuality's vulnerability when faced with the
     destructive release of unintegrated passion, which he counters with the
     release of imagination carried to other objects of love.

309   BLANCHARD, J. MARC. "The Tree and the Garden: Pastoral Poetics and Milton's Rhetoric of Desire." *MLN* 91 (1976):1540-68.

Milton selects a pastoral setting for *Comus* because such a setting is traditionally associated with both harmony and violence. The pastoral setting and genre reveal an ambivalence of mimesis because they raise and exorcise the power of sex, violence, and death. Only the expulsion of Comus resolves the masque's semiotic conflict between rhetoric (form of expression) and desire (form of content). Milton uses Comus to retain the pastoral context associated with Circe's progeny and to emphasize the orgiastic aspect of the Dionysiac tradition. Comus places his desire within rhetoric, thus making his sexual instincts formal and normal. Rhetoric becomes the outlet for sexual gratification. Language fails in the debate between the Lady and Comus, so she must appeal to magic. If the object of desire never materializes in *Comus*, the temptation scene in Book 9 of *Paradise Lost* shows desire's tacit victory over the sign.

310   BREASTED, BARBARA. "*Comus* and the Castlehaven Scandal." *Milton Studies* 3 (1971):201-24.

Because the Bridgewater family, for whom *Comus* is first performed in 1634, has relatives who were recently involved in a sex scandal, the masque expresses their need to see their last unmarried daughter portray sexual virtue. *Comus* may be intended to help repair the reputation of a family whose cousins were involved in rape, homosexuality, and turning a young girl (Lady Alice Egerton's cousin) into a whore. The five principal cuts in the Bridgewater manuscript, particularly the omission of the Lady's speech on chastity, are required to avoid clear allusions to the scandal and to present Lady Alice Egerton in a pure manner, an innocence that provides a contrast--even without the omitted lines--with her cousin. See entries 316, 339.

311   BROCKBANK, PHILIP. "The Measure of *Comus*." *Essays and Studies*, n.s. 21 (1968):46-61.

Only when our ears are alert to certain effects and our eyes are accustomed to certain perspectives can we see *Comus*'s unity and its ability to satisfy the ethical imagination. Rather than restrict the masque's argument, we should note that it is about "a choice of enchanted states" (49) and that its setting signifies sometimes the whole mortal condition and sometimes that precarious part of it called

Comus

adolescence. Comus's poetic dialect has a sensuous music, which the Elder Brother tries to displace with a moral music. Other characters, such as the Attendant Spirit and Lady, use a music of transfigured, sublimated sensuality. Each of these three musics has its own measure.

312 BROWN, CEDRIC C. *John Milton's Aristocratic Entertainments*. Cambridge: Cambridge University Press, 1985, 222 pp. 14 illustrations.

Arcades and *Comus* are idealistic and reformist in spirit. With the Countess Dowager's grandchildren at the center, *Arcades* may be dedicated to her in recognition of her holding the family together during a trying time. Michaelmas, when *Comus* is probably performed in 1634, has both secular associations as the day of the election of new magistrates and governors, and religious associations as a day in a holy festival that celebrates heaven's conquering of evil forces. The journey motif links Milton's two entertainments, and both are originally staged indoors. In them, Milton presents a radical Arcadianism that is exemplary for the young aristocrats and their nation. His reformist program in the aristocratic entertainments does not preach but outlines the refinements, both moral and literary, for an ideal ruling class, which leads to *Lycidas*'s theme of spiritual leadership and Milton's clear sense of vocation.

Appendix: "The Authenticity of the Bridgewater Manuscript and the Idea of the Censor."

313 CALHOUN, THOMAS O. "On John Milton's *A Mask at Ludlow*." *Milton Studies* 6 (1974):165-79.

Comus deals with three age groups: the adolescents, the Lady and Comus, are concerned with problems of erotic love, while children (the Brothers) and adults (the Attendant Spirit and Egerton parents) join forces "not to solve, but to suppress the erotic dilemma of adolescence" (167). Inhabiting the youths' interior landscape, Comus is part of their rite of passage. The Lady's virginity is tested, and the boys are tested on faith in doctrine, patience, and the ability to follow orders. Each trial is appropriate for the individual's age. Two families, Bacchus-Circe and the Egertons, are opposed in the masque. Family unity wins out over eros for the Lady.

314   CARRITHERS, GALE H., Jr. "Milton's Ludlow *Mask*: From Chaos to Community." *ELH* 33 (1966):23-42. Reprinted in *Critical Essays on Milton from "ELH"* (Baltimore, Md., and London: Johns Hopkins Press, 1969), pp. 103-22.

Comus has as its center the idea of an established community reinforcing itself by a precarious recruitment process. Initially, the apparent community of the three young people is centrifugal, idiosyncratic, and extremist. This group disintegrates, and its members then undergo trials. Comus's speeches point toward chaos; endorsing society and fertility, Sabrina is in the world of vocal communication. The Attendant Spirit defines the final vision as one of reunion, familial initiation, and social responsibility. Yet the Spirit leaves for another world.

315   COX, JOHN D. "Poetry and History in Milton's Country Masque." *ELH* 44 (1977):622-40.

The typical Caroline masque transforms history into myth in order to compliment the monarch by comparing him to God, but Milton's *Comus* does so in order to state a moral imperative. Milton praises Bridgewater only insofar as the Earl aspires to the values of the masque. The antagonism between England's court and country grows under Charles, and Milton associates his masque with the country and its values. Through the masque's journey to Ludlow, Milton shows the Egertons' triumph over the events of the Castlehaven scandal, for the journey symbolizes the rejection of the court's values. The historical view of England's division into court and country relies on the traditional pastoral idea of evil courtiers and virtuous country dwellers. Transforming history into poetry, Milton uses Sabrina to parallel the Egertons' family history and the split between court and country.

316   CREASER, JOHN. "Milton's *Comus*: The Irrelevance of the Castlehaven Scandal." *Notes and Queries*, n.s. 31 (1984):307-17.

That King Charles I would nominate Bridgewater to the Lord Presidency when the Castlehaven scandal is at its height indicates that the Earl and his family are not directly touched by it--indeed, they are exonerated. Bridgewater's assumption of office is not delayed, though his official residence is, but not because of the scandal. Furthermore, there is no necessary causal link between the scandal and Milton's selection of the theme of chastity for *Comus*. Rather than being a

Comus

reaction to the scandal, the revisions in the Bridgewater manuscript are not Milton's, while some of the other revisions are done to avoid having the Lady speak about sex. These indecorous passages appear in the 1637 printed text, however, at a time when the memory of the scandal has not faded, which suggests that the Egerton family wishes to show that its members are above suspicion. See entries 310, 339.

317 CREASER, JOHN. "'The Present Aid of This Occasion': The Setting of *Comus*." In *The Court Masque*. Edited by David Lindley. The Revels Plays Companion Library. Manchester and Dover, N.H.: Manchester University Press, 1984, pp. 111-34.

Commissioned by one of the richest men in England, the Ludlow production of *Comus* uses spectacle, machinery, and a perspective stage. Bridgewater is appointed Lord President by King Charles during his personal rule, which--with its centralist tendencies--lessens the power of the Earl and his Council. *Comus* represents one of the Earl's moves to reaffirm the authority of the Lord President, whose family appears to be royalist rather than Puritan. It is ironic that Milton, future defender of regicide, should write for a royalist family in a form that embodies the Stuarts' absolutist claims. In 1634, however, Milton is not troubled by current theological and political developments. *Comus* is in part highly complimentary to the Egertons and Lawes, but in part an attempt to shift the audience's perspective away from self-glorification and toward traditional values. Seen in light of heavenly strength, human strength is relative or qualified.

318 DEMARAY, JOHN G. *Milton and the Masque Tradition: The Early Poems, "Arcades," and "Comus."* Cambridge, Mass.: Harvard University Press, 1968, 200 pp. 8 illustrations.

Jonson is the first within the masque tradition to give prominence to the grotesque dance. His *Hymenaei* establishes the structural pattern of the court masque in England: prologue, antimasque, main masque speeches and spectacle, *deus ex machina* resolution, and epilogue. As a stage presentation, *Comus* generally follows this structure. The descriptions in *Nativity Ode* are related to masque figures and scenic designs; its structure resembles that of a masque. *L'Allegro* shows Milton's awareness of the wanton antimasque, the country folks' dance, and a main masque dancing song. *Arcades* is an entertainment, a work not used to introduce an evening of indoor dancing, which pays tribute to the Countess Dowager of Derby. The debates in *Comus* are not inconclusive: the Lady refutes Comus's views, and the Elder Brother is wiser than the Younger Brother. Rather than resolving issues raised in the masque, the epilogue clarifies and supplements the virtuous characters' statements.

Demaray provides a hypothetical reconstruction of *Comus*'s first performance.

319 DIEKHOFF, JOHN S. "A Maske at Ludlow." In *"A Maske at Ludlow": Essays on Milton's "Comus."* Edited by John S. Diekhoff. Cleveland, Ohio: Press of Case Western Reserve University, 1968, pp. 1-16.

As a collaborator, Lawes requires Milton to move or omit lines from *Comus*; few of Lawes's (Thyrsis's) own lines are cut. The older children must receive big parts in order to show off. By maintaining the children's relationships to each other and to Lawes, the masque emphasizes players rather than the parts they play. Omitted lines reflect Lawes's emphasis on the performance over Milton's moral. Never cut from the text, compliments flatter members of the Egerton family.

320 DYSON, A. E. "The Interpretation of *Comus*." *Essays and Studies*, n.s. 8 (1955):89-114. Reprinted in *"A Maske at Ludlow": Essays on Milton's "Comus*," ed. John S. Diekhoff (Cleveland, Ohio: Press of Case Western Reserve University, 1968), pp. 102-25.

By asserting the value of reason, the Lady gives the right perspective, while Comus's speeches about passion offer the wrong one. Tempters in Milton's poems have strong arguments, some plausibility, and intellectual and emotional appeal; they really tempt. Real and allegorical, the Lady is both a rarefied mortal and chastity (or virtue) incarnate. The Attendant Spirit synthesizes Platonism and Christianity in his concern to help some people ascend the ladder of love to virtue. Descending, the victims of Comus's cup journey into degradation through bestial sensuality. Contrary to Woodhouse's view (see entries 357-58) of the Lady's being composed of temperance and continence from the order of nature, chastity from the orders of nature and grace, and virginity from the order of grace, nature and grace are two ways of responding to the human situation. Comus speaks for the pagan order of nature, the Lady for the order of Christian grace.

Comus

321 FINNEY, GRETCHEN LUDKE. *"Comus, Dramma per Musica."*
     Studies in Philology 37 (1940):482-500. Reprinted in *Musical
     Backgrounds for English Literature: 1580-1650* (New Brunswick, N.J.:
     Rutgers University Press, 1962), pp. 175-94; reprinted (Westport,
     Conn.: Greenwood Press, 1976).

The form of *Comus* differs from that of the typical masque
because Milton is working with a musical dramatic form now called
opera. These *drammi per musica* are a Roman attempt, soon after 1620,
to relieve the monotony of early Florentine sung drama. To the
Florentine form's serious plot and preponderance of recitative, the
Romans add song, dance, and spectacle to produce sung drama. In
many ways, *Comus* resembles Tronsarelli and Mazzocchi's *La Catena
d'Adone* (1626), which is based on Marino's *L'Adone*. See entries 15,
22, 142, 290, 337, 370, 430, 861.

322 FISH, STANLEY E. "Problem Solving in *Comus*." In *Illustrious
     Evidence: Approaches to English Literature of the Early Seventeenth
     Century*. Edited by Earl Miner. Berkeley, Los Angeles, and London:
     University of California Press, 1975, pp. 115-31.

Comus moves us to ask questions, as it encourages us to take
one attitude toward a person or action and then apparently endorses
the opposite attitude. Although the masque's theme is the superiority of
virtue over vice, during much of *Comus* we learn where virtue's
superiority does not reside: in physical strength, invulnerability, or
delicacy of perception. In the masque, values are not, as we might
assume, properties (or accidents) of things; Milton teaches us to use a
double perspective with which we can discard accidents and
comprehend essences. *Comus* is static, but its experience is not, for it
leads us to a conversion.

323 FLETCHER, ANGUS. *The Transcendental Masque: An Essay on
     Milton's "Comus."* Ithaca, N.Y., and London: Cornell University
     Press, 1971, 275 pp. 16 illustrations.

A transcendental form is any poetic structure that includes
more than its traditional generic limits would allow. In writing *Comus*,
Milton assumes the role of magus and the responsibility of envisioning
chastity in the most sacred of languages. *Comus*, a drama of initiation,
has a philosophical plot that is allegorical and a magical plot that is
mimetic and centered on song, which emerges triumphant. Attempting

to present the conditions of true vision, Milton insists on the Lady's enforced solitude. Virginity, the Lady's special grace, transcends chastity. In the act of recognizing Comus in her final harangue, the Lady recognizes herself and her Orphic power. While chastity leads to an awareness of others and the world around the self, virginity leads to an interior knowledge of the inner life. "The *Maske at Ludlow* is a ricercare, a figure searching out its thematic implications, on the theme of atonement" (228-29).

324   GUILLORY, JOHN. "'Some Superior Power': Spenser and Shakespeare in Milton's *Comus*." In *Poetic Authority: Spenser, Milton, and Literary History*. New York: Columbia University Press, 1983, pp. 68-93.

   Comus alludes to previous literary works, which *L'Allegro* and *Il Penseroso* start to organize, and then develops a dichotomy between two kinds of poetic aspiration, represented by Shakespeare and Spenser. When Milton deals with daemonic agents (or mediation), desire and imagination, and metamorphosis or the effectuality of art in *Comus*, he rewrites Shakespeare's plays about imagination (*Midsummer Night's Dream*) and the artist's relationship to the world (*Tempest*). The Lady's struggle to stand independently assumes the burden of Milton's struggle "to justify his authority in relation to prior '*auctors*'" (84). After banishing the strong Shakespearean spirits, Milton uses Spenser to halt the temptation to regress into Shakespearean plenitude.

325   HALPERN, RICHARD. "Puritanism and Maenadism in *A Masque*." In *Rewriting the Renaissance: The Discourses of Sexual Difference in Early Modern Europe*. Edited by Margaret W. Ferguson, Maureen Quilligan, and Nancy J. Vickers. Chicago, Ill., and London: University of Chicago Press, 1986, pp. 88-105.

   In *Comus*, Milton's ideological plan is "to trace the line that leads from virginity to married chastity" (88), a line that wanders and is filled with tension in his age. But Milton's masque wanders from this ideology because its myth is ambivalent and has surplus meanings that the allegory cannot contain. The myth thus subverts the allegory's linearity. Just as Dionysus's female followers, the maenads, dismember Orpheus, Comus threatens only men or beasts; a chaste figure, like the bacchantes, the Lady cannot be harmed, but the poet can be threatened, so the masque's key opposition (Comus versus the Lady) is

Comus

questioned from the start. The god of contradictions, Dionysus leads us to see that the supposed oppositions in *Comus*, such as virginity and promiscuity, are in fact doubles. Again with the image of Dionysus at the center, Milton's masque is ambiguous or contradictory about social classes. Ultimately, patriarchy and imperialism triumph.

326 HAUN, EUGENE. "An Inquiry into the Genre of *Comus*." In *Essays in Honor of Walter Clyde Curry*. Vanderbilt Studies in the Humanities, 2. Nashville, Tenn.: Vanderbilt University Press, 1954, pp. 221-39.

There is no established definition of the masque form: Renaissance masques have little in common except for the random use of music and dance. Using elements that appear in other masques, *Comus* fits into the pattern of the form's steady evolution. Milton's masque originally contained more music than is usually assumed-- indeed, it used music from start to finish--and we might see *Comus* as a transitional work acting as an anticipation of opera in England.

327 HUNTER, WILLIAM B., Jr. *Milton's "Comus": Family Piece*. Troy, N.Y.: Whitston Publishing Co., 1983, 109 pp. 8 illustrations.

Because masques are commissioned and occasional, Milton receives directions concerning the subject of *Comus*, which is surprisingly not about the installation of Wales's Lord President but about his family. *Arcades*, written earlier in the year for the Earl of Bridgewater's mother-in-law, is probably performed on Saturday, 3 May 1634, to celebrate the Countess Dowager's seventy-fifth birthday. Three years earlier, she and the Earl of Bridgewater were horrified by the Castlehaven scandal in their family, and *Comus* must have recalled the event, probably according to the Egertons' wishes. Milton may have responded too enthusiastically to their instructions about the masque's subject. *Comus*'s first performance probably occurs in the inner bailey rather than the Great Hall of Ludlow Castle, and we can reconstruct much of that performance.

Hunter prints "A Tentative Promptbook for *Comus*."

328 HYMAN, LAWRENCE W. "*Comus* and the Limits of Interpretation." *Structuralist Review* 2 (1981):68-77.

Rather than continue to offer endless individualistic interpretations of *Comus*, we should recognize both our role in the interpretive process and the limits of interpretation. The meaning that is not in *Comus* is its allegorical meaning, by which we attempt to create a pattern from images and actions. We find discrepancies between the work's ostensible Christian allegory or theme and the resistance to allegory that appears in its images and actions. Meaning appears and disappears, so a reader should not look for consistency or a coherent morality.

329   JAYNE, SEARS. "The Subject of Milton's Ludlow *Mask.*" *PMLA* 74 (1959):533-43. Revised in *Milton: Modern Essays in Criticism*, ed. Arthur E. Barker (London, Oxford, and New York: Oxford University Press, 1965), pp. 88-111; reprinted in "*A Maske at Ludlow*": *Essays on Milton's "Comus*," ed. John S. Diekhoff (Cleveland, Ohio: Press of Case Western Reserve University, 1968), pp. 165-87.

The Attendant Spirit emanates from God to the outermost circle of the Platonic world soul. Following Ficino, Milton has Jove represent divine providence and a governor of people; natural providence is represented by the masque's actions that occur in Neptune's realm. The two realms and kinds of providence are in harmony, though the Lady must choose between them. *Comus* is concerned with the soul's achievement of Platonic chastity, with the narrative action divided into three scenes corresponding to the soul's three motions: descending from God, stopping, and ascending to God. By exercising temperance and gaining Christian philosophical knowledge (represented by haemony), Reason (the Lady) achieves regeneration. The Mind (Sabrina) then leads Reason to God; together, Mind and Reason form the soul. In *Comus*, virtue is Platonic *castitas*.

330   KIRKCONNELL, WATSON, trans. *Awake the Courteous Echo: The Themes and Prosody of "Comus," "Lycidas," and "Paradise Regained" in World Literature with Translations of the Major Analogues.* Toronto and Buffalo, N.Y.: University of Toronto Press, 1973, 360 pp.

Kirkconnell lists thirty-nine analogues for *Comus*, 102 for *Lycidas*, and twenty-five for *Paradise Regained*. Many of the analogues are translated in whole or in part. Kirkconnell includes appendixes

Comus

discussing meter, listing biblical epics, and mentioning Thomas Ellwood's *Davideis* (1712).

331 LAGUARDIA, ERIC. "Milton's *Comus*." In *Nature Redeemed: The Imitation of Order in Three Renaissance Poems*. Studies in English Literature, vol. 31. London, The Hague, and Paris: Mouton, 1966, pp. 126-47.

    Comus imitates a two-dimensional nature whose guises are passion (or the lawless) and purity (or the lawful), which come into harmony and lead to nature's redemption as it moves into alignment with the divine world. Like the love quests of Spenser's knights, the Lady's journey is from the disorder of sensual experience to the order of chaste innocence. With its reference to the marriage of Cupid and Psyche, the epilogue, rather than rejecting sensual pleasure as the masque proper does, shows sensuality's purification and role in chaste love. Comus perverts nature, but the masque reveals through the image of chastity that nature has its proper use as it conforms to eternal law.

332 LERNER, LAURENCE. "Farewell, Rewards and Fairies: An Essay on *Comus*." *JEGP: Journal of English and Germanic Philology* 70 (1971):617-31.

    Syncretists believe that pagans see a good deal of truth through the light of revelation, but Puritans argue that, because unredeemed wisdom is at best devilish, pagan myth opposes Christian myth. Milton never resolves the conflict between these two views. Like the Elder Brother's speech about chastity's power, the Attendant Spirit in *Comus* is very pagan, both being associated with a world filled with natural magic. The world to which the Attendant Spirit descends is not Christian but prepared for Christianity. The Lady, however, sees a different world, one shaped by morality. Not surprisingly, she experiences no real conflict with Comus, the play's most pagan character. Rejecting paganism, Milton's masque "enacts the cultural change that came over England in the seventeenth century" (629).

333 McGUIRE, MARYANN CALE. *Milton's Puritan Masque*. Athens: University of Georgia Press, 1983, 219 pp.

    Milton, a Puritan, appropriates a royalist form when he writes *Comus*, whose historical context is the recreation debates of the 1630s.

The *Declaration of Sports* approves rural pastimes on Sunday and Charles's court holds Sunday theatricals, but the Puritans see these actions as diversions from spiritual responsibility. Although Milton generally agrees with the Puritan arguments against recreation, his view of Christian liberty calls for freedom from such restraints so the individual can grow morally and intellectually. Comus presents the royalists' main arguments in favor of festivities; the counterarguments show a sympathy with Puritan attitudes. *Arcades, Comus,* and *Of Education* reconcile sports and serious responsibility, for Milton comes to see study and recreation as nearly identical: both prepare young men for responsible Christian lives in society. He argues for reformed, moral recreation. *Comus* celebrates the limitations of government, forces its audience to unlearn lessons derived from conventional masques, and reforms the masque to make it a vehicle for Puritan concerns.

334 MARCUS, LEAH SINANOGLOU. "The Milieu of Milton's *Comus*: Judicial Reform at Ludlow and the Problem of Sexual Assault." *Criticism* 25 (1983):293-327.

When the Privy Council calls on Sir John Egerton to investigate the case of Margery Evans's abduction and rape in 1631, he is Lord President of the Council in the Marches of Wales, a powerful but lax and corrupt court of law. *Comus* investigates the administration of justice--its difficulties, importance, and obstacles. Criticizing the Council for negligence and for prejudging Evans, the masque provides a mirror for the judges and allows them to measure their principles against those they view in the performance. *Comus* praises Egerton for pursuing justice and acknowledges the limits of what he can accomplish. Milton's masque focuses on the liturgical subject of Michaelmas, the humbling and edification of judges. The Lady's predicament often parallels that of Margery Evans, and Sabrina is an ideal figure of judicial humility who has much to teach the judges on Egerton's Council.

335 MARCUS, LEAH S. "Milton's Anti-Laudian Masque." In *The Politics of Mirth: Jonson, Herrick, Milton, Marvell, and the Defense of Old Holiday Pastimes.* Chicago, Ill., and London: University of Chicago Press, 1986, pp. 169-212.

Comus

Comus symbolically undoes royal power as it appears in the Earl of Bridgewater's Council in the Marches of Wales. Milton creates a distance between the Earl and the King, between Ludlow and Whitehall, and between the Earl's goals and the images of authority portrayed in court masques. Insofar as public mirth can be independent of Laud, whom the Earl and Milton oppose, *Comus* defends it. Milton uses the Anglican ritual against the Anglican establishment of Laud. When Milton requires us to see that episodes can be interpreted not in terms of the Stuart politics of mirth but in terms of free judgment, he shows that traditional pastimes and the masque do not need to be seen as an encoding of Stuart authority.

336 MARTIN, JEANNE S. "Transformations in Genre in Milton's *Comus*." *Genre* 10 (1977):195-213.

Jonson defines the very conventions or standards of a masque from which Milton departs. While Jonson shows the antimasque's participants in action and then allows the hero to discover them, Milton first has the Attendant Spirit describe and judge them, which deprives the Lady of the hero's conventional duty. The antimasque concludes not because of the Lady's keen perceptions, but because Comus detects the approach of virtue. Contrary to the conventions of the masque form, in *Comus* the villain's power is increased and the heroine's power is decreased. She is vulnerable. The conventional masque shows the main masque's world to be an ideal, which is then communicated to the courtly audience. But the audience at Ludlow Castle learns that, in the masque and in the real world, evil can disguise itself as good and attempt to corrupt virtue. Unlike Jonson's masques, *Comus* merges masquer and audience in a world of mutability and deceptive appearances.

337 MARTZ, LOUIS L. "The Music of *Comus*." In *Illustrious Evidence: Approaches to English Literature of the Early Seventeenth Century*. Edited by Earl Miner. Berkeley, Los Angeles, and London: University of California Press, 1975, pp. 93-113.

Because of additions, deletions, and revisions, no extant version of *Comus* presents the work in its ideal state. The Bridgewater manuscript shows that Lawes wants to begin *Comus* with a fourteen-line song, which--in other versions--appears at the opening of the Attendant Spirit's epilogue. All versions indicate that additional music, some just instrumental and some with vocal parts as well, is at least planned for the masque. Furthermore, allusions to and descriptions of music develop the theme of disorder versus harmony. Haemony may be an image of poetic inspiration. We should view *Comus* as something analogous to an opera. See entries 15, 22, 142, 290, 321, 370, 430, 861.

338 MAXWELL, J. C. "The Pseudo-Problem of *Comus*." *Cambridge Journal* 1 (1948):376-80.

Virginity as a blessed state or one that receives protection is not a central issue in *Comus*. Instead of moving beyond chastity to the religious level, the epilogue sums up the entire poem's moral. The Lady's virtue is neither narrow nor one-sided. Because the whole poem is about virtue, there is no contradiction between Milton's doctrine in the epilogue and the speeches of the Lady and Elder Brother.

339 MUNDHENK, ROSEMARY KARMELICH. "Dark Scandal and the Sun-Clad Power of Chastity: The Historical Milieu of Milton's *Comus*." *Studies in English Literature, 1500-1900* 15 (1975):141-52.

In 1631, Mervyn Touchet, the Second Earl of Castlehaven, is executed for sexual offenses. When Milton writes *Comus*, he seeks to honor the Earl of Bridgewater and to deliver the Countess Dowager (Touchet's sister) and her family from embarrassment. The themes of chastity and incontinence, and reason and passion are especially appropriate. Alice Egerton and her brothers, along with their music instructor, Henry Lawes, never lose their identities by assuming parts in the masque. Since no family member can be a villain, an outsider must play Comus. The Castlehaven scandal may be behind a few of the textual differences between the Trinity and Bridgewater manuscripts. With the publication of *Comus* in 1637, the work reaches a wider audience and anyone can play the Lady, so--while Milton does not need to overstate Alice Egerton's virtue--he adds dialogue that strengthens the Lady's characterization as a chaste maiden. See entries 310, 316.

340 NEUSE, RICHARD. "Metamorphosis and Symbolic Action in *Comus*." *ELH* 34 (1967):49-64. Reprinted in *Critical Essays on Milton from "ELH"* (Baltimore, Md., and London: Johns Hopkins Press, 1969), pp. 87-102.

Comus

The Lady's original clash with Comus initiates a complication and resolution when she is paralyzed and released by Sabrina. Even after being changed to the shepherd Thyrsis, the Attendant Spirit cannot release the Lady from Comus's enchantment. The solution to her problem lies lower: in Sabrina, who has been changed to a goddess of the river. She symbolizes a person's lower nature transformed to be in harmony with spirit and reason. Comus is a threat because he represents a nature disjoined from spirit. In *Comus*, there is a dual metamorphosis to restore the golden world: the Platonic forms change into active participants in the human arena, and the social world of masquers and audience changes as the two merge in the final dance. The epilogue is a form of verbal action, pointing out that the masque has its origin deep within the mind.

341 ORAM, WILLIAM A. "The Invocation of Sabrina." *Studies in English Literature, 1500-1900* 24 (1984):121-39.

Although the masque form emphasizes closure, the first 800 lines of *Comus* avoid it by stressing uncertainties. With the invocation of Sabrina, an image of truth, comes the end of suspension and the beginning of resolution. If Comus and the Attendant Spirit reveal opposing views of the world and its services, Sabrina reconciles opposites as she embodies a proper understanding. The Lady gradually learns to value and use the creation correctly. Milton balances two rites, an invocation of Cotytto and another of Sabrina, to show the evolution from pagan to Christian, and from the opposition of passion and reason to their reconciliation. The Lady is in a self-induced ecstatic state caused by rejecting her own physical nature as represented by Comus. Immobilized and isolated, she cannot participate in the trials of this world. Sabrina's ascent symbolizes the Lady's reconciliation to herself. Her success prefigures her father's political success.

342 PATTERSON, ANNABEL. "*L'Allegro, Il Penseroso* and *Comus*: The Logic of Recombination." *Milton Quarterly* 9 (1975):75-79.

As the third work in a sequence of three companion pastorals, *Comus* contains many echoes of *L'Allegro* and *Il Penseroso*. The antitheses of the earlier companion poems are recombined in *Comus* to give the masque "a more complex ethical solution" (75). Comus is a false Allegro and a false Penseroso, while the Lady must debate (by acting out) the ethical abstractions of the latter. The Attendant Spirit reconciles L'Allegro with Il Penseroso.

343 ROLLINSON, PHILIP B. "The Central Debate in *Comus*." *Philological Quarterly* 49 (1970):481-88.

Because critics do not examine the Lady's logical handling of Comus's argument, her views are frequently considered inadequate. In the first part of the debate, Comus urges the Lady to drink from his magic cup. She responds with a logical argument based on the authority of the New Testament. The Lady recognizes that only the testimony of an unreliable character, Comus, indicates that the potion is beneficial. In the second part of the debate, Comus's argument--that the Lady should stop being chaste and instead be used immediately--reveals his limited perception of reality. As in the first part, her response shows her ability to argue logically and evaluate arguments carefully. Though Comus's dazzling rhetoric never misleads the Lady, it does mislead critics.

344 SAGE, LORNA. "The Coherence of *Comus*." *Yearbook of English Studies* 1 (1971):88-99.

Even as *Comus* invites interpretation as a dramatic event and as an allegory, it confounds that interpretation because we do not define allegory as Milton does. Milton uses details of poetic texture to play off "knowledge against experience, masquers against actors, stage against audience" (90). An enveloping tone prevents moral value from conflicting with aesthetic values. If the Lady and her brothers begin as high members in the world of the audience, but are unaware of that audience, they eventually attain their true position. The Attendant Spirit reverses this movement by assuming his identity as Thyrsis, thus losing knowledge that he had at the start and relying on human resources. Established as fictions, Comus and his crew belong to the stage, for they know of no other mode of existence. The fictionality of Comus reveals his moral negativeness, while other characters reach full reality, with Thyrsis's help, by understanding and creating fictions.

345 SAVAGE, J. B. "*Comus* and Its Traditions." *English Literary Renaissance* 5 (1975):58-80.

Comus

    Comus must be read as a masque, which is not a dramatic but an expository form, for it presents moral ideals brought to life. As a literary form, the masque is not Christian but allegorical, philosophical, and Platonic, which are also the three ways in which Milton approaches the theme of chastity. His subject, however, is the soul's incorruptibility rather than sexuality, because for Plato in the *Phaedo* chastity means the purification of the soul through a renunciation of the world. The Lady must reject Comus because his sensuality is an obstacle to the soul's journey. Evolving from within the soul and the Lady, Sabrina is both a figure of what the Lady discovers and a character associated with immortality and immutability. Even the paralysis that Comus induces in the Lady is a stage in the process of reaching her destiny.

346   SCOUFOS, ALICE-LYLE. "The Mysteries in Milton's *Masque*." *Milton Studies* 6 (1974):113-42.
    By Milton's time, the apocalyptic dramas that conclude morality cycles are no longer performed in England. But Milton is aware of the structures of these plays, as we see in *Comus*, where he uses the plot of the medieval Advent plays of the Antichrist, as they are revived during the Reformation, for a structure and stock medieval characters for certain attributes of the main characters. The central woman in *Comus* is modeled on the Lady Wandering in the Wilderness, who is nameless and a symbol of the visible church of true believers. As such, Milton's Lady expresses his concern for contemporary ecclesiastical problems. Her brothers represent two factions of Puritan ministers. Milton merges the figures of Comus with the Antichrist and the prelates, while the Attendant Spirit is analogous to the angel Michael, who will conquer the Antichrist.

347   SENSABAUGH, G. F. "The *Milieu* of *Comus*." *Studies in Philology* 41 (1944):238-49.
    We should interpret *Comus* in the context of contemporary views about Platonic love, which the Stuart court promotes and which sees women as the objects of men's devotion, and marriage, which the Puritans consider a sacred bond with the male responsible and the female submissive. While Platonic lovers praise chastity, they pursue carnality, thus challenging the traditional values of love and marriage, which the Puritans defend. When Milton praises chastity in *Comus*, he runs the risk of having his views confused with the court's. So Comus

embodies the false view of chastity, beauty, and love as it is preached at court. The Lady exposes his casuistry and presents the true doctrine.

348 SMITH, GEORGE WILLIAM, Jr. "Milton's Revisions and the Design of *Comus*." *ELH* 46 (1979):56-80.

 Comus has a pyramidic structure as it moves from its outermost to its innermost members and back again, with a symmetry in which song balances song, debate balances debate, and dance balances dance. Milton's revisions in the central debate between Comus and the Lady connect it to the orations of Comus and the Elder Brother, thus inviting the audience to decide the issue. Making his masque more dramatic, Milton turns the temptation scene between Comus and the Lady into a vigorous debate. Later revisions emphasize the contrast between the Elder Brother's and Comus's speeches, and between the Younger Brother's and the Lady's speeches. In the conclusion, the various views are not synthesized or arranged to form a hierarchical reconciliation; they are left unresolved.

349 STEADMAN, JOHN M. "Iconography and Renaissance Drama: Ethical and Mythological Themes." *Research Opportunities in Renaissance Drama* 13-14 (1970-71):73-122. 15 illustrations. Part reprinted in *Nature into Myth: Medieval and Renaissance Moral Symbols* (Pittsburgh, Pa.: Duquesne University Press, 1979), pp. 213-40.

 Working within the same ethical and mythological traditions, Renaissance poets and painters share basic aesthetic principles, use the same technical devices and subjects, and converge in certain "synaesthetic" art forms. Although the parallels between Milton's Comus and the iconography of Cartari and de Vigenere are not impressive, the iconographic tradition helps us understand the significance not only of Comus's mother Circe but especially his father Bacchus. Milton uses the lexicographers' tradition of defining "Comus" as "reveling," particularly holding a nocturnal drinking party or banquet; associates Comus with erotic pleasures and a band of revelers; but undercuts the tradition by altering some of its conventional values.

350 SWAIM, KATHLEEN M. "Allegorical Poetry in Milton's Ludlow Mask." *Milton Studies* 16 (1982):167-99.

Comus

     Comus is and is about allegorical poetry. Denying allegory and true poetry, the enchanter imitates the Attendant Spirit, who acts as a true pastor and instructor about allegory's methods and ends. The Lady shares in the Attendant Spirit's role of true poet. Memory, the basis for all teaching in *Comus*, works with the imagination to redeem nature at the end of the masque.

351   TREIP, MINDELE ANNE. "*Comus* as 'Progress.'" *Milton Quarterly* 20 (1986):1-13.
     While the 1637 and later texts of *Comus* represent the work becoming increasingly literary, the 1634 version is the most vivid acting text. The 1634 performance of *Comus* may have started outdoors and moved into (or at least to the entrance of) the Great Hall of Ludlow Castle. If this is true, then *Comus* is performed like *Arcades*, as a progress. Fusing the masque and progress forms, *Comus* presents a journey that emulates the Earl's own travels.

352   WELSFORD, ENID. "The Influence of the Masque on Poetry." In *The Court Masque: A Study in the Relationship between Poetry and the Revels*. Cambridge: Cambridge University Press, 1927, pp. 302-23. Reprint. New York: Russell and Russell, 1962.
     Because Spenser transmutes masques and pageants into poetry, writers who are influenced by him, such as Milton, show the same characteristic. Influenced by the elaborate court masque developed by Jonson and Jones, Milton's poetry often alludes to masques or dancing. *Paradise Lost* turns to the masque for dance imagery, details of landscape and architecture (such as Pandemonium), and supernatural machinery. Greatly indebted to Jonson, *Comus* does not fit neatly into the masque form, for it lacks masquers and its concluding speeches and dances are hardly essential to the unity of the work. Dance does not play an explicitly key role in *Comus*, which shifts its climactic moment away from the presentation of the youths to their parents, and toward the Lady's refusal to take Comus's cup. Milton frees the masque from its banqueting hall atmosphere and from the usual compliment and gallantry, which are replaced by moralizing.

353   WILCHER, ROBERT. "Milton's Masque: Occasion, Form and Meaning." *Critical Quarterly* 20 (1978):3-20.

Rather than expanding the masque form, *Comus* unifies aristocratic entertainment and academic disputation with a moral theme appropriate to both. Debates, a regular feature of Milton's education, are divided into disputations (arguing back and forth) and declamations (presenting quotations from classical authors to support a point). In *Comus*, the Attendant Spirit acts as the moderator who introduces the opponents and the key issue for consideration. The opponents, Comus and the Lady, then outline their positions. The brothers do not hold a debate because, at their age, they have not mastered the method, but the Elder Brother's speech on chastity is a declamation. When the Lady and Comus square off, we should expect not the drama of real temptation but "a disputation conducted from two firmly entrenched debating positions" (11). Their arguments have logical structures.

354   WILDING, MICHAEL. "Milton's *A Masque Presented at Ludlow Castle, 1634*: Theatre and Politics on the Border." *Trivium* 20 (1985):147-79. Revised in *Dragons Teeth: Literature in the English Revolution* (Oxford: Clarendon Press, 1987), pp. 28-88.

In *Comus*'s opening lines, the Attendant Spirit draws an analogy between Jove's court and the Court in the Marches. The political context of England's repression of Wales is both suppressed and expressed in Milton's masque. Though Puritans and the middle class oppose them, the pagan pastimes that Comus promotes are endorsed by the Stuart court and are popular in Wales. In *Comus*, chastity (a private virtue) replaces the public virtue of charity, which declines in Milton's age and would be unnecessary in an economically and politically just society. Milton thus points to the need for charity by showing social injustice. Comus sees everything in terms of currency. Apparently praising the Egertons, Milton uses ambiguous signification to criticize them and to replace their hierarchy based on aristocracy with one based on virtue.

355   WILKENFELD, ROGER B. "The Seat at the Center: An Interpretation of *Comus*." *ELH* 33 (1966):170-97. Reprinted in *Critical Essays on Milton from "ELH"* (Baltimore, Md., and London: Johns Hopkins Press, 1969), pp. 123-50.

The sudden change in the masque's action comes from the concrete, visual emblem of the Lady paralyzed in Comus's seat. This

Comus

image is at the center of the masque's two motions: the horizontal, literal movement of the three young people to their father, and the vertical, symbolic movement that explores the nature of freedom. All of the variations on prisons and imprisonment are dramatically resolved when the Attendant Spirit cannot free the Lady from Comus's seat. With Sabrina's entrance, the play's movement shifts from horizontal to vertical, as Sabrina descends and the Lady rises, so the characters may shift to the horizontal motion of the Lady's return to her father's house. The end of *Comus* reveals a conjunction of natural and supernatural events.

356 WILLIAMSON, GEORGE. "The Context of *Comus*." In *Milton and Others*. London: Faber and Faber, 1965, pp. 26-41.
        In writing *Comus*, Milton gives us another form of the play he once proposed about the destruction of Sodom, "Cupids Funeral Pile." He creates a doctrine of continence or temperance by harmonizing chastity and love. Much of Milton's early poetry bears fruit in *Comus*: his Latin elegies show the susceptibility to love and sensitivity to moral discipline that the masque responds to; we may also see the masque as *Il Penseroso*'s sober music in opposition to a licentious form of *L'Allegro*. The themes of *Comus* are best defined in the context of Milton's work.

357 WOODHOUSE, A. S. P. "The Argument of Milton's *Comus*." *University of Toronto Quarterly* 11 (1941):46-71. Reprinted in *"A Maske at Ludlow": Essays on Milton's "Comus*," ed. John S. Diekhoff (Cleveland, Ohio: Press of Case Western Reserve University, 1968), pp. 17-42; *The Heavenly Muse: A Preface to Milton*, ed. Hugh MacCallum, University of Toronto Department of English Studies and Texts, no. 21 (Toronto and Buffalo, N.Y.: University of Toronto Press, 1972), pp. 55-98; *Milton: "Comus" and "Samson Agonistes,"* a *Casebook*, ed. Julian Lovelock (London and Basingstoke: Macmillan, 1975), pp. 41-70.
        The doctrine of chastity, which exists in the orders of nature and of grace, is the central theme of *Comus*'s argument. Found only in the order of nature, temperance and continence are treated briefly and subordinated to chastity. Virginity, the highest virtue, is found in the order of grace. Influenced by Spenser, particularly *Faerie Queene*, Books 2 and 3, *Comus* shows the necessity of ascending from the

doctrines of temperance and continence (nature) to the doctrine of chastity (nature and grace combined). But Spenser then progresses to chastity as wedded love, while Milton leads to virginity (in the order of grace). The Attendant Spirit's closing allusion to the Spenserian garden of Adonis symbolizes life on the natural level. In *Comus*'s final lines, Milton raises the doctrine of Christian liberty and takes us into the level of grace alone. See entry 320.

358 WOODHOUSE, A. S. P. "*Comus* Once More." *University of Toronto Quarterly* 19 (1950):218-23. Reprinted in *"A Maske at Ludlow": Essays on Milton's "Comus,"* ed. John S. Diekhoff (Cleveland, Ohio: Press of Case Western Reserve University, 1968), pp. 72-77; *The Heavenly Muse: A Preface to Milton*, ed. Hugh MacCallum, University of Toronto Department of English Studies and Texts, no. 21 (Toronto and Buffalo, N.Y.: University of Toronto Press, 1972), pp. 55-98.

The argument of *Comus* is based on an intellectual frame of reference that posits three realms: nature (the wild wood and Comus's palace), nature and grace combined (Ludlow and the castle), and grace (Ludlow as the parents' home). With a kind of pilgrimage at its center, the masque portrays an ascent through these realms. Sabrina symbolizes chastity as a positive virtue, a principle of action in the realm of grace. Sabrina and the power of grace destroy evil to free the good. See entry 320.

For the variorum, see entry 35; for analogues, see entry 330. See also entries 7, 15, 30, 43-44, 47, 49, 55, 57-59, 63, 65, 67-68, 71-72, 87-88, 91-93, 103, 105, 107-9, 111, 123, 126-27, 129-30, 134-35, 137-40, 142, 147, 150, 152, 155, 159, 163, 165, 169, 172, 175, 177, 179-83, 185-88, 190, 193-94, 197, 199-200, 205, 207-8, 211, 214, 216-20, 222, 224, 228, 230, 233, 236, 238, 245-48, 250-51, 289, 366, 416, 462, 480, 498, 504, 560, 563, 592, 596, 599, 614, 682, 789, 942, 1005, 1013.

LYCIDAS:

EDITION

359   Le COMTE, EDWARD, ed. *"Justa Edovardo King": A Facsimile Edition of the Memorial Volume in which Milton's "Lycidas" First Appeared*. Norwood, Pa.: Norwood Editions, 1978, 147 pp.
      Le Comte's facsimile of the 1638 volume of *Justa Edovardo King* and *Obsequies* includes notes and translations from the Latin.

ANTHOLOGY OF CRITICISM

360   ELLEDGE, SCOTT, ed. *Milton's "Lycidas": Edited to Serve as an Introduction to Criticism*. New York and London: Harper and Row, 1966, 352 pp.
      After printing the 1638 text of *Lycidas*, Elledge presents excerpts from other works that establish the poem's context in various ways: as a pastoral elegy (works by Theocritus, Bion, Moschus, and Virgil); as a consolation (Seneca and Statius); as a pastoral (Petrarch, Boccaccio, and Marot); and as a monody (Scaliger and Puttenham). Elledge also prints other Stuart elegies, selections from *Justa Edovardo King* and *Obsequies*, Milton's autobiographical statements about his training and aspirations, observations about England in 1637, and critical comments from such writers as Warton, Hurd, Hallam, Graves, and Auden.

CRITICISM

361   ABRAMS, M. H. "Five Types of *Lycidas*." In *Milton's "Lycidas": The Tradition and the Poem*. Edited by C. A. Patrides. New York: Holt, Rinehart and Winston, 1961, pp. 212-31. Rev. ed. (Columbia: University of Missouri Press, 1983), pp. 216-35.
      The traditional reading of *Lycidas* sees the poem as a conventional elegy mourning Edward King's death. Then, distinguishing between the poem's "nominal" and "real" subjects, Tillyard (see entry 216) concludes that *Lycidas* is about Milton himself. Ransom (see entry

390), on the other hand, says the poet stays out of his verse and writes an exercise in technique. In Brooks and Hardy's view (see entry 30), the poem is about neither King nor Milton, but about water and the theme of nature's lack of concern for poetry. Finally, Adams (see entry 362) and Frye (see entry 375) find archetypal patterns in *Lycidas*. If one applies a literal reading to the monody, none of the five preceding interpretations deals with the poem's essential concerns. The poem presents a nameless shepherd (not Milton), who laments and celebrates Lycidas (not King) while fearing the insecurity of his own life. The style moves from above the pastoral norm at the beginning, when the speaker introduces sympathetic nature, nymphs, and Orpheus's death, to Christian when Peter appears; it concludes by descending to the solitary piper's plain utterance. See entry 30.

362   ADAMS, RICHARD P. "The Archetypal Pattern of Death and Rebirth in Milton's *Lycidas*." *PMLA* 64 (1949):183-88. Revised in *Milton's "Lycidas": The Tradition and the Poem*, ed. C. A. Patrides (New York: Holt, Rinehart and Winston, 1961), pp. 120-25; rev. ed. (Columbia: University of Missouri Press, 1983), pp. 111-16.

    Lycidas follows the conventional movement of the pastoral, beginning with a friend's death and descending into sorrow and despair; comfort then leads to heavenly joy. The poem uses such images of immortality as evergreens and the metamorphosis of a mortal into a plant. Flower imagery symbolizes both mourning and the promise of rebirth. Edward King's death is blamed on a man-made ship rather than on water, which is a principle of life. Milton's monody contains no digressions. See entry 361.

363   ALPERS, PAUL. "*Lycidas* and Modern Criticism." *ELH* 49 (1982):468-96.

    The very nature and peculiar difficulties of *Lycidas* lead to criticism that tries to substitute the scholar's poem for Milton's. Even excellent critics write weakly or perversely about *Lycidas*, often misunderstanding the pastoral convention and perpetuating Dr. Johnson's claim that the poem is the antithesis of personal and individual expression. From the Latin *convenire*, to come together, "convention" is the practice of a community of previous poets, which enables the individual poet as he responds to and challenges this community. *Lycidas* traces the emerging voice of a narrator who begins

Lycidas

by speaking in the poet's voice and then, through loss and separation, develops into an individual shepherd who participates in the pastoral elegy's topoi. This speaker is open, responsive, and willing to identify with real, remembered, and imagined things. In *Lycidas*, "social" truth, the kind sanctioned by discursive conventions, is more important than ontological or epistemological truth.

364 BAKER, STEWART A. "Milton's Uncouth Swain." *Milton Studies* 3 (1971):35-53.
     Through a reductive analogy, *Lycidas*'s *commiato* restates the relevance of the elegiac themes in the life of a swain who gains a redemptive vision in the face of death. Milton presents an uncouth swain to express pastoral's double vision, which reduces experience to innocence. When the swain uses motifs from pastoral's subgenres, he brings them into thematic conflict. The swain's point of view transvalues naturalistic or libertine pastoral motifs into the motifs of allegorical or Christian pastoral. His perspective brings this variety into a unity. According to Scaliger, pastoral works through inverse reduction (great subjects should be reduced more than small ones), a process that operates in Lycidas's elevation or St. Peter's and Christ's reduction. Written in what Scaliger calls the florid mode, *Lycidas* modulates from low to high levels of style within that mode.

365 BERKELEY, DAVID SHELLEY. *Inwrought with Figures Dim: A Reading of Milton's "Lycidas."* De Proprietatibus Litterarum, Series Didactica, vol. 2. The Hague and Paris: Mouton, 1974, 233 pp.
     Lycidas's structure is based on Christian typology, which unites the Old and New Testaments. Although Milton's swain never comprehends types, Lycidas appears more and more on the antitypological level as the poem progresses. Figures and forces adumbrating Christ and heaven are opposed to those of Satan and hell. In the middle are figures of judgment to heaven or hell, along with the supreme judge. Milton portrays Cambridge University as a type of the heavenly paradise and Britain as an Edenic place of supreme felicity where the golden age is in progress. A symbol of sin and death, and subject to diabolic control, the sea is an unredeemed region in *Lycidas*. The poem's sunken bark is the providentially ordained wreck of the state church.

366 BRETT, R. L. "Milton's *Lycidas*." In *Reason and Imagination: A Study of Form and Meaning in Four Poems*. London, New York, and Toronto: Oxford University Press, 1960, pp. 21-50.

Although nature appears to lead to grace in *Comus*, the two may be opposed. Milton is influenced by two movements that divide experience into separate orders: repudiating knowledge based on sensory experience, Puritanism favors faith, while scientific rationalism favors reason. Through Platonism, Milton links humanism and rationalistic Puritanism. For his prelapsarian audience, Raphael in *Paradise Lost* explains the connection between the sensory and spiritual worlds, but *Paradise Regained* and *Samson Agonistes* show that poetry must approximate rational discourse, and avoid the sensory, if it is to approach divine truth. Dualism is strong in these two last works. Milton does not use Platonism to connect humanism and Christianity in *Lycidas*.

367 CREASER, JOHN. "*Lycidas*: The Power of Art." *Essays and Studies*, n.s. 34 (1981):123-47.

In *Lycidas*, Milton uses the pastoral elegy form, though it is anachronistic and unfashionable, because it frees him from shows of wit and allows him to celebrate fellowship based on art. Written during a troubled decade in England's history, the poem introduces a sense of communal grief for nature, the nation, church, and university. The pastoral elegy form also contributes to the monody's heightened artificiality, but Milton renews the tradition instead of merely imitating it. Milton's artful writing expresses his love of the pastoral community's traditional values and what Lycidas's death means to that community. With the cry of "Weep no more," despair turns to exultation because of the purging of false surmise, the implication of providential concern, and the self-conscious artistry. Art has the power to restore faith.

368 ELLIOTT, EMORY. "Milton's Uncouth Swain: The Speaker in *Lycidas*." In *Milton Reconsidered: Essays in Honor of Arthur E. Barker*. Edited by John Karl Franson. Salzburg Studies in English Literature, Elizabethan and Renaissance Studies, vol. 49. Salzburg, Austria: Institut für Englische Sprache und Literatur, Universität Salzburg, 1976, pp. 1-21.

In the penultimate stanza of *Lycidas*, there is some irony in the speaker's fusion of pagan and Christian images, and this irony

Lycidas

reinforces the contrast between him and Lycidas. The uncouth swain has neither the faith nor the will to achieve true consolation, so he settles for a compromise Christianity based on superstition. According to the decorum of the pastoral elegy, the swain should conclude by emphasizing "the life of virtuous Christian deeds which lies ahead for him" (7), while reaffirming his faith in God's justice. In contrast to Lycidas, the swain fails to lead a life of virtuous self-sacrifice and faith. The New Testament's call to perform good works pulls the swain's conscience in one direction, but his will pulls him in another. While this speaker dwells in a world of both Christianity and paganism, the poet enters in the last stanza to dissociate himself from such a perspective.

369 EVANS, J. MARTIN. *The Road from Horton: Looking Backwards in "Lycidas."* ELS Monograph Series, no. 28. [Victoria, B.C.]: English Literary Studies, University of Victoria, 1983, 90 pp.

For Milton, the composition of *Lycidas* marks "an Age Thirty Transition" (7). The monody is filled with repetitions of itself and of other poems in the pastoral tradition, yet these repetitions often invert their antecedents, which means that *Lycidas* opposes the pastoral elegy tradition. Reluctance marks Milton's attitude from the first line on. Consolation comes only when the resurrected King joins the saints in their love and Dionysiac ecstasy. Bipartite in structure, the poem contains contrasting movements that conclude by comparing King and the uncouth swain. At the beginning of the poem, Milton does not distinguish himself from the swain, for they are identical; as the monody progresses, Milton slowly loses his historical identity and emerges as a fictional character who finally becomes a figment of the poet's imagination.

370 FINNEY, GRETCHEN. "A Musical Background for *Lycidas*." *Huntington Library Quarterly* 15 (1952):325-50. Reprinted in *Musical Backgrounds for English Literature: 1580-1650* (New Brunswick, N.J.: Rutgers University Press, 1962), pp. 195-219; reprinted (Westport, Conn.: Greenwood Press, 1976).

Lycidas has clear structural parallels with sung poetry of Milton's age. Divided into three sections, the monody contains two kinds of recitative styles, one for the shepherd-narrator and another for the characters he introduces. With its foundation in the pastoral eclogue, the new Italian musical drama of the seventeenth century, which alone uses recitative style, influences *Lycidas*, though the middle of the poem suggests oratorio. Orpheus is a popular musical subject in the period. In the seventeenth century, "monody" denotes music sung by a solo voice in the new recitative style. See entries 15, 22, 142, 290, 321, 337, 430, 861.

371 FISH, STANLEY E. "*Lycidas*: A Poem Finally Anonymous." In *Glyph: Johns Hopkins Textual Studies* 8 (1981):1-18. Reprinted in *Milton's "Lycidas": The Tradition and the Poem*, rev. ed., ed. C. A. Patrides (Columbia: University of Missouri Press, 1983), pp. 319-40.

While some critics frequently challenge the unity of *Lycidas*, others defend its unity, usually by domesticating or explaining away its discontinuities. All of these readings assume that *Lycidas* is about the emergence of the ego. Suppressing the personal voice is the poem's achievement; the forces that undermine that voice and challenge its fictive control account for *Lycidas*'s energy. As the pastoral's authority falls, the speaker's rises. His claims to spontaneity and to independence as a maker are compromised; his solution is to rewrite or misread Phoebus's challenge by setting the god against the pastoral. As he exposes the false surmises of pastoral consolation, the poem exposes the surmise that allows him (he thinks) to do so. With the call to "Weep no more," the speaker disappears for the last time. If he is heard again, it is only as a member of a chorus. *Lycidas* achieves its victorious vision by suppressing and then silencing the speaker.

372 FOWLER, ALASTAIR. "'To Shepherd's Ear': The Form of Milton's *Lycidas*." In *Silent Poetry: Essays in Numerological Analysis*. Edited by Alastair Fowler. London: Routledge and Kegan Paul, 1970, pp. 170-84.

Some of the poems accompanying *Lycidas* in the 1638 *Justa Edovardo King* and *Obsequies*, as well as the whole volume, follow numerological patterns of organization. *Lycidas* is composed of eleven stanzas, the number of mourning, or ten full stanzas plus a *commiato*. Each of the ten full stanzas, except the tenth, is broken by a six-syllable line. The unbroken tenth stanza signals an end to mourning and a transition to Christian consolation. All of the stanzas that lack unrhymed lines (stanzas 3, 8, 10, and 11) deal with harmony. The day that the monody charts represents the day of human life, King's or the poet's. Phoebus occupies the central position in the poem.

Lycidas

373 FRENCH, ROBERTS W. "Voice and Structure in *Lycidas*." *Texas Studies in Literature and Language* 12 (1970):15-25.

In line 164 of *Lycidas*, the speaker says that his friend is dead, only to assure us in the next twenty lines that he is not dead. The shift is abrupt. A poet, the uncouth swain speaks lines 1-185 in two voices: the swain feels no grief for he knows the ending when he sings a song in which a speaker mourns in lines 1-164. In these lines, the speaker hears but does not understand the Christian message; after line 164, he drops his mask and speaks to his audience about Christian consolation. Having created a role, the swain cancels it. He leads us away from Christian assertions and, just when despair seems the only alternative, returns us to Christian consolation. The poem makes us whole again.

374 FRIEDMAN, DONALD M. "*Lycidas*: The Swain's Paideia." *Milton Studies* 3 (1971):3-34. Revised in *Milton's "Lycidas": The Tradition and the Poem*, rev. ed., ed. C. A. Patrides (Columbia: University of Missouri Press, 1983), pp. 281-302.

Milton's persona in *Lycidas* is carefully chosen to express the poem's central attitude of questioning. The persona struggles, fighting against the knowledge that enters his mental landscape. Because of the transformation of reality, the swain must define what is by what was; he concludes only that death is inimical to beauty and the potential for creation. While his poetic calling does not change, his awareness of it and its rewards does. Using the flower passage to recall a healing, literary pastoral, he tries to evade Peter's speech and the knowledge it brings. A "false surmise," the evasion fails just as the poetic imagination fails to shape experience. By admitting his inadequacy, the swain receives an answer: Michael's guardianship of Lycidas's body. In *Lycidas*, answers do not come from questions; they come unexpected, when the questioner finds himself most ignorant. *Lycidas* dramatizes a key tension in Milton's mind between the will to create a poetic proof of his abilities and the belief that poetry comes, in its own time, through divine inspiration.

375 FRYE, NORTHROP. "Literature as Context: Milton's *Lycidas*." In *The Proceedings of the Second Congress of the International Comparative Literature Association*. Edited by W. P. Friederich. University of North Carolina Studies in Comparative Literature, no. 23. Chapel Hill: University of North Carolina Press, 1959, pp. 44-55.

Reprinted in *Milton's "Lycidas": The Tradition and the Poem*, ed. C. A. Patrides (New York: Holt, Rinehart and Winston, 1961), pp. 200-11; rev. ed. (Columbia: University of Missouri Press, 1983), pp. 204-15; *Fables of Identity: Studies in Poetic Mythology* (New York: Harcourt, Brace, 1963), pp. 119-29.

The pastoral name Lycidas is equivalent to Adonis and is associated with nature's cyclical rhythms: the sun's movement across the sky, the yearly cycles of seasons, and the movement of water from wells and fountains through rivers to the sea. As a clergyman, Edward King is associated with the archetypes of poet (Orpheus) and priest (Peter). *Lycidas* is organized in an ABACA form, with the main theme --the drowning of Lycidas--appearing three times and two other episodes intervening and stressing premature death. The Adonis myth shapes the structure of *Lycidas*. See entry 361.

376 HANFORD, JAMES HOLLY. "The Pastoral Elegy and Milton's *Lycidas*." *PMLA* 25 (1910):403-47. Reprinted in *John Milton, Poet and Humanist: Essays by James Holly Hanford* (Cleveland, Ohio: Press of Western Reserve University, 1966), pp. 126-60; revised in *Milton's "Lycidas": The Tradition and the Poem*, ed. C. A. Patrides (New York: Holt, Rinehart and Winston, 1961), pp. 27-55; rev. ed. (Columbia: University of Missouri Press, 1983), pp. 31-59.

Lycidas and *Epitaphium Damonis* are indebted to the first idyl of Theocritus. By lamenting the death of an actual person conceived as a shepherd, Moschus's *Lament for Bion* transforms a genre of erotic verse into a personal elegy in pastoral form. In Virgil's hands, the pastoral eclogue has an epic quality in style, an elevation of tone, and a willingness to include a range of material. Virgil exerts the greatest influence on Milton's pastoral poems. Political, religious, and moral ideas dominate the vernacular pastorals of Petrarch and Boccaccio, who influence Mantuan, Marot, and Spenser. Milton displays his vast power of assimilation in *Lycidas* and *Epitaphium Damonis*.

377 HUNT, CLAY. *"Lycidas" and the Italian Critics*. New Haven, Conn., and London: Yale University Press, 1979, 206 pp.

When he writes the pastoral *Lycidas* as a subspecies of the genus lyric, Milton wants to refashion the genre of the pastoral elegy to make it produce effects found in epic and tragedy. Many works by Tasso, Sannazaro, and Spenser provide hints for Milton's practice in his

Lycidas

monody. The lyric joins music and poetic language, as in the canzone, which Dante claims to be the preeminent poetic form that mixes rough and smooth sounds, deals with tragic matter, and permits metrical improvisation. If *Lycidas* follows a musical structure, Milton arranges its sections according to tonal effects rather than logical content. In *Lycidas*, he "has taken the 'base' form of the eclogue, transformed it into the kind of lyric which will permit him to write in both the middle and the lofty style, and imposed on the whole poem a musical structure" (151) and a tragic mode. The poem is what Milton tells us it is: a monody.

378 JOHNSON, BARBARA A. "Fiction and Grief: The Pastoral Idiom of Milton's *Lycidas*." *Milton Quarterly* 18 (1984):69-76.

The narrator's search for Lycidas's corpse, an unprecedented act in the pastoral elegy tradition, tests the pastoral mode, which results in the rejection of conventional patterns of consolation. Exhausted, the pastoral's imagery is not equal to the task the narrator has given it. Corporeal imagery transforms the conventional apotheosis in the monody's conclusion by emphasizing that Lycidas's corporeal nature is in heaven. As early as 1637, Milton may be working toward the mortalist position, or the view of the body's and soul's indivisibility. His use of the pastoral succeeds because he demonstrates its inadequacy or failure to respond to King's death.

379 LAMBERT, ELLEN ZETZEL. "*Lycidas*: Finding the Time and the Place." In *Placing Sorrow: A Study of the Pastoral Elegy Convention from Theocritus to Milton*. University of North Carolina Studies in Comparative Literature, no. 60. Chapel Hill: University of North Carolina Press, 1976, pp. 154-86.

When Milton shatters the leaves in the opening lines of *Lycidas*, he simultaneously pays tribute to the dead in the traditional act of scattering leaves and shatters the pastoral elegy convention. He is torn between apparently contrary impulses that parallel the conflict between nature's cyclical pattern and the uncertainty of human life, including his own. Milton finds the harmony between these patterns. Of all pastoral elegy writers, only Milton disorients the reader by omitting an opening frame while including a closing one: he discovers order instead of imposing it, for his consolation is not assured from the start. In terms of theme and prosody, *Lycidas* follows the wayward pattern of mourning as it moves backward and forward and repeats itself. When the poet searches for a world to console him, one landscape replaces another. His pastoral world has room for rage and grief, which become healing forces.

380 LAUTERMILCH, STEVEN J. "'That Fatal and Perfidious Bark': A Key to the Double Design and Unity of Milton's *Lycidas*." *Renaissance Quarterly* 30 (1977):201-16. 3 illustrations.

Milton advances the double design in *Lycidas* by using the image of a ship that is divinely blessed but weakened or ruined by human corruption. This image is associated with Noah's ark (the type of the church) and transformed in the New Testament to the Apostles' vessel (the new church), which Christ preserves by calming the Sea of Galilee. Using this traditional image of the church in an unconventional way, Milton "attacks the traditions that the Reformation scorned in order to attack the Reformers themselves" (208). This is consistent with his use of the same image in *Doctrine and Discipline of Divorce* and *Of Civil Power*. *Lycidas* is thus designed as both satire and elegy. Milton's satiric point is that Lycidas died in a "fatal and perfidious Bark," a church and body that deserve blame; his elegiac point is that Lycidas's new life, given by "him that walk'd the waves," is connected to a grace and strength that deserve praise.

381 LAWRY, JON S. "'The Faithful Herdman's Art' in *Lycidas*." *Studies in English Literature, 1500-1900* 13 (1973):111-25.

In the beginning of *Lycidas*, the speaker suffers from mortal despair and needs to be nearly resurrected from it by viewing the bad deeds of false herdsmen and the shepherd death. The divine herdsmen Apollo, Peter, and Michael oppose the mortal doubt and assert the herdsman's art. The speaker nearly abandons the herdsman's art, so--if he is to become an agent of salvation--he must first be its object. He has a great temporal range from which he can choose to remain in past despair, look to future mortal consolation, or advance into the present and eternal. Guiding the speaker toward consolation and faith, Apollo, Peter, and Michael judicially defeat sin and death by condemning them to the past. Lycidas and the speaker become shepherds who perfectly practice the faithful herdsman's art.

Lycidas

382 LIEB, MICHAEL. "Milton's 'Unexpressive Nuptial Song': A Reading of *Lycidas*." *Renaissance Papers* (1982):15-26.

Lycidas transforms the amatory tradition of classical bucolic verse into a Christian perspective. Presented as a lover, Milton's poet-shepherd loves poetry yet believes he will be a bad lover who plucks berries and shatters leaves. He does not initially know what it means to write a love song, such as *Lycidas*, and he must gain this knowledge. First, he has to encounter failed love relationships based on the destructive classical notion of *amor*: Arethuse and Alpheus, Hyacinth and Apollo. A Christian pastoral poem, *Lycidas* concludes with a vision of *amor* as an eternal, celestial, and creative force that is part of a never-ending wedding.

383 LIEB, MICHAEL. "'Yet Once More': The Formulaic Opening of *Lycidas*." *Milton Quarterly* 12 (1978):23-28.

The formulary "Yet once more," having analogues in Moschus, Theocritus, and Sannazaro, is part of the pastoral elegist's basic vocabulary. Through these three words, Milton invokes the entire tradition of the pastoral. He also recalls Hebrews 12:26-29, which in turn echoes Haggai 2:6-7, both passages being concerned with the passing of ephemera in the wake of what will endure. The New Testament author recasts and reinterprets Old Testament prophecy to accord with New Testament ideology. Milton associates "Yet once more" with Christ's redemptive mission, the Last Judgment, and the enjoyment of heavenly bliss by the saved. When Milton summons the elegiac, he shatters it; yet the monody's opening phrase implies its own consolation in "Weep no more," another formulary.

384 MacCAFFREY, ISABEL G. "*Lycidas*: The Poet in a Landscape." In *The Lyric and Dramatic Milton*. Edited by Joseph H. Summers. Selected Papers from the English Institute. New York and London: Columbia University Press, 1965, pp. 65-92. Reprinted in *Milton's "Lycidas": The Tradition and the Poem*, rev. ed., ed. C. A. Patrides (Columbia: University of Missouri Press, 1983), pp. 246-66.

Neither the argument nor the introductory section of *Lycidas* allows us a broad view of where the poem will end. Instead, the speaker, not initially identified as an uncouth swain, dramatically hastens into the midst of things and into a fictive pastoral geography. The poem's true landscape is the speaker's consciousness, for he records how a death led to his unwelcome movement from innocence to experience. To imitate this movement, the poem shifts tone, setting, and temporal planes. In the opening paragraphs, passages of reminiscence, focusing on a world before the appearance of death and change, exist only in memory. Pastoral perfection recedes into the past and is then contrasted with a harsh present; these two movements lead to a wiser innocence in the end.

385 MAYERSON, CAROLINE W. "The Orpheus Image in *Lycidas*." *PMLA* 64 (1949):189-207. Revised in *Milton's "Lycidas": The Tradition and the Poem*, rev. ed., ed. C. A. Patrides (Columbia: University of Missouri Press, 1983), pp. 116-28.

Renaissance mythographers and exegetes understand Orpheus to be a musician and teacher who exerts a civilizing force over society. Associated with Orpheus, Lycidas assumes these roles. But Orpheus's and Lycidas's deaths suggest that the civilizing force is vulnerable to attacks by man's own anarchic nature. Disturbed by these deaths, parts of an unintelligible universe, the poet searches for answers and stability. Although he initially finds no solution and instead indulges in escapism, the poet finally recognizes Christ's power to turn chaos into cosmos. The Orpheus myth reveals cycles of barbarism and civilization, of death and rebirth.

386 MULRYAN, JOHN. "Milton's *Lycidas* and the Italian Mythographers: Some Suggestive Parallels in Their Treatment of Mythological Subjects." *Milton Quarterly* 15 (1981):37-44.

Possibly providing the raw material for the imagery of Milton's monody, Conti's *Mythologiae* and Cartari's *Imagini* contain passages that parallel some of *Lycidas*'s images: the muses, Orpheus, the Fates, Arethusa and Alpheus, and the dolphin.

387 NELSON, LOWRY, Jr. "Milton's *Lycidas*." In *Baroque Lyric Poetry*. New Haven, Conn., and London: Yale University Press, 1961, pp. 64-76.

In *Lycidas*, the speaker establishes two time planes: his present and the remote past of a youth he shared with Lycidas. The time of Lycidas's drowning is placed on a separate plane, as is the procession of mourners. Moving from the remote past to the present, the poem

Lycidas

shows an increasing intensity of grief over Lycidas's death. Then the speaker finds a new present and a gesture toward the future, in which Lycidas is mounted high. But this baroque work ends in the past tense, emphasizing serenity and poem as performance or fiction.

388   NELSON, LOWRY, Jr. "Milton's *Lycidas* Again." In *Baroque Lyric Poetry*. New Haven, Conn., and London: Yale University Press, 1961, pp. 138-52.

   Lycidas's three-part rhetorical structure first establishes the speaker, reader, and audiences through which the speaker's grief evolves (lines 1-84). Then the procession of mourners signals that no one audience is defined, for the grief is public and formal (lines 85-164). In the third section (lines 165-85), the audience is composed of the mourners closest to Lycidas, the shepherds, who mark the climax of grief. The speaker becomes a comforter. He progresses from despair to a kind of pagan hope and finally to a Christian solution. In the final lines, his self-objectification is complete; he is a new person looking back at his old self. A baroque poem, *Lycidas* reconciles pagan and Christian traditions.

389   POGGIOLI, RENATO. "Milton's *Lycidas*." In *The Oaten Flute: Essays on Pastoral Poetry and the Pastoral Ideal*. Cambridge, Mass.: Harvard University Press, 1975, pp. 83-104.

   The opening vegetation imagery proclaims *Lycidas* to be both funeral elegy and pastoral of friendship. Just as his friend's death is premature, so Milton considers his poem immature but timely. The prelude reaches a climax with its emphasis on death, and a shift in tone brings an invocation to the muses and a sign of Milton's concern about his own death. In the lines about Amaryllis and Neaera, he rejects the pastoral of love from the genre of the funeral elegy. *Lycidas* adheres to and deviates from many of the traditional pastoral motifs. After Phoebus's speech transcends the pastoral's formal and thematic limits, the poet attempts to proceed in his humble style. But he does so only intermittently, because silence intrudes, and he listens to the voices of others. Breaking the pastoral and acting as a poem within a poem, the allegorical pastoral used to discuss the corrupted clergy is a literary error unique to *Lycidas*.

390 RANSOM, JOHN CROWE. "A Poem Nearly Anonymous." *American Review* 1 (1933):179-203, 444-67. Reprinted in *The World's Body* (New York: Charles Scribner's Sons, 1938), pp. 1-28; *Milton Criticism: Selections from Four Centuries*, ed. James Thorpe (New York: Rinehart & Co., 1950), pp. 225-38; *Milton's "Lycidas": The Tradition and the Poem*, ed. C. A. Patrides (New York: Holt, Rinehart and Winston, 1961), pp. 64-81; rev. ed. (Columbia: University of Missouri Press, 1983), pp. 68-85.

   Lycidas is originally printed with no title and only two initials to indicate its authorship; as a poet, Milton always seeks this anonymity. A literary exercise that flaunts its craftsmanship, Milton's monody shows little raw grief and much mourning with technical piety. The form of *Lycidas* is derived from the Italian canzone as modified by the irregular stanzas of Spenser's *Epithalamion*, to which Milton adds unrhymed lines as a gesture of rebellion against his art's formalism. Milton's work is highly eclectic, yet it surpasses its predecessors in the pastoral elegy genre. There is a breach in the logic of *Lycidas*'s composition: it begins as a monologue, but--in a calculated departure from convention--this is repeatedly broken by narrative. See entry 361.

391 SACKS, PETER M. "Milton's *Lycidas*." In *The English Elegy: Studies in the Genre from Spenser to Yeats*. Baltimore, Md., and London: Johns Hopkins University Press, 1985, pp. 90-117. Reprinted in *John Milton*, Modern Critical Views, ed. Harold Bloom (New York, New Haven, Conn., and Philadelphia, Pa.: Chelsea House Publishers, 1986), pp. 267-92.

   An extension of church tyranny provides the historical context for *Lycidas*, as the Stuarts and Laud increase the repression of Puritanism. In his elegy, Milton presents a displaced, verbal revenge for King's death, while creating a transcendent context to sanctify that revenge. If Milton believes that renunciation brings its own reward and self-sacrifice guards against mortality, he cannot continue to hold these views after King's death. Spiritualized sexual energy must triumph over the castrative moment of submission to death and the deflection of desire. The poem prepares us for loss and forces us to reexperience its reality, even as--by analogy--Milton offers self-critical rejections of the poem's indulged fictions. The inexplicable tragedy of King's death finds a place in the Christian scheme of sin, fall, and redemption.

Lycidas

392 SHUMAKER, WAYNE. "Flowerets and Sounding Seas: A Study in the Affective Structure of *Lycidas*." *PMLA* 66 (1951):485-94. Reprinted in *Milton: Modern Judgements*, ed. Alan Rudrum (London: Macmillan, 1968), pp. 94-103; *Milton's "Lycidas": The Tradition and the Poem*, ed. C. A. Patrides (New York: Holt, Rinehart and Winston, 1961), pp. 125-35; rev. ed. (Columbia: University of Missouri Press, 1983), pp. 129-39.

The images of vegetation suggest a frustration in nature, for the laurel's and myrtle's berries are "harsh" and "crude," a condition that balances the human frustrations at the center of *Lycidas*. The flower catalogue develops the theme of depression while subduing it to contrast with the ease the poet seeks. All the flowers wear "sad embroidery," but the early emphasis on brown changes to "a thousand hues." Lifted and brightened, grief is made tolerable; the reader now imagines nature in something other than a state of decay and death. The theme of water, prominent and often menacing in *Lycidas*, fixes the Irish Sea in the reader's mind. But the image of a tossed, ruined body leads to the image of a redeemed, joyous soul. Purified, the flower and water themes lead to an apotheosis that resolves the poem's tensions.

393 WALLERSTEIN, RUTH. "Iusta Edouardo King." In *Studies in Seventeenth-Century Poetic*. [Madison]: University of Wisconsin Press, 1950, pp. 96-114.

Lycidas brings to final realization both the Continental humanists' forms and attitudes, and the religious feeling of such minor elegists as Beaumont and Cleveland, whose work accompanies Milton's in the volume to Edward King. Milton defines poetry as simple (that is, *simplex*, a unified living essence that reflects nature), sensuous (implying the immanence of spiritual meaning, grasped first through the senses), and passionate (able to affect the rectified imagination and will). For Milton, the love of nature is an expression of a religious sentiment. *Lycidas* transforms an indefinable grief and the world of nature into transcendent consolation and the realm of grace.

394 WILLIAMSON, GEORGE. "The Obsequies for Edward King." In *Seventeenth Century Contexts*. London: Faber and Faber, 1960, pp. 132-47. Rev. ed. (Chicago, Ill.: University of Chicago Press, 1969); (London: Faber and Faber, 1969).

Lycidas

The English poems in *Justa Edovardo King*, including *Lycidas*, present water imagery, allusions prompted by King's drowning, and mythological and biblical allusions. While the other elegists use the drowning episode to praise King or to blame the sea, Milton uses it to strain the pastoral fiction until it breaks. Unlike the other contributors to the volume, Milton and Henry King (Edward's brother) stress not just the loss of a scholar but of a prospective priest. Of all King's poetic mourners, only Milton combines pagan and Christian myth in his consolation; only King's brother gives more emphasis to the personal relationship with the deceased.

395   WOODHOUSE, A. S. P. "Milton's Pastoral Monodies." In *Studies in Honour of Gilbert Norwood*. Edited by Mary E. White. *The Phoenix: Journal of the Classical Association of Canada*, Supplementary vol. 1. [Toronto]: University of Toronto Press, 1952, pp. 261-78. Reprinted in *The Heavenly Muse: A Preface to Milton*, ed. Hugh MacCallum, University of Toronto Department of English Studies and Texts, no. 21 (Toronto and Buffalo, N.Y.: University of Toronto Press, 1972), pp. 55-98.

Those poems by Milton that use extra-aesthetic experience as a starting point do so in one of two ways: when the poem deals with no problem or emotional tension, the aesthetic pattern is imposed on experience only to confirm Milton's feeling and thought; or the poem faces a problem and uses the aesthetic pattern to transform feeling and thought. *Lycidas* and *Epitaphium Damonis* belong to the latter group, and both use the traditional pattern of moving from pagan lament to Christian consolation.

For the variorum, see entry 35; for analogues, see entry 330. See also entries 30, 43-44, 46-47, 49, 55, 58-60, 63, 65, 68, 71-72, 87, 92-83, 103, 107-9, 123, 129-32, 135, 137-39, 142, 149-50, 154-55, 160, 163-64, 168-69, 171-72, 176, 179-90, 192, 193-94, 197-98, 200, 207-8, 211, 213-17, 219-20, 222, 227-30, 232-33, 236-38, 244, 247-48, 260, 270, 272, 274, 312, 432, 480, 560, 592, 599, 605, 614, 617, 636, 709, 723, 789, 899, 942, 1005, 1013.

Sonnets and "Canzone"

SONNETS AND "CANZONE":

EDITIONS

396 HONIGMANN, E. A. J., ed. *Milton's Sonnets*. London: Macmillan; New York: St. Martin's Press, 1966, 220 pp.

Honigmann discusses the battles of the Anglicans, Presbyterians, and Independents, which occur when Milton writes most of his sonnets. Elizabethan sonnets suffer from excessive mellifluousness, but Milton's classical restraint gives new life to an outmoded form. His greatest debt is to Della Casa's "magnificent" style, which uses enjambment to dissociate syntax and metrics. When Milton's subject requires gracefulness, he turns to a Petrarchan style. His sonnets include a wide range of topics, from lamentation to praise or execration. The four sonnets published in Milton's *Letters of State* (1694) contain variants from a manuscript that predates the Trinity manuscript. Organized not chronologically but by groups connected by threads, Milton's sonnets are arranged like Horace's *Odes* or Shakespeare's *Sonnets*: an idea or image in one is juxtaposed by ideas or images in the poems that precede and follow it. The Italian sonnets may date from 1638 rather than 1629.

397 SMART, JOHN S., ed. *The Sonnets of Milton*. Glasgow: Maclehose, Jackson & Co., 1921, 205 pp. Reprint. Oxford: Clarendon Press, 1966.

Deeply influenced by Italian literature, Milton returns to the abandoned literary fashion of writing sonnets while avoiding the familiar sentiments and conceits that accompany the form for centuries. His classical standards lead to precise diction and a lack of ornamentation, yet he uses the form and prosody of the Italian sonnet. In some of Milton's sonnets, the division into quatrains and tercets does not correspond to the thoughts expressed; he follows Della Casa in breaking with the Petrarchan tradition. The notion that the Italians define a principle for using the *volta* or turn as a break between octave and sestet is unfounded. Milton's Italian sonnets are an autobiographical record of his first love. When Milton publishes his sonnets, he keeps them in chronological order.

Sonnets and "Canzone"

CRITICISM

398   BOOTH, STEPHEN, and FLYER, JORDAN. "Milton's 'How Soon Hath Time': A Colossus in a Cherrystone." *ELH* 49 (1982):449-67.
Sonnet 7 is a great poem--both very good and big. Its final two lines move in two directions, as the "All is" assertion promises to simplify and be broad, while the parenthetical "if" clause points to a precision in the general claim it interrupts. As an act of faith, a reader believes these lines, though they do not reveal their truth; or a reader can accept a paraphrase of these lines--any paraphrase--because this sonnet demonstrates "that a whole range of sub-lunary distinctions of the sort by which we maintain and define sanity need not matter" (453). In a way, Sonnet 7 is a sustained exercise in imitating, illustrating, and justifying the parable of the vineyard, or its principle. Raising incidental distinctions (such as less or more, soon or late, fast or slow) only to neutralize them, this sonnet shows that such distinctions are insignificant.

399   CHENEY, PATRICK. "Alcestis and the 'Passion for Immortality': Milton's *Sonnet XXIII* and Plato's *Symposium*." *Milton Studies* 18 (1983):63-76.
Neoplatonic readings of Sonnet 23 point to the theme of how human mortality prevents man from uniting with the ideal. In Plato's *Symposium*, as scholars note, Phaedrus calls Alcestis a figure of self-sacrificial love and resurrection. But in the same dialogue Diotima refers to Alcestis as one who loves the eternal and, by connecting her with spiritual procreation, discusses how humans can become immortal in this life and ascend the Platonic ladder. These ideas inform each part of Sonnet 23's tripartite structure. In the final couplet, Milton exposes the truth about Platonic love: it does not make humans immortal, but instead leads them to see their mortality and separation from the ideal world. Participation in Platonic love requires disembodying the beloved. The persona's vision of the beloved, through an ascent of the Platonic ladder, leads to anguish produced by separation.

400   COLACCIO, JOHN J. "'A Death Like Sleep': The Christology of Milton's Twenty-Third Sonnet." *Milton Studies* 6 (1974):181-97.

Sonnets and "Canzone"

Sonnet 23 shows man's ascent to God through love of him (the vertical movement of a Christian Neoplatonic journey) and through life in history (the horizontal movement of Christian typology). As a brief drama about "the salvation continually offered to and lost by man" (183), Sonnet 23 uses the image of the late espoused saint to fulfill the sacrifice ethos, which is perfected by Christ's redemptive self-sacrifice. Suffering from mortal blindness, the poet does not recognize the revelation that the veiled saint offers, and he overvalues her as a reflection of virtue and beauty. Her love parallels Christ's love for man, so she descends the Neoplatonic ladder to elevate the poet. But she fails to purify her husband's faculties. His dream offers clarity, while his wakening offers spiritual confusion.

401 FINLEY, JOHN H., Jr. "Milton and Horace: A Study of Milton's Sonnets." *Harvard Studies in Classical Philology* 48 (1937):29-73.
    Horace influences the Petrarchan sonnets of Milton's youth and the Christian sonnets of his mature years. In his eight sonnets praising such people as Ley, Fairfax, and Skinner, Milton usually describes the person's parentage and achievements, writes in a simple style and structure, and presents a moral judgment. These sonnets show that he defines the poet's social function according to classical ideas. Milton makes the style, purpose, form, and subject matter of the sonnet approximate those of the Horatian ode.

402 HEINZELMAN, KURT. "'Cold Consolation': The Art of Milton's Last Sonnet." *Milton Studies* 10 (1977):111-25.
    We interpret Sonnet 23 while the poet interprets a vision of his saint as being like Alcestis and her story as being like Christian myth. The poet realizes not the saint's resurrected body but an image that resembles Alcestis and herself; though the poet wants to identify her as herself, he cannot because he does not know whether she is a saint in the likeness of his wife or his wife in the likeness of a soul in heaven. The poet must face the limitations of his desire, vision, and speech. By explaining what "Methought I saw," Sonnet 23 affirms the image-making powers of the poet's thought, which in the end is consumed by a far greater thought: the vision "proves itself true by being so much more vivid and distinct than what follows it" (123). In the Alcestis story is an analogue of Christian salvation.

Sonnets and "Canzone"

403   HUNTLEY, JOHN. "Milton's 23rd Sonnet." *ELH* 34 (1967):468-81.
      Sonnet 23 uses the "late espoused Saint" not as a subject but as
an occasion that provokes the narrator "to conceive and feel
metaphysical relationships and spiritual possibilities with unusual
vividness" (470). Unlike Admetus, he is particularly alert to the
relationship between nature and grace. In the middle of the poem, the
woman who is saved from "spot of child-bed taint" cannot be identified
with a historical wife of Milton or a traditional literary symbol. Sonnet
23 expresses but does not successfully communicate a very private
experience. Milton succeeds in communicating a tone of conditionality
and in imitating a mind as it tries to regain a vision of uncertain feature.

404   LAWRY, J. S. "Milton's Sonnet 18: 'A Holocaust.'" *Milton Quarterly*
      17 (1983):11-14.
      Sonnet 18's protests against the massacre are linked to and
opposed by objective reflections on that event. The octave addresses
the atrocity, while the sestet elevates the martyrs' moans to heaven.
After the passion of the first part comes something approaching
resurrection in the second. As the poem moves through patterns of
speech acts and witnessings, curse turns to prayer, which turns to
prophecy. The evangelistic example of the Waldensians alters history
instead of transcending it. Sonnet 18 justifies God to men.

405   McCARTHY, WILLIAM. "The Continuity of Milton's Sonnets."
      PMLA 92 (1977):96-109.
      Milton's sonnets fall into a pattern describing the three phases
of a paradigmatic career: youth (the love sonnets, 2-6, and "Canzone"),
maturity (Sonnets 8-18), and old age (Sonnets 20-23). The implied
author, who is both like and unlike Milton, develops as a poet should,
awakening and serving love in the first six poems, serving a great
taskmaster in Sonnet 7, and--in Sonnets 8-18--giving a sense of the
various ways in which a Renaissance poet serves God. He retires in the
next group, learns to be content, and reviews his life. From another
perspective, his life is a microcosm of the Christian pattern of history,
moving from a fall to bondage and then to a struggle and hope for
redemption.

Poetry

Sonnets and "Canzone"

406 MENGERT, JAMES G. "The Resistance of Milton's Sonnets."
English Literary Renaissance 11 (1981):81-95.
   If the conclusion of a typical sonnet by Milton recalls the opening and thus leads to a sense of unity, this movement is countered by the particular negative or resistant conclusion, especially the final word or words. The sense of unity lets us recognize how Milton uses the sonnet to organize experience; the resistant conclusion acknowledges that the experience is intransigent. Milton's sonnets resist resolution, forcing the will to affirm order while disallowing the permanence or completeness of that affirmation.

407 MUELLER, JANEL M. "On Genesis in Genre: Milton's Politicizing of the Sonnet in 'Captain or Colonel.'" In *Renaissance Genres: Essays on Theory, History, and Interpretation.* Edited by Barbara Kiefer Lewalski. Harvard English Studies, vol. 14. Cambridge, Mass., and London: Harvard University Press, 1986, pp. 213-40.
   Genre studies of Milton's sonnets fail to illuminate genesis in genre--that is, why a poet chooses a particular genre at a particular time and what transformations the genre undergoes. Milton's Sonnet 8 inaugurates the political sonnet in English, and from 1642 to 1655 this kind of sonnet dominates his writing in the form. During this period, Milton's sonnets and prose form a complementary relationship. Unlike the diffuse phrasing of the prose, the style of these sonnets is based on brevity. The political sonnets consider the role of human agency in public affairs, but the postpolitical sonnets (18, 22, and 23) reassign the agency from the political to the theological sphere. With Sonnet 8, Milton's poetry becomes a form of public, political action. When his political activity stops, so does his writing of political sonnets.

408 MUELLER, MARTIN. "The Theme and Imagery of Milton's Last Sonnet." *Archiv für das Studium der Neueren Sprachen und Literaturen* 201 (1964):267-71.
   In Sonnet 23, the images of Alcestis, the purified woman, and the saint (veiled and unveiled) appear in ascending order with the contrasts growing greater as the poem progresses. Analogous to the progression of images of women is the progression from Greece to Judaism to Christianity. The rhymes lead us to expect a movement toward "light," but this is checked by the concluding word "night." Structurally, Sonnet 23 is both Petrarchan because of its rhyme scheme

176

Sonnets and "Canzone"

(the octave has "a" rhymes, the sestet "i" rhymes) and Elizabethan because Milton provides a syntactic stop between lines twelve and thirteen. The sonnet expresses hope and despair, as suggested by the veil image.

409   NARDO, ANNA K. *Milton's Sonnets and the Ideal Community.* Lincoln and London: University of Nebraska Press, 1979, 225 pp.
    Milton's sonnets are unified not by the traditional idea of the *donna angelicata* but by "the ideal of a godly community" (4). The sonnets portray an ideal community with a free and virtuous individual at the center, surrounded by a society that extends from a beloved woman to a Protestant Europe: like the rest of Milton's canon, these poems show the engagement of self with an "other," along with the historical or transcendent perspective on that engagement. "As a whole, Milton's sonnet sequence suggests an ideal progress of man in a community from perfection of the individual, to earthly love and service, to attainment of the Kingdom of God" (137). Such Italian poets as Bembo, Della Casa, and Tasso are Milton's primary models when he writes sonnets, though the form of his later ones reveals an Elizabethan influence. *Paradise Lost*'s submerged sonnets show Milton's exploration of the lyric's potential within epic form. Satan's fourteen-line speeches are parodies of the sonnet.

410   PEQUIGNEY, JOSEPH. "Milton's Sonnet XIX Reconsidered." *Texas Studies in Literature and Language* 8 (1967):485-98.
    If we begin by regarding Sonnet 19's protagonist as fictional, we see him defined by condition (the blind servant), character (a good man), and crisis (a disabling affliction has frustrated his religious duty). He now experiences a greater desire to serve God, as the octave shows, but also despondency and a fear of personal waste. That the bartering imagery is omitted from the sestet shows both that the speaker is mistaken to use it in the octave and that he is willing to criticize the parable of the talents. The sestet introduces patience, and the theology of patience emphasizes kingliness and patience. In the final line, "wait" carries two meanings and produces two interpretations: "attend" (readiness is all) and stay expectant (resignation to inactivity constitutes appropriate service to God). We see the seeds of renewal in the speaker, along with the direction of his spiritual growth. His suffering leads to consolation and restoration.

Sonnets and "Canzone"

411 SLOANE, THOMAS O. "Reading Milton Rhetorically." In *Renaissance Eloquence: Studies in the Theory and Practice of Renaissance Rhetoric*. Edited by James J. Murphy. Berkeley, Los Angeles, and London: University of California Press, 1983, pp. 394-410.

    Inventio, choosing the appropriate ideas, is a key part of rhetoric because it systematizes part of the writer's creative process and assists the reader's interpretive process. Author-based stylistic analysis and reader-based affective stylistics are shortsighted insofar as they ignore the function of *inventio* and its connection to *elocutio*. In "On Time" and Sonnet 18, Milton creates certain expectations to which the reader will respond as the poet fulfills or thwarts them.

412 SPITZER, LEO. "Understanding Milton." *Hopkins Review* 4 (1951):16-27. Reprinted in *Essays on English and American Literature*, ed. Anna Hatcher (Princeton, N.J.: Princeton University Press, 1962), pp. 116-31.

    One can understand Sonnet 23 without any knowledge of Milton's biography because its key poetic patterns--including the poet who lives in darkness without his beloved--are used by other Renaissance poets and the tradition of the *dolce stil nuovo*. In this Platonic poem, Milton describes the barriers between the living and the dead, between the fallen world and the ideal. Other poems by Milton, rather than his biography, tell us about his blindness, a significant piece of information that he wants us to learn about from his verse. According to this perspective, his inner eyes cannot fully perceive his saint, but in heaven he will have full sight of her. Sonnet 23 has a tripartite structure as the ancient pagan tradition leads to the ancient Jewish tradition, and from thence to the Christian tradition.

413 STROUP, THOMAS B. "'When I Consider': Milton's Sonnet XIX." *Studies in Philology* 69 (1972):242-58.

    Sonnet 19 deals with such matters as temptation, pride, good works, faith, acceptance, consolation, and grace, which Milton develops in detail in later works. Structured like a syllogism, the poem is also a meditation or interior drama in which doubt and despair lead to strength. The parable in Matthew 25:24-30, on which the sonnet is based, is concerned with distrust and the use of faith to produce good works. As in Milton's later works, Sonnet 19 shows the greater heroism

Sonnets and "Canzone"

of patience, which in the sonnet is a manifestation of prevenient grace descending. Written in about late 1651, the sonnet presents a miniature of the problem of the testing of a hero such as Job or Christ, with trial and passion leading to despair, suffering, and triumph. Milton's one talent is his civil and political ability.

414 STULL, WILLIAM L. "Sacred Sonnets in Three Styles." *Studies in Philology* 79 (1982):78-99.
Cicero argues that a plain style is best for teaching, a middle style for delighting, and a high style for moving people to action. Petrarchan sonneteers use the middle style to please a courtly mistress, while such religious sonneteers as Donne, Greville, and Milton use a full rhetoric of all three styles and goals. Written in a grand style, Milton's sonnets are influenced by the Italian heroic sonneteers, including Bembo and Della Casa.

415 ULREICH, JOHN C. "Typological Symbolism in Milton's Sonnet XXIII." *Milton Quarterly* 8 (1974):7-10.
Because "old Law" alludes to Luke and Leviticus, "Purification" in Sonnet 23 is spiritual rather than merely ritualistic. The poem moves in lines 5-6 from the letter or law to the spirit or covenant of faith, just as the imagery develops on a larger scale from classical through Hebraic, and then to Christian. Because Milton's experience in the sonnet is mythic, he identifies himself with Orpheus.

416 WENTERSDORF, KARL P. "Images of 'Licence' in Milton's Sonnet XII." *Milton Quarterly* 13 (1979):36-42.
Accused of advocating licentiousness in his divorce tracts, Milton uses classical allusions and animal imagery in Sonnet 12 to turn the charge back on his detractors. The creatures of line 4, for example, can all symbolize lechery. His opponents' "barbarous noise" resembles both the dissonance of Comus's monsters and the noise of Bacchus and his revelers in *Paradise Lost*.

417 WILLIAMSON, MARILYN L. "A Reading of Milton's Twenty-Third Sonnet." *Milton Studies* 4 (1972):141-49.

Sonnets and "Canzone"

Throughout Sonnet 23, Milton insists on the fragile, dream quality of the experience he conveys. The rites of purification after childbirth, interpreted typologically, prefigure Christian salvation. The idea that day brings night to the poet need not imply blindness; it alludes to his separation from his saint. Sonnet 23's structure is based on "a progressive definition of salvation from death and of the human condition in this world" (147), moving from pagan legend to ritual salvation under the Law, and finally to true Christian salvation.

For the variorum, see entry 35; for a concordance to the Italian poems, see entry 79. See also entries 30, 43-47, 49, 53, 58-60, 65, 67, 79, 87, 93, 95, 132, 167, 169, 175, 180, 183, 194, 205, 215-16, 221, 234, 236, 247, 251, 449, 723, 899, 1005.

OTHER INDIVIDUAL SHORT ENGLISH POEMS:

CRITICISM

418   BALDWIN, EDWARD CHAUNCEY. "Milton and the Psalms." *Modern Philology* 17 (1919):457-63.
Milton's translation of Psalms 80-88 is an experiment in accurate translation directly from the Hebrew (though influenced by the Vulgate), while his translation of Psalms 1-8 is an experiment in versification. The translation of Psalms 80-88 shows his urge to expand upon the original and the flaw of choosing less concrete diction. His knowledge of Hebrew is not unusual in an age when it is considered a learned language. See entry 431.

419   BODDY, MARGARET. "Milton's Translation of Psalms 80-88." *Modern Philology* 64 (1966):1-9.
Milton may have planned his translation of Psalms 80-88 to be a response to Henry Lawes's royalist work, *Choice Psalms*, and then realized it could be used at the army's 1648 prayer meeting at Windsor. His metrical Psalms do not attack King Charles, but Milton rejects the reading of the Psalms as a defense of the King against all attacks. This work may have reached Henry King, Bishop of Chichester, whose translation includes lines, phrases, and rhymes that duplicate Milton's.

Other Individual Short English Poems

420 CHAMBERS, A. B. "Milton's 'Upon the Circumcision': Backgrounds and Meanings." *Texas Studies in Literature and Language* 17 (1975):687-97.

Biblical lessons from the Book of Common Prayer assigned for reading on 1 January, Circumcision Day, link the naming of Jesus with the first shedding of his blood; recall God's imposition of circumcision when he makes a covenant with Abraham in Genesis 17; and show that circumcision is a metaphor for obedience to God. Contemporary poems about the circumcision by such authors as Herrick, Wither, and Quarles consider it an act of sacrifice and of the Son's definition of his dual nature. Milton's poem is consistent with the liturgical themes of heroism (which he emphasizes), pathos, and identity.

421 COLLETTE, CAROLYN P. "Milton's Psalm Translations: Petition and Praise." *English Literary Renaissance* 2 (1972):243-59.

The Psalms that Milton translates between 1648 and 1653 have thematic connections with his prose and the Civil Wars. The reformers emphasize the Psalms because of their importance for the earliest Christians and, as the Westminster Assembly believes, because they establish a model for prayer. Rejecting formal prayer, Puritans use the Psalms as a prayer book to provide comfort during strife. In 1648, the radical army and Independents face trouble from the Scots, who are poised to invade England, where the Presbyterians unite with the royalists, on King Charles's behalf. The Presbyterians try to pass a bill involving forced conformity. So Milton deals with the bond between church and state by connecting Israel and England in his Psalm translations of 1648. His Psalm translations of 1653 bring to the foreground the theme of the lamentation of a man wronged by his enemies and uncertain of his relationship with God.

422 COPE, JACKSON I. "Fortunate Falls as Form in Milton's 'Fair Infant.'" *JEGP: Journal of English and Germanic Philology* 63 (1964):660-74.

"Fair Infant" uses movement as a symbolic vehicle for the idea of the fortunate fall, because its action is embedded in allusions to a syncretic mythology. Using the allusions to recall narratives that contain similar promises, Milton presents an Ovidian rape when winter descends to take the victim's soul through the motive of pride, an action that parallels Satan's fall and temptation of man. Though it involves

Other Individual Short English Poems

seasonal repetition rather than permanence, the Hyacinthus myth suggests resurrection for the child. The reader, unlike the persona, sees that the infant's fate recapitulates mankind's infancy, including the fortunate fall and its pattern of descent and ascent, which lead us toward Astraea. Rape turns to rapture, with the promise of a new spring in Christ.

423 DEMARAY, JOHN G. "*Arcades* as a Literary Entertainment." *Papers on Language and Literature* 8 (1972):15-26.

Arcades presents a tension between the fatalistic pagan world of the disguising and the redeemed Christian world in which the participants live. Arcady, the rural queen's realm, is threatened by the evils of fate and death, which pagan figures attempt to overcome. Though they remain trapped on the fictive level, the entertainment genre works also with another level, that of real life, where individuals have social and symbolic identities. The performers unmask just enough to reveal a glance at a Christian social reality behind the pagan artifice. In this Christian realm, the performers are released from the domination of fate and death.

424 GALLAGHER, PHILIP J. "Milton's 'The Passion': Inspired Mediocrity." *Milton Quarterly* 11 (1977):44-50.

The eight stanzas of "Passion" amount to a prologue or invocation to a poem about the Passion, not that poem itself. As a poem about poetry, a prologue such as this has one purpose: "to show the futility of attempting to write a divine poem in the absence of divine inspiration" (44). That failure is the occasion for a successful poem about such failures. Regularly committing the pathetic fallacy, the egocentric persona creates outrageous metaphysical conceits that serve no purpose. The poem's deliberate failure is a mark of its aesthetic success.

425 HESTER, M. THOMAS. "Typology and Parody in 'Upon the Circumcision.'" *Renaissance Papers* (1985):61-71.

Although "Upon the Circumcision" is modeled in some ways (such as stanzaic form) on Petrarch's poem to the Virgin (*Canzoniere* 366), Milton uses music imagery and metaphysical paradoxes. Petrarch's poem offers a literary type for Milton's; both poets present sacred parodies of their earlier amatory language, attitudes, and poetic self-fashionings. Milton's poem elaborates on the Book of Common Prayer's readings for the Feast of the Circumcision. Celebrating divine typology, Milton's poem glances backward at the Nativity and forward at the Crucifixion. It is a prayer for and meditative enactment of the circumcision of the spirit that the Feast celebrates. Christ's disfigurements are transfigured as embodiments of the transcendent and historical texts of God's Word. Petrarch's final canzone and Milton's "Upon the Circumcision" extend and recreate the search for and response to the divine type presented in the authors' earlier sonnets. Milton's poem is about typological transformations.

426 HUNTER, WILLIAM B., Jr. "Milton Translates the Psalms." *Philological Quarterly* 40 (1961):485-94.

Because metrical translations of the Psalms frequently borrow from their predecessors, the authors produce an almost communal poetry. Participating in this tradition when he translates Psalms 80-88, Milton consults many earlier metrical versions. He begins his translations just when authorities are making decisions about adopting a new psalter. One might conjecture that he is working indirectly for the Church of Scotland.

427 JACOBUS, LEE A. "Milton Metaphrast: Logic and Rhetoric in Psalm I." *Milton Studies* 23 (1987):119-32.

After attempting in 1648 to produce an accurate, public translation of certain Psalms to be sung and to be in accord with the 1644 Ordinance about using the Psalms as a cornerstone of worship, Milton in 1653 has a private motive for translating Psalms in an idiosyncratic meter. In the latter group, Milton seeks to begin with the original language and write the finest poetry possible. Psalm 1 attracts Ramists because its imagery can convince in an argument. More concrete than other translations and featuring a greater emphasis on imagery, Milton's version of Psalm 1 clarifies the structure or logical implications uncovered by the Ramists Richard Bernard and William Temple.

428 McGUIRE, MARY ANN. "Milton's *Arcades* and the Entertainment Tradition." *Studies in Philology* 74 (1978):451-71.

Other Individual Short English Poems

Arcades is Milton's version of "the entry episode of an estate entertainment" (452), the tradition that it draws on. While retaining the form's images and structural patterns, Milton replaces the conventional mythology with a theological framework. Conventional motifs in the estate entertainment include dealing with the royal progress as a fictional journey, using the country house as a literal and mythic focal point as well as a *locus amoenus*, offering compliments, and presenting the theme of order as a reflection of the estate's owners. In *Arcades*, Milton changes the journey to a spiritual quest, focuses on the estate's spiritual values, and does not give humans the divine power to transform an estate into a paradise. The Countess Dowager and her estate thus reveal a level of excellence that we can attain in a fallen world.

429   MACLEAN, HUGH N. "Milton's 'Fair Infant.'" *ELH* 24 (1957):296-305. Reprinted in *Milton: Modern Essays in Criticism*, ed. Arthur E. Barker (London, Oxford, and New York: Oxford University Press, 1965), pp. 21-30.
      In terms of relating classical ideas and images to Christian ones, "Fair Infant" represents an intermediate stage between two elegies--*Elegy 3* and "In Obitum Praesulis Eliensis"--and *Nativity Ode*. The earlier, Latin elegies allow Christian joy to supersede but not banish the classical imagery. "Fair Infant" attempts to show classical and Christian elements in harmony, even if the Christian must dominate. While the bishops in the elegies are passive and do not act on behalf of humanity, the infant intercedes for people on earth; Christ in *Nativity Ode* is the ultimate mediator. "Fair Infant" is divided into stanzaic groups of three (emphasizing incompleteness and mistake), three (on transformation and creation), four (with a descent and, eventually, color), and one (which corrects the impression of stanza 1).

430   PECHEUX, MOTHER M. CHRISTOPHER. "'At a Solemn Musick': Structure and Meaning." *Studies in Philology* 75 (1978):331-46.
      The structural divisions in "At a Solemn Music" occur at lines 8, 16, and 24, numbers that suggest the musical octave, which symbolizes the human and divine harmony that is the poem's theme. Matching verbal and musical phrases is common in Milton's age, and he may also attempt it in "On Time." Specialized musical terminology

appears throughout "At a Solemn Music." In the first octave, the pure music of the spheres (the archetype of music) is balanced by the heavenly hymns and songs of the second octave, with man's prelapsarian answer completing the chord in the third octave. The poem concludes with a four-line prayer that recapitulates the poem's divisions in reverse sequence and uses light imagery to capture the harmony of man's return to the source of being. See entries 15, 22, 142, 290, 321, 337, 370, 861.

431   STUDLEY, MARIAN H. "Milton and His Paraphrases of the Psalms." *Philological Quarterly* 4 (1925):364-72.

Between 1600 and 1653, 206 metrical versions of the complete psalter and twenty-seven metrical versions of excerpts are published. It is a popular kind of writing, so one should expect Milton to attempt it. His 1648 group of Psalms 80-88 may constitute a sample of what he might write to supersede other psalters in public worship. Milton's 1648 and 1653 translations resemble contemporary psalmody in diction, theological interpretation, and relation to contemporary versions of the Bible. Rather than depending too heavily on the Vulgate, as Baldwin argues (see entry 418), Milton relies on the style of contemporary psalmody as he leans on all available texts.

432   TROMLY, FREDERIC B. "Milton's 'Preposterous Exaction': The Significance of 'The Passion.'" *ELH* 47 (1980):276-86.

In "Passion," Milton finds value in the dynamics of failure based on the conflict between his desire to write and his emotional or spiritual unreadiness. Trying to force the poem's direction and predestine its end, he anxiously wrestles with matters of decorum and the proper instruments in an attempt to compensate for the imaginative argument that he lacks. His writing becomes fanciful and hyperbolical, and disengaged and ironic in the end. Milton fails in his attempt to will a poem, to work with a kind of automatic writing. If we see the connection between "Passion" and *Lycidas* in the 1645 *Poems*, the monody begins at the point of failure where "Passion" breaks off; both poems fall into fragments, for in *Lycidas* the speaker experiences a number of failures as he tries to find a poetic response to death. The use of a persona in *Lycidas* allows Milton to objectify and explore imaginative inadequacy.

Other Individual Short English Poems

433   VIA, JOHN A. "Milton's 'The Passion': A Successful Failure."
Milton Quarterly 5 (1971):35-38.
Though Milton knows that "Passion" is a failure, he publishes it
in 1645 and 1673 because it represents a normal reduction in the
intensity of an individual's religious involvement. The regenerate
person must anticipate such fluctuations.

434   WALLACE, JOHN MALCOLM. "Milton's *Arcades.*" *JEGP: Journal
of English and Germanic Philology* 58 (1959):627-36. Reprinted in
Milton: Modern Essays in Criticism, ed. Arthur E. Barker (London,
Oxford, and New York: Oxford University Press, 1965), pp. 77-87.
The key to understanding a masque is the symbolism applied
to the person or persons whom the work is written to honor. Married to
patrons of literature and being one herself, Lady Alice Egerton,
Countess Dowager of Derby, is an aged gentlewoman whom Milton can
praise for her wit. When the shepherds approach her at the beginning
of *Arcades* to praise and envy her fame, Milton alludes to the Queen of
Sheba's amazement at Solomon's wisdom (1 Kings 10:6-7), an episode
often interpreted as the soul's journey to divine revelation. Milton
transforms the Countess into Solomon or Sapience. As Latona, she is
that isolated goodness in a world of peril that hopes to reach the
celestial beauty; as Cybele, she is linked to intelligence and protective
powers. Milton moves Arcadian myth into a Christian landscape and
converts the pagan world. *Arcades* shows a pilgrimage from the pagan
to the Christian.

For the variorum, see entry 35. See also entries 30, 43, 46, 49, 53, 65, 67, 71-
72, 91, 96, 103, 107-8, 115, 129, 132, 135-37, 139, 157, 161, 163, 168, 172, 178-
80, 182-83, 185-86, 188-89, 192, 194, 196, 199-200, 205, 208, 211, 213, 216, 219,
223, 227, 229, 232, 234, 236-37, 244, 247-48, 251-52, 266, 308, 312, 318-19, 327,
333, 339, 351, 411, 462, 592, 789, 819, 899, 918, 942, 1005.

PARADISE LOST:

TEXTUAL STUDIES

435   DARBISHIRE, HELEN, ed. *The Manuscript of Milton's "Paradise Lost," Book I.* Oxford: Clarendon Press, 1931, 121 pp.

The first edition of *Paradise Lost* (1667) is set from this manuscript, which an amanuensis writes and several people correct. Most of the changes in the manuscript are made according to Milton's instructions, and the printer follows it closely. The corrections are generally concerned with spelling and punctuation, for Milton has his own orthography based on sound, meter, and a love of Italian spellings; he is equally meticulous about punctuation. The manuscript does not resolve the issue of whether editors should prefer the first or second edition.

Appendix: "Milton's Spelling of the Word *Their*."

436   ELLEDGE, SCOTT, ed. *Paradise Lost.* A Norton Critical Edition. New York: W. W. Norton & Co., 1975, 575 pp.

Following a substantial introduction, the text of *Paradise Lost* is accompanied by brief but thorough annotations. A section on Backgrounds and Sources includes Milton's autobiographical passages about his literary program, selections from the Bible, and notes on such key concepts in *Paradise Lost* as the universe, the scale of nature, and the fortunate fall. The volume concludes with selections from nine modern critics, excerpts from such early critics as Voltaire, Johnson, and Coleridge, and a selected bibliography.

437   MOYLES, R[OBERT] G[ORDON]. *The Text of "Paradise Lost": A Study in Editorial Procedure.* Toronto, Buffalo, N.Y., and London: University of Toronto Press, 1985, 198 pp.

Although *Paradise Lost* appears with title-pages dated 1667, 1668, and 1669, the poem's text in all three instances is printed as one edition--with about one-hundred minor and four major variants--in 1667 (except for two sheets that contain as many variants as the rest of the text and that are reprinted for one of the 1669 title-pages). Some of

Paradise Lost

the alterations are improvements, some are in error, and the majority are open to debate. All of the changes are within the capacity of a proof corrector or printing-house master. Milton is not concerned with the minutiae of *Paradise Lost*'s printing. Since the Columbia edition of 1931-38 (see entry 39), editors have practiced "reasoned eclecticism" (77). Milton uses conventional spelling rather than phonetic principles. Because a printer usually establishes his own practices about punctuation, it is as difficult to restore Milton's punctuation as it is to restore his spelling. "An uncompromising reliance on the universal authority of either the 1667 or 1674 edition of *Paradise Lost* is totally unacceptable and unwarranted" (138). Editorial eclecticism should govern substantives; within reason, copy-text determines accidentals.

438   SHAWCROSS, JOHN T. "Orthography and the Text of *Paradise Lost*." In *Language and Style in Milton: A Symposium in Honor of the Tercentenary of "Paradise Lost*." Edited by Ronald David Emma and John T. Shawcross. New York: Frederick Ungar Publishing Co., 1967, pp. 120-53.
      Edward Phillips is not a careful corrector of *Paradise Lost*'s manuscript, from which the first edition (1667) is printed with a few changes. The second edition (1674) is set from the first, with unreliable corrections. Because scribes, correctors, and compositors alter the orthography of *Paradise Lost*--sometimes in accordance with Milton's practices, sometimes not--the manuscript and printed text do not reproduce his spelling at all points. Milton does not care about spelling as much as critics often assume.

See also entries 33, 115, 460, 477.

GENERAL CRITICISM

439   BAKER, C. H. COLLINS. "Some Illustrators of Milton's *Paradise Lost* (1688-1850)." *Library* 5th ser., 3 (1948):1-21, 101-19.
      The illustrations to *Paradise Lost* can be divided into five groups: J. B. de Medina's work (1688); Thornhill and Cheron's work (1720); Francis Hayman's illustrations (1749); the academicians' work (1794-1802); and the works of Blake and Martin (1806-50). The first illustrations are on the fringes of gothic-baroque art; by 1850, the

resources of mezzotint reveal Milton's world as no other engraving process could.

Baker lists the main illustrators from 1688 to 1850 and provides brief descriptions of their illustrations.

440 BARKER, ARTHUR. "Structural Pattern in *Paradise Lost*." *Philological Quarterly* 28 (1949):17-30. Reprinted in *Milton: Modern Essays in Criticism*, ed. Arthur E. Barker (London, Oxford, and New York: Oxford University Press, 1965), pp. 142-55.

In *Paradise Lost*, Milton modifies the structural pattern of the *Aeneid*. But *Paradise Lost*'s original ten-book form suggests a comparison with the drama; in its 1667 form, *Paradise Lost* is a five-act epic whose focus is on the fourth act, in which Satan turns God's design and causes the fall. The 1674 division into twelve books does not change the structure, but it offsets the tragic implications of Satan's deeds by emphasizing man's restoration and the events following Satan's defeat in heaven. The 1667 edition presents five groups of two books each and two groups of five books; in 1674, the divisions are into six groups of two books each, three groups of four, and two groups of six. Like the *Aeneid*, *Paradise Lost* in 1674 stresses foreshadowings of triumph.

441 BENNETT, JOAN S. "God, Satan, and King Charles: Milton's Royal Portraits." *PMLA* 92 (1977):441-57.

Milton's portrayal of Satan's tyranny in *Paradise Lost* is consistent with his interpretation of the monarchy of King Charles, himself Milton's literary creation in *Eikonoklastes*. Examples of false heroism, Satan and Charles are usurpers of divine power, as the politically charged sun image indicates in both *Paradise Lost* and *Eikonoklastes*. Milton's God, unlike Satan and Charles, rules primarily through the attribute of goodness, not omnipotence. Charles and Satan are tyrants, not defenders of liberty.

442 BERCOVITCH, SACVAN. "Three Perspectives on Reality in *Paradise Lost*." *University of Windsor Review* 1 (1965):239-56.

Paradise Lost presents three perspectives in its three main settings. Truth emerges in heaven through a dialectic of love and justice, while self-deceit that oscillates between pride and despair is the outlook in hell. Shifting between obedience and temptation, the human

Paradise Lost

perspective finally reaches a "unique postlapsarian synthesis" (239). God occupies *Paradise Lost*'s stable center, a point he outlines in his speech about sufficiency and free will. But because the Father speaks from the limited viewpoint of justice, we must combine his perspective with the Son's viewpoint of mercy in order to see reality in its fullest meaning. In their prelapsarian state, Adam and Eve have a limited but right point of view that needs to be demonstrated through free choice. They assume a Satanic perspective based on pride and illusion after the fall.

443   BERGER, HARRY, Jr. "Archaism, Vision, and Revision: Studies in Virgil, Plato, and Milton." *Centennial Review* 11 (1967):24-52.
      Seeing a regressive or archaic quality in the search for recurrent, universal archetypes, Virgil, Plato, and Milton prefer the act of revision, which denies the finality of a total vision and remains open to the future. *Paradise Lost* recapitulates cultural history in its development as an individual work. As it moves from a spatial and atemporal pattern in the first half to a temporal pattern in the second half, Milton's epic reproduces the movement from old to new law, from the extensive, external stresses to the intensive, internal stress of historical experience. In Book 3, God, unlike the narrator in Books 11 and 12, sees history as a series of archaically determined repetitions of the original sin. The Incarnation changes the relationship between God and man, for man takes on the burden of ruling himself from within. The entire poem and events within it (creation, fall, and history) imitate the pattern of moving from the childlike to the mature image of relationship.

444   BLESSINGTON, FRANCIS C. "'That Undisturbed Song of Pure Concent': *Paradise Lost* and the Epic-Hymn." In *Renaissance Genres: Essays on Theory, History, and Interpretation.* Edited by Barbara Kiefer Lewalski. Harvard English Studies, vol. 14. Cambridge, Mass., and London: Harvard University Press, 1986, pp. 468-95.
      The ideal genre in *Paradise Lost* is the hymn, which comes in opposition to the epic genre, for the epic is narrative and thus oriented toward action while the hymn pauses "to acknowledge the ideal toward which the epic struggles" (472). Satan and the rebel angels use mockery and antihymns to express contempt for the hymn. In his invocations, the

narrator uses both hymn and prayer, the request within a hymn. The pure hymn exists in heaven and, to a lesser extent, in prelapsarian Eden. After the fall, Adam and Eve lapse into antihymns and prayers of request. Although the inset hymn is a feature of Roman epic, it retains its independence; in *Paradise Lost*, Milton uses the hymn to challenge the epic's claim to be the highest genre.

445 BODKIN, MAUD. *Archetypal Patterns in Poetry: Psychological Studies of Imagination*. London: Oxford University Press, 1934, pp. 91-92, 96-100, 108-9, 150, 153-58, 165-70, 230-52, 261-63, 298. Reprint. 1963.

In the invocation to Book 7, Milton's inspiration comes from a muse-mother figure who must work with the poet's infantile fear and dependence. The situation is different in Book 1's invocation, where the muse's poetic power is masculine and the poet is the receptive female. Eve receives inconsistent treatment in *Paradise Lost*: at times, she is responsible for actions; at other times, when she is associated with Proserpine, she is a helpless, innocent victim. As an example of the devil archetype, Satan moves us by displaying those forces, internal and external, that threaten our supreme values. When we see the Promethean Satan of the early books, we join his party; later, after we witness human innocence and see it shattered, we abhor Satan as God's enemy and ours. Self-assertion and abasement, two forces in Milton's mind, appear respectively in Satan's imaginative aspiration and defeat.

446 BOWRA, C. M. "Milton and the Destiny of Man." In *From Virgil to Milton*. London: Macmillan, 1945, pp. 194-247.

Milton transforms epic conventions by using them with a subject outside of the main epic tradition. Where Virgil's epic is secular, Milton's subject is theological, true, and more heroic because it is concerned with the relationship between man and God, not power. Heroism is goodness. In *Paradise Lost*, Milton's grand style is the grandest of all styles, consistently sublime and apparently cold. His God stands for order, law, and justice, concepts that carry the author's intellectual conviction, if not his emotional and imaginative powers. Satan stands for disorder, hatred, and passion, and his heroic spirit seems to contradict his corrupt motives. He exemplifies the old heroism, which is based on pride. Milton substitutes a new heroism in

Paradise Lost

the character of Abdiel, the defender of truth. Within him is a conflict between Puritan and humanist values.

447 BOYETTE, PURVIS E. "Milton and the Sacred Fire: Sex Symbolism in *Paradise Lost*." *Literary Monographs* 5 (1973):63-138.

In his epic of married love, Milton celebrates eros, for romantic love can transform flesh to spirit. The epistemology of the male-female principle, on which Milton bases *Paradise Lost*'s poetic, is part of his larger attempt to deal with apparent differences, without eliminating them, by forming a unity out of opposites. Human sexuality corresponds to divine and cosmic fertility in *Paradise Lost*. Just as language allows us to move between the phenomenal and nonphenomenal worlds, sexual imagery--a metaphoric action--links biology and metaphysics. The male and female principles in *Paradise Lost* are associated with specific images, such as Adam with the sun and Eve with the moon. Passion in Milton's epic is lust, not eros, which leads to God. Eve is the vehicle that leads to revelation, and in Book 9 Adam confuses these two elements. As an agent of perverted sexuality, Satan as a serpent is a phallic symbol, though he brings sterility and the rejection of being.

448 BROADBENT, J. B. *Some Graver Subject: An Essay on "Paradise Lost*." London: Chatto and Windus, 1960, 312 pp. Part reprinted in *Milton's Epic Poetry: Essays on "Paradise Lost" and "Paradise Regained*," ed. C. A. Patrides (Harmondsworth: Penguin Books, 1967), pp. 132-56; part reprinted in *Paradise Lost*, ed. Scott Elledge (New York: W. W. Norton & Co., 1975), pp. 460-68.

Stuart England sees a reading audience that extends beyond the court and demands a Christian epic in its Protestant version. By the time of the Restoration, the possibility of a divine epic seems to be slipping away from England's culture; the public no longer wants such a work. *Paradise Lost* is reactionary in content. Milton's flaw is not that he creates beauty or laments its loss, but that, having created it, he denies it and imposes a strenuous rationality on his material. The inability to portray an immaterial, real Sin and Death is a sign of his unwillingness to understand his own soul. Rather than approach God in a mystical way, Milton makes an intellectual effort to bring God down to his level for a debate. The Father's arguments to cleanse himself of blame in the fall are dramatically ineffectual and theologically vicious.

Milton's mood is split--partly idealistic and heroic in his wish to write a lasting poem, yet partly realistic and resigned to "the recalcitrant data of human existence" (287).

449 BUDICK, SANFORD. "Milton's Epic Reclamations." In *Poetry of Civilization: Mythopoeic Displacement in the Verse of Milton, Dryden, Pope, and Johnson.* New Haven, Conn., and London: Yale University Press, 1974, pp. 41-80.

The Augustans succeed in reaffirming the poet's public role because Milton provides a paradigm for the supremacy of logos and reason over mythos and Satanic idol-making. In Sonnet 18 (on the Piemont massacre), Milton shows his prophetic strain by abstracting the murdered Vaudois from temporality and detaching them as the orthodox religion's eldest practitioners. In *Samson Agonistes*, the protagonist's revenge and reawakening are most significant as symbols of the national progress that absorbs Samson. Placing Hebrew and Philistine mythologies in opposition, Milton reveals the causal connection between continence and faith, and sexuality and idolatry. Peripeteia in *Samson Agonistes* means reversing the Philistine idolatry and returning to covenant, which is present in latent form throughout. *Paradise Lost*'s power comes from the meeting of "the narrative of desolation" and "a scaffolding of reconstruction" (58). The epic redeems language from Satan's grasp, reason from fancy, and mythic thought (especially epic heroism) from its classical heritage.

450 BURDEN, DENNIS H. *The Logical Epic: A Study of the Argument of "Paradise Lost."* Cambridge, Mass.: Harvard University Press, 1967, 215 pp.

By basing *Paradise Lost* on Genesis, Milton must scrutinize his biblical source with an eye to its rationality and logic. Certain issues-- how to reconcile God's goodness with the existence of evil or God's foreknowledge with man's free will--can lead to skepticism; Milton's narrative works through these problems to leave the reader reassured about the logic behind providential wrath and piety. In order that the temptation of the senses follow that of the heart, the forbidden fruit in *Paradise Lost* must be a thing indifferent, neither provocative nor unattractive. It becomes provocative for Eve only when her judgment is in abeyance: she is not compelled to sin; she chooses to disobey God's command. After she falls, the poem moves into a Satanic mode.

Paradise Lost

Adam's sense of surrender is a Satanic response, presented with poor logic. The providential design is just as evident after the fall as before it.

451   BUSH, DOUGLAS. *"Paradise Lost" in Our Time: Some Comments*. Ithaca, N.Y.: Cornell University Press, 1945, 126 pp. Part reprinted in *Milton: Modern Essays in Criticism*, ed. Arthur E. Barker (London, Oxford, and New York: Oxford University Press, 1965), pp. 156-76; part reprinted in *Milton: A Collection of Critical Essays*, ed. Louis L. Martz (Englewood Cliffs, N.J.: Prentice-Hall, 1966), pp. 109-20; part reprinted in *Milton's Epic Poetry: Essays on "Paradise Lost" and "Paradise Regained,"* ed. C. A. Patrides (Harmondsworth: Penguin Books, 1967), pp. 33-54.
     Milton stresses the principles of an intellectual and thoughtful attitude, a Christian society, a broad tolerance for the expression of diverse views, right reason, and the individual's Christian liberty. In *Paradise Lost*, God exercises the sovereignty of right reason and the law of nature, not the arbitrary tyranny of absolute will. Christ is virtually identified with right reason, along with divine love and the divine beauty of order. As the fall indicates, the root of man's sin is pride; his greatest need is religious humility. Milton's epic contains very little that is specifically Puritan. Although he has such heroic qualities as bravery, strength, and prudence, Satan--not God--is the tyrant of *Paradise Lost*. Adam errs in subordinating reason to sense and himself to Eve, who displays pride and presumption. But Milton's poem is a divine comedy. See entries 111, 609.

452   CARNES, VALERIE. "Time and Language in Milton's *Paradise Lost*." *ELH* 37 (1970):517-39.
     Before the fall, time in *Paradise Lost* is an aspect of order, but in postlapsarian life it reflects disintegration of the cosmic order. Time then changes by restoring the original order and becoming a potential instrument of redemption. Like time, language--a vehicle for expressing poetic irony in *Paradise Lost*--alters with the fall. God's speech remains plain, ritualistic, compressed, and typological. Raphael and unfallen man use language to try to draw themselves closer to God. Seeing time as static, Satan is a literalist in his use of language, for he can perceive only physical phenomena in the present and the immediate past and future. For Adam and Eve, like Satan, linguistic disintegration suggests

progressive moral degeneration. With the fall, man leaves analogical (or spatial) symbolism and uses figurative (or temporal) symbolism.

453 CIRILLO, ALBERT R. "Noon-Midnight and the Temporal Structure of *Paradise Lost*." *ELH* 29 (1962):372-95. Reprinted in *Milton's Epic Poetry: Essays on "Paradise Lost" and "Paradise Regained*," ed. C. A. Patrides (Harmondsworth: Penguin Books, 1967), pp. 215-32; *Critical Essays on Milton from "ELH"* (Baltimore, Md., and London: Johns Hopkins Press, 1969), pp. 210-33.

In *Paradise Lost*, Milton uses a double time scheme in which events are expressed in temporal terms while they occur in the eternal present that is the poem's central setting. Time in this dual aspect becomes a basis for structure as the temporal is the metaphor for the eternal. The Platonic Great Year envisions all heavenly bodies in an eternal noon, and almost every event of thematic significance in *Paradise Lost* happens at noon or midnight, polarities that exist in the single noon of the Great Year. Satan seduces Eve at noon, the closest earthly approach to the eternal, because effective temptation must occur under the appearance of good.

454 COLIE, ROSALIE L. "Time and Eternity: Paradox and Structure in *Paradise Lost*." *Journal of the Warburg and Courtauld Institutes* 23 (1960):127-38. Reprinted in *Paradoxia Epidemica: The Renaissance Tradition of Paradox* (Princeton, N.J.: Princeton University Press, 1966), pp. 169-89; *Milton: Modern Judgements*, ed. Alan Rudrum (London: Macmillan, 1968), pp. 189-204.

Readers of *Paradise Lost* must accept certain paradoxes of Christian faith in order to comprehend the poem. As one way of rendering the paradox of a God who creates in time but exists in eternity, Milton uses epic similes and begins *in medias res*, which allows him to establish Satan's motivation and rebellion as occurring outside of time and the creation of the world as beginning time. Then the drama of Adam and Eve starts, stretching into the future under the aspect of eternity. God, Adam and Eve, and Satan have different perspectives of time in *Paradise Lost*. Writing his epic, Milton shares an aspect of foreknowledge with God. The poet has free will to choose his poetic material, ornamentation, and arrangement. Milton does not explain paradoxes, for they are not logical; *Paradise Lost* allows the reader to experience them.

Paradise Lost

455 COPE, JACKSON I. *The Metaphoric Structure of "Paradise Lost."*
Baltimore, Md.: Johns Hopkins Press, 1962, 189 pp.
In Milton's age, the advance of Ramism brings in a spatial
logic that supplants dialogue in favor of an expositor's monologue
pointing out the connections among parts. As a symbol in *Paradise
Lost*, space is the vehicle of pain and imperfection; man and Satan
attempt to transcend space in their own ways. Even time becomes space
in Milton's epic, because space is the creature and symbol of the fall.
Space becomes time in the historical view presented in *Paradise
Regained*. The motion of falling, rising, and resurrection--or moving
from darkness to light--appears in miniature in each scene in *Paradise
Lost* and is the symbol of the entire poem's "great argument." This
vertical spatial organization along a scale of luminosity is contained by
the circle of God's eternity, which looks upon time as space. In the
dialogue in heaven, the Son's words are highly rhetorical. Assimilating
the rhetoric of repetition, the Father adds other rhetorical schemes,
especially paradox, which is "the miniature mimesis of both structure
and theme" in *Paradise Lost* (175).

456 CROSMAN, ROBERT. *Reading "Paradise Lost."* Bloomington and
London: Indiana University Press, 1980, 273 pp.
Milton addresses a universal reader who can respond to the
confusion of *Paradise Lost*'s many paradoxes, such as evil's (or even
God's and our own) attractiveness and repulsiveness, because the
dialectical struggle of opposites leads to higher spiritual meaning. After
presenting an initial view of things to the reader, Milton repeatedly
undermines that perspective, collapsing it into its opposite. By learning
to distrust the narrator and his poem, the reader unlearns in order to
learn. In *Paradise Lost*, multiple points of view represent choices for the
reader to make. When Adam and Eve appear, the poem's narrative
center shifts away from a Satanic perspective to one that the reader is
happier to share. In Books 11 and 12, we enter the epic, while Adam
enters and learns to read the paradoxical world that we inhabit. See
entry 500.

457 CRUMP, GALBRAITH M., ed. *Approaches to Teaching Milton's
"Paradise Lost."* New York: Modern Language Association of
America, 1986, 211 pp. 9 illustrations.

In the section on materials, Crump surveys editions of Milton and aids to teaching. The section on approaches moves from general overviews (which include Elizabeth McCutcheon's "Getting To Know *Paradise Lost*" and essays on teaching *Paradise Lost* at a variety of institutions). In a section on specific approaches, Ellen S. Mankoff discusses reading *Paradise Lost* in the context of Milton's sonnets; Eugene D. Hill presents *Paradise Lost*'s metrics; Robert W. Halli, Jr., considers *Paradise Lost* as part of a survey course; Virginia Tufte presents a visual approach to *Paradise Lost* through illustrations by Medina, Blake, and Doré; Joan E. Hartman raises the issue of gender and teaching *Paradise Lost*; and Herman Rapaport brings together *Paradise Lost* and the novel. The final section, on backgrounds and contexts, contains Hugh M. Richmond's essay on "Milton Contexts" and William Malin Porter's on Milton's allusions.

458   CRUMP, GALBRAITH MILLER. *The Mystical Design of "Paradise Lost."* Lewisburg, Pa.: Bucknell University Press; London: Associated University Presses, 1975, 194 pp.

   A vast hieroglyph of divine abundance and love, and of man's response to them, *Paradise Lost* embodies the symbol of the circle in its syntax and structure. Milton's epic is written in the allegory of the theologian, in which historical fact has mystical (or anagogical) significance. The poet sings of the creative acts of God and man, and of the Satanic perversion of creativity. As the verse pushes forward, its imagery and Latinate syntax enact a circular motion. *Paradise Lost* is structured in concentric rings that surround its central image: Christ's victory in the war in heaven. By making minor revisions and turning *Paradise Lost*'s ten books into twelve, Milton clarifies relationships between its halves, suggests numerological readings, and balances styles.

459   CURRY, WALTER C. *Milton's Ontology, Cosmogony, and Physics.* Lexington: University of Kentucky Press, 1957, 233 pp. Reprint. 1966.

   Christian Doctrine formulates two ways to consider God that are echoed in *Paradise Lost*: in his metaphysical subsistence and in his operational existence. Milton believes that the Son is neither coessential nor coeternal with the Father. The finite, created worlds are emanations within God's infinity. A numerical unity, God is indivisible

Paradise Lost

and omnipresent. In a process of transformation in *Paradise Lost*, the sun constantly turns inflowing exhalations from earth into sol and luna, but Milton is not interested in the physics of light transmission back to earth. Milton creates a vast stage for his epic by specifying times, directions, distances, and limits, though none of these exists in a cosmos that is contained in God's infinity and eternity. According to Milton's view, the scale of nature implies that all created things are formed from a homogeneous matter, which emanates from God and deteriorates as it is transmitted farther from him. See entries 6, 18, 212, 476, 489, 512, 521, 579, 728.

460   DARBISHIRE, HELEN. *Milton's "Paradise Lost."* London, New York, and Toronto: Oxford University Press, Geoffrey Cumberlege, 1951, 51 pp.

Literary fashions may change, but *Paradise Lost* remains "a central force among forces" (6). Bentley's astringent comments on Milton's epic are refreshing, for he alerts us to important aspects of its diction, though he complains about the slightest deviations from logic, a sign of his deficient poetic imagination. Furthermore, he smooths out Milton's fluid blank verse. When Bentley decides to emend *Paradise Lost* independent of any manuscript, which he claims is not extant, he is being a rogue, for he has seen and collated the manuscript of Book 1. Dr. Johnson also draws attention to important matters in Milton's epic. Man's fall in *Paradise Lost* is in a sense a rise.

461   DAVIES, STEVIE. *Images of Kingship in "Paradise Lost": Milton's Politics and Christian Liberty.* Columbia: University of Missouri Press, 1983, 248 pp.

Milton assures us that, when kings reign, they are merely pausing on the road to execution; they belong to a family whose traits Milton describes in *Eikonoklastes*. By illustrating the descent of Satanic kingship into human history, *Paradise Lost* urges readers to repudiate kings of this world. Charles I's ancestors include Satan and Nimrod, conquerors coated in blood. Christ and God are portrayed as the rare good emperors of history; Satan is the forerunner of the typically corrupt ruler, such as Nero, Caligula, or Tiberius. When he uses accommodation to discuss the leadership of God, Christ, and Adam, Milton transfers to an innocent context the images of kingship in a corrupt world, including titles, ritual, and coronation. God rules as heaven's feudal lord, Adam as earth's. The English constitution defines the relationship between king and subject as the equivalent of father and child, a view that turns regicides into parricides. Milton denies that the king is the people's father; rather, the people father the king.

462   DEMARAY, JOHN G. *Milton's Theatrical Epic: The Invention and Design of "Paradise Lost."* Cambridge, Mass., and London: Harvard University Press, 1980, 180 pp. 16 illustrations.

   Paradise Lost is composed of a series of scenes, each having a structural unity. Taken together, they form a visionary *sacra rappresentazione*. The Trinity manuscript shows Milton's use of the sacred representation form for biblical episodes, and the 1674 revision of *Paradise Lost* into twelve books reveals his constant awareness of theatrical matters organized around a narrator. In *Paradise Lost*, the residents of hell act out a "masquelike ritual of idolatry" (64) in a realm of disguise, excess, and fragmentation. Prelapsarian life in Eden takes the form of a revel of love or an idealized masque of Hymen. Hell stands as an antimasque to the masque of heaven, where light and triumphs dominate. In Books 11-12, the visions are patterned after sixteenth-century *sacre rappresentazioni* and processional masques and pageants.

463   DIEKHOFF, JOHN S. *Milton's "Paradise Lost": A Commentary on the Argument.* New York: Columbia University Press; London: Oxford University Press, 1946, 161 pp. Reprint. New York: Humanities Press, 1958, 1963.

   Milton believes that poetry should delight, teach, and inspire action. A form of rhetoric, poetry is related to oratory in its use of appeals to an audience. The autobiographical remarks in Milton's prose and in the invocations to *Paradise Lost* act as proofs to gain the audience's attention and approval by revealing the writer's probity and authority. Those who see Satan as an admirable figure or as *Paradise Lost*'s central character are literary heretics. In artistic terms, the figure of Satan is a great, convincing creation; in moral terms, he is evil, as his soliloquies and the poet's comments indicate. He disintegrates as the narrative proceeds. Although the testing of virtue by trial is a fundamental Miltonic idea, it applies to the fallen world, not to the prelapsarian world in which Satan persuades Eve to test her virtue. She falls because she departs from reason. Adam's uxoriousness, another

Paradise Lost

departure from reason, produces his fall. *Paradise Lost* presents an example for our fallen world; readers learn that, for Milton, faith and obedience to God's will provide the foundation for virtuous action.

464   DYSON, A. E., and LOVELOCK, JULIAN. "Event Perverse: The Epic of Exile." In *Milton: "Paradise Lost," a Casebook*. Edited by A. E. Dyson and Julian Lovelock. London and Basingstoke: Macmillan, 1973, pp. 220-42.

   Paradise Lost's three perspectives--original perfection, perfection lost, and perfection regained--are present simultaneously only in God's consciousness, but readers must recognize them from the first line to the last. Milton's epic is a divine comedy mixed with controlled tragic effects. As a son of Eve, the narrator responds to her fall with tragic pity and reserves his hatred for Satan. God never withdraws freedom from any character, but the state of freedom, which requires active love, may contain the seeds of evil. Only with Satan's appearance can paradise be tested and know its full potential. We fall into a Satanic reading of *Paradise Lost* if we see Adam's decision after Eve's fall as the conflict of love and law as antithetical forces. An epic of exile, Milton's poem holds in balance certain tensions of structure and language.

465   EMPSON, WILLIAM. "Emotion in Words Again." *Kenyon Review* 10 (1948):579-601. Reprinted in *The Structure of Complex Words* (London: Chatto and Windus, 1951), pp. 101-4; reprinted (Ann Arbor: University of Michigan Press, 1967).

   The prominence of the word "all" in *Paradise Lost*, where it appears some 612 times, is not surprising since the poem is about all time, space, men, and angels, and since Milton is an absolutist, a believer in all-or-none. A self-centered person is not interested in the world's variety, so he lumps it all together as "all." Whenever there is any serious emotional pressure in *Paradise Lost*, Milton uses "all." A useful ambiguity arises from this word, for it provides confusion at the deep level.

466   EMPSON, WILLIAM. "Milton and Bentley: The Pastoral of the Innocence of Man and Nature." In *Some Versions of Pastoral*. London: Chatto and Windus, 1935, pp. 149-91. Reprinted as *English*

Pastoral Poetry (New York: W. W. Norton, 1938); reprinted (Harmondsworth: Penguin, 1966); *Milton: A Collection of Critical Essays*, ed. Louis L. Martz (Englewood Cliffs, N.J.: Prentice-Hall, 1966), pp. 19-39.

Although English critics condescendingly view Richard Bentley as "the Man who said the Tactless Thing" (149), he asks important questions that still require answers. Zachary Pearce's more rational comments make Bentley appear less stupid. Both men emphasize the meaning of *Paradise Lost*'s lines, but--because Bentley and Pearce often fail to resolve their confusion--modern critics learn the wrong lesson: that we should not bother about the sense of Milton's verses. Milton frequently relies on abstract expression and shoddy thinking. Bentley worries that the poet uses generous language when describing Satan, vilifies Eve, and makes pagan myth imply a doubting of Eden. He is correct, but these are not errors to be emended away; rather, they point to the uncertainties and contradictions at the center of Milton's myth.

467   EVERETT, BARBARA. "The End of the Big Names: Milton's Epic Catalogues." In *English Renaissance Studies Presented to Dame Helen Gardner in Honour of Her Seventieth Birthday*. [Edited by John Carey.] Oxford: Clarendon Press, 1980, pp. 254-70.

Eliot (see entries 89, 239) believes that poetry must be not only great (or weighty) but good and that *Paradise Lost*'s geographical catalogues are grand and solemn games but neither great nor good. Yet Milton's verse combines sound and meaning. Geographical catalogues appear densely in Book 1, less so in Books 2-4, and they disappear until the description of the serpent, vanishing again until Michael's revelation of the fallen world to Adam in Book 11. That they are absent from God's speech in the beginning of Book 3 and from Eden in Book 4 signals a simplification or purification of style. The context of the geographical catalogues is the intoxicating illusion of Satan's vision, which is why the catalogue of Book 11 is detached and cool--it reflects the disillusioning fact of what the Satanic mind has done.

468   FISH, STANLEY EUGENE. *Surprised by Sin: The Reader in "Paradise Lost."* New York: St. Martin's; London: Macmillan, 1967, 355 pp. Reprinted (Berkeley, Los Angeles, and London: University of California Press, 1971); part reprinted in *Milton: Modern Judgements*, ed. Alan Rudrum (London: Macmillan, 1968), pp. 104-

Paradise Lost

35; part reprinted in *Milton: "Paradise Lost," a Casebook*, ed. A. E. Dyson and Julian Lovelock (London and Basingstoke: Macmillan, 1973), pp. 152-78; part reprinted in *Paradise Lost*, ed. Scott Elledge (New York: W. W. Norton & Co., 1975), pp. 422-33.

Milton harasses the reader into realizing that he is unable to read *Paradise Lost* with confidence in his perception; this is the poem's focus, and the technique is revealed in part through the poet's intrusions to comment on characters' speeches. The poet's judgment of the characters challenges the reader's judgment, forcing the reader to criticize himself by recognizing his misreading. *Paradise Lost* provides a "good temptation" by exposing corruption and making the reader more fit to resist less benevolent tempters. When Milton uses a prelapsarian vocabulary to describe Adam, Eve, and Eden, such words as "fall," "wandering," "wanton," and "loose" reveal the reader's fallen nature, for the corrupt meanings that he sees cannot exist in a prelapsarian universe; they must exist in the reader. The reader projects his own inadequacies onto pure characters and settings. Forced to recognize his corruption, the reader must over-moralize and exclude meanings that are not properly there. Satan, according to the morality of stylistics, demoralizes language by misusing some words and avoiding others. After making mistakes and correcting them, the reader is instructed. His goal is to attain clear vision and reassemble truth's perfect form, which the fall violated. See entry 500.

469   FIXLER, MICHAEL. "Milton's Passionate Epic." *Milton Studies* 1 (1969):167-92.

A devotional poem as well as an epic, *Paradise Lost* worships the mystery of providence's hidden ways even as its argument justifies God's ways to men. The poem intends to involve some few readers as if they were "participants in an extraordinary act of extemporary liturgical service" (172), as we see in the angelic chorus of Book 3. For another group of readers, the bulk of sinning humanity, the worship that *Paradise Lost* offers is a means of evangelical edification. The impulse to pray and to know inspires the poetic ascent. In the invocation to Urania in Book 7, the poet excludes profane readers, that bulk of humanity in Book 3, from his act of offering a sacramental gesture.

470   FRANK, JOSEPH. "John Milton's Movement toward Deism." *Journal of British Studies* 1 (1961):38-51.

Milton's use of the verb "justify" generally carries negative, defensive implications, and the choice of this word in *Paradise Lost*'s opening ("And justify the ways of God to men") is an apology for traditional religion and a sign of his movement toward deism. Starting as an orthodox Anglican and Trinitarian, Milton breaks with the episcopacy in the 1640s and embraces Presbyterianism; he continues his journey to the political left by endorsing the Independents and then what we might call the congregationalists. His major poems are concerned not with theology but ethics. In *Paradise Lost*, he shrinks the Old Testament God and makes him both a remote and an internal figure. Again shunning the supernatural, Milton in *Paradise Regained* humanizes Christ. *Samson Agonistes* lacks hope, emphasizes failure, and raises more dark questions than it answers. A deist in the end, Milton does not succeed in justifying God's ways if by that expression we mean whatever is, is right. Justification for Milton means freedom to choose.

471 FRYE, NORTHROP. *The Return of Eden: Five Essays on Milton's Epics*. Toronto and Buffalo, N.Y.: University of Toronto Press, 1965, 151 pp. Part reprinted in *Milton: Modern Essays in Criticism*, ed. Arthur E. Barker (London, Oxford, and New York: Oxford University Press, 1965), pp. 429-46; part reprinted in *Milton's Epic Poetry: Essays on "Paradise Lost" and "Paradise Regained*," ed. C. A. Patrides (Harmondsworth: Penguin Books, 1967), pp. 301-21; parts reprinted in *On Milton's Poetry*, ed. Arnold Stein (Greenwich, Conn.: Fawcett Publications, 1970), pp. 89-96, 228-36; part reprinted in *Paradise Lost*, ed. Scott Elledge (New York: W. W. Norton & Co., 1975), pp. 405-22.

Milton understands the epic to be long, narrative, and encyclopedic, qualities displayed in *Paradise Lost*. A twelve-book division of the poem maintains its true proportions, but Milton first publishes it in ten books to show his contempt for tradition. Like the *Odyssey*, the *Aeneid*, and Exodus, *Paradise Lost* is divided into a quest theme and a theme of settling a social order, though Milton reverses the sequence. His epic's structure forms an ascending spiral whose ending is the starting point after it has been renewed and transformed by Christ's heroic quest. While *Paradise Lost*'s content is human, its narrative movement is provided by God, yet he often sounds like an unconvincing, "smirking hypocrite" (99). One of the key themes in Milton's work is the externalizing of the demonic and the internalizing

Paradise Lost

of the divine. His style is simple and direct. In *Paradise Regained*, Christ's temptation forms part of his mental process of separating the law that is to be overthrown from the law that is to be fulfilled and internalized. As a brief epic, *Paradise Regained* lacks both predecessors and descendants.

472   FRYE, ROLAND MUSHAT. *Milton's Imagery and the Visual Arts: Iconographic Tradition in the Epic Poems*. Princeton, N.J.: Princeton University Press, 1978, 433 pp. 269 illustrations.

That Milton is blind when he writes his epics does not imply that he retains no visual imagination. During his Italian journey, such friends as Gaddi, Dati, Manso, and Frescobaldi--all interested in art and architecture--could gain him admission to almost any collection of art. When in *Paradise Lost* Milton depicts spiritual beings in heaven (as in the war or the expulsion of the rebels) or in hell, and when he writes of Adam and Eve in Eden, he works not just within a literary tradition but also within an artistic one that includes landscapes, paintings, sculptures, tapestries, maps, mosaics, and architecture. This also applies to *Paradise Regained*. Like his use of earlier writers, Milton's use of art is eclectic. To understand this aspect of his epic verse, we need to recover the visual lexicon that he employs.

473   FRYE, ROLAND MUSHAT. "*Paradise Lost* and the Christian Vision." In *God, Man, and Satan: Patterns of Christian Thought and Life in "Paradise Lost," "Pilgrim's Progress," and the Great Theologians*. Princeton, N.J.: Princeton University Press, 1960, pp. 21-91.

According to Christianity, evil is good in its created intention but perverted from its proper ends; totally subordinated to God, evil aspires to Godhead and seeks to enjoy itself rather than God, as Milton's Satan illustrates. When he denies the fact of his own creation by God, Satan becomes the first Manichee, arguing for the existence of independent deities, good and evil. *Paradise Lost* emphasizes the conflict between Christ and his opposite, Satan the Antichrist. The gifts of reason, wisdom, and companionship show God's respect for Adam and Eve's integrity, which they fail to respect by repudiating God's image and aspiring to Godhead. The fall leads to alienation from God, self, and others. *Paradise Lost* is far more concerned with the triumph of grace than with the commission of sin.

474 GARDNER, HELEN. *A Reading of "Paradise Lost."* The Alexander Lectures in the University of Toronto, 1962. Oxford: Clarendon Press, 1965, 141 pp.

   Although the argument over Milton's style is dead, the debate over his choice of subject is still important. Rather than being obtusely unconscious of his purpose in writing *Paradise Lost*, Milton faces it directly: God is responsible for the world as we know it. Milton attempts to combine the concentration of drama and the discursiveness of epic. Developing the slight action of *Paradise Lost* requires Milton to expand the character and role of Satan. The poet can afford to present Satan grandly because he is doomed. Milton's theme is great but impersonal, and into it he infuses intense, personal feeling through the ever-present narrator. The stricture against eating the apple is irrational so that it may be religious. There are no reasons for or against this command; it cannot be the subject of an argument; Satan's skill lies in suggesting to Eve that the command is reasonable and arguable. On the cosmic level, the providential scheme is to bring good out of evil. On the human level, however, Milton celebrates only the inner victory of the "upright heart and pure" and the prospect of a "paradise within."

   Appendixes: "Milton's Satan and the Theme of Damnation in Elizabethan Tragedy" (reprinted in *Milton: Modern Essays in Criticism*, ed. Arthur E. Barker [London, Oxford, and New York: Oxford University Press, 1965], pp. 205-17); "Milton's First Illustrator."

475 GIAMATTI, A. BARTLETT. "Milton." In *The Earthly Paradise and the Renaissance Epic*. Princeton, N.J.: Princeton University Press, 1966, pp. 295-355.

   Paradise Lost is built on ironies and paradoxes. While the poet writes of the good and the beginning, he must implicate the experience of an audience that possesses knowledge of evil and the end. Milton uses an allusive, elusive style filled with verbal ambiguities when he writes of Satan, Adam and Eve, and Eden. This style maintains multiple perspectives and suspense; Milton uses it to prepare Adam and Eve for sin while keeping them innocent, and to make us suspicious of the innocence of the garden and its residents. When Satan, the artist and actor, enters Eden, the corrupt perspective is balanced with the innocent one. The fallen Eve is both victim and creator of the split between illusion and reality. Milton's Eden sums up all previous images of an earthly paradise.

Paradise Lost

476 GILBERT, ALLAN H. "Milton and Galileo." *Studies in Philology* 19 (1922):152-85.

Galileo, Milton's only contemporary to find a place in *Paradise Lost*, acts as a symbol for free thought and for the poet's desire for truer scientific teaching than decadent Aristotelianism. Although Milton wants Galileo's views to be tolerated, he deals with Copernicus's cosmology as though it were not established and probably teaches Ptolemaic astronomy to his students. But *Paradise Lost* derives details from Galileo: the explanation of sun spots, the shining earth, and Venus's phases. The mixed cosmology of *Paradise Lost* points to Milton's uncertainty. He often speaks in Ptolemaic terms in *Paradise Lost* because the average educated person of his day is more familiar with them. Yet Milton does not care whether the Copernican or Ptolemaic system proves true. See entries 6, 18, 212, 459, 489, 512, 521, 579, 728.

477 GILBERT, ALLAN H. *On the Composition of "Paradise Lost": A Study of the Ordering and Insertion of Material.* Chapel Hill: University of North Carolina Press, 1947, 195 pp.

Handicapped by his blindness, Milton composes *Paradise Lost* in small units of about twenty lines over a number of years, during which time he is interrupted by writing prose tracts. There are many inconsistencies between the arguments and the poem they describe, indicating that the arguments form part of an outline, which is not thoroughly revised before the epic reaches its final state. Milton's narrative initially follows a chronological sequence, beginning with the war presented directly by the narrator; the story of the creation also appears early in the original work. The poem contains numerous narrative inconsistencies and insertions.

Gilbert provides a table showing the tentative sequence of *Paradise Lost*'s composition. See entry 250.

478 GILBERT, SANDRA M. "Patriarchal Poetry and Women Readers: Reflections on Milton's Bogey." *PMLA* 93 (1978):368-82. Reprinted in *The Madwoman in the Attic: The Woman Writer and the Nineteenth-Century Literary Imagination*, by Sandra M. Gilbert and Susan Gubar (New Haven, Conn., and London: Yale University Press, 1979), pp. 187-212.

When Virginia Woolf writes that literate women must "look past Milton's bogey, for no human being should shut out the view," she may be referring to Milton himself or to *Paradise Lost*'s inferior and Satanically inspired Eve, both of whom intimidate women and block their view of real and literary possibilities. To deal with the misogyny of Milton's epic, with its emphasis on a Father God as the creator and only legitimate model for authors, such women writers as Charlotte Brontë and Mary Shelley define revisionary myths and metaphors, sometimes by transforming Satan into a Promethean Eve. *Paradise Lost*, according to Woolf, speaks for the western literary patriarchy and for female subordination. Eve parallels Satan and Sin in many ways throughout the epic, and there are important connections among Satan, rebellious Romanticism, and incipient feminism. Milton's Satan is like women in some key ways, and he is also very attractive to them.

479 GOSSMAN, ANN. "The Ring Pattern: Image, Structure, and Theme in *Paradise Lost*." *Studies in Philology* 68 (1971):326-39.

One key image in *Paradise Lost* is the Christian Platonic ring pattern, which Milton uses by contrasting good rings with circular mazes of error. The positive ring imagery, like the image of Jacob's ladder, implies a moral process and a pattern of return; attempting to counterfeit the ring, the complex maze is a treadmill of futility. Satan's pattern of aspiration and descent illustrates the wrong moral process, just as his rhetoric and motion as a serpent reveal the workings of a maze. But man proceeds from God, falls, and returns to God. *Paradise Lost*'s structure shows a balance of becoming and being. Christ is the exemplary model of the ring pattern in the epic.

480 GROSE, CHRISTOPHER. *Milton's Epic Process: "Paradise Lost" and Its Miltonic Background*. New Haven, Conn., and London: Yale University Press, 1973, 279 pp.

Avoiding the tendency to make poetry become a mere image or verbal icon, Milton exploits the process that articulates a poem or image. He stages a poem's origins and its emergence from them. His poetic theory is primarily concerned with the truth of poetry; from *Nativity Ode* onward, he seeks to use poetry as a vehicle, to transcend mere poetry and arrive at truth. *Art of Logic* indicates that Ramist logic, distinct from words and things, is serviceable for a poetry of wisdom. *Paradise Lost*'s formal similes signal perceptual crises in which the

Paradise Lost

narrator appears in his most casual pose, as the maker and expositor of images. His similes merely pretend to refer, taking us outside the poem to explain or establish the world within the poem; they also emphasize the artifice of his work and the poem's secondary status. The epic's invocations suggest the discreteness of poem and poetic process.

481 GROSSMAN, MARSHALL. "Milton's Dialectical Visions." *Modern Philology* 82 (1984):23-39.

Paradise Lost thematizes its narration by including it within an eschatological framework of our present imperfect earthly knowledge and our future complete divine knowledge. Revelation allows the interpretation of the former through the latter. In his epic, Milton uses the sacrifice of Christ and the universal history presented in the Bible to mediate the dialectical antithesis of becoming (historical appearance) and being (eternal essence). There is an ontological progression revealed by the dialectical progression from metaphor (analogy) to synecdoche (identity). In *Paradise Lost*, Milton presents an apocalyptic revision of history.

482 HALE, JOHN K. "The Significance of the Early Translations of *Paradise Lost*." *Philological Quarterly* 63 (1984):31-53.

Early translations of *Paradise Lost* give an indication of how its first readers receive it. As a sign that it is immediately viewed as a classic, there are more Latin translations, and they appear earlier, than Greek, German (and Dutch), French, or Italian ones. Joseph Trapp publishes a complete Latin version of *Paradise Lost* (1740-44), as does William Dobson (1750-53). The first translation of *Paradise Lost* is in German, and the epic is translated into verse and prose in German, Dutch, and French. All Italian translations are in verse, and this language seems especially well suited to Milton's high style.

483 HALEWOOD, WILLIAM H. "*Paradise Lost*" and "Milton's Arianism and Arminianism." In *The Poetry of Grace: Reformation Themes and Structures in English Seventeenth-Century Poetry*. New Haven, Conn., and London: Yale University Press, 1970, pp. 140-67, 168-75.

The meaning of *Paradise Lost* is contained in part in its two arguments based on two perspectives: from God's point of view, man's disobedience is of great importance; from the human point of view, the consequence of disobedience is crucial. That the two views are never joined in *Paradise Lost* is both an event in the epic and a cause for it. Man's perspective continues to exclude the divine and then see his justice as unjust; God sees that he has asked little of man, provided the ability for man to stand, and been disobeyed. As an illustration of the theologically defined condition of fallen man, Satan appears heroic to some readers. The themes of fellowship and solitude are important in *Paradise Lost*, and they explain why Adam chooses to sin.

The supposed theological liberties in *Christian Doctrine* actually take place within Reformation limits. See entries 962, 967-68, 989-90.

484 HALLER, WILLIAM. "The Tragedy of God's Englishman." In *Reason and the Imagination: Studies in the History of Ideas, 1600-1800*. Edited by J. A. Mazzeo. New York: Columbia University Press; London: Routledge and Kegan Paul, 1962, pp. 201-11.

Although Milton takes a long time to discard the idea of writing an epic about England's vocation and destiny, *Paradise Lost* still springs from his early devotion to that theme. The idea of Britain's ascent from Troy's ashes is transformed in Milton's prose to the dream of a new Jerusalem rising on English soil. The historian's duty is to understand and reveal the providential design of events, the conclusion of which is prophesied as the Lord's calling of his saints to battle Satan and thus restore the true church. This battle, the Puritans believe, will occur in England; the very idea fills Milton's imagination. But "antichrist did not meet his doom on English ground. God's Englishmen did not keep covenant with God" (208), so in *Paradise Lost* Milton stresses man's first disobedience and its consequences rather than Christ's final victory.

485 HAMLET, DESMOND M. *One Greater Man: Justice and Damnation in "Paradise Lost."* Lewisburg, Pa.: Bucknell University Press; London: Associated University Presses, 1976, 224 pp.

The justice of Milton's God in *Paradise Lost*--a restorative, righteous attribute--is an integral part of his omnipotence, creative purpose, and love. Because Satan perverts all of these qualities, he is damned. Although moralistic and theocratic excesses reinforce the idea of God's justice as distributive and retributive during Milton's age, he

Paradise Lost

avoids such positions, repudiates Calvinism, and turns to the Bible to define God's justice. The Old Testament often parallels God's justice or righteousness and salvation. In this context, divine justice is restorative. The New Testament reinterprets the Old Testament's view of divine justice, sees it as both positive and negative, and reveals Christ as divine justice itself, a conjunction of God's mercy and justice. There is no dichotomy in *Paradise Lost* between the Father's justice and the Son's mercy. Everything in Milton's epic turns in on and is defined by the paradoxical significance of the Son.

486   HANFORD, JAMES HOLLY. "The Dramatic Element in *Paradise Lost.*" *Studies in Philology* 14 (1917):178-95. Reprinted in *John Milton, Poet and Humanist: Essays by James Holly Hanford* (Cleveland, Ohio: Press of Western Reserve University, 1966), pp. 224-43.

   Although the sensuous and aesthetic essence of Elizabethan drama grows less important as Milton moves from *Paradise Lost* to *Paradise Regained* and *Samson Agonistes*, his sympathy with the moral, philosophical, and human phases of the English Renaissance becomes deeper. In *Paradise Lost*, the epic and dramatic impulses meet on equal terms. The dramatic element is revealed in dialogues and soliloquies, which show the psychology of the speakers. Milton also uses the tragic principles of irony and hubris.

487   HANFORD, JAMES HOLLY. "Milton and the Return to Humanism." *Studies in Philology* 16 (1919):126-47. Reprinted in *Milton Criticism: Selections from Four Centuries*, ed. James Thorpe (New York: Rinehart & Co., 1950), pp. 143-68; *John Milton, Poet and Humanist: Essays by James Holly Hanford* (Cleveland, Ohio: Press of Western Reserve University, 1966), pp. 161-84.

   The audience that Milton ideally intends for *Paradise Lost* does not exist when it is published. The wits rather than the Puritans first write about it, and the major critical issue in the eighteenth century is the basis of Milton's aesthetic theory because, for these readers, his ideas are dead. Valued primarily for style, *Paradise Lost* is frequently imitated in the eighteenth century as a phase of classicism. Late in that century and into the nineteenth, critics emphasize Milton's epic as a work of the imagination and stress his radical politics. They still do not value his ideas. Twentieth-century readers agree with Raleigh (see entry 66) that *Paradise Lost* is "a monument to dead ideas," though more recent criticism evaluates *Paradise Lost* in terms of humanism, with its claims for the spiritual dignity of man.

488   HARDISON, O. B., Jr. "*In Medias Res* in *Paradise Lost.*" *Milton Studies* 17 (1983):27-41.

We can view *Paradise Lost* from two perspectives: its inclusive plot begins with Christ's elevation and ends with the Last Judgment; the use of the convention of *in medias res* gives the epic a dramatic plot focused on a single action, the fall. Material from the inclusive plot is introduced into, and subordinated to, the dramatic plot by characters who act as narrators. When Milton begins *Paradise Lost* with Satan's soliloquy to the sun, now in Book 4, he aims the dramatic plot directly at its major crisis, the temptation; in the early stages of composition, Milton sees the fall in terms of Elizabethan revenge tragedy, which marks an alternative to the next stage: the Trinity manuscript's plans for more chronological classical dramas on the fall. Although the addition of Books 1-2 diverts attention from the primary action, presents fictional material, comes from the narrator rather than from another character, and confuses readers about Satan's status, it does make Satan a credible example of evil, to be offset only later by God's benign power.

489   HARRIS, NEIL. "Galileo as Symbol: The 'Tuscan Artist' in *Paradise Lost.*" *Estratto da Annali dell'Istituto e Museo di Storia della Scienza di Firenze* 10 (1985):3-29.

During his Italian journey, Milton meets Galileo, whose discoveries lead Italian heroic poets to equip their heroes with telescopes and to write digressions about astronomy. Milton's simile about the Tuscan artist in Book 1 of *Paradise Lost* may not allude to Galileo, for it is applied to Satan, is associated with Homeric descriptions of shields, and locates the Tuscan artist's residence at the opposite side of Florence from where Galileo is imprisoned. When he mentions Fiesole, Milton evokes a city of stargazers (according to Dante), an evil city that struggles against Florence. The Tuscan artist is thus "a Satanic image" (16). The simile casts doubt on the direction the modern world, as introduced by Galileo, is taking. Milton connects himself as poet to Dante, each an example of the single individual seeking truth. See entries 6, 18, 212, 459, 476, 512, 521, 579, 728.

Paradise Lost

490 HARTMAN, GEOFFREY. "Milton's Counterplot." *ELH* 25 (1958):1-12. Reprinted in *Milton: Modern Essays in Criticism*, ed. Arthur E. Barker (London, Oxford, and New York: Oxford University Press, 1965), pp. 386-97; *Milton: A Collection of Critical Essays*, ed. Louis L. Martz (Englewood Cliffs, N.J.: Prentice Hall, 1966), pp. 100-108; *Critical Essays on Milton from "ELH"* (Baltimore, Md., and London: Johns Hopkins Press, 1969), pp. 151-62; *Beyond Formalism: Literary Essays, 1958-1970* (New Haven, Conn., and London: Yale University Press, 1970), pp. 113-23.

God's imperturbability, based on his knowledge that the creation will outlive death and sin, constitutes part of the counterplot of *Paradise Lost*. It is also made up of our view of Satan as real and terrible, yet never irresistible. While Milton's similes provide an aesthetic distance, they reveal both Satanic destruction and the imperturbable order of the creation.

491 HOWARD, LEON. "'The Invention' of Milton's 'Great Argument': A Study of the Logic of 'God's Ways to Men.'" *Huntington Library Quarterly* 9 (1946):149-73.

According to Milton's Ramist *Art of Logic*, "artificial" invention is subdivided until one arrives at the first of all arguments, cause, which forms *Paradise Lost*'s great argument. The first efficient cause, as *Art of Logic* argues, works with and through other causes, and they are also efficient. Aided by instrumental causes, man is the principal cause of his first disobedience. The proegumenic cause is Adam's lack of self-sufficiency, which leads to the creation of Eve. By dividing the cause of Adam's sin into two parts, Milton shows that his innocence is the "matter" from which original sin comes; the "form" of that sin is the change in human nature that accompanies the fall. The "end" or final cause of this sin is God's demonstration of his love and mercy, a cause we should not overemphasize.

492 HUGHES, MERRITT Y. "Beyond Disobedience." In *Approaches to "Paradise Lost."* The York Tercentenary Lectures. Edited by C. A. Patrides. London: Edward Arnold, 1968, pp. 181-98.

Because Milton's use of the word and concept of disobedience is vague, we should think of piety and impiety as one of *Paradise Lost*'s many dichotomies. In *Paradise Lost*, two great acts of disobedience to divine commands (Satan's, and Adam and Eve's) are balanced by two great acts of obedience (the Son's and Abdiel's). After Book 9's invocation, the word "disobedience" disappears from the poem's vocabulary because Milton finds it inadequate and defines the fall as a sin against reason. Rather than emphasizing apocalyptic possibilities in the final books of *Paradise Lost*, Milton indicates that personal perfection is attained by restoring the broken image of God in man.

493   HUGHES, MERRITT Y. "Milton's *Eikon Basilike.*" In *Calm of Mind: Tercentenary Essays on "Paradise Regained" and "Samson Agonistes" in Honor of John S. Diekhoff.* Edited by Joseph Anthony Wittreich, Jr. Cleveland, Ohio, and London: Press of Case Western Reserve University, 1971, pp. 1-24.

Milton works on four royal images: human (Charles I), diabolic (Satan), and two divine ones (Christ and God). Because he does not respect the mind mirrored in King Charles I's *Eikon Basilike*, Milton dislikes writing *Eikonoklastes*. In the Satan of *Paradise Lost*, he finds an intelligent aspirant to kingship who behaves in a tyrannical fashion; the poet satirizes Satan as he sacrifices rational rule of the soul to become a mere image and idol, "the false *eikon basilike*" (5). The Son in the epic, with the unfallen angels, demonstrates loyalty through obedience based on love; in *Paradise Regained*, he shows no sense of independent royal power. He is the supreme epiphany of magnanimity. If God in *Paradise Lost* sounds cold, legalistic, and unpoetic, that is appropriate because his first attribute is truth. An *eikon basilike*, he is righteous and royal.

494   HUNTER, G. K. *Paradise Lost.* Unwin Critical Library. London: George Allen and Unwin, 1980, 222 pp.

With patriotism and religion in the front of his mind, Milton joins the epic tradition in order to transform it, even to save it. *Paradise Lost* praises true heroism as "the saving creativity which redeems what is lost" (24). Combining opposite movements, the narrative uses both the Hellenic-Hebraic episodic view of history and the Christian one in which all events are causally related insofar as they lead to or from the Incarnation. The heroism Milton defines, the glory of failure and repentance, opposes the traditional kind even while using its language. Since space and conquest appear in a moral geography, Satan's odyssey is actually a type of standing still. *Paradise Lost* culminates in Adam and Eve's relationship. While some readers worry about Eve's inferior

Paradise Lost

status, Adam's lesson to be "lowly wise" is an indication that he should be more like Eve.

495   IDE, RICHARD S. "On the Uses of Elizabethan Drama: The Revaluation of Epic in *Paradise Lost.*" *Milton Studies* 17 (1983):121-40.

Although Satan acts the role of the Elizabethan stage villain in *Paradise Lost*, Adam and Eve and their descendants will have the final revenge, through Christ, at the Resurrection. Satan is an impenitent "tragic hero in a tragedy of damnation" (123). The story of Adam and Eve holds the same potential, but divine retribution and penitence turn it into a heroic argument. Milton thus overturns the classical epic's subject matter by asserting that these characters are tragic rather than heroic. Aspects of Elizabethan tragic theory and practice show why we should condemn Satanic heroism, while the principles of Elizabethan tragicomedy (particularly forgiveness and patience) help Milton depict the new heroism of Adam and Eve.

496   JACOBUS, LEE A. *Sudden Apprehension: Aspects of Knowledge in "Paradise Lost."* Studies in English Literature, vol. 94. The Hague and Paris: Mouton, 1976, 225 pp.

In the contemporary controversy involving the values of reason and faith, Milton holds that human reason should be used in religious matters. Self-knowledge, which implies knowledge of God and is necessary to gain wisdom, appears in its distorted form in *Paradise Lost* in Satan's soliloquy to the sun: he appears to understand himself and God, but he knows neither. Adam, on the other hand, has sure self-knowledge before the fall. As the episode at the pool indicates, Eve may not have been created fully self-knowing: unable to see beneath the surface of physical and natural beauty, she feels its pull and is also interested in Adam's higher knowledge. Milton's theory of knowledge in *Paradise Lost* is monistic, with reason joining or disjoining the perceptions of the senses or imagination. In the temptation and fall scenes, as well as in the crucial episodes surrounding them, Adam and Eve use formal and informal logic to determine a course of action. Perception, reason, and understanding do not lead to knowledge of God in *Paradise Lost*, but faith, love, and obedience do.

497 KERMODE, FRANK. "Adam Unparadised." In *The Living Milton: Essays by Various Hands*. Edited by Frank Kermode. London: Routledge and Kegan Paul, 1960, pp. 85-123. Reprinted in *On Milton's Poetry*, ed. Arnold Stein (Greenwich, Conn.: Fawcett Publications, 1970), pp. 134-50; *Milton: "Paradise Lost," a Casebook*, ed. A. E. Dyson and Julian Lovelock (London and Basingstoke: Macmillan, 1973), pp. 179-203; *Paradise Lost*, ed. Scott Elledge (New York: W. W. Norton & Co., 1975), pp. 490-507.

   Paradise Lost embodies "life in a great symbolic attitude" (86). Milton's epic is not a theological treatise, for its immediate goal is to delight rather than to explain; poetry, in his view, appeals to the reason through the senses. Yet he uses a circuitous, counterlogical route (which includes a twisted syntax, rhyme, and pseudo-rhyme) to the mind by means of delighting the reader's perturbed senses. The tragic theme of *Paradise Lost* is the power of joy and its loss. So that we may understand the gap between possible and actual physical pleasure in our fallen world, Milton forces us to experience Eden and all delight through Satan's eyes.

498 KERRIGAN, WILLIAM. *The Sacred Complex: On the Psychogenesis of "Paradise Lost."* Cambridge, Mass., and London: Harvard University Press, 1983, 355 pp.

   As Milton revises *Comus* between 1634 and 1637 in his father's country homes, his experiences parallel the Lady's. He goes through a period of stasis not because he feels guilty about preferring a poetic to a priestly vocation, but because he can conceive of no desirable career. "Transformations of the lady in Milton are in effect the history of his poetic identity from *Comus* to *Paradise Lost*" (50). In the figure of Comus, Milton overcomes the Oedipal temptation; his incest wish is directed at his sister and especially at his mother. In his major poems, Milton reconciles the Oedipus complex in the sphere of religion, thus composing ambition's terrors and ecstasies while giving life to the symbols of his faith. *Paradise Regained* dramatizes the work of redemption as the sacred complex, through which an Oedipal marriage is transcended through its latent repetition. An epic of genesis, *Paradise Lost* lets us revisit and observe many acts of creation, the first of which is God's creation of light, not of the Son.

Paradise Lost

499   KNIGHT, G. WILSON. *Chariot of Wrath: The Message of John Milton to Democracy at War.* London: Faber and Faber, 1942, 194 pp. Part reprinted in *Poets of Action* (London: Methuen, 1967), pp. 70-162.

Milton records the agony of civil disruption in his age and foresees recovery; we must similarly analyze the conflict of our age and begin to see a new civilization's creation. The basic opposition in Milton's life and work, that between Christian virtue and pagan lust, appears in *Paradise Lost* on a vast scale much like today's conflict. After Parliament and Cromwell fail him, Milton comes to believe in Christ as king. The hero of *Samson Agonistes*, an autobiographical work, corresponds to the English people as they move toward recovery and control over their destiny. Samson displays active virtue. In *Paradise Regained*, Milton attempts to give Christ's personality both calm and volcanic power. Like Christ, Milton's Britain prefers a policy of international morality over might or statecraft. See entry 118.

500   KNOTT, JOHN R., Jr. "*Paradise Lost* and the Fit Reader." *Modern Language Quarterly* 45 (1984):123-43.

In order to help us understand the meaning of a "fit" reader, the idea of authorial intent is worthy of examination. Fish's reader-response approach (see entry 468) allows the sinful reader only a narrow range of responses, while Crosman's approach (see entry 456) defines the bewildered reader too loosely. Rather than seeing the reader's experience almost exclusively as dramatic and transforming, we should view Milton's fit readers, as defined by the invocation to Book 7, as a select group that sympathizes with his radical position on reformation and the rule of the saints--not exactly a very sinful or confused audience. Milton wants his readers to recognize the brilliance and power of divine majesty and the foolishness of challenging it. We must experience a variety of emotions in *Paradise Lost*, ranging from delight to horror.

501   LABRIOLA, ALBERT C. "The Aesthetics of Self-Diminution: Christian Iconography and *Paradise Lost*." *Milton Studies* 7 (1975):267-311. 7 illustrations.

Using typology, Christian iconography connects the creation, fall, and Crucifixion (and the settings of these events) as Christ is depicted as the new Adam, Mary as the new Eve, and the cross as the new tree of knowledge. Milton develops the same perspective in *Paradise Lost* and celebrates the theme of humility.

502 LABRIOLA, ALBERT C. "The Medieval View of Christian History in *Paradise Lost*." In *Milton and the Middle Ages*. Edited by John Mulryan. Lewisburg, Pa.: Bucknell University Press; London and Toronto: Associated University Presses, 1982, pp. 115-32.

Milton uses the main events of the Paschal triduum--the suffering and death of Christ, the harrowing of hell, and the Resurrection--as a frame of reference to interpret much of *Paradise Lost*'s action and characterization. Satan is the demonic counterpart who parodies Noah's role in the second creation and first salvation after the flood, which in turn prefigure Christ's Paschal triumph and the second coming. Noah and Christ have three roles--creator, redeemer, and judge--that Satan enacts ironically, for he plans earth's uncreation.

503 LANDY, MARCIA. "Kinship and the Role of Women in *Paradise Lost*." *Milton Studies* 4 (1972):3-18.

Not a misogynist, Milton is a representative seventeenth-century poet who believes in the centrality of marriage and the traditional roles of men and women. In *Paradise Lost*, he recreates the myth of the fall from his own perspective and that of his age. Adam is the author, teacher, and ruler; Eve, the creation, student, and ruled. They are siblings, in one sense, before being husband and wife. Satan and Sin provide a perverted analogue by reenacting these relationships. In the relationships of God, the Son, and Satan, which parallel Adam and Eve's relationship, Milton explores obedience, disobedience, and dominance-submission. Woman is excluded from heaven, and she is denied the principle of creativity in the rest of the cosmos. The family structure is the basis for models of authority, social order, and proper behavior.

504 LEWALSKI, BARBARA K. "Milton on Women--Yet Once More." *Milton Studies* 6 (1974):3-20.

Female Miltonists do not write feminist analyses of *Paradise Lost* because they do not share feminists' assumptions about how we experience and what we value in this epic. Transcending the way gender affects our perceptions, great art speaks to our common humanity.

Paradise Lost

Besides substituting sociological for literary analysis, feminist criticism forgets that poets are in some ways bound to their own ages. "Few writers of any era--including our own--have taken women so seriously as Milton does" (5-6). In the prelapsarian state, Eve participates in the full range of human activities, not just the domestic and maternal ones. Many critics fail to notice that Eve is present for most of Raphael's lesson. Adam receives epithets alluding to paternity as often as Eve receives ones alluding to maternity. In *Paradise Lost*, Milton shows both Adam and Eve as they take responsibility for choices. Adam uses his role as leader correctly when it enhances Eve's freedom of choice.

505   LEWALSKI, BARBARA KIEFER. *"Paradise Lost" and the Rhetoric of Literary Forms*. Princeton, N.J.: Princeton University Press, 1985, 389 pp.

Milton incorporates a complete spectrum of literary forms and genres in *Paradise Lost* because the epic is defined as encyclopedic in its subjects, forms, and styles; such a spectrum will be most exemplary to a nation; and he wants to examine the values embodied by those forms. The three prophet-poets in *Paradise Lost*--the narrator, Raphael, and Michael--dramatize "the process, the problems, and the purposes of creating divine poetry" (26), along with the functions of accommodation and education. In Satan's narrative, Milton includes the genres of epic, heroic tragedy, romance quest epic, Ovidian epic, and epic of Exodus. To portray God, Milton uses an even wider range of forms, avoids a resolution of paradigms in a scene of closure, and provides multiple perspectives on God to hint at his divine totality. Angelic society appears in the pastoral, georgic, and heroic modes, which Milton associates with prophetic dialogue and lyric hymns. Prelapsarian life in Eden is portrayed in the pastoral mode, not as a low form but as it is linked to epic. Books 9 and 10 shift to a tragic mode that includes the genres of lament, complaint, and elegy. Books 11 and 12 use the prophetic and Christian heroic modes.

506   LEWIS, C. S. *A Preface to "Paradise Lost."* London: Oxford University Press, 1942, 150 pp. Frequently reprinted; part reprinted in *Milton Criticism: Selections from Four Centuries*, ed. James Thorpe (New York: Rinehart & Co., 1950), pp. 267-88; part reprinted in *Milton: Modern Essays in Criticism*, ed. Arthur E. Barker (London, Oxford, and New York: Oxford University Press, 1965), pp. 196-204;

part reprinted in *Milton: A Collection of Critical Essays*, ed. Louis L. Martz (Englewood Cliffs, N.J.: Prentice-Hall, 1966), pp. 40-55; part reprinted in *Milton: "Paradise Lost," a Casebook*, ed. A. E. Dyson and Julian Lovelock (London and Basingstoke: Macmillan, 1973), pp. 85-105.

The primary epic (such as the *Iliad* and *Odyssey*) is tragic, true, aristocratic, ceremonial, concerned with man, and recited in the court. Poetic diction in an oral work describes language that is familiar because it is part of every poem, but unfamiliar because it is not used elsewhere. Since the experience of a secondary epic is not part of a public ritual, the author's style must provide the solemnity of such an occasion. Milton does this with unfamiliar words and constructions, proper names, and continued allusion to sensory experience. His complex syntax prevents the reader from pausing, but it is balanced with simple imaginative effects presented in a natural sequence. Milton intends his style to sound, not spontaneous, but as though he were doing something out of the ordinary. It conveys ritualistic deliberation and solemnity. *Paradise Lost* suffers from a serious structural flaw--"the untransmuted lump of futurity" contained in Books 11-12 (129). The presentation of God is unsatisfactory because of its anthropomorphic details. See entries 116, 118, 609, 657, 661, 683.

507 LIEB, MICHAEL. *The Dialectics of Creation: Patterns of Birth and Regeneration in "Paradise Lost."* [Amherst]: University of Massachusetts Press, 1970, 263 pp.

A dialectical struggle between truth and falsehood, leading to a higher knowledge, characterizes Milton's view of argumentation in his prose works, but it applies--in a more nearly universal and sublime way --to *Paradise Lost*. God's creative power can create or uncreate, and Satan's frustration arises in part from imitating the latter. As a fallen man, the poet-prophet "must confront the uncreative aspects of the fall in order to create positively" (37). Milton's dialectical stance involves the resolution of creation and uncreation with recreation in heaven, when a return to the source occurs, things are reduced and brought into a union, and God shall be all in all. Satan's relationship to Sin and Death, as well as his temptation of Eve, is based on the concept and imagery of generation. Countering Satan's temporary success, the reunion and redemption of Adam and Eve are acts of creation. We fulfill *Paradise Lost*'s dialectical process with the completion of our lives.

Paradise Lost

508   LIEB, MICHAEL. "*Paradise Lost* and the Twentieth Century Reader." *Cithara* 9 (1969):27-42.

Not just scholarly and aesthetic, our appreciation of *Paradise Lost* also involves extraliterary elements because the poem states a moral imperative and urges us to action. Modern readers should extend themselves to see that *Paradise Lost*, written in an age as troubled as our own, shows the justice of the providential design and encourages hope. Besides allowing us to view the universal form of man's tragic fate, *Paradise Lost* is celebrative as it shows the comic or positive meaning in tragic events. As the triumphant Books 11 and 12 indicate, human suffering provides a purifying trial, which culminates in the Apocalypse. Although we may think that *Paradise Lost* says nothing to our age, it and Eliot's work preach discipline, the power of elemental forces, and charity.

509   LIEB, MICHAEL. *Poetics of the Holy: A Reading of "Paradise Lost."* Chapel Hill: University of North Carolina Press, 1981, 463 pp.

As a visionary poet of "the other," Milton writes *Paradise Lost* as a sacral document that manifests divine realities. The poet has a priestly role as a discloser of mysteries. Hierophanies, numinous visions, occur regularly in Milton's poems. When Adam and Eve eat the apple, they disobey God's prohibition, which involves violating a sacred thing and breaking prescribed boundaries that establish one's place in the creation. In *Paradise Lost*, the war in heaven is portrayed as a holy war. Accounts of English Civil War battles create "a holy war mythos that transforms history into vision and accords epic status to isolated events" (262). Milton believes that the Civil Wars are just, for they are undertaken to promote a righteous cause.

510   MacCAFFREY, ISABEL GAMBLE. "*Paradise Lost*" *as* "*Myth.*" Cambridge, Mass.: Harvard University Press, 1959, 235 pp. Part reprinted in *Paradise Lost*, ed. Scott Elledge (New York: W. W. Norton & Co., 1975), pp. 508-12.

In the Renaissance, all myths are seen as versions of the one true history, and Milton assumes a kind of literalness when he presents his myth in *Paradise Lost* to embody "the Christian pattern of human destiny" (26). Milton's poems often follow the circular pattern of loss (or fall), journey of life in death, and recovered paradise. The fall produces a retreat from truth and a movement into metaphoric language, and myth recovers truth and knowledge--or reality itself. The plan of *Paradise Lost* is spatial, with ascending or descending motion occurring against a static background and historic time radiating away from and back to the background. Milton's elevated diction works toward a single effect, while his descriptions combine physical and abstract or moral qualities. In *Paradise Lost*, imagery reinforces theme. Satan enacts the archetypal myth of exile, the dark voyage that prefigures fallen man's state.

511   McCANLES, MICHAEL. "*Paradise Lost* and the Dialectic of Providence." In *Dialectical Criticism and Renaissance Literature*. Berkeley, Los Angeles, and London: University of California Press, 1975, pp. 120-55.

By admitting that he cannot presumptuously make himself God, Milton acknowledges that the dialectic of *Paradise Lost* fails to mirror divine providence. Instead, the epic mediates the divine vision in a discursive movement through time. The mirroring of God, which results from the creation's separation from the creator, leads to two dialectical functions: idolatry, in which God is seen as a mirror of the creature, and worship, in which the creature reflects God. Bearing his share of the first couple's failures of reason, the narrator must deal with fallen language, which acts as a barrier to his understanding of the providential dialectic of human history. After the narrator's journey into hell in Books 1 and 2 of *Paradise Lost*, written in a parody of the epic style, he is inoculated against Satanic perversion of the journey and aware of the limitations of his language and vision, which then receive a renewed grace. In a dialectical movement, strength comes from weakness; moral self-recognition, the awareness of one's Satanic characteristics, can lead to repentance and the cessation of one's identity with Satan.

512   McCOLLEY, GRANT. "The Astronomy of *Paradise Lost*." *Studies in Philology* 34 (1937):209-47.

Although scholars often assume that in *Paradise Lost* Milton compares the Ptolemaic and Copernican theories, his era sees a multitude of astronomical hypotheses, along with the commonplace theory of the diurnal rotation of central earth (which appears in Book 8) and the theory of the plurality of worlds. During Milton's age, Copernicus's heliocentric theory receives credible support, though the

Poetry

Paradise Lost

antiquated description in *Paradise Lost* of earth's triple motion is in favor only before 1630. The epic ignores the important Tychonic or geo-heliocentric theory, even though it has a much stronger reputation than the Ptolemaic, because Milton is not interested in it or because he finds it insignificant. He shares his age's views on the doctrine of the plurality of worlds. Retaining a geocentric cosmos, Milton still accepts as much of the new astronomical thought as possible. See entries 6, 18, 212, 459, 476, 489, 521, 579, 728.

513 McCOLLEY, GRANT. "*Paradise Lost.*" *Harvard Theological Review* 32 (1939):181-235.
     Designed as a non-sectarian epic, *Paradise Lost* is modeled on a conservative tradition of hexameral literature. Milton includes a number of ideas that are not conventional in his age: the angels' existence before the creation of the world; God's revelation of the future Incarnation to the angels; and Christ's, rather than Michael's, battle in heaven against Satan. But Milton's descriptions of the war in heaven, the nature of spiritual beings, and the demonic council are all conventional. When he describes the temptation and fall in order to justify God's ways, Milton again follows tradition. Angels, such as Raphael and Michael in *Paradise Lost*, are traditionally the vehicles by which God conveys knowledge to man. Milton follows many of the commentaries on Genesis by making marriage a key theme and Satan the opponent of marriage in *Paradise Lost*. Because Milton's contemporaries are interested in amplified paraphrases of biblical history, they would not agree with modern readers who dislike Books 11 and 12.

514 McQUEEN, WILLIAM A. "Point of View in *Paradise Lost*: Books I-IV." *Renaissance Papers* (1967):85-92.
     After the opening invocation and argument, *Paradise Lost*'s point of view shifts for two books to the carefully limited and distorted view from hell mixed with the narrator's abstract and omniscient voice, which insists on a broader vision. In order to establish Satan as a formidable adversary, Milton uses point of view to let us hear only the devil's voice and opinions (the narrator is not a dramatized character). Satan describes himself as malevolent and his war career as almost successful. With Book 3, the focus on Satan shifts to the total perspective that God offers: all characters are visible, action stops, and

the Father comments on the whole poem. Not a dramatically successful character, God must appear so Satan does not become the epic's hero. The Father validates the narrator's statements in Books 1 and 2. Point of view gradually expands in *Paradise Lost*, becoming complete only in Book 12.

515 MARESCA, THOMAS E. "Milton: *Paradise Lost.*" In *Three English Epics: Studies of "Troilus and Criseyde," "The Faerie Queene," and "Paradise Lost."* Lincoln and London: University of Nebraska Press, 1979, pp. 75-142.

In our sense of the word "act," *Paradise Lost* begins with the first act or motion, a fall or differentiation from God that imitates all other acts we can comprehend. Satan and the rebels undergo a parody of the Neoplatonic descent, conversion (or illumination), and ascent, each based on supposed self-sufficiency. Adam and Eve begin life by ascending, and Milton uses the triple motion of the *descensus* primarily as an analogue to God. From its smallest unit to its largest patterns, *Paradise Lost* follows the *descensus* structure. Departing from this pattern, the Son in Raphael's narrative takes steps toward the time when God will be "All in All." With the fall, Adam and Eve illustrate the soul's descent into body and matter, and the world of epic--with its movement of exile, return, and restoration--begins at this moment.

516 MARTZ, LOUIS L. "*Paradise Lost*: The Journey of the Mind." In *The Paradise Within: Studies in Vaughan, Traherne, and Milton.* New Haven, Conn., and London: Yale University Press, 1964, pp. 103-67.

Paradise Lost's narrator emphasizes the theme of recovery and encourages us to read the poem as a journey to the soul. Extending the poem's geography, literary allusions and epic similes relate all the action to the fallen human world. The result is a double movement: while the narrator moves from hell to chaos, to heaven and then to earth in the first four books, the action simultaneously shifts toward the inward light that illuminates a paradise at the center of the poem and of the mind. *Paradise Lost* as a whole appears as a picture with a dark border but a bright center. The opening and closing books portray our world, in flames and ruins, but the center contains creativity. Adam in Book 11 learns the worst about the fallen world, yet the rainbow of God's covenant soon appears. Theologically successful, this pattern is a

Paradise Lost

poetic disaster because Michael's statements about grace are brief, cold, defensive, and abstract.

517 MERRILL, THOMAS F. "*Paradise Lost* and the Hazards of Semantic Idolatry." *Neuphilologische Mitteilungen* 77 (1976):387-410.
As a piece of distinctly religious expression, a holy thing, and a work of art, *Paradise Lost* is inaccessible to readers who do not understand the peculiarities of religious language. God, for example, is always accommodated and never predicated like a conventional noun. Semantic idolatry stalls religiously unattuned readers before they reach the revelation of mystery that the religious work is intended to evoke. In the meetings of Satan and Abdiel, and in the quarrel between Adam and Eve, Milton shows the confrontation between natural reason based on observable evidence and right reason based on God's decrees. Satan and Eve offer logical views, but Abdiel and Adam speak from the religious foundation of Christian liberty and the logic of obedience. Before her real fall, Eve undergoes a linguistic fall and relies on empiric objectivity.

518 MILLER, MILTON. "*Paradise Lost*: The Double Standard." *University of Toronto Quarterly* 20 (1951):183-199.
Although the idea of right reason permeates *Paradise Lost*, its signs are not as straightforward as they might be for readers whose right reason is unsure. By exalting false splendor in terms of the true, Milton creates a contrast by which hell and its residents appear even more false, while heaven and its residents receive greater glory. Readers may well have difficulty seeing this double contrast, for the loyal and rebel angels often perform the same kinds of actions. When Milton introduces characters, he differentiates them by applying standards of judgment that may be termed heroic. Despite Satan's exaltation, readers should use a broader standard--the super-heroic one, which calls for patience, martyrdom, and right reason--to see him as less admirable than the other demons. Especially in *Paradise Lost*'s described action, Milton does not send readers clear signals about when to apply the heroic or the super-heroic standard.

519   MINER, EARL. "Milton's Laws Divine and Human." In *The Restoration Mode from Milton to Dryden*. Princeton, N.J.: Princeton University Press, 1974, pp. 198-287.

Although the fall will prove fortunate only for the few who are saved, Milton and *Paradise Lost* redeem us as we grow closer to union with three elect characters--Adam, Eve, and the narrator. As Milton's spiritual journey takes him from the Calvinist Anglican church to the Presbyterians, and then from Independency to his own church of one, at each crisis he holds ideals that are betrayed by something central to the past. He needs to justify God's ways to man, especially to himself. With the failure of the prose epic of England, Milton defines England as something more than a nation and turns to God's, not just England's, history as he writes *Paradise Lost*. In his way of honoring the classical epic tradition by transforming it, Milton effectively destroys it. *Paradise Regained* conveys four related perspectives--Satan's, the Son's, the narrator's, and the reader's--which are ultimately reduced to two clear choices. Dominated by an air of uncertainty, the brief epic reveals that knowing is not essential, but faith is.

520   MINER, EARL. "The Reign of Narrative in *Paradise Lost*." *Milton Studies* 17 (1983):3-25.

Narrative, a literary resource of the fallen world as well as the appropriate genre for dealing with the fall, rules over *Paradise Lost*'s other main elements, the lyric and dramatic. Milton's epic contains as many narrators as characters, but they are not all equally reliable. By displacing and enlarging part of the classical prophecy in Books 11-12 and the descent to the underworld in Books 1-2, Milton renovates epic narrative. He creates a new narrative by poising the dramatic against the lyric in *Paradise Lost*.

521   NICOLSON, MARJORIE. "The Discovery of Space." *Medieval and Renaissance Studies* (1965):40-59.

Shakespeare, as Masson says, lives in a world of time, Milton in a universe of space. The new stars that appear in 1572 and 1604 are "a prelude to the change from a closed world to an infinite universe" (45). Combined with Giordano Bruno's philosophy, the work that Galileo publishes in 1610 changes astronomy and the literary imagination by making people aware of the vastness of the universe. These men discover space. With Galileo's announcement that the moon

Paradise Lost

is a world much like ours, authors write works featuring moon voyages. *Paradise Lost* contains many references to Galileo's discoveries, including the moon to which Milton compares Satan's shield and, in the creation scene, the sun, moon, Milky Way, and phases of Venus. We feel the vast sense of space throughout *Paradise Lost*, especially in its cosmic voyages. See entries 6, 18, 212, 459, 476, 489, 512, 579, 728.

522 NICOLSON, MARJORIE H. "Milton and Hobbes." *Studies in Philology* 23 (1926):405-33.

Hobbes's philosophy points to Renaissance naturalism based on man as he is, a selfish creature, and to political and ethical authoritarianism required by the arbitrary nature of morality. Many authors from 1650 to 1670 respond to Hobbes's materialism, atheism, and views on liberty and necessity. The most magnificent of these responses, *Paradise Lost* shows that Milton develops an ethical system based on Plato, Plotinus, and especially Renaissance Neoplatonism and cabbalism. To justify God's ways, Milton must refute Hobbes's ethics. In *Paradise Lost*, he thus argues that choice is not an act of the will, moved by instinct to pursue the individual's good; for him, instincts are not evil, but they should lead to a higher good than self-preservation and other egotistical goals. Reason occupies a higher place in Milton's ethics than in Hobbes's. Hobbes's ultimate good is the law of nature, but Milton believes in an eternal and immutable law of nature.

523 NORFORD, DON PARRY. "'My Other Half': The Coincidence of Opposites in *Paradise Lost*." *Modern Language Quarterly* 36 (1975):21-53.

The universe's harmony, according to Heraclitus, comes from a balance of opposites, whose separateness exists for man but not for God. A number of pairs of opposites--good and evil, spirit and matter, male and female--are central to *Paradise Lost* and to Milton's use of the Great Chain of Being. Adam and Eve's association with solar and lunar imagery suggests an analogy between their relationship and that of God and Satan. Furthermore, the sun is often linked to spirit and the moon to matter. If the number two belongs to the devil, female, and matter, the principle of division is also the source of creation. Evil appears to be inherent in creation. God's actions in *Paradise Lost* become clearer when we see that he is attempting to overcome the dark side of himself that he has projected into the created universe.

524 NYQUIST, MARY. "The Father's Word/Satan's Wrath." *PMLA* 100 (1985):187-202.

Although beginnings and endings often carry implications about each other in Milton's poems, *Paradise Lost* and *Paradise Regained* clearly begin with God's revelation of himself in his Word, which occurs at an assembly, initiates a new order, and incites Satan to rebellion, starting with his own counter-assembly. Under attack, the Logos is transformed by Satan into mythos or plot, a kind of death consciousness. When he transforms himself into the Word, Milton's God condemns himself to rule an order divided by an opponent who appropriates the Word only as a negative and alienating force. The temptations of Eve in *Paradise Lost* and the Son in *Paradise Regained* have affinities with the Reformation view of temptation as the trial of the Word: succumbing to temptation is a participation in the subversive interpretation of the Word, and resisting temptation is a defense of the Word with a refusal to participate in Satan's plots.

525 ONG, WALTER J., S.J. "Milton's Logical Epic and Evolving Consciousness." *Proceedings of the American Philosophical Society* 120 (1976):295-305.

Any example of Ramist logic, including Milton's *Art of Logic*, emphasizes method to prescribe the organization of the logic and of all thought. The old formulaic and heroic noetics gives way to abstract or logical analysis, which extends into *Paradise Lost* as a means of managing knowledge. Compared to Spenser's use of epithets, Milton's in *Paradise Lost* is sparse. And while epithets in the *Faerie Queene* fit into the oral tradition by requiring no literary knowledge, Milton uses anti-epithets, for they require a reader's full attention and a store of bookish knowledge. *Paradise Lost* thus illustrates a development in the conscious organization of knowledge through the epic and logic traditions. Consciousness usurps what had been, in the oral tradition, the territory of the unconscious. A rise in consciousness destroys the epic tradition.

526 PARKER, PATRICIA A. "Milton." In *Inescapable Romance: Studies in the Poetics of a Mode*. Princeton, N.J.: Princeton University Press, 1979, pp. 114-58.

Moments of suspension that lead to a turning appear frequently in *Paradise Lost*, and characters may go up toward dawn or

Paradise Lost

down into night. In the image of the "evening," the threshold state of time is united with the threshold of choice. As *Paradise Lost* moves from evening to morning, it progresses from shadowy types to truth. To remain in the realm of shadows or signs is to stay or stray. Milton's poetic line breaks down as we read it, and he creates invisible turning points in his syntax; both techniques make the ruin of error lead to truth. *Paradise Lost* participates in a tension associated with the uncertain middle realm of romance, where meaning and error exist, and the shadowy and ambiguous place of wandering becomes the instability of linguistic signs and the attraction of their variety. Because the crucial moment of decision in *Paradise Lost* is beyond language, Milton writes a narrative of graduated continuity and radical discontinuity. Though our minds crave resolutions, he provokes us with suspensions or moments of misprision.

527   PECHEUX, MOTHER MARY CHRISTOPHER, O.S.U. "The Second Adam and the Church in *Paradise Lost*." *ELH* 34 (1967):173-87.

   Paradise Lost contains a Holy Trinity, an unholy trinity (Satan, Sin, and Death), an earthly trinity (Eve, Adam, and the human race or Messiah), and an eschatological or anagogical trinity (the church or bride of Christ, the Savior, and the elect). This fourth trinity helps explain the artistic significance of the description of Eve's creation and helps justify the allegory of Sin and Death. Many parallels connect the four trinities in *Paradise Lost*.

528   PETER, JOHN. *A Critique of "Paradise Lost."* New York: Columbia University Press; London: Longmans, 1960, 181 pp.

   We tend to think of *Paradise Lost*'s God as the embodiment of perfect strength and majesty and of the loyal angels as paragons, even though some passages faintly qualify these notions. The problems with Milton's God are rooted in an imperfect anthropomorphic presentation, and readers are encouraged to have a divided response to him, disliking him but admiring the creative and redemptive acts of his Son. Milton handles Satan and the devils more adroitly, though sometimes these characters reveal contradictory appearances. Even if the devils' logic is incoherent, the narrator's intrusions do not square with the scenes they are meant to illuminate. Adam and Eve appeal to us because, though they are prototypes, they resemble us. But we do not know why they fall. God seems almost pleased by the fall as he distorts its facts and turns to the pleasant duty of judgment.

529 QUILLIGAN, MAUREEN. *Milton's Spenser: The Politics of Reading.* Ithaca, N.Y., and London: Cornell University Press, 1983, 249 pp.

Spenser and Milton are connected by a reader who sees reading as a protopolitical activity and by their attitude toward him or her, which is to reach the reader's will so he or she will act for the public good. In *Areopagitica*, Milton presents his rhetoric of reading, which is based on the reader's active knowing, abstaining, and choosing. If Spenser's language is self-conscious about its fallenness, Milton asks us to unpun words as he makes punning language work against itself. Milton, like Spenser, warns readers about poetry's power to mislead. He replaces a masculine stance of heroic defiance with a feminine posture of supplication. *Paradise Lost* handles sexuality in a fundamentally political way. Urania renders readers fit, but those who lack this inspiration are figured in the bacchic revelers. Milton gives Eve a mediator position, since her relationship to God must proceed through Adam. To be a fit reader of *Paradise Lost*, a female must accept a similar role in a hierarchy. Milton rewards such submission.

530 QUINT, DAVID. "Epilogue: From Origin to Originality." In *Origin and Originality in Renaissance Literature: Versions of the Source.* New Haven, Conn., and London: Yale University Press, 1983, pp. 207-20.

By invading the Edenic source, the fountain beside the tree of life, which is associated with the originary dispensation of the Word, Satan emblematically reenacts his first, paradigmatic sin: the denial of his secondary nature as a creature of God and his desire to be self-begot like God. By denying the linear concept of history and substituting a cyclical one, Satan hopes to refute all claims of authority based on originary dispensation. When Satan as author treats chaos as an autonomous system of signification, the result is a Babelic confusion. *Paradise Lost* uses revisionary strategies in an attempt to "correct" earlier texts, reveal a true narrative of sacred history, and recover original events. In a process that is analogous to but satirized in Satan's search for origin, Milton desacralizes the literary tradition and claims a unique authority for himself as author because of his poem's divine origin.

Paradise Lost

531 QVARNSTRÖM, GUNNAR. *The Enchanted Palace: Some Structural Aspects of "Paradise Lost*." Stockholm: Almqvist and Wiksell, 1967, 189 pp.

From the generation of Christ to Michael's revelation of man's future, the epic action of *Paradise Lost* stretches over thirty-three days. Milton presents careful symmetries: the creation of the sun, for example, occurs on day 17, at the chronological midpoint; the enthronement of Christ, in the 1667 edition of *Paradise Lost* (6.761-62), occurs in the epic's central line, for the same number of lines precede and follow it. *Paradise Lost* is based on a Christocentric structure. Many of its epic speeches are structured according to numerological principles. The time scheme in the direct action of *Paradise Lost*'s first edition divides into blocks: Books 1-4; 5-7; 8-9; and 10. This descending numerical organization from four books to three, two, and then one, inverts the Pythagorean *progressio quaternaria*, "thus pointing to nought and to the loss of Paradise" (143). When Milton divides *Paradise Lost* into twelve books, the numerological patterns remain, but in a less precisely defined way.

532 RAJAN, BALACHANDRA. *"Paradise Lost" and the Seventeenth Century Reader*. London: Chatto and Windus, 1947, 171 pp. Frequently reprinted; part reprinted in *Milton: "Paradise Lost," a Casebook*, ed. A. E. Dyson and Julian Lovelock (London and Basingstoke: Macmillan, 1973), pp. 106-21.

Milton writes *Paradise Lost*, not only for posterity, but for readers of his own age. Unlearned contemporaries can readily grasp the poem's essentials while being invited to learn about the various disciplines and cultures that lead to its creation. *Paradise Lost*, unlike *Christian Doctrine*, subordinates heretical ideas. Though almost three centuries of scholars find Books 11-12 dull and pessimistic, Michael does not think that his presentation displays these qualities. There is in Milton's age a general agreement that man's sinfulness does not dominate God's mercy but is balanced with it until, in a spirit of optimism, divine redemption and internal liberty are victorious. The weight of *Paradise Lost*'s poetry is thrown on the side of Satan, giving the dramatic illusion of equality between the contending forces of God and Satan. But this illusion is temporary; Satan is reduced in stature as the poem progresses. The style of *Paradise Lost* is not dramatic. It is clear, forceful, simple, and assertive. Sound and sense usually work together in Milton's verse. See entries 116, 657.

533   RAJAN, BALACHANDRA. *"Paradise Lost*: The Uncertain Epic." *Milton Studies* 17 (1983):105-19. Revised in *The Form of the Unfinished: English Poetics from Spenser to Pound* (Princeton, N.J.: Princeton University Press, 1985), pp. 104-27.

According to the two-poem theory of *Paradise Lost*, there is another poem, beyond the official one, in which we find Milton's real accomplishment: the creation of a Satanic hero. If we reverse this view, the true poem (an epic) and the other poem (a tragedy) confront each other as icon and idol or as reality and parody. *Paradise Lost* is a mixed-genre poem with a different protagonist for each of its main genres. Originating as a tragic drama, Milton's epic carries a tragic weight that the twelve-book version corrects somewhat by emphasizing creative forces, Christ, and Adam and Eve's repentance. The two structures, two genres, and at least two heroes of *Paradise Lost* point not to artistic confusion but to the valuable conflict and uncertainty that we observe in the relationship among the providential epic, the human pastoral, and the demonic and fallen human tragedy.

534   RANSOM, JOHN CROWE. *God without Thunder: An Unorthodox Defense of Orthodoxy.* New York: Harcourt Brace, 1930, pp. 127-45. Reprint. Hamden, Conn.: Archon Books, 1965.

To prevent the Edenic life in *Paradise Lost* from seeming empty, Milton complicates it. Adam and Eve fall by adopting a secular attitude, viewing nature passively rather than romantically, and having too much belief in the powers of human science. Milton's portrait of Satan makes use of the myth of Prometheus, whose gift of fire (science) would make mortals independent of the despotic Zeus; but this story of the conflict between science and religion ends with the punishment of Prometheus for encouraging the folly of secularism and science, which cannot fulfill their promises. Milton sees that the new science or enlightenment of his age is just the old Prometheus or Satan. In *Paradise Lost*, sensuality is the false benefit of applying science too hard. If Satan is the half-god who aspires to be God, Christ in *Paradise Regained* is the Son who does not wish to take his Father's seat. Milton's Christ is man reaching his highest potential and refusing to secularize himself.

535   ROBSON, W. W. *"Paradise Lost*: Changing Interpretations and Controversy." In *From Donne to Marvell.* Rev. ed., ed. Boris Ford.

Paradise Lost

New Pelican Guide to English Literature, vol. 3. Harmondsworth: Penguin Books, 1982, pp. 239-59.

As a poet, Milton makes a very small impression during his lifetime, and his long poems receive attention only after his death. His poetic fame is always connected to his political stance of defender of English liberty. *Paradise Lost* gains a strong reputation at the end of his century because of Dryden's attitude toward it, the contemporary emphasis on works of literature, and a longing for a Christian epic. But uncertainties emerge, and they become dominant in the twentieth century. While Dr. Johnson sees orthodoxy in *Paradise Lost*, some Romantic poets appreciate a subversive Milton. The Victorians do not find Milton interesting because, they say, he paraphrases orthodox commonplaces and has an unpleasant personality. The twentieth century resumes Johnson's dislike of Milton's personality and the Romantic interest in his heterodox views. In our century, scholars study Milton's thought, milieu, and sources, but they render ambiguous his presence as a human force and great poet.

536 ROLLIN, ROGER B. *"Paradise Lost*: 'Tragical-Comical-Historical-Pastoral.'" *Milton Studies* 5 (1973):3-37.

An "encyclopedic drama-epic" (4), *Paradise Lost* is most successful when it adheres to three of the generic forms of drama: tragedy (Satan's drama), tragicomedy (Adam and Eve's pastoral drama), and history (the Son's drama). Each genre in *Paradise Lost* has a plot and hero of its own, yet the narrator's role remains consistent throughout. Like a stage manager, he provides exposition, establishes moods, and gives moral explications of events in the poem. He thus resembles the prologues, choruses, and epilogues of Renaissance drama. His plot is concerned with the victory of writing an epic poem; he is that plot's hero.

537 ROSTON, MURRAY. *Milton and the Baroque*. London: Macmillan; Pittsburgh, Pa.: University of Pittsburgh Press, 1980, 201 pp. 12 illustrations.

Paradise Lost uses the baroque because of its new vision of the cosmos and of the Christian's place in it. Just as baroque cathedrals open up to the infinite vastness of the universe, so *Paradise Lost* requires a vast cosmos as its setting, which requires Milton to transcend the epic's traditional limits. A baroque artist is intrigued by the physical forces in the universe and attempts to convey them visually as they meet in combat; to demonstrate the victor's strength, he wins by a narrow margin over an otherwise invincible opponent. Thus Milton establishes Satan's immensity and vigor in *Paradise Lost*'s early books so we can later appreciate the magnitude of God's victory. Milton writes *Paradise Lost* in a variety of styles, the baroque in its most typical form appearing in the first six books when the subject involves force, vastness, or great energy. See entries 138, 147, 178, 206.

538   RUMRICH, JOHN PETER. *Matter of Glory: A New Preface to "Paradise Lost."* Pittsburgh, Pa.: University of Pittsburgh Press, 1987, 220 pp.

Before matter is created, it is chaos; after its creation, if it reaches the final cause, it is glory. Milton's idea of glory is based on the Hebrew word *kabod*, which is associated with the idea of weight and means both great reputation and a substantial entity's very being. For the Greeks, glory as a potency is *areté*, *kleos* when accomplished. Glory and death are opposites and terms that mutually define each other. In the New Testament, *kabod* is translated *doxa* (or opinion), substituting the subjective human view for the objective fact of glory or very being of God. For the Romans, glory is conferred according to community values and applies to few people. Revising the idea of glory, Milton synthesizes *kabod* and Homeric glory. The creature can be transformed, as are Adam and Eve before the fall, through love and proper nutrition to reach the glory of apocalyptic harmony; hate and malnutrition lead to shame and death, the fate of the rebel angels.

539   RYKEN, LELAND. *The Apocalyptic Vision in "Paradise Lost."* Ithaca, N.Y., and London: Cornell University Press, 1970, 250 pp.

For Milton, the theory of accommodation is the foundation for *Paradise Lost*'s presentation of the apocalyptic vision, which contains physical and human details (thus reflecting his humanism) even as it describes a realm located above the earthly. To describe his apocalyptic vision, Milton uses contrasts involving time and quality; adjectives denoting apocalyptic qualities linked with empirical nouns; diction having unfallen meanings but also, through our experience, negative associations; oxymorons; and the theological tradition of negation. In *Paradise Lost*, analogies show the similarities and differences between earthly life and the apocalyptic vision. Through a number of techniques,

Paradise Lost

including the use of internal narrators, Milton maintains apocalyptic distancing (both spatial and temporal) throughout *Paradise Lost*. His apocalyptic imagery depends on three techniques: the frequent use of conceptual rather than visual imagery, generic terms instead of specific images, and sensory nonvisual images.

540 SAMUEL, IRENE. "Milton on Learning and Wisdom." *PMLA* 64 (1949):708-23.

In *Paradise Lost* and *Paradise Regained*, statements about learning expand Milton's views on the place of studies in one's life. Raphael, speaking at a critical moment, appropriately tells Adam to be pragmatic about knowledge; Michael's goal is to prepare Adam to leave Eden, so the angel discusses the value of moral habit; Christ in *Paradise Regained* rejects learning and other things as good in themselves, for the human spirit does not need certain books to gain knowledge of the good life. These characters' views are consistent with *Of Education* and Milton's theory of learning throughout his life: learning should be useful, one must integrate it as a way of life, and theology and ethics are the first and last branches of learning. For Milton, learning can lead to wisdom, but they are not synonymous.

541 SAMUEL, IRENE. "*Paradise Lost*." In *Critical Approaches to Six Major English Works: "Beowulf" through "Paradise Lost*." Edited by R. M. Lumiansky and Herschel Baker. Philadelphia: University of Pennsylvania Press, 1968, pp. 209-53.

Since about 1942, commentaries on *Paradise Lost* multiply uncertainties about its subject, genre, and structure. Studying *Paradise Lost*'s style, critics often use their ideas about the poem's purpose to determine what stylistic elements they perceive. Attention shifts from the epic's main action to its central patterns, which critics see as tragic, comic, or mixed. Emphasizing the theological nature of *Paradise Lost*, commentators discuss the poem's orthodoxy or heterodoxy and focus on the center and final books. Other scholars emphasize *Paradise Lost* as *paideia* and show its movement toward renewal and a new dispensation.

Paradise Lost is a tragic epic designed as a *paideia*. The epic's central thesis is that man has free choice, and choices have consequences. Though commentators do not often notice, the poem has much to say not just about grace but also about gracefulness, not just about the desire for salvation but also about the desire for beauty. Milton's epic contains a humanizing richness.

542   SENSABAUGH, G. F. "Milton on Learning." *Studies in Philology* 43 (1946):258-72.

Milton's cries for free inquiry in *Areopagitica* and *Of Education* cannot be reconciled with Raphael's speech in *Paradise Lost* or Christ's speech in *Paradise Regained,* which both argue for limits on knowledge. Milton is disillusioned. With the failure of the revolution, he changes his mind about his aspirations for the individual and society. *Christian Doctrine* may hold the key to Milton's change in attitude, for it implies that the individual gains salvation through Scripture alone. His earlier prose works are dominated by a secular, humanist approach to knowledge; later, in the major poems, he turns to Christianity's major tenets.

543   SHAWCROSS, JOHN T. *With Mortal Voice: The Creation of "Paradise Lost."* Lexington: University Press of Kentucky, 1982, 208 pp.

Milton writes *Paradise Lost* in his role as God's minister emulating the creation. But the epic is a joint creation of God and man, with sexual imagery surrounding their relationship: God and the Spirit appear as male forces impregnating a receptive poet. The poem has two symmetrical climaxes, a Satanic one (the fall of man) and a divine one (God's assertion of redemption, through Christ, for man in Book 3), which are transcended by a third (the Son's ascent, in Book 6, to defeat Satan). The epic's theme is love. Satan functions as the prototype antihero who seeks to change the world, the Son is the prototype hero, and Adam and Eve act as "the protagonist in the drama of life" (35). *Paradise Lost*'s hero may be the reader. The epic is a comedy because it rebukes vice, especially as displayed by ordinary people; shows the driving out of evil in a universe whose order insists on perfection; follows the process of temptation, sin, and redemption. Not written in a single style, *Paradise Lost* covers a range of styles as decorum requires.

544   SHULLENBERGER, WILLIAM. "Wrestling with the Angel: *Paradise Lost* and Feminist Criticism." *Milton Quarterly* 20 (1986):69-85.

Paradise Lost

Paradise Lost's promise of authority and identity is not bound by gender, though feminist critics assume that a woman's proper response is to be a resisting reader. Feminist criticism may do just what it accuses Milton of doing: cutting women readers off "from the 'spaciousness of possibility' afforded by the poet" (70). An author who supports a patriarchal view is not necessarily a misogynist. *Paradise Lost*'s subtext encourages a feminist reading. In the process of criticizing its own values, Milton's epic raises feminist questions and responds to them. God recognizes that his patriarchy is anomalous, so he is willing to surrender power; Eve acts in a creative capacity as the archetypal woman poet; Satan rejects patriarchy and substitutes a narcissistic supposed heroism. In Adam's diatribe after the fall, Milton criticizes antifeminist thinking.

545 SHUMAKER, WAYNE. *Unpremeditated Verse: Feeling and Perception in "Paradise Lost."* Princeton, N.J.: Princeton University Press, 1967, 241 pp.

As myth, *Paradise Lost* records divine events that shaped the world and the human situation. It is "an enormous 'tell-me-why' story" (6) whose ability to explain at the level of myth precedes explanation at the level of rationalization. The weightiness and good sense of *Paradise Lost* appeal to our intellect, which helps our subconscious minds take the myth seriously. Milton's narrative has problems, chiefly in the transition from innocence to sin: no myth stands up well to searching scrutiny. His descriptions sometimes describe very little and instead present attitudinal qualities. Precise visual images fill in the foregrounds in *Paradise Lost*, while general ones sketch in the backgrounds. Books 11 and 12 require brevity, forcing Milton to neglect visual development. When Michael instructs Adam, the affective content of the poem illustrates the angel's confident authority and the human's submissiveness.

546 STAPLETON, LAURENCE. "Perspectives of Time in *Paradise Lost.*" *Philological Quarterly* 45 (1966):734-48.

While acknowledging the Aristotelian definition of time as the measure of motion, *Paradise Lost* defines time in heaven as the measure of durable things by the sequence in which they occur. Some episodes, such as the war in heaven followed by the fall of the rebels, receive a clear chronology, which gives them realism, but other events, such as the creation and God's statement that he will create another world, occur at unspecified times. Universal matters, especially those implying the spread of good or evil, or those that contain the theme of turning evil to good, include time rather than being included in time. Raphael's visit brings Adam to view the unknown past from the perspective of the present that it generated. Not only are the fall and its consequences related in a careful chronology, but Adam and Eve's consciousness of time is essential to the narrative. Michael's narrative extends the time of *Paradise Lost* into the future while uniting immediate and cosmic time.

547 STEADMAN, JOHN M. *Epic and Tragic Structure in "Paradise Lost."* Chicago, Ill., and London: University of Chicago Press, 1976, 200 pp.

The principal action of *Paradise Lost, Paradise Regained,* and *Samson Agonistes* is based on sacred history; the poet's craft deals with structuring events and the interaction of thought, character, and action. Because Milton replaces physical combat and the use of arms with spiritual battles and moral crises, the isolated protagonist's dianoia (thought) and ethos (character) are central to mythos (plot). Not caused by fate, the hero's apparent change of fortune (peripeteia) is governed by providence through divine laws or voluntary, human actions. Milton retains the classical epic's form and motifs, but replaces its values with those of the Judeo-Christian tradition. *Paradise Lost's* argument, protagonist, and emotional effects display the "tragic illustrious" as conceived by Aristotelian poetic theory. Some Renaissance critics argue that a rapid peripeteia in a single location, such as Adam and Eve's fall in one morning in paradise, more effectively arouses passion and admiration. Comprehending good and evil agents and resulting in justice, Milton's plot mirrors God's design; plot becomes the vehicle of a logical argument.

548 STEADMAN, JOHN M. *The Wall of Paradise: Essays on Milton's Poetics.* Baton Rouge and London: Louisiana State University Press, 1985, 163 pp.

Milton's views about the art of poetry are shaped by the rhetorical needs of the context. An instrument of moral education, eloquence must be subordinated to religious ends. Milton follows the concept of "ideal" imitation, delineating abstract concepts "in and

Paradise Lost

through sensuous forms that have themselves been abstracted from nature and idealized by art" (23). His three major poems focus on kingdoms that turn away from justice and the worship of God, but in *Paradise Lost* this becomes an emphasis on mankind's fall through Adam's fall. *Samson Agonistes* shows the individual on a divinely appointed mission. Milton's discussion of tragic purgation in *Samson Agonistes*'s Preface conflates Aristotle's definition of tragedy with the views on catharsis in the *Politics*. In *Samson Agonistes*, internal and external causes are interwoven and, when they come together in the catastrophe, reveal the logic of a providential design, which appears probable or necessary in retrospect.

549   STEIN, ARNOLD. *Answerable Style: Essays on "Paradise Lost."* Minneapolis: University of Minnesota Press, 1953, 175 pp. Reprinted (Seattle and London: University of Washington Press, 1967); part reprinted in *Milton: Modern Essays in Criticism*, ed. Arthur E. Barker (London, Oxford, and New York: Oxford University Press, 1965), pp. 264-83; part reprinted in *Milton: A Collection of Critical Essays*, ed. Louis L. Martz (Englewood Cliffs, N.J.: Prentice-Hall, 1966), pp. 148-55; part reprinted in *Milton's Epic Poetry: Essays on "Paradise Lost" and "Paradise Regained,"* ed. C. A. Patrides (Harmondsworth: Penguin Books, 1967), pp. 92-120.

Neither a tragic hero nor an absurd villain, Satan expresses his pride chiefly in his role as leader. His loyalty is directed only toward his inferiors, for like most leaders he depends on their dependence. Part of Satan's penalty is a self-punishment, while much of it is the realization of his own failure. Like Adam and Eve after the fall, Satan reasons from a special position--self. The action of the war in heaven exists not for its literal, independent meaning, but as part of a complex metaphor. Ridicule, an important attitude of both sides in the conflict, approaches epic farce in the war and appears in psychological, verbal, and intellectual forms. Both "carefully elevated and sensitively graduated" (129-30), Milton's diction is often familiar and simple yet not natural. The ornate style of a Mammon or a Satan is not representative of the epic; rather, it is a style from which Milton can easily descend for most of *Paradise Lost*. To see the sound of Milton's verse echo its sense is not to see much. In *Paradise Lost*, the structure of sound shapes the image. The "very exacting exactness" of his complexity creates "the true clarity" (154).

550 STEVENS, PAUL. "Milton and the Icastic Imagination." *Milton Studies* 20 (1984):43-73. Reprinted in *Imagination and the Presence of Shakespeare in "Paradise Lost"* (Madison and London: University of Wisconsin Press, 1985), pp. 46-79.

Milton is suspicious only of that kind of poetry that merely lulls the sense; otherwise, imagination for Milton is a God-given means to lead to knowledge of the deity. One must use images to gain such knowledge. Produced by the fancy, icastic poetry creates, procreates, or reflects the good. This poetry, at its highest potential, moves prophecy. In Book 8 of *Paradise Lost*, Adam learns about the limits of knowledge, mainly knowledge based on speculative reason. Revelation must aid reason. Knowledge before the fall arrives through images that are duplicates of reality; revelation works through the imagination to enter intuitive reason. This process applies to Adam's dream and to the icastic imagination in prophecy and poetry. The icastic imagination is thus the ground of faith.

551 STOLL, ELMER EDGAR. "Milton Classical and Romantic." *Philological Quarterly* 23 (1944):222-47.

Anticipating the Romantics, Milton presents enchanting views by distancing them with mythology, superstition, and vague description. Milton's Satan owes something to the classical tradition, but the romantic view dominates in the extremes used to portray the devil-- elevation and degradation, good and evil, tenderness and cruelty. Though he is no romantic, Milton shares with the Romantics the classical spirit and an interest in rebellion.

552 STOLL, ELMER EDGAR. "Milton, Puritan of the Seventeenth Century." In *Poets and Playwrights: Shakespeare, Jonson, Spenser, Milton*. Minneapolis: University of Minnesota Press, 1930, pp. 241-95. Frequently reprinted.

Because modern readers see themselves as humanists, they prefer to count Milton as one of their number, even if this means transforming him into a sixteenth- or twentieth-century man. He is instead a Puritan and a great poet-prophet. Unlike the humanist, Milton is somewhat melancholic, wary of pleasure, and firm in his faith. But he is not a complacent bore. A Puritan document composed in a range of tones and styles, *Paradise Lost* is nearly drama; as such, the weak and sinful (devils and woman) are the most fully realized

Paradise Lost

characters because they belong to our world. Insubordination and self-confidence cause Eve to fall. Milton's style emphasizes the vast, vague, and remote. His work is mysterious, with a picturesque and romantic aspect.

553 SUMMERS, JOSEPH H. *The Muse's Method: An Introduction to "Paradise Lost."* Cambridge, Mass.: Harvard University Press; London: Chatto and Windus, 1962, 227 pp. Reprinted (Binghamton, N.Y.: Center for Medieval and Early Renaissance Texts, 1981); part reprinted in *Milton: A Collection of Critical Essays*, ed. Louis L. Martz (Englewood Cliffs, N.J.: Prentice-Hall, 1966), pp. 183-206; part reprinted in *Milton's Epic Poetry: Essays on "Paradise Lost" and "Paradise Regained,"* ed. C. A. Patrides (Harmondsworth: Penguin Books, 1967), pp. 179-214.

The style of *Paradise Lost* differs from the norm of English less than do its subject, intent, and scope. Creative life in heaven and fulfilled life in Eden imply fruitful motion. Satan imagines a static order, violated only by his aspirations; motion in hell is a destructive parody of divine and Edenic motion. In the original version of *Paradise Lost* (1667), Abdiel occupies the center; at the middle of the twelve-book version are the war in heaven and the creation. These events serve the dramatic function of warning Adam about danger and advising him of his "happy state" and shift the epic's focus away from human experience, actions, and participants, while repeating the epic's motif of falling and rising. Books 11 and 12 do not emphasize human happiness without horror because Milton insists that readers accept life. *Paradise Lost* is constructed upon a few themes: love, creation, battle, fall, and praise, each implying its opposite. The poem traces the patterned relationship of God and man throughout time and eternity.

554 TESKEY, GORDON. "From Allegory to Dialectic: Imagining Error in Spenser and Milton." *PMLA* 101 (1986):9-23.

Because he separates error from truth and thus acts as an interpreter and relater, Spenser is Milton's original. Milton represents error dialectically, as the willful negation of good, but Spenser's diagetic view of error allows for moral complexity. Characters in *Paradise Lost* are free to choose their own story or not to engage in the story's action. Allegory denies that we can state truth in a positive way, so Milton rejects it and creates a boundary region to draw error out of his narrative.

555   THOMPSON, ELBERT N. S. "The Theme of *Paradise Lost*." *PMLA* 28 (1913):106-20.

The theme of *Paradise Lost* is that man, with his great potential for good, is able to transform each virtue into a corresponding vice; he determines his own destiny. If *Christian Doctrine* interprets the Bible literally, *Paradise Lost* presents such episodes as the creation, rebellion in heaven, and fall of man as symbols of moral truth. Good in Milton's epic is self-creative, ever growing; evil is destructive, self-annihilating. Symbolizing the many stages of sin, Satan is neither heroic nor a martyr for liberty. In the heavenly realm, Christ is the hero; on earth, Adam repents and emerges victorious with Christ. *Paradise Regained* presents *Paradise Lost*'s fundamental thought in a more concrete form.

556   TILLYARD, E. M. W. "Milton." In *The English Epic and Its Background*. New York: Oxford University Press, 1954, pp. 430-47. Reprint. 1966.

Ignoring the contemporary cultural shift from Italy to France, Milton embraces the older kind of neoclassicism and Italian epic theory. He accepts the Tudor myth, but--after the Civil Wars--he gives his patriotism a contemporary turn: *Paradise Lost* celebrates not the nation's destiny but the establishment of a community of saints on earth. Milton's subject of Adam, Eve, and the fall is medieval, with Renaissance and classical elements carefully selected for inclusion. His choice of blank verse is radical, even defiant, as is the move to domesticate the poem's crisis. The epic's real climax occurs after the fall, in the reconciliation and regeneration of Adam and Eve. *Paradise Regained* has no place in the epic tradition.

557   ULREICH, JOHN C., Jr. "Milton on the Eucharist: Some Second Thoughts about Sacramentalism." In *Milton and the Middle Ages*. Edited by John Mulryan. Lewisburg, Pa.: Bucknell University Press; London and Toronto: Associated University Presses, 1982, pp. 32-56.

Concerning sacramentalism, the notion that a physical act may be a vehicle of grace or that the spirit may be made flesh, Milton is not

Paradise Lost

as antipathetic as critics have believed. Nor does he completely accept it. The iconoclastic view expressed in *Christian Doctrine* opposes sacramentalism, while the iconic poetry of *Paradise Lost* offers a compromise by linking spirit and matter through consubstantiality. In *Paradise Lost*, as Raphael explains, human nature is sacramental as material and spiritual growth are joined. The word "transubstantiate" (*Paradise Lost*, 5.438) secularizes one of the sacred mysteries of the mass, exalts the digestive process into a sacramental act, and endorses the idea of the participation of body in spirit. Milton believes in a figurative meaning of the sacramental experience, in which spirit is implied or shadowed but not contained or manifested. Only the mind, will, and imagination participate in the sacrament. For Milton, the sacraments express imaginative energy.

558 WALDOCK, A. J. A. *"Paradise Lost" and Its Critics*. Cambridge: Cambridge University Press, 1947, 156 pp. Frequently reprinted; part reprinted in *Milton: A Collection of Critical Essays*, ed. Louis L. Martz (Englewood Cliffs, N.J.: Prentice-Hall, 1966), pp. 77-99; part reprinted in *Milton's Epic Poetry: Essays on "Paradise Lost" and "Paradise Regained,"* ed. C. A. Patrides (Harmondsworth: Penguin Books, 1967), pp. 74-91.

By ignoring Milton's statement that *Paradise Lost* is about man's first disobedience and the fall, and by asking instead about "the real theme," twentieth-century scholars subordinate the poem's primary concerns and stress lesser themes. The subject Milton chooses, the original state of featureless happiness, runs contrary to his belief in testing virtue to prove it strong. Because it denies him the chance to express his deepest concerns, Milton's central theme never profoundly interests him. His deepest concerns do appear in *Paradise Lost*, but often in inappropriate places. Milton is unaware of the discrepancy between authorial pronouncement and narrative action. He uses literary cheating when he deals with Satan, whom he seeks to make interesting and whose rebellion must appear credible. But Milton repeatedly puts glorious speeches in Satan's mouth, only to step in and neutralize or damper them with an authorial comment. We should grant more authority to the poem's actions and the characters' speeches, which reveal the poet's true intentions, rather than to Milton's interruptions. See entries 110, 116, 657.

559 WEBBER, JOAN MALORY. "The Politics of Poetry: Feminism and *Paradise Lost.*" *Milton Studies* 14 (1980):3-24.

Milton generally prepares the way for feminist thinking when he defines the direction in which humanity must move. Although *Paradise Lost* appears superficially as a conservative work, Milton overturns the traditions of the biblical epic's form and content. His epic presents something very different from simple patriarchal rule, for God, handing power to his Son, is in the process "toward full realization of the higher state imagined in the images of light" (9). When Milton describes heavenly reproduction and creativity, he does not allow the sexes to fall into contraries. The epic tradition links men with process (seeking and fighting, for example) and women with goals (deceiving and inspiring). Eve, officially Adam's inferior, is a strong, human woman who enacts both epic functions with her roles in falling and repenting. Marriage is *Paradise Lost*'s main theme and subject, and Milton shows that Adam and Eve must balance self-sufficiency and mutual need. Adam and Eve's harmony based on disjunction is the principle at the center of the creative process, whose goal is unity (when "God shall be all in all").

560 WHITING, GEORGE WESLEY. *Milton and This Pendant World.* Austin: University of Texas Press, 1958, 279 pp. 2 illustrations.

The stairs in Book 3 of *Paradise Lost* illustrate the traditional principle that one must go up to reach one's goal, God. Milton describes a spiritual ladder leading to salvation. While he cites the Authorized Version of the Bible in his prose, the epic's interpretation of Scripture frequently coincides with the Geneva Bible's commentary. Both Milton's epic and this Bible commentary are Protestant in their conception of divine power and grace, the creation, man, Satan, the devils, the fall, and redemption. The survey of history in Books 11-12 of *Paradise Lost* follows the conventional structure outlined by commentators on the Bible's time scheme. *Samson Agonistes* is clearly Hebraic in spirit or tone, and--because it emphasizes dynamic individual action--Protestant or Puritan in character. Some of the ideas in the Geneva Bible's commentary on Samson appear in Milton's drama. In form, *Samson Agonistes* is Greek, except for the choruses, which blend Greek and Italian styles.

Paradise Lost

561 WIDMER, KINGSLEY. "The Iconography of Renunciation: The Miltonic Simile." *ELH* 25 (1958):258-69. Reprinted in *Milton's Epic Poetry: Essays on "Paradise Lost" and "Paradise Regained,"* ed. C. A. Patrides (Harmondsworth: Penguin Books, 1967), pp. 121-31; *Critical Essays on Milton from "ELH"* (Baltimore, Md., and London: Johns Hopkins Press, 1969), pp. 75-86.

In *Paradise Lost* and *Paradise Regained*, Milton uses the disparate simile--comparing pagan things with Christian or small things with great--to show obvious similarities and, especially, ironic differences. Many of the similes indicate that Satan is a multiplicity, not a person; he reflects the transitory values that are worshiped in life but not in heaven. Milton inverts the mythology of regeneration into one of renunciation.

562 WILDING, MICHAEL. *Milton's "Paradise Lost."* Sydney, Australia: Sydney University Press, 1969, 128 pp.

Contrasts and comparisons, not events that we already know from the Bible, create *Paradise Lost*'s narrative principle. Everything about Satan that is traditionally heroic is also corrupt, an ambiguity that implies that the two are inseparable. A liar and a deceiver, Satan comes to believe his own lies and deceits. By presumptuously attempting to imitate heaven, the devils reveal their need to regain it and their distance from it. Images of light and order (or hierarchy) show that Milton's God is omnipotent and omniscient; Satan has a dualistic view of the cosmos. Milton's God seems touchy, egotistic, and legalistic; the Son, gentle and selfless; the Holy Spirit, almost absent. The war in heaven is intentionally ridiculous and morally confusing. Both rich and simple, paradise contains elements that foreshadow the fall. Before the fall, Adam and Eve have emotional states--his passion, her potential vanity--that can lead to sin, but they remain innocent.

563 WILKENFELD, ROGER B. "Theoretics or Polemics? Milton Criticism and the 'Dramatic Axiom.'" *PMLA* 82 (1967):505-15.

Milton criticism analyzes his long poems in the light of one axiom: "*Milton was not a dramatist and his poems are not dramatic*" (505). By starting with the assumption that in *Paradise Lost* he is writing a drama rather than an epic, critics have no difficulty concluding that it is undramatic when Satan is offstage. A few critics find everything Milton writes dramatic, but most agree that *Comus* has no real dramatic range, though some hold the masque form more responsible than the author for this liability. Generally uniform, criticism of *Paradise Regained* argues that the brief epic is undramatic, though critics rarely articulate their criteria for reaching this conclusion. In critical works about Milton's long poems, "dramatic" usually means nothing--and will continue to mean nothing until critics distinguish between the modal and vocal definitions of the dramatic.

564   WILKES, G. A. *The Thesis of "Paradise Lost."* Parkville, Australia: Melbourne University Press; London and New York: Cambridge University Press, 1961, 42 pp.

We must examine *Paradise Lost* itself, rather than the author's intentions or his original audience's preconceptions, to determine whether it does what it promises--to justify the ways of God to men. Furthermore, we must take Milton's whole scheme into account and not focus exclusively on certain characters or episodes. Not just a poem about the fall and obedience, *Paradise Lost* deals with the operation of providence through the celestial cycle, from the war in heaven to the final judgment. Satan, despite the evil that we see in him, has our admiration as well as our disapproval of the policies he promotes. However admirable the attributes of omniscience and omnipotence may be, they are awkward, as Milton's God shows, when translated to literary terms. Though the official view of Adam's fall states that female charm is responsible, *Paradise Lost* does not support this. He falls because of selflessness in love, so we cannot condemn him.

565   WITTREICH, JOSEPH. *Feminist Milton*. Ithaca, N.Y., and London: Cornell University Press, 1987, 196 pp.

According to the female perspective from 1700 to 1830, *Paradise Lost* seeks to dethrone authority and form new gender paradigms. Milton is the women's ally as they rise up against the patriarchal tradition of Scripture. Modern criticism, feminist and otherwise, that finds misogyny in him and his poem repeats a male-dominated, establishmentarian phase of the critical tradition. The female readership of this period approaches Milton's work with the methods that we call deconstructionism and new historicism. During the eighteenth century, *Paradise Lost* is gradually opened to a female readership that alters the premises and ideology of Milton criticism by seeing the link between his prose and poetry, and looking suspiciously

Paradise Lost

at *Paradise Lost*, the narrator, and scriptural allusions. Unlike others, early female readers see that in Books 11 and 12 *Paradise Lost* shifts from the oppression to the power and agency of women. *Samson Agonistes* records a misogynistic phase of human consciousness that *Paradise Regained* revises.

566 WOODHOUSE, A. S. P. "Pattern in *Paradise Lost*." *University of Toronto Quarterly* 22 (1953):109-27. Reprinted in *The Heavenly Muse: A Preface to Milton*, ed. Hugh MacCallum, University of Toronto Department of English Studies and Texts, no. 21 (Toronto and Buffalo, N.Y.: University of Toronto Press, 1972), pp. 176-207.

In *Paradise Lost*, Milton develops themes through rhetorical patterns and image patterns, the latter appearing when he distinguishes spiritual light from the inferior physical light. The classical view recognizes only the order of nature and the natural virtues, but the Christian view adds the intersecting order of grace and the heroic virtues of love, piety, and humility. When the Christian view includes tragedy, it does so only in the larger perspective of a divine comedy. By moving toward a significant end with a providential purpose and by using a structural pattern, *Paradise Lost* builds on the *Aeneid* rather than the *Iliad*. The broad structural pattern of *Paradise Lost* places the human subject in between the past and future: Christ defeats Satan in heaven; Satan conquers Adam on earth; and then Christ the second Adam defeats Satan. Adam is *Paradise Lost*'s human protagonist, Christ its divine protagonist. Satan asserts classical heroism and tries to deny the validity of Christian heroism.

567 WRIGHT, B. A. *Milton's "Paradise Lost."* London: Methuen; New York: Barnes and Noble, 1962, 210 pp.

Paradise Lost presents an orthodox view of life and of Christian theology. Although Milton succeeds in portraying God indirectly, he fails by making God argue and justify himself rather than simply pronounce. Readers must see that Satan is "a towering genius" (53), but we must always remember that his genius is Satanic. Unlike most people of his age, Milton credits women with being capable of providing emotional and intellectual companionship in marriage. His style is original yet plain, based on the educated speech of his day. Not consistently grand, this style changes levels to suit the subject matter and mood. The fall is preceded by a narrative sequence that leads directly to the crisis. Although Books 11 and 12 show Milton in command of his epic style, he does not--and cannot--bring their subject within the action of *Paradise Lost*.

For analogues, see entry 577; for *Paradise Lost*'s relation to *Paradise Regained*, see entries 232, 524, 555, 803, 815-16, 843, 871, 890, 899. See also entries 3, 9, 15, 23, 25, 43-47, 49, 53, 57-58, 60, 63, 65-69, 71-72, 87-88, 90-99, 104-111, 114-17, 120-23, 125-30, 133-35, 138, 140-42, 144-47, 149-51, 153-60, 162-71, 173-83, 186-90, 192-93, 198-99, 201-9, 211-18, 221-25, 228, 230-33, 270, 278, 309, 320, 333, 352, 366, 409, 416, 807, 815-16, 829, 831, 841, 867, 874, 899, 901, 906, 923, 951, 967-70, 972, 988-90, 1001.

PARADISE LOST AND THE BIBLICAL AND EPIC TRADITIONS

568 BERRY, BOYD M. *Process of Speech: Puritan Religious Writing and "Paradise Lost."* Baltimore, Md., and London: Johns Hopkins University Press, 1976, 316 pp.

Because such reformers as the Presbyterians, Prynne, and Cartwright precede Milton, he can adopt their style while extending his protest in more radical directions, including the unpuritanic idea that Christ merits his exaltation. In *Paradise Lost*, he bases his battle scenes on the Puritans' unheroic militarism, which emphasizes not fighting and winning but following providential plans and organizing troops in a church-like pattern. Milton's God repeatedly sends angels on missions that remain inconclusive. Since the constraints defining the sphere of action for a Puritan soldier in Christ's service also apply to Satan, we experience difficulty telling the fallen from the unfallen in *Paradise Lost*. The problem of locating the epic's hero comes from its accurate reflection of the incoherence at the center of Puritan ideology. After Adam and Eve admit their guilt, loops of spiritual calling and repentance bring them to a state of spiritual regeneration.

569 BLOOM, HAROLD. "Milton and His Precursors." In *A Map of Misreading*. New York: Oxford University Press, 1975, pp. 125-43.

Milton uses allusions in *Paradise Lost* as an individual, original defense against poetic tradition, allowing him to distance his epic from "its most dangerous precursor" (125), the *Faerie Queene*. In *Areopagitica*, when Milton discusses Guyon's journey into Mammon's cave, he offers a powerful misinterpretation that increases his distance

Paradise Lost

from his poetic father, Spenser. By troping upon his precursors' tropes, Milton argues for the priority of interpretation and insists on his own uniqueness and accuracy. He uses transumptive schemes to reverse literary tradition, to make his predecessors moderns and himself an ancient.

570   BUSH, DOUGLAS. "Ironic and Ambiguous Allusion in *Paradise Lost*." *JEGP: Journal of English and Germanic Philology* 60 (1961):631-40. Reprinted in *Milton Studies in Honor of Harris Francis Fletcher*, ed. G. Blakemore Evans, et al. (Urbana: University of Illinois Press, 1961), pp. 23-32.

If we recognize them, *Paradise Lost*'s ironic and ambiguous allusions to the Bible and classical works quickly reveal that Milton is not a Satanist, for Satan is the victim of many of these allusions. Irony appears in allusions applied to Adam and Eve, primarily because they are unaware of their future. These allusions point to the potential weaknesses that lead to their fall and state of sin.

571   COHEN, KITTY. *The Throne and the Chariot: Studies in Milton's Hebraism*. Studies in English Literature, vol. 97. The Hague and Paris: Mouton, 1975, 203 pp.

Judaism emphasizes a religious and national identity, while Hebraism stresses cultural values relevant to the Hebrew language and Old Testament. Milton's description of hell is classical in its diction and structure, Christian in its moral conception of evil, and Hebraic in its imagery and geography. Hebraic references provide norms against which we measure hell's values. By referring to the fallen angels by their Hebrew names, Milton shows the ironic distance between these characters' magnificent exteriors and their corrupted morals. The Hebrew elements in *Paradise Lost*'s portrayal of God make him a convincing character. Michael's role unifies the epic's allusions to the Old Testament while validating Milton's view of man in terms of the Hebraic idea of history.

Appendix: "Milton's Editors from Hume to Hughes."

572   DOBBINS, AUSTIN C. *Milton and the Book of Revelation: The Heavenly Cycle*. Studies in the Humanities, no. 7, Literature. University: University of Alabama Press, 1975, 176 pp.

From Milton's perspective, the Son's begetting and exaltation, *Paradise Lost*'s chronological starting point, are theological truths, as *Christian Doctrine* makes clear. The Son's begetting as the Son of God produces Satan's pride and rebellion. Milton has scriptural evidence, largely from Revelation, for most of the heavenly cycle in *Paradise Lost* (Books 1-6 and 9), which includes the begetting of the Son, the war in heaven (its structure, details, and outcome), the expulsion of the rebels, and the location and description of hell. A literal reading of Revelation also provides the authority for Sin and Death's placement at the gates of hell. Although both Abdiel and Satan lust, only the latter turns it to an evil end.

Appendixes: "The Structure of the Heavenly Cycle"; "The Binding of Satan."

573   EVANS, J. M. *"Paradise Lost" and the Genesis Tradition*. Oxford: Clarendon Press, 1968, 328 pp.

The opening chapters of Genesis raise many questions and answer few of them when they are considered as a narrative. In order to deal with pagan myths, Christian writers show how to read the stories as support for Christian doctrine and how to write Christian poems using pagan motifs to describe the creation, Eden, and the fall. *Paradise Lost* marks the culmination of the myth of the fall of man in its many traditions. When Milton chooses what to include or emphasize, he does so for literary rather than doctrinal reasons. The explanation for Satan's rebellion, for example, is an original idea included for dramatic purposes. Milton makes Eden less stable and more dependent on human maintenance than do traditional versions. Unlike many traditional narratives of the fall, which rely on tragic coincidence or bad luck to separate and ruin Adam and Eve, Milton insists that they fall by free choice.

574   FIORE, PETER A. *Milton and Augustine: Patterns of Augustinian Thought in "Paradise Lost."* University Park and London: Pennsylvania State University Press, 1981, 128 pp.

Milton follows Augustine's philosophy that all created nature is good, while evil is nothing. As a creature, Satan, even when fallen, partakes of this good, revealing an excellence of character. The central irony of *Paradise Lost* is that the perversion of the best nature becomes the worst, from which God brings forth the best. By portraying Adam and Eve as genuinely human, though perfect, Milton adheres to Augustine's concept of preternatural life. Augustine and Milton agree that the one divine prohibition in Eden was easy to observe, which makes its violation more grave. Violating the prohibition, Adam and Eve commit not only disobedience but also an act of defiance against the entire divine plan. Books 11 and 12 complete *Paradise Lost*'s plan of salvation, just as redemption completes God's. If man is free to fall, he is also free to choose salvation through Christ's merits.

575   GREENLAW, EDWIN. "'A Better Teacher than Aquinas.'" *Studies in Philology* 14 (1917):196-217.
    Spenser does not influence the plot, style, or structure of *Paradise Lost*; rather, Milton shares with him "a far deeper and more intimate relationship of the spirit" (197). Milton follows Spenser's interpretation of classical and Renaissance idealism. Both are Platonists, and both believe that the poet is a teacher who instructs through examples that test active virtue through an exercise of free will, as one can see from the parallel situations in Book 2 of the *Faerie Queene* and Milton's two epics. Milton's Eden resembles Spenser's Bower of Bliss; Adam and Raphael's relationship parallels that of Guyon and the Palmer; Adam's life--beginning in innocence, falling into sin, and then going through repentance--is similar to the career of Red Cross Knight. Both characters must learn temperance. The ethical system of *Paradise Lost* is derived from Spenser's work.

576   GREENLAW, EDWIN. "Spenser's Influence on *Paradise Lost*." *Studies in Philology* 17 (1920):320-59.
    Milton's poetry is largely concerned with the scheme of salvation, a theme developed by the medieval mystery cycles. But *Paradise Lost*, unlike any of its sources or analogues, stresses man's place in nature and presents a complete structure of the universe. Milton's work shows similarities with Spenser's theory of the origin of animal and vegetable life, as it appears in the garden of Adonis; his theory of chaos and night; and his cosmology, which is Ptolemaic and Aristotelian. After 1642, Milton moves beyond imitating Grotius or Andreini and, because of Spenser's influence, turns to a greater theme and a vaster cosmology.

577   KIRKCONNELL, WATSON, trans. *The Celestial Cycle: The Theme of "Paradise Lost" in World Literature with Translations of the Major Analogues*. Toronto: University of Toronto Press, 1952, 728 pp. Reprint. New York: Gordian Press, 1967.

Kirkconnell prints a descriptive catalogue of 329 analogues of *Paradise Lost* (from the eighteenth-century B.C. to 1946) and translates twenty-four of the most significant ones.

578   KURTH, BURTON O. *Milton and Christian Heroism: Biblical Epic Themes and Forms in Seventeenth-Century England*. University of California Publications, English Studies, 20. Berkeley and Los Angeles: University of California Press, 1959, 160 pp.

A participant in the cosmic drama, the Christian hero is fallen but uses Christ as his model for conduct. In Milton's view, this hero has free will as he struggles and suffers to bring good out of evil. Milton opposes contemporary writers who believe that biblical subjects cannot be used for invented action or mixed with pagan matter. In *Paradise Lost*, Milton combines the key elements of three types of subjects-- hexameral, Old Testament, and New Testament--and focuses on the entire cosmic drama implied by the fall of man. Christ's true heroism is contrasted with Satan's false heroism. If Adam and Eve are not heroic, they begin to seek salvation, and their descendants will display heroism by struggling with Satan in the world. Milton turns to Christ's most human aspect to define Christian heroism in *Paradise Regained*. Samson in Milton's play is an example of tragic heroism, in which divine support resolves an internal conflict with evil.

579   McCOLLEY, GRANT. *"Paradise Lost": An Account of Its Growth and Major Origins, with a Discussion of Milton's Use of Sources and Literary Patterns*. Chicago, Ill.: Packard & Co., 1940, 373 pp. 4 illustrations.

Beginning in the first century, the hexameral tradition is *Paradise Lost*'s most important single source, though Milton's epic gives more attention to the war in heaven and less to the creation than do conventional hexameral works. When Raphael explains astronomy, he refers to geocentric, heliocentric, and triple-motion theories but ignores the geo-heliocentric theory that mid-seventeenth-century astronomers usually advocate. The opening two books constitute *Paradise Lost*'s most and least original section, for Milton uses a

251

Paradise Lost

traditional scene and characters but gives the demons diverse roles. Eden's geography is also traditional and innovative in Milton's hands, just as his account of the creation adds an initial, unsuccessful temptation of Eve. While Books 11 and 12 may bore modern readers, they are based on commentaries on Genesis, the most popular book for commentary in Milton's age. The sources of the dialogue on astronomy are John Wilkins and Alexander Ross. Having started to write one of Satan's soliloquies, Milton begins composing the rest of *Paradise Lost* in 1652-53, reaches the midpoint by 1660, and completes it in 1663. See entries 6, 18, 212, 459, 476, 489, 512, 521, 728.

580 NEWMAN, JOHN KEVIN. "The English Tradition: Chaucer and Milton." In *The Classical Epic Tradition*. Wisconsin Studies in Classics. Madison and London: University of Wisconsin Press, 1986, pp. 339-98.

    The classical tradition teaches Milton many lessons: great poetry tends toward drama; other arts--particularly painting and music --help the word; logic in an epic must be subservient to the pity and terror aroused by projecting the imagination into objective form; a single hero is not crucial (though a tragedy requires a hero with hamartia); classical models provide extra resonance; imagery unifies a poem; and a poem's language must be intelligible yet not shocking. In *Paradise Lost*, but especially in the climactic Book 9, Milton mixes such styles as the tragic, the Euripidean or pantomimic, the Ovidian metamorphic, and the comic or joyful. Satan's approach to Eve and the temptation scene are theatrical and operatic. Following the Italian epic tradition, Milton places love, the relationship between man and woman, at the epic's center.

581 PATRIDES, C. A. *Milton and the Christian Tradition*. Oxford: Clarendon Press, 1966, 318 pp. Part reprinted in *On Milton's Poetry*, ed. Arnold Stein (Greenwich, Conn.: Fawcett Publications, 1970), pp. 111-33.

    Paradise Lost is neither Arian nor subordinationist in its portrayal of the Godhead, which is far more orthodox than the subordinationist *Christian Doctrine*. In the epic, Milton maintains the unity of the Godhead even when he differentiates between Father and Son for dramatic reasons. The character of Christ links love and obedience in *Paradise Lost*. Milton's view of grace is in accord with the balanced view of St. Paul, St. Augustine, and the Christian tradition. Unlike the cyclic Greco-Roman view of history, the Jewish tradition sees history as unfolding under God's eye and expressing his will. All of the Bible, except Ecclesiastes, envisions history's linear progress to the day of the Lord, which is Michael's perspective in Books 11-12 of *Paradise Lost*. A long tradition of believing in mortalism leads to Milton's adoption of it in *Christian Doctrine*.

582   RYKEN, LELAND. "*Paradise Lost* and Its Biblical Epic Models." In *Milton and Scriptural Tradition: The Bible into Poetry*. Edited by James H. Sims and Leland Ryken. Columbia: University of Missouri Press, 1984, pp. 43-81.

By replacing the epic tradition's heroic values with pastoral and domestic ones (as Genesis instructs him to do), emphasizing divine greatness and human smallness instead of human greatness (the message of Exodus), and spiritualizing such motifs as warfare and kingship that are traditionally earthly (an idea found in Revelation), Milton in *Paradise Lost* reconciles the philosophical-theological definition and the literary portrayal of the hero. His use of the Bible as a literary model accounts for his redefinition of the heroic. *Paradise Lost* does not fulfill the classics; it corrects or even refutes them.

583   SAMUEL, IRENE. *Dante and Milton: The "Commedia" and "Paradise Lost."* Ithaca, N.Y.: Cornell University Press, 1966, 309 pp.

Of all English poets, Milton is apparently the first to get at the *Divine Comedy*'s heart and "to adapt its techniques of instruction through narrative to his own purposes" (45). Eve's dream, the angels, light and dark imagery, the epic subject, and invocations in *Paradise Lost* have parallels in Dante's *Comedy*. Like Dante, Milton presents heaven and Eden in order to give examples of what earthly life could be. *Purgatorio*'s theme, the search for liberty (or free will) through re-education, and the entire *Comedy*'s goal, "the communion of saints" (218), are both relevant to *Paradise Lost*, as we see in the lessons of Raphael and Michael. Milton's poem gives more emphasis to right reason. From Dante, Milton may have learned about the problem with rhyme and the value of writing in the vernacular, issues raised in the *Convivio*. His style may owe something to Dante's, especially in terms of repetition and diction.

Paradise Lost

584 SHUMAKER, WAYNE. *"Paradise Lost* and the Italian Epic Tradition." In *Th'Upright Heart and Pure: Essays on John Milton Commemorating the Tercentenary of the Publication of "Paradise Lost."* Edited by Amadeus P. Fiore, O.F.M. Duquesne Studies, Philological Series, vol. 10. Pittsburgh, Pa.: Duquesne University Press, 1967, pp. 87-100.

By rejecting an Arthurian, chivalric subject, Milton dismisses the only epic tradition that demonstrates an ability to earn popularity and critical esteem in Europe. He thus embraces a simple rather than a complex plot with a limited number of characters. Instead of multiplying incidents, as Boiardo, Ariosto, and Spenser do, Milton gives the epic a new focus by exploring a problem. His complex world demands that a single work confront a single segment of experience. Milton also excludes certain ruling interests (such as valor, romantic love, and magic) because he, unlike the Italian epic poets, does not believe in them.

585 SIMS, JAMES H. *The Bible in Milton's Epics.* Gainesville: University of Florida Press, 1962, 290 pp.

In *Paradise Lost* and *Paradise Regained*, Milton uses the Bible to provide stories and biblical allusions to make characters and events seem probable and real, as if they have scriptural authority. This is true even when he invents episodes or characters because they are logical extensions of Scripture. Milton uses the Greek, Hebrew, and Latin Bibles in three ways to provide sources for allusions: transliterating Greek or Hebrew into English, and placing a translation nearby; quoting variant translations of certain texts; and following the Latin Bible's words or phrasings. As the medieval mystery plays give Renaissance dramatists the technique of using biblical allusions for dramatic effect, so Milton adapts this technique from the Elizabethans to create aspects of *Paradise Lost*'s and *Paradise Regained*'s settings and actions, and to add dramatic force to the language and chief characters.

Sims includes an "Index of Biblical References" in *Paradise Lost* and *Paradise Regained*, as identified by him and by eighteen of Milton's foremost editors and commentators from the eighteenth century to the twentieth century.

586 STEADMAN, JOHN M. "The Arming of an Archetype: Heroic Virtue and the Conventions of Literary Epic." In *Concepts of the*

Hero in the Middle Ages and the Renaissance. Edited by Norman T. Burns and Christopher J. Reagan. Albany: State University of New York Press, 1975, pp. 147-96.

Epic calls to imitate heroic action and moral archetypes are divergent. Once the Homeric epic is written down, it becomes "the cultural heritage of less martial classes in more literate societies" (151), so the epic has to be moralized to accommodate newer, more spiritual ideals. Rejecting the martial argument, Milton in *Paradise Regained* presents not an epic hero or an embodiment of heroic ideals but the heroic archetype itself. *Paradise Lost*'s generic designation as a heroic and a divine poem is perhaps paradoxical. By focusing on a human act of moral choice, Milton defies his readers' expectations about the heroic exemplar, Adam. The regenerate Christian hero is heroic only by grace. Not Adam but the superhuman combatants, Christ and Satan, perform the heroic enterprise. With the fall in *Paradise Lost*, the heroic pattern is obliterated; as in so many Renaissance epics, the hero breaks down because of the strain of his quest for perfection.

587 STEADMAN, JOHN M. *Milton and the Renaissance Hero*. Oxford: Clarendon Press, 1967, 229 pp.

While the epic tradition emphasizes courage and strength (*fortezza*), ethical and theological traditions find heroism in reason, justice, and piety. Since Milton conceives the goal of epic poetry as teaching, delighting, and moving through images of heroic virtue, he recognizes that the traditional hero's character contradicts his ethical intent. *Paradise Lost* presents old heroic patterns as foils for the new. In his portrait of Satan, Milton discredits the *fortezza* formula. *Paradise Regained* shows displays of might to be frail, and the plight of *Samson Agonistes*'s hero implicitly indicts the *fortezza* ideal. In his three major poems, Milton criticizes other patterns (vain prudence, false wisdom, false love, evil leadership, hubristic magnanimity, and apparent constancy) by similarly dissociating them from piety and associating them with evil characters or deeds. Ignoring secular monarchs as models for his heroes, he spiritualizes the epic's traditional argument and political structure.

588 WEBBER, JOAN MALORY. *Milton and His Epic Tradition*. Seattle and London: University of Washington Press, 1979, 258 pp.

Paradise Lost

Every epic is subversive, rejecting the assumptions of its predecessors while maintaining its ties to them. Rather than celebrating a previous age, an epic poet displays his culture and undermines it by showing its vulnerability. The hero strives to understand the unconscious, to reject madness and suicide, and to accept consciousness and self-consciousness, which includes an awareness of his mortality. Unlike other epics, *Paradise Lost* begins in a cave (of hell), locating the reader in the confines of the human condition; instead of seeing the cave from the outside, we are in it because our consciousness is identified with Satan's. As fallen creatures, we are the threat. Milton's God, the Son, Adam, and Eve illustrate the epic hero's solitude that creates and changes human consciousness. Milton needs to write *Paradise Regained* in order to bring epic history back to human nature, which *Paradise Lost* does only in Books 11 and 12. Rejecting the founding of an empire, the Son regards the usual epic tasks as delusive activities of fallen man. Milton makes the epic internal.

589   WILLIAMS, ARNOLD. "Renaissance Commentaries on 'Genesis' and Some Elements of the Theology of *Paradise Lost*." *PMLA* 56 (1941):151-64.
       Renaissance commentaries on Genesis form the foundation of hexameral literary works. Presenting the unorthodox idea of creation from pre-existing matter in *Paradise Lost*, Milton agrees with the commentaries' view of the nature of chaos, though they argue that it is created *ex nihilo*. He disagrees with the orthodox view that time begins with the world and vice versa; *Paradise Lost* and *Christian Doctrine* indicate that time exists before the creation. Milton also believes that the angels are created at an earlier date than the commentaries allow.

See also entries 131, 208, 446, 506, 519, 538, 540, 547, 556, 594, 601, 638, 748.

PARADISE LOST AND CLASSICAL LITERATURE

590   BLESSINGTON, FRANCIS C. *"Paradise Lost" and the Classical Epic*. Boston, Mass., London, and Henley: Routledge and Kegan Paul, 1979, 139 pp.
       Milton does not regard the classical epic tradition as evil. Rather than embodying the old heroism, Satan perverts Homer's and Virgil's values. The frame of reference for Satan in hell is the *Aeneid*; in

the war in heaven, the *Iliad*; in his journey to and appearance on earth, the *Odyssey*. Satan parodies Aeneas, Achilles, and Odysseus. All characters in Milton's heaven, except the rebels, synthesize classical and Christian elements, illustrating a purified version of Homer's and Virgil's theology. Adam, Eve, and the narrator combine pagan and Christian values. Adam is a perfected Odysseus who bases his heroism on reason but later becomes, like Achilles, a deathbringer. Eve, although she is analogous to Dido, Circe, and Penelope, participates in the heroic action and shares its consequences. Adam and Eve fall from epic into tragedy, the corrupt classicism of Satan, and the pagan world of mortality. Instead of watching a reenactment of the Greeks destroying Troy, in *Paradise Lost* we see God (through Michael) destroy Eden, the city of man.

591 COLLETT, JONATHAN H. "Milton's Use of Classical Mythology in *Paradise Lost*." *PMLA* 85 (1970):88-96.

Throughout his life, Milton attacks pagan mythology while recognizing its poetic value and making extensive, original use of it. His youthful poems use myth as ornament. In *Paradise Lost*, however, Milton uses myth in three ways: some "fabl'd" myths consider the gods and goddesses to be fallen angels in a new guise; the sensual beauty of some "feign'd" myths is used to describe Eden and its residents; and in Book 11, a few myths are types of the revelation that Adam receives.

592 DuROCHER, RICHARD J. *Milton and Ovid*. Ithaca, N.Y., and London: Cornell University Press, 1985, 241 pp.

Early in his career, Milton imitates Ovid; later, Milton associates his characters with Ovid's imagery, diction, and rhetoric of those characters who are emotionally or ethically unstable. The postscript to Milton's Ovidian elegies marks his departure from the Ovid of the *Amores* and *Ars Amatoria*, and toward the *Metamorphoses*, as is seen in *Comus*. In *Paradise Lost*, Eve goes through incremental changes that reveal weaknesses and potentialities, and the stages are marked by allusions to Narcissus and Echo, Pomona, Medea, and Pyrrha. While maintaining Satan's semblance of heroism, Milton shows his degeneration by making him an analogue of apparently heroic but finally debased characters in the *Metamorphoses* and by assigning him stylistic features and rhetorical strategies of Ovid's epic. In order to revalue the metamorphic epic, and to distinguish *Paradise Lost* from it,

Paradise Lost

Milton imitates and transforms it, as Ovid does to Homer's and Virgil's epics. Milton thus allows pagan and Christian values to compete for the reader's approval. If Virgil contributes structural components to *Paradise Lost*'s design, Ovid helps Milton in the transvaluation of those structures.

Appendix: "Verbal Echoes of Ovid's *Metamorphoses* in *Paradise Lost*."

593 GALLAGHER, PHILIP J. "*Paradise Lost* and the Greek Theogony." *English Literary Renaissance* 9 (1979):121-48.

If the Greek writers present a cosmic struggle leading to a divine patriarchy, Milton corrects them in *Paradise Lost* by showing the event as "an internecine strife in which fallen angels fight among themselves to secure worship at various heathen shrines" (122). The titanomachia, he argues, is a Satanically inspired distortion of the war in heaven. Satan's lies become the material for Hesiod's *Theogony* and Aeschylus's *Prometheus Bound*, whose errors in the divine succession myth Milton wants to expose. Compared to the war in heaven, the titanomachia is consistently belittled in *Paradise Lost*. The narrative of the war in heaven includes allusions that mock Zeus's stratagems and what amounts to a pro forma battle in Hesiod. Milton indicates that the Greek poetry, as a vehicle for Satan's autobiographical lies, undercuts God's omnipotence and overstates his reliance on force.

594 GRANSDEN, K. W. "*Paradise Lost* and the *Aeneid*." *Essays in Criticism* 17 (1967):281-303.

Paradise Lost's classicism is reflected in its structure, language, and syntax, through which Milton creates a teleological epic of Christian heroism that supersedes Virgil's epic of Roman heroism. Both the *Aeneid* and *Paradise Lost* are about time. Because of the classical allusions, chiefly Ovidian, that describe Eve, she is surrounded with ambivalence in *Paradise Lost*. Milton repeatedly turns to Virgil to transform false accounts into true ones, and *Paradise Lost*'s style is indebted to that of the *Aeneid*. When Anchises speaks to Aeneas, we also hear Virgil addressing Rome and thus merging the two ages. Certain books in Milton's epic (5-8 and 11-12) form its teleological center, for indirect narration dominates here, and, as Adam listens to Raphael and Michael, we listen to and learn from Milton. Again, two ages are brought together.

595   HARDING, DAVIS P. *The Club of Hercules: Studies in the Classical Background of "Paradise Lost."* Illinois Studies in Language and Literature, vol. 50. Urbana: University of Illinois Press, 1962, 145 pp.

In *Paradise Lost*, Satan embodies the old heroism, which Milton discredits and exposes. As indicated by classical allusions and analogies, Satan deserves credit for leadership and courage, while his strength and desire for revenge are undercut. The fall poses a problem for Milton: from a theological perspective, he must maintain Adam and Eve's innocence; from a poet's point of view, however, he must provide a motivation for the fall, a frailty that leads to sin. His solution is to make the reader tentatively uneasy about Adam and Eve while maintaining the illusion of their sinlessness. Milton writes *Paradise Lost* in blank verse, though rhyme is fashionable, because of its flexibility, loftiness, and remoteness from ordinary speech. Trying to make English do the work of Latin, Milton strains the bonds of language. He uses Virgilian principles to revolutionize English blank verse. The style used in scenes in hell is concrete; in heaven, it is abstract, while unfallen Adam and Eve mix these styles.

596   HARDING, DAVIS P. *Milton and the Renaissance Ovid*. Illinois Studies in Language and Literature, vol. 30, no. 4. Urbana: University of Illinois Press, 1946, 105 pp.

During Milton's lifetime, rationalists and Puritans hold myth and allegory in disfavor. Ovid's poetry has an established position in the curriculum of English Renaissance grammar schools. Though he is always influenced by the *Metamorphoses*, after deciding to become a Christian epic poet in late 1629, Milton is far less indebted to Ovid's amatory verse, which is not a good model for someone with Milton's aspirations. In *Paradise Lost*, he is most indebted to Ovid's epic when writing about the creation, chaos, Eden, and the flood. Satan is often associated with Typhon (or Typhoeus) and Phaethon. As Milton grows older, he becomes increasingly skeptical about the ability of pagan myth to contain moral or religious truths, so his last works show little Ovidian influence.

597   KNOESPEL, KENNETH J. "The Limits of Allegory: Textual Expansion of Narcissus in *Paradise Lost*." *Milton Studies* 22 (1986):79-99.

Paradise Lost

Approaching Ovid as an equal, Milton in *Paradise Lost* silently imitates the Narcissus story to give psychological depth to Satan, Adam, and Eve (especially when she gazes into the pool). The Ovidian fable about love turns into a fable about understanding and its need to rely on guidance. In Ovid's tale, an unheard narrator warns Narcissus when he begins to love an extension of his own image, but Satan experiences pain when he falls in love with thought or self-reflection itself and gives birth to Sin. Unlike Narcissus, Eve approaches the pool with a desire for knowledge, does not recognize the reflected image, and is led away by an audible divine voice. Adam's call to Eve, when she begins to return to the reflection, parallels Narcissus's call to his disappearing image. As a sign of his weak understanding, Adam does not heed Raphael's warning about being attracted to his own image in Eve. Ovid stresses the attractiveness of visual phenomena, Milton of aural phenomena.

598   LABRIOLA, ALBERT C. "The Titans and the Giants: *Paradise Lost* and the Tradition of the Renaissance Ovid." *Milton Quarterly* 12 (1978):9-16.
       Milton follows the tradition of the Renaissance Ovid, in which the Typhon myth is Christianized, for an allegorical technique that "correlates classical mythology with a Christian frame of reference" (10). In *Paradise Lost*, the traditional resemblances among the Titans and Typhon, the fallen angels and Satan, and the giants of Genesis 6:2-4 are developed in terms of characterization, theme, imagery, and structure.

599   LOW, ANTHONY. "Milton and the Georgic Ideal." In *The Georgic Revolution*. Princeton, N.J.: Princeton University Press, 1985, pp. 296-352.
       Like his life, Milton's poetry embodies the Virgilian georgic values of long labor, heroism based on daily care, and dedication to one's civilization and people. Georgic elements are present even when Milton celebrates pastoral beauty, leisure, and play, as in *L'Allegro*, *Comus*, and *Lycidas*. Moving from pastoral to georgic, *Paradise Lost* leaves mankind in a world of labor that ends with the nightfall of death and a return to paradise at the end of time. Just as Milton qualifies prelapsarian pastoralism, so he qualifies his approval of postlapsarian georgic in order to exclude Satanic imperial labors. The georgic spirit

receives a new and more hopeful significance in *Paradise Regained*: the georgic agent, Christ sacrifices labor and gives humanity the chance to help in the divine job of planting and harvesting to create an internal paradise. *Paradise Regained*'s dominant mode is georgic, its dominant genre a mixture of narrative and drama.

600 MARTINDALE, CHARLES. "Paradise Metamorphosed: Ovid in Milton." *Comparative Literature* 37 (1985):301-33.

An admirer of Ovid and English Ovidian poets even when they are out of fashion after the Restoration, Milton knows four ways of reading Ovid's *Metamorphoses*: as moral, allegorical, rhetorical, and amoral poetry. *Paradise Lost* shows significant signs of all four versions of Ovid, and Milton's double view of pagan myth--it is both powerful and untrue--anticipates certain aspects of the Romantic sensibility. Two episodes in particular do not draw our attention to Ovid through allusion or imitation, but still show his presence: Adam's entertainment of Raphael and the fallen angels' transformation into serpents.

601 MUELLER, MARTIN. "*Paradise Lost* and the *Iliad*." *Comparative Literature Studies* 6 (1969):292-316.

Like the *Iliad*, which is concerned with the wrath of Achilles, *Paradise Lost* focuses on an action (disobedience) rather than a person, which is the focus of the *Odyssey* and *Aeneid*. The action is further linked to Homer's and Milton's main theme of destruction, as wrath and disobedience lead to death. The tragic destruction in the *Iliad* and *Paradise Lost* is balanced by a movement toward reconciliation; each ends quietly. Not linear but episodic, the structures of the *Iliad* and *Paradise Lost* are analogous, for in each the whole is subordinated to one part. Both epics' plots are most successful when they use the dramatic devices of anagnorisis and peripeteia. In the *Iliad* and *Paradise Lost*, hero and reader share emotions and perspective to some extent. Like Virgil's relation to Homer, Milton's relation to the epic tradition is based not just on revaluation but also on careful imitation of the Homeric epic's plot patterns and formal conventions.

602 NORTHRUP, MARK D. "Milton's Hesiodic Cosmology." *Comparative Literature* 33 (1981):305-20.

Paradise Lost

Plato's *Timaeus* and Neoplatonic thought influence Milton's cosmology in *Paradise Lost* less than does Hesiod's *Theogony*. Chaos and the war in heaven owe much to Hesiod, as does the theme of justifying God's ways to men. Just as Hesiod exalts Zeus by showing his invincibility in battle and further discusses his attributes by dividing them among his wives and children, so Milton's God is victorious in battle and is a complex character made up of three persons with different attributes. Hesiod's Chaos is a passive, personified nothingness, his daughter Night an active, creative source of evil things. Their incestuous marriage parodies those of Satan and Sin, and Sin and Death in *Paradise Lost*. The contrast between Chaos and Night, and Zeus and God emphasizes the highest powers' most positive attributes. *Paradise Lost*'s invocation to Book 1 has a double ancestry, going back to the Bible and to the classical literature that Milton promises to transcend.

603   PORTER, WILLIAM MALIN. "A View from 'Th'Aonian Mount': Hesiod and Milton's Critique of the Classics." *Classical and Modern Literature* 3 (1982):5-23.

In *Paradise Lost*'s prologues and war in heaven, Milton pays close attention to Hesiod's text and encourages him "to respond to the apparent 'critique' of him articulated in *Paradise Lost*" (6). Milton's Aonian Mount in the prologue to Book 1 is Helicon, where Hesiod's theophany occurs in the *Theogony*. Like Moses, Hesiod is the divinely inspired poet-shepherd, and, like Moses and Milton, Hesiod in the *Theogony* and *Works and Days* justifies divine ways. Milton does not discredit Hesiod's inspiration or contrast it with his own. Having reworked the *Theogony* in parts of Books 1 and 2 of *Paradise Lost*, Milton in the war in heaven episode ambushes Hesiod by creating an analogy between Satan's attributes and Zeus's combination of knowledge and power. Milton thus contradicts the *Theogony* by revealing Zeus's knowledge to be fraudulent and his rule a tyranny based on force. When Milton alludes to another work, he always creates a dialogue in which that work responds to his allusions.

604   REVARD, STELLA P. "Vergil's *Georgics* and *Paradise Lost*: Nature and Human Nature in a Landscape." In *Vergil at 2000: Commemorative Essays on the Poet and His Influence*. Edited by John D. Bernard. New York: AMS Press, 1986, pp. 259-80.

Once we recognize that Virgil's *Georgics* is a brief philosophical epic that deals with the human condition, man's relationship with the enduring aspects of the world, and a divine plan-- in short, it justifies God's ways to man--we can see how *Paradise Lost* is indebted to it. Virgil's just farmer is the model for Milton's prelapsarian Adam, and Milton follows Virgil's view of man's degeneration after the golden age or, in Christian terms, the fall. By insisting that nature's beauty and order come from a divine source and inspire man's reverence and virtue, both poets adopt a clear moral tone. Like Virgil, Milton shows that war threatens the peaceful georgic life. Obedience to God or Jove is imperative for continued happiness. After the loss of Eden or the golden age, man lives in a hostile world, and Milton and Virgil sound pessimistic notes. Milton turns to Virgil's Orpheus for the model of the tragic human and tragic lover. Milton sees the epic potential of Virgil's *Georgics*.

605   TILLYARD, E. M. W. "Milton and the Classics." *Transactions of the Royal Society of Literature of the United Kingdom*, 3d ser., n.s. 26 (1953):59-72.

Milton has a deep knowledge of classical literature and great respect for classical ethics. But we do him great harm if, adhering to our superstitious reverence for the classics, we think of him as having "the soul of an ancient in the body of a modern" (61). Readers overestimate Milton's Latinate diction: just as Shakespeare does in his work, Milton plays off Latin against Saxon vocabulary in *Paradise Lost*. He is "a completely English poet" (63). In *Lycidas*, *Paradise Lost*, and *Samson Agonistes*, he owes much to the classics, but he transforms his borrowings into something contemporary.

See also entries 20, 127, 130-31, 182, 187, 207-8, 256, 443, 446, 506, 519, 538, 540, 547, 556, 570-71, 580, 636, 644-45, 660, 712, 780.

STYLE

606   BEREK, PETER. "'Plain' and 'Ornate' Styles and the Structure of *Paradise Lost*." *PMLA* 85 (1970):237-46.

For the fit reader, God's unpoetic doctrinal speeches in Book 3 of *Paradise Lost* create standards for the use of language by which we can shape our response for the rest of the poem. Satan believes that

Paradise Lost

words are entities with an independent value and existence; his speech lacks logical coherence but gives the appearance of sense. God's speech, on the other hand, does not manipulate words to mean what he wants or entice us with sound patterns. Bridging the distance between the Father's speech and our fallen language, the Son introduces emotion to Book 3. He is our paradigm for speaking and acting. In prelapsarian Eden, Adam and Eve's speech shows similarities with divine language; after the fall, they use language in a Satanic manner, thriving on ambiguity and slippery reasoning. Adam and Eve's language parallels the Son's when they are reconciled to each other and to God.

607 BEUM, ROBERT. "So Much Gravity and Ease." In *Language and Style in Milton: A Symposium in Honor of the Tercentenary of "Paradise Lost."* Edited by Ronald David Emma and John T. Shawcross. New York: Frederick Ungar Publishing Co., 1967, pp. 333-68.

Because Milton is not a foot prosodist, his verse should be discussed as accentual-syllabic, accounting for both number of syllables and number and positions of accents. Readers should balance their prosodic analysis of the line with an examination of its context. In his choice not to rhyme the verse of *Paradise Lost*, Milton is influenced by the blank verse of Elizabethan drama and by the belief that plainness and sublimity are impossible in rhyme. Alliteration and assonance are moderate and unobtrusive in his epic. To create tension, Milton uses a great deal of enjambment along with heavy line termination in stress. He eschews terminally hypermetrical lines, or feminine endings. Not mellifluous, Milton's verse is somewhat harsh.

608 BROADBENT, J. B. "Milton's Rhetoric." *Modern Philology* 56 (1959):224-42. Reprinted in *Milton: Modern Judgements*, ed. Alan Rudrum (London: Macmillan, 1968), pp. 270-95.

Books 3 and 9 of *Paradise Lost* contain the most prosodic and verbal rhetoric, indicating the relevance of figures to theological context. Satan's rhetoric of temptation parodies God's rhetoric, which relies more on formal schemes than on iterations. The relativism of Satan's values appears in his lack of schematic rhetoric and question-begging ploys. When Eve is tempted, her rhetoric imitates Satan's. Celebratory and argumentative rhetoric disappears in Books 11 and 12 of *Paradise Lost* and in *Paradise Regained* as Milton comes to trust art less and less. Never flamboyant, his rhetoric serves a structural function.

609   BROOKS, CLEANTH. "Milton and Critical Re-Estimates." *PMLA* 66 (1951):1045-54.

Because Lewis (see entry 506) and Bush (see entry 451) misunderstand the opposition to Milton, they fail to rehabilitate his reputation as an artist. Only a misguided student of Milton's style would praise it for just its picturesque images and sonorous music. In fact, *Paradise Lost*'s style exemplifies many of the principles sought by modern critics. Milton's power as an artist comes from his ability to use myth, as when he places the garden of Eden between the city of God and Satan's city of Pandemonium or when he makes Satan the colonizer who wants to civilize Adam and Eve, the happy savages on earth.

610   DAVIS, WALTER R. "The Languages of Accommodation and the Styles of *Paradise Lost*." *Milton Studies* 18 (1983):103-27.

The many styles of *Paradise Lost* become a major part of its plot. In the first six books, Milton's epic style and language are difficult, forcing the reader to work with images, symbols, and reified concepts to understand the foreign worlds of hell, heaven, and paradise. But in the last six books, the human style is smoother because *Paradise Lost* follows the narrative history we know, from creation to fall to aftermath, including our world. Books 5-6, in which Raphael visits earth, show the intersection of divine and human language, as well as the naturalness of understanding. His speech on cosmic order works through both typology and analogy, as does his narrative of the war in heaven, which contains three thematic sections (true Christian heroism, the vanity of false Christian heroism, and salvation by Christ) presented in different styles. Like the language of traditional scriptural exegesis, Raphael's speech moves from allegory to analogy.

611   DiCESARE, MARIO A. "Advent'rous Song: The Texture of Milton's Epic." In *Language and Style in Milton: A Symposium in Honor of the Tercentenary of "Paradise Lost."* Edited by Ronald David Emma and John T. Shawcross. New York: Frederick Ungar Publishing Co., 1967, pp. 1-29.

Paradise Lost

When Satan first sees Adam and Eve, Milton creates a contrast between the tempter's moment of self-definition as a solitary, fragmented being and the couple's wholeness. Satan reacts by proposing an alliance that is in fact an absorption or devouring. The passage's rhythms mimic this logical structure. In many places, the sinuosity of the verse and labyrinth image is apt for describing Satan's self-embrace and coiling motion. Adam echoes Satan's logic, rhythms, and images when he despairs in Book 10. Hand images symbolize a creative force, power, or relationship.

612   DOBRÉE, BONAMY. "Milton and Dryden: A Comparison and Contrast in Poetic Ideas and Poetic Method." *ELH* 3 (1936):83-100.

As adolescents, Milton and Dryden are both greatly influenced by Sylvester's translation of Du Bartas, but Milton appreciates its religious subject and Dryden its style. Neither Milton nor Dryden is interested in writing metaphysical poetry to embody the emotional apprehension of thought. Although they attempt to write metaphysical conceits, Dryden uses and develops the metaphysical tradition, while Milton develops his own diction. Milton thus "made the language stiff and tortuous, even distorted, unuseable in that form by other poets"; "he injured our poetry" (89). Compared to Milton's almost innate sense of mission, Dryden's urge to reform poetry is self-imposed. Milton cannot turn an abstract idea into great poetry; Dryden can. Their ideas are comparable even if their methods differ.

613   FRASER, RUSSELL. "On Milton's Poetry." *Yale Review* 56 (1966):172-96.

Milton's Platonism leads him to reject sensory, physical perception and even higher perception in favor of the excellent perception by which the soul apprehends God. His poetry is thus abstract because he wishes to convey the totality of truth and to be delivered from poetry. In *Paradise Lost*, descriptions of characters and places are weak, for Milton wants "to obliterate the surface of things" (177). The epic's imagery and similes are often irrelevant. Milton's rushing verse leads to a sameness of tone and voice in such works as *Paradise Lost* and *Samson Agonistes*. By reforming the language of English poetry in this way, Milton inaugurates a decline.

614 LEAVIS, F. R. "Milton's Verse." *Scrutiny* 2 (1933):123-36. Reprinted in *Revaluation: Tradition and Development in English Poetry* (London: Chatto and Windus, 1936), pp. 42-67; *Milton's Epic Poetry: Essays on "Paradise Lost" and "Paradise Regained,"* ed. C. A. Patrides (Harmondsworth: Penguin Books, 1967), pp. 15-32.

    Readers of Milton should dislike the thud that comes inevitably with his verse, for when one reads *Paradise Lost* one must resist the verse's movement. But Milton wears us down, and we surrender to the monotony of his epic ritual. His verse suffers from a sensuous poverty. Although Milton has a command of sensuous details, dramatic speech, and the English language as a native medium when he writes *Comus*, all of these are missing from *Paradise Lost*, where he renounces the English language in favor of a Latinate diction that leads to obscurity. Milton's vast undertaking in *Paradise Lost*'s myth exposes him as single- and simple-minded. The verse of *Samson Agonistes* is stiff. See entries 110, 116-17, 621.

615 LEAVIS, F. R. "Mr. Eliot and Milton." *Sewanee Review* 57 (1949):1-30. Reprinted in *The Common Pursuit* (London: Chatto and Windus, 1952), pp. 9-32; frequently reprinted.

    Milton's use of language does emphasize sound, but--contrary to Eliot's claim (see entries 89, 239)--poetic sound is different from musical sound. Intoxicating readers with the sound of words, Milton forces us to relax our standards of force and consistent meaning. He has no ability to analyze ideas clearly or to use language precisely. Pride and self-confidence encourage him to select a form and subject that are beyond his abilities. Too much of the argumentative and suffering John Milton enters *Paradise Lost*.

616 PARTRIDGE, A. C. "*Paradise Lost* and *Samson Agonistes*." In *The Language of Renaissance Poetry: Spenser, Shakespeare, Donne, Milton*. London: Andre Deutsch, 1971, pp. 290-312.

    Paradise Lost's grand style, appropriate for a transcendent subject, remains high until the fall in Book 9. Its style is based on the expanded simile rather than on metaphor. In order to achieve sublimity, Milton makes the rhythm and the word fit the sensuous impression. If *Samson Agonistes*'s realistic phrasing echoes Euripides's work, the play's dramatic conception follows the spirit of Sophocles.

Paradise Lost

This play is unsuitable for the stage because it lacks a dramatic crisis, has an unheroic figure at the center, and champions passivity.

617 PATRICK, J. MAX. "Milton's Revolution against Rime, and Some of Its Implications." In *Milton and the Art of Sacred Song*. Edited by J. Max Patrick and Roger H. Sundell. Madison and London: University of Wisconsin Press, 1979, pp. 99-117.

After completing *Paradise Lost* by about August, 1665, Milton dictates *Samson Agonistes* from 1665 to 1667. The rhymed passages in *Samson Agonistes* persuade him to cease rhyming. As early as *Lycidas*, Milton sees rhyme as something to retreat from, so he softens his rhymes by distancing rhyming words from each other, enjambing lines, and creating patterns of assonance. The note on the verse in the fourth issue of *Paradise Lost*'s first edition acknowledges that, from 1625 to 1659, Milton had made the mistake of rhyming according to custom. A baroque artist, he masters the tradition of rhyming verse in order to exploit it. Although Milton's last work is *Paradise Regained*, he publishes the three major poems in the sequence in which he wants us to read them: *Paradise Lost*, *Paradise Regained*, and *Samson Agonistes*.

618 PATRIDES, C. A. "*Paradise Lost* and the Language of Theology." In *Language and Style in Milton: A Symposium in Honor of the Tercentenary of "Paradise Lost."* Edited by Ronald David Emma and John T. Shawcross. New York: Frederick Ungar Publishing Co., 1967, pp. 102-19.

The essence of theological language combines an appropriate "oddness" with a certain logical behavior. Although *Christian Doctrine* is a failure, both in its theology and language, *Paradise Lost* employs accommodation to expound the very metaphors for the deity that the prose work avoids. When Milton uses a myth, a metaphor that draws a spiritual truth within the range of our fallen apprehension, the incident appears odd when taken out of context; but, in context, it has its own logical significance, especially as it gathers echoes from throughout *Paradise Lost*. Neither negative nor abstract, the language of the epic is concrete and earth-bound, yet we must hear its affinities with apocalyptic literature.

619   PEARCE, DONALD R. "The Style of Milton's Epic." *Yale Review* 52 (1963):427-44. Reprinted in *Milton: Modern Essays in Criticism*, ed. Arthur E. Barker (London, Oxford, and New York: Oxford University Press, 1965), pp. 368-85.

   Paradise Lost displays the stylistic qualities of great theological and philosophical prose. Milton's style draws on artificial classic prose and on his own prose, rather than on common speech. In *Paradise Lost*, classic eloquence distances the reader from the poem's events and guarantees precision of statement. The appeal of Milton's epic verse lies in the silence among its images, not in its sound.

620   RICKS, CHRISTOPHER. *Milton's Grand Style*. Oxford: Clarendon Press, 1963, 160 pp. Frequently reprinted; part reprinted in *Milton's Epic Poetry: Essays on "Paradise Lost" and "Paradise Regained,"* ed. C. A. Patrides (Harmondsworth: Penguin Books, 1967), pp. 249-75; part reprinted in *On Milton's Poetry*, ed. Arnold Stein (Greenwich, Conn.: Fawcett Publications, 1970), pp. 167-82; part reprinted in *Milton: "Paradise Lost," a Casebook*, ed. A. E. Dyson and Julian Lovelock (London and Basingstoke: Macmillan, 1973), pp. 204-19; part reprinted in *Paradise Lost*, ed. Scott Elledge (New York: W. W. Norton & Co., 1975), pp. 442-59.

   The anti-Miltonists argue that Milton's verse is governed by sound instead of sense. On the contrary, his grand style achieves elevated dignity without sacrificing sense. His style is not just grand: it is simultaneously grand, subtle, evocative, and sensitive. Although Milton's syntax is occasionally twisted simply because he is in the habit of writing in that style, he usually uses un-English inversions to convey a tortuous thought or psychological state, to encompass a grand subject, or to provide a forward and spinning movement to the verse. When one considers Milton's use of metaphor, one must offer more concessions to the anti-Miltonists. To give the label Latinate to some of his diction is to state only half of the truth, for his Latinate words retain their English meanings. Milton's word-play calls attention to a word's etymology. By using words in their proper and primary sense, he attempts to recreate, at least in part, the prelapsarian state of language. Most Miltonic epic similes have considerable relevance to the narrative, though some point to an unlikeness between vehicle and tenor. See entry 110.

Paradise Lost

621   RICKS, CHRISTOPHER. "Sound and Sense in *Paradise Lost*."
*Essays by Divers Hands: Being the Transactions of the Royal Society
of Literature*, n.s. 39 (1977):92-111. Reprinted in *The Force of Poetry*
(Oxford: Clarendon Press, 1984), pp. 60-79.
        In *Paradise Lost*, we do not relive the experiences of the poem.
Rather, where Shakespeare presents the immediacy of experience,
Milton mediates it and asks us to contemplate it. Milton's poetry is, as
Leavis observes (see entry 614), external. But a poem that works from
the outside is not inferior or lacking in its presentation of experience.

622   SHAKLEE, MARGARET E. "Grammatical Agency and the
Argument for Responsibility in *Paradise Lost*." *ELH* 42 (1975):518-
30.
        To see oneself as the agent of one's actions and to assume
responsibility for them constitute moral viability in *Paradise Lost*.
Grammatical evidence, such as the agent's role as the subject of a
sentence in which he or she performs the action of the verb (and the
agent's commitment to truth in uttering the sentence), makes a claim
for moral viability. Through passive voice structures and
nominalization, agents can attempt to shift or delete agency and thus
evade responsibility. God uses many such constructions in *Paradise
Lost*, speaking in passives and abstractions because he is the judge who
reads the law. More than any other character, Satan deletes the agent
from his sentence structures, attempting to clear himself of
responsibility or to see himself as victim or object. Eve is ignorant of
agency not only at the pool and in her dream, but when she accepts the
serpent and the apple as viable agents. She turns to agent-deleted
constructions after the fall.

623   SHERRY, BEVERLEY. "Speech in *Paradise Lost*." *Milton Studies* 8
(1975):247-66.
        Tudor and Stuart writers frequently note that God gives pure
and eloquent speech to Adam and Eve, but that it is corrupted with the
fall and later repaired; eloquence has a regenerative effect on fallen
humans. The various styles of speech in *Paradise Lost*--infernal and
Edenic, pre- and postlapsarian, for example--display different rhythms
as Milton connects eloquence and virtue. Originally pure, Adam and
Eve's conversation deteriorates after the fall, and they later reestablish

communication with reason and love. With Orphean abilities, the narrator speaks to and receives praise from God.

624   SMITH, GEORGE WILLIAM, Jr. "Iterative Rhetoric in *Paradise Lost.*" *Modern Philology* 74 (1976):1-19.

Not used to embellish or conceal meaning, iteration in *Paradise Lost* appears both from line to line (prosodic iteration) and, more frequently, from one grammatical unit to the next (clausal iteration). In the dialogue in heaven in Book 3, God and the Son use more extensive iteration than anywhere else in the poem. Critics are wrong when they state that the Father's speeches use a great deal of iterative rhetoric because Milton is mimicking the Logos or that Satan's seduction speech to Eve uses extensive iteration to distract her from his faulty logic. Only in the dialogue in Book 3 is the Father's speech filled with iterative rhetoric, and the frequency of iteration in Satan's speeches is fairly consistent throughout *Paradise Lost*. Iterative rhetoric appears regularly to emphasize the themes of mercy and justice in God's speeches. Rhetorical schemes reinforce meanings.

625   SMITH, HALLETT. "No Middle Flight." *Huntington Library Quarterly* 15 (1952):159-72.

We now recognize that *Paradise Lost* is firmly rooted in the hexameral tradition. Milton's claims that his "advent'rous song" has never been attempted may be based on both its style and content--that is, the merging of poetic fiction and doctrine makes *Paradise Lost* new. The style of the epic can be baroque as descriptive details press against the boundaries of the medium that contains them. In general, his style mediates between the extremes of Elizabethan luxury and neoclassical restraint.

626   STEADMAN, JOHN M. "*Ethos* and *Dianoia*: Character and Rhetoric in *Paradise Lost.*" In *Language and Style in Milton: A Symposium in Honor of the Tercentenary of "Paradise Lost."* Edited by Ronald David Emma and John T. Shawcross. New York: Frederick Ungar Publishing Co., 1967, pp. 193-232.

Critics frequently ignore Aristotle's warning against confusing ethos (character) and dianoia (thought). In *Paradise Lost*, a speaker's remarks are often an index of thought, not of character. Argument

Paradise Lost

implies thought; what a speaker seeks or avoids reveals character. Deliberative oratory, a form of moral persuasion that urges a listening character and reader to do or not to do something, forms a substantial part of *Paradise Lost* and *Paradise Regained*. Judicial rhetoric is also prominent in *Paradise Lost* because of its emphasis on defense and accusation, and justice and injustice. Demonstrative rhetoric fixes the responsibility for sin on man rather than on God. The various speakers' main oratorical tool in the epics is the enthymeme. Satan often employs fallacious arguments, particularly equivocation, *secundum quid*, *ignoratio elenchi*, and false cause. Opposing these, Christian rhetoric is divinely inspired and emerges from the speaker's virtue, truth, and clarity.

627   STEIN, ARNOLD. "Milton and Metaphysical Art: An Exploration." *ELH* 16 (1949):120-34.
       The ideal description in Renaissance rhetoric is a speaking picture, in which the writer seems to have painted a work and the reader seems to have viewed it. In some of *Paradise Lost*'s descriptive passages, Milton achieves the effect of a painting as he carefully controls verb tenses to create depth, blur and focus details, and suspend time. He even conveys music in the manner of painting. If Milton's verse is stylistically complex, he does not allow complex expression to dominate ideas or use craftsmanship as its own end. His poetic complexity is inner and functional.

628   TOLIVER, HAROLD E. "Complicity of Voice in *Paradise Lost*." *Modern Language Quarterly* 25 (1964):153-70.
       In *Paradise Lost*, God's linguistic scheme creates a variety of decorums for speech; this becomes even more complex when Satan introduces ironies and lies. The narrator must fashion a human decorum from this range, using his voice to take in human experience and to create a dialectic of lies and truth. Wandering demonic speech and the program of heroism in collapse foreshadow the voice and perspective of man after the fall. Before the fall, Adam's language, though limited, participates in the Word's creative power; after the fall, Eve learns how to use irony, illusion, and inflated language.

629   WATERS, LINDSAY. "Milton, Tasso, and the Renaissance Grand Style: Syntax and Its Effect on the Reader." *Stanford Italian Review* 2 (1981):81-92.

By using a purposefully obscure style in *Paradise Lost*, Milton confuses the reader with difficult syntax but, as a reward, suggests that deeper meanings lurk beneath the text's surface. The analogue for Milton's grand style appears in the "parlar disgiunto" of Tasso's work. According to Italian literary theory, rhetoric can merely prove or persuade; poetry must overwhelm and enrapture readers so they will submit themselves to the poem. The main goal of Milton's sublime style is not the reader's rational comprehension of what the poem states; rather, he uses a stylistic strategy based on obscurity and emotional effect.

See also entries 49, 66, 89-90, 93, 109-11, 126, 129, 165, 171, 217, 235, 237-43, 245-46, 248, 250-51, 253, 409, 455, 457, 497, 549, 553, 595, 918, 942, 1010.

THE NARRATOR, HIS INVOCATIONS, AND HIS MUSES

630   ADELMAN, JANET. "Creation and the Place of the Poet in *Paradise Lost*." In *The Author in His Work: Essays on a Problem in Criticism*. Edited by Louis L. Martz and Aubrey Williams. New Haven, Conn., and London: Yale University Press, 1978, pp. 51-69.

Concerned with varieties of and attitudes toward creation, including the process of writing poetry and its sources, *Paradise Lost* frequently implicates Milton in its subject. The structure of imitation is everywhere in the epic--in the reflections of God, the Son, heaven, and Satan. God is the great creator; the poet imitates him and "explores the status of his own poetic creation as imitative act" (52). But Milton's inspiring spirit has connections to both God and Satan. Only by acknowledging the muse's gifts does the poet avoid participating in the Satanic model. In his invocations, the poet mixes self-denial and self-assertion. Just as Eve is created by God and through Adam, so *Paradise Lost* is created by God through Milton. When Adam misunderstands his relationship to Eve and becomes a victim of self-love, he illustrates one temptation that Milton faces with respect to his poetic creation.

Paradise Lost

631   BARUCH, FRANKLIN R. "Milton's Blindness: The Conscious and Unconscious Patterns of Autobiography." *ELH* 42 (1975):26-37.

In *Paradise Lost*, Milton introduces autobiographical concerns only when they suit the poem's larger aesthetic and intellectual purposes. When he writes about his blindness in Book 3, it shows his sharing in the woe of postlapsarian life, a woe that Adam and Eve suffer; yet it also shows providence working in time, the very lesson Michael gives Adam. By writing the poem and bringing up the torment of his blindness, Milton hopes to gain emotional insulation, to lessen the pain, and to understand his woe. Passive verbs and the flight to a spiritual realm alleviate his sense of being threatened; action is possible and holy for him in a spiritual arena. Unconsciously, he wishes to escape the fact of his blindness. The poet and blind man unconsciously become separate individuals. Located at the moral center of *Paradise Lost*, the poet figure must be tested and make choices. His actions continue to parallel Adam and Eve's when he gains a paradise within.

632   BERRY, BOYD M. "Melodramatic Faking in the Narrator's Voice, *Paradise Lost*." *Milton Quarterly* 10 (1976):1-5.

The narrator of *Paradise Lost* pumps melodrama into situations that are not melodramatic, briefly deluding the reader and then denying the delusion. At the beginning of the war in heaven, when God uses his golden scales, and also when Satan does not recognize Death, the outcomes clash directly "with the expectations which the narrator's voice has aroused" (3). We lose confidence in the narrator's authority.

633   CIRILLO, ALBERT R. "'Hail Holy Light' and Divine Time in *Paradise Lost*." *JEGP: Journal of English and Germanic Philology* 68 (1969):45-56.

Although Milton seeks to justify eternal providence in *Paradise Lost*, his narrative requires a beginning, middle, and end. He gives certain symbols characteristics of the poem's cumulative movement, thus transforming a narrative restriction into a metaphor of providence. He blurs sequential distinctions in *Paradise Lost*. In the invocation to Book 3, Milton reconciles the apparently opposite lights, one the first-born of heaven and the other of the eternal coeternal beam. Through Christ, man's created or material light is linked to God's uncreated or essential one. Milton uses the light of divine inspiration to approach the essential light of Book 3. As a temporal metaphor for the eternal, light encompasses Milton's twofold time scheme. With the separation of the Godhead into Father and Son in the dialogue in heaven, we see how time and first-born light emanate from God and flow back to him. In the invocation to Book 3, Milton uses light imagery to conflate the realms of time and eternity under the aspect of eternity.

634   DIEKHOFF, JOHN S. "The Function of the Prologues in *Paradise Lost.*" *PMLA* 57 (1942):697-704.
       Not digressions but part of *Paradise Lost*'s ethical proof, the prologues attempt to gain the audience's good will by persuading us of the poet's character. Because the poet also acts as a teacher, he must live up to high standards. In part an argument, Milton's epic contains many examples of logical, pathetic, and ethical proofs.

635   FERRY, ANNE DAVIDSON. *Milton's Epic Voice: The Narrator in "Paradise Lost."* Cambridge, Mass.: Harvard University Press, 1963, 202 pp.
       In the opening invocation of *Paradise Lost*, the narrator establishes his relation to the audience and its identity as Adam's heirs who participate in the narrative. The narrator shares our fallen state, but like a bird he can soar beyond our fallen vision because he is a blind bard who has received illumination. Forming part of the action's pattern, his comments are indications of his double perspective, composed of fallen knowledge and inspired vision. Milton's narrator uses complex, artful similes to show contrasts between our fallen world and the prelapsarian world that we cannot see. Rather than showing fragmentation, the narrator's metaphors use double reference to recreate our lost vision and show the unity of divine truth. The argument of *Paradise Lost* is the conflict of forces within the unity of divine creation.

636   FIXLER, MICHAEL. "Plato's Four Furors and the Real Structure of *Paradise Lost.*" *PMLA* 92 (1977):952-62.
       In Milton's view, which parallels Plato's, a divine force inspires the poet, whose verse moves the reader's mind and heart back toward God. The four Platonic raptures--the *furor poeticus* and the others associated respectively with Dionysus, Apollo, and Eros--provide the

Paradise Lost

structure for the four invocations in *Paradise Lost*. As these raptures are assimilated into Christian thought, they involve the soul's awakening (the invocation to Book 9), purification (Book 7), illumination (Book 3), and apotheosis or united vision with God (Book 1). The pattern is a descent followed by an ascent, which parallels the epic's narrative structure.

637 GREGORY, E. R. "Three Muses and a Poet: A Perspective on Milton's Epic Thought." *Milton Studies* 10 (1977):35-64. 5 illustrations.

For Milton, Calliope is the prime and general representative of poetry; Clio, the muse of fame, glory, and heroic poetry because of their relation to the Renaissance concept of history; and Urania, the muse of divine poetry. Milton's allusions to Clio in *Ad Patrem*, *Elegy 6*, and *Mansus* point to his early definition of poetry in the Spenserian tradition. After the early 1640s, Clio disappears from his poetry, for her values cannot be reconciled with Christianity. Invoking Urania, *Paradise Lost* turns out to be a different epic from the one Milton considers earlier. Urania, unlike Clio, has Christian values and renounces the things of this world, the latter being an antiheroic perspective. By emphasizing Uranian values, *Paradise Lost* and *Paradise Regained* reject the heroic tradition.

638 HARDISON, O. B., Jr. "Written Records and Truths of Spirit in *Paradise Lost*." *Milton Studies* 1 (1969):147-65.

Book 1 of *Paradise Lost* links the muse with the Spirit that presided over the creation. Unlike its scriptural precedents, Milton's epic uses the dove--an image for the Holy Spirit--in an erotic image in which creation resembles the sexual impregnation of chaos by the spirit, a sensuous image by which God's world is connected to man's. In the creation scene in Book 7, a tension develops between creation described in sexual terms (a Neoplatonic approach) and in terms that follow Genesis with a literal approach. *Paradise Lost*'s creation is initiated when Christ calms part of chaos, but the process then becomes a compromise between creation as an autonomous or organic process and as a process in which God is the fabricator. When he describes the creation of heaven, Milton portrays the latter process. The command "Be fruitful" links human eros to the erotic creative forces that appear in every level of the created world.

639   HUGHES, MERRITT Y. "Milton and the Symbol of Light." *Studies in English Literature, 1500-1900* 4 (1964):137-62. Reprinted in *Ten Perspectives on Milton* (New Haven, Conn., and London: Yale University Press, 1965), pp. 63-103.

Light imagery is central to *Paradise Lost*, especially in its invocations. Deprived of God's physical epiphany in the book of nature, the blind poet must seek internal, divine illumination. Milton's muse is neither the Greek patron of astronomy nor the Christianized muse of Neoplatonic writings, often called Wisdom or Sapience. Rather, Milton says that Urania is Wisdom's sister, both born of God yet uncreated and always existing, according to Augustine. Robert Fludd provides little help in understanding the invocation to Book 3. We should interpret "Light" in the opening line of Book 3 as physical light, which is connected to the key metaphor of "Celestial light."

640   HUNTER, WILLIAM B., Jr. "Milton's Urania." *Studies in English Literature, 1500-1900* 4 (1964):35-42.

In *Paradise Lost*'s four invocations, Milton calls to the Son to mediate with God on behalf of the poet. He means the Son even in Book 7, where he calls to Urania. The older Venus is called Uranian, and she is interpreted as the principle of heavenly beauty, mind, or intelligence. Milton refers to the Greek Urania and Hebrew Wisdom as sisters, perhaps because each name applies to the second person of the trinity in her own culture. Milton's images for the Father and Son's relationship imply a subordinationist view.

641   LORD, GEORGE de F. "Milton's Dialogue with Omniscience in *Paradise Lost*." In *The Author in His Work: Essays on a Problem in Criticism*. Edited by Louis L. Martz and Aubrey Williams. New Haven, Conn., and London: Yale University Press, 1978, pp. 31-50.

More than other western epic writers, Milton projects himself into *Paradise Lost* as the heavenly muse's collaborator, "a quasi-divine poet of omniscience" (31), and the representative man who is the poem's hero. To dramatize his contrary interior workings, he uses the meditative process of epic creation. He balances faith and doubt, the objective and subjective, and the impersonal and autobiographical by establishing a dialogue between the divinely inspired, omniscient voice (in the invocation to Book 1, for example) and the voice of the fallen, limited poet (in the other three invocations). An Odyssean character,

Paradise Lost

Paradise Lost's narrator parallels Satan in some ways and recognizes the demonic potential of the poetic act. The epic is the instrument of Milton's deliverance through the reassertion, not the submission, of ego.

642 MOLLENKOTT, VIRGINIA R. "Some Implications of Milton's Androgynous Muse." *Bucknell Review* 24, no. 1 (Spring, 1978):27-36. Special issue: *Women, Literature, Criticism*, edited by Harry R. Garvin.

After the invocation to Book 1, the reader of *Paradise Lost* assumes that the muse is masculine, but in Book 7 the muse is identified with the female Urania. The muse's androgyny is clear in the opening, where it broods over the abyss, a verb meaning breed and hatch. Its sexual identity is indeterminate in Book 3's invocation, though the light associates it with the sun-Son as well as the androgynous dove of Book 1. When Milton refers to his "Celestial Patroness" in Book 9, we connect her to the Son, pictured as female in Book 3's invocation. Milton even portrays himself as poet in a female role, waiting to be spiritually impregnated or inspired by a female muse playing a male role. Milton's God is both a great father and mother. With its male and female imagery for God, the Bible is the main source for *Paradise Lost*'s androgynous imagery.

643 MULDER, JOHN R. "The Lyric Dimension of *Paradise Lost*." *Milton Studies* 23 (1987):145-63.

Readers should view *Paradise Lost* "as the picture of a great poet's tentative and faltering search for certitude" (145). In the epic, we experience the process of surrendering to the lack of human certainties. We should not attribute to Milton a confidence or lifelong consistency of principles that is not present. By using a dramatic mode of presentation, Milton lets characters speak, which leads to multiple points of view and the narrator's different perspectives on the speakers. Milton's epic shows his recantation of aspiration through a reenactment of that aspiration: he presents a double pattern of affirming and denying his character, aim, and achievements. As *Paradise Lost* progresses, the prologues grow less religious as the poet's suffering and instruction become his argument. He undergoes not the change he asks for in Book 1's prologue, but a decline and an ascent.

644   PORTER, WILLIAM MALIN. "Milton and Horace: The Post-
       Bellum Muse." *Comparative Literature* 35 (1983):351-61.
       The opening words of Book 7 of *Paradise Lost*, "Descend from
Heav'n," create a political allusion by translating the beginning of one
of Horace's *Odes*. Milton's relationship to the muse is more complex
than Horace's, and it is not always positive; the Orpheus example casts
doubt on Horace's confidence in the muse's patronage. Political
material appears at the end of Book 6, where Milton's version of the
war in heaven is analogous to Horace's notion about celestial combat as
a political event; at the time Horace and Milton write their poems, each
poet's nation has just concluded a civil war. If Horace links inspiration
and celestial revolt because of his need to advise the prince, Milton
separates and reverses them, while dismissing Calliope, to show his
rejection of the restored King Charles II. Milton refuses to assume the
classical poet's role of spokesman for the civic community.

645   REVARD, STELLA P. "Milton's Muse and the Daughters of
       Memory." *English Literary Renaissance* 9 (1979):432-41.
       In *Paradise Lost*, Milton could invoke no muse (as in *Paradise
Regained*) or a Christian spirit (as do other Renaissance epics).
Although he insists that his muse is a divine descendant of God rather
than one of the nine muses on Olympus, she retains the latter
association because of her name, gender, haunts, habits, and relation to
her poet. Milton and his muse have a mystical communion that
"established and sustained the poet's dedication to his vocation of
poetry" (432). His muse has a close resemblance to that of Hesiod, who
receives the gift of divine song, as do Isaiah, Ezekiel, and Moses.
Attempting to restore poetry to its ancient place of honor, Milton's
invocation thus combines the Greek and Hebrew traditions.

646   RIGGS, WILLIAM G. *The Christian Poet in "Paradise Lost."*
       Berkeley, Los Angeles, and London: University of California Press,
       1972, 202 pp.
       In *Paradise Lost*'s four invocations, Milton's encounters with
Satan, Adam and Eve, the angels, and the Son explore what it means to
be a Christian poet who exemplifies the relevance of his epic to fallen
man. Seeking to contrast himself with Satan, Milton does not ignore the
similarities. He parallels his poetic flight, an exploration of truth, with
Adam's education at the hands of God's various representatives.

Paradise Lost

Guided by the urge to assert eternal providence, the poet pursues knowledge even as he admits the possibility of self-deception or Satanic inspiration. Providing a more perfect pattern of the Christian poet, the angelic ministry in *Paradise Lost* reveals the range and limits of Christian poetry. Raphael and Michael replace Milton and assume the role of epic narrator, which suggests that the mortal poet follows angelic precedent. As a poet, Milton imitates the Son, a servant of mankind and of God's Word who speaks as a mediator. Imitating Christ is a precarious act for Milton, because it carries the danger of Satanic overreaching. Not an anticipatory work, *Paradise Regained* has as its subject an actual recovery of paradise.

647 ROLLIN, ROGER B. "Milton's 'I's': The Narrator and the Reader in *Paradise Lost*." In *Renaissance and Modern Essays in Honor of Edwin M. Moseley*. Edited by Murray J. Levith. Saratoga Springs, N.Y.: Skidmore College, 1976, pp. 33-55.
　　　The narrator of *Paradise Lost* is a developing character who acts as the protagonist in a dramatic subplot that frames *Paradise Lost* and centers on his struggle to write a great poem. His play occurs in four acts (the four invocations) and a denouement in the epic's final lines, which give the evidence that he has completed his task. As readers, we do not perform physical or verbal acts; we react to *Paradise Lost* as we partially suppress the moral ego-function of reality-testing while extending our mental and emotional ranges. We experience literary characters both by taking in some of their traits and by projecting some of our own onto them. Because the narrator says the epic's genesis occurs in dreamlike states, his poem has some qualities of dreams. Readers will find *Paradise Lost* pleasurable insofar as they can correlate it with their idiosyncratic psychical personalities, especially their unconscious fantasies.

648 ROSENBLATT, JASON P. "The Mosaic Voice in *Paradise Lost*." *Milton Studies* 7 (1975):207-32.
　　　The Mosaic voice is present throughout *Paradise Lost*. While critics place Moses in a Neoplatonic context and elevate him to nearly a godlike status, we should also see that, in Books 10-12, Milton stresses Moses's fallen condition and brings him into a closer relationship with the narrator. Typologically related to Christ, Moses has a role in the mediated process of accommodation that leads to the Savior. Christ

completes Moses's meaning and the purpose of his mission. *Paradise Lost*'s narrator calls on the Holy Spirit to transform Moses's narrative by showing its Christian significance and thus to transform the poem, reader, and poet.

649   SHAWCROSS, JOHN T. "The Poet in the Poem: John Milton's Presence in *Paradise Lost.*" *CEA Critic* 48-49 (1986):32-55.
        The poet in *Paradise Lost*, or "the elements of the poem that indicate a poetizing mind behind it" (37), appears in his theme of the need for and means of obedience, which is conveyed by language, rhetorical devices, allusions, structure, and content. The image of the lake in Book 1, along with many words from Satan's early speeches, reappears frequently in different forms and contexts, all controlled by the poet. Too many of the twentieth-century's negative comments about *Paradise Lost* appear when a critic presents a dictum and evaluates Milton's epic according to it. Milton continues to be a living presence in modern poetry.

650   SIMS, JAMES H. "The Miltonic Narrator and Scriptural Tradition: An Afterword." In *Milton and Scriptural Tradition: The Bible into Poetry.* Edited by James H. Sims and Leland Ryken. Columbia: University of Missouri Press, 1984, pp. 192-205.
        Because Milton uses his internal spirit to guide his reason in interpreting Scripture, he rejects some canonical and human authorities but accepts others. Guided by the muse, the epic narrator of *Paradise Lost* and *Paradise Regained*, like Milton when he is led by the Holy Spirit, has to distinguish truth from falsehood or mere opinion. Milton's narrator presents more alternatives subject to one's opinion than alternatives based on truth and falsehood. He and the reader may exercise their judgment about things indifferent. The poems present this struggling of choice.

651   STEIN, ARNOLD. *The Art of Presence: The Poet and "Paradise Lost."* Berkeley, Los Angeles, and London: University of California Press, 1977, 199 pp.
        The presence of the dedicated poet is formally admitted into *Paradise Lost*, but he reveals and conceals many aspects of it to satisfy the purposes and pleasures of his art. Throughout the epic, the poet is

Paradise Lost

on trial as the truth of his inspiration and the merit of his action are subject to judgment. As Milton tells the story of Adam and Eve at the center of *Paradise Lost*, he must prevent the reader's fallen experience from providing the basis by which to evaluate the first couple. Heavenly events provide the pattern for what should occur on earth, which always returns to God's love, the supreme example of creative action. When Adam gives Eve permission to work alone, he commits an error of will and judgment that we deplore yet applaud, because the fall that occurs must appear in the story, and this result limits Adam's involvement in Eve's temptation. The poet's presence appears as detachment or reticence in some places and more involved and accepting of authority in others.

652   SUNDELL, ROGER H. "The Singer and His Song in the Prologues of *Paradise Lost*." In *Milton and the Art of Sacred Song*. Edited by J. Max Patrick and Roger H. Sundell. Madison and London: University of Wisconsin Press, 1979, pp. 65-80.
Together, the four prologues in *Paradise Lost* form a single poem with its own voice, progression, and themes and purpose. The prologues to Books 1 and 7 are similar in their style of formal invocations; the prologues to Books 3 and 9 do not act as invocations but are "in part literary progress reports and in part commentaries on subjects introduced in the opening prologue" (69). We need to distinguish the poet's voice in the prologues from that of the omniscient, editorial narrator. The poet's tone moves from confidence to presumption and then from apprehension to a more mature confidence.

See also entries 181, 189, 208, 443-45, 448, 454, 456, 463, 468-69, 474, 478, 480, 494, 500, 505, 514, 516, 520, 528-29, 533, 536, 590, 602, 709, 798.

HELL (WITH CHAOS AND LIMBO OF VANITY)

653   ADAMS, ROBERT M. "A Little Look into Chaos." In *Illustrious Evidence: Approaches to English Literature of the Early Seventeenth Century*. Edited by Earl Miner. Berkeley, Los Angeles, and London: University of California Press, 1975, pp. 71-89.
In *Paradise Lost*, before the rebel angels fall, the cosmos is only heaven and chaos. God, in order to create hell, subtracts part of

chaos. We do not know whether heaven is created from chaos (though we know it is created), but the rest of the cosmos is ordered chaos, which can return to its original state. Chaos "represents a very deeply felt image of evil as essential weakness" (76), neutrally poised between good and evil, but inclining toward the latter. Satan serves God in many ways that involve their enmity of chaos. By taking up residence in hell, Satan structures the cosmos and creates a range of moral and physical potential for man. His most important function is in terms of *Paradise Lost*'s argument, for his independence from God prevents the Father from receiving the responsibility for evil in the world. Satan even takes much of Adam and Eve's burden of guilt. As God and Satan parallel each other, Milton risks having chaos prevail.

654 BRODWIN, LEONORA LEET. "The Dissolution of Satan in *Paradise Lost*: A Study of Milton's Heretical Eschatology." *Milton Studies* 8 (1975):165-207.

Although *Christian Doctrine* argues that the fallen angels are condemned to a punishment of everlasting death in hell, *Paradise Lost* takes the heretical view that Satan, the creatures he perverts (both human and angelic), and hell itself will undergo a final dissolution while the just will be resurrected to eternal life. Milton is indebted to the Socinian eschatology for this heresy.

655 CHAMBERS, A. B. "Chaos in *Paradise Lost*." *Journal of the History of Ideas* 24 (1963):55-84.

Christian Doctrine says that matter is good, but in *Paradise Lost* chaos is "unmistakably opposed to God" (55). The sources of Milton's thoughts about chaos are Genesis, Plato, Greco-Roman atomism, and--most importantly--Hesiod. In terms of its physical properties of confusion ruled by chance, Milton's chaos resembles that of Plato's *Timaeus* more closely than any other antecedent. These properties also help account for the enmity between God and chaos. Milton views chaos and night as eternal, having always resided with the infinite extension of God but being preceded by a "material" God and "incorporal," passive matter (possibly the prime matter, night). Chaos or chance is the reigning power of the realm through which Satan travels. Only with God's power can the passive principle of matter take on the first rudiments of form and become chaos. We must consider chaos one of the important settings in *Paradise Lost*.

Paradise Lost

656   FALLON, STEPHEN M. "Milton's Sin and Death: The Ontology of
       Allegory in *Paradise Lost*." *English Literary Renaissance* 17
       (1987):329-50.

           Using an Augustinian ontology of evil, Milton in *Paradise Lost*
       creates Sin and Death as allegorical characters who have a lesser reality
       because they negate substance rather than expressing it. Moral evil,
       thus deprived of any ontological status, is appropriately described in
       allegorical characters who, as abstractions or universals, lose much
       reality. As we follow Milton's poetic career, we see that he grows
       increasingly dissatisfied with allegory. Sin and Death measure the
       negative ontological distance between Lucifer and Satan--the turning
       from God and the result of that turning. In the episodes involving chaos
       and the limbo of vanity, Milton again uses allegory to describe
       characters who have a lesser reality.

657   FIORE, AMADEUS P., O.F.M. "Satan Is a Problem: The Problem
       of Milton's 'Satanic Fallacy' in Contemporary Criticism." *Franciscan
       Studies* 17 (1957):173-87.

           Twentieth-century critics say that we must respond to *Paradise
       Lost*'s Satan in two ways: artistically and aesthetically or morally and
       theologically. If we follow Rajan's view (see entry 532), which favors the
       former but also insists on the latter, Satan cannot be the poem's hero.
       Waldock's aesthetic evaluation (see entry 558) finds a division between
       the heroic Satan of the opening books and the Satan of the rest of
       Paradise Lost, who does not emerge as a hero. Using a historical
       perspective, Lewis (see entry 506) finds Satan an ass, while Tillyard (see
       entries 216, 218) sees a great irony in Satan's portrait. When we read
       Paradise Lost, we should recognize that the narrator's voice is always
       inferior to the assumed voices of his characters. The narrator and his
       characters offer consistent views in Books 3-12, but even in Books 1-2
       we should not be seduced by Satan, who ironically exposes himself as
       unheroic when he speaks.

658   FLESCH, WILLIAM. "The Majesty of Darkness." In *John Milton*.
       Modern Critical Views. Edited by Harold Bloom. New York, New
       Haven, Conn., and Philadelphia, Pa.: Chelsea House Publishers,
       1986, pp. 293-311.

           In order to claim poetry's prerogative as the one human
       endeavor that is adequate to the God of *Paradise Lost*, the epic

dramatizes a series of erroneous interpretations of God, who derives his authority from the one thing that Milton believes is antipathetic to idolatry: poetry. Satan's iconoclastic traits, which lead him to rebel against a tyrant, are admirable, though he shares some of God's tyrannical tendencies. Because Satan wishes to be worshiped as an icon, his iconoclasm is not sustained. His understanding of God is better than that of the other angels (loyal or rebel) since it is less iconic. Only Abdiel recognizes a sharp discontinuity between the highest angels and the Son. Raphael attributes God's apparent invisibility to a weakness in angelic vision, not to one of God's attributes; similarly, Adam and Eve think they cannot see God because of their place in the chain of being. The fall is fortunate because it allows a greater understanding of God.

659   FOLEY, JACK. "'Sin, Not Time': Satan's First Speech in *Paradise Lost*." *ELH* 37 (1970):37-56.
       If we exclude the narrator, Satan utters the first word in *Paradise Lost*, "If," and the following speech contains his first words as Satan, not as Lucifer. His early speeches present points that become true or explicit, often in ways Satan does not intend, only later in the epic. Contrasted with the narrator's confident voice, Satan's is initially uncertain and ignorant; his personality is on the brink of nothingness. The first speech shows the birth of the Satanic mentality, which includes a gift for euphemism, blaming the wrong party, and defiance.

660   GALLAGHER, PHILIP J. "'Real or Allegoric': The Ontology of Sin and Death in *Paradise Lost*." *English Literary Renaissance* 6 (1976):317-35.
       When Milton presents Sin and Death in *Paradise Lost*, he argues that they are consistently real (historical and physical), offers a systematic critique of Hesiodic cosmology, and reconstructs the origins of the Greek myth. Even when Milton personifies Sin and Death in order to adhere to his scriptural source (James 1:15), he insists that they are still real characters. He believes that Hesiod's myth of the birth of Athena from Zeus's head cannot be a distortion of St. James's epistle, of which the Greek poet could not know; rather, in Milton's view, Hesiod tells a true story that is actually a version of the conception and birth of Sin, but that becomes distorted by Satan.

Paradise Lost

661   GILBERT, ALLAN H. "Critics of Mr. C. S. Lewis on Milton's Satan." *South Atlantic Quarterly* 47 (1948):216-25.

Although such critics as Hamilton (see entry 663) and Stoll (see entry 683) raise legitimate concerns about Lewis's discussion of Satan (see entry 506)--Lewis does exaggerate and display faulty taste--they end up agreeing that Milton's Satan is both absurd and a grand poetic achievement. Unlike some scholars, Lewis rediscovers *Paradise Lost*'s final books, which clarify our double perspective of Satan.

662   GRIFFIN, DUSTIN. "Milton's Hell: Perspectives on the Fallen." *Milton Studies* 13 (1979):237-54.

In Books 1 and 2 of *Paradise Lost*, we see the lesser angels from different perspectives and distances. They thus appear at times as "spiteful fiends" and at other times as "comic bustlers" (237) who are related to postlapsarian humans. These presentations prevent readers from making easy and final judgments of those characters, especially when we realize that judging them is equivalent to judging ourselves. Combining the three parts of Virgil's underworld, Milton modifies the portrait of hell, which in *Paradise Lost* resembles our world and features activities that parallel ours. We sympathize with the residents.

663   HAMILTON, G. ROSTREVOR. *Hero or Fool? A Study of Milton's Satan*. London: George Allen and Unwin, 1944, 41 pp.

When we read about Satan in *Paradise Lost*, two radically different responses are possible: we may identify completely with his party, or we may be so committed to the loyal angels that we cannot give Satan his due. As an abstraction, he is evil; as an imaginary creature, however, he is composed of good and evil, heroism and folly. His speeches and actions in *Paradise Lost* reveal a mixture of magnificence and vice, but the narrator uses epithets and intrusive comments to emphasize the latter. Milton the moralist thus tries to control Milton the poet, who triumphs. Not a fool, Satan is heroic because he seeks to overthrow a God of power and vengeance who does not often show his capacity for love. But Satan's heroism is perverted by his selfishness and pride. See entry 661.

664   HUCKABAY, CALVIN. "The Satanist Controversy of the Nineteenth Century." *Studies in English Renaissance Literature*.

Edited by Waldo F. McNeir. Louisiana State University Studies, Humanities Series, no. 12. Baton Rouge: Louisiana State University Press, 1962, pp. 197-210.

While many eighteenth-century commentators are repelled by Satan, Dryden anticipates Blake's elevation of him to the role of *Paradise Lost*'s hero. The young Romantics embrace Blake's view, but some orthodox critics, though they agree with him, seek to justify or explain away Satan's heroism, often by focusing on only Books 1 and 2, by removing Satan from the context of *Paradise Lost*, or by ignoring the epic tradition. Anti-Satanists in the nineteenth century include Landor and Morris. Raleigh's study (see entry 66) is the culmination of the nineteenth-century's Satanist criticism of *Paradise Lost*. The debate continues in our own century.

665 HUGHES, MERRITT Y. "Milton's Limbo of Vanity." In *Th'Upright Heart and Pure: Essays on John Milton Commemorating the Tercentenary of the Publication of "Paradise Lost."* Edited by Amadeus P. Fiore, O.F.M. Duquesne Studies, Philological Series, vol. 10. Pittsburgh, Pa.: Duquesne University Press, 1967, pp. 7-24.

The paradise of fools passage is linked to Michael's presentation of the consequences of the fall in Books 11-12 of *Paradise Lost*. Milton uses the example of Empedocles (3.471) to show the vain human hope of fame, and the example of Cleombrotus (3.473) to illustrate the surrendering to pagan teaching of the right to individual judgment about immortality and other great issues. Milton's limbo of vanity episode draws on Ficino's commentary on Plato's Er.

666 HUGHES, MERRITT Y. "'Myself am Hell.'" *Modern Philology* 54 (1956):80-94. Reprinted in *Ten Perspectives on Milton* (New Haven, Conn., and London: Yale University Press, 1965), pp. 136-64.

The hell of *Paradise Lost* is both an imaginatively realized version of the Neoplatonists' psychological and moral hell (a microcosm) and a place consistent with Milton's belief that hell exists outside our universe (a macrocosm), created by God for evil beings. When Satan is punished by being transformed into a serpent and banished to a place where everything reflects the monstrosity of the evil in the demons' hearts, the truths of allegory and history are barely distinguishable.

Poetry

Paradise Lost

667   HUGHES, MERRITT Y. "Satan and the 'Myth' of the Tyrant." In *Essays in English Literature from the Renaissance to the Victorian Age Presented to A. S. P. Woodhouse.* Edited by Millar MacLure and F. W. Watt. [Toronto and Buffalo, N.Y.]: University of Toronto Press, 1964, pp. 125-48. Reprinted in *Ten Perspectives on Milton* (New Haven, Conn., and London: Yale University Press, 1965), pp. 165-95.

   In *Paradise Lost*, Satan is the archetypal tyrant whose influence shapes the political process that Michael describes in Books 11-12. Not a representation of King Charles or of Cromwell, Satan is a classic paranoiac and an idol in Plato's and Bacon's meanings of the word.

668   HUNTER, WILLIAM B., Jr. "The Heresies of Satan." In *Th'Upright Heart and Pure: Essays on John Milton Commemorating the Tercentenary of the Publication of "Paradise Lost."* Edited by Amadeus P. Fiore, O.F.M. Duquesne Studies, Philological Series, vol. 10. Pittsburgh, Pa.: Duquesne University Press, 1967, pp. 25-34.

   In *Paradise Lost*, Satan expounds heretical views, yet no other characters (or the narrator) point to this. Satan denies God's omnipotence, parodies the Trinity's mystical union and the Incarnation, and ignores the Son's existence, probably to display his monarchianism, which rejects a triune Godhead. Of the two kinds of monarchianism, dynamic and modalistic, *Paradise Regained* indicates that Satan believes in the former, meaning that he denies the Son's very existence. If Milton were an Arian, he would adopt this position.

669   HUNTLEY, FRANK L. "A Justification of Milton's 'Paradise of Fools' (*P.L.* III, 431-499)." *ELH* 21 (1954):107-13.

   The simile that introduces the paradise of fools episode is appropriate for the midpoint of Satan's journey from hell to Eden, for it describes a vulture traveling from a snowy mountain range to the fertile ground of India. In the paradise of fools episode, Milton presents friars and priests, the future victims of Satan's sin of pride, who reverse Satan's direction by moving from earth to the wind-swept plain. The key images in the limbo episode are connected to pride or monstrous births, which link this passage to others in *Paradise Lost*.

670   LAW, JULES DAVID. "Eruption and Containment: The Satanic Predicament in *Paradise Lost*." *Milton Studies* 16 (1982):35-60.

Satan's punishment in *Paradise Lost* is a freedom that compromises his energies and that he cannot fill. Many loyal angels and many scholars misunderstand his punishment by assuming that it involves restriction or captivity, but breaking through such restraints would allow Satan some measure of heroism. Although Satan and his followers seek containment, freedom and self-extension lead him to wander (physically and rhetorically) and ultimately to dissolve. Only God and chaos need no boundaries to define their identities, so any desire to go beyond one's limitations must take one of those two forms.

671   LEONARD, JOHN. "'Though of Thir Names': The Devils in *Paradise Lost*." *Milton Studies* 21 (1985):157-78.
      Although Milton assigns names to the devils in *Paradise Lost*, and Raphael uses the ones they will acquire, the narrator insists that these are not the names they had in heaven. Satan and his troops never call each other by the names Milton gives them. The demons have no names in *Paradise Lost*. In Satan's career, there are two major changes in his relation to his name: the loss of his unfallen name in the rebellion and the acceptance of his new name, Satan.

672   LOW, ANTHONY. "The Image of the Tower in *Paradise Lost*." *Studies in English Literature, 1500-1900* 10 (1970):171-81.
      Bracketing *Paradise Lost*, two buildings--Pandemonium in Book 1 and the tower of Babel in Book 12--symbolize the culmination of evil's attempt to rival and create its own reality. But the buildings are merely parodies of God's creative power, and they are connected to the epic's metaphors of ascent and descent. Babel expresses pride, the most perverse kind of sinfulness, until it is humbled in a mixture of the tragic catastrophe of worldly greatness and the comic ridicule of foolish presumption. Treated more seriously, Pandemonium is associated with the tragedies of fallen, great empires. Besides acting as a unifying image for heaven, earth, and hell, the tower image functions proleptically in *Paradise Lost*, for it is often linked to Satan and prophesies his disaster.

673   MERRILL, THOMAS F. "Milton's Satanic Parable." *ELH* 50 (1983):279-95.

Paradise Lost

According to Christian hermeneutics, the parable is an incarnational instrument that stretches language to merge divine and worldly realities. Central to the use of parable is the delegated sensibility, a character who shares the postlapsarian perspective as well as the bliss of prelapsarian life and who can mediate between them, create a sense of mystery by evoking religious knowledge, and use the medium of human language. Satan is "the glass in *Paradise Lost* through which we see God darkly" (285). A source of more profound religiosity than God, Satan utters hermeneutically affective language. In the Satanic parables in *Paradise Lost*--such as his opening speech and soliloquy in Book 4--the sacred interpenetrates the secular. The demon's parables give us an awareness of God's presence.

674 MUSGROVE, S. "Is the Devil an Ass?" *Review of English Studies* 21 (1945):302-15.

By allowing Books 1 and 2 of *Paradise Lost* to convince them of Satan's glory, romantic critics start at the wrong point. Milton does not need to prove that Satan is evil; he assumes this, and so must every reader approaching *Paradise Lost*. Romantic critics judge Satan by his early appearances and by his words alone, while ignoring context. In the opening books, he does seem magnificent, but this trait appeals to our unregenerate nature. Milton presents narratorial comments and Satan's own denigrating episodes to undercut the apparent splendor. Satan lies to others and to himself, and feels sexual jealousy. Neither a nincompoop nor a Prometheus, Satan shrinks and darkens after we leave Books 1 and 2; he proceeds in a general downward direction.

675 PECHEUX, SISTER M. CHRISTOPHER. "The Council Scenes in *Paradise Lost*." In *Milton and Scriptural Tradition: The Bible into Poetry*. Edited by James H. Sims and Leland Ryken. Columbia: University of Missouri Press, 1984, pp. 82-103.

While the Bible, in its earliest stages, shows Yahweh presiding over the lesser gods (the gods of the nations), commentators soon demythologize this pagan concept by presenting the council members as angels and then as men, particularly as prophets. Milton's council in hell corresponds to the earliest view by referring, as Milton almost always does, to the rebel angels as gods. *Paradise Lost*'s infernal councils contain ironic allusions to the biblical council tradition. As we move through the four scenes portraying infernal councils, for example, we see Satan gradually discarding the pretense of democracy. The many heavenly councils show loyal angels instead of gods. But heaven needs not even the expectation of democracy, for its councils exist only to receive and execute God's decrees. Heavenly gatherings are characterized by spontaneity, harmony, and access to God; demonic councils display uncertainty, fear, and anxiety over gaining prestige.

676 RADZINOWICZ, MARY ANN. "Psalms and the Representation of Death in *Paradise Lost*." *Milton Studies* 23 (1987):133-44.

In *Christian Doctrine*, Milton finds evidence in eighteen Psalms to support a heterodox but reasonable idea of death. In *Paradise Lost*, those Psalms form a drama showing the process by which death comes to be understood, beginning with allegorized Semitic myth and ending with a demythologized rationality. Book 1 reveals the process in miniature, and the remaining books recapitulate it, turning to the eighteen death Psalms for ideas, images, structure, and energy. Milton consistently uses the power of art to rationalize death synecdochically; one can deprive death of its power by understanding it: as a physical phenomenon, death is merely sleep; on the metaphysical level, as Michael teaches Adam, it is first a positive force and then a nullity. Death in *Paradise Lost* is an ethical state; its lesson is one of patience and temperance. Two Psalms authorize Milton's allegory of Sin and Death.

677 REBHORN, WAYNE A. "The Humanist Tradition and Milton's Satan: The Conservative as Revolutionary." *Studies in English Literature, 1500-1900* 13 (1973):81-93.

According to Satan's political vision and twisted logic, heaven is a divine monarchy in which order and degree give him preeminence before he falls. The hierarchy exists, Satan believes, yet it does not depend on God, who is only a king who rules by custom but is ruled by fate. From Satan's perspective, God is thus a tyrant who practices nepotism, and the rebels are conservative defenders of the traditional order. Satan sees the war in heaven and against man as ways to show his merit and overcome his shame by rising to the place of pride that he and his followers deserve. But the war is a parody of revolution as the Christian humanist tradition understands the concept. Although the portrayal of heaven as a divine monarchy and God as the supreme king appears paradoxical because of Milton's stand in the English

Paradise Lost

Revolution, we must recognize that, despite their similarities, earthly and heavenly monarchies are different and that Milton is applying political metaphors to the eternal.

678 ROSENBLATT, JASON P. "'Audacious Neighborhood': Idolatry in *Paradise Lost*, Book I." *Philological Quarterly* 54 (1975):553-68.

Based on the Pauline Christian tradition, moral opposites act as a structural device in *Paradise Lost*. The idolatry described in Book 1, lines 387-91, has its source in the antitheses found in 2 Corinthians 6:14-17. Milton uses antitheses and Pauline precedent to stress Satan's and hell's separation from heaven and the difference between past and present. The Exodus story heightens the effects of the devils' victories. While emphasizing the invasions of Jerusalem, the catalogue of demons (*Paradise Lost*, 1.376-521) has a broad temporal range of allusion as well as a wide variety of biblical sources. In the catalogue, the pattern of the holy's contamination by the profane can be connected to the fall and many other events in *Paradise Lost*. According to *Doctrine and Discipline of Divorce*, the union of a Christian and an idolatrous heretic is an act of contagion, like those in Book 9 of *Paradise Lost*, that leads to alienation from God. Even in a happy marriage, a husband should divorce his idolatrous spouse, a theme that helps us better understand Adam's sin.

679 SCHANZER, ERNEST. "Milton's Hell Revisited." *University of Toronto Quarterly* 24 (1955):136-45.

Because the macrocosm and microcosm are so closely related in *Paradise Lost*, the setting in which characters appear is a sign of their current spiritual state. Created by God, hell is ordered and evil, yet in some ways it resembles chaos; the minds of hell's residents show an analogous mixture of evil and chaos produced by passion and the conflict of their dual nature, formerly angelic (of which vestiges remain) but now demonic. Hell's perverted order appears most clearly in its political state of tyranny. To stress the differences between the demonic and divine positions, Milton establishes parallels between hell and heaven. The devils have an urge to turn their new geography into a facsimile of heaven.

680   SCHWARTZ, REGINA. "Milton's Hostile Chaos: '. . . And the Sea was No More.'" *ELH* 52 (1985):337-74.
        Created in a disordered state by God, chaos is good, according to *Christian Doctrine*; but the chaos of *Paradise Lost* is hostile. It resembles Satan, with whom it has its only encounter, in being boundless, evil, and a violator of order in the epic. Even if one believes that chaos is neutral, this does not point to its moral ambiguity, since indeterminacy may be more dangerous in *Paradise Lost* than the choice of disobedience. Milton blurs the distinction between chaos and hell, using synonyms for chaos interchangeably for hell. Chaos is further paralleled with the war in heaven. In *Paradise Lost*, chaos is fallen but also fortunate since it issues in creation; in the drama of salvation, repeated throughout history, God turns evil to good in order to frustrate Satan.

681   STEADMAN, JOHN M. "The Idea of Satan as the Hero of *Paradise Lost*." *Proceedings of the American Philosophical Society* 120 (1976):253-94.
        Critics go to extremes by praising or vilifying Satan. Milton's contemporaries view ethical intent as implicit in the definition of the heroic genre, which leads some to doubt *Paradise Lost*'s status as a heroic poem. Neoclassical critics connect the problem of Satan with questions about *Paradise Lost*'s formal regularity, while many romantic critics identify the duality in Satan's character. A consistent character who manages to be both an Achilles and an Odysseus, Satan in all of his guises is motivated by the will to glory and dominion. He greatly resembles a Machiavellian prince. Satan is the *eidolon*, Christ the true image of divine majesty.

682   STEADMAN, JOHN M. "Milton's Rhetoric: Satan and the 'Unjust Discourse.'" *Milton Studies* 1 (1969):67-92.
        Milton's poetry contains debates between characters using true rhetoric and false rhetoric, or logic and sophistry. When we read the speech of a deceiver such as Satan, the narrator's commentary exposes the adversary's false rhetoric. In *Paradise Lost*, there is no disparity between the narrative and the narrator's commentary. Satan's deceptive oratory is a sign of his ethos (character), not dianoia (thought). Fraudulence is the key theme by which Milton makes Satan's character plausible and consistent, even as he slips from one disguise to the next.

Paradise Lost

Satan generally displays a false ethos, which he deliberately changes to suit the occasion. In *Paradise Lost, Paradise Regained, Samson Agonistes*, and *Comus*, dianoia is prominent: the emphasis on the temptation motif, with its verbal battles, and on wisdom leads Milton to assign key roles to just and unjust discourse.

683   STOLL, ELMER EDGAR. "Give the Devil His Due: A Reply to Mr. Lewis." *Review of English Studies* 20 (1944):108-24.
        Lewis's interpretation of Satan's character is not flattering to the might and cleverness of God, whose enemy is seen to be silly (see entry 506). Lewis insists on applying common sense to the story of Satan, a supernatural creature. Although we should not consider *Paradise Lost*'s hero or Milton a member of the devil's party, we should grant that Satan commands admiration because of his active nature, courage, and pity. Milton disapproves of Satan, but the wicked and terrible are beautiful in *Paradise Lost*. Eve's gift of the apple to Adam expresses not a murderous drive, but jealousy and love. See entries 661, 684.

684   STOLL, ELMER EDGAR. "A Postscript to 'Give the Devil His Due.'" *Philological Quarterly* 28 (1949):167-84.
        See entry 683. Scholars who belittle Satan's personality and accomplishments in *Paradise Lost* are too inflexible and theological to enter into the poem's dramatic situation. In certain areas, Satan deserves our admiration and sympathy. The successful construction of Satan's character leads to a conflict between the poet and moralist in Milton. When Satan disappears from the narrative, *Paradise Lost* is far less interesting.

685   SWIFT, JOHN N. "Similes of Disguise and the Reader of *Paradise Lost*." *South Atlantic Quarterly* 79 (1980):425-35.
        Shape-shifting in *Paradise Lost* is closely connected to Satanic evil. For Satan, metamorphosis is a false freedom that leads to self-discovery. In the early books, Milton uses the extended simile to disguise Satan and allow him temporarily to escape God's and the reader's judgments. The distinction between figurative transformations through similes and literal ones is not always clear in *Paradise Lost*, especially in hell, where form and definition are subjectively fluid.

Milton tempts us to mistake signs for things, especially in the complex similes, almost all of which appear in books dominated by Satanic activity (1, 2, 4, and 9). A reader can penetrate Satan's disguises in complex similes by understanding the interrelationships of allusions in the similes. Recognizing that a simile points to likeness rather than equality, the reader sees it as typology and is drawn to God.

686   WERBLOWSKY, R. J. ZWI. *Lucifer and Prometheus: A Study of Milton's Satan*. London: Routledge and Kegan Paul, 1952, 139 pp. Part reprinted in *Milton: "Paradise Lost," a Casebook*, ed. A. E. Dyson and Julian Lovelock (London and Basingstoke: Macmillan, 1973), pp. 129-51.

The Promethean elements in Milton's Satan account for his appeal, which harms *Paradise Lost*'s unity and purpose. Although Satan is sinful, he also represents the aspiration, basically Greek and unregenerate, toward higher levels of existence. Even as he detests Satan, Milton invests him with courage, steadfastness, and loyalty. We presume but cannot feel God's love in *Paradise Lost*, just as Satan's splendor dominates our awareness of his evil. The *Paradise Lost* that Milton means to write is not the one he produces; his epic demands responses that do not match our genuine ones. Suffering from a Greek type of pride, which is connected to his sensuality, Milton sometimes does not make Satan's pride sufficiently reprehensible. The myth of Prometheus is ambivalent, as *Paradise Regained* dramatizes, pointing toward Christ and toward Satan, with Milton's emphasis on the latter.

687   WILLIAMS, ARNOLD. "The Motivation of Satan's Rebellion in *Paradise Lost*." *Studies in Philology* 42 (1945):253-68. Reprinted in *Milton: Modern Judgements*, ed. Alan Rudrum (London: Macmillan, 1968), pp. 136-50.

Biblical commentaries and literature provide unsatisfactory explanations of Satan's rebellion, the accepted version being that he falls through pride. For Milton's purposes in *Paradise Lost*, this is too abstract and leads to more questions than it resolves. So Milton begins *in medias res*, allowing us to see the start of Satan's rebellion in Book 5 through our perceptions of his fulfilled evil, which appears clearly in Books 1 and 2. The main motivation of Satan is envy at the Son's exaltation, not at man's creation.

Paradise Lost

688 WITTREICH, JOSEPH. "'All Angelic Natures Joined in One': Epic Convention and Prophetic Interiority in the Council Scenes of *Paradise Lost*." *Milton Studies* 17 (1983):43-74.

In an attempt to break the boundaries of the traditional epic form, Milton's "epic undertaking is absorbed into a prophetic vision" (43), and one genre's conventions are altered to suit the purpose of another. The genre of Christian prophecy contains the purified state of all literary forms; it is the containing form of *Paradise Lost*, in which prophetic history chronicles events to explore the interior, spiritual life of every person. In the infernal council of Book 2 and the divine council of Book 3, the poem turns toward allegory and contemplation, thus moving inward to the natures of evil and good. God is the true prophet and Satan the false, and each is further revealed by those loyal to and identified with him.

689 WOOTEN, JOHN. "The Metaphysics of Milton's Epic Burlesque Humor." *Milton Studies* 13 (1979):255-73.

Based on a systematic letdown that travesties a careful buildup of expectations, burlesque debunks. From a theological perspective, burlesque exists in *Paradise Lost* only to be removed at the end of time; from a dramatic perspective, it uses juxtaposition to create tragicomic discords that complicate our experience of the poem's action, as is clear in the limbo of fools episode and in the allegory of Satan, Sin, and Death. Burlesque satire exposes fraud and evil, as it helps people deal with doubts and build new norms where the old ones crumble.

690 WOOTEN, JOHN. "Satan, Satire, and Burlesque Fables in *Paradise Lost*." *Milton Quarterly* 12 (1978):51-58.

Degrading an elevated subject or elevating in order to degrade, burlesque invades other modes in its effort to debunk by mixing high and low. The satiric burlesque of *Paradise Lost* accounts for the tone and manner in the presentation of Satan (and Sin and Death), the paradise of fools, the war in heaven, hell, and the fallen angels in hell.

See also entries 86, 441-42, 448, 450, 459, 462, 529, 533, 549, 562, 589, 596, 602, 774, 778, 796, 972, 988.

EARTH

691 AMOROSE, THOMAS. "Milton the Apocalyptic Historian: Competing Genres in *Paradise Lost*, Books XI-XII." *Milton Studies* 17 (1983):141-62.

In their apocalyptic, millenarian presentation of history, Books 11-12 show how God will lead mankind back to him by destroying "patterns of behavior that obstruct his freeing mankind from fallen history" (141). Milton rejects the cyclical idea of history as the Greco-Roman tradition conceived it, but he also subverts the linear structure of the Judeo-Christian tradition. Although he does not believe in the imminence of millenarian reform, Milton locates that reform in the future, beyond human comprehension yet subject to the choices that people make. Genres collide in Books 11-12, with the prophetic mode prevailing as offering a valid perspective on human events; Milton undercuts both the epic perspective and the view presented in history written without prophecy. The prophet emerges as the new hero, for normal and even epic action produces insignificant results.

692 ANDERSON, DOUGLAS. "Unfallen Marriage and the Fallen Imagination in *Paradise Lost*." *Studies in English Literature, 1500-1900* 26 (1986):125-44.

Milton's treatment of unfallen love and sexuality is carefully restrained because he knows that *Paradise Lost*'s success depends on the impact of the vision of paradisal life. The accommodation of Adam and Eve's marriage places great demands on the reader's imagination. In *Paradise Lost*, hell is more physical and heaven more organized than paradise. As the closest metaphorical approximation of "the union between God and all created beings" (139), paradise is demanding in its use of metaphors, such as marriage, the fruit, and the single prohibition that the Father issues. But the presence in Eden of a sexual hierarchy threatens to compromise this metaphor, as Eve is inferior to Adam. Hierarchy allows the completion of the highest marital promise.

693 BARKER, ARTHUR E. "*Paradise Lost*: The Relevance of Regeneration." In "*Paradise Lost*": *A Tercentenary Tribute*. Edited by Balachandra Rajan. [Toronto and Buffalo, N.Y.]: University of Toronto Press, 1969, pp. 48-78.

Paradise Lost

Milton's career has the appearance of "three-act tragic discontinuity" (52): early poetic promise, controversial prose, and major poetry. Even in *Paradise Lost*, there is a disjunction or discontinuity between mythological or classical naturalistic elements and supernatural Christian ones, and between dogma and drama. Milton's frustrating experiences translate into a tone of despair in some of *Paradise Lost*; but the epic demands that we face the inhuman and weakly human realities of the human condition, which persists in turning favorable opportunities into misery. Responding to despair and misery, Milton's poem asserts the dignity of regenerated human nature. *Paradise Lost* focuses on the human couple and their innocence, which is never static. Its most demanding theme is regeneration, the responsible effort necessary for responsible liberty. Satan's actions are significant only for what they parody.

694   BELL, MILLICENT. "The Fallacy of the Fall in *Paradise Lost*."
       PMLA 68 (1953):863-83.
              The transition between the unfallen and the fallen states simply occurs, though the mind demands a motivation or cause. If the temptation bridges the two conditions, it can be explained only by man's fallen motivations. Disobedience, for example, must be a result rather than a cause of the fall. In *Paradise Lost*, prelapsarian Eden shows symptoms of fallen nature. By distributing indications of Adam and Eve's humanity throughout the epic, Milton makes them susceptible to corruption from the start; perhaps there is no fall in *Paradise Lost* and, thus, no need to search out its causes: "the Fall is only the climax of self-realization reached by humankind already fallen" (878).

695   BELL, ROBERT H. "'Blushing like the morn': Milton's Human
       Comedy." *Milton Quarterly* 15 (1981):47-55.
              If one appreciates the perspective of Adam as narrator when he speaks with Raphael in Book 8 of *Paradise Lost*, one can appreciate the episode's comedy. Adam, briefly self-conscious as a storyteller, relates the domestic epic in which he is the comic hero--larger than life, yet human; bewildered and new-born, yet triumphant and self-confident in God's reassuring grasp. The scene's comedy comes from immediate incongruities (Adam's fear that he will dissolve to his former state or be deprived by God of a partner) that lead to ultimate unities. As in all

archetypal comedies, the hero faces an obstacle, here a debate with a graciously condescending God. The comedy humanizes Adam, leaving readers to resist and resent the angel's "heavy-handed priggishness" when Raphael hears Adam speak adoringly of Eve (52).

696 BENNETT, JOAN S. "'Go': Milton's Antinomianism and the Separation Scene in *Paradise Lost*, Book 9." *PMLA* 98 (1983):388-404.

Antinomianism holds that the coming of Christ abrogates the whole Mosaic Law, which is replaced by Christ's spirit to act as a guide for the believer. In the separation scene in Book 9 of *Paradise Lost*, Milton deals with the antinomians' key concern of how, if one lacks external laws, one knows the difference between action based on personal desire from action based on God's spirit in one's heart. Guided by right reason, Adam and Eve must wrestle with total spiritual liberty, which is more difficult than our responsibility of keeping the law in a fallen world. Milton's antinomianism indicates that Eve must freely decide whether to remain at Adam's side; she should not accept someone else's authority. By letting her go, Adam fails as her governor, for he substitutes his authority for her free decision.

697 BOWERS, FREDSON. "Adam, Eve, and the Fall in *Paradise Lost*." *PMLA* 84 (1969):264-73.

Narrative pressures require *Paradise Lost*'s fall to be believable and inevitable, so Milton makes Adam and Eve's love an act of imperfection (each seeks fulfillment in what he or she is not) within perfection (their love exemplifies the creatures' love of God). More than a foreshadowing of vanity, Eve's episode at the pool shows that she does not ratiocinate but learns by reflection; similarly, Raphael's lesson about sensuality, besides foreshadowing future events, reveals Adam's lack of self-esteem and need to exercise wisdom in judgment. Although Eve expels the evil that Satan introduces in her dream, he succeeds in poisoning her animal spirits and thus rouses discontented thoughts that breed pride. Adam fails by relieving himself of the responsibility of acting as Eve's protector when he says, "thy stay, not free, absents thee more" (9.372). Milton creates narrative probability in Adam's and Eve's actions, which lead them to the fall.

Paradise Lost

698   BROOKS, CLEANTH. "Eve's Awakening." In *Essays in Honor of Walter Clyde Curry*. Vanderbilt Studies in the Humanities, 2. Nashville, Tenn.: Vanderbilt University Press, 1954, pp. 281-98. Reprinted in *Milton: Modern Judgements*, ed. Alan Rudrum (London: Macmillan, 1968), pp. 173-88.

When she wakes after her creation, Eve in *Paradise Lost* immediately shows her powerful intellect. She is charmingly feminine, for Milton uses the traditional concept of woman in his poetry. A sensitivity to beauty is her main difficulty. *Paradise Lost* tells of the creation of many characters--Satan, Death, Eve, and Adam--and we need to compare these episodes and their key images. In the creation of Adam and Eve, Milton implies the nature of the fall: Eve should continue to use her intellect and not be obsessed with her own beauty; Adam too should not be overcome with Eve's image. Self-consciousness, Adam and Eve's knowledge that they have a certain kind of knowledge, comes with the fall and destroys that knowledge.

699   BRYAN, ROBERT A. "Adam's Tragic Vision in *Paradise Lost*." *Studies in Philology* 62 (1965):197-214.

When Michael shows Adam a vision of the world in Book 11 of *Paradise Lost*, Milton uses the traditional idea of the movement of civilization or learning, starting in China and moving to Europe and the new world. But Milton ironically reverses the convention by revealing the progress of sin and corruption in terms of tyranny. The geographical and human names in Books 11-12 come from contemporary travel literature, most of which tells of man's passions ruling his reason in a reenactment of the fall. Adam receives a tragic vision of the fall's consequences.

700   BUDICK, SANFORD. "Milton and the Scene of Interpretation: From Typology toward Midrash." In *Midrash and Literature*. Edited by Geoffrey H. Hartman and Sanford Budick. New Haven, Conn., and London: Yale University Press, 1986, pp. 195-212.

Milton's poetry emphasizes neither percept nor concept, but rather the interpretive process that relates them. In *Paradise Lost*, the first fifty lines of Book 11 draw attention to themselves as a network of interpretation, and they comment on the subject of typological interpretation. By using the mercy seat, the Logos moves the edified heart in Book 11's opening through a deconstruction and reconstruction, which continue until the poem's conclusion. When he ends the epic by referring to man's "solitary way," Milton indicates that we live with individual interpretations of the world--interminable interpretations, misinterpretations, and reinterpretations.

701   BUNDY, MURRAY W. "Milton's Prelapsarian Adam." *Research Studies of the State College of Washington* 13 (1945):163-84. Reprinted in *Milton: Modern Judgements*, ed. Alan Rudrum (London: Macmillan, 1968), pp. 151-72.

In the 1674 edition of *Paradise Lost*, Milton divides the original Book 7 at line 640 in order to clarify his intention. Book 8, in its final form, begins with Adam's criticism of the providential plan and ends with his criticism of Eve's creation, thus shifting the focus from God's creation of the universe to man's comprehension and acceptance of the divine plan. Book 8 studies Adam alone so that we may understand his ability to reason on the eve of the temptation. The contrasts between Adam's and Eve's experiences show that Adam, when created, is not susceptible to the kind of temptation to which Eve is prone. By criticizing God's creation of a beautiful Eve and arguing that beauty and appetite overthrow wisdom, Adam displays a lack of faith in himself and in God's ways.

702   BUNDY, MURRAY W. "Milton's View of Education in *Paradise Lost*." *JEGP: Journal of English and Germanic Philology* 21 (1922):127-52.

Milton's prose links education, ethics, and politics. Whether he believes that the goal of education is to repair the ruins of Adam and Eve or to train the individual in the public and private offices of peace and war, two approaches that Milton never reconciles, his view of education is pragmatic. In *Paradise Lost*, Raphael teaches Adam the latter lesson, Michael the former. The angels' lessons are complementary, focusing on preserving and regaining liberty. Adam, an ideal pupil, displays a curiosity that the angels satisfy by exercising his rational powers. Raphael strengthens Adam's reason; Michael gives him the materials with which to contemplate virtue and vice. The final lesson is of an education that leads man to liberty through obedience to law.

Paradise Lost

703   CAVANAGH, MICHAEL. "A Meeting of Epic and History: Books XI and XII of *Paradise Lost*." *ELH* 38 (1971):206-22.

Milton brings together Adam and history in Books 11 and 12 of *Paradise Lost*, which adopt Augustine's view of providence. If all men question providence's justice, as they should, they will learn through a proper presentation of history that God's ways are just. Though a figure of historical authority, Adam is remote, which is appropriate for epic. In Books 11 and 12, he gains the knowledge and experience to know why he lost paradise, to see how this loss affects the future, and to develop the courage to call the consequences just. This makes Adam heroic; this is why Books 11 and 12 are necessary.

704   CHAMBERS, DOUGLAS. "'Discovering in Wide Lantskip': *Paradise Lost* and the Tradition of Landscape Description in the Seventeenth Century." *Journal of Garden History* 5 (1985):15-31. 9 illustrations.

For Milton and his contemporaries, the word "landscape" refers to a picture of inland natural scenery. Landscape is a painterly term, and the description of Eden in *Paradise Lost* is painterly. Many aspects of Milton's description of Eden, such as its airy softness, elegiac atmosphere, and river, are consistent with those elements in early seventeenth-century Italianate Dutch landscape artists, particularly Adam Elsheimer.

705   CHEUNG, KING-KOK. "Beauty and the Beast: A Sinuous Reflection of Milton's Eve." *Milton Studies* 23 (1987):197-214.

In iconography and literature, Eve is traditionally associated with the serpent, which in *Paradise Lost* is to some extent her image: both are deceived and self-deceived, and their names are etymologically related. By blurring the line between tempter and tempted, Milton emphasizes Eve's moral responsibility and culpability. Foreboding implications appear in the unfallen Eve's actions and description, and when Milton describes Satan, he repeats words and images that he applies to Eve. Ultimately, she wants to copy the serpent.

706   CLARK, MILI N. "The Mechanics of Creation: Non-Contradiction and Natural Necessity in *Paradise Lost*." *English Literary Renaissance* 7 (1977):207-42.

In Book 3 of *Paradise Lost*, God states the paradigm of sufficiency and falling, but does not point to a cause or principle that bridges the two contradictory terms. Milton never overcomes this contradiction. According to his mechanics of creation, sin is naturally propagated after the fall, though virtue is not, and God's interference by reestablishing man's sufficiency merely slows the rate of humanity's decay. *Paradise Lost* displays and defends the traditional law of non-contradiction, according to which any proposition is either true or false; God is thus not two gods, one self-sufficient and the other a creator because he needs creatures to realize his perfection. God's alone, this Neoplatonic principle bridges sufficiency and falling, and it also introduces the inevitability of the failure of God's creatures, who participate not in the law of non-contradiction but rather in its finest version, natural necessity, by which the creature communicates its deficiency.

707   COFFIN, CHARLES MONROE. "Creation and the Self in *Paradise Lost*." *ELH* 29 (1962):1-18. Reprinted in *Kenyon Alumni Bulletin* 20 (1962):11-17.
      Paradise Lost is concerned with the prelapsarian relationship between the human and the divine outside of history and with this relationship as it applies, in postlapsarian life, to the personal and private within history. The human-divine relationship follows a pattern of "association, dissociation, and preparation for reassociation" (2). Although God differentiates everything from himself, he is still "all," and the all of creation will one day merge with the all of God, with no loss of identity. The self (such as Adam) in *Paradise Lost* knows it exists, enjoys physical sensations, recognizes that another being exists (God, for example), and completes the process of self-realization by defining a relationship, which includes some separateness, with that other being. But Eve has difficulty acknowledging an other and defining a stable relationship. Her separateness is precarious.

708   DANIELLS, ROY. "A Happy Rural Seat of Various View." In *"Paradise Lost": A Tercentenary Tribute*. Edited by Balachandra Rajan. [Toronto and Buffalo, N.Y.]: University of Toronto Press, 1969, pp. 3-17.
      The garden of Eden is enclosed, but various elements--variety of landscape, structured yet flexible spatial planning, and images that

Paradise Lost

appeal to all senses--prevent it from being claustrophobic. Adam and Eve share each other's company as well as that of Raphael, whose pictorial and narrative skills bring a pageant into Eden. Within Adam's and Eve's minds is a paradise that parallels the external garden.

709   DAVIES, STEVIE. "Milton." In *The Feminine Reclaimed: The Idea of Woman in Spenser, Shakespeare and Milton*. Lexington: University Press of Kentucky, 1986, pp. 175-247.

Given the complexity of Milton's response to women in his life and poetry, he deserves to be called a misogynist and its opposite. His attitudes are produced by thwarted idealism. In *Paradise Lost*'s invocations, Milton explores his relationship with the feminine "as the elusive counterpart of his own nature" (186). His bisexual muse offers more and more protection as the poem progresses. The Hermetic model of *Paradise Lost*'s female principle, along with Milton's sense of the beauty and power of sexual love, helps him avoid misogyny. Eve is Adam's source of knowledge, and when he refuses to accept their separation, he remains loyal to his earliest emotional commitment, a link to the feminine that fulfills his human nature. By assimilating Christ and Eve to the terms of the myth of Ceres and Proserpina, Milton makes *Paradise Lost* a fertility myth.

710   DEMARAY, HANNAH DISINGER. "Milton's 'Perfect' Paradise and the Landscapes of Italy." *Milton Quarterly* 8 (1974):33-41.

Milton follows Italian painting and landscape convention by placing "controlled irregularities and artificial elements" in *Paradise Lost*'s prelapsarian Eden (33). His paradise reconciles nature's wildness and art's refinements.

711   DIEKHOFF, JOHN S. "Eve, the Devil, and *Areopagitica*." *Modern Language Quarterly* 5 (1944):429-34.

When Eve argues with Adam (*Paradise Lost*, 9.322-41), she paraphrases a section from *Areopagitica* that also asks, "what is Faith, Love, Virtue unassay'd?" Because we should find her argument wrong, some critics note that this stand contradicts *Areopagitica*'s position. But Eve's criticism of a cloistered virtue and her assertion that temptation leaves a stain fail to answer Adam's objections and furthermore do not apply to prelapsarian life, though they are relevant to Milton's England.

Eve uses arguments from *Areopagitica* to rationalize her desire for temptation.

712   DUNCAN, JOSEPH E. *Milton's Earthly Paradise: A Historical Study of Eden*. Minneapolis: University of Minnesota Press, 1972, 338 pp.

Milton includes most of the details from Genesis, retains much of its language, and expands it. Other sources for *Paradise Lost*'s garden include the description of the golden age or Islands of the Blest in Homer, Hesiod, and Virgil, and the Christianized gardens of Justin Martyr and Lactantius. Patristic writers and poets develop the idea of original righteousness and assign literal and symbolic meanings to Eden, but Renaissance rationalists dismiss these allegorical interpretations. Milton relies more on the church fathers than on medieval authors' fanciful discussions of Eden. Like many Renaissance writers, Milton seeks a real Eden that existed at a precise time and in a precise place. Two of his most significant departures from literary tradition are the portrayal of Adam and Eve's clearing Eden's growth (rather than plowing or planting) and worshiping together. Many Protestant authors, including Milton, believe that Eden was destroyed. The earthly paradise that Adam and Eve lose is typologically related to the celestial one into which Christ welcomes the redeemed.

713   DURKIN, SISTER MARY BRIAN. "Iterative Figures and Images in *Paradise Lost*, XI-XII." *Milton Studies* 3 (1971):139-58.

In Books 11 and 12 of *Paradise Lost*, Michael prepares Adam to live in a world unparadised; prosody and rhetorical devices show Michael increasing the lesson's instructional value. His tone--serious, restrained, and hortatory in places, reproachful and sorrowful in others --matches his theme: Adam's life must be guided by reason and illumined by faith and love. The final books are not lacking in figurative language; metaphors for fruit and seed are important.

714   FROULA, CHRISTINE. "When Eve Reads Milton: Undoing the Canonical Economy." *Critical Inquiry* 10 (1983):321-47. Reprinted in *Canons*, ed. Robert von Hallberg (Chicago, Ill., and London: University of Chicago Press, 1984), pp. 149-75.

When Eve awakes in Book 4 of *Paradise Lost*, we witness a scene of canonical instruction in which she consigns her authority to

Paradise Lost

Adam and, through him, to God and to Milton's poem and finally to "the ancient patriarchal tradition" (327). The episode at the pool, however, lacks patriarchal indoctrination. But the voice tells Eve that the reflection is herself--she has no substance. By insisting that Eve can read the world in only one way, Adam colonializes her imagination and teaches her that she is part of him. She becomes patriarchal woman. Adam needs to possess Eve and to appropriate her creative power, because he feels inadequate and recognizes her perfection. Repressing the mother figure, Milton invokes the creator rather than a muse. See the exchange between Froula and Edward Pechter in *Critical Inquiry* 11 (1984):163-70, 171-78.

715 FRYE, NORTHROP. "The Revelation to Eve." In *"Paradise Lost": A Tercentenary Tribute*. Edited by Balachandra Rajan. [Toronto and Buffalo, N.Y.]: University of Toronto Press, 1969, pp. 18-47.

In *Paradise Lost*, the relation of man to woman dramatizes the relation of creator to creature. The male principle in the natural world is linked to sky, sun, wind, or rain, the female principle to earth, caves, trees, and flowers. Eve, in her Satanic dream, experiences sexual sensations of flying and falling, just as Adam, during Michael's revelation, is elevated. The two levels of nature in *Paradise Lost* are the lower, which is nature's physical or created aspect (Eden), and the higher, which is intellectual or creative (the music of the spheres). As Milton sees the poet's ascent of eros, he moves from "the love of the sensuous toward the love of God" (36).

716 GALLAGHER, PHILIP J. "Creation in Genesis and in *Paradise Lost*." *Milton Studies* 20 (1984):163-204.

In *Paradise Lost*'s creation scenes, Milton shows that the creation myths of Genesis are "thoroughly rational and mutually compatible" (163). Milton's devotion to a Logos-cosmogony leads him to insist, contrary to Genesis, on creation *ex Deo* and on the Logos as the force behind all creative acts, including the creation of heaven and earth. Furthermore, Milton reconciles chronological inconsistencies in the two creation accounts of Genesis. He expands, rearranges, and clears up ethical ambiguities in Genesis.

717   GRANSDEN, K. W. "Milton, Dryden, and the Comedy of the Fall."
      Essays in Criticism 26 (1976):116-33.

  In *Paradise Lost*, the fall is theologically fortunate because it
produces a Christocentric universe. Seeing the fortunate fall as a
doubtful proposition that is justified and comprehended only in God's
terms, Milton attempts to reconcile divine and human logic and time.
God foresees events that have already occurred and that he chooses not
to render uncompleted, a perspective that makes the epic a comedy.
Milton tries to make *Paradise Lost* tragic, a view that comes only
through partial vision. When Dryden rewrites Milton's work in the *State
of Innocence*, he highlights the absurdity and comedy of Adam's
situation at the fall. Dryden exposes the contradictions and weaknesses
in the links that lead up to the fall. Concerning free will, Dryden faces
what Milton tries to avoid: to know that he has free choice, Adam must
test it; if he tests it, he will fall. Free will is an illusion in *Paradise Lost*.

718   GREENE, THOMAS. "Milton." In *The Descent from Heaven: A
      Study in Epic Continuity*. New Haven, Conn., and London: Yale
      University Press, 1963, pp. 363-418. Part reprinted in *On Milton's
      Poetry*, ed. Arnold Stein (Greenwich, Conn.: Fawcett Publications,
      1970), pp. 200-214.

  Paradise Lost, unlike any other epic, incorporates the celestial
descent into a larger pattern of rising and falling imagery that includes
Satan's and Adam's falls. Lowness can mean humility or despair;
height, spiritual eminence or pride. A sign of divine compassion for
man, Raphael's descent is opposed to Satanic aspiration. Raphael's
mission differs from those of his epic predecessors because they prod
or punish, while he simply expounds the truth. When Milton shifts the
definition of heroism from violence to morality, he rejects part of the
very foundation of epic. He prepares the conventional epic for
destruction by internalizing the action, questioning the hero's
independence, and detaching heroism from the community.

719   GROSSMAN, MARSHALL. "Dramatic Structure and Emotive
      Pattern in the Fall: *Paradise Lost* IX." *Milton Studies* 13 (1979):201-
      19.

  With its prologue, soliloquies, domestic agon, and narrator-
chorus, Book 9 follows the decorum of a drama. It observes the unities
of time, place, and action, and its five-act structure associates it with

307

Paradise Lost

classical drama, whose theme--that a mixture of accident and fate directs our lives--is at the center of Book 9.

720 GUILLORY, JOHN. "Ithuriel's Spear: History and the Language of Accommodation." In *Poetic Authority: Spenser, Milton, and Literary History*. New York: Columbia University Press, 1983, pp. 146-71.

When Ithuriel touches Satan, who "squat like a toad" next to Eve, the angel undoes the simile by revealing it as literal. The spear "represents an ideal relation between the object and the process of representation" (149). Although Milton touches history with Ithuriel's spear in order to produce a univocal interpretation by turning the figurative into the literal or restoring a more essential likeness, nothing happens. Milton believes that the muse accommodates the language of *Paradise Lost* before it reaches the poet. This process leaves the poet with no intentions. In his epic, the accommodating telescope of Galileo reveals uncertainty (the moon) and its inferiority to Raphael's vision. Reformation, seen from *Paradise Lost*'s perspective, is a Satanic error, for it is based on historical repetition. In Milton's view, authority is messianic.

721 HARTMAN, GEOFFREY. "Adam on the Grass with Balsamum." *ELH* 36 (1969):168-92. Reprinted in *Beyond Formalism: Literary Essays, 1958-1970* (New Haven, Conn., and London: Yale University Press, 1970), pp. 124-50; *On Milton's Poetry*, ed. Arnold Stein (Greenwich, Conn.: Fawcett Publications, 1970), pp. 215-27.

Surrounded by the fruitfulness of the cosmos, Adam and Eve have troubled consciences even if they cannot articulate their problem. Satan exploits man's need to share the divine vision, while Raphael's mission is to lead Adam from ignorant bliss to full knowledge of happiness. But innocent knowledge feeds on created things without wounding or taking anything from them. Although Adam readily converts sign to symbol, he must learn to know with reflective vision what he sees. "Narrative conduct, in Milton, is subordinated to hermeneutic structure: inner light, the divining rod of the interpreter, sounds Scripture out. Narration becomes, in fact, a kind of concordance" (191).

722   HUNTER, WM. B., Jr. "Eve's Demonic Dream." *ELH* 13 (1946):255-65.

Based on contemporary dream and demon lore, Eve's dream in Book 4 of *Paradise Lost* anticipates the fall, reveals Satan's machinations, and provides an argument against current ideas about materialism. Phantasms exist, yet we can sense them only during sleep, when there are no distractions. Using one theory about the cause of dreams, Adam blames Eve's dream on the previous day's labor, though he is troubled because he shared the labor but not the dream. During the dream, Satan shows the demonic power to work from within a victim; during the temptation, he acts from without.

723   KERRIGAN, WILLIAM, and BRADEN, GORDON. "Milton's Coy Eve: *Paradise Lost* and Renaissance Love Poetry." *ELH* 53 (1986):27-51.

Petrarch's lyrics affirm that obsessive, unrequited love is an ideal, which--as Renaissance sonneteers and Milton's "Canzone" argue --leads not to consummation but to poetry and fame. Turning back to Ovid, the libertine tradition sees a cause in the very design of sexual love and often focuses on antifruition as a means of prolonging desire. The Renaissance uses Ovidian premises to reinvent Petrarchan frustration. Milton presents Adam and Eve's sexual connection in terms of the dominant sexual fantasy of the Renaissance: men chase; women are chaste before they yield. Eve experiences a double loss of virginity, at the pool and with Adam, who chases as she flees and later yields. The goal is to save desire and prevent it from decaying through long frustration or quick consummation. Satan, the hunter and arch-Petrarchist, symbolically leads Eve back to the solitude of her image in the pool, Adam's rival. Adam's fall is associated with the medieval attitude toward identity, which is found in courtly love.

724   KNIGHT, DOUGLAS. "The Dramatic Center of *Paradise Lost*." *South Atlantic Quarterly* 63 (1964):44-59.

Acting as the main means to pull readers into *Paradise Lost*, its similes force us to engage in intellectual action in order to comprehend the narrative, settings, and characters. We must understand the highly allusive similes as well as their relation to the events of *Paradise Lost*; this leads us to see that the poem's action is part of us. The most problematic books (3, 6, 11, and 12) force us to think the most. In Book

Paradise Lost

6, at the poem's mid-point, we recognize Satan for what he actually is and see that his power over man is increasing. The dramatic center of *Paradise Lost* occurs when Adam and Eve discover a character and course of action.

725 KNOTT, JOHN R., Jr. *Milton's Pastoral Vision: An Approach to "Paradise Lost."* Chicago, Ill., and London: University of Chicago Press, 1971, 195 pp.

An epic with a pastoral center, *Paradise Lost* broadens the scope of pastoral and gives it a new seriousness. Milton places the Arcadian ideal on a foundation of theological reality. Pastoral and epic exist harmoniously in heaven, the former revealing God's peace and the latter his love. In Eden, there is a conflict between the epic and pastoral modes. Milton follows Virgil in using pastoral values to test the epic hero's traditional virtues. Milton's Edenic landscape is sensuous and dynamic, yet Adam and Eve may securely wander there without becoming disoriented. Even Milton's portrayal of heaven is in part pastoral; unlike Revelation, *Paradise Lost* gives greater significance to heaven as paradise than as city of God. For Milton, the only valid pastoral vision is based upon the unification of the redeemed with God in heaven. Eve's literary pastoral ancestry includes Flora, Shakespeare's Perdita, and Spenser's Pastorella. In Milton's late works, one key symbol of evil is the city, which cannot exist with paradise on earth.

726 KOEHLER, G. STANLEY. "Milton and the Art of Landscape." *Milton Studies* 8 (1975):3-40.

Milton's Eden influences the "picturesque" style of natural beauty that characterizes the eighteenth-century landscape tradition. Various elements are common to Milton's description and to eighteenth-century prescriptions for landscape design: an elevated site, which provides both openness and seclusion; the division into three areas (a central formal garden, park, and wilder area); and the handling of the wall, trees, flowers, and water. The bower is the thematic and artistic center of Milton's garden. By including elements of the terrible and the surprising in *Paradise Regained*'s setting, Milton points to a darker pastoral vision. His descriptions of hell and heaven lack significant detail.

727 LOVEJOY, ARTHUR O. "Milton and the Paradox of the Fortunate Fall." *ELH* 4 (1937):161-79. Reprinted in *Essays in the History of Ideas* (Baltimore, Md.: Johns Hopkins Press, 1948), pp. 277-95; *Milton's Epic Poetry: Essays on "Paradise Lost" and "Paradise Regained,"* ed. C. A. Patrides (Harmondsworth: Penguin Books, 1967), pp. 55-73.

In *Paradise Lost* (12.469-78), Milton states the paradox of the fortunate fall: Adam's violation of the divine command is infinitely sinful, yet without this act, the Incarnation and Redemption will not occur. This paradox gives Milton's view of history the character of a comedy, for a happy ending is implicit in and made possible by it. The paradox has a long tradition, including works by such authors as Du Bartas, Giles Fletcher, St. Ambrose, and Wyclif (and the Roman liturgy). Although the fortunate fall in *Paradise Lost* stresses the redemptive process, it also places the fall in an ambiguous light.

728 LOVEJOY, ARTHUR O. "Milton's Dialogue on Astronomy." In *Reason and the Imagination: Studies in the History of Ideas, 1600-1800.* Edited by J. A. Mazzeo. New York: Columbia University Press; London: Routledge and Kegan Paul, 1962, pp. 129-42.

Adam's doubt about the design of the cosmos (*Paradise Lost*, 8.15-38) is based on the Copernican principle of nature's economy, simplicity, and reasonableness, which runs counter to the principle of plenitude. Rather than seeing cosmic bodies serve some other purpose besides warming and lighting the earth, and thus wasting no motion, Adam assumes that these are their sole purposes and that they are thus arranged efficiently in a Copernican structure. Raphael's suggestion that other worlds are inhabited is never refuted, which is odd because *Paradise Lost*'s logic is based on a single earth's history, with its fall, Incarnation, and Crucifixion. If other worlds exist, these events would need to be duplicated there. Milton rejects the idea of the infinity of the universe and its worlds, and he attacks not one astronomical theory but the very study of astronomy. See entries 6, 18, 212, 459, 476, 489, 512, 521.

729 McCOLLEY, DIANE. "Subsequent or Precedent? Eve as Milton's Defense of Poesie." *Milton Quarterly* 20 (1986):132-36.

Paradise Lost

Partly because Eve in *Paradise Lost* embodies many of the properties and performs many of the processes that Milton attributes to poetry, she is the epic's interpretive center. Her relationships with God, the creatures, and the creation figure poetic graces and imagination as the work of the fancy. Eve's gardening and commentary about looking into a mirror link her with Milton's poesy. The method of her vocation, imagery associated with her, and her work all personify poetry.

730   McCOLLEY, DIANE KELSEY. *Milton's Eve*. Urbana, Chicago, and London: University of Illinois Press, 1983, 240 pp.
    Before Milton, painters and writers present an Eve who is deficient in virtuous behavior. The iconographic tradition generally portrays Eve as a temptress; the literary tradition continues this dualistic theme by showing female concupiscence ruining male virtue, or passion (body) dominating reason (soul). The literary Eve is mindless and lacking a sense of responsibility. Faced with an antifeminine tradition, Milton--if he is to assert eternal providence--has to form an Eve that a just and provident God actually creates. In *Paradise Lost*, she is Adam's subordinate, but this does not mean she is inferior. They are moving toward perfection together and, before they fall, they are equal in sanctitude. When Eve stares into the pool and when she dreams, she undergoes good temptations through which she and Adam learn to separate truth from illusion and correctly to use poetic imagination. Unlike the Eve of tradition, Milton's character takes her work seriously--it is a figure of the poet's work.

731   MARILLA, E. L. *The Central Problem of "Paradise Lost": The Fall of Man*. Essays and Studies on English Language and Literature, vol. 15. Upsala: A.-B. Lundequistska Bokhandeln; Copenhagen: Ejnar Munksgaard; Cambridge, Mass.: Harvard University Press, 1953, 36 pp. Reprinted in *Milton and Modern Man: Selected Essays* (University: University of Alabama Press, 1968), pp. 27-55.
    Without theorizing or moralizing in a vacuum, Milton in *Paradise Lost* uses the fall to show how the world can be lost by disregarding divine laws. Satan proposes and Eve accepts a defiance of the divine plan. Her view of human self-sufficiency echoes the foundations of the new science and such thinkers as Bacon and Hobbes. Adam deliberately acquiesces to Eve's defection; he sacrifices ultimate good for present benefits, thus acting as a negative example for all

people. The fundamental crime against humanity always follows the pattern of the willful surrender of intellectual perception to the pressure of sentiment. In the episode of the fall, Milton shows the results of following ideologies that ignore or misunderstand man's nature, man's needs, or the laws of nature.

732   MARSHALL, WILLIAM H. "*Paradise Lost: Felix Culpa* and the Problem of Structure." *Modern Language Notes* 76 (1961):15-20. Reprinted in *Milton: Modern Essays in Criticism*, ed. Arthur E. Barker (London, Oxford, and New York: Oxford University Press, 1965), pp. 336-41.

Disagreement about whether the fall in *Paradise Lost* is fortunate points to a kind of failure by Milton because didactic literature should not leave readers confused. Until midway through Book 10, *Paradise Lost*'s main method is irony: Satan's evil produces good, and man finds grace but Satan does not. We recognize and accept this balance. Only when Satan returns to hell in Book 10 are our emotional and intellectual responses to *Paradise Lost* fused. In Books 11 and 12, we move from the dramatic, devotional treatment of these matters to Michael's intellectual handling of them for Adam's education. Since we understand this point from the beginning, we cannot share Adam's joy in Book 12. For almost ten books, Satan is the center of attention in an anthropocentric poem; in the final books, Adam is the object of attention in a theocentric poem.

733   MERRILL, THOMAS F. "Miltonic God-Talk: The Creation in *Paradise Lost*." *Language and Style* 16 (1983):296-312.

Logical context determines how words are used, so religious language--particularly God-talk in *Paradise Lost*--demands to be trusted not as descriptive but as prescriptive discourse that is not empirically based. Raphael carefully points out that his story of the creation is a matter of revelation rather than plain empirical information; God-talk conveys not data but a relationship. Religious language is always untidy because it bears the logical stress of expressing the inexpressible. Speaking a parable, Raphael accommodates and encourages Adam (and the reader) to use Christian rather than aesthetic priorities when he interprets God-talk.

Paradise Lost

734   MINER, EARL. *"Felix Culpa* in the Redemptive Order of *Paradise Lost." Philological Quarterly* 47 (1968):43-54.

If the fall is portrayed as fortunate in Books 11 and 12 of *Paradise Lost,* then these books contradict the rest of the poem. But Milton's view is more complex. He indicates that the fall is fortunate because it displays God's greater glory and mercy for the few who are saved, and only in the last days; the many more who are not redeemed will experience God's wrath and damnation. When Adam expresses his joy about the *felix culpa,* Michael's silence implies assent, though he may find Adam overly enthusiastic, for the *felix culpa* has terms attached to it, including the need for patience and Christian fortitude. The tone of *Paradise Lost*'s conclusion mixes joy and sorrow.

735   MOLLENKOTT, VIRGINIA R. "The Cycle of Sins in *Paradise Lost,* Book XI." *Modern Language Quarterly* 27 (1966):33-40.

Adam's five visions of the future in Book 11 of *Paradise Lost* appear in a cyclic pattern. Elaborations of the sins of Satan (the vision of Cain and Abel), Eve (the lazar house), and Adam (the tents of many hues) form the first three visions. The fourth vision (the cities of the plain) returns to the first, and the fifth vision (luxury and riot) returns to the second. By placing the episode on a hill, Milton connects it with *Paradise Lost*'s opening invocation, Moses's receiving of the Law on Mount Sinai, and Christ's temptation on the mountain. Book 11 removes any glamor from sin in *Paradise Lost,* and it ends with the flood and Noah's salvation, thus emphasizing redemption and grace.

736   MOLLENKOTT, VIRGINIA R. "Milton's Rejection of the Fortunate Fall." *Milton Quarterly* 6 (1972):1-5.

In *Paradise Lost,* Milton indicates that man--had he not fallen-- would have progressed toward a magnificent goal. An assertion of the paradox of the fortunate fall comes only from Adam, who doubts its validity. If Adam had decided to rejoice because of his sin (since it leads to the Incarnation and Redemption), he would have favored the idea of a fortunate fall. But he does not know whether to rejoice or repent. Milton gives this paradox short shrift in *Paradise Lost.*

737   MOORE, C. A. "The Conclusion of *Paradise Lost." PMLA* 36 (1921):1-34.

Some eighteenth-century critics find *Paradise Lost*'s conclusion too bleak for a proper heroic poem, but Milton carefully balances sorrow and hope in a conclusion that he has in mind from the start of the poem. The epic is concerned less with the results of sin, including death, than with the cure. Milton's liberal doctrinal views do not mix well with ancient creed, though he generally succeeds in making the biblical story logically consistent. If Milton appears to glorify Satan, he does so only to reveal the immensity of God's triumph. At the end of *Paradise Lost*, Milton does not leave Adam in a state of despair or joy.

738   OGDEN, H. V. S. "The Crisis of *Paradise Lost* Reconsidered." *Philological Quarterly* 36 (1957):1-19. Reprinted in *Milton: Modern Essays in Criticism*, ed. Arthur E. Barker (London, Oxford, and New York: Oxford University Press, 1965), pp. 308-27.

Before they fall, Adam and Eve--though not perfect--are sinless, innocent, and liable to temptation. They are not already fallen. The fall is *Paradise Lost*'s theological turning point and the narrative's climax.

739   OTTEN, CHARLOTTE F. "'My Native Element': Milton's Paradise and English Gardens." *Milton Studies* 5 (1973):249-67.

The garden in *Paradise Lost* is based on contemporary, often English, analogues and influences. Drawing material from herbals, gardening manuals, and real gardens, including reconstructed "paradises" of his own age, Milton blends traditions to create his vision of Eden.

740   PATRICK, J. MAX. "A Reconsideration of the Fall of Eve." *Études Anglaises* 28 (1975):15-21.

Much of *Paradise Lost*, including most of Milton's account of Adam and Eve in Eden, is didactic fiction. Although no one, not even God, has absolute free will, Adam and Eve exercise limited free will by choosing good or evil. Rather than comparing Eve to Narcissus when she looks in the pool, we should see the differences between them. Her mistake at the pool is innocent, and she learns from it. The word "perfect" applies to Adam and Eve only in its meaning of complete, not infallible or ideal. While her dream gives Eve knowledge, it does not lessen her free will or precondition her to fall. She is a sophisticated

315

Paradise Lost

and knowledgeable woman when Satan approaches her. Her fall is the result of the failure to use her faculties properly, particularly reason and memory.

741 PECORINO, JESSICA PRINZ. "Eve Unparadised: Milton's Expulsion and Iconographic Tradition." *Milton Quarterly* 15 (1981):1-10.

While traditional iconography shows Eve as the first to leave paradise because she is the first to sin and as more distant than Adam from the escorting angel because of her worldliness, Milton indicates that Eve's sin is no greater than Adam's and that Michael leads the way out of the garden, with neither sinner taking the lead and asserting moral superiority.

742 PECZENIK, F. "Fit Help: The Egalitarian Marriage in *Paradise Lost*." *Mosaic* 17 (1984):29-48.

Only if we ascribe fallen values to the prelapsarian state will we perceive inequality between Adam and Eve. Milton summons our conventional beliefs about women to explain those views, to test our understanding of prelapsarian life, and to allow the first couple freely to ponder and reject them. Adam asks for and receives an equal, Eve, a status that God confirms. Raphael explains something that Satan never understands: reciprocity supersedes hierarchy. The line in Book 4 that seems to characterize the relationship between man and woman ("He for God only, she for God in him") in fact describes God's centrality to their relationship. In *Paradise Lost*, contempt for women comes from Satan and the Satanic point of view. At the moment of the fall, Adam and Eve lose their equality and conjugal reciprocity; God institutes a domestic hierarchy, Eve lives in a subordinate role, and Adam has no equal for a mate.

743 PRINCE, F. T. "On the Last Two Books of *Paradise Lost*." *Essays and Studies*, n.s. 11 (1958):38-52. Reprinted in *Milton's Epic Poetry: Essays on "Paradise Lost" and "Paradise Regained*," ed. C. A. Patrides (Harmondsworth: Penguin Books, 1967), pp. 233-48.

Not merely historical or theological statement, Books 11 and 12 of *Paradise Lost* follow Milton's usual method of dramatization: they contain a revelation for Adam, and his reactions should renew our vision of human life and Christian faith. These books, as part of Adam's story, are also part of the evolution of consciousness. A mirror image of its beginning *in medias res*, an epic's conclusion should imply much more to come. When we reach the end of Book 10, our interest may flag as we realize that all the great events are over. Milton uses this attitude and counts on our sober concentration for the remaining two books.

744 RADZINOWICZ, MARY ANN. "'Man as a Probationer of Immortality': *Paradise Lost* XI-XII." In *Approaches to "Paradise Lost."* The York Tercentenary Lectures. Edited by C. A. Patrides. London: Edward Arnold, 1968, pp. 31-51.

Concerned with the theme of man's education in liberty, Books 11 and 12 of *Paradise Lost* are carefully constructed and neither harsh nor pessimistic. They redefine what is noble, heroic, and hopeful, while proposing to Adam a clear action involving the public struggle of good and evil. The concluding books bring into final focus the epic context and inner system of ethics based on work (or works) as a sign of loving obedience to God. Michael teaches Adam how righteous men may alter the course of history through ethics and politics, private and public actions.

745 RADZINOWICZ, MARY ANN NEVINS. "Eve and Dalila: Renovation and the Hardening of the Heart." In *Reason and the Imagination: Studies in the History of Ideas, 1600-1800.* Edited by J. A. Mazzeo. New York: Columbia University Press; London: Routledge & Kegan Paul, 1962, pp. 155-81.

A bad choice or fall does not ruin one forever, as Milton's divorce tracts argue by pointing to one area of remediable error. A fall can be mended, but this does not imply that God turns all losses into good by defeating evil; rather, as *Christian Doctrine* indicates, people may do battle in their own hearts and gain victory if their wills are resolute. Eve shows the process of renovation; Dalila, of the hardening of the heart. Both women fall from their created natures, but they then pursue opposite courses: every rejection of renovation by Dalila is matched by Eve's affirmation of the process. The marriage relationship in each case is an epitome of God's ways toward man.

Paradise Lost

746 REICHERT, JOHN. "'Against His Better Knowledge': A Case for
     Adam." *ELH* 48 (1981):83-109.

          If we are to take seriously the claim that Adam falls "not
     deceiv'd" and its source (1 Timothy 2:14), we must believe that his
     knowledge does not fail him until he eats the fruit. He has great
     intuitive knowledge, though it can be degraded because of his view of
     Eve. Adam and Eve's discussion about laboring apart creates growth in
     their knowledge and virtue. In this scene, Adam also fulfills his place in
     the hierarchy and rightly lets Eve go off alone. After she falls, he is not
     persuaded to join her; he simply chooses to do so, without the aid of
     her arguments or his own. "Adam does the wrong thing for good
     reasons" (98). His love for Eve is both selfless and selfish.

747 REVARD, STELLA P. "Eve and the Doctrine of Responsibility in
     Paradise Lost." *PMLA* 88 (1973):69-78.

          The narrative voice in *Paradise Lost* does not assign greater
     blame to either Adam or Eve. God in Book 3 says he is not to blame,
     and Adam and Eve later arrive at the idea of divided responsibility
     when they define the turning point as the events of the morning rather
     than the sin at noon. Because the fall is not determined by their
     morning conversation, they thus attempt to evade responsibility. Adam
     allows Eve to accept her responsibility, while he tries to implicate her
     and thus avoid responsibility. The Son calls on Adam to stand alone
     and accept responsibility for himself and Eve, but not for allowing Eve
     to go off alone. Adam's proper role is not to deprive Eve of free choice
     but to give advice, as Raphael explains. This is exactly what Adam does
     in the morning conversation. If Eve is Adam's inferior, she is not
     therefore incomplete or liable to sin. She resembles Abdiel in many
     ways.

748 ROSENBLATT, JASON P. "Adam's Pisgah Vision: *Paradise Lost*,
     Books XI and XII." *ELH* 39 (1972):66-86.

          Although Virgil and Du Bartas exert an incidental influence on
     Adam's vision in Books 11-12 of *Paradise Lost*, Milton models this
     episode on Moses's vision of Canaan, the promised land from which he
     is excluded, from the mountain of Pisgah (Deuteronomy 34).
     Typological interpretations view the Pisgah vision as the Mosaic Law's
     experience of a glimpse of the Gospel. When Michael presents the
     vision, Adam, also excluded from sacred ground, is linked with Moses

in receiving a glimpse of Christian salvation. Milton exploits the typological links between Moses's vision and Christ's temptation by Satan. Preventing Adam from being aloof, Michael forces him to see his relationship to his descendants and the necessity of Christ's salvation. If Moses's vision and death at the end of the Pentateuch shadow forth the vision of the heavenly Jerusalem in Revelation, Milton's use of this episode at the end of *Paradise Lost* gives the epic a sense of comfort and closure.

749 SASEK, LAWRENCE A. "The Drama of *Paradise Lost*, Books XI and XII." *Studies in English Renaissance Literature*. Edited by Waldo F. McNeir. Louisiana State University Studies, Humanities Series, no. 12. Baton Rouge: Louisiana State University Press, 1962, pp. 181-96. Reprinted in *Milton: Modern Essays in Criticism*, ed. Arthur E. Barker (London, Oxford, and New York: Oxford University Press, 1965), pp. 342-56; *Milton: Modern Judgements*, ed. Alan Rudrum (London: Macmillan, 1968), pp. 205-18.

     Our knowledge of the epic convention of revealing the future may lead us to misread Books 11 and 12 of *Paradise Lost*. Although Milton, like his epic predecessors, uses this convention to broaden the scope of the action, the differences are more significant. Homer and Virgil describe the future as it appears on a shield; Milton, like Du Bartas, narrates future episodes to conclude the events of the epic. But the dialogue of Books 11 and 12 provides a more dramatic quality than does Du Bartas's work. Milton focuses not on biblical scenes but on the process Adam goes through, moving from initial despair to a series of hopes and fears, in order to attain new insight and peace.

750 SAVAGE, J. B. "Freedom and Necessity in *Paradise Lost*." *ELH* 44 (1977):286-311.
     Milton sees freedom as a moral act and as perhaps the most important idea of all. If we approach *Paradise Lost* by thinking in terms of causation, we are using terms of necessity rather than free will. A belief that the fall occurs through free will requires our ignorance about its causes, but we habitually think in terms of causality, and dispensing with it makes the poem's action inexplicable. Uncaused actions occur by chance, ending any argument for free will, which is a tenuous idea. Man's freedom in *Paradise Lost* is always limited, dependent, and provisional, "relative to the circumstances in which it first was given"

Poetry

Paradise Lost

(291). When the soul acts in harmony with God and itself, we have Milton's definition of freedom. The supposed antecedents of the fall in *Paradise Lost*, the falls before the fall, affirm Adam and Eve's freedom, though we must entertain the contradictory view that these episodes carry the seeds of the fall. We must think about the prelapsarian state and, after the fall, revise our thoughts. At the end of Book 8, the fall is inevitable.

751 STOLL, ELMER EDGAR. "From the Superhuman to the Human in *Paradise Lost*." *University of Toronto Quarterly* 3 (1933):3-16. Reprinted in *From Shakespeare to Joyce: Authors and Critics; Literature and Life* (Garden City, N.Y.: Doubleday, Doran & Co., 1944), pp. 422-35; *Milton Criticism: Selections from Four Centuries*, ed. James Thorpe (New York: Rinehart & Co., 1950), pp. 211-24.

   Paradise Lost's concluding books, but not its final lines, share with *Paradise Regained* a dry, concise style. *Paradise Lost*'s conclusion reconciles opposites, making them acceptable: good comes from evil, and death becomes a cure. When Milton deals with heaven and hell, his grand style is sublime and noble without being inflated; in the scenes concerned with prelapsarian earthly life, his tone descends, and the style conveys tenderness. In the temptation scene, *Paradise Lost* becomes drama. Adam and Eve's style grows more complex after the fall, as suits the complexities of human nature.

752 STOLL, ELMER EDGAR. "Was Paradise Well Lost?" *PMLA* 33 (1918):429-35. Reprinted in *Poets and Playwrights: Shakespeare, Jonson, Spenser, Milton* (Minneapolis: University of Minnesota Press, 1930), pp. 203-9; frequently reprinted.

   The conclusions of Milton's three major poems feature a simple style and "a quiet note of reconciliation with life" (429). Ending without anger or a denunciation of sin that brings death, *Paradise Lost* provides a portrait of Adam and Eve as a symbol of the life they enter and of the life their children will lead. The magnanimous conclusion is consistent with the increasingly humanized tone and the new point of view after the temptation of Eve. Superhumans in the beginning, Adam and Eve gradually join our level of humanity. Milton's assertions about death as both curse and blessing are similarly consistent, for death in *Paradise Lost* is both. Milton does not indicate that paradise was well lost.

753 SVENDSEN, KESTER. "Adam's Soliloquy in Book X of *Paradise Lost*." *College English* 10 (1949):366-70. Reprinted in *Milton: Modern Essays in Criticism*, ed. Arthur E. Barker (London, Oxford, and New York: Oxford University Press, 1965), pp. 328-35.

Adam's soliloquy marks a crucial stage in his development and provides a justification for Books 11 and 12. Resulting from the fall and acting as a prelude to his emotional maturity, his soliloquy is cathartic: "he purges off the grosser corruption of his will" (366), an act that leads to the growth of faith. The speech mixes emotional progress and the debate form, as Adam's reason battles his passion. When he speaks of marriage, he blusters in ridiculous generalizations. He focuses in the soliloquy on the themes of death and immortality, and the speech is structured according to the idea of the four degrees of death.

754 SWAIM, KATHLEEN M. *Before and After the Fall: Contrasting Modes in "Paradise Lost."* Amherst: University of Massachusetts Press, 1986, 305 pp.

Milton contrasts the pre- and postlapsarian states in terms of small details and large structures, such as Raphael's lectures about a unified, harmonious universe and Michael's exegesis of a fragmented, contradictory one in which appearance and reality are dichotomous. Their two epistemologies--Raphael gives Adam vicarious experience, while Michael fortifies his faith--are complementary. The texts from which the explicating angels work are similarly complementary, for Raphael reads Adam the book of God's works (nature), and Michael shows him the book of God's word (Scripture or grace). *Paradise Lost* also presents the explicit contrast, through Raphael's and Michael's speeches, between pre- and postlapsarian language, imagery (shifting from fruit to seed, for example, and from sun to Son), Ramist logic (as Raphael guides Adam in invention, Michael in disposition, method, and memory), and poetics (the Platonic Raphael uses a creative poetic of analogy, the Aristotelian Michael a critical poetic of typology).

755 TAYLOR, DICK, Jr. "Milton and the Paradox of the Fortunate Fall Once More." *Tulane Studies in English* 9 (1959):35-51.

Milton does not believe in the fortunate fall, and *Paradise Lost* never argues that the fallen struggler, however successful, receives a greater reward for regaining what he loses needlessly. In Milton's view, related through contrasts between pre- and postlapsarian life and

Paradise Lost

through parallels between the devils' and man's falls, the fall is a catastrophe with disastrous consequences. The plan of God and Christ to save humanity is balanced by Satan's destructive plan; hell and the war in heaven are connected to postlapsarian life. In Book 12, when Adam seems to state the doctrine of the fortunate fall, he actually displays excessive enthusiasm concerning Michael's message, which contains steadily building hope. Parts of Adam's speech discredit the idea of a fortunate fall, while God's speech near the beginning of Book 11 denies this doctrine.

756 TAYLOR, DICK, Jr. "Milton's Treatment of the Judgment and the Expulsion in *Paradise Lost.*" *Tulane Studies in English* 10 (1960):51-82.

Milton's treatment of Adam and Eve's experiences after they sin is more hopeful and compassionate than that of his predecessors. Like Milton, previous biblical commentators and hexameral writers divide the first postlapsarian events into three phases: God's approach and questioning of Adam and Eve, the judgment, and the expulsion. But, unlike Milton, they portray these as harsh episodes with a fierce God. Besides mixing in hopeful events to mitigate severe ones, Milton shows God's leniency and man's own ability to attain regeneration. No other author gives the Atonement so much scope or has the Son deliver the judgment.

757 THOMPSON, ELBERT N. S. "For *Paradise Lost,* XI-XII." *Philological Quarterly* 22 (1943):376-82.

In Books 11-12 of *Paradise Lost,* Milton selects and orders historical details with care and writes in a style much like that of the rest of the epic. These books are also necessary, for Adam lacks a sense of history and has very little personal experience. He learns that history is an expression of God's will, and that--as a sinner--he must accept responsibility for what the human race will inherit from his sin. He conforms to heaven's ways, just as heaven accommodates itself to the earthly scene.

758 TOLIVER, HAROLD. "Symbol-Making and the Labors of Milton's Eden." *Texas Studies in Literature and Language* 18 (1976):433-50.

As namers, botanists, interpreters of dreams, and so on, Adam and Eve engage in their central occupation of symbol making. Poetry in Eden is occasional and a household function. For Adam, who shares in "the Word's original creative ordinance" (434-35), symbol making leads to establishing the relationships among things. Life unfolds harmoniously for Adam, so he unifies poetry and science--and perception, reason, and intuition--in a spontaneous hymnal mode that takes a circular, upward motion. But Raphael points to a potential danger when Adam presents the linear narrative of his marital status: Eve might become the center of his attention. With the fall, disintegration occurs, and the mediating role of symbol making becomes crucial. New genres of moral poetry and a wealth of language come from the fortunate fall.

759 TOLIVER, HAROLD E. "Milton's Household Epic." *Milton Studies* 9 (1976):105-20.

By placing a married couple at the center of *Paradise Lost*, Milton creates an important deviation from the epic tradition. When Milton evaluates previous epics, one criterion is his proposition that civil power should remain only the executive arm of spiritual reform. The portrait of Adam and Eve provides a model for restoring dignity, based on both masculine and feminine dignity, to Restoration households. Prelapsarian Edenic life is domestic-heroic; postlapsarian life introduces redemption for Adam and Eve, while Christ, growing in a manger and being tested in the desert, completes the pattern of domesticity in the restored image of God.

760 TURNER, JAMES GRANTHAM. "Love Made in the First Age: Edenic Sexuality in *Paradise Lost* and Its Analogues." In *One Flesh: Paradisal Marriage and Sexual Relations in the Age of Milton*. Oxford: Clarendon Press, 1987, pp. 230-309. 4 illustrations.

In his confrontation with Genesis, Milton links sexuality to perception, interpretation, the politics of gender, and the struggle between the poetic and the iconoclastic. His vision of the Word includes sexuality, egalitarianism, and the efforts of the imagination; *Paradise Lost* gives life to all of these and creates a vision of eros based on Milton's reading of Genesis. Allowing eros to see again and joining it to submission, the epic reverses the incompatibility and hatred depicted in the divorce tracts. Filled with eroticism, *Paradise Lost*

Paradise Lost

attempts to redeem marital sexuality from libertinism and repression by expropriating the delights of licentious texts. Satan expropriates pagan and Solomonic eroticism and punctuates *Paradise Lost* with pornographic responses. The discovery of the human capacity for egalitarian love leads to self-knowledge in Milton's epic. In its postlapsarian form, eros retains and parodies its prelapsarian characteristics.

761   ULREICH, JOHN C., Jr. "A Paradise Within: The Fortunate Fall in *Paradise Lost*." *Journal of the History of Ideas* 32 (1971):351-66.
        Rather than wanting us to find the fall and its consequences acceptable or necessary, Milton makes it fortunate only if we recognize our guilt, which comes from our free choice. Although the good that results from the fall outweighs the woe, the benefits for man will not be greater than if he had remained unfallen. God does not require evil so he can produce good. When Michael says that Adam and Eve have "A paradise within thee, happier far," we see that "*in spite of* the Fall, man has it in his power to become happier than he *had been* in Paradise" (358). If man were to have been happier than he now is, we cannot conclude that man was and was to have been happier than he has become or might have become. Raphael's speech (*Paradise Lost*, 5.493-99) about man's potential for improvement helps us understand the fortunate fall.

762   WADDINGTON, RAYMOND B. "The Death of Adam: Vision and Voice in Books XI and XII of *Paradise Lost*." *Modern Philology* 70 (1972):9-21.
        Books 11 and 12 of *Paradise Lost* follow a figural pattern that moves from a world destroyed to one restored, from the first Adam's sins to the second Adam's prophecies. Although the division of the final two books reveals an asymmetrical structure, with the first Adam and the first of seven historical ages receiving as much space as the second Adam and the last six ages, each of Book 11's six visions corresponds to one of the six ages in Book 12. Each book ends with a redemptive revelation. Biblical commentators argue that Adam's death occurs during the fifth age, just before the recession of the flood, which is seen as a type of baptism. Adam responds to the vision of the flood and the corresponding episode in Book 12, the description of Christ's death, with repentance, purification, and spiritual renewal. In the flood, Adam

drowns; his physical death typologically anticipates his resurrection in the second Adam. Michael turns from vision to narration at the point where Adam's life ends.

763   WERMAN, GOLDA. "Repentance in *Paradise Lost*." *Milton Studies* 22 (1986):121-39.

Dealing with a pre-Christian Adam and Eve, the Bible and Christian hexameral writers avoid the subject of repentance. Milton rejects Calvin's doctrine of total depravity, allows Adam and Eve to retain free will and some spiritual strength after the fall, and makes their repentance a central theme in *Paradise Lost*. These views agree with Midrash, ancient rabbinical commentaries on the Bible, though Milton's thinking does not correspond with contemporary Protestant theology, which denies free will to the fallen, argues for predestination, and gives God the full responsibility for salvation through Christ. After the fall in *Paradise Lost*, as in midrashic commentaries, Adam and Eve need to learn by exercising choice based on free will. Milton also shares the midrashic writers' belief that a repentant sinner reaches a higher spiritual level than that of a righteous person who never sins.

764   WILKES, G. A. "'Full of Doubt I Stand': The Final Implications of *Paradise Lost*." In *English Renaissance Studies Presented to Dame Helen Gardner in Honour of Her Seventieth Birthday*. [Edited by John Carey.] Oxford: Clarendon Press, 1980, pp. 271-78.

While one can demonstrate that the linear structure of *Paradise Lost* shows the providential design of turning evil to good, we imaginatively experience the fortunate fall as too theoretical. The sense of loss is stronger than the sense of gain or redemption. Neither the occasionally limp style nor the undramatic nature of Books 11-12 accounts for this; rather, Milton wants the epic to present a disturbing vision. Unrealized, the new Eden and the defeat of Satan belong to the remote future. We leave the poem not with a blinding vision of God but in our fallen world. Adam never accepts Christ as his Redeemer in truly human terms. Despite assurances that the fall is fortunate, the fact of its irreversibility contributes greatly to *Paradise Lost*'s troubling vision, for perfection cannot be replaced by itself.

Paradise Lost

765   WILLIAMSON, GEORGE. "The Education of Adam." *Modern Philology* 61 (1963):96-109. Reprinted in *Milton and Others* (London: Faber and Faber, 1965), pp. 42-65; *Milton: Modern Essays in Criticism*, ed. Arthur E. Barker (London, Oxford, and New York: Oxford University Press, 1965), pp. 284-307.

Adam receives his education in two installments: in Books 5-8, Raphael prepares him for temptation and helps him explore the potential of human nature that the fall will reveal; in Books 11-12, Michael explains the consequences of the fall. After his creation, Adam expresses a fear of solitude, which is the basis of his fall, when he realizes that, if happiness is impossible without love, he faces a tragic dilemma in choosing between God and Eve.

766   WOODHOUSE, A. S. P. "Notes on Milton's Views on the Creation: The Initial Phases." *Philological Quarterly* 28 (1949):211-36. Reprinted in *The Heavenly Muse: A Preface to Milton*, ed. Hugh MacCallum, University of Toronto Department of English Studies and Texts, no. 21 (Toronto and Buffalo, N.Y.: University of Toronto Press, 1972), pp. 145-75.

In many respects, Milton's view of the creation in *Paradise Lost* and *Christian Doctrine* is orthodox: the creation is an article of faith, a voluntary act (though God's goodness is a necessitating force), and for God's glory and diffusive goodness. His views are unorthodox when he rejects creation *ex nihilo*, argues for creation *de Deo*, and states that creation begins with the preparation of matter to receive form. Milton's theistic monism resembles that of stoic thought; his conception of the creation as a voluntary act, in which God puts forth himself, resembles Fludd's thinking on the subject. For Milton, unlike Fludd, matter is inherently good.

767   WORDEN, WARD S. "Milton's Approach to the Story of the Fall." *ELH* 15 (1948):295-305.

If we look for a logical motivation or a psychological state to account for the fall, we run the risk of explaining it out of existence as a theological idea. Milton in *Paradise Lost* gives Eve sufficient "reason and excuse" to make the fall the prototype of all future human sinning. And the inadequacy of her motives demonstrates evil's basically irrational nature. The speed with which Satan succeeds is more meaningful. If the fall of man is mysterious, Satan's fall is unknowable, but Milton tries to solve this problem by presenting Sin and Death to bridge the gap between the spiritual and physical realms. Sin and Death help us understand Satan's fallen conduct and essence, even as Milton's use of allegory removes the fall from human experience and restores its eschatological nature. But readers may experience difficulty as they move among the three levels portrayed in *Paradise Lost*: real or historical (God, Christ, angels), human (Adam, Eve), and allegorical (Sin, Death).

768   ZIMMERMAN, SHARI A. "Milton's *Paradise Lost*: Eve's Struggle for Identity." *American Imago* 38 (1981):247-67.
        If we look beyond the imposed visions of Eve conveyed to us by *Paradise Lost*'s male narrator, Adam, and Satan, we find a complex character who seeks to regain the separate, secure identity that she surrenders at the outset. She must balance paradoxical drives: the urge for separateness, which leads to isolation, and the urge for union, which leads to fusion. *Paradise Lost* describes an ambivalence that is the foundation of all human identity. Eve's sense of self begins to emerge as she gazes into the pool. However, a voice asks her to give up her image and become Adam's. Her dream continues the journey toward selfhood, independent of Adam. When her relationship with Adam becomes stifling, Eve wants autonomy; but her acceptance of Satan's view, which denies human interdependence, leaves her lost in isolation. She then seeks to recover her link to Adam.

See also entries 94, 442, 448, 450, 462, 466, 475, 494, 507, 533, 549, 562, 573-74, 596, 630, 953.

HEAVEN

769   BLESSINGTON, FRANCIS C. "Autotheodicy: The Father as Orator in *Paradise Lost*." *Cithara* 14 (1975):49-60.
        No wooden spokesman of theological dogma, Milton's God is a rhetorician who defends himself. As a justification of God's ways, the very theme of *Paradise Lost* moves the poem into the realm of forensic oratory and theological controversy. If we judge God's speeches according to Aristotle's criteria for oratory--appeal to the orator's character (ethos), the audience's emotions (pathos), and rhetorical proof (pistis)--the Father shows his good will toward man and hatred of

Paradise Lost

Satan, identifies himself with his angelic audience and moves the reader to feel gratitude, and reasons in enthymemes and rhetorical examples. Satan, on the other hand, reveals his hatred of humanity, manipulates his demonic audience during their council and alienates the reader, and reasons badly with contradictions and hypocrisy.

770   CHRISTOPHER, GEORGIA B. "The Improvement of God's 'Character' in *Paradise Lost.*" *Renaissance Papers* (1982):1-8.
        Milton's God speaks English, though the Reformation tradition holds that some analogies exist between human and divine speech, but divine language is not related to human language with respect to sacramental power and expressive function. As the limit and medium of revelation, God's speech can receive only a selective gloss from humans, for we do not share his apprehension, language, or experience. Milton's God can speak in a loving or mean-spirited manner, each voice determined by how the human listener perceives him. Thus, as the narrator's religious experience progresses in *Paradise Lost*, moving from rebellion to understanding and then to love, God's character develops.

771   DANIELSON, DENNIS RICHARD. *Milton's Good God: A Study in Literary Theodicy.* Cambridge: Cambridge University Press, 1982, 303 pp.
        Milton believes in a material God and in creation *ex Deo*. In *Paradise Lost*, creation occurs in a threefold pattern. He joins Arminius and the Remonstrants in rejecting certain Calvinist doctrines. Furthermore, he adopts the Arminian view of predestination, grace, and free will. Because Milton presents divine justice in a dramatic way, he must make the fall appear plausible but not predetermined. Although critics try to make Milton a compatibilist, one who believes that free will does not preclude determinism and vice versa, he constructs incompatibilist models to deal with issues. His presentation of foreknowledge in *Paradise Lost* shows the conflicts of theoretical considerations and literary demands. The notion of a fortunate fall-- fortunate because it needs to occur to produce the Incarnation and Redemption--runs counter to Milton's presentation of free will and his avoidance of absolute predestination.

772 EMPSON, WILLIAM. *Milton's God*. London: Chatto and Windus; Norfolk, Conn.: New Directions, 1961, 280 pp. Rev. ed. 1965. Reprinted (Cambridge: Cambridge University Press, 1981); part reprinted in *Milton's Epic Poetry: Essays on "Paradise Lost" and "Paradise Regained*," ed. C. A. Patrides (Harmondsworth: Penguin Books, 1967), pp. 157-78; part reprinted in *Paradise Lost*, ed. Scott Elledge (New York: W. W. Norton & Co., 1975), pp. 478-90.

In *Paradise Lost*, Milton expresses the contemporary European mind by showing the bad effects of making a legalistic God whose actions may even parody legalistic behavior. Milton's epic "is an impressive example of one of the more appalling things the human mind is liable to do" (12-13; rev. ed.). Once we realize that the Father schemes, lies, and cheats his troops in order to bolster power that the Son will inherit, then God appears less selfish. If Raphael had not visited Adam and Eve, they would not have fallen, for he tempts them to speculate about God's ways. In *Samson Agonistes*, Jehovah's religion has no moral superiority over Dagon's. Milton makes a strong case for Dalila as a great lady who loves a dangerous lunatic. At the end of both of their careers, Milton and Samson stand as examples of the independent conscience.

773 FIXLER, MICHAEL. "All-Interpreting Love: God's Name in Scripture and in *Paradise Lost*." In *Milton and Scriptural Tradition: The Bible into Poetry*. Edited by James H. Sims and Leland Ryken. Columbia: University of Missouri Press, 1984, pp. 117-41.

When the word "all" in *Paradise Lost* becomes "All" or "All in All," it signifies the Father's transcendence as it is associated with the Son's "identifiable name and function as Love" (119). The use of "Love" as a name for the Son and "all" for any aspect of God's transcendence has an enigmatic quality associated with the names assigned to God in Scripture and tradition. Satan, and to some extent the fallen reader, cannot perceive the divine attributes that a name veils. Adam has an instinctual understanding of the essence of God's name. In Book 8, God demonstrates that he is Love even while refusing to answer Adam's questions about the Father's name. God's name is the argument of *Paradise Lost*.

Paradise Lost

774 FREEMAN, JAMES A. *Milton and the Martial Muse: "Paradise Lost" and European Traditions of War*. Princeton, N.J.: Princeton University Press, 1980, 272 pp. 27 illustrations.

Unlike Milton, almost all Renaissance artists and politicians argue that men's efforts should lead to a holy or just war. *Paradise Lost* attacks "the notion of desirable conflict" (5) even as it meets the learned audience's conventional expectations. Throughout his life, Milton feels the pressure to treat war positively, an attitude he sees in treatises, news, pictures, and propaganda. Although war occasionally seizes his imagination, particularly after he returns from Italy, Milton studies and mistrusts it. Satan in *Paradise Lost* reacts in a way consistent with martial treatises. Milton's portrayal of Satan marks the first time in literature that his military role is presented with such accuracy and in so sustained a manner. As a warrior, Satan often parodies epic conventions.

775 GILBERT, ALLAN H. "Form and Matter in *Paradise Lost*, Book III." *JEGP: Journal of English and Germanic Philology* 60 (1961):651-63. Reprinted in *Milton Studies in Honor of Harris Francis Fletcher*, ed. G. Blakemore Evans, et al. (Urbana: University of Illinois Press, 1961), pp. 43-55.

When God and the Son converse in Book 3 of *Paradise Lost*, they are looking down on Satan as he approaches earth; the dramatic situation involves the contrast between heaven's theology, which defines the triumph of good, and Satan's preparations, which are negated by the dialogue. Milton accommodates the heavenly dialogue by making God act as an earthly ruler and the Son as a prudent courtier. They conduct a debate about royal policy.

776 HAMILTON, GARY D. "Milton's Defensive God: A Reappraisal." *Studies in Philology* 69 (1972):87-100.

The Father's theology in *Paradise Lost* is our best guide to understanding Milton's God. If the mid-seventeenth century produces an important dispute between the Arminians and Calvinists about absolute predestination, Milton's God, when he defends himself, reflects the age's doubts about the goodness of a Calvinist deity. God defends himself against certain aspects of Calvinism by presenting himself as a God of goodness, rather than of power, who is not the author of sin. Milton uses the Calvinists' language to deny their positions: the Calvinist God's immutable decree is predestination; in *Paradise Lost* (3.122-28), God's unchangeable decree is freedom. A reasonable being, Milton's God states Arminian views.

777 HANFORD, JAMES HOLLY. "Milton and the Art of War." *Studies in Philology* 18 (1921):232-66. Reprinted in *John Milton, Poet and Humanist: Essays by James Holly Hanford* (Cleveland, Ohio: Press of Western Reserve University, 1966), pp. 185-223.

The military study and discipline prescribed in *Of Education* are part of an educational program based on the humanistic ideal. Given the struggles of Milton's age and his role as their interpreter, he must have studied the art of war by reading classic technical treatises and accounts of ancient wars. There is no evidence that he ever undergoes military training, though he does practice using a sword and perhaps a bow and arrow. His study, observation, and practice--along with the Christian habit of applying martial terms to spiritual conflicts-- allow him to bring military details into *Paradise Lost* and *Paradise Regained*. In *Paradise Lost*'s descriptions of arms and battles, Milton mixes romance and science. He uses the art of war in *Paradise Regained* to represent the civilized world at the beginning of Christ's ministry.

778 HUCKABAY, CALVIN. "The Beneficent God of *Paradise Lost*." In *Essays in Honor of Esmond Linworth Marilla*. Edited by Thomas Austin Kirby and William John Olive. Louisiana State University Studies, Humanities Series, no. 19. Baton Rouge: Louisiana State University Press, 1970, pp. 144-57.

Milton's God is credible in the dramatic framework of *Paradise Lost*, and he offers a positive alternative to Satan's negative, stoic autonomy. If Satan is linked to hate, destruction, and disorder, God is associated with love, creation, and order. They are in an antithetical relationship, and the poet's sympathies are with God, whom we see from the perspectives of the demons, fallen and unfallen humans, and loyal angels--and as a speaking character.

779 HUGHES, MERRITT Y. "The Filiations of Milton's Celestial Dialogue (*Paradise Lost*, III.80-343)." In *Ten Perspectives on Milton*. New Haven, Conn., and London: Yale University Press, 1965, pp. 104-35.

Paradise Lost

In the medieval morality tradition, the four daughters of God--justice and truth, mercy and peace--debate the future of man, with mercy always prevailing. The heavenly dialogue in Book 3 of *Paradise Lost* transcends the courtroom, and the demonic council provides a useful context for the heavenly one. Satanic egotism is contrasted with the Son's sacrifice of ego. In the heavenly dialogue, Milton tactfully presents the Father's and Son's contrasting emphases--justice and love, respectively--while preparing for a final union of their wills. The dialogue reveals that God is not responsible for man's sin and that the finite will has freedom only when it obeys God's will.

780   HUGHES, MERRITT Y. "Milton's Celestial Battle and the Theogonies." In *Studies in Honor of T. W. Baldwin*. Edited by Don Cameron Allen. Urbana: University of Illinois Press, 1958, pp. 237-53. Reprinted in *Ten Perspectives on Milton* (New Haven, Conn., and London: Yale University Press, 1965), pp. 196-219.

Though the war in heaven is beyond the comprehension of human sense, Milton conceives it as real and finds evidence of the event, and a model of accommodation, in Hesiod's *Theogony* and other classical titanomachies. The classical myths, in Milton's view, contain fragments of authentic biblical history.

781   HUNTER, W. B. "Milton on the Exaltation of the Son: The War in Heaven in *Paradise Lost*." *ELH* 36 (1969):215-31. Reprinted in *Bright Essence: Studies in Milton's Theology*, by W[illiam] B. Hunter, C. A. Patrides, and J. H. Adamson (Salt Lake City: University of Utah Press, 1971), pp. 115-30.

The Son's exaltation or "begetting" occurs, in the traditional view (as *Christian Doctrine* indicates), at his Resurrection. This is one of the few discrepancies between *Christian Doctrine* and *Paradise Lost*: in the epic, the exaltation is the first explicit event in the poem's true chronology. As a subordinationist who believes that the Son's divinity is subordinate to the Father's and thus can be exalted, Milton accepts the idea that the Son is exalted, in his human and divine natures, by applying some of the Father's merits to himself. With the begetting of the Son and the war in heaven, Milton telescopes time to narrate these events (the fall of the rebel angels, the defeat of Satan and his devils in Revelation, and the exaltation of the Son, which occurs concomitantly at the Resurrection) from three points of view.

782 HUNTER, WM. B., Jr. "Milton's Materialistic Life Principle." *JEGP: Journal of English and Germanic Philology* 45 (1946):68-76.

According to Milton's physics, everything in the universe--including the life principle or soul--is created from intrinsically good matter. Milton believes in monism or materialism, arguing in *Christian Doctrine* that the soul, complete with original sin, is propagated from parent to child. In the creation scene in *Paradise Lost*, unformed matter receives form and vital power from God, through light. After death, the soul, like the body from which it cannot be separated, decays and returns to its original elements (in the sun) as part of the universal order. The flow of the life principle is thus circular.

783 IDE, RICHARD S. "On the Begetting of the Son in *Paradise Lost*." *Studies in English Literature, 1500-1900* 24 (1984):141-55.

Functioning in the opposite way from what Raphael intends, his accommodation of heaven makes it appear to be the shadow of earth, as heavenly events mirror Christian history on earth. Heavenly and earthly time are continuous and Christocentric. Milton connects the begetting of the Son to three interpretations of Psalm 2:7: the generation of the Son in his divine nature, in his human nature, and in his metaphorical exaltation on the third day when he fulfills the purpose of his begetting. In *Paradise Lost*, the pattern of earthly life--humiliation followed by exaltation--applies as well to the Son's begetting, Incarnation, and victories in heaven and on earth.

784 LABRIOLA, ALBERT C. "'God Speaks': Milton's Dialogue in Heaven and the Tradition of Divine Deliberation." *Cithara* 25 (1986):5-30. 2 illustrations.

Of the two main topics included in the iconographic and theological traditions of divine deliberation, the redemption and the creation of mankind, Milton in *Paradise Lost* uses the former almost exclusively. He presents the dialogue in heaven as a religious drama, with the Father and Son acting as the main characters and the angelic choir as spectators, with whom the narrator joins his voice. After the argument to Book 3 defines the narrator's role, he establishes the dialogue's setting, further delineates the participants' personalities, comments on the discourse, and provides transitions between speeches. The dialogue presents and interprets the various parts of God's biblical

Paradise Lost

statement at the Transfiguration. Not just an external event, the dialogue dramatizes a debate in God's mind and a dilemma in his will.

785   LABRIOLA, ALBERT C.   "'Thy Humiliation Shall Exalt': The Christology of *Paradise Lost*." *Milton Studies* 15 (1981):29-42.

In order to elaborate *Paradise Lost*'s Christology, Milton presents the interrelation of Moses, the Son, and Satan in terms of images of ascent and descent, light and dark, and disclosure and concealment. The exaltation of the Son's angelic nature is also his humiliation, for he is subject to the limitations of a lesser nature. Satan cannot acknowledge that all angels are thereby exalted by the deity's sharing their nature. The Son's self-abnegation is the antithesis of Satan's proud effort to become a deity.

786   Le COMTE, EDWARD. "Dubious Battle: Saving the Appearances." *English Language Notes* 19 (1982):177-93.

Milton's contemporaries praise *Paradise Lost*'s war in heaven, though a few worry that readers may accept the episode as doctrine. From Milton's age to our own, apologists for Book 6 justify the war in terms of epic precedents. With regard to the view of Book 6 as comic, there are problems with perspective. Some critics see typology and others detect topical references to the Civil Wars in the heavenly battle, while still others view Milton's denigration of war as a sign of his pacifism. Milton denies that the war in heaven is a symbol.

787   LIEB, MICHAEL. "Milton's 'Dramatick Constitution': The Celestial Dialogue in *Paradise Lost*, Book III." *Milton Studies* 23 (1987):215-40.

Not some abstract being, Milton's God belongs in a dramatic environment and should use the discourse of dialogue. He struggles with himself, and we should struggle with him. Anticipated by the outlines in the Trinity manuscript and the tradition of the four daughters of God, *Paradise Lost*'s dialogue follows a five-act structure, complete with a prologue and epilogue. Milton's heavenly dialogue embodies the drama of the Godhead's personalities, a drama characterized by conflict and wrath as God struggles with his own theology. The Son contributes contentiousness and energy to the scene.

By showing how the Son questions God's greatness and goodness, Milton radicalizes dialogue.

788   LOW, ANTHONY. "Milton's God: Authority in *Paradise Lost.*" *Milton Studies* 4 (1972):19-38.

The modern reader's problem with Milton's God comes from a flaw in *Paradise Lost* or from the reader's bias, probably against authority figures. But Milton stands firmly opposed to arbitrary authority--any authority involving one person over another--as distinguished from divine authority. In *Paradise Lost*, he contrasts the perfect rule of God and the Son with the tyrannies of Satan and humans. God's plain, logical style is the opposite of Satan's obfuscating, persuasive style. If readers worry that the Son is *Paradise Lost*'s main conveyer of love and mercy, they forget that the source of these qualities is the Father. Milton's God is defined by what he does: he creates the world and is reflected in the book of nature, especially in Adam and Eve.

789   MacCALLUM, HUGH. *Milton and the Sons of God: The Divine Image in Milton's Epic Poetry.* Toronto, Buffalo, N.Y., and London: University of Toronto Press, 1986, 335 pp.

Milton's epics explore the three kinds of divine sonship suggested by Scripture: divine sonship between God and the Son; sonship for all believers, extending from God through the Son; and sonship for all men, who are created in God's image. Insisting on a distinction among the members of the Trinity, *Christian Doctrine* advances subordinationist views of the Son, monotheistic views of the Father, and (as *Paradise Lost* and *Paradise Regained* reinforce) a view of the Holy Spirit as God's power extended through the Son or an angel. Never explicitly heterodox, *Paradise Lost* and *Paradise Regained* are not divisive or polemical works. In prelapsarian Eden, Adam and Eve progressively realize God's image before the fall, in actions that parallel their regeneration. The Son provides a model and guidance for them. Adam and Eve's repentance, another act of growth, proceeds as each contributes to a dialectic. In *Paradise Regained*, which recalls Nestorianism, Christ combines the divine and human natures, though they are highly unequal in essence; Milton stresses Christ's unity of being.

Paradise Lost

790 MILLER, GEORGE ERIC. "Stylistic Rhetoric and the Language of God in *Paradise Lost*, Book III." *Language and Style* 8 (1975):111-26.
      While Milton's God may echo Scripture in Book 3 of *Paradise Lost*, he does not quote it. The Father's speech in Book 3 is full of rhetorical figures, with approximately one scheme or trope in each line, creating a distinctive style that gives him the illusion of authority. Characterized by figures of word play, repetition, and balance, God's speech is plain not because it lacks literary resources but because it creates a sense of coherence and clarity.

791 MURRIN, MICHAEL. "The Language of Milton's Heaven." *Modern Philology* 74 (1977):350-65. Revised in *The Allegorical Epic: Essays in Its Rise and Decline* (Chicago, Ill., and London: University of Chicago Press, 1980), pp. 153-71.
      By not allegorizing *Paradise Lost*'s war in heaven, Milton signals the end of the allegorical tradition, though he avoids it for theological rather than artistic reasons. He turns to Exodus for the image of God's mountain, to Ezekiel for the Son's chariot, and to Revelation for heavenly ritual. To protect his heavenly scenes from literalist readings, Milton invents a special language, one derived from the Bible. In the descriptions of heaven, similes explain familiar matters by referring to the unknown, the reverse of the usual method and a procedure that makes the scene stranger and stranger. The terms used to describe heaven refer to each other, as Milton constructs a complete world that we cannot enter. His descriptive method reflects his iconoclastic theology, for dispensing with or multiplying images leads to the same end: his heavenly scenes resist analysis.

792 NORFORD, DON PARRY. "The Devouring Father in *Paradise Lost*." *Hebrew University Studies in Literature* 8 (1980):98-126.
      As a negative force that divides the heavenly substance against itself so that it creates the world and man, Satan is essential to God. In *Paradise Lost*, God is the devouring father, the world his body, chaos his belly or womb, and hell his bowels. God digests everything except what he cannot assimilate into spirit (and all else he rejects). But he is also the source of all things, including matter. Because Milton sees human accomplishment as demonic, there are tensions in his view of his own creative process. He is the poet of the Logos, yet he realizes that the dark and chaotic are essential to creativity, so he tries to

reconcile the devouring and the prolific. Satan, the principle of individuation, leads Adam and Eve to gain consciousness through the tree of knowledge. Recognizing the darkness within himself, God secretly wants the fall to occur so man can become like the Father; God's other side insists that man be punished for this. Evil originates in God's decision to create.

793   PATRIDES, C. A. "The Godhead in *Paradise Lost*: Dogma or Drama?" *JEGP: Journal of English and Germanic Philology* 64 (1965):29-34. Reprinted in *Bright Essence: Studies in Milton's Theology*, by W[illiam] B. Hunter, C. A. Patrides, and J. H. Adamson (Salt Lake City: University of Utah Press, 1971), pp. 71-77.

    Christian Doctrine and *Paradise Lost* do not agree at all points in their presentations of the Father and Son. Instead of being an Arian work, *Paradise Lost* asserts the Godhead's unity and makes distinctions between the Father and the Son only in their dialogues. The narrative requires drama, which the dialogue provides; the epic's theological framework requires clear dogma, so the Father and the Son are not mentioned as separate in any action that occurs outside of heaven.

794   REVARD, STELLA PURCE. *The War in Heaven: "Paradise Lost" and the Tradition of Satan's Rebellion*. Ithaca, N.Y., and London: Cornell University Press, 1980, 315 pp.

    The war in heaven is caused by Satan's intellective sin of pride, a wrong choice made by a good creature. When the Son is exalted, Satan envies his heavenly kingship and chooses to be separate from him, an act synonymous with alienation and damnation. Satan controls or chooses pride in Book 5, where it is an intellectual error; in Book 1, however, pride becomes an emotional force that controls him. Contemporaries interpret Revelation, particularly Michael's combat with the dragon, as a description of modern crises, including the Civil Wars. The war in heaven, though it has a long literary tradition, receives detailed treatment only in Renaissance works, which make it a real war and use a structure, images, and characterization similar to those in *Paradise Lost*. Milton discredits the ethic of heroic war by giving his angels the demeanor of classical warriors. Unlike most previous poems, Milton's epic assigns the Son a major role in the war.

Paradise Lost

795 ROSENBLATT, JASON P. "Structural Unity and Temporal Concordance: The War in Heaven in *Paradise Lost.*" *PMLA* 87 (1972):31-41.

Because the war in heaven occurs at the beginning of time, in the middle of *Paradise Lost*, and at the end of Revelation, readers should look for a temporal concordance in Milton's episode. The Book of Exodus, with its climax of Israel's redemption from Egypt, provides such a concordance. In analogies between Pharaoh and Satan, and between Moses and Abdiel, and in the emphasis on the themes of liberty and servitude, Milton gives parallels that never turn into a typological pattern. Allusions to the climax of Exodus also appear in Books 1 and 12 of *Paradise Lost*, so the war in heaven radiates meaning in both directions and provides a structural unity for the epic.

796 SAMUEL, IRENE. "The Dialogue in Heaven: A Reconsideration of *Paradise Lost*, III.1-417." *PMLA* 72 (1957):601-11. Reprinted in *Milton: Modern Essays in Criticism*, ed. Arthur E. Barker (London, Oxford, and New York: Oxford University Press, 1965), pp. 233-45; *Paradise Lost*, ed. Scott Elledge (New York: W. W. Norton & Co., 1975), pp. 468-78.

If we read the dialogue in heaven as dogma rather than drama, and if we fail to see how central the episode is to the whole epic, we run the risk of joining critics who find the Father a bore. Milton's God is "Being, infinitely beyond all created things" (603), so the tonelessness of his first speech is appropriate, since he is not just a person. No mere echo of God's logical views, the Son's voice is different: compassionate and loving. God's voice has range, including more warmth and love than the Son's. Even in its smallest details, the dialogue in heaven stands in contrast with events in hell, and it is related to what might have occurred in the temptation scene.

797 SCHIFFHORST, GERALD J. "Patience and the Humbly Exalted Heroism of Milton's Messiah: Typological and Iconographic Background." *Milton Studies* 16 (1982):97-113. 2 illustrations.

Milton uses typology to show that the Son's triumph in the war in heaven fulfills his divine exaltation and prepares for his humiliation on the cross. Because he is both *Christus victor* and *Christus patiens*, these events are connected. Patience, an active virtue central to

Paradise Lost's definition of Christian heroism, is Adam's lesson in Book 12.

798   SWAIM, KATHLEEN M. "The Mimesis of Accommodation in Book 3 of *Paradise Lost*." *Philological Quarterly* 63 (1984):461-75.
     To mediate between divine mysteries and human limitations in Book 3 of *Paradise Lost*, Milton uses the image of light as a mimesis of accommodation. Book 3 uses two kinds of accommodation, one lowering truth to earth's inhabitants and the other raising the human mind to heaven. If the poet at the beginning of Book 3 stresses his blindness, we too have only a limited ability to see light unless we receive God's help. Accommodation is thus necessary from the start. Light is next used to portray the Father and Son, whose actions--like accommodation--work in two directions: creative (downward) and redemptive (upward). Finally, the description of the sun's site compliments readers whose imaginations can grasp such radiance, even as the passage encourages them to wonder at the deity behind it.

799   TUNG, MASON. "The Abdiel Episode: A Contextual Reading." *Studies in Philology* 62 (1965):595-609.
     When Raphael tells Adam the story about Abdiel, the lessons are clear: like Abdiel, Adam and Eve are happy and have the free will to remain so, if they choose, even against great odds or a great foe; one needs to control one's inner self, as Abdiel does; reason triumphs; anyone's fall is evitable. We learn from the Abdiel episode, as in *Paradise Lost* as a whole, that God's ways are just.

800   WEST, ROBERT H. *Milton and the Angels*. Athens: University of Georgia Press, 1955, 246 pp.
     Works on angelology are abundant in the middle of the seventeenth century, when Milton composes *Paradise Lost*, with Puritan thinkers accepting angelic operations but limiting their extent by arguing that angels, as God's retainers, guide and punish humans. In some of *Paradise Lost*'s discussions of angels, Milton bases his thoughts on classical works and the Bible, which brings him to the fringes of angelology. Milton's angelology is consistent and clear, its flaws being inherent in the traditional material. *Christian Doctrine* contains none of *Paradise Lost*'s heretical, extremely independent assertions about

Paradise Lost

angelic eating and love-making, which Milton introduces to reinforce thematic points, though the two works share a great deal of angelology, both heterodox and orthodox.

801   WINN, JAMES A. "Milton on Heroic Warfare." *Yale Review* 66 (1976):70-86.

In *Paradise Lost*, Milton has an ambiguous attitude toward the heroism of warfare, though earlier in his life he advocates military training for young men and serves a military government. Even his political pamphlets downgrade the traditional glory of war in favor of the better fortitude, mental accomplishments. *Paradise Lost* later reveals war to be "an evil, post-lapsarian necessity" (75) because Milton's view of war changes when he does not see the Commonwealth move from martial victory to acts of creation. In the war in heaven episode in *Paradise Lost*, God's Logos battles uncreation. Milton here mocks all warfare, but for the loyal angels such submission to mockery is a sign of obedience. The Son's arms are allegorical objects.

802   WOOTEN, JOHN. "The Comic Milton and Italian Burlesque Poets." *Cithara* 22 (1982):3-12.

Burlesque poetry, especially its Italian roots (including Pulci's work), influences Milton when he writes about the war in heaven in *Paradise Lost*. Elevating a subject in order to debunk it, burlesque appears in epic-comic episodes, such as when the angels hurl parts of heaven's landscape, and in the mock-romance attitude used to discuss chivalric trappings (such as the rebels' cannon in Book 6 or the beginning of Book 9).

See also entries 225, 441-42, 448, 462, 533, 562, 572, 579, 593, 602, 606, 675, 677, 679, 688, 858, 967-69, 972, 989-90, 1001.

PARADISE REGAINED:

803   BARKER, ARTHUR E. "Calm Regained through Passion Spent: The Conclusions of the Miltonic Effort." In *The Prison and the Pinnacle*. Papers To Commemorate the Tercentenary of *Paradise Regained* and *Samson Agonistes*. Edited by Balachandra Rajan.

Toronto and Buffalo, N.Y.: University of Toronto Press, 1973, pp. 3-48.

Milton's poetry, like his prose, seeks "to allay the perturbations induced by a desperate sense of irreversible pollution in human affairs" (6) and to help human affections attain the harmonious state necessary for reform. *Paradise Regained* shows Satan's efforts to introduce perturbation to a imperturbable mind, which is thus energized; *Samson Agonistes* shows the hero's perturbations followed by purgation and action based on faith. That these works repeat the purgative and restorative movement of Books 11-12 of *Paradise Lost* indicates how valuable Milton finds this pattern. We usually assume that *Paradise Regained*'s structure is formed according to the temptations, a delusion that Satan encourages; yet he is asymmetrical, his temptations spilling over book-divisions and the middle being overblown. A better structural guide is the end of each book, where Christ confirms his knowledge and develops his awareness of how identity shapes responsibility. *Samson Agonistes* transcends the Hellenistic and Hebraic sense of fallibility.

804   CHAMBERS, A. B. "The Double Time Scheme in *Paradise Regained*." *Milton Studies* 7 (1975):189-205.

Paradise Regained's structure is based on Milton's handling of the two concepts of religious time: the linear concept using the idea of *kairos* and the cyclic concept using the idea of *chronos*. The wilderness temptation emphasizes the former to indicate that the precise moment for Christ's actions, most of which Satan suggests, has not yet arrived. The Son must wait. But the repetition of events and allusions illustrates the movement of *chronos*. Milton portrays Christ as only a man before the pinnacle scene; at the beginning of *Paradise Regained*, he is confused and potentially culpable. He finally resumes his status as God. Man must model his *chronoi* on God's *kairoi*, for the two schemes must be compatible if salvation is to occur.

805   CLARK, IRA. "*Paradise Regained* and the Gospel According to John." *Modern Philology* 71 (1973):1-15.

Although John is the only Gospel that lacks the temptation in the wilderness, *Paradise Regained* alludes to it more than to any other Gospel except Matthew. The explanation of Christ's nature in *Paradise Regained*, as the Messiah and the Logos incarnate, is based on John.

Paradise Regained

Besides dogma, John provides *Paradise Regained*'s key vocabulary terms and the signs that identify the Son. Just as John reveals the Messiah by signs, so Milton uses a similar structure in *Paradise Regained*.

806   COX, LEE SHERIDAN. "Food-Word Imagery in *Paradise Regained*." *ELH* 28 (1961):225-43.

In Matthew and even more clearly in Luke, Christ rejects Satan's temptations by turning to the Word: "It is written" and "It is said" begin his responses to Satan. Milton's only alteration of scriptural dialogue in *Paradise Regained* involves Satan's attempt to imitate or appropriate the Word, though ironically he cannot even recognize the Word as it speaks to him. Throughout the poem, Milton is concerned with "the nature and office of the Word Incarnate and of the Word" (226). Word and food images are interwoven in *Paradise Regained*, as true Word and food, the sources of life, and as Satan, who offers the false word (lies) and false food. On the first day, there is a temptation of the food of the spiritual life, divine bread; on the second day, of the food that supports the senses, imagination, and reason; and on the third day, of all foods--physical, mental, and spiritual.

807   DYSON, A. E. "The Meaning of *Paradise Regained*." *Texas Studies in Literature and Language* 3 (1961):197-211.

Paradise Lost contains a tension between the literal heroic level, concerned with battle and power, which conflicts with the allegorical level, concerned with the suffering and peaceable battles of Christ, who is thus not a heroic figure. The force of Milton's poetry is behind the former, for he is incapable of writing effectively about humility, love, or forgiveness. He is fascinated by courage and power, as we see in his portraits of Christ and Satan in the two epics. In *Paradise Regained*, Christ's victory is marked by pride and superior strength rather than compassion and moral insight. Inevitably doomed, Satan offers unreasonable arguments and appears ridiculous, though in terms of arrogance and aspiration he is much like Christ (and like Milton's Samson). Milton is a great heroic poet.

808   ELLIOTT, EMORY. "Milton's Biblical Style in *Paradise Regained*." *Milton Studies* 6 (1974):227-41.

In *Paradise Regained,* Milton uses scriptural words and phrases "to draw into the poem essential details of the encircling framework of Christ's total career and teachings" (228). The poem insists that we overcome the limitations of Satan's perspective and see the temptations in context, as part of Christ's mission of salvation. Allusions to Hebrews emphasize the young Christ's humanity, years of preparation, and exemplary role, and they are relevant to the theme of the correct use and interpretation of Scripture. Like the reader but unlike Satan, Christ exercises critical principles to understand the new covenant. Allusions to Romans and Ephesians point to the need for restraint and self-discipline, while allusions to Revelation in *Paradise Regained*'s closing passages stress the extremes of woe or joy in the next world.

809 ETTIN, ANDREW V. "Milton, T. S. Eliot, and the Virgilian Vision: Some Versions of Georgic." *Genre* 10 (1977):233-58.

Despite their differences, Virgil's *Georgics,* Milton's *Paradise Regained,* and Eliot's *Four Quartets* share many elements: a belief in the possibility of progress through difficult labor and a belief that humans misconstrue the meaning of progress; the affirmation of inner, heroic qualities achieved in private; the poet's urge to break with current thought and return to the source of belief; and the use of nature as a hostile or attractive setting to which we must not yield.

810 FISH, STANLEY E. "Inaction and Silence: The Reader in *Paradise Regained.*" In *Calm of Mind: Tercentenary Essays on "Paradise Regained" and "Samson Agonistes" in Honor of John S. Diekhoff.* Edited by Joseph Anthony Wittreich, Jr. Cleveland, Ohio, and London: Press of Case Western Reserve University, 1971, pp. 25-47.

By refining or purging the reader, Milton's art seeks to lose the self in a union with God, to exchange human values for divine. Thus the narrative action progressively narrows the arena in which the self is preeminent or active, while the verbal action reveals a corresponding decrease in language's complexity and volubility until--when the self unites with God--silence reigns. *Paradise Regained* is based on the pattern of a reader's expectation (of what one assumes will be a Christian action in the face of a problem or temptation) followed by disappointment when the action (response) is withheld, and--finally-- perplexity when one finds an issue left unresolved or a confrontation avoided. By doing God's will, the character himself does nothing.

Paradise Regained

Paradise Regained, by provoking the wrong response, leads us to the correct one: the self's admission of dependence on God.

811   FISH, STANLEY. "Things and Actions Indifferent: The Temptation of Plot in *Paradise Regained*." *Milton Studies* 17 (1983):163-85.
        Action in Milton's poems is not something one does but it is interiorized as something one is: "for Milton being *is* an action" (165). Continual and never inconsequential, action is not the result of one climactic event. His mature poetry illustrates the tension between narrative and the continuing obligation of obedience. In *Paradise Regained*, Satan tries to persuade the Son that he is a character in a plot that offers new riches and opportunities; the Son's response is his inability or unwillingness to recognize a plot that offers him different objects and actions. Accepting or rejecting temptation is inappropriate, since one's attitude toward externals is crucial while the externals themselves are not. *Paradise Regained* works out the doctrine of things indifferent.

812   FORSYTH, NEIL. "Having Done All To Stand: Biblical and Classical Allusion in *Paradise Regained*." *Milton Studies* 21 (1985):199-214.
        In *Paradise Regained*, Milton uses layers of allusion and parallel images to prepare us for the final image of a hero standing firm, which is typical of his poetry. Allusions to Hercules versus Antaeus emphasize the opposition of standing and falling; allusions to Psalm 91, Ephesians 6, and Antaeus and the Sphinx reveal that the temptation of Christ is part of a larger combat. Milton adapts biblical allusions to classical forms, particularly those based on Homer and Virgil. Applied to Christ, these allusions are faint, but applied to Satan, they are explicit.

813   FORTIN, RENÉ. "The Climactic Similes of *Paradise Regained*: 'True Wisdom' or 'False Resemblance'?" *Milton Quarterly* 7 (1973):39-43.
        Given Milton's ambivalence toward classical culture, we should be suspicious when we examine the similes at the end of *Paradise Regained* comparing Christ's triumph to those of Hercules and Oedipus. Milton equivocates in these similes, which do not precisely

match the action at the poem's conclusion. The similes are distorted to point to the distance between classical and Christian cultures.

814 GRANT, PATRICK. "Time and Temptation in *Paradise Regained.*" *University of Toronto Quarterly* 43 (1973):32-47.

A contemporary iconography of time provides both a useful background for interpreting *Paradise Regained* and a principle for poetically motivating the temptations. The poem's main characters view time through different iconographic traditions, with Christ trusting time the revealer and Satan relying on time the destroyer. Satan begins by assaulting Christ's faith, for it is logically prior (in fact, it is eternal) and preparative to the following temptations because they are produced within the realm of time. Following the three divisions of time the destroyer, Satan tempts Christ to lust (suggesting the wolf and time past); to wealth, glory, and fame (suggesting the dog and future); and to anger and pride (suggesting the lion and time present).

815 GUSS, DONALD L. "A Brief Epic: *Paradise Regained.*" *Studies in Philology* 68 (1971):223-43.

Paradise Regained is not an assertion of doctrine but a narrative, which means that we must consider the context--the "time, place, audience, antecedents, and motive" (224)--of each speech and action. The brief epic presents a historical example of extraordinary human virtue and divine providence, which combine to create its epic subject and purpose. Christ's firmness is heroic, and it produces the desired epic effects of praise, wonder, and emulation. *Paradise Regained* fulfills all the criteria of the Renaissance epic, though it is an example of the brief epic and not, like *Paradise Lost*, the diffuse epic. While the central action of *Paradise Regained*, the temptation, is much longer than that of *Paradise Lost*, in the brief epic all inessential matter is greatly condensed. Like the holy simplicity of biblical eloquence, *Paradise Regained*'s style must be judged according to how it suits its subject.

816 HAMILTON, GARY D. "Creating the Garden Anew: The Dynamics of *Paradise Regained.*" *Philological Quarterly* 50 (1971):567-81.

Paradise Regained

By acting out what Adam and Eve could have become, Christ in *Paradise Regained* develops as he moves toward the inner paradise that Michael discusses in *Paradise Lost*. The human Christ undergoes a process of purification by trial that leads him to start changing earth to heaven. Christ's responses rather than Satan's temptations define *Paradise Regained*'s structure: Christ reveals faith in Book 1, temperance in Book 2, patience in Book 3, and "the sum of wisdom" in Book 4, and these are the stages that Michael outlines in *Paradise Lost* (12.575-87). Only after he perfects his human nature does Christ go above the human in the episode on the pinnacle.

817   HUGHES, MERRITT Y. "The Christ of *Paradise Regained* and the Renaissance Heroic Tradition." *Studies in Philology* 35 (1938):254-77. Reprinted in *Ten Perspectives on Milton* (New Haven, Conn., and London: Yale University Press, 1965), pp. 35-62.

Medieval and Renaissance romance epics influence the allegorical atmosphere and *contemptus mundi* theme of *Paradise Regained*. Colored very little by stoic doctrine, Milton's portrait of Christ is shaped by writings (particularly Italian epic theory) that Christianize Aristotle's concept of the magnanimous man. Heroism, in the Neoplatonists' hands, becomes a contemplative quality. The Christ of *Paradise Regained* is an epic hero because of his attributes as the redemptive, creative Word.

818   HUNTER, WILLIAM B., Jr. "The Obedience of Christ in *Paradise Regained*." In *Calm of Mind: Tercentenary Essays on "Paradise Regained" and "Samson Agonistes" in Honor of John S. Diekhoff*. Edited by Joseph Anthony Wittreich, Jr. Cleveland, Ohio, and London: Press of Case Western Reserve University, 1971, pp. 67-75.

The events of Christ's life reveal his active obedience to his Father's will; this recovers eternal life for mankind. His death shows his passive obedience, which releases mankind from punishment for sin. Satisfying divine justice for mankind requires both kinds of obedience. *Paradise Regained*'s subject is active obedience to the Law, indicating that the paradise to be regained is mankind's eternal life with God. To illustrate Christ's passive obedience, Milton introduces nonbiblical material into *Paradise Regained*.

819 HUTTAR, CHARLES A. "The Passion of Christ in *Paradise Regained*." *English Language Notes* 19 (1982):236-60.

For three centuries, defenders of *Paradise Regained* have had to answer one theological objection: paradise is regained through Christ's death and Resurrection, not his temptation. But *Paradise Regained*'s title is appropriate because the Redemption by the cross is an implicit theme that forms an essential part of the poem. The brief epic may be the work that Milton does not complete at age twenty-one, "Passion," which fails because grief is not yet natural to him. Two symbolisms of the Passion--a majestic Christ or a suffering Christ--are available to Milton, and in "Passion" he turns to the latter, though it does not suit his personality. In *Paradise Regained*, the temptation is seen as a true, though lesser, instance of Christ's conquest by humiliation in the Passion, to which the temptation is figurally linked. *Paradise Regained* contains many allusions to the Passion, particularly in the pinnacle episode, where the doctrine of the cross receives a full presentation.

820 JORDAN, RICHARD DOUGLAS. "*Paradise Regained* and the Second Adam." *Milton Studies* 9 (1976):261-75.

If Christ acts as the second Adam in *Paradise Regained*, Milton also uses their typological relationship to stress their differences. Adam is fallible; Christ is incapable of falling, for his success is predestined, and the poem's focus remains on God's will, not the Son's. This makes dramatic interest difficult to sustain. On the pinnacle, Christ makes no assertion about his nature; rather, he quotes Matthew 4:6. Not a response to a revelation of Christ's identity, Satan's fall is the symbolic antithesis of the Son's stand. *Paradise Regained* is a biblical, ritual drama.

821 KERMODE, FRANK. "Milton's Hero." *Review of English Studies*, n.s. 4 (1953):317-30.

Blending valor and contemplation, Milton aspires to heroism, seeing himself as resembling the Christ of *Paradise Regained*. In the brief epic, the poet shows the hero as he faces the primary crisis of emerging from seclusion. Milton tries to define the Christian heroic virtue as something distinct from the pagan; the former receives heavenly rewards while the latter gains earthly ones. Christ in *Paradise Regained* transcends or confutes all the known kinds of heroism.

Paradise Regained

822 KERRIGAN, WILLIAM. "The Riddle of *Paradise Regained*." In
Poetic Prophecy in Western Literature. Edited by Jan Wojcik and
Raymond-Jean Frontain. Rutherford, N.J., Madison, Wi., and
Teaneck, N.J.: Fairleigh Dickinson University Press; London and
Toronto: Associated University Presses, 1984, pp. 64-80.

   Discursive and symbolic, *Paradise Regained* becomes prophetic
when Christ, on the pinnacle, speaks ambiguously for the first time. At
various points in the poem, the symbolism brings Christ and Satan into
a single identity, which is reinforced by Milton's subordinationism (for
both figures are sons of God), just as Oedipus in the final simile is the
Sphinx's double. Undone by his mother and father, Oedipus is
connected to Christ, who is man through Mary and God through the
Father. The joining of Christ and Satan is done through myth and
symbol because Milton cannot otherwise articulate it. The Hercules
and Oedipus similes at the end of *Paradise Regained* show the
importance of separation from the first mother. In the wilderness,
Christ symbolically relives the history of the libido, and at the end of
the brief epic he solves the tragedy of Oedipus with the superego. The
consistent psychological strategy of Milton's work and life involves
dividing the imago of the father in order to depose one and obey the
other.

823 LEWALSKI, BARBARA KIEFER. *Milton's Brief Epic: The Genre,
Meaning, and Art of "Paradise Regained."* Providence, R.I.: Brown
University Press; London: Methuen & Co., 1966, 448 pp. Part
reprinted in *Milton's Epic Poetry: Essays on "Paradise Lost" and
"Paradise Regained,"* ed. C. A. Patrides (Harmondsworth: Penguin
Books, 1967), pp. 322-47.

   The seventeenth century accepts a tradition that sees the Book
of Job as a heroic poem resembling the classical epic in meter, subject,
and narrative technique. Job's encounter with Satan is interpreted as a
heroic combat. Although no classical epics fit Milton's conception of
the brief epic, *Paradise Regained*'s ancestors come from European
biblical poetry written between the fourth and seventeenth centuries.
The opening lines of *Paradise Regained* assert its generic identity as an
epic with a more noble and heroic subject than that of *Paradise Lost*.
They also contain typological allusions to Adam and Job, which indicate
that Christ will relive and reverse Adam's temptation and repeat and
surpass Job's victory. These typological traditions help Christ pursue a
definition of self. The narrator of *Paradise Regained*, whose voice and

stance are not the same as those in *Paradise Lost*, has an easy, confident tone because he has already sung one successful epic and his new poem uses more familiar material and settings. Contrary to many critics' assertions, *Paradise Regained* contains many epic stylistic features.

824 LEWALSKI, BARBARA [KIEFER]. "Time and History in *Paradise Regained*." In *The Prison and the Pinnacle*. Papers To Commemorate the Tercentenary of *Paradise Regained* and *Samson Agonistes*. Edited by Balachandra Rajan. Toronto and Buffalo, N.Y.: University of Toronto Press, 1973, pp. 49-81.

Milton's God acts within the temporal process, not in an eternal present, as the God of history. In *Paradise Regained*, Christ works within the providential plan to recapitulate, surpass, and fulfill the types that precede him. Satan assumes that what happened must happen again. Though aware of God's providence, Satan attributes all ordinances and events to the workings of fate, a blind perspective that affects all who devote themselves to evil. Faced with Satan's Machiavellian principles, Christ responds with Machiavelli's own view that a virtuous character provides a better foundation than fortune for establishing a kingdom. Satan frequently resembles and takes on the cyclical or astrological premises of classical historians.

825 LORD, GEORGE de FOREST. "Folklore and Myth in *Paradise Regain'd*." In *Poetic Traditions of the English Renaissance*. Edited by Maynard Mack and George de Forest Lord. New Haven, Conn.: Yale University Press, 1982, pp. 229-49. Reprinted in *Trials of the Self: Heroic Ordeals in the Epic Tradition* (Hamden, Conn.: Archon Books, 1983), pp. 93-109.

Like the young redeemer of a folk tale, Christ at the beginning of *Paradise Regained* shows ignorance, submissiveness, and a lack of power. He leaves home, like the hero of a fairy tale, to enter a supernatural world and to return victorious with rewards for mankind. From the public's perspective, however, Christ accomplishes nothing in his microcosmic, internal adventures; from his perspective, he achieves self-discovery. As the supposedly wiser older brother of such tales, Satan attempts to subvert the younger brother's secret strength, his identity and mission. *Paradise Regained*'s chastened style is reflected in the deprivation and privacy of Christ's ordeal. Time and place are

Paradise Regained

interior concerns, oracles irrelevant. As an epic, *Paradise Regained* radically modifies that form, in part through its use of Christ as the heroic antihero.

826 McADAMS, JAMES R. "The Pattern of Temptation in *Paradise Regained.*" *Milton Studies* 4 (1972):177-93.

The second temptation (*Paradise Regained*, 2.245-4.431), which dominates the poem, contains nine episodes, of which the discussion of Israel is central. It also constitutes the thematic center because it brings together and focuses *Paradise Regained*'s themes, exposing Christ's and Satan's natures, and foreshadows the conclusion. The four episodes before and the four after the exchange about Israel mirror each other, the first being linked to the last and so on. The night scenes isolate the second temptation, which relies on deviousness, and the Israel episode's emphasis on distrust parallels the first and third days' temptations.

827 MARTZ, LOUIS L. "*Paradise Regain'd*: The Interior Teacher." In *The Paradise Within: Studies in Vaughan, Traherne, and Milton*. New Haven, Conn., and London: Yale University Press, 1964, pp. 169-201. Reprinted in *Milton's Epic Poetry: Essays on "Paradise Lost" and "Paradise Regained,"* ed. C. A. Patrides (Harmondsworth: Penguin Books, 1967), pp. 348-77.

Like Virgil's *Georgics*, *Paradise Regained* is a poem of about 2,000 lines divided into four books and written in the middle style; these poems share the praise of a temperate life as opposed to the grandeur of empires. Milton in *Paradise Regained* converts Virgil's georgic mode "into a channel for religious meditation" (175). Engaged in personal meditation on the Gospel, the brief epic's narrator is a plain man, not the bard of *Paradise Lost*. The style of *Paradise Regained* resembles that of *Paradise Lost*, yet it is muted. The hero learns what it means to be called the Son of God. Milton avoids naming him Christ because he is writing not about the unique being, but about "a composite generalized being" (181). *Paradise Regained* contains a battle of styles, with the Son's temperance revealed in a middle style that defeats Satan's self-indulgent, elaborate one.

828 NOHRNBERG, JAMES. "*Paradise Regained* by One Greater Man: Milton's Wisdom Epic as a 'Fable of Identity.'" In *Centre and*

Paradise Regained

Labyrinth: Essays in Honour of Northrop Frye. Edited by Eleanor Cook, Chaviva Hosek, Jay Macpherson, Patricia Parker, and Julian Patrick. Toronto, Buffalo, N.Y., and London: University of Toronto Press, 1983, pp. 83-114.

Each of Milton's dramatically structured poems from *Nativity Ode* to *Paradise Regained* and *Samson Agonistes* presents the poet and protagonist with a crisis that is developed and resolved. In *Paradise Regained*, the poet's and Christ's egos receive a calling and ascend from darkness to the promised land of identity. Milton's brief epic is based on an archetypal fable of identity for Christ, who is tried by the future. The temptations represent the ego's regressions from or presumptions on that future. Satan's and Christ's personalities have much in common with that of Oedipus, whose life cycle also parallels theirs in the rebellion against the father and the redeeming of a wasteland. By such events as the exaltation in heaven, Nativity, and acknowledgment at the baptism, Christ is differentiated from the Father. Like the poet, the Son is perfected by an acceptance of life on the terms offered by the Father.

829 PATTERSON, ANNABEL M. "*Paradise Regained*: A Last Chance at True Romance." *Milton Studies* 17 (1983):187-208.

Between *Il Penseroso* (?1631) and *Apology for Smectymnuus* (1642), Milton's attitude toward romance changes, for the genre in the 1630s becomes associated with King Charles and his wife. Milton thus deemphasizes it in his political plans to reconstitute the crusading ideal in the English Revolution. In *Eikonoklastes* (1649 and 1650), he indicts most European romance. *Paradise Lost* shows only one type of romance, the pastoral kind, as capable of authenticity. *Paradise Regained* appears to be constructed on an antiromantic foundation, which dismisses romance's wandering narrative structure and use of fictions. But Satan presses for a narrative structure after Book 1, while the Son learns to read Christian narrative whose rules are not yet revealed. The allusion to Tasso's "Hippogrif" (4.542) indicates that in *Paradise Regained* Milton's attitude to the marvelous is neither antiromantic nor romantic.

830 POPE, ELIZABETH MARIE. "*Paradise Regained*": The Tradition and the Poem. Baltimore, Md.: Johns Hopkins Press, 1947, 151 pp.

Although Milton follows the Gospel of Matthew in narrating *Paradise Regained*, he introduces two new episodes, the banquet and

Paradise Regained

storm scenes. Unlike most medieval and Renaissance writers, Milton makes an unusual shift and follows the Gospel of Luke's sequence of temptations. The Christ of *Paradise Regained* is treated primarily in his human nature of an exalted, perfect man, a portrayal that does not make the poem an Arian document. Milton follows one traditional view by making Satan undertake the temptation to determine Christ's identity as the only Son of God. *Paradise Regained* presents a triple equation, which reveals parallels among Adam's, Christ's, and the world's temptations. In the banquet scene, Satan tempts Christ to commit a sin of sensuality and to admit or claim his divinity. The offer of kingdoms is an appeal to worldly power; the tower scene is a temptation to vainglorious presumption, which corresponds to Adam's wish to be as God. Milton thus alters the usual sequence and presents Christ facing the flesh, world, and devil.

831   RAJAN, BALACHANDRA.   "'To which is Added *Samson Agonistes--*.'" In *The Prison and the Pinnacle*. Papers To Commemorate the Tercentenary of *Paradise Regained* and *Samson Agonistes*. Edited by Balachandra Rajan. Toronto and Buffalo, N.Y.: University of Toronto Press, 1973, pp. 82-110.
    When Adam and Eve repent in the final books of *Paradise Lost*, the existential perspective reveals the free and full exercise of responsibility as they move from despair to God, while the cosmic perspective shows that Adam does not understand or initiate grace. Milton balances "an ethic of self-reliance" and "a theology of dependence" (89). If the events of *Paradise Regained* and *Samson Agonistes* are connected by typology, Milton never reminds us of this relationship. *Paradise Regained* and *Samson Agonistes* portray perfection and fallibility, respectively; in the brief epic, Christ possesses the pattern and sees as from a hill, but in Milton's play the protagonist gropes for the pattern on a dark subjected plain. Milton juxtaposes two poems containing multiple temptations and two examples of temptation resisted. The two works contain parallels and contrasts in phrasing, action, and theme.

832   REVARD, STELLA P. "Milton and Classical Rome: The Political Context of *Paradise Regained*." In *Rome in the Renaissance: The City and the Myth*. Edited by P. A. Ramsey. Medieval and Renaissance

Texts and Studies, vol. 18. Binghamton, N.Y.: Medieval and Renaissance Texts and Studies, 1982, pp. 409-19.

Like other "classical" republicans of the 1640s and 1650s, Milton admires the ancient Roman republic and sees it as the exemplar of the free Commonwealth that the Puritans attempt to construct in England. Milton endorses the Roman senate, concept of liberty, and ideas about executing tyrants. He appears to reverse his views in *Paradise Regained* when Christ rejects earthly glory and offers a critique of what leads to that glory. Rome, according to Christ, fails to reach its political destiny of nurturing the pattern of a commonwealth that it establishes for the world. Perhaps Rome's failure and reversion to tyrants are lessons for Milton, his fellow revolutionaries, and all Englishmen. With republican principles, Christ in *Paradise Regained* dismisses Rome's history, which resembles that of Milton's England. The people may lose liberty by surrendering to tyrants. In *Paradise Regained*, Milton does not reverse his earlier political views but extends them.

833   RICKS, CHRISTOPHER. "Milton: Part III. *Paradise Regained* and *Samson Agonistes*." In *English Poetry and Prose, 1540-1674*. Edited by Christopher Ricks. Vol. 2, *Sphere History of Literature in the English Language*. London: Sphere Books, 1970, pp. 299-316. Revised in *English Poetry and Prose, 1540-1674*, ed. Christopher Ricks, vol. 2, *The New History of Literature* (New York: Peter Bedrick Books, 1987), pp. 293-309.

Because its moral purpose is too direct, *Paradise Regained* is less vivid and morally effective than *Paradise Lost*. Rather than creating beliefs, it transmits them. If parts of the brief epic are written in a plain style, much--including some of Christ's speeches--is overemphatic and repetitious. In *Paradise Regained*, a diminished Satan offers Christ temptations that are easy to refuse. Dr. Johnson recognizes that *Samson Agonistes*'s episodes affect Samson's psychological state, but he does not believe that justifies them, for the work requires other structural principles. By discussing Milton's play in terms of such antitheses as spiritual versus physical and plot versus character, we acknowledge its limitations, for it depends on antitheses that great tragedies reveal to be simplifications.

Paradise Regained

834 SACKTON, ALEXANDER H. "Architectonic Structure in *Paradise Regained*." *University of Texas Studies in English* 33 (1954):33-45.

Based on parallelism and balance, the structure of *Paradise Regained* carefully presents multiple perspectives of the opening baptism scene, shifts from earth to mid-air to heaven and finally to earth, and contrasts the main speeches in each setting. The first temptation (which uses persuasion) and the last (using force) are respectively an introduction and an epilogue, while the second temptation fills the poem with increasingly complex appeals to Christ as a human being. Milton creates strong parallels and contrasts between the first and second temptations; the third is connected to the baptism scene.

835 SAMUEL, IRENE. "The Regaining of Paradise." In *The Prison and the Pinnacle*. Papers To Commemorate the Tercentenary of *Paradise Regained* and *Samson Agonistes*. Edited by Balachandra Rajan. Toronto and Buffalo, N.Y.: University of Toronto Press, 1973, pp. 111-34.

Paradise Regained asks not about one's identity but about how one is to live. When Christ says, "Tempt not the Lord thy God" in Book 4, he means that he will not call on God to help with a miracle, which is the common Renaissance understanding of the passage in Luke and Matthew. An example for all people, Christ in *Paradise Regained* receives no revelation, experiences no anagnorisis, but remains wisely ignorant about his identity. His exemplary responses provide a complete pattern for the reader to regain Eden. Satan is defeated precisely because Christ stands not on his social nature but on his bond with all humanity. *Paradise Regained*'s main interest, which some call "just talk," prepares us for action: "saying is itself a doing" (131).

836 SCHULTZ, HOWARD. "Christ and Antichrist in *Paradise Regained*." *PMLA* 67 (1952):790-808.

Rather than showing signs of a late developing pietism or asceticism, *Paradise Regained* defines the kingdom of Christ, the true and invisible church. Milton sees the Antichrist as corruption in any community, including contemporary Christendom; his goal is to reform the church. The brief epic is an antiprelatical work.

837 SHAWCROSS, JOHN T. "The Genres of *Paradise Regain'd* and *Samson Agonistes*: The Wisdom of Their Joint Publication." *Milton Studies* 17 (1983):225-48.

    Paradise Regained is a brief epic because its whole subject, the combat of hero and antagonist, is the climax of the more usual epic; not diffuse, though it does mix genres, this poem lessens the complexities of action, character, time, and setting. While not typical of any drama, *Samson Agonistes* is "a distillation . . . of the prototypical Greek drama" (234). In terms of genre, *Samson Agonistes*'s form and characteristics make it a drama; its execution and structure make it a poem. It is thus a kind of poem, a dramatic poem. The comic mode of *Paradise Regained* implies "futural significance, . . . life and continuance" (239), while *Samson Agonistes*'s tragic mode reveals the waste in achieving the fairer paradise. Samson shows us Christ's potential fate had he succumbed to temptation; Christ shows us what Samson's role as great deliverer should have been. Forming a whole for man, the two works are complementary.

838 STEIN, ARNOLD. *Heroic Knowledge: An Interpretation of "Paradise Regained" and "Samson Agonistes."* Minneapolis: University of Minnesota Press, 1957, 251 pp. Parts reprinted in *Twentieth Century Interpretations of "Samson Agonistes*," ed. Galbraith M. Crump (Englewood Cliffs, N.J.: Prentice-Hall, 1968), pp. 63-73, 104-6; part reprinted in *On Milton's Poetry*, ed. Arnold Stein (Greenwich, Conn.: Fawcett Publications, 1970), pp. 247-56.

    When he writes *Paradise Regained*, Milton chooses (and increases) certain handicaps: a heroism based on superior wisdom; the negative action of a hero who must reject temptations that do not tempt him; and a dramatic stage that is the hero's mind. In response to these difficulties, Milton shifts the weight of the poem to Satan, who becomes tempter and tempted. Temperance, the virtue of self-mastery, is important in this Platonic poem. *Samson Agonistes* begins with the major theme of the promise ruined, evolves with Samson's responses to that theme, and then abandons it in favor of an independent expression of the dependent response. Seeing the tragic experience, Manoa offers a purified human reaction; the Chorus, filled with awe and pity, finds the message of a medieval tragedy. Samson's moral growth reaches its high point just when his psychological retreat is lowest. After a descent into the self, the source of being, Samson emerges into the realm of practical action.

Paradise Regained

839   SUNDELL, ROGER H. "The Narrator as Interpreter in *Paradise Regained*." *Milton Studies* 2 (1970):83-101.

In *Paradise Regained*'s prologue, the narrator establishes his relationship to the reader by pointing to the poem's themes, the Son's transition from the human to the divine side of his dual nature, the authority of the singer who wrote *Paradise Lost* and who claims the Holy Spirit as his only inspiration, and the brief epic's unique and superior subject. Later, the narrator introduces all of the major characters and provides the reader with the fallen human perspective through which to view the poem's divine events. In the temptation scenes, Christ assumes the narrator's interpretive role; besides outlining the theological framework of *Paradise Regained*, God also interprets the Son's nature and mission. As the interpreter during the temptation scenes, Christ reorients Satan's material concerns so the reader may see the spiritual import of the Son's mission for all mankind. *Paradise Regained*'s various kinds of internal commentaries guide the reader toward appropriate responses.

840   SWAIM, KATHLEEN M. "Hercules, Antaeus, and Prometheus: A Study of the Climactic Epic Similes in *Paradise Regained*." *Studies in English Literature, 1500-1900* 18 (1978):137-53.

At the climax of *Paradise Regained*, Satan is compared to Antaeus and the Sphinx, Christ to Hercules and Oedipus. Satan is a riddler in *Paradise Regained*, and Christ solves the riddle. Grasping the allusion to the Sphinx's riddle for Oedipus, the reader knows that "man" is the answer and recognizes its relevance to the issue of Christ's identity. More explicit, the linking of Hercules and Antaeus with Christ and Satan emphasizes wrestling (though it is internalized in *Paradise Regained*) and the superiority of Christ's victory compared to that of Hercules. The reader must also recall two main episodes in Hercules's life, his choice and his death and resurrection. In the Renaissance, Hercules is seen as the temperate moral man. That he kills Antaeus while going to free Prometheus reveals a parallel with Christ's role for humanity.

841   WILLIAMSON, GEORGE. "Plot in *Paradise Regained*." In *Milton and Others*. London: Faber and Faber, 1965, pp. 66-84.

Paradise Regained is Milton's epic of obedience; *Paradise Lost*, his epic of love. In *Paradise Lost*, Christ in his divine aspect defeats

Satan, so in *Paradise Regained* we witness Satan's trial of man. Christ prepares the way from law to love. Satan's temptation of Christ is, in terms of plot, a developing exploration of human nature; Christ's resistance is, in terms of the poem's ethical meaning, a lesson for human nature.

842 WOLFE, DON M. "The Role of Milton's Christ." *Sewanee Review* 51 (1943):467-75.

Seeking a heaven on earth to replace the one Adam and Eve lost, Milton believes that the instrument to reach this goal is Christ in one of his three aspects: the temperate and self-disciplined Christ, the judge and punisher, or the mild and patient Christ. But each aspect leads to a different means and a separate philosophy of reform. In *Paradise Regained*, Christ initially appears temperate, then becomes the judge of Satan, and at various points shows his character to be patient and persuasive, though this last portrait never dominates.

843 WOODHOUSE, A. S. P. "Theme and Pattern in *Paradise Regained*." *University of Toronto Quarterly* 25 (1956):167-82. Revised in *The Heavenly Muse: A Preface to Milton*, ed. Hugh MacCallum, University of Toronto Department of English Studies and Texts, no. 21 (Toronto and Buffalo, N.Y.: University of Toronto Press, 1972), pp. 320-44.

Paradise Regained focuses on the episode that closely parallels and contrasts the crisis of *Paradise Lost*. Both poems deal with Christian heroism, as an active virtue in *Paradise Lost* and as the Son's period of waiting or Passion in *Paradise Regained*. By following Luke's account of the temptation, Milton can portray the theme of Christ's nature and office by presenting the temptations in a sequence with a clear climax. The important structural divisions in *Paradise Regained* occur not between books but between the falling of night and the dawning of a new day. Because of Christ's obedience and trust, his experience in the poem leads him to a deeper awareness of his nature and God's plan. Christ moves from the Jewish view of his role as Messiah to a Christian (actually Miltonic) view. The Son rejects secular knowledge, a thing indifferent, because it here serves evil and is far inferior to divine revelation. In the temptation on the temple, Christ gives his greatest display of obedience and trust.

Paradise Regained

844 ZWICKY, LAURIE. "Kairos in *Paradise Regained*: The Divine Plan." *ELH* 31 (1964):271-77.

According to the divine plan, everything will occur at its proper moment or *kairos*. *Paradise Lost* promises that, in the fullness of time, Christ will redeem mankind, a promise on which *Paradise Regained* is based. In the brief epic, Milton contrasts Christ's awareness of time with Satan's kind of time. Satan attempts to make Christ act before his time, thus ruining God's plan. Cyclicism, the Greek view of history, is the demonic approach, while the Judeo-Christian view is linear. When Christ enters and begins to save mankind at the end of *Paradise Regained*, the *kairos* has come.

For the variorum, see entry 35; for analogues, see entry 330; for *Paradise Regained*'s relation to *Paradise Lost*, see entries 232, 524, 555, 803, 815-16, 843, 871, 890, 899; for *Paradise Regained*'s relation to *Samson Agonistes*, see entries 232, 803, 831, 837, 890, 899, 901, 923-24. See also entries 3, 9, 23, 43-44, 46-47, 49, 53, 58, 60, 63, 65, 67-69, 71-72, 87, 91, 95, 105, 107, 111, 115, 117, 123, 125, 128-30, 133-35, 138, 140-41, 144, 146-47, 150-51, 153-54, 156-57, 159-60, 162-64, 166, 168-69, 173, 176, 179-81, 183, 187, 190, 192-93, 198, 201-9, 211, 213-14, 216, 218, 224-25, 230-33, 235-36, 242-43, 245-46, 250-51, 253, 278, 333, 366, 455, 470-72, 484, 486, 493, 498-99, 519, 534, 540, 542, 547-48, 556, 559, 561, 563, 565, 578, 581, 585-88, 599, 606, 617, 626, 637, 646, 668, 682, 686, 726, 752, 759, 777, 789, 853, 855, 865, 901, 906, 908, 918, 923, 990, 1001.

SAMSON AGONISTES:

845 ARTHOS, JOHN. "Milton and the Passions: A Study of *Samson Agonistes*." *Modern Philology* 69 (1972):209-21.

Characters urge Samson to do what God elected him to do, yet in *Samson Agonistes* they produce contrary effects. His changes appear natural, his final deeds miraculous. When his passions are ordered, he may go to the temple, but this ordering takes on the new sense of the renewal of his role as God's servant. The warrior moves out of retirement and prepares to become a martyr. As Samson calms his passions and becomes part of the divine order of things, we see the play's primary movement as representing the alteration from one state of feeling to another. *Samson Agonistes*'s conflict occurs when divine grace and nature's restorative powers meet Samson's inertia. *Dispositio*, the logical arrangement of persuasive material, operates in the play's structure, which can be divided into an exordium, exposition and refutation, and peroration.

846 ASALS, HEATHER. "In Defense of Dalila: *Samson Agonistes* and the Reformation Theology of the Word." *JEGP: Journal of English and Germanic Philology* 74 (1975):183-94.

Dalila is both the cause of Samson's fall and the agent of his regeneration, two events that are similar because the Word has an important function in both: by uttering his secret, Samson sins; the "honied words" of Dalila associate her with the Word and Gospel. When she comes to Samson for forgiveness, she becomes an example of an act of faith. She elicits a new man from the old one; Samson will adumbrate the folly of Christ. As an opponent of faith, Harapha gives Samson a good opportunity to show what he has learned. Manoa entertains hope without evidence from the Word. Samson's salvation starts with his fall.

847 ASALS, HEATHER. "Rhetoric Agonistic in *Samson Agonistes*." *Milton Quarterly* 11 (1977):1-4.

When Samson's three tempters come to him, they act as three different kinds of orators in terms of debate rhetoric: epideictic (Manoa), deliberative (Dalila), and forensic (Harapha). Each character uses the subject matter, temporal direction, and rhetorical devices appropriate to his or her mode. The Chorus mimics each tempter. *Samson Agonistes*'s substance is the agony of debate.

848 BARUCH, FRANKLIN R. "Time, Body, and Spirit at the Close of *Samson Agonistes*." *ELH* 36 (1969):319-39.

In *Samson Agonistes*'s *kommos* (lines 1660-1758), Milton shows Samson's growth in spiritual insight and power, and the limited effect it has on the Chorus and Manoa. The burden of trial is passed on to others, including the Chorus, who do not yet recognize their need for the illumination that comes only through direct spiritual activity. Milton indicates that, while it is good to admire an example such as Samson, one must merely admire because vicarious regeneration is a foolish idea. Seeing act as act, Manoa at the end cannot penetrate outward

Samson Agonistes

form to find inner truth. Samson's strength and physical deed are signs of his internal state, yet the Chorus and Manoa never understand this.

849   BAUM, PAULL FRANKLIN. "*Samson Agonistes* Again." *PMLA* 36 (1921):354-71.
      Of all the elements that Aristotle requires in a tragedy, *Samson Agonistes* does not need song or spectacle because it is a closet drama; it succeeds with thought and character (particularly in the portraits of Samson and Dalila); and, despite Johnson's critical remarks, it has a "simple" plot with no true recognition or distinct reversal. Uniting the play are the dual motifs of the effects of previous incidents on Samson and the gradual approach of a catastrophe. The plot, which operates on a spiritual level, satisfies Aristotle's criteria of unity, relevance, and necessity or causal arrangement of incident. But if the plot lacks conflict and is too linear, even sluggish, the theme is *Samson Agonistes*'s greatest weakness, for Samson, rather than falling from prosperity to adversity through an unconscious error, exhibits a moral weakness. His failure is not quite tragic.

850   BENNETT, JOAN S. "Liberty under the Law: The Chorus and the Meaning of *Samson Agonistes*." *Milton Studies* 12 (1978):141-63.
      Our understanding of *Samson Agonistes* is shaped by the tension created by the contrast between Samson's and the Chorus's religious experiences. Representing the whole Hebrew people, the Chorus is bound by the Mosaic Law, like many of Milton's Christian contemporaries, while Samson acts as a model for the regenerate. Liberty is possible even before Christ, though the chosen people live in a divinely imposed bondage, if the individual uses reason to comprehend the Law in the spirit of love in which it is given. The Law can accomplish only two things: the discovery of sin, which is all the Chorus does, and the transcendence of its own limitations through grace. Samson does both, moving away from a state of bondage that he shares with the Chorus and into sonship and liberty. Meeting Manoa, Samson confesses his guilt because he gains insights that the Chorus cannot grasp. The meeting with Dalila teaches him about the universality of God's justice.

851   BENNETT, JOAN S. "'A Person Rais'd': Public and Private Cause in *Samson Agonistes*." *Studies in English Literature, 1500-1900* 18 (1978):155-68.

Dalila's and Harapha's political stands are parodies of Samson's commitment to the public good. Once we recognize that a good act in the public interest means training citizens to lead free lives based on virtue and wisdom, we see that relativism does not apply in *Samson Agonistes*: Samson's use of his marriages to battle the Philistines is not equivalent to Dalila's use of her marriage to ruin Samson. Betraying himself to Dalila, Samson can no longer uphold the public good. To undo that act is to serve the public good, while Dalila serves a tyranny. Harapha believes those with superior means should rule; Samson argues that a wise and virtuous God sees power only as a means. Milton uses many of the same arguments to support Parliament and to attack King Charles.

852   BOWERS, FREDSON. "*Samson Agonistes*: Justice and Reconciliation." In *The Dress of Words: Essays on Restoration and Eighteenth Century Literature in Honor of Richmond P. Bond*. Edited by Robert B. White, Jr. University of Kansas Publications, Library Series, 42. Lawrence: University of Kansas Libraries, 1978, pp. 1-23.

The pattern of Samson's life--sin, punishment, and reconciliation with God--includes an apparently harsh estrangement from the Father that is difficult to grasp since he is a loving God. *Samson Agonistes* shows that no agent chosen by God can thwart his divine purpose, though Samson must learn how his role changes after disobedience. Redemptive justice works by punishment that leads, through mercy, to an understanding of God's will. When Samson rejects the views of Manoa, Dalila, and Harapha, he performs the correct action but has no conscious understanding of it. Samson goes through the stages of repentance by showing patience and acceptance of guilt when he talks to the Chorus; sorrow and penance with Manoa; and forgiveness but a refusal to sin again with Dalila. Facing Harapha, Samson now knows that his punishment is corrective not retributive, so he brings his purpose into harmony with God's and turns from a private to a public role.

853   BOWRA, C. M. "*Samson Agonistes*." In *Inspiration and Poetry*. London: Macmillan; New York: St. Martin's Press, 1955, pp. 112-29.

Poetry

Samson Agonistes

In *Paradise Regained*, Christ is not moved by Satan's temptation of literature (particularly Attic tragedy) and philosophy because readers must be equal or superior to their reading materials, an attitude that parallels Milton's after the revolution fails. Milton thus denies the literature that he loves. But with *Paradise Regained* appears *Samson Agonistes*, written in the manner of Attic tragedy, which signals Milton's recovery of confidence after defeat, his renewed belief in action over passivity. *Samson Agonistes* is indebted to Sophocles's *Oedipus at Colonus*, though the plays differ about the question of personal responsibility, with Samson's faults (pride and concupiscence) causing his fall and the gods causing Oedipus's fall. Unlike Sophocles, Milton begins his drama after his hero has finished committing errors and has almost paid for them; this allows the play to focus on the exaltation of a humbled man while omitting the humbling of a proud man.

854 CHAMBERS, A. B. "Wisdom and Fortitude in *Samson Agonistes*." *PMLA* 78 (1963):315-20.

When Samson develops from a muscle-bound figure in the Bible to a tragic figure in *Samson Agonistes*, Milton relies on the tradition of *sapientia et fortitudo* to shape his protagonist's personality. Fortitude, as discussed by Plato, Aristotle, and Aquinas, comes to mean not brute strength but "heroic magnitude of mind." Milton believes that this marks the true heroism, so he stresses the quality of Samson's mind. At the end of the play, Samson achieves the heroism of wisdom and fortitude.

855 CIRILLO, ALBERT R. "Time, Light, and the Phoenix: The Design of *Samson Agonistes*." In *Calm of Mind: Tercentenary Essays on "Paradise Regained" and "Samson Agonistes" in Honor of John S. Diekhoff.* Edited by Joseph Anthony Wittreich, Jr. Cleveland, Ohio, and London: Press of Case Western Reserve University, 1971, pp. 209-33.

Milton's vision presents time and place as all time and placelessness, indicating that *Samson Agonistes*'s drama occurs in the human soul and moves toward possessing God in a human moment through Samson's struggle and internal motions. That *Samson Agonistes* and *Paradise Regained* are published together is remarkable because the brief epic deals with moral struggle as defined for the

362

Christian dispensation, while the closet drama deals with it "in a context that precedes yet prefigures that dispensation" (213). *Samson Agonistes* portrays man's triumph over despair by recognizing God's plan. Occurring between daybreak and noon on the day of the feast of Dagon, the temporal span of *Samson Agonistes* is a compression of a moral lifetime placed in the context of ritualistic enactment that moves from darkness to light, from time and despair to eternity and grace, and from death to life. The phoenix simile summarizes the poem's entire movement.

856   COX, LEE SHERIDAN. "Natural Science and Figurative Design in *Samson Agonistes*." *ELH* 35 (1968):51-74.

In *Samson Agonistes*, Milton uses imagery of the four elements to define Samson's change from one quality to another. Each element in *Samson Agonistes* has a twofold nature, reflecting an ambivalence and conflict between good and evil, but different elements may appear identical, and they are all interrelated. Storm imagery shows the alternatives, ambivalence, and paradox in elemental imagery. Using images of plants, ships, and winged creatures, Milton examines the relation between the microcosm and geocosm. Sense imagery teaches us that the proper use of the senses is connected to freedom and life; the improper use leads to imprisonment.

857   DAMICO, HELEN. "Duality in Dramatic Vision: A Structural Analysis of *Samson Agonistes*." *Milton Studies* 12 (1978):91-116.

Located at the center of *Samson Agonistes*, the meeting between Dalila and Samson marks a shift in the play's imagery, tone, style, and narrative elements. The play follows a bipartite structure, for it is patterned on antitheses and fuses comic and tragic forms. Old Comedy's agon--the encounter of agonist and antagonist, who remain irreconcilable--is duplicated when Samson and Dalila engage in a dialectical argument. These characters are antithetical in every way, though Dalila also functions as Samson's other self: merged on a symbolic level, they become a single antagonist of God. Unlike its counterpart in Old Comedy, Milton's agon scene shows no one as victor. But in Attic comedy, the antagonist's double (in *Samson Agonistes*, Harapha and the Public Officer) emerges victorious, for the agon falls again (Samson displays hubris). Samson's "rousing motions" are impulsive, sensuous, and internal rather than divine in origin. A

Samson Agonistes

disobedient sinner in the end, Samson does not fulfill his divine mission.

858   DI SALVO, JACKIE. "'The Lord's Battells': *Samson Agonistes* and the Puritan Revolution." *Milton Studies* 4 (1972):39-62.
       We may read *Samson Agonistes* in light of Milton's allusions to Samson in *Areopagitica* and *First Defence*, where he appears as a revolutionary, national champion opposing an unjust order. Samson, a culture hero of the Puritan revolution, acts in a play expressing the main interior drama of the Puritans who had to form a new church, society, and ethos of activism. As a saint with a military vocation, Samson conducts a holy war that resembles both the Puritan effort and *Paradise Lost*'s war in heaven, both spiritually motivated as Harapha's acts are not. Cromwell, like Samson, knows the value of waiting in an active posture until God reveals his plans.

859   ELLIS-FERMOR, UNA. "*Samson Agonistes* and Religious Drama." In *The Frontiers of Drama*. London: Methuen, 1945, pp. 17-33. Reprinted with an introduction by Allardyce Nicoll and a bibliography by Harold Brooks (London: Methuen, 1964).
       We expect a tragedy to balance pain or terror with illumination or triumph. But in *Samson Agonistes*, the latter gradually subdues the former. Milton's play is a religious drama that cannot be tragic. Like much modern psychological drama, *Samson Agonistes* presents the action that occurs in the theatre of the soul. Samson begins in a state of almost complete despair and inertia, as the slow opening rhythms indicate, but the appearance of the Chorus helps lessen his doubts and mental divisions. Manoa's lament pushes Samson to defend heaven's decrees and take responsibility for his own actions. Dalila brings out his self-determination and wrath, while the encounter with Harapha takes the play from its focus on internal event to a display of external event. When Harapha leaves, Samson is rehabilitated. *Samson Agonistes* concludes in the mood of beatitude. Throughout the play, Samson's internal state is mirrored in poetic rhythms.
       Appendix: "A Note on the Dramatic Function of the Prosody of *Samson Agonistes*."

860 FELL, KENNETH. "From Myth to Martyrdom: Towards a View of Milton's *Samson Agonistes*." *English Studies* 34 (1953):145-55.

Starting as a remote, unpromising legend, the Samson story is ennobled as it evolves. The legend must be discarded in order to fulfill the story. In the Book of Judges, Samson and his story are closely associated with sun imagery. Later interpretations, emphasizing Samson as one of the elect, deal with his relation to Christ. Milton departs from tradition by showing the purification of Samson so he can act as God's instrument.

861 FINNEY, GRETCHEN LUDKE. "Chorus in *Samson Agonistes*." *PMLA* 58 (1943):649-64. Reprinted in *Musical Backgrounds for English Literature: 1580-1650* (New Brunswick, N.J.: Rutgers University Press, 1962), pp. 220-37; reprinted (Westport, Conn.: Greenwood Press, 1976).

The Preface to *Samson Agonistes* indicates that a contemporary form of Italian drama imitates the Greek drama's use of a chorus. Most contemporary dramatists in England and France omit the chorus, but--while this also tends to be true of Italian drama to be spoken or read--the Italian *melodramma* uses a chorus until at least the mid-seventeenth century. In sixteenth- and seventeenth-century Florence, dramatists believe that all Greek drama is sung, but the current contrapuntal style obscures the words, so recitative is developed, with the chorus chanting in unison. *Samson Agonistes*'s unusual character comes from Milton's use of a chorus even though he never intends to include music. When the use of a chorus starts to decline in the Italian musical drama, the oratorio, which is very popular when Milton visits Rome, continues to use it. See entries 15, 22, 142, 290, 321, 337, 370, 430.

862 FISH, STANLEY. "Question and Answer in *Samson Agonistes*." *Critical Quarterly* 11 (1969):237-64. Reprinted in *Milton: "Comus" and "Samson Agonistes," a Casebook*, ed. Julian Lovelock (London and Basingstoke: Macmillan, 1975), pp. 209-45.

Samson's spiritual regeneration is not necessarily linked to pulling down the temple. The experience of *Samson Agonistes* is the experience of the mystery at the heart of Samson's action, whether this is his first marriage, his betrayal of himself to Dalila, or his arbitrary decision to go to the temple. In *Samson Agonistes*, where the

Samson Agonistes

connection between cause and effect is always ambiguous, discursive reasoning cannot open up the phenomena of experience, so one is left wondering what one should do. Manoa says one will be mocked no matter what one does because events confound expectations; the Chorus philosophizes, articulating our confusion and concerns. The play does not contain a middle describing a process of despair and regeneration. Using the only standard for evaluating action, Samson finally interprets his action as a reading of God's will. If he, and we, were God, we would understand more.

863   FLOWER, ANNETTE C. "The Critical Context of the Preface to *Samson Agonistes*." *Studies in English Literature, 1500-1900* 10 (1970):409-23.
       Milton's justification of tragedy parallels Sidney's treatment of the genre. Closely connected to the moral purpose of a play, catharsis in Milton's view is the tempering of all passions--those that exist in overabundance as well as those that are deficient--to a mean. Milton does not wish to teach an attitude but to change the reader's emotional constitution. While Dryden and Howard debate the use of mixed genres and rhyme, the Preface to *Samson Agonistes* agrees with Howard. Milton's Preface discusses all of the key issues of neoclassical dramatic theory.

864   FOGLE, FRENCH. "The Action of *Samson Agonistes*." In *Essays in American and English Literature Presented to Bruce Robert McElderry, Jr.* Edited by Max F. Schulz with William D. Templeman and Charles R. Metzger. Athens: Ohio University Press, 1967, pp. 177-96.
       Although Samson does indeed change, moving from private despair to public victory, the text of *Samson Agonistes* does not support the critics who see his regeneration as a steady psychological process. Milton defines regeneration in *Christian Doctrine* as being applicable to pre-Christians and as the operation of the Word and Spirit to destroy the old man and regenerate the new one by bringing his understanding, will, and works into harmony with those of God. Milton's three major poems discuss the will in its various states, functions, and relationships-- free and enslaved, passive and active, and obedient and rebellious. Even in his opening state of despair and spiritual death, Samson retains some remnants of the divine will and its liberty. He is not unaware that God

366

once ordained that he do heroic deeds, but his will and mind are incapable of action. When the Chorus suggests Samson's choices, he has the occasion to exercise his will. Samson's mind is enlightened and it responds with rousing motions that urge actions. His and God's wills are united.

865   FRYE, NORTHROP. "Agon and Logos: Revolution and Revelation." In *The Prison and the Pinnacle*. Papers To Commemorate the Tercentenary of *Paradise Regained* and *Samson Agonistes*. Edited by Balachandra Rajan. Toronto and Buffalo, N.Y.: University of Toronto Press, 1973, pp. 135-63.

In *Samson Agonistes*, as in *Paradise Lost*, an act is the accomplishing of God's will, and tragedy occurs when human reason recognizes God's will in the form of law or justice. Samson is initially tormented by nemesis when his folly leads to disaster. Moving away from nemesis-tragedy, *Samson Agonistes* presents the higher kind of tragedy, which is part of the analogy of the Law. Once Samson is freed from the machinery of nemesis, it is transferred to the Philistines, whose pagan worship focuses on a static visual symbol or idol. Christian revelation, by contrast, arrives through the Word and initiates action. Because of its emphasis on Samson's internalized action, *Samson Agonistes* is "a kind of visual anti-play" (150). Unlike Samson, the Chorus sees the play as a melodrama featuring a hero (Jehovah) and a villain (Dagon). *Paradise Regained* and *Samson Agonistes*, like Christianity, are revolutionary.

866   FURMAN, WENDY. "*Samson Agonistes* as Christian Tragedy: A Corrective View." *Philological Quarterly* 60 (1981):169-81.

In neither the Old nor the New Testament are Samson's deeds criticized; rather, he struggles for God's glory and sets aside his sin by faith. Even if God in the Bible and in Milton's works prefers peace over war, in the mire of fallen human history vengeance may be the only kind of justice. Milton takes liberties with the Book of Judges in order to make Samson more palatable, but he never distorts the biblical narrative's tone or movement of providence. Milton in *Samson Agonistes* does not adhere closely to Aristotle's theory of tragedy and Greek precedents. The play is a Christian tragedy in which the hero gains some partial awareness; it is not a grim Greek tragedy.

Samson Agonistes

867 GILMAN, ERNEST B. "Milton's Contest "Twixt God and Dagon.""
In *Iconoclasm and Poetry in the English Reformation: Down Went
Dagon*. Chicago, Ill., and London: University of Chicago Press, 1986,
pp. 149-77. 2 illustrations.

A complex agonistic relationship exists between the visual and
the verbal Milton. Like the true warfaring Christian, he confronts the
temptations of his own pictorial forms with his obligation to write as a
militantly reforming Christian. The prose, such as *Eikonoklastes*, is
antagonistic less toward idolatry than toward an inner contamination
that leads to lust for the visible. Michael's "new Speech" in Book 12 of
Paradise Lost contains a new knowledge that does not rely on Adam's
visual imagination. When Samson brings down the temple of idolatry,
he strikes out at the sighted world, including the Philistines, their
English counterparts, the "audience" of *Samson Agonistes*, and the very
form of tragedy insofar as it offers the satisfactions of spectacle. The
experience of witnessing the final spectacle is denied to the Philistines
and us. We must abstain in order to achieve salvation. An iconoclast,
Milton purifies the classical genre by removing its appeal to the eye.

868 GRENANDER, M. E. "*Samson*'s Middle: Aristotle and Dr.
Johnson." *University of Toronto Quarterly* 24 (1955):377-89.

Contrary to Dr. Johnson's view, if we examine *Samson
Agonistes* from the perspective of Aristotle's *Poetics*, it has a beginning,
middle, and end, and its various incidents are related by probability or
necessity. Johnson differs from Aristotle by defining the beginning,
middle, and end according to the representation of the plot instead of
the action imitated. The latter view makes an allowance for action that
occurs outside of the play. A thorough understanding of *Samson
Agonistes* must deal with four sets of relationships--between Samson
and God (the most important), Samson and the Philistines, Dagon and
the Philistines, and God and Dagon. The play begins by establishing
Samson as preeminent and admirable, an Aristotelian tragic hero.
What follow, through necessity or probability (or both), are his
marriage to Dalila, his capture and blinding by the Philistines, and the
play's opening, which appears well into the middle of the action.

869 GROSE, CHRISTOPHER. "'His Uncontrollable Intent': Discovery
as Action in *Samson Agonistes*." *Milton Studies* 7 (1975):49-76.

Milton believes that a "virtuous wisdom" joins word and action, a union that helps us connect Samson's final act and the drama we read. His opening speech almost creates the voices, if not the persons, of the other characters, who materialize and awaken griefs. Transcending the limitations of the Chorus's thoughts, Samson thinks in a dialectical manner by imagining the Philistine perspective. From this point on, Samson assumes more and more of the choric mask, articulates to himself what the Chorus cannot say, and thus leads himself to repentance. He is victorious over himself and his own nation, figured in the Chorus.

870   GUILLORY, JOHN. "Dalila's House: *Samson Agonistes* and the Sexual Division of Labor." In *Rewriting the Renaissance: The Discourses of Sexual Difference in Early Modern Europe.* Edited by Margaret W. Ferguson, Maureen Quilligan, and Nancy J. Vickers. Chicago, Ill., and London: University of Chicago Press, 1986, pp. 106-22.

With the emergence of bourgeois society in the sixteenth and seventeenth centuries, a conjunction occurs between the sexual division of labor and the subjection of women. *Samson Agonistes* represents an intervention, on behalf of divorce, into the social circumstances that determine the circumstances of that intervention. As he must, Samson rejects Dalila's offer to return to her house; the other alternative is his father's house. This choice produces a social contradiction that can be solved, as Milton sees in the 1640s, with divorce. Showing the division between public and private, Milton in *Samson Agonistes* indicates that the hero's patriotic vocation is far superior to idle confinement in a household, Samson's true antagonist. He is threatened because Dalila, while advocating a domestic resolution, acts as his double by pursuing the vocation of delivering her people. Samson's sexual crisis thus becomes his political crisis. *Samson Agonistes* is "the prototype of the bourgeois career drama" (120).

871   HANFORD, JAMES HOLLY. "*Samson Agonistes* and Milton in Old Age." In *Studies in Shakespeare, Milton and Donne.* By Members of the English Department of the University of Michigan. New York and London: Macmillan, 1925, pp. 167-89. Reprinted in *John Milton, Poet and Humanist: Essays by James Holly Hanford* (Cleveland, Ohio: Press of Western Reserve University, 1966), pp. 264-86;

Poetry

Samson Agonistes

Twentieth Century Interpretations of "Samson Agonistes," ed. Galbraith M. Crump (Englewood Cliffs, N.J.: Prentice-Hall, 1968), pp. 14-32.

Paradise Lost discusses the scheme of salvation, but the theological foundation for this plan, which involves discipline and trial in a world of evil, appears in the pattern of Christ's life in *Paradise Regained*. In *Samson Agonistes*, Milton portrays frail humanity, once sinful but now repentant, restored to strength and experiencing a trial. That Samson attains salvation before the time of Christ indicates that the Son's sacrifice is not a necessary part of Milton's scheme of salvation. The character of Samson contains a great deal of Milton's personality. Milton gives an Aristotelian diagnosis, complete with a catharsis, of Samson's state and of his own.

872 HARRIS, WILLIAM O. "Despair and 'Patience as the Truest Fortitude' in *Samson Agonistes*." *ELH* 30 (1963):107-20.

If Samson struggles with the sins of *tristitia* and despair, fortitude is the virtue traditionally opposed to them. Fortitude's highest manifestation is patience; its lesser and complementary manifestation is *magnanimitas*, the "heroic magnitude of mind." This is a traditionally Christian perspective, as shown in iconography and literature. Milton's Samson attains regeneration through patience, though the Danite Chorus does not perceive its superiority to magnanimous conduct.

873 HASKIN, DAYTON, S.J. "Divorce as a Path to Union with God in *Samson Agonistes*." *ELH* 38 (1971):358-76.

Having chosen Dalila above God, Samson can attain regeneration only by removing obstructions to his union with God and placing that union above all else. He must leave Dalila and the temporal perspective that she maintains. According to the divorce tracts' criteria for a good marriage--which include spiritual fitness, physical fitness, and love--Dalila is not a good helpmeet for Samson; she impedes his spiritual growth. He ought to divorce her, though, from God's perspective, she is part of the scheme to deliver Israel from the Philistines. Samson and Christ stand as two exceptions to Milton's idea that humans normally attain salvation through married love.

874   HAWKINS, SHERMAN H. "Samson's Catharsis." *Milton Studies* 2 (1970):211-30.

The redemptive catharsis, conveyed through dramatic scenes in Books 11 and 12 of *Paradise Lost*, acts upon the audience, Adam, while in *Samson Agonistes* it acts upon the hero. To purge Samson's sin, the catharsis functions as "the tragic or dramatic counterpart of what theology calls repentance and regeneration" (216). By translating *katharsis* as *lustratio* in *Samson Agonistes*'s epigraph, Milton includes the word's religious and medical meanings, which are complementary parts of the tragic, redemptive process. Samson's cure is to use like against like to purge passion. Representing aspects of Samson as he is or was, Manoa increases Samson's grief, Dalila asks for his pity, and Harapha and the Philistine Officer try to excite his fear. But all three passions are reduced and made moderate. Samson is cleansed by blood. Through the imagery of purgation, he is related to Adam; through the imagery of lustration, to Christ.

875   HOFFMAN, NANCY Y. "Samson's Other Father: The Character of Manoa in *Samson Agonistes*." *Milton Studies* 2 (1970):195-210.

Manoa is our human connection with a distant, mythic Samson and his story's beginning, middle, and end. The relationship between Manoa and Samson has suggestive parallels with the relationship of God and the Son and with Adam and his posterity. In the character of Manoa, Milton stresses the frailty of the human relationship, for this father is awestruck at his son's transcendence of everyday life. We see in Manoa "a searching psychological study of the demands and limitations of parental love" (198). Attempting to take Samson's sins upon himself, Manoa finds that he cannot do it, so he pities his son and finds God unjust. Father and son then exchange roles. At the end, Manoa alternates between rejoicing in Samson's union with God and mourning his loss, which leaves the father lonely. Although Samson's life is a glorious example to youth, his life and death are tragic in Manoa's eyes.

876   HUNTLEY, JOHN. "A Revaluation of the Chorus' Role in Milton's *Samson Agonistes*." *Modern Philology* 64 (1966):132-45.

Samson Agonistes's Chorus begins in a state of spiritual darkness like Samson's, but then moves from a position of vanity that expresses platitudes to a state of knowledge ready for action. After

Samson Agonistes

their decline and his rise in spiritual terms, the Chorus's progress parallels Samson's movement toward regeneration. Both the Chorus and Samson display a discrepancy between noble words (such as admitting responsibility for errors) and far less noble deeds (acting as victims who avoid the guilt associated with errors). Though they do not recognize the contradiction within themselves, the Chorus urges Samson to face this discrepancy and begin to change. Ironically, their intention is to perpetuate his bondage, but the outcome is to initiate his movement toward freedom. After the Dalila episode, Samson begins to be released from bondage and blindness; after the Harapha episode, the Chorus's worldly attitudes start to weaken. Finally, the Chorus learns to do God's will and to see themselves in terms of Samson's experience.

877   JEBB, Sir R. C. "*Samson Agonistes* and the Hellenic Drama." *Proceedings of the British Academy* 3 (1907-8):341-48. Reprinted in *Milton: "Comus" and "Samson Agonistes," a Casebook*, ed. Julian Lovelock (London and Basingstoke: Macmillan, 1975), pp. 175-84.
       The language and structure of *Samson Agonistes* are classical, even if Milton makes the Chorus's measures arbitrary rather than dividing them into strophe, antistrophe, and epode. Though the play's action is "a still action" (342), the drama makes a clear progress between start and finish. Milton's mind is Hebraic, given to action and direct intensity and controlled by a strict conscience and earnest faith; he sees the Civil Wars in these terms, with the English people holding a covenant with God. *Samson Agonistes*'s spirit is thoroughly Hebraic.

878   JOSE, NICHOLAS. "*Samson Agonistes*: The Play Turned Upside Down." In *Ideas of the Restoration in English Literature, 1660-71.* Cambridge, Mass.: Harvard University Press, 1984, pp. 142-63.
       Samson Agonistes is a political drama about a spiritual restoration that opposes the political one and falsifies its claims and values. After opening with Samson apparently deprived of God and the creation, the Chorus reminds him that he cannot use his experience to draw conclusions about the world's end. At the close, Samson undergoes a vast restoration, which brings back the creation, spiritual life, and God's true history. Milton sees the return of King Charles, like the rule of the Philistines in *Samson Agonistes*, as a deviation from God's providential plan. In his play, Milton inverts plays of restoration

by celebrating the active vengeance of a powerless hero and showing the lords, who typically work for restoration, achieve annihilation. If the drama of restoration usually shows the woman's marriage to a hero, which leads to regeneration, in *Samson Agonistes* the separation of man and woman produces spiritual growth. In Milton's work, Samson is the new, true monarch.

879 KAUFMANN, R. J. "Bruising the Serpent: Milton as a Tragic Poet." *Centennial Review* 11 (1967):371-86.

A weak writer when he gives dramatic treatment to myth, Milton shows a tension between his memories of suffering and his conviction that such pain has ultimate significance. In *Samson Agonistes*, we see both the protagonist's inner agonies and the larger context that reduces our concern for his pain because it leads to his regeneration. Tragedy portrays the glorification and diminution of humanity by its own imaginative powers and the restriction of humanity by its necessary and costly choices. Combining divinely sanctified revenge with the urge to let God make the decision, Milton in *Samson Agonistes* refuses to face the imbalance of desire and power, of capacity and opportunity. A great dramatist must have the qualities of forgiveness and charity that Milton lacks. *Samson Agonistes* displays the urge for revenge and the absorption of human choices by divine ones. Samson's dramatic life is pragmatic, for he acts as an instrument of God's will. Strictly speaking, the play is neither a tragedy nor a Christian tragedy.

880 KERRIGAN, WILLIAM. "The Irrational Coherence of *Samson Agonistes*." *Milton Studies* 22 (1986):217-32.

Samson Agonistes and *Paradise Regained* illustrate the alliance between God and will at special moments in sacred history. Critics who view Milton as a Christian humanist have difficulty recognizing that, in his last two poems, reason has only a protective role, guarding heroes against the temptation to premature action. The pattern of Samson's marriage choices, in which he defies his father in order to follow his own "intimate impulse" and God's will, offers a sketch of his "rousing motions" and final victory. Excessive feelings of guilt, which parallel Milton's unconscious reaction to his blindness, help Samson earn the favor of the motions. Once he regains his spiritual virginity, Samson must paradoxically lose it in the scene in Dagon's temple.

Samson Agonistes

881 KIRKCONNELL, WATSON, trans. *That Invincible Samson: The Theme of "Samson Agonistes" in World Literature with Translations of the Major Analogues*. Toronto: University of Toronto Press, 1964, 236 pp.

Kirkconnell lists over 100 analogues (from the twelfth-century B.C. to 1944) and translates all or part of five significant ones: Hieronymus Zieglerus's *Samson, Tragoedia Nova* (1547); Marcus Andreas Wunstius's *Simson, Tragoedia Sacra* (1600); Theodorus Rhodius's *Simson* (1600); Vincenzo Giattini's *Il Sansone: Dialogo per musica* (1638); and Joost van den Vondel's *Samson, of Heilige Wraeck, Treurspel* (1660).

882 KRANIDAS, THOMAS. "Dalila's Role in *Samson Agonistes*." *Studies in English Literature, 1500-1900* 6 (1966):125-37.

Sexuality constitutes only part of Dalila's complex personality, for she also has a tough unreasonableness that accompanies her lyric grace, a variety of voices suited to different audiences and arguments, and an ability to lie. In her scene with Samson, she is culpable, self-deluding, and "in general quite deliberately wrong" (126). She begins speaking in a wavering manner and shifts to a legal one, but both styles are devious. She argues from love, patriotism, and religion. Analyzing each tactic, Samson exposes its fallaciousness. The end of her last speech is a sophisticated hymn that honestly reveals how an awareness of her infamy leads her to crave glory.

883 KROUSE, F. MICHAEL. *Milton's Samson and the Christian Tradition*. Princeton, N.J.: Princeton University Press for University of Cincinnati, 1949, 167 pp. Part reprinted in *Twentieth Century Interpretations of "Samson Agonistes,"* ed. Galbraith M. Crump (Englewood Cliffs, N.J.: Prentice-Hall, 1968), pp. 46-50.

There is a disparity between Samson in the Old Testament and in the New Testament. Allegorical interpretation gives nearly every episode in Samson's life a figurative significance that foretells the story of Christ. In the Renaissance, rationalistic interpretation flourishes, with some tropological and anagogical interpretation. Since commentators often repeat earlier commentators, Milton knows all of these interpretations of Samson. Milton's contemporaries see Samson's tragedy as a failure in high calling, so they stress his spiritual ruin. He is a tragic hero. In *Samson Agonistes*, Milton follows these traditions and interprets the story with rationalistic literalism, while subordinating the hero's earlier exploits in favor of his tragic, heroic end. Keeping with the tradition, Milton portrays Samson as physically strong but not intellectually gifted. Not an image of Milton's first wife, Dalila reflects the antifeminist element in the tradition. Like many commentators, Milton regards Samson as a repentant, great man whose final act is a self-sacrifice willed by God.

884 LABRIOLA, ALBERT C. "Divine Urgency as a Motive for Conduct in *Samson Agonistes*." *Philological Quarterly* 50 (1971):99-107.
The "impulse" that leads Samson to marry the woman of Timna is analogous to the urge that leads him to marry Dalila, and neither one is the kind of inspiration (the "rousing motions") that signals his spiritual renewal and causes the destruction of the Philistines' temple. In his Philistine marriages, Samson experiences what Milton considers evil temptation: God inclines someone who conceives evil and who is vulnerable because of pride to behave in an evil manner. Though Samson proudly thinks that each of his marriages will help Israel, God will accomplish the same deed when and how he chooses. Aided by the good temptations provided by Manoa, Dalila, and Harapha, Samson must undergo renovation to lead him into a state of grace. He is renewed and thus regains his former liberty.

885 LANDY, MARCIA. "Language and the Seal of Silence in *Samson Agonistes*." *Milton Studies* 2 (1970):175-94.
Samson passes through the limits of speech and beyond them into noise and, finally, silence. At the beginning of *Samson Agonistes*, the hero is in the bondage of words, for when Manoa speaks they hurt and remind him of what he was and has become. His bond with God is symbolized by a vow of silence concerning the sources of his strength; when Samson breaks silence, he reveals his lack of awareness about the power of language. Some characters--Manoa and Dalila, for example-- use legalistic language that reflects their world views; they see language as reality. Harapha's taunts reveal the increasing distance between Samson and the world of external values that he once cherished. The play's last movement contains an intensification and acceleration of noises, through which Samson passes to arrive at the calm silence of liberation.

Samson Agonistes

886   LEWALSKI, BARBARA K. "*Samson Agonistes* and the 'Tragedy' of the Apocalypse." *PMLA* 85 (1970):1050-62.

By pointing to the Book of Revelation as one of *Samson Agonistes*'s models as a tragedy, Milton follows an exegetical tradition that identifies Revelation as a tragedy in which the elect people of every age are the protagonists, and the dragon (Satan), the whore of Babylon, and the Beast (Antichrist) are the enemies. The tragedy comes from the agon of the elect people, who win a spiritual victory. Typological relationships exist among Revelation, the Book of Judges, and the elect in the world during all ages, including the period of the English Civil Wars. Samson is thus the type of which the Christian spiritual elect is the antitype, for both experience the paradigmatic pattern of "Vocation, Fall, Regeneration, Temptation, Trial, [and] Growth in spiritual perfection" (1055). *Samson Agonistes* is closely connected to the Apocalypse.

887   LOCHMAN, DANIEL T. "'If There be Aught of Presage': Milton's Samson as Riddler and Prophet." *Milton Studies* 22 (1986):195-216.

When the "presage" in Samson's mind tells him that the day will be remarkable because of some act or that it will be his last day, he displays a mixture of logic and prophecy. We recognize that life is not made up of dualities (either-or propositions), but instead it is complex and ambiguous. The "If" ("If there be aught of presage") begins to leave room for such ambiguity, while Samson's final act is unwittingly prophetic. Prophecy breaks into his opening state of despair, allowing him to transcend his preoccupation with past sins and their result, present suffering. Prophecy joins his personal future to providence, as he learns to avoid restrictive human thought processes. He moves from an interest in the past to an interest in the future, from passive despair to active hope, and from riddles rooted in the past to the beginnings of prophecy, which connects past to future.

888   LOW, ANTHONY. *The Blaze of Noon: A Reading of "Samson Agonistes*." New York and London: Columbia University Press, 1974, 245 pp.

The Greek form and Hebrew content of *Samson Agonistes* are veils for its Christian, tragic meaning. Living before Christ is Samson's tragedy; Samson must act without a full understanding of his typological role as sacrificial victim or of Christian life after death. The many ironic reversals in *Samson Agonistes* involve the constant frustration of each character's intentions. A new type of irony, the irony of alternatives, appears when a character posits a hypothetical choice only to find that both options occur, though they are supposed mutually exclusive. Characters who can see become more blind to Samson's inner state as it changes and as the blind hero gains spiritual vision. Dalila's character and motivations remain inscrutable. Not an entirely comic character, Harapha reveals an arrogance that is satirized until he leaves as a coward. He is also Samson's parodic double, whose faults Samson must recognize in himself and purge. Causation in *Samson Agonistes* is internalized because it consists of the various steps in Samson's regeneration.

889 MacCALLUM, HUGH. "*Samson Agonistes*: The Deliverer as Judge." *Milton Studies* 23 (1987):259-90.
Samson Agonistes shows a process of discovery that reaches only a partial, and therefore tragically incomplete, resolution between the Mosaic Law as external prescription and the rational, inner freedom best fulfilled in the Gospel. As judge or interpreter as well as deliverer, Samson provides an incomplete judgment and deliverance. In *Christian Doctrine* and elsewhere, Milton downplays the value of the Mosaic Law by arguing that its promise of life applies to temporal rather than eternal life. During Samson's age, Milton sees just the beginning of the process by which people are educated so they can move from the works of Law to those of faith. Given a culture shaped by Law and limited in its view of God, *Samson Agonistes* shows the evolution of that society's idea of freedom. Samson never understands that love alone fulfills the Law, and this limitation contributes to his tragic imperfection.

890 MARILLA, ESMOND L. "*Samson Agonistes*: An Interpretation." *Studia Neophilologica* 29 (1957):67-76. Reprinted in *Milton and Modern Man: Selected Essays* (University: University of Alabama Press, 1968), pp. 68-77.
Paradise Lost shows man's loss of a world through human weakness, concluding with the prerequisite for regeneration. *Paradise Regained* portrays man's efforts to regain the ideal society, though his faith will always be challenged. *Samson Agonistes* unifies these works. Samson's crime is basically the same as Adam's; Samson faces

essentially those temptations that Christ rejects in *Paradise Regained*. In Samson's final act, we see him assert the moral obligation called for from sinning man by the challenges of life.

891   MOLLENKOTT, VIRGINIA R. "Relativism in *Samson Agonistes*." *Studies in Philology* 67 (1970):89-102.
       When Milton shifts from a concern with ultimate categories in his epics, he avoids absolute terms when dealing with human categories and points of view in *Samson Agonistes*. Only when Samson enters God's battle with Dagon are absolute terms of truth versus falsehood relevant to the play. On the human level, *Samson Agonistes* shows the validity of the hero's private inspiration or "rousing motions," but we also see the limitations of each character's perspective, especially Samson's when he judges Dalila. Although she does wrong by acting as an agent of Dagon, on the human level Dalila's betrayal of Samson has valid reasons behind it. But Samson's marriage to her is based on sound reasons from his perspective. The validity of limited points of view gives way to obedience to the true God.

892   MUELLER, MARTIN E. "*Pathos* and *Katharsis* in *Samson Agonistes*." *ELH* 31 (1964):156-74.
       Samson Agonistes's pathos, the act of violence that constitutes the catastrophe, is relevant not to human relationships (and therefore need not be probable and necessary) but to the final event in Samson and God's relationship. When Samson severs his ties to his countrymen, the isolation produces a pathos that is, in Aristotelian terms, anti-tragic. Only his relationship to God matters to him, and the play reestablishes that connection at the expense of tragic conflict. Samson develops with respect to hamartia, ignorance leading to the fatal deed, and catharsis as the play moves from reason to faith. Manoa's purgation represents the audience's. Catharsis might be defined as a state of equilibrium at the end of a work, which is how *Samson Agonistes* closes. The tragedy is accepted, not resolved.

893   MUELLER, MARTIN. "Sixteenth-Century Italian Criticism and Milton's Theory of Catharsis." *Studies in English Literature, 1500-1900* 6 (1966):139-50.

Milton learns a great deal about literary theory during his Italian journey of 1638-39. His definition of catharsis combines purgation and the Aristotelian mean, uses a homeopathic analogy, and shows a complex relationship of imitation, purgation, and pleasure. Milton's views about catharsis correspond closely to Giacomini's.

894 MULRYAN, JOHN. "The Heroic Tradition of Milton's *Samson Agonistes*." *Milton Studies* 18 (1983):217-34.

Contrary to some critics' views, recent biblical scholarship sees Samson as intelligent, resourceful, and motivated not by vengeance but, in a more accurate translation, by deliverance. Milton uses the traditional depictions of Heracles, particularly those by Sophocles, Euripides, and Seneca, as models for only Samson's most redeeming features. The cerebral orientation of Samson may be derived from mythographers and emblem books. Milton's Samson also has parallels with Sisyphus and the hero of Sophocles's *Oedipus at Colonus*. In *Samson Agonistes*, Milton integrates the Hebrew and Greek traditions.

895 MUSTAZZA, LEONARD. "The Verbal Plot of *Samson Agonistes*." *Milton Studies* 23 (1987):241-58.

Samson moves from a "shameful garrulity" before the play begins to a heroic silence at the conclusion. Following a tripartite structure, *Samson Agonistes* shows the protagonist's use of language to assess the errors of the past when he speaks with the Chorus and Manoa; to reveal his acquired resistance to verbal attacks with Harapha and the relationship between words and deeds with Dalila; and to present prudent speech and ultimately silence in his final conflict with the Philistines. After Samson brings together words and deeds in a verbal action, his silence is a sign that he reaches the right relationship with God.

896 PARKER, WILLIAM RILEY. *Milton's Debt to Greek Tragedy in "Samson Agonistes."* Baltimore, Md.: Johns Hopkins University Press; London: Humphrey Milford for Oxford University Press, 1937, 276 pp. Part reprinted in *Twentieth Century Interpretations of "Samson Agonistes,"* ed. Galbraith M. Crump (Englewood Cliffs, N.J.: Prentice-Hall, 1968), pp. 33-45.

Samson Agonistes

Greek tragedy, the Book of Judges, Milton's personal experience, and dramatic invention account for virtually all of *Samson Agonistes*. Milton uses almost half of the biblical account, omitting material that diverts attention from Samson or that turns him into a coarse, grimly humorous character. Like many Greek tragedies, Milton's play is named after its hero plus the epithet *agonistes*, meaning wrestler, advocate, actor, and champion. *Samson Agonistes*'s plot moves with an Aeschylean directness. In avoiding the spectacular, however, the play is Sophoclean. While Aristotle prescribes that a tragic hero must be highly renowned, Milton gives Samson an exalted spiritual position as God's agent on earth. But, like a Sophoclean hero, Samson is a splendid human; like a Euripidean hero, he is the portrait of a soul at war with itself; like an Aeschylean hero, he is cold and forbidding. *Samson Agonistes* is Judeo-Christian in content and theme, but Greek in form and spirit. The play's themes are regeneration and reward, which are possible only after Samson accepts responsibility for his ruin.

897 PATRIDES, C. A. "The Comic Dimension in Greek Tragedy and *Samson Agonistes*." *Milton Studies* 10 (1977):3-21.
Milton the prosaic author argues in *Samson Agonistes*'s Preface that a play should not mix comic and tragic matter, a view upheld by critical tradition but not by dramatic practice. Milton the dramatist promptly violates this principle. Not only do Aeschylus, Sophocles, and Euripides write satyr-plays but they also write tragedies that contain comic elements. In *Samson Agonistes*, Harapha's literary relatives (the braggarts of comic Continental literature) and Manoa's similarities to the comic Oceanus in Aeschylus's *Prometheus Bound* point to the play's comic potential. Manoa is comic because, as the world moves onward about him, he remains immobile. Samson's supposed friends in the vulgar Chorus are his worst enemies, for they misunderstand the ways of providence.

898 RADZINOWICZ, MARY ANN. "The Distinctive Tragedy of *Samson Agonistes*." *Milton Studies* 17 (1983):249-80.
The beginning episode of *Samson Agonistes* features two bold moves: presenting the hero at a moral nadir but a zenith of tragic passions, and apparently denying any doubt or conflict, for "Just are the ways of God." Milton also separates the catastrophe from the denouement, creating a double catharsis in the first section. Through

dramatic suspension, he emphasizes not physical action but intellectual conflict and the themes of distributive justice and moderative catharsis. *Samson Agonistes*'s recapitulative structure contains a number of subgenres appropriate for philosophical speculation.

899 RADZINOWICZ, MARY ANN. *Toward "Samson Agonistes": The Growth of Milton's Mind*. Princeton, N.J.: Princeton University Press, 1978, 459 pp. Part reprinted in *Milton: "Comus" and "Samson Agonistes," a Casebook*, ed. Julian Lovelock (London and Basingstoke: Macmillan, 1975), pp. 198-208.

   Samson Agonistes's "complex" structure, which conforms to Aristotelian principles and Renaissance practice, presents dialectical patterns in which, one by one, characters oppose Samson in the Chorus's presence and elicit a resolving definition from him. Beginning with a protagonist ill in mind and body, *Samson Agonistes* portrays his restoration to health. The drama interprets contemporary history by justifying God's ways in light of the concept of patience, which is history's main lesson. Samson's example presents the historical lesson that each person must be his own deliverer. A "drama of the English revolution" (113), *Samson Agonistes* shows how an individual may be a nation's representative and encapsulate its political existence. Milton uses the Psalms' repeated patterns and structures (lament, wisdom, trust, and thanksgiving) to shape his play. Published together, *Paradise Regained* and *Samson Agonistes* are closely connected in their themes and relationship to *Paradise Lost* and to the Book of Job. Written in 1667-70, *Samson Agonistes* reveals Milton's most advanced theological position and enacts his most revolutionary poetics.

900 SADLER, LYNN VEACH. "Coping with Hebraic Legalism: The Chorus in *Samson Agonistes*." *Harvard Theological Review* 66 (1973):353-68.

   Samson Agonistes's Chorus interprets Samson's experience by turning to Old Testament traditional wisdom, which leaves them spouting platitudes. But Old Testament legalism cannot explain his life. Samson also grasps at various frames of reference (often legalistic) for consolation. Though the Chorus usually does not know it, its legalistic Hebraism is reoriented throughout, and this helps Samson develop a correct understanding of the Law. Both Samson and, to a lesser extent, the Chorus comprehend more at the end. As Samson moves from a

Samson Agonistes

self-centered heroism, which separates him from his people, to true heroism, he and the Chorus come together.

901   SADLER, LYNN VEACH. "Regeneration and Typology: *Samson Agonistes* and Its Relation to *De Doctrina Christiana, Paradise Lost,* and *Paradise Regained.*" *Studies in English Literature, 1500-1900* 12 (1972):141-56.
      Milton's typology emphasizes continuity between dispensations: through Christ, all types can receive regeneration. Samson's experience in *Samson Agonistes* follows the sequence of Law, prophets, and finally Gospel. Milton uses types as exemplars, the patterns of actions. In *Paradise Lost,* as in *Samson Agonistes,* sin produces some of what *Christian Doctrine* defines as the four degrees of death, including guiltiness and spiritual death. Samson resembles Adam in Book 10, for both experience regeneration, with which they overcome the distortion of experience produced by sin. By making correct choices, Christ in *Paradise Regained* is exemplary. In *Paradise Lost,* Satan parodies the Son's loving response to God. Regeneration requires that an individual perceive the Father as the God of both mercy and justice.

902   SADLER, LYNN VEACH. "Typological Imagery in *Samson Agonistes*: Noon and the Dragon." *ELH* 37 (1970):195-210.
      Samson's experience fulfills the figural and revelatory regenerative pattern of Scripture, which represents the outline of the individual experience. Through faith, Samson acquires prophetic liberty. Genesis is the prologue of the dispensatory drama, while the Gospel is the noon of the revelatory process, and Revelation is the midnight. In *Samson Agonistes,* the hero's experience is that of noon, as he moves from its dark side (God's wrath) to the consolation of Revelation. The image of the dragon made to devour the foul birds symbolizes Christ's and Samson's power over Satan. If the epithet *agonistes* can mean "feigning," *Samson Agonistes* shows how God feigns weakness before his enemies so his servants can respond to grace and understand providential ways.

903   SAMUEL, IRENE. "*Samson Agonistes* as Tragedy." In *Calm of Mind: Tercentenary Essays on "Paradise Regained" and "Samson*

Agonistes" in Honor of John S. Diekhoff. Edited by Joseph Anthony Wittreich, Jr. Cleveland, Ohio, and London: Press of Case Western Reserve University, 1971, pp. 235-57.

Samson Agonistes does not demonstrate the hero's election in a final vengeance on God's enemies, for Milton associates revenge with tyrannical rather than divine power. Following Aristotle, Milton prefers a flawed tragic agent whose shortcomings lead to his downfall. *Samson Agonistes* is not a martyr play. Samson repeatedly calls for his own death and displays continued garrulity and hubris. Neither a villain nor an enchanter, "Dalila is surely the most bird-brained woman ever to have gotten herself involved in major tragedy" (248). The conclusion of Samson's life leaves the impression of horror, not of shallow comfort. That Samson kills the Philistines indicates that his is not divinely illuminated conduct. Although he is of superior stature, he also comes to accept and employ Philistine values of combat between his God and their Dagon, thus reducing the divinity to the scale of a tribal deity.

904 SELLIN, PAUL R. "Milton's Epithet *Agonistes.*" *Studies in English Literature, 1500-1900* 4 (1964):137-62.

Since the mid-eighteenth century, most critics interpret *agonistes* to mean one who wrestles or competes in athletic contests. In the biblical account of Samson, the ambiguous Masoretic Hebrew verbs may indicate that, while the Philistines ask Samson to "play" for them, they unwittingly demand that he "mock" them; when he deceives them, they are the ironic victims of their own laughter. Samson may be seen as a passive or active figure. The verbs in the Greek of the Septuagint stress his active role as the performer of "sports" (in the Vatican codex), his passive role as the butt of mockery (in the Alexandrine codex), or his role as deceiver or mocker. Milton includes all three interpretations in *Samson Agonistes.* Adding a fourth interpretation, the epithet *agonistes* most appropriately refers to Samson "dissembling," "assuming a mask," or "acting a part."

905 SHAWCROSS, JOHN T. "Irony as Tragic Effect: *Samson Agonistes* and the Tragedy of Hope." In *Calm of Mind: Tercentenary Essays on "Paradise Regained" and "Samson Agonistes" in Honor of John S. Diekhoff.* Edited by Joseph Anthony Wittreich, Jr. Cleveland, Ohio, and London: Press of Case Western Reserve University, 1971, pp. 289-306.

Samson Agonistes

We should see Samson ironically as a hero who acts out of his faith to commit a deed whose metaphoric and spiritual significance he does not understand. More than revenge, Samson's action is a metaphor of the uselessness of such deeds because it has no lasting effect. Regeneration is an individual experience that recurs throughout history. At the end of *Samson Agonistes,* we join the Chorus in achieving purgation and hope, but only with respect to Samson; like the Chorus, we are shortsighted, so we fail to see the play's conclusion as a symbolic action. The irony comes from our realization that Samson's accomplishment seems to have no meaning in history because it is limited and no one understands its full implications. The play contains Samson's tragedy of man's hope, which blinds man to reality and prevents lasting achievements if it is not based on faith in God. Manoa's and the Chorus's tragedy is that they wait for God to act alone. Hope is tragic when it replaces truth and action.

906 SLIGHTS, CAMILLE W. "A Hero of Conscience: *Samson Agonistes* and Casuistry." *PMLA* 90 (1975):395-413. Revised in *The Casuistical Tradition in Shakespeare, Donne, Herbert, and Milton* (Princeton, N.J.: Princeton University Press, 1981), pp. 247-96.

For Milton, the use of inquiry and right reason, not the rigid application of prescribed law, helps one resolve doubts. In his treatises on divorce, religion, and politics, he consistently argues that doubtful actions based on the individual's conscience, rather than breaking divine law, in fact fulfill its intention. *Paradise Lost* uses cautionary and exemplary models to dramatize the process of making moral choices. In *Paradise Regained* and *Samson Agonistes,* issues are not as clear. Christ and Samson learn how to know God's will for them in particular circumstances.

907 STOLLMAN, SAMUEL S. "Milton's Samson and the Jewish Tradition." *Milton Studies* 3 (1971):185-200.

Jewish tradition defines Samson as virile, divinely guided, and judged three times by the law of measure for measure. In *Samson Agonistes,* Milton agrees with Jewish tradition that Samson and Dalila are married but indicates that a prohibition is suspended so she can remain a Gentile. Contrary to the standard Hebraic view of the Mosaic Law as immutable, Milton's position is that right reason or the natural law may supersede it. Milton, unlike the Jewish commentators, stresses the decline in Samson's reason, not the growth of his sensuality, as the cause of his fall. By ascribing a servile personality to the Jewish people, Milton again differs from the normative Hebrew tradition. He understands Samson from the perspective of "the Christian canonization of Old Testament saints whose spiritual calling and conversion is not far different from the experience of the regenerate" (196). Samson, in Milton's rationalistic interpretation, is a Christianized hero.

908 STOLLMAN, SAMUEL S. "Milton's Understanding of the 'Hebraic' in *Samson Agonistes*." *Studies in Philology* 69 (1972):334-47.

Because Milton differentiates between Judaic and Hebraic, Samson is not a Judaic or Jewish figure. The Hebrew refers to what is, in effect, Christian or at least compatible with Milton's Christian doctrine. Milton uses such a perspective when he presents the Mosaic Law in *Samson Agonistes* as neither eternal nor immutable, but as an external force that the hero can abrogate in favor of an internal impulse, the equivalent of the Christian Holy Spirit within the regenerate. If the Jews are inclined to servitude, Milton's Hebraic view presents Samson as a fighter for liberty. Action (or works) is also central to Milton's Christian doctrine and to his Hebraic view of Samson's career. Like Christ in *Paradise Regained*, Samson is a Hebrew hero who performs works of faith. Milton does not place Hebraism and Christianity in opposition.

909 SUMMERS, JOSEPH H. "The Movements of the Drama." In *The Lyric and Dramatic Milton*. Edited by Joseph H. Summers. Selected Papers from the English Institute. New York and London: Columbia University Press, 1965, pp. 153-75.

If *Samson Agonistes* moved simply from Samson's degradation and suffering to his triumph, the play might not raise the pity and fear that are part of Milton's requirement for tragic purgation. Milton complicates the play by introducing ironic and paradoxical movements. We begin by wondering about Samson's identity, a concern throughout, and by seeing him as an unlikable hero. The play presents double images and perspectives, as well as mutually exclusive alternatives that are both true. By repeating or developing emotions that Samson has already expressed, the temptations lead him to grow to a heroic,

Samson Agonistes

triumphant self. The Chorus, though it is sometimes in error, is closest to our level of understanding, but we are expected to correct its mistakes. We share the Chorus's realization that God's will holds the resolution. When Samson understands heroic freedom, he defeats the Chorus, which is incapable of understanding or exercising it. Samson recreates the self.

910   SWAIM, KATHLEEN M. "The Doubling of the Chorus in *Samson Agonistes.*" *Milton Studies* 20 (1984):225-45.
        Doubleness is everywhere in *Samson Agonistes*, from small images to large issues and even in the hero's name, whose Hebrew etymology is "there is a second time." If the play is dominated by the epistemological distinction between experience and faith, Samson acts on the former for most of the play. The experiential view, based on the individual ego and the evidence of the material world, leads him to a sense of failure and despair. In between the Officer's first and second visits, Samson changes, turning to the future and faith. His language becomes silence or riddling, itself a form of doubleness. Manoa, Dalila, and Harapha act as Samson's doubles or mirrors, in which he can see various aspects of himself and correct them. The Chorus's suffering and changes of mind parallel those of Samson. As the second semichorus (lines 1687-1707) presents the Chorus's altered vision and expression, so Samson makes a transcendental move into silence. The Chorus undergoes a process of revelation; Samson's victory effects a new dispensation.

911   TINKER, CHAUNCEY B. "*Samson Agonistes.*" In *Tragic Themes in Western Literature*. Edited by Cleanth Brooks. New Haven, Conn.: Yale University Press, 1955, pp. 59-76.
        Unimpressed by the riddle, harlot at Gaza, and feminine wiles of Dalila in the biblical account of Samson, or unable to use these materials, Milton is interested in the noble matter of Samson's broken bond with God. We can love Milton's Samson because he is a more serious character whose fate is connected to that of his nation and whose movement is a fall from high estate to misery. Like the Book of Judges, *Samson Agonistes* asks us to take delight in the destruction of Israel's enemies. If Milton develops Manoa's role, he also turns Dalila into a living woman. It is a mistake to read *Samson Agonistes* as

autobiography. Because Samson reaches the very end that providence intends, the play may not be strictly tragic.

912 TIPPENS, DARRYL. "The Kenotic Experience of *Samson Agonistes*." *Milton Studies* 22 (1986):173-94.

Milton's life and art are shaped by the theme of kenosis, the emptying out of divine attributes. But his definition stresses descent and ascent: the humiliation Christ experiences in his Incarnation and then his exaltation to glory. Milton's heroes must follow this pattern, though the unfaithful (such as Dalila) undergo a pseudo-kenosis, an ironic imitation of God's plan. Clothing imagery permeates *Samson Agonistes*, as garments are linked to sinfulness and rags or undress to spirituality. Once he stops grasping for glory and trying to avoid blame, Samson experiences spiritual and physical journeys that follow the kenotic parabola.

913 TUNG, MASON. "Samson Impatiens: A Reinterpretation of Milton's *Samson Agonistes*." *Texas Studies in Literature and Language* 9 (1968):475-92.

The middle of *Samson Agonistes*'s plot is not characterized by the hero's gradual regeneration. Until the climactic reversal, Samson is impatient; then, in a sudden conversion, he moves from hypocritical patience and stoical apathy to true patience. Milton uses the choral odes to stress Samson's need for patience. When confronted by Dalila's initial patience, Samson responds with wrath and impatience rather than a fear of female charms. His impatience is equally evident when Manoa and Harapha visit him. After the climactic "rousing motions," Samson's speech and actions change as he becomes the patient martyr for God.

914 ULREICH, JOHN C., Jr. "'Beyond the Fifth Act': *Samson Agonistes* as Prophecy." *Milton Studies* 17 (1983):281-318.

An example of tragic prophecy, *Samson Agonistes* transforms catastrophe into revelation; as a Christian prophecy whose model is the Book of Amos, the play becomes tragicomic. *Samson Agonistes* shows two problems of development: the literal action focuses on the classical heroism of Samson's triumph, while the spirit of its argument deals with the Hebraic martyrdom that leads to God's triumph. Although they

Samson Agonistes

produce the same catastrophe, these patterns are irreconcilably opposed. Both are subsumed in the play's Christian meaning as a religious parable about Christ that asserts Samson's self-discovery and redemption. *Samson Agonistes* fulfills and refutes the Book of Amos. Instead of appearing within the play, prophetic recreation remains a potential for the audience to attain.

915 ULREICH, JOHN C., Jr. "'This Great Deliverer': *Samson Agonistes* as Parable." *Milton Quarterly* 13 (1979):78-84.

   Samson Agonistes's many paradoxes--the hero is a deliverer of Israel who delivers himself to his oppressors and a judge who cannot rule himself--lead us to read it figuratively as a parable of deliverance. In the Bible, Samson's story is enigmatic, since it appears to be a religious tale lacking religious meaning, a primitive myth of redemption. The tension of Milton's drama comes from the conflict between its literal sense, which carries a repellent religious significance, and its spiritual meaning, conveyed in Samson's heroic martyrdom. Although the classical and Hebraic meanings are incompatible, a Christian message subsumes and reconciles them. The play's movement is that of Samson's self-discovery, as he eventually "enacts a parable of Redemption" (83).

916 WADDINGTON, RAYMOND B. "Melancholy Against Melancholy: *Samson Agonistes* as Renaissance Tragedy." In *Calm of Mind: Tercentenary Essays on "Paradise Regained" and "Samson Agonistes" in Honor of John S. Diekhoff*. Edited by Joseph Anthony Wittreich, Jr. Cleveland, Ohio, and London: Press of Case Western Reserve University, 1971, pp. 259-87.

   Milton surely knows the etymology that derives Samson's and Hercules's names from "sun"; he also considers Hercules a type of Christ in *Nativity Ode* and *Paradise Regained*. In *Samson Agonistes*, he links the hero and Hercules as Adams who exhibit "effeminate slackness." Another tradition that helps shape *Samson Agonistes* is Hercules's madness as an excess of melancholy. At the opening of the play, Samson's despair comes from pervasive religious melancholy. The imagery of sterility, imprisonment, disease, and shipwreck supports this. *Samson Agonistes*'s Preface explains those elements of the drama most relevant for comprehending it (for example, the pattern of like curing like). Through thematic and character parody, Samson is faced with images of himself that he must repudiate in order to control the excesses of his own passions. Milton's medical analogy is based on Paracelsian theory.

917   WEBER, BURTON J. "The Schematic Design of the *Samson* Middle." *Milton Studies* 22 (1986):233-54.

The middle of *Samson Agonistes* follows a bipartite structure in which two pairs of characters enter: the Chorus and Manoa, and Dalila and Harapha. The first two receive comfort rather than give it, though they unwittingly cause Samson's atonement; the latter two, Samson's enemies, ironically revive his self-respect. Milton contrasts Samson with Dalila and Harapha, for Samson recognizes the difference between his state and Dalila's complete moral depravity, and between his condition and Harapha's more thorough state of shame and dishonor. Through them, Samson finds regeneration.

918   WEISMILLER, EDWARD. "The 'Dry' and 'Rugged' Verse." In *The Lyric and Dramatic Milton*. Edited by Joseph H. Summers. Selected Papers from the English Institute. New York and London: Columbia University Press, 1965, pp. 115-52.

We see in Milton's later verse, and especially in *Samson Agonistes*, his eagerness to use any prosodic resource that gives variety to his syllabic lines. In *Samson Agonistes*, many of the Chorus's lines remain metrically ambiguous: though they may suggest the rhythms of classical tragedy's verse, they are loose English heroic blank verse. Two of Milton's early poems written in the form of monostrophic rhymed odes, "On Time" and "At a Solemn Music," show affinities with the meter of *Samson Agonistes*'s choral parts. In Cowley's *Pindarique Odes* (1656), we find lines with all of the variety in length and meter that we see in *Samson Agonistes*'s choral odes.

919   WEST, ROBERT H. "Samson's God: 'Beastly Hebraism' and 'Asinine Bigotry.'" *Milton Studies* 13 (1979):109-28.

Characters in *Samson Agonistes* point often to God's power, far less often to his goodness, which is roughly their view of Samson. But rage and turbulence may be valid means by which to express moral principles. Ultimately, we should judge Samson's God and good and recognize that the protagonist's doubt about providence disappears in

Samson Agonistes

the end, even as he acknowledges that the Father's ways are mysterious and arbitrary.

920   WILKENFELD, ROGER B. "Act and Emblem: The Conclusion of *Samson Agonistes*." *ELH* 32 (1965):160-68.
      Samson Agonistes is concerned with the individual's transformation that leads to the recovery of freedom implicit in the recovery of God. Samson moves from being the Philistines' fool to become his own fool, at which point he can begin to act. If Manoa lives in and can think only about the past, Samson eliminates it after the Officer's arrival. The phoenix emblem unifies the poem's motifs and establishes the central themes of freedom and transformation.

921   WILKES, G. A. "The Interpretation of *Samson Agonistes*." *Huntington Library Quarterly* 26 (1963):363-79.
      In response to Dr. Johnson, modern critics define *Samson Agonistes* as a drama of regeneration, a view the text does not support. Even at the beginning of the play, Samson no longer blames God but instead accepts responsibility for his downfall. He does not vanquish his weaknesses as various characters meet him, with Harapha's visit serving as the supposed climactic encounter. Instead, the play begins with Samson's realization that, though he is chosen by God, he has failed; but there is a hint that the providential pattern can still be realized. Samson rejects the plans of action proposed by others, though he has none of his own. He experiences neither trial nor regeneration; he receives grace.

922   WILLIAMSON, GEORGE. "Tension in *Samson Agonistes*." In *Milton and Others*. London: Faber and Faber, 1965, pp. 85-102.
      The incidents of *Samson Agonistes* are external, and the hero has no power over them. Action can come from Samson only when he figures out how to turn his limitations to his own ends. He faces a conflict between spiritual and physical redemption, though the latter leads to the former. In many ways, the blind Samson is the antithesis of the blind Milton. But *Samson Agonistes* does show Milton's distressed challenge to faith. With the exception of Manoa, the visitors arrive in a clear order from most sympathetic to least, with Dalila's ambivalent appearance providing the transition. Providence guides Samson to his

redemption as he moves from a passive role to an active one within the limits of his punishment.

923   WITTREICH, JOSEPH. *Interpreting "Samson Agonistes."* Princeton, N.J.: Princeton University Press, 1986, 425 pp.

The controversy over *Samson Agonistes* always has a political aspect, which is appropriate because the play is polemical. Although Samson's story is appropriated by all political sides in Renaissance England, the dominant view of Samson during the 1650s and 1660s is negative. Because Milton wishes to decode the Samson story by correcting the fraudulent outline that history imposes on it, he foregrounds some episodes from the Book of Judges, excises others, and makes some peripheral. His revisions of the biblical account accent Samson's guilt and subvert his heroism. The Samson story, decontextualized in order to make way for New Testament contextualizers, is recontextualized in the Renaissance, largely through new typological symbolism. Both political parties reclaim Samson in the 1640s as an elect member of God's army. But, with the execution of the King and the failure of the revolution, Samson's heroism is diminished, and his story undergoes an interiorization. We must take *Paradise Regained* and *Samson Agonistes* together, for they form a totality and have a hidden intertextuality between them. The 1671 volume that contains these two works is thus structured according to principles of contrast, irony, and opposition.

924   WOODHOUSE, A. S. P. *"Samson Agonistes* and Milton's Experience." *Transactions of the Royal Society of Canada* 3d ser., 43 (1949):section 2, 157-75. Reprinted in *The Heavenly Muse: A Preface to Milton*, ed. Hugh MacCallum, University of Toronto Department of English Studies and Texts, no. 21 (Toronto and Buffalo, N.Y.: University of Toronto Press, 1972), pp. 292-319.

The date of *Samson Agonistes*'s composition is uncertain, but 1660-61, a period of political disaster and personal danger for Milton, is probable. In *Paradise Lost* and *Paradise Regained*, he divides between Adam and Christ the themes of "temptation, disobedience, repentance, obedience, restoration" (161); Samson experiences the entire series of events. In part a retrospective view of Milton's experience, *Samson Agonistes* touches deeper issues than an autobiography would. The play deals with regeneration and the harmony of the human and divine views

Samson Agonistes

of Samson's tragedy. In a state of despair at the opening, Samson acknowledges his fault and begins his recovery. The play's catharsis works first on the human level, because that is the level on which we know Samson. There are many parallels between Samson and Milton, including the confession of sin and error, which for Milton include his first marriage and proud spirit.

925 WOODHOUSE, A. S. P. "Tragic Effect in *Samson Agonistes*." *University of Toronto Quarterly* 28 (1959):205-22. Reprinted in *Milton: Modern Essays in Criticism*, ed. Arthur E. Barker (London, Oxford, and New York: Oxford University Press, 1965), pp. 447-66; part reprinted in *Twentieth Century Interpretations of "Samson Agonistes*," ed. Galbraith M. Crump (Englewood Cliffs, N.J.: Prentice-Hall, 1968), pp. 110-13; *The Heavenly Muse: A Preface to Milton*, ed. Hugh MacCallum, University of Toronto Department of English Studies and Texts, no. 21 (Toronto and Buffalo, N.Y.: University of Toronto Press, 1972), pp. 292-319.

Presenting the tension between human freedom and God's providence, *Samson Agonistes* is an example of Christian rather than Greek or Hebrew tragedy, though the Chorus provides commentary from the Hebrew perspective. Samson begins the play in a state of self-centered remorse and despair, which starts his movement back to God, even if the meeting with Manoa initially takes him lower. When Samson encounters Dalila, he wins his first victory, over himself. This gives him the courage to state something hopeful when Harapha enters, for remorse turns into repentance. At the end of *Samson Agonistes*, the tragic effect is presented on two levels, human and providential, and we do not need to choose between them. Samson's return to God is also his catastrophe, which gives the play its tragic irony and Christian perspective. The play's conclusion mitigates the tragedy's disaster.

For analogues, see entry 881; for *Samson Agonistes*'s relation to *Paradise Regained*, see entries 232, 803, 831, 837, 890, 899, 901, 923-24. See also entries 3, 9, 43-47, 49, 53, 58, 60-61, 63, 65, 67-69, 71-72, 87, 90, 92, 105, 107-9, 117, 122-23, 125, 129-30, 134-35, 138, 140-42, 147, 150-51, 153-54, 156-57, 160, 162-64, 167-69, 173-74, 176, 179-81, 183, 186, 190, 192-93, 198, 201-3, 205, 207-9, 211, 213-14, 216-17, 221, 224, 228, 230-33, 235-36, 242, 245-46, 248, 250-51, 333, 366, 449, 470, 484, 486, 499, 519, 547-48, 560, 563, 565, 578, 587, 605-6, 613-14, 616-17, 620, 682, 745, 752, 772, 789, 803, 831, 833, 837-38, 951, 1001, 1005.

Prose

BIBLIOGRAPHY

926 SHAWCROSS, JOHN T. "A Survey of Milton's Prose Works." In
     Achievements of the Left Hand: Essays on the Prose of John Milton.
     Edited by Michael Lieb and John T. Shawcross. Amherst: University
     of Massachusetts Press, 1974, pp. 291-391.
         "This survey of Milton's prose attempts to pull together all
     known information about editions, dates of composition, public
     reaction to and knowledge of the works, and general scholarly
     discussions of them" (291).

CRITICISM

927 AUKSI, PETER. "Milton's 'Sanctifi'd Bitternesse': Polemical
     Technique in the Early Prose." *Texas Studies in Literature and
     Language* 19 (1977):363-81.
         Cultivating the literary tradition of nonconformist controversy
     in his five antiprelatical tracts, Milton speaks as a prophet for
     continuing reformation, and "his regenerative prose forces the reader to
     evaluate both the literary act and its inspired agent" (366). The speaker
     claims to resemble earlier prophets and church reformers, and he uses
     apocalyptic metaphors, anachronistic epithets, and vehement rhetoric.
     Milton's antiprelatical attacks rely on the congruence of speaker and

Criticism

discourse. His polemic establishes his fitness as a speaker and reflects the prelatical party's carnal acts.

928   AYERS, ROBERT W. "Milton's *Letter to a Friend* and the Anarchy of 1659." *Journal of Historical Studies* 1 (1968):229-39.

When Cromwell dies and is succeeded by his son, the King's cause is thought hopeless, yet within one year Milton writes *Letter to a Friend*, in which he sees the royal enemy as an immediate threat. During that year, the army attempts to be free of civilian control, some of its leaders grow disaffected, and lieutenant general Charles Fleetwood seeks greater power. The army's Commonwealthsmen want to end the Protectorate; along with civilian groups of Republicans, the army's rank and file wishes to restore the Rump Parliament; most army field officers want to control the government but keep Richard Cromwell as a figurehead. The Rump alienates its supporters and the army. Royalist plans are in action to regain power. Milton's *Letter* recognizes the chaotic events of the preceding year and the dangers at hand. As an indication of his realistic perspective, his proposal to establish an interim government matches what actually occurs days after he writes *Letter*.

929   BANSCHBACH, JOHN. "Ethical Style in Milton's *The Readie and Easie Way*." *Language and Style* 17 (1984):79-91.

Ready and Easy Way has two prose styles: a monarchy style, with long and complex sentence structures, and a Commonwealth one, with shorter, more coherent sentence structures. When Milton writes about the monarchy, he uses a digressive, associative style whose logical connections and syntax are at best loosely constructed. This is a style of attack, and its intensity suggests the unpopularity of Milton's cause.

930   BARKER, ARTHUR. "Christian Liberty in Milton's Divorce Pamphlets." *Modern Language Review* 35 (1940):153-61.

Based on Galatians and developed by Calvin, the doctrine of Christian liberty states that believers must not think of justification by the Law; must obey the Law out of the freedom by which they voluntarily obey God's will; and must be free to use or omit the observance of external things. Puritans of the left broaden the interpretation to deny all human authority in religious matters. Only in his divorce tracts does Milton reinterpret the doctrine, pushing it in the heretical direction of individual or private liberty, especially in the revised edition of *Doctrine and Discipline of Divorce* and *Tetrachordon*. By considering the issue of divorce between 1643 and 1645, Milton arrives at the radical interpretation of Christian liberty that he uses in *Christian Doctrine*.

931 BOEHRER, BRUCE. "Elementary Structures of Kingship: Milton, Regicide, and the Family." *Milton Studies* 23 (1987):97-117.

The Stuarts continue to create a myth of monarchy, and King Charles I's trial and execution have a theatrical and rhetorical character. Turning to the system of natural law, royalists define a king's relationship to his subjects as that of father to a glorified family; to kill the king is to violate paternal dignity in the form of God, king, and father. Milton, having disrupted sexual and familial identity by advocating divorce, is seen in the same terms when he defends parricide. His attack on the *Eikon Basilike* in *Eikonoklastes*, unlike his attack on Salmasius or More in *First* and *Second Defence*, cannot succeed because traditional rhetoric does not apply to an adversary who is a figure of God, king, and father, the very begetter of the people Milton wishes to persuade. Milton fails to understand the *Eikon Basilike*'s rhetorical situation, in which he must address not Salmasius or More but God, king, and father.

932 BOWERS, A. ROBIN. "Milton and Salmasius: The Rhetorical Imperatives." *Philological Quarterly* 52 (1973):55-68.

In order to understand the structure, rhetorical arguments, and sequence of subjects in Milton's *First Defence*, we must examine those elements in the work he refutes, Salmasius's *Defensio Regia*. Salmasius addresses the emotions, turns to appeals to reason in discussions of the nature of the right of kings and whether subjects should oppose their rulers, and treats the injustice of the execution of Charles I. He mixes syllogistic, oratorical, classical, and Ramist methods of argument. Turning all of these practices to his own advantage, Milton offers argument-by-argument refutations, using Salmasius's structure and persuasive techniques and writing a concise work to answer Salmasius's prolix one. When Salmasius attacks the character of the Independents, Milton assaults the life of his one opponent. If Salmasius's reputation is based on his rhetorical skills, Milton undermines that very strength.

Criticism

933   CABLE, LANA. "Shuffling up Such a God: The Rhetorical Agon of Milton's Antiprelatical Tracts." *Milton Studies* 21 (1985):3-33.

Milton's antiprelatical tracts are characterized by their conflict between rational argumentative purpose and the vivid language that illuminates it, disrupts it, and exercises a rhetorical tyranny over it. In these works, Milton shifts between two rhetorics: that of the temporal world of "polemical activity and 'clubbing quotations'" (5) and that of truth, revealed through the free use of images. Although he wants the images of the moral realm to gain authority from their relationship, their power actually comes from their sensuous nature. They overwhelm the argument. Because Milton cannot separate or reconcile the realms of fact and truth, and the modes they imply, the tracts display a rhetorical agon with no victor.

934   CAMPBELL, GORDON. "*De Doctrina Christiana*: Its Structural Principles and Its Unfinished State." *Milton Studies* 9 (1976):243-60.

Christian Doctrine represents Milton's attempt to create a systematic exposition of Christian teaching, systematized according to the method proposed in *Art of Logic*, which includes such Ramist principles as a dichotomous structure and formal transitions. This process of systematization remains incomplete. The chaotic state of Book 1, chapters 29-33, where the use of dichotomies and transitions breaks down, indicates that the work is unfinished. Milton probably intends to write a work with a ten-part division, but he never revises one of the sections.

935   CAMPBELL, GORDON. "Milton's *Accedence Commenc't Grammar*." *Milton Quarterly* 10 (1976):39-48.

Although it implements the initial stages of the principles outlined in *Art of Logic*, Milton's *Accedence Commenc't Grammar* omits a discussion of the parts of a word, so his endorsement of Ramist methods is qualified. Milton's grammar book opposes the contemporary trend of learning language by reading and defies the traditional scholastic kind of grammar book constructed on Lily's method. Milton believes in learning a language through the Ramist principles of the art of grammar.

936　CONKLIN, GEORGE NEWTON. *Biblical Criticism and Heresy in Milton.* New York: Columbia University, King's Crown Press, 1949, 148 pp.

　　A revolution in biblical interpretation replaces the medieval emphasis on allegory and mystic paraphrase with a sacred philology. Milton's deviations from orthodoxy derive from the philological approach (combined with liberal Puritan hermeneutics) rather than from patristic, Renaissance, or rabbinical sources. Milton's hermeneutics is based solely on the doctrine of Scripture. In *Christian Doctrine*, "Divine revelation alone by perusal of Scripture, dependent upon neither the faith nor judgment of any other is the axiom of method" (31). The Socinians' exegesis comes closest to Milton's in terms of heresies, but his adherence to divine guidance deviates from their ideas. He knows enough Hebrew to be a good general scholar but no more. Medieval rabbinical exegesis has a very doubtful relevance to Milton studies. Milton finds philological authority for denying creation *ex nihilo* and for affirming the soul's mortality.

937　CORNS, THOMAS N. *The Development of Milton's Prose Style.* Oxford: Clarendon Press, 1982, 132 pp.

　　In the antiprelatical tracts (1641-42), Milton's use of synonyms produces a large vocabulary, while his final tracts (1659-73) repeat words or word groups and thus have a smaller vocabulary. His prose, like that of his contemporaries, incorporates many neologisms, though neologisms, especially those of foreign origin, are perhaps more frequent in his early prose. There is no evidence that Milton uses Latinate words to recall their etymological meanings. His early tracts reveal a wit and sparkle that distinguish them from contemporary tracts and his later ones. Milton's sentence structure, even with its peculiarities, is not remarkable in light of contemporary practice. His early prose uses more imagery than do works by his contemporaries and his later prose. In many areas of style, *Ready and Easy Way* is atypical of Milton's late prose. As a prose stylist, Milton moves from being a flamboyant, innovative writer to a plain-style writer.

938　CORNS, THOMAS N. "Milton's Quest for Respectability." *Modern Language Review* 77 (1982):769-79.

　　Polemicists who favor a centrally determined ecclesiastical doctrine and discipline create an archetype of the opposing sectary.

397

Criticism

Though his enemies seek to smear Milton by associating him with radical groups in the 1640s, he does not deny the association but discusses the sectaries only in ambiguous terms. According to Milton, the sects are a necessary prelude to the spiritual revolution he predicts, but--after the reformation is accomplished--the sects will disappear. He uses this polemical strategy to reach orthodox Puritans who hold power and to give his support for a temporary toleration for heterodox views that he shares. In *Colasterion*, Milton meets his opponents' strategy by presenting himself not as a wild sectary but as a man of quality. He continues to distance himself from the sectaries in *Judgement of Martin Bucer* and *Poems* (1645).

939 DUHAMEL, P. ALBERT. "Milton's Alleged Ramism." *PMLA* 67 (1952):1035-53.

 While Ramism distrusts the human thought processes and stresses the simple, intuitive perception of logical relations, Milton's rationalism frequently deviates from Ramist logic. Ramus's *Dialectic* presents principles and examples, bridged only by the reader's intuition, but Milton's *Art of Logic* inserts explanations of the principles. Furthermore, Milton adds examples, again showing his movement away from intuition and toward artificial or Aristotelian logic. Milton's conception of art and definition of what constitutes an argument are also closer to Aristotle's. When discussing the parts of logic, Milton disagrees with Ramus. Milton's argumentative method in his prose works, especially when he uses syllogistic techniques, never implies an agreement with Ramus's definition of logical reasoning.

940 DUVALL, ROBERT F. "Time, Place, Persons: The Background for Milton's *Of Reformation.*" *Studies in English Literature, 1500-1900* 7 (1967):107-18.

 Milton's Puritanism is closely related to his efforts as a prose writer who seeks reformation. If *Of Reformation*'s roots appear in Foxe's work, its immediate context is the religious revolution of the 1640s; Milton's idea of the future is contained in a vision of a reformed English Commonwealth.

Prose

941   EGAN, JAMES. *The Inward Teacher: Milton's Rhetoric of Christian Liberty*. Seventeenth-Century News Editions and Studies, vol. 2. University Park: Pennsylvania State University, 1980, 103 pp.

Attentive to the genres of his prose works, Milton uses the oration, disputation, history, and homiletic forms, moving in each from logical to affective arguments and from public to personal rhetorical stances. Ciceronian rhetoric serves Christian prophecy in *Areopagitica* and *Tenure of Kings and Magistrates*, which are deliberative orations intended to promote different kinds of liberty. In *History of Britain*, Milton's plain, neutral style, with which he relates the events of his country's past, is accompanied by increasingly complex statements of moral evaluation that illustrate the intervention of providence into human events. Milton transforms the academic debate form of disputation in *Of Prelatical Episcopacy* and *Tetrachordon*, where he uses dialectic to create antitheses from which the reader must choose. The plain style dominates in *Treatise of Civil Power*, *Likeliest Means To Remove Hirelings*, and *Ready and Easy Way*.

942   EKFELT, FRED EMIL. "The Graphic Diction of Milton's English Prose." *Philological Quarterly* 25 (1946):46-69.

Milton's prose style develops from his low opinion of pamphleteering. In the English pamphlets, he takes his sub-poetic diction from such varied sources as slang, Elizabethan English (for archaisms and dialect words), and "unbookish borrowings from French, Dutch, and German" (47). The graphic words of daily experience contribute most to the style of Milton's English prose. If *Paradise Lost*'s poetry is elevated and Milton's prose is low, certain minor poems--*Comus*, *Lycidas*, and the Hobson poems--occupy a middle ground and use graphic diction. Such prose works as *Areopagitica*, *Apology*, and *Animadversions* use graphic diction to make generalizations concrete. Milton's prose style develops from opulent in *Of Reformation* to the more economical diction of later tracts.

943   EVANS, JOHN X. "Imagery as Argument in Milton's *Areopagitica*." *Texas Studies in Literature and Language* 8 (1966):189-205.

Essential to the development of *Areopagitica*'s argument, images of life and death, health and illness through food, commerce, the military, and light and dark form a rhetorical structure.

Criticism

944 FINK, Z. S. "The Theory of the Mixed State and the Development of
     Milton's Political Thought." *PMLA* 57 (1942):705-36.
         Articulated by Polybius, the idea of a mixed or balanced state,
     in which democratic, aristocratic, and monarchial elements share
     power, is influential in Milton's England. In *Of Reformation*, Milton
     sees his country as having such a mixed constitution--made up of the
     people, an aristocracy of virtuous men, and a king--though it is being
     corrupted by the power of the episcopacy. Milton attempts for many
     years to reconcile the idea of a return to old English principles and an
     imitation of classical mixed states. When this reconciliation fails, he
     tries to combine the ideas of mixed state and popular sovereignty, but--
     as he becomes disillusioned with Cromwell, Parliament, and the
     people--he never believes that his goal has been attained. *Ready and
     Easy Way* presents Milton's most fully developed ideas about
     restructuring government to form a mixed state.

945 FIRTH, C. H. "Milton as an Historian." *Proceedings of the British
     Academy* 3 (1907-8):227-57. Reprinted in *Essays Historical and
     Literary* (Oxford: Clarendon Press, 1938), pp. 61-102.
         Long interested in British history, Milton is unsure about
     whether to write an epic or dramatic poem. When he writes *History of
     Britain*, he is initially more concerned with story telling than with the
     truth of events. Holinshed's *Chronicles* is an important source for
     History of Britain, though Milton's independent mind dismisses some
     assertions and theories made by chroniclers. He exercises skepticism
     about King Arthur and the events of Arthur's age, and he combines and
     compares the statements of many authorities. *History* is a work of real
     research, but the style of the early sections is more polished than that of
     the later ones. Milton's prejudices become apparent when he discusses
     women or church matters.

946 FISH, STANLEY E. "Reason in *The Reason of Church
     Government*." In *Self-Consuming Artifacts: The Experience of
     Seventeenth-Century Literature*. Berkeley, Los Angeles, and London:
     University of California Press, 1972, pp. 265-302.
         While asserting the value of rational processes, *Reason of
     Church-Government* simultaneously asks the reader to recognize the
     superfluity of reason in a discussion of spiritual matters. The treatise's
     rhetorical strategy forces the reader to choose where no choice is

possible: either one does not heed the direction of Christian belief or one finds self-evident the assertion that presbyters and deacons, rather than prelates, should run church government. Because the tract never moves from this position, the experience of reading it is a static one. Reason is associated with prelacy, and both are subverted in favor of a higher wisdom. Outwardly, the treatise presents reasoned arguments; in fact, it merely makes points that some readers recognize they have always known to be true. *Reason of Church-Government* is not written to change minds, but to validate certain people's true vision.

947 FLETCHER, HARRIS FRANCIS. *The Use of the Bible in Milton's Prose.* University of Illinois Studies in Language and Literature, vol. 14, no. 3. Urbana: University of Illinois, 1929, 176 pp. Reprint. New York: Haskell House, 1970.

Excluding *Christian Doctrine*, which contains over 7,000 references to Latin biblical passages, Milton's prose contains about 500 citations or quotations of scriptural origin. He uses Scripture in four ways: he gives citations without quotations; he uses Scripture but does not indicate the material's origin; he quotes in English and follows a specific text, usually the King James Version; and he quotes but the wording differs from any recognized text. Milton has an extensive knowledge of the original texts of the Old and New Testaments. In *Christian Doctrine*, he almost always relies on the Junius-Tremellius Latin text for quotations. Before going blind, Milton feels free to alter scriptural passages as he quotes them; but after losing his sight, he has to depend on an amanuensis, so there are far fewer alterations.

Fletcher prints a chronological list of biblical citations in Milton's works published during his lifetime; an index of biblical quotations and citations in the prose works (except *Christian Doctrine*); and an index of quotations and citations in *Christian Doctrine*.

948 FOGLE, FRENCH R. "Milton as Historian." In *Milton and Clarendon.* Two Papers on Seventeenth Century English Historiography Presented at a Seminar Held at the Clark Library, 12 December 1964, by French R. Fogle and H. R. Trevor-Roper. [Los Angeles]: William Andrews Clark Memorial Library, University of California, Los Angeles, 1965, pp. 1-20.

Milton studies history extensively because he feels it provides the best preparation for his work as poet or pamphleteer. Classical

Criticism

writers give him models for style and manner; Christian writers teach him that history's purpose is to show the providential design in human events. Although Milton thinks he sees God's plan during the 1640s, and the final ends are always clear to him, many disappointments reveal that intermediate ends are not predictable. For Milton, history is more important as an art than as a science, so his search for general truths leads him to be uncritical in his handling of primary materials. He uses few of the new historical methods and materials available to him. *History of Britain* is structured according to a moral pattern of divine reward and punishment that follows no steady progression.

949   FRENCH, J. MILTON. "Milton as a Historian." *PMLA* 50 (1935):469-79.
        A reluctant poet, Milton finds verse writing difficult; his mind tends naturally toward prose criticism. He also turns to prose for other reasons: poetry is held in low esteem in his age; he is absorbed in study; and his critical powers are growing. *History of Britain* shows his skeptical spirit, scholarly precision, and concern with material that is accurate rather than merely interesting. Milton writes a poem of the creation only after he ceases to believe in Arthur and other fabulous characters. His mind remains "essentially critical rather than creative" (476). For many years, he feels the lure of the world and its controversies. His blindness forces him to turn back to himself and his creative abilities.

950   FRENCH, J. MILTON. "Milton as Satirist." *PMLA* 51 (1936):414-29.
        A good conversationalist who enjoys a jest, Milton defends the use of satire in such works as *Apology for Smectymnuus* and *Animadversions*. His satiric abuse of opponents takes the form of epithets, irony, and puns. Satire allows the author certain prerogatives, so we should recognize, and not apologize for, Milton's accomplishments in this vein. In the history of satire, Milton is an important figure.

951   GILBERT, ALLAN H. "Milton on the Position of Woman." *Modern Language Review* 15 (1920):7-27, 240-64.

Arguing that man is generally the head of the household, with woman subordinate, Milton grants the female some independence. Marriage exists for the mutual benefit of husband and wife. In Milton's view, mental and emotional satisfaction is more important than physical satisfaction in marriage, so incompatibility is grounds for divorce. The wife has the same rights as the husband with respect to divorce, though --as a male--Milton often speaks from the husband's perspective. His prose illuminates his poetry, for these views of how men and women treat each other are exemplified in *Samson Agonistes* and *Paradise Lost*. Given her nature, Dalila cannot be a true wife; she is treacherous, and only when Samson rejects her is he free. As the male, Adam is superior to and more rational than Eve, so when they fall his sin is greater.

952 GILMAN, WILBUR ELWYN. *Milton's Rhetoric: Studies in His Defense of Liberty*. University of Missouri Studies, vol. 14, no. 3. Columbia: University of Missouri, 1939, 193 pp. Reprint. New York: Phaeton Press, 1970.

Areopagitica follows a classical structure and uses a deductive method of argument, which mixes logical and emotional appeals. Lacking rhetorical incentive and subordinating its logical proofs, *Of Education* is another work of deduction, but its method is to compare and contrast traditional educational practices with those advocated by the humanists. *Of Reformation* uses logical proofs, deliberative rhetoric, and a tripartite structure of inductive proof, statement of proposition, and deductive proof. *Of Civil Power* states its key proposition early and supports it with deliberative rhetoric and logical proof based on scriptural citations. *Tenure of Kings and Magistrates*, another example of deliberative rhetoric, presents an elaborate logical argument to justify the punishment of King Charles. Organized according to classical divisions, *Ready and Easy Way* uses both deduction and induction to assert two points: a monarchy is undesirable; a commonwealth is feasible. In all six pamphlets, Milton employs the principles of classical rhetoric.

953 HALKETT, JOHN. *Milton and the Idea of Matrimony: A Study of the Divorce Tracts and "Paradise Lost."* Yale Studies in English, 173. New Haven, Conn., and London: Yale University Press, 1970, 171 pp.

Criticism

Milton's divorce tracts spring primarily from the objective purpose of arguing for a cause or defining the nature of marriage, which he does according to his Puritan religious training as well as his reading of Plato and Spenser. In *Doctrine and Discipline of Divorce*, his view of marriage differs from that of many previous writers: though he claims an affinity with them, Milton rearranges the objectives of marriage to become religious, social, and physical companionship. Earlier authors emphasize the last aspect. More than any other writer on the subject, Milton stresses mutual solace in marriage and describes an unfit mate as being spiritually or mentally unclean. His argument for divorce contains the two traditional concepts of feminine virtue, compliance (passive) and helpfulness (active), though he emphasizes the latter. We can apply the divorce tracts' definitions of marriage to Adam and Eve's relationship in *Paradise Lost*.

954 HALLER, WILLIAM. "Before *Areopagitica*." *PMLA* 42 (1927):875-900.

London tracts published in 1644, immediately before *Areopagitica* appears, argue for freedom with respect to thought, discussion, printing, and religious and secular matters, a view to which *Areopagitica* has little to add. All of the authors of these tracts, including Milton, want to win freedom because it is a prerequisite for other achievements that they anticipate. Like others, Milton does not want to hand authority over to the Presbyterian Westminster Assembly, whose members oppose toleration and seek to control the public's thinking. *Areopagitica* restates the principle of free conscience as it is articulated by Henry Robinson, John Goodwin, and others. Apparently, few people paid any attention to Milton's tract.

955 HALLER, WILLIAM. "'For the Liberty of Unlicenc'd Printing.'" *American Scholar* 14 (1945):326-33.

Though Milton has no reason to fear that his opponents will invoke the recently adopted printing ordinance against him or his cause, he writes *Areopagitica* to tell Parliament that the flow of printed material permanently alters the conditions under which the English government must operate. Rigid enforcement of censorship is impossible, and the contemporary religious revolution points to the reading of a book as the key spiritual experience in an individual's life.

For some time, England has already enjoyed extensive liberty of the press, a freedom Milton wants the state to implement.

956 HANNAY, MARGARET. "Milton's Doctrine of the Holy Scriptures." *Christian Scholar's Review* 5 (1976):339-49.

According to Milton's doctrine of Scripture, expressed in *Christian Doctrine*, salvation is a matter for the individual rather than the church. One's knowledge, not that of professional scholars, leads one to interpret the Bible by using Christian charity as a guide. A reader of the Bible must recognize that God accommodates truth to our understanding, work in the original languages, keep each passage in context, and distinguish the literal from the figurative. The Spirit of God works in the Christian's heart to guide interpretation and prevent deception. See entries 12, 25, 166, 176.

957 HENRY, NATHANIEL H. "Milton's Last Pamphlet: Theocracy and Intolerance." In *A Tribute to George Coffin Taylor*. Edited by Arnold Williams. [Chapel Hill]: University of North Carolina Press, 1952, pp. 197-210.

Of True Religion argues only for limited toleration, primarily for Milton's own party. Written to protest Charles II's Declaration of Home Policy (1672), which is seen as a subterfuge for giving toleration to Catholics, Milton's tract is consistent with all of his thinking after 1640, particularly after *Of Civil Power* (1659). He argues for Protestant intellectualism in *Of True Religion*, which presents no more restrictions than does *Areopagitica*.

958 HOFFMAN, RICHARD L. "The Rhetorical Structure of Milton's *Second Defence of the People of England.*" *Studia Neophilologica* 43 (1971):227-45.

Second Defence fits the formal classical pattern of oratory, though not as strictly as *Areopagitica* does. According to Quintilian's classifications, *Second Defence* is a laudatory or demonstrative oration, which praises the famous (the Commonwealth government) and blames the wicked (Salmasius and More). If Salmasius and More face Milton as counselors in a lawsuit, Milton defends the accused English people and Cromwell, and the learned populace of Europe acts as judge. The tract is thus also a forensic or judicial oration. Seeking to win a friendly

Criticism

hearing, Milton's exordium takes on some functions of the narration, which follows it and states the facts of the case. Then come the partition, showing how the orator will treat the case; the refutation, the longest section, with digressions on Bradshaw and Fairfax and a panegyric on Cromwell; and the peroration, a deliberative oration that offers advice to the citizens of England.

959 HUGHES, MERRITT Y. "The Historical Setting of Milton's *Observations* on the *Articles of Peace*, 1649." *PMLA* 64 (1949):1049-73.

Responding to the royalist support offered by Charles's lord lieutenant in Ireland through an agreement with the Catholic Confederacy of Kilkenny, Parliament orders Milton to prepare *Observations* on the *Articles of Peace* and other documents. Milton expresses resentment about the Confederates' threat to English sovereignty, for the *Articles of Peace* appear to be no more than "articles of treasonable surrender" (1052). Ironically, Milton uses the principles of religious toleration to attack the lord lieutenant, Catholicism, and Presbyterianism.

960 HUGHES, MERRITT Y. "Milton's Treatment of Reformation History in *The Tenure of Kings and Magistrates*." In *The Seventeenth Century: Studies in the History of English Thought and Literature from Bacon to Pope*. By Richard Foster Jones, et al. Stanford, Calif.: Stanford University Press, 1951, pp. 247-63. Reprinted in *Ten Perspectives on Milton* (New Haven, Conn., and London: Yale University Press, 1965), pp. 220-39.

The first edition of *Tenure of Kings and Magistrates* says little about Reformation history, but Milton promises to marshal authorities in another edition to prove the legality of resisting a tyrant in defense of liberty. In *Tenure*'s second edition, he adds an appendix, which contains quotations from various reformers, as a response to the Presbyterian position that Scripture does not sanction tyrannicide and to the broader Protestant view that the regicides are traitors to the Reformation heritage. Milton's use of evidence from Luther, Paraeus, Calvin, and Bucer gives fair representation to their ideas about resisting unworthy kings.

961 HUGUELET, THEODORE L. "The Rule of Charity in Milton's Divorce Tracts." *Milton Studies* 6 (1974):199-214.

In his divorce tracts, Milton needs a clear hermeneutic principle with which to show that Christ, in Matthew 5:31-32 and 19:8-9, does not uncharitably deny all hope of remarriage after divorce or divorce based on mental incompatibility alone. This principle, the rule of charity, is intended to correct centuries of biblical misinterpretation. Although the rule of charity appears in works by Augustine, Erasmus, Calvin, Zanchius, Bullinger, and Grotius, it is essentially Milton's own concept. With the help not of specific sources but the Ramist method, Milton arrives at this principle.

962 HUNTER, WILLIAM B., Jr. "Milton's Arianism Reconsidered." *Harvard Theological Review* 52 (1959):9-35. Reprinted in *Bright Essence: Studies in Milton's Theology*, by W[illiam] B. Hunter, C. A. Patrides, and J. H. Adamson (Salt Lake City: University of Utah Press, 1971), pp. 29-51.

Although the appearance of *Christian Doctrine* in 1825 leads many critics to reread *Paradise Lost* and find heresies, Milton's work never supports Arius and, while Milton knows that his conception of the Son is unusual, he does not seem to acknowledge that he is advancing heretical views. He never denies Christ's divinity, but he does see the Son as different from and inferior to the Father and as generated at the beginning of creation. Agreeing with Philo and Tertullian, Milton asserts that God freely wills the creation of the Son. Milton uses "beget" and "create" as synonyms because the Greek words for these terms are identical. His views of the Trinity are similar to those of such Cambridge Platonists as Henry More and Ralph Cudworth, though there are also some disagreements. Milton is no Arian. See entries 483, 967-68, 989-90.

963 HUNTER, WILLIAM B., Jr. "The Theological Context of Milton's *Christian Doctrine*." In *Achievements of the Left Hand: Essays on the Prose of John Milton*. Edited by Michael Lieb and John T. Shawcross. Amherst: University of Massachusetts Press, 1974, pp. 269-87.

In the latter part of the 1650s, Milton develops his theological outline of biblical texts into *Christian Doctrine* as we know it. Written in Latin, *Christian Doctrine* is addressed to "members of the various

Criticism

branches of the Reformed or Calvinistic churches" (270), particularly on the Continent, in an attempt to unify these groups and bring them into harmony with Milton's own branch of Independency. Patterned after works by reformed scholastics, *Christian Doctrine*'s structural framework, the first part concerned with faith and the second with works, indicates that Milton expects to find readers in centers of Calvinistic orthodoxy. His use of biblical proof texts also shows that he is addressing the French school of Saumur as well as the reformed scholastics. Milton's subordinationist views are indebted to Episcopius, de Courcelles, and the school of Amsterdam. In his views on Christology, Milton is an Arminian, though he disagrees with that theology in many other areas.

964   HUNTLEY, JOHN F. *"Proairesis, Synteresis,* and the Ethical Orientation of Milton's *Of Education." Philological Quarterly* 43 (1964):40-46.
     When Milton refers to ethics or *proairesis* in *Of Education*, he means a conscious operation of the mind that one performs to some degree by nature and that can be developed through education. It refers not to good habits of moral judgment but to "the incipient capacity for contemplating moral choice" with judgment (41). He significantly avoids the concept of *synteresis*, which refers to the dictates of conscience. In Milton's age, the term *proairesis*, which applies to Christians and pagans, is rarely used, while *synteresis*, applied only to Christians, appears frequently. Milton's emphasis is thus on the rational and moral rather than the disciplinary and pietistic.

965   HUNTLEY, JOHN F. "The Images of Poet and Poetry in Milton's *The Reason of Church-Government."* In *Achievements of the Left Hand: Essays on the Prose of John Milton.* Edited by Michael Lieb and John T. Shawcross. Amherst: University of Massachusetts Press, 1974, pp. 83-120.
     The Preface to Book 2 of *Reason of Church-Government*, in which Milton discusses poetry, is an ethical proof for the main argument. Developing from a young man at the tract's outset, the narrator becomes a spokesman for rationality and knowledge; in the final chapters, he finds his prophetic voice. His reader is also elevated as the oration proceeds. Placed at the argument's midpoint, the discussion of poetry balances the carefully structured work, which

moves from church government's general theory in Book 1 to its specific operation in Book 2, each book posing two questions and providing two answers about ecclesiastical administration. In 1642, Milton thinks of poetry in allegorical and moral terms, seeing its affinities with sermons and histories. But his thinking evolves before he turns to his three major poems: he eventually recognizes only a small audience; indicates that saving truth comes from within rather than from above; abandons seductive eloquence (such as rhyme); and redefines appropriate subjects to include biblical matters while making each poem maintain its fictive character. Finally, in 1659, Milton views the religious teacher not in terms of formal preparation but in a simpler role.

966   ILLO, JOHN. "The Misreading of Milton." *Columbia University Forum* 8 (1965):38-42. Reprinted in *Radical Perspectives in the Arts*, ed. Lee Baxandall (Harmondsworth and Baltimore, Md.: Penguin Books, 1972), pp. 178-92.

For three centuries, many people's approval or disapproval of *Areopagitica* has been based on their misunderstanding of it. The tract does not call for complete freedom of expression or popular liberty. Rather than pointing to a judicial forum of learned Athenians, the work's title alludes to the Areopagus's role, by the time of Aeschylus, of controlling the private and public lives of all Athenians. Milton believes that book printing should be supervised, preferably by regenerate Protestants, so dissenting counter-revolutionary ideas can be suppressed. He advocates revolutionary censorship.

967   KELLEY, MAURICE. "Milton and the Trinity." *Huntington Library Quarterly* 33 (1970):315-20.

Referring not only to followers of Arius's views, Arianism can mean any rejection of orthodox Trinitarianism, which is a definition Milton uses and a position he holds. *Christian Doctrine* does not present a two-stage conception of the Logos, an unorthodox position even if Milton were to accept it. In the last period of his life, after about 1658, Milton consistently takes an anti-Trinitarian stand in *Christian Doctrine*, *Art of Logic*, *Of True Religion*, and *Paradise Lost*. *Christian Doctrine* is clearly an Arian document. See entries 483, 962, 968, 989-90.

Criticism

968   KELLEY, MAURICE. "Milton's Arianism Again Considered."
      Harvard Theological Review 54 (1961):195-205.
            Contrary to Hunter's argument (see entry 962), Milton's views
      on the Trinity, as expressed in *Christian Doctrine*, do not agree with the
      Nicene Creed. The Creed states that the Father and Son are of the
      same essence and that there was never a time when the Son did not
      exist, but Milton follows Arius in disagreeing. Milton belongs with
      those who are anathematized in the concluding part of the Creed.
      Rather than restricting Arianism to refer only to the immediate
      followers of Arius, we should define it as a kind of anti-Trinitarianism
      that is still closer to orthodoxy than are Socinianism and Unitarianism.
      Milton is an Arian, though anti-Trinitarian is a more precise term for
      his doctrine. From the time Milton starts composing *Paradise Lost*, in
      about 1655, and *Christian Doctrine* in about 1658, until *Of True
      Religion*'s appearance in 1673, his views on the Son do not change.
      Christian Doctrine illuminates our understanding of the Trinity in
      Paradise Lost, and both works are anti-Trinitarian. See entries 483, 967,
      989-90.

969   KELLEY, MAURICE. *This Great Argument: A Study of Milton's
      "De Doctrina Christiana" as a Gloss upon "Paradise Lost."* Princeton
      Studies in English, vol. 22. Princeton, N.J.: Princeton University
      Press, 1941, 283 pp. Reprint. Gloucester, Mass.: Peter Smith, 1962.
            Christian Doctrine's manuscript shows that the work existed in
      two states: relying on a fair copy, Jeremie Picard wrote out the basic
      version in ca. 1658-ca. 1660, just before or during the period when
      Milton dictated *Paradise Lost*, and in the following years Daniel
      Skinner was the scribe for Milton's revisions, which were minor (usually
      adding documentation or clarifying a point). From start to finish, there
      is no essential change in dogma in *Christian Doctrine*. A study of
      parallel passages demonstrates that *Paradise Lost*'s dogma agrees with
      that of *Christian Doctrine*: despite its introduction of fictional material,
      the epic frequently offers a concrete and poetic rendering of concepts
      found in Milton's systematic theology.

970   KEPLINGER, ANN. "Milton: Polemics, Epic, and the Woman
      Problem, Again." *Cithara* 10 (1971):40-52.
            Milton's divorce tracts turn doctrine and history (sacred,
      British, and personal) into polemics and satire, and his views of the

relationship between man and woman mark the climax of humanistic-Reformation thought, while heralding a new rationalistic approach to social relationships and morals. For his contemporaries, Milton wishes to recapture the husband-wife relationship of the Old Testament and the male-female experience of Eden. The liberal Hebraic view stresses the unity or wholeness of man-woman and the subjectivity in their relationship, and thus sees no need for a particular cause to terminate it. Milton's polemic contains a double standard, in which the bulk of humanity, but not Milton or his intelligent readers, will break the natural law and God's law. In Book 4 of *Paradise Lost*, Milton uses many of the polemical tactics that appear in the divorce tracts.

971 KIRBY, R. KENNETH. "Milton's Biblical Hermeneutics in *The Doctrine and Discipline of Divorce.*" *Milton Quarterly* 18 (1984):116-25.

Christ's remark about divorce in Matthew 19 forces Milton to develop a new system of hermeneutics, the rule of charity, according to which no New Testament precept can regulate happiness more strictly than do Old Testament precepts. By the second edition of *Doctrine and Discipline of Divorce*, Milton emphasizes human reason over scriptural prescription as a guide to human good. He probably is not aware of taking liberties with his own interpretive principles in order to make the argument work.

972 KRANIDAS, THOMAS. *The Fierce Equation: A Study of Milton's Decorum*. Studies in English Literature, vol. 10. The Hague, London, and Paris: Mouton, 1965, 165 pp. Part reprinted in *On Milton's Poetry*, ed. Arnold Stein (Greenwich, Conn.: Fawcett Publications, 1970), pp. 190-99.

In his antiprelatical tracts, Milton adjusts the intensity of his language to fit the situation; he thus can be scurrilous, retain decorum, and seek to glorify God. Decorum, in the form of harmony and unity, is one of the themes of these tracts, as Milton argues against the excesses of language, tradition, and the body. His divorce tracts share the antiprelatical works' emphasis on decorum as the highest unity as well as their assault on its opposites. Both *First* and *Second Defence* find a decorum in the congruity of the revolutionaries' characters, words, deeds, and situation. *Paradise Lost*'s clearest vision of order, unity, and harmony appears in heaven. With its decreasing stature, Satan's

Criticism

character fits the decorum of consistency. Because God is not a person, the requirements of the decorum of a consistent personality do not apply to him.

973 KRANIDAS, THOMAS. "Milton's *Of Reformation*: The Politics of Vision." *ELH* 49 (1982):497-513.
    Before 1641, Milton transforms literary genres and personal experience to make them appropriate to his role as "the emerging great poet" (497). Then he defers his progress by returning from Italy and writing *Of Reformation*, which attempts to merge history and his career, his Christian vocation as a poet and the deferral of that vocation by writing prose. Exhausting and exploding its genre, *Of Reformation* fuses politics and vision as Milton's images present the interaction and final confluence of history and eternity. The tract moves horizontally through a survey of history, but vertically in the descent of God and ascent to vision. Although there is an apparent tension between these motions, they are identical and both conclude in the apocalyptic vision of God. Reason in *Of Reformation* must surrender to faith at the moment of enlightenment.

974 KRANIDAS, THOMAS. "Polarity and Structure in Milton's *Areopagitica*." *English Literary Renaissance* 14 (1984):175-90.
    Besides using a deliberative oratorical structure, *Areopagitica* follows a second structure based on polarization and subsumption. The English Commonwealth is the heir of Greek intellectual liberty and the opponent of Roman repression, to which Milton attaches the prelacy. He often appropriates his adversaries' images for Puritan controversy and turns them against his opponents.

975 KRANIDAS, THOMAS. "Style and Rectitude in Seventeenth-Century Prose: Hall, Smectymnuus, and Milton." *Huntington Library Quarterly* 46 (1983):237-69.
    Animadversions contains two stylistic lines, peevish and sublime, and a rational, patterned argument in which the personal "digressions" are appropriate. If Milton establishes himself as righteous, his opponent, Bishop Hall, cultivates the image of a gentle "authoritative peacemaker" (239), though his invective can be quite sharp. Each author uses style to express rectitude: Hall is a standard

and elegant edition of truth, the established text; Milton is a living text, his *Animadversions* an organism that feeds on old and new ideas. Seeking to expose and eliminate the danger that Hall poses, Milton finds a style to suit this opponent. By accurately quoting and paraphrasing Hall's books, Milton in effect places all of the evidence-- Hall's and Milton's arguments--before the reader, who can freely study and judge. Milton defines this pamphlet war as a battle between his persona and Hall's.

976 LEWALSKI, BARBARA KIEFER. "Milton: Political Beliefs and Polemical Methods, 1659-60." *PMLA* 74 (1959):191-202.

At the close of the Interregnum, England's political scene is chaotic. Milton's political arguments and models for government are varied, even contradictory, because they reflect and adapt to the confusion around him. He supports the Protectorate, then denounces it and praises the Rump Parliament; next he praises the army that deposes the Rump and then calls for the Rump's return. He proposes two apparently contradictory theories of government: in one, a worthy minority forms a ruling aristocracy; in the other, the people have the right to choose and alter their government. Always based on practical considerations, his political thought still emerges from principles, including the preservation of religious and civil liberty and the rule of a virtuous aristocracy. Unlike the millenarians, Milton argues that the virtuous have political privilege, but that--while the regenerate manifest these virtues--they are attainable by natural man.

977 LEWALSKI, BARBARA KIEFER. "Milton on Learning and the Learned-Ministry Controversy." *Huntington Library Quarterly* 24 (1961):267-81.

Addressing the issue of tithes and ministers' learning (the former compensates preachers for the latter), *Likeliest Means To Remove Hirelings* argues both for a ministry dependent on personal illumination rather than learning (the position of the left, which includes Quakers, Baptists, and Fifth Monarchists) and for a learned ministry (the Presbyterian position). Milton's contradictory views may be based on two kinds of human learning: it may mean "the subject matter of the arts, sciences, and philosophies" (278), which are useless to anyone seeking spiritual knowledge; or it may refer to the methods, such as languages and textual analysis, that can be applied usefully to

Criticism

Scripture and that schools should teach. Like the Accommodating Independents, a centrist group, Milton in the late 1650s does not doubt the value of a secular university education to deal with matters of the natural order, though it is useless for matters of grace.

978 LIMOUZE, HENRY S. "Joseph Hall and the Prose Style of John Milton." *Milton Studies* 15 (1981):121-41.

Milton's battle with Hall is more than a match between Ciceronian and Senecan styles: Hall's style and argumentative technique manipulate readers to assume the author's position, while Milton distances us so we become judges. Milton does not dictate to us as we make decisions. Through stylistic parody, he exposes Hall.

979 LIMOUZE, HENRY S. "'The Surest Suppressing': Writer and Censor in Milton's *Areopagitica*." *Centennial Review* 24 (1980):103-17.

If Milton in *Areopagitica* appears to contradict himself by advocating toleration and then restricting its beneficiaries in a move toward anti-toleration, this occurs because he is deliberately vague about stating alternatives and clarifying limits. The image of a "mortal glass wherein we contemplate" is paradoxical and requires a moral choice for we decide whether to limit the search for truth in a mirror (ourselves) or through a telescope (which takes us outward to "the utmost prospect"). Public forces must not interfere with the individual's private acts of discovery. Joining the public and private spheres by writing and printing words, an author should not be hindered as he sends truth forward. Regulation must be an internal force, a liberating act of the author's private authority over the self. Milton in *Areopagitica* attempts to engage our interior censor by making us use it on this very treatise.

980 McGUIRE, MARY ANN. "'A Most Just Vituperation': Milton's Christian Orator in *Pro Se Defensio*." *Studies in the Literary Imagination* 10 (1977):105-14.

Shunning a lukewarm approach and the Anglican *via media*, Puritan polemicists use abusive language when castigating opponents. Milton's *Pro Se Defensio* belongs in this Puritan tradition. As the tract progresses, Milton slowly reveals More's evil character and his persona's personality, which is initially virtuous but fallible and in need of enlightenment. The persona thus allows readers to identify with him, and he soon realizes that his conflict with More is a psychomachia or holy war that calls for an adherence to one's cause and a Christian response to the enemy's evil. Vituperation suits the decorum of Milton's persona and the treatise's context.

981 MACK, JESSE F. "The Evolution of Milton's Political Thinking." *Sewanee Review* 30 (1922):193-205.

Not characterized by consistency or steady maturing, Milton's political thought evolves as events change. But liberty, as an energizing force, is always the key word for him. Milton starts as a moderate constitutionalist. When he publishes *Areopagitica*, he believes the nation can reform everything from intellectual and political theories to morality. *Tenure of Kings and Magistrates* shows Milton's attraction to Republicanism, but not the most radical kind. He still does not despise the monarchy itself. With the next tracts, *Eikonoklastes* and *First Defence*, comes Milton's disillusionment, for the people do not deserve to have responsibility. So he turns to radical Republicanism and breaks with the monarchy. In *Ready and Easy Way*, Milton's despair extends to Cromwell's rule. Throughout his career as a pamphlet writer, Milton has the habit, when one idea fails, of suggesting another that is even more impracticable.

982 MELCZER, WILLIAM. "Looking Back without Anger: Milton's *Of Education*." In *Milton and the Middle Ages*. Edited by John Mulryan. Lewisburg, Pa.: Bucknell University Press; London and Toronto: Associated University Presses, 1982, pp. 91-102.

As he greatly reduces the humanist emphasis on man-oriented subjects, except languages, Milton in *Of Education* lets the applied sciences dominate. He also reintroduces theology and, given his emphasis on martial matters, sees education as the final step in the militant Protestant Reformation. If his view of learning is humanistic, it is a highly pragmatic version. Milton's tract has affinities with Comenius's work, particularly in the area of methodology. Milton is influenced by Aristotelianism as the middle ages, not the Renaissance, reinterprets it. The formal elements of his educational scheme come from the Renaissance, while the substance is medieval in origin.

Criticism

983   MINEKA, FRANCIS E. "The Critical Reception of Milton's *De Doctrina Christiana.*" *Studies in English* (Department of English, University of Texas, 1943), 115-47.

When the manuscript of *Christian Doctrine* is discovered in 1823, periodical writers are enthusiastic about its publication, but it causes a "shock to English religious sensibilities" (116) because for 150 years few suspect Milton of holding unorthodox beliefs. While orthodox periodicals express outrage and print refutations of Milton's heterodox views, the unorthodox are delighted by the publication of *Christian Doctrine*. Reviews of Sumner's translation show an unwillingness, which extends well into the nineteenth century, to see any heterodoxy in *Paradise Lost*; evidence of Milton's strong reputation, despite charges of heresy; a new tone in Milton criticism; and the religious and secular periodicals' movement toward the standard view of *Christian Doctrine*.

984   MOHL, RUTH. *John Milton and His "Commonplace Book."* New York: Frederick Ungar, 1969, 341 pp.

Commonplace books form part of a training in logic and rhetoric, giving their compilers evidence from works they read to use in speaking or writing. Although it does not reflect all of his reading, Milton's *Commonplace Book* contains entries from ninety-two authors and about 110 of their works. Milton makes use of his *Commonplace Book*'s three divisions--ethical, economic, and political--in his poetry and prose.

985   MORKAN, JOEL. "Wrath and Laughter: Milton's Ideas on Satire." *Studies in Philology* 69 (1972):475-95.

In his antiprelatical tracts, Milton issues *apologiae* for the use of satire as well as theoretical statements about its nature. Many of his statements are conventional, except that his *apologiae* for satire are heroic and contain direct invocations to God, thus linking "the destructive intentions of his dark rhetoric with the cleansing, apocalyptic fury of the wrathful Lord" (478). In *Animadversions*, he finally sees that satire, which produces an intellectual and wrathful laughter, is compatible with religious virtue. In such works as *Apology* and *Reason of Church-Government*, Milton creates a persona by merging the medieval *vir bonus* and the religious Renaissance satiric speaker. Milton believes that the satirist has a divine mission and that his satire works for religious and social reformation.

986   NEUMANN, JOSHUA H. "Milton's Prose Vocabulary." *PMLA* 60 (1945):102-20.

In such areas as orthography and linguistic change, Milton shows the standardizing and rationalizing tendencies that become apparent in the eighteenth century. In terms of syntax, sentence structure, and vocabulary, however, he displays the Elizabethan sense of versatility and extravagance. His prose vocabulary is not as different from his poetic vocabulary as some scholars suppose. He coins many words, and when he borrows words, he usually turns to Latin or Greek, though his diction is not excessively colored by these languages. He seems to prefer introducing a new native compound instead of a simple borrowing. His prose rarely uses archaisms.

987   PARKER, WILLIAM R. "On Milton's Early Literary Program." *Modern Philology* 33 (1935):49-53.

The famous passage in *Reason of Church-Government* that refers to models for the epic form and heroes is not an assertion of a literary program but Milton's appeal to religious readers. He suggests a religious sanction for the most important literary forms (epic, drama, and ode) and argues that a Christian God provides the poetic gifts of all great pagan authors.

988   PATRICK, J. MAX. "Significant Aspects of the Miltonic State Papers." *Huntington Library Quarterly* 33 (1970):321-30.

Not a policy maker but a clerk-secretary, Milton as Secretary for Foreign Tongues in the 1650s checks, rewords, and translates into Latin papers prepared by others. Of the thousands of such letters addressed to foreign powers, he is connected to about three hundred. One-third of Milton's letters involve routine correspondence. Their rhetoric is often significant because Milton must persuade foreign states of the legitimacy of the Commonwealth government, and the letters "reveal how true to life and how solidly based on realities was the machiavellianism of Milton's Satan" in *Paradise Lost* (325). From the letters, we learn about *Paradise Lost*'s contemporary audience, made up in part of politicians from various social ranks who are knowledgeable about the arts of rhetoric and persuasion. In the state papers, we see Milton's skill in condensing the verbose writing of politicians and in handling details with care.

Criticism

989 PATRIDES, C. A. "Milton and Arianism." *Journal of the History of
    Ideas* 25 (1964):423-29. Reprinted in *Bright Essence: Studies in
    Milton's Theology*, by W[illiam] B. Hunter, C. A. Patrides, and J. H.
    Adamson (Salt Lake City: University of Utah Press, 1971), pp. 63-70.
        Milton agrees with Arius's orthodox idea of the creation as an
    act of God's free will, though he disagrees with every other Arian tenet.
    Milton is a subordinationist. See entries 483, 962, 967-68, 990.

990 PATRIDES, C. A. "Milton and the Arian Controversy; or, Some
    Reflexions on Contextual Settings and the Experience of
    Deuteroscopy." *Proceedings of the American Philosophical Society*
    120 (1976):245-52.
        An arid, scholastic, and inconsistent work, *Christian Doctrine*
    does not illuminate *Paradise Lost* except insofar as Milton's
    dissatisfaction with the solutions he reaches in the prose work leads to
    the poem's fertility. Arianism denies the Son's divinity and separates
    him, as a created being, from the Father; subordinationism asserts the
    Father's priority over the Son in terms of a shared divine substance, a
    flexible, metaphorical view that produces the orthodox doctrine of the
    Trinity. The mind behind *Christian Doctrine* is literal, but the mind
    behind *Paradise Lost* explores the full implications of metaphors for the
    Trinity. The dispute between the Father and the Son in *Paradise Lost* is
    a sign not of their division but of the universality of the principle of free
    will, which applies even in heaven. In *Paradise Lost* (or *Paradise
    Regained*) and *Christian Doctrine*, the same ideas appear in such
    radically different contexts that we dare not equate those ideas. See
    entries 483, 962, 967-68, 989.

991 PATTERSON, ANNABEL. "The Civic Hero in Milton's Prose."
    Milton Studies 8 (1975):71-101.
        If Milton's major poems present a heroism of passive fortitude,
    his pamphlets develop the heroic ethos of civic fortitude, which blends
    action and contemplation. He adopts this mixed heroic persona for
    himself--defensively in the divorce tracts, actively in *Areopagitica*, and
    triumphantly in *Second Defence*. In *Pro Se Defensio*, the synthesis
    collapses before Milton, for he loses confidence and realizes that this
    persona offers no protection.

992 PRITCHARD, JOHN PAUL. "The Fathers of the Church in the Works of John Milton." *Classical Journal* 33 (1937):79-87.

Milton's tracts oppose writers who rely on the authority of the fathers, yet he accepts his opponents' choice of weapons, sometimes turning their citations against them by questioning their credibility, ascription, availability, or orthodoxy. As one who believes in the supreme authority of the Bible, Milton in *Of Reformation* finds early Christian authors who share his view and others whose views are unreliable or heretical. In *Of Prelatical Episcopacy*, he turns primarily to the ante-Nicene fathers to prove that *episkopos* and *presbyteros* refer to the same rank of clergy rather than to different grades. The church fathers also help Milton justify the resistance to a tyrant and the act of regicide in *First Defence*. When Milton discusses divorce, he often uses the fathers as authorities to refute.

993 RAJAN, BALACHANDRA. "*Areopagitica* and the Images of Truth." In *The Form of the Unfinished: English Poetics from Spenser to Pound*. Princeton, N.J.: Princeton University Press, 1985, pp. 85-103.

Even as the poetic imagination seeks beauty and proclaims it as truth, the imagination questions this very process because truth must engage the world without repudiating or replacing it as reality. The responsible imagination should not subvert experience by inhabiting the fictive world; rather, it must mediate between the actual world of experience and the authentic world of truth. In his early works, such as *Comus* and *Of Reformation*, Milton argues that truth is self-evident, synchronically revealed, and final. Later, he adopts more evolutionary views: turning to the principles of the search and vision, *Areopagitica* introduces to the field of inquiry an evolving consciousness that consolidates its past and creates a relationship between the eternally present and the historically attained.

994 ROSENBERG, D. M. "Parody of Style in Milton's Polemics." *Milton Studies* 2 (1970):113-18.

In order to expose his adversaries' attitudes, Milton in his prose parodies their styles and uses the language of living speech to assert his own views. In *Areopagitica*, he ridicules corrupt pastors and merchants by imitating the language of commerce. He can be crude or

Criticism

indecent, as in *Animadversions* or *Apology for Smectymnuus*, and he attacks Hall by distorting his diction.

995 ROSENBERG, D. M. "Style and Meaning in Milton's Anti-Episcopal Tracts." *Criticism* 15 (1973):43-57.
     Drawing his styles from the pulpit, the polemical pamphlet, and the biblical prophets, Milton in his early antiprelatical tracts attempts to synthesize such forces as church and state, revelation and reason. But his eclectic style instead reveals ideological conflicts. In his pulpit style, Milton achieves a ceremonial voice through Latinate diction and complex syntax, even though he sees the Bible as a work in the plain style. He resolves this dilemma by locating emotive, ambiguous sections in the Bible and by turning to the plain colloquial language of the pamphlet. When the pulpit style clashes with the pamphleteering style, we see a dramatization of the clash between the ideologies of reform and liberty. The transcendent prophetic style resolves the conflict.

996 ROSENBERG, D. M. "Theme and Structure in Milton's Autobiographies." *Genre* 2 (1969):314-25.
     Milton regains his past in his autobiographical works, using it to discover himself and the meaning in his life. In *Reason of Church-Government*, he presents the autobiography of a writer, as he examines his conscience and resolves doubts about his vocation. His identity as an author is associated with the Puritan cause. This work's form mimics the writer's division between politics and poetics. More retrospective, the spiritual autobiography in *Apology* imposes greater order on Milton's life because it attempts to see it from its end. His proposal of church reformation is paralleled by his individual spiritual progress, through which he emphasizes the themes of liberty and discipline. The idealized political autobiography in *Second Defence* takes the form of forensic oratory to advance the theme of virtue.

997 SAMUEL, IRENE. "Milton and the Ancients on the Writing of History." *Milton Studies* 2 (1970):131-48.
     The young Milton at Cambridge sees historical writing as a branch of epideictic oratory or as a kind of *narratio*. A form of literature, history is written to entertain and produce emotional

responses. In the 1650s, Milton's views change as he repudiates the rhetorical precepts for writing history: he defines the historian's duty as telling the truth, preferably in a terse style that abandons maxims, narrative, and proof. Although he once believed that the memory of deeds could be diminished by the stylistic art of the historian who reported them, as he writes *History of Britain*, Milton concludes that a "civilization gets the historians it deserves" (145): an era filled with glorious acts will also produce historians to record them.

998 SAMUEL, IRENE. "Milton on the Province of Rhetoric." *Milton Studies* 10 (1977):177-93.

Regarding rhetoric as an ancillary, organic art that should produce something beyond itself, Milton shows the influence of Ramism when he makes logic the foundation of all coherent discourse. In his prose, he prefers deliberative or persuasive rhetoric over the rhetoric of praise or blame associated with controversy; logical over pathetic proof; artistic or artificial proof over inartistic proof. Milton never condemns rhetoric, but he does condemn its abuse.

999 SÀNCHEZ, REUBEN MÀRQUEZ, Jr. "'The Worst of Superstitions': Milton's *Of True Religion* and the Issue of Religious Tolerance." *Prose Studies* 9 (1986):21-38.

The Clarendon Code's prohibitions against nonconformist Protestants are made less severe by Charles II's Declaration of Indulgence in 1670, though its main goal is toleration of Catholicism. An angry Parliament responds with the 1673 Test Act, mandating that any prospective holder of civil or military office in England must take the sacrament by the Church of England's rites. Milton writes *Of True Religion* in this context. He uses a devious rhetorical strategy with which he seeks to establish a common ground with Parliament while arguing for toleration for all Protestants. Although Milton's countrymen vehemently believe that Catholicism should be repressed, he holds that the people should discover (with his help) how to avoid Catholicism, a step that requires liberty. In *Of True Religion*, the persona's contradictions and inconsistencies urge us to be skeptical about his uncompromising assertions, particularly about the lack of toleration for Catholics.

Criticism

1000   SASEK, LAWRENCE A. "Milton's Patriotic Epic." *Huntington Library Quarterly* 20 (1956):1-14.

Milton's plan to write a patriotic work, perhaps an Arthuriad, is fulfilled by his prose writings, for he is not determined to write in a certain genre, such as epic. The reasons usually presented for his abandonment of an Arthuriad--distrust of romance, doubt about the story's veracity, adherence to Virgil's plan of poetic development, repudiation of monarchy--do not resolve the issue. In *Second Defence*, Milton invites comparison with Homer and Virgil, citing their epics as precedents for how he handles material in his defenses. For Milton, *First* and *Second Defence* form a kind of epic. The prose works are thus essential parts of his literary career.

1001   SEWELL, ARTHUR. *A Study in Milton's Christian Doctrine.* London: Oxford University Press, 1939, 227 pp. Reprint. Hamden, Conn.: Shoe String Press, 1967.

The first two stages in the composition of *Christian Doctrine* start in 1640 and 1658-60; the third stage, involving revision and reshaping, occurs after the Restoration. It remains unpublished during Milton's lifetime not because he fears prosecution but because it is not finished or because he becomes less confident about the truth of his views. Since Milton's ideas change, we must be careful about using *Christian Doctrine* to interpret the theology of *Paradise Lost*. After working on *Christian Doctrine*, Milton realizes that argument does not nourish the spirit and that his heterodox positions are not necessary for salvation. His three major poems give him deeper satisfaction and report the integral truth of his spiritual development. The early books of *Paradise Lost* are completed before Milton addresses the question of anti-Trinitarianism in *Christian Doctrine*, which is not a systematic or thorough statement of Milton's theology. *Paradise Regained* and *Samson Agonistes*, rather than searching for or defining a system of belief, accept what Scripture asserts.

1002   SHAWCROSS, JOHN T. "The Higher Wisdom of *The Tenure of Kings and Magistrates*." In *Achievements of the Left Hand: Essays on the Prose of John Milton*. Edited by Michael Lieb and John T. Shawcross. Amherst: University of Massachusetts Press, 1974, pp. 142-59.

Tenure argues not against royalists but against those who, while agreeing with the reformers, hesitate to perform the necessary actions that reason dictates: removing King Charles and instituting a more representative government. Milton recognizes that the "resistance to reasonable outcomes" (145), motivated by self-interest and tradition, persists through all times. Taking a radical position, he rejects compromise and the past. His argument uses idealism and logic, which rarely sway opponents.

1003   SHULLENBERGER, WILLIAM. "Linguistic and Poetic Theory in Milton's *De Doctrina Christiana.*" *English Language Notes* 19 (1982):262-78.

A poetic treatise, *Christian Doctrine* explicates a theory of language and a theory of metaphor because of Christ's centrality as word and image. The theological difference between Father and Son in *Christian Doctrine* characterizes language's formal structure: through the Son, the Father accomplishes the divine performative speech of creation and redemption. Based on a linguistic model of the Godhead, the Father's relationship to the Son is analogous to the relationship between language (an implicit system of rules and conventions) and speech (the actualization of those rules in a specific situation). Through the metaphor of the *Sermo* (Word), the Son entails a theory of representation that allows a reading of God's ways in terms of linguistic structures. As prophet, Christ renovates fallen speech; as priest, he is a sacrifice, a metaphorical substitute for sinners; as king, he expresses his structural power in the formation of human identity.

1004   SIRLUCK, ERNEST. "Milton Revises *The Faerie Queene.*" *Modern Philology* 48 (1950):90-96.

Milton errs in *Areopagitica* by saying that Spenser's Palmer accompanies Guyon into Mammon's cave. Spenser excludes the Palmer from this episode because he would serve no function, for Guyon here illustrates the Aristotelian relationship of virtue and habit: acting as the habitually temperate man, Guyon is immune to Mammon's offers. Milton does not share this view of the ethical significance of habit. As his misremembering of Spenser's episode shows, Milton believes that choice, to be correct, always depends on reason. Habit never protects anyone.

Criticism

1005 SIRLUCK, ERNEST. "Milton's Idle Right Hand." *JEGP: Journal of English and Germanic Philology* 60 (1961):749-85. Reprinted in *Milton Studies in Honor of Harris Francis Fletcher*, ed. G. Blakemore Evans, et al. (Urbana: University of Illinois Press, 1961), pp. 141-77.

Although in *Second Defence* Milton encourages us to believe that he works without rest on prose tracts, in fact the years from 1641 to 1660 are characterized by cycles in which bursts of activity are followed by periods (sometimes years) of silence. He is not, despite his claims in *Reason of Church-Government*, a reluctantly interrupted poet during the Civil Wars. Some of his silence in the 1650s may be attributed to ill health, the death of a wife and child, and work on *Christian Doctrine*; but during the 1640s, he is doing nothing urgent. When his marriage falls apart, Milton must wonder whether he is being punished for offering God a pledge of chastity and then withdrawing it; because he wanted to serve God with chastity and poetry, his sense of calling and inspiration ends. When he regains his sense of mission as a poet, the new symbol of inspiration is his blindness. *Samson Agonistes* is Milton's last work. Sonnet 7 is written in 1631, and *Ad Patrem* is not in chronological sequence in *Poems* (1645).

Appendix: "Some Recent Suggested Changes in the Chronology of Milton's Poems: *Samson Agonistes*, Sonnet 7, *Ad Patrem*."

1006 SIRLUCK, ERNEST. "Milton's Political Thought: The First Cycle." *Modern Philology* 61 (1964):209-24.

Between 1649 and 1654, Milton formulates a theory of natural law for the political arena, displays ambivalence toward his theory, and retreats into an alternative one. The secondary law of nature, that part of original perfection accessible to fallen man, binds him, along with special revelations that apply to certain groups (the Old Testament for the Israelites or the Gospel for Christians). Because the Gospel contains no pattern of civil government, Christians must rely on the secondary law of nature. *Tenure of Kings and Magistrates* makes law dependent on justice, which shares sovereignty with the popular will. In *Eikonoklastes*, Milton adds an emphasis on Parliament, which exercises the people's sovereignty, though his promotion of the public's will turns into a promotion of the public's good--even if that position is a minority view--in *First Defence*. *Second Defence* repudiates this theory, arguing instead for the theocratic view of a providentially guided state.

Contradicting his earlier political tracts, Milton ends up defending the authority of a regenerate minority.

1007 SMALLENBURG, HARRY R. "Contiguities and Moving Limbs: Style as Argument in *Areopagitica*." *Milton Studies* 9 (1976):169-84.

Areopagitica's style, which features disjunctive sentences and syntactic dislocations, corresponds to the very nature of truth, whose energy cannot be subjected to the limits imposed by fallen humans. After presenting an organizational scheme and a generalized summary of the issues, Milton violates our expectations: we find that inspired truths encourage a breakdown of the predicted organization. *Areopagitica* is itself an image of Truth's scattered limbs; we must become the searchers of unity.

1008 STAVELY, KEITH W. *The Politics of Milton's Prose Style*. Yale Studies in English, 185. New Haven, Conn., and London: Yale University Press, 1975, 145 pp.

The exalted poetic texture of Milton's prose limits its political effectiveness, interfering with each tract's correspondence to political reality and participation in social and political life. Legislating by imaginative fiat is an admirable poetic aspiration, so Milton's prose often succeeds as literature; but this is not an effective political strategy. When he discusses divorce in *Tetrachordon* and *Doctrine and Discipline of Divorce*, Milton removes it from a realistic, domestic context and brings it into a literary one. The political failure of these tracts is thus entirely predictable, as is the failure of *Areopagitica*, a great poem but a poorly calculated political statement. With the English people's defection from the cause of liberty in the 1650s, the split between social reality and ideals becomes final in the rational arguments of such tracts as *Of Civil Power*, *Likeliest Means To Remove Hirelings*, and *Ready and Easy Way*.

1009 STEWART, STANLEY. "Milton Revises *The Readie and Easie Way*." *Milton Studies* 20 (1984):205-24.

The anonymous author of *Censure of the Rota* (1660) criticizes the writer of *Ready and Easy Way*'s first edition for being too much the rhetorician. Milton's revisions of this treatise point to his diminishing interest in parts of the contemporary political scene and to an

Criticism

increasing interest in its fictional or mythical potential. Although he
starts his prose career as a rhetorician, by the time Milton writes
Paradise Regained, Satan is the master of rhetoric. Addressed to
Parliament, the first edition of *Ready and Easy Way* responds to
Harrington's ideal political system, which in turn deals with Hobbes's
ideas; but Milton's second edition looks to a wider audience, the
electorate, and uses biblical allusions (particularly to Jeremiah) to take
the form of prophecy rather than of argument.

1010 SVENDSEN, KESTER. "Milton's *Pro Se Defensio* and Alexander
More." *Texas Studies in Literature and Language* 1 (1959):11-29.
　　　　Because *Second Defence* erroneously attacks More as the
author of *Regii Sanguinis Clamor* in the controversy that leads to *Pro Se
Defensio*, Milton is forced to take some extraordinary steps in his
argument: he simultaneously admits, denies, and defends his mistake.
Pro Se Defensio contains vituperative language because Milton is
defending his government, people, and character. He learns a great
deal about More, and many of the charges he raises against him in
1654-55 are substantiated by the Synod of Tergou in 1659. Milton writes
of More as if his readers are familiar with the facts of his scandalous
life. The style of *Pro Se Defensio* is "incipient or half-formed poetry"
(25), filled with allusions, puns, and echoes, and characteristic of certain
aspects of *Paradise Lost*.

1011 THOMPSON, ELBERT N. S. "Milton's Prose Style." *Philological
Quarterly* 14 (1935):1-15.
　　　　Since Milton disparages prose style, one would not expect his
prose works to be polished, though he gives them more careful
consideration than one might think. His goal is to assert his views and
to attack those of others. In English or Latin, the syntax of his
sentences is loose, with many of his English sentences sounding like
spoken language. His diction is always resourceful, vigorous, and
precise; he has a good ear for homely English words, metaphors, and
expressions. But his eloquence is not constant.

1012 TURNER, JAMES GRANTHAM. "The Intelligible Flame:
Paradisal Eros and Old Testament Divorce in Milton's Prose." In

One Flesh: Paradisal Marriage and Sexual Relations in the Age of Milton. Oxford: Clarendon Press, 1987, pp. 188-229.

Milton's divorce tracts call for the restoration of the essence of marriage, as defined in Genesis and Plato, and of Deuteronomy's law that allows a husband to divorce a wife who is unclean, which Milton reinterprets in light of the Edenic ideal as psychological or spiritual incompatibility. He wants to lead us back to paradisal happiness by recognizing that we lack the strength to return. In his view, divorce, not love, has a primordial creative power. Milton knows that he is vulnerable to attack because of the tracts' almost libertine combination of mental life and erotic excitement that he projects into marriage. He uses the divorce tracts to try to reinvent prelapsarian voluntary sexuality, and he believes in the subordination of women in marriage.

1013   VIA, JOHN A. "Milton's Antiprelatical Tracts: The Poet Speaks in Prose." *Milton Studies* 5 (1973):87-127.

Dominated by an awareness of corruption as well as of regeneration, *Prolusion 6, Comus, Lycidas*, and *Epitaphium Damonis* anticipate Milton's antiprelatical tracts, which attack "the characteristics and effects of disharmony, degeneracy, and corruption" (88-89). Although the prose contains concrete images of evil and ugliness, Milton's uncertainty about the proper form of church government leads to less clear images of goodness and beauty. His early poems have a balance between corruption and regeneration that these prose tracts lack, for Milton cannot transfer his vision of the regenerate man's apotheosis to England's reformation.

1014   WEBBER, JOAN. "John Milton: The Prose Style of God's English Poet." In *The Eloquent "I": Style and Self in Seventeenth-Century Prose*. Madison, Milwaukee, and London: University of Wisconsin Press, 1968, pp. 184-218.

In his antiprelatical tracts, though he rarely uses the first-person pronoun, Milton often presents evidence that he is worthy to be heard, to represent his cause, and someday to be a great poet. His qualifications, which are signs of grace, always lead back to his art. Typically Puritan, his "I" is "preconceived and rigid, controversial and time-bound, active and literal, relatively humorless, devoted to nationalism and progress" (185). The antiprelatical tracts attempt to reform England, in part so the nation is worthy of the product of

Criticism

Milton's dearest vocation, poetry. His salvation and that of his country are parallel events. Milton casts himself as both prophet and thing prophesied, as artist and art. In *Apology*, he links such opposites as action and contemplation, time and eternity. As Milton fights back, he does not allow the reader to be a mere spectator. He writes in an impersonal personal voice, for he accepts his role as God's instrument.

1015 WHITAKER, JUANITA. "'The Wars of Truth': Wisdom and Strength in *Areopagitica*." *Milton Studies* 9 (1976):185-201.
    Advanced by its language and imagery, *Areopagitica*'s epistemological argument is that wisdom and strength are ideals of human endeavor leading to knowledge and action. Milton's choice of title, role as modern Isocrates, and comparison of England and Athens are all ironic. Books, the dominant metaphor in the tract, are both strong and wise, while censorship is misdirected strength and perverted wisdom. Intellectual freedom produces positive strength.

1016 WILDING, MICHAEL. "Milton's *Areopagitica*: Liberty for the Sects." *Prose Studies* 9 (1986):7-38. Reprinted in *The Literature of Controversy: Polemical Strategy from Milton to Junius*, ed. Thomas N. Corns (London: Frank Cass, 1987), pp. 7-38.
    Milton may say that Parliament honors truth, but printing was regulated since 1486, shortly after being introduced in England. *Areopagitica*'s images of mangling and tearing apart are vivid reminders of the punishments of people who write or import unapproved books. Milton argues not just for freedom of the press but for freedom to print radical spiritual and political ideas to effect social change--that is, the democratization of access to and expression of ideas. Radical schismatics and sectaries, according to his anti-elitist view, will help build the lord's temple, and he is committed to their radicalism. While Milton indicts the Stationers' Company, his position on commerce is to oppose monopolies and favor free trade if it will break the stranglehold on truth and lead to the free exchange of ideas. Couched in complex negatives, Milton's apparent endorsement of punishment for offending books is in fact a distanced, tactical concession.

1017 WILLIAMS, ARNOLD. "*Areopagitica* Revisited." *University of Toronto Quarterly* 14 (1944):67-74.

We often try to judge *Areopagitica* by tests appropriate to our age, which indicates that we find it a vital document, even if it fails to live up to our standards. Milton has a specific, limited purpose in *Areopagitica* (to persuade Parliament to repeal the June 1643 licensing act), and he selects his evidence with this audience in mind. Punishment for publishing divorce tracts is not his main concern, though he does identify himself with the universal cause he presents. *Areopagitica* is relevant today, during a world war and three-hundred years after its first appearance, precisely because of the universality of its principles, their permanent implications, and the work's magnificent rhetoric. Although Milton does not want the destroyers of freedom to enjoy a free press, he does not wish to discuss too many limits on freedom of the press. He recognizes that freedom implies responsibility, and he finds truth more valuable than a free press.

1018   WITTREICH, JOSEPH ANTHONY, Jr. "'The Crown of Eloquence': The Figure of the Orator in Milton's Prose Works." In *Achievements of the Left Hand: Essays on the Prose of John Milton.* Edited by Michael Lieb and John T. Shawcross. Amherst: University of Massachusetts Press, 1974, pp. 3-54.
    Influenced by Cicero's and Quintilian's ideas, Milton projects the image of an orator who possesses all human knowledge and wishes to give it to a nation in preparation for the Apocalypse. Yet he also wants to transcend the classical oratorical tradition by surpassing its subjects and themes. In Christ and St. Paul, Milton finds a precedent for his revolutionary stance in the prose tracts. He defines a fit audience as a majority, which is the regenerate, spiritual elite of Europe. When Milton addresses Parliament in many treatises, he indicates that he is an orator of the highest standing who speaks as the people's liberator. By using a variety of styles in a tract or from one treatise to the next, Milton deals with a range of audiences. In the defenses, he allows each oration to take the form of the treatise to which it responds. He adopts the persona of the true orator and casts his opponents as false ones.

1019   WITTREICH, JOSEPH ANTHONY, Jr. "Milton's *Areopagitica*: Its Isocratic and Ironic Contexts." *Milton Studies* 4 (1972):101-15.
    The title of *Areopagitica* establishes correspondences between Milton and Isocrates, and between Parliament and the General

Criticism

Assembly. By introducing a biblical allusion to St. Paul, Milton provides a foundation for an inversion of these correspondences, equating himself with the General Assembly and Parliament with Isocrates. Milton misrepresents Isocrates's failed attempt to persuade the Athenian assembly to impose restrictions, thus revealing his suspicion that Parliament will deny the liberty for which he pleads. Filled with irony and equivocation, along with emotional extravagance, the peroration shifts from a licensing exemption for any book to requiring licensing of Catholic books. Men of principle will see that Catholic books deserve no different treatment, a point Parliament will miss as it swallows the ironic concession.

1020   WITTREICH, JOSEPH ANTHONY, Jr. "Milton's Idea of the Orator." *Milton Quarterly* 6 (1972):38-40.
        The title page of *First Defence*, which portrays one shield containing a cross and the other a harp, points to Milton's conception of the orator as Christian warrior and as king. Milton views the orator as a prophet and priest, roles that he shares with the poet.

1021   WOOLRYCH, AUSTIN. "Milton and Cromwell: 'A Short but Scandalous Night of Interruption'?" In *Achievements of the Left Hand: Essays on the Prose of John Milton*. Edited by Michael Lieb and John T. Shawcross. Amherst: University of Massachusetts Press, 1974, pp. 185-218.
        The reasons behind Milton's apparent change of allegiance to Cromwell raise questions about Milton's consistency of thought and conception of civil and spiritual liberty. Although *Second Defence* eulogizes Cromwell, Milton's brief treatment of two events--the ejection of the Rump and the failure of the Barebones Parliament-- suggests his doubt. But since the goal of *Second Defence* is to support the regicides in the face of a European attack, Milton can use the occasion only to give Cromwell pages of advice and exhortation, almost defining the criteria by which the Protector's performance will be judged. From Milton's perspective, Cromwell is a disappointment. Milton in the late 1650s has an increasing allegiance to the Rump's republican leaders, who oppose the Protectorate. *Of Civil Power* turns not to the new Protector, Richard Cromwell, but to Parliament with an appeal to reverse the Protectorate's ecclesiastical policies. Parliament does not change course. When *Likeliest Means To Remove Hirelings*

refers to the "night of interruption," we see the inconsistency in Milton's thought.

For editions, see entries 36-37, 39, 42; for a concordance to the English prose, see entry 85. See also entries 2, 5, 9-10, 16, 19-20, 23, 27-29, 43-47, 49, 51-52, 58, 60, 63, 65-66, 68-72, 85, 91, 96-97, 99-100, 112, 122, 125, 129, 133, 141, 143-46, 151, 153, 156, 163-64, 166, 169-71, 176-77, 180-81, 183, 188, 192, 199, 201-4, 212, 216, 223, 226, 228, 240-41, 249, 270, 377, 379, 441, 459, 461, 463, 470, 480, 483, 491, 493, 498, 502, 519, 525, 540, 542, 557, 569, 572, 574, 581, 589, 599, 618-19, 638, 654, 678, 680, 686, 693, 702, 711, 745, 754, 763, 766, 771, 777, 781-82, 789, 793, 800, 829, 858, 864, 867, 873, 889, 899, 901, 906, 923.

Index

439

Index